DESIGN
AND ANALYSIS
A Researcher's
Handbook

Second Edition

GEOFFREY KEPPEL

Department of Psychology
University of California, Berkeley

Prentice-Hall, Inc., *Englewood Cliffs, New Jersey 07632*

Library of Congress Cataloging in Publication Data

KEPPEL, GEOFFREY.
  Design and analysis.

  Bibliography: p.
  Includes index.
  1. Social sciences—Statistical methods. 2. Factorial
experiment designs. 3. Social sciences—Research.
I. Title.
HA29.K44 1982   300'.72   81–15419
ISBN 0–13–200048–2   AACR2

Editorial/production supervision by
  Alison D. Gnerre and Dee Amir Josephson
Cover design by Martha Geering
Manufacturing buyer: Edmund W. Leone

Printed in the United States of America

10 9 8 7 6

Prentice-Hall International, Inc., *London*
Prentice-Hall of Australia Pty. Limited, *Sydney*
Prentice-Hall of Canada, Ltd., *Toronto*
Prentice-Hall of India Private Limited, *New Delhi*
Prentice-Hall of Japan, Inc., *Tokyo*
Prentice-Hall of Southeast Asia Pte. Ltd., *Singapore*
Whitehall Books Limited, *Wellington, New Zealand*

Contents

Chapter 4
The Sensitivity of an Experiment *66*

Chapter 5
Assumptions and Other Considerations *80*

Chapter 6
Analytical Comparisons Among Treatment Means *103*

Chapter 7
Analysis of Trend *127*

Chapter 8
Correction for Multiple Comparisons *144*

III
FACTORIAL EXPERIMENTS WITH TWO FACTORS

Chapter 9
Introduction to the Factorial Design *169*

Chapter 10
Rationale and Rules for Calculating the Major Effects *185*

Chapter 11
Detailed Analysis of Main Effects and Interaction *208*

Chapter 12
Other Types of Two-Factor Designs *246*

IV
HIGHER-ORDER FACTORIAL EXPERIMENTS

Chapter 13
The Three-Factor Design: The Basic Analysis *275*

Chapter 14
The Three-Factor Design: Simple Effects and Interaction Comparisons *302*

Chapter 15
Analysis of the General Case *334*

V
WITHIN-SUBJECTS DESIGNS

Chapter 16
Introduction to Within-Subjects Designs *367*

Chapter 17
The Single-Factor Within-Subjects Design *381*

Chapter 18
The Mixed Two-Factor Design *408*

Chapter 19
Other Common Within-Subjects Designs *451*

VI
ADDITIONAL TOPICS: ANALYSIS OF COVARIANCE AND GENERALIZING RESULTS

Chapter 20
Analysis of Covariance *481*

Chapter 21
Generalizing Results and Other Theoretical Considerations *516*

Chapter 22
Concluding Remarks *538*

Appendix A
Statistical Tables *541*

Appendix B
Answers to the Chapter Exercises *560*

Appendix C-1
A Comparison of Notational Systems *613*

To Sheila

Preface

My major purpose in writing this book was to present the design and analysis of experiments from a researcher's point of view. The book was not intended to be a primary statistical reference, but rather to be a useful source of information and explanation of design and statistical matters rarely touched on by more mathematically sophisticated books. I wrote the book with a particular reader in mind, namely, a student who is about to engage in experimental research, but who possesses only the most fundamental of mathematical skills and has little or no formal statistical background. What I offer in effect are *research tutorials* that provide the basic information necessary to design and to analyze meaningful experiments in the behavioral, social, and biological sciences. The emphasis is on the use of *the experiment as an inferential tool,* which a researcher employs to test theory and to build an empirical base for the science. Thus, a large proportion of the book is devoted to a detailed discussion of matters of experimental design and to the practical use of statistical procedures that will assist researchers in drawing inferences from experimental data. Statistical arguments are not neglected, however, but are covered in the context of data analysis and data interpretation; references to more mathematically oriented sources are liberally provided.

The major difference between my book and others at this level is its coverage of the detailed analysis of experiments. The book considers the reasons behind these analyses and provides numerous illustrations of their creative application to experimental problems. In contrast, most books focus on the standard information available from experiments and spend very little time discussing the procedures which tailor the analysis to satisfy a researcher's specific needs. This book covers all of the major designs commonly utilized by psychologists. I present these designs and the analyses appropriate to them in considerable detail. As a result, the book will provide you with a thorough appreciation for the richness of information obtainable from different experimental designs, and you should be in the position to take advantage of these procedures to plan your analyses in order to maximize the discovery and statistical assessment of this information.

The organization of this sort of book is dictated largely by the nature of the subject matter. I begin, therefore, with the simplest material and progress logically to the more complex. Because the analysis of variance consists of a number of design "building blocks" (a blending of simpler designs into more complex ones), I devote approximately 30 percent of the book to the analysis of the simplest experimental design, the completely randomized single-factor design, and about 20 percent to the completely randomized two-factor design. This unique depth of coverage makes it possible for students and researchers to extend this knowledge to the analysis of the more complex designs.

Each chapter begins with an outline of the major subdivisions. This outline can be used as a preview before you begin each chapter and as a summary of the material after you complete the chapter. The outlines also function as a useful reference to specific sections. Major sections are numbered to make it easier to find particular discussions.

This second edition represents an extensive revision. Approximately 70 percent of the text consists of either new material or material from the first edition that has been rewritten. Very little material from the original book has been dropped; instead, rewriting consisted largely of recasting chapters, removing redundancy, and of tying together previously separate discussions. The pages thus saved permitted the introduction of new topics and material into the second edition. I will list several of these:

1. Power, estimation of sample size, and the use of replications are introduced in an early chapter (Chapter 4), in the context of the completely randomized single-factor design. Omega squared and other measures of treatment magnitude are also considered at an early point in the second edition (Chapter 5). (Previously, these topics were covered in the final chapters of the first edition.)
2. The linear model is presented in conjunction with each major experimental design, and there is a better integration of the theoretical underpinnings with the testing procedures. Procedures for deriving expected mean squares are presented in an appendix (Appendix C–4).
3. The analysis of trend is now presented in a separate chapter (Chapter 7).
4. The discussion of post-hoc testing has been revised and different strategies for dealing with the problem of inflated familywise type I error are discussed.
5. Certain specialized designs, e.g., randomized blocks, nested designs, and factorial designs with "outside" control groups, are included in a new chapter (Chapter 12) that follows the presentation of the completely randomized two-factor design.
6. Latin square designs are now treated in the book with particular emphasis on their use in repeated-measures, or within-subjects, designs. In addition, there is a treatment of single-df comparisons for Latin square designs, which is not presented in as useful a form in any other book.
7. Random effects and problems of generalizing experimental findings are presented in a new chapter (Chapter 21) containing a thorough discussion of analyses appropriate for crossed and nested random independent variables. This includes discussions of between- and within-subjects designs.
8. Two new appendices have been added. One appendix (Appendix C–1) explains the rationale behind the notational system adopted for this book, and the other (Appendix C–4) brings together in one place a set of rules outlining the analysis of variance for a wide variety of experimental designs and structural models.
9. New problems and exercises have been added. Collections of problems have been placed at the end of most chapters. Complete answers to the exercises are presented in Appendix B.

The instructor who might wish to simplify some of the material for his or her students, and readers either who are a bit rusty on the "basics" usually taught at the undergraduate level or who have not been exposed to a course on experimental design as a sophomore or junior in college, can consult my introductory statistics text.[1] The use of the same notational system and of the same general approach to experimental analysis in the two texts permits them to serve as supplements to each other.

This book is intended for use in a one-semester course or a two-quarter sequence in experimental design and statistical analysis. For a one-quarter course, I usually cover in detail Chapters 1-11, 13, and 16-20, which represent what I consider the basic knowledge graduate students should have mastered before becoming productively involved in experimental research. Because students require little supervision in working through most of the early chapters, instructors do not have to duplicate the presentation of the analyses in lecture. Instead, they are able to supplement the various topics with a development of statistical theory or with an amplification of the problems of experimental design—topics that are often neglected when an instructor must present the details of the analyses in class.

I wish to thank the American Statistical Association, *Biometrics,* the *Biometrika* Trustees, and *Psychometrika* for their permission to reproduce statistical tables in this book.

I am indebted to a number of individuals who provided advice and other assistance in the preparation of this book. I should mention first the useful comments I have received over the years from readers of the first edition, including students in my undergraduate and graduate courses and individuals who have written to me with questions and ideas for improving the book. Helpful suggestions concerning possible directions that the revision might take were offered by John L. Wasik, University of North Carolina at Chapel Hill; Dan Roenker, Western Kentucky University; and Geoffrey R. Loftus, University of Washington. I am particularly grateful to Dr. Thomas Wickens, University of California, Los Angeles, who prepared detailed comments on the first edition and who read critically the first draft of the present edition. His considerable knowledge of statistics and experimental design and his long-term experience in teaching this material to graduate students contributed in innumerable ways to the final version of this book. The assistance of others in the production of this book should be mentioned. Dr. William H. Saufley, Jr. helped with a major portion of the proofreading. John Isley, the Psychology editor for Prentice Hall, provided helpful advice and support at various stages of the project. Alison Gnerre and Dee Amir Josephson skillfully guided the manuscript through the many details of production. Melissa Keppel helped prepare bibliographical material, typed the tables, and assisted with the proofreading. Peter Keppel remodeled my study to accommodate my reference materials and microcomputer. Martha Geering was responsible for the design of the jacket cover.

Geoffrey Keppel

---

[1] Keppel, G., and Saufley, W. H., Jr. *Introduction to Design and Analysis: A Student's Handbook.* San Francisco: W. H. Freeman, 1980.

INTRODUCTION

This book was written for a relatively diverse audience—one ranging from advanced undergraduates to graduate students and professional researchers. As a result, some sections of the book, especially in the earlier chapters, may safely be omitted by the "seasoned" investigator, just as some sections in the later chapters may not be relevant to the immediate needs of the undergraduate. This first section is intended for less experienced investigators.

A science is built upon a large body of reliable facts and information. As most of you have discovered, or soon will discover, these facts are not easy to come by. They are established through many hours of patient observation, recording, and analysis of the behavior generated during the observation periods. A common method for establishing facts is the **experimental method.**

Basically, the experimental method consists of the contrast between two treatment conditions. The subjects in both of these conditions are treated identically, except for one feature that is different. I will refer to this difference as the **experimental treatment** or more commonly as the **independent variable.** (In this latter designation, **independent** stresses the point that the manipulation is under the control of the experimenter and **variable** indicates that the manipulation may take on two or more values.) Some aspect of the performance of the subjects in the two treatment conditions is measured and recorded after the treatment has been administered. This critical feature of the behavior of the subjects is referred to variously as the **dependent variable,** the **response variable,** or the **criterion variable.** Any difference between these two conditions that we observe on the dependent variable is called the **treatment effect** and is usually assumed to have been *caused* by the experimental treatment.

The experimental method is not the only method with which reliable scientific facts may be discovered. It is possible, for example, to show that two bits of behavior tend to appear together in nature and to use this fact to predict the occurrence of one from a knowledge of the other. Although relationships obtained by this **correlational approach** may be reasonably accurate in their predictions, e.g., the prediction of success in a job by means of scores on an aptitude test, we have not established a *causal* relationship with this procedure. For instance, to establish that cigarette smoking and the incidence of lung cancer tend to be related does not necessarily mean that smoking *caused* the cancer, as the cigarette manufacturers have maintained for years. There is always the possibility that some other factor, a chemical imbalance, say, will account both for the smoking and for the occurrence of cancer as well.

The most important feature of the experimental method is that it *is* possible to infer a cause-effect relationship. That is, we can conclude that the difference we observe in the performance of the subjects in our two conditions was caused by the experimental treatment. This book will be concerned exclusively with the analysis of data obtained from such controlled experiments. Chapter 1 describes the important features that must be considered in the design of an experiment.

I

Design of Experiments

An experiment consists of a carefully worked-out and executed plan for data collection and analysis. Treatment conditions are chosen to focus on particular features of the testing environment. These conditions are administered to subjects in such a way that observed differences in behavior can be unambiguously attributed to critical differences existing among the various treatment conditions. In essence, a well-designed experiment permits the inference of *causation*. This chapter describes a number of important features of experimentation—to place all readers on an equal footing. The steps required to establish causation are complicated, however, and will be considered in later chapters. Many of the points discussed in this chapter will be amplified and additional ones introduced throughout the remainder of the book. I will continually consider problems of experimental design along with the presentation of the formal statistical procedures. The design and statistical analysis of experiments are mutually serving and interdependent activities.

1.1   COMPONENTS OF EXPERIMENTATION

Experimentation begins by formulating a number of research hypotheses. These hypotheses may represent deductions or derivations from a more or less formal theoretical explanation of the behavioral phenomenon you wish to study, or they may represent simply hunches or speculations that you tentatively hold concerning this phenomenon. You may merely feel the need to collect additional facts about the behavior before developing a theory and deriving hypotheses from it. Research hypotheses are the questions you hope to answer by means of the experiment. They are what motivates your research. The introduction to a journal article generally contains the background information needed to set the experiment in proper theoretical and empirical perspective as well as an elaboration of the research hypotheses that are tested by the study.

The next stage in experimentation is the translation of the different research hypotheses into a set of treatment conditions and the selection of an appropriate experimental design within which to embody the different treatment conditions. The major requirement is that the particular treatment conditions chosen be capable of testing the research hypotheses. Are the treatment conditions relevant? Do the differences among the treatment conditions reflect the features of the experiment that we intended or have other features changed as well? The first question involves a consideration of the logical connection between the theory, the research hypotheses, and treatment conditions. The second question refers to a serious problem known as **confounding**, which I will discuss shortly. The details of the experimental design are presented in the methods section of a journal article.

The experiment is conducted, and the data are collected. We now have the two important tasks of summarizing the outcome of the experiment by means of statistical indices and procedures and evaluating the status of the research hypotheses. Our goal in this stage is to extract as much meaningful information as we can from the experiment. Our efforts at summarizing and analyzing the results of our experiment form the basis of the results section in a research report.

Since most of our time in this book will be spent in considering the statistical analysis of data, I should say a few more words about its place in experimentation. The statistical analysis provides a way of determining the *repeatability* of any differences observed in an experiment. If the same outcome is found when an experiment is repeated (or replicated) over and over again, we really do not need a statistical analysis to convince us that these differences are "real." A repeatable finding is really what we mean by a *fact* or a *phenomenon*. But rarely do we see replication used as a means for verifying the repeatability of findings, mainly because of the cost of conducting the same experiment more than once. Instead, we usually conduct a *single* experiment, and then we use the statistical analysis to help us to decide whether it is likely that these same differences *would* be found *if* we repeated the experiment.

The final stage of experimentation, which is reported in the discussion section of an article, involves either the assimilation of the outcomes of the statistical tests of the research hypotheses into the theory that generated the hypotheses originally or the creation of a theoretical explanation if none is available in the literature. This process is a *reconstructive* phase, where facts that were not known before the experiment was conducted are now integrated into the research literature. If the experiment was conducted to test a theory and the outcome of the experiment is favorable to the theory, further tests of the theory (i.e., new experiments) may be proposed. If the outcome is negative, the effect upon the theory is a bit more complicated. At first glance, we might expect the theory either to be discarded, or revised, or perhaps even brought to further test. Actually, theories are much more entrenched than this suggests, and what happens is that the adequacy of the *experiment* is usually questioned instead! For example, its methodology may be re-examined; its supposed relation to the theory is reevaluated; a search for possible contaminating variables may be conducted; and so on. Only after considerable examination of the experiment is there much consideration of changing the theory. When it occurs, however, this complete sequence—research hypothesis, experiment, assimilation, research hypothesis—corresponds to the familiar **deductive** and **inductive** roles of science, namely, theory testing and theory building.

The completion of the assimilation stage is usually the beginning of another cycle, however. That is, your theoretical interpretations of these new findings now form the basis for a new set of research hypotheses, and a new research endeavor is launched.

1.2 PRINCIPLES OF EXPERIMENTAL DESIGN

The basic requirements of an experiment are simple: Differential treatments are administered to different groups of subjects (or to the same subjects in different orders) and performance on some response measure is observed and recorded following the administration of the treatments. In this section, I will elaborate upon this relatively simple idea.

The Independent Variable

Identifying Critical Features. An experiment is composed of two or more treatment conditions that in turn are characterized by a particular combination of potentially critical features. In an experiment, we compare the performance of subjects in the different treatment conditions and attempt to attribute differences in behavior to the feature (or features) that is (or are) different—i.e., that vary—across the conditions. The independent variable is usually defined by the nature of the critical differences systematically varied among the treatment conditions. I will refer to an independent variable in a number of ways; for example, as a manipulated variable, a treatment variable, or a factor.

As an example, suppose that condition 1 consisted of a

SATIATED ADULT RAT given FOOD reward for solving a DIFFICULT maze.

In addition to the potentially critical features of this treatment condition, written in capital letters, I could list other features as well, such as the characteristics of the testing room, the apparatus, and the experimenter, the time of testing, and so on. What can we conclude by studying subjects in this single condition? Very little, except to *describe* the situation. We can infer nothing about the relative importance of the various characteristics listed above in influencing the speed with which the maze in learned.

On the other hand, let's add a second condition, which consists of a

SATIATED *YOUNG* RAT given FOOD reward for solving a DIFFICULT maze.

While this condition suffers from the same problem as the first when the behavior of the subjects is considered alone, the purpose of the experiment springs immediately into focus when we *compare* the two treatment conditions. More specifically, the critical difference between the two conditions is the *age* of the rats, and any difference observed between the two conditions will be attributed to this particular difference (adult versus young). Age is the independent variable.

Additional illustrations of independent variables are presented in Table 1-1, where separate experiments are defined by contrasting condition 1 with a different condition 2. Condition 2a, for example, focuses on a contrast between rats on the one hand (condition 1) and hamsters (condition 2a) on the other; any difference observed between the two conditions will be attributed to this particular difference. *Species* (rats versus hamsters) constitutes the independent variable. Condition 2b studies the effect of *food deprivation* (satiated versus hungry); condition 2c studies the effect of *type of reward* (food versus water); and condition 2d studies the effect of *maze difficulty* (difficult versus easy).

Each pair of conditions (condition 1 and one of the other conditions) constitutes an experiment. In each case the two conditions are identical except for one critical difference. This critical difference defines the independent variable. Re-

Table 1-1   Examples of Treatment Conditions

Condition 1	A satiated adult rat given food reward for solving a difficult maze
Condition 2	A satiated YOUNG rat given food reward for solving a difficult maze
Condition 2a	A satiated adult HAMSTER given food reward for solving a difficult maze
Condition 2b	A HUNGRY adult rat given food reward for solving a difficult maze
Condition 2c	A satiated adult rat given WATER reward for solving a difficult maze
Condition 2d	A satiated adult rat given food reward for solving an EASY maze

searchers usually refer to the different treatment conditions—"treatments" for short—in terms of the critical *difference* between conditions. Thus, for the experiment defined by the contrast between conditions 1 and 2, the treatments are *adult* and *young*. For the remaining experiments, the treatments would be *rat* and *hamster, satiated* and *hungry, food* and *water*, and *difficult* and *easy*, respectively.

Multiple Conditions. Most experiments consist of more than two treatment conditions. If we were interested in comparisons among species in a given learning task, for example, we might design an experiment where various types of animals are represented, e.g., rats, hamsters, mice, kangaroo rats, and so on. The choice of animal would be dictated by the questions we wanted to ask. If we were interested in the effects of food deprivation on learning, we would probably include several treatment conditions varying in the amount of time the animals have been without food, e.g., 0, 12, 24, and 36 hours. Each one of the independent variables represented by the experiments specified in Table 1-1 could be expanded in a similar fashion.

Quantitative independent variables are variables that represent variation in *amount*—amount of food deprivation, variations in dosage, loudness of the masking noise, length of the learning task. Variables of this sort usually include treatment conditions that represent the full range of variation of the independent variable as well as several intermediate conditions to provide a picture of the effects of the variable in between the two extremes. **Qualitative independent variables,** on the other hand, represent variations in *kind* or in *type* rather than in amount. Experiments designed to study species differences or the effects of type of reward or of different kinds of drugs are all examples of qualitative independent variables.

Qualitative manipulations can often be viewed as a collection of *miniature* experiments included within the context of a more general experiment. Suppose an experiment is designed to study the effects of different rewards on the speed of learning. Rats that have been deprived of food and water for a period of time are given one of the following three conditions:

Condition 1—food reward for solving the maze
Condition 2—water reward for solving the maze
Condition 3—food *and* water for solving the maze

A comparison between conditions 1 and 2 concentrates on the relative effects of food and water as rewards for learning. A comparison between conditions 1 and 3, on the other hand, focuses on the addition of water to the food reward. And a comparison between conditions 2 and 3 permits a similar determination of the effects of the addition of food to the water reward. Most experiments involving a qualitative independent variable can be analyzed as a set of smaller, more focused experiments. The primary characteristic of these miniature experiments is that they focus on a meaningful contrast between two (and sometimes more) treatment conditions. I will discuss the analysis of such manipulations in Chapter 6.

The effects of quantitative independent variables are usually analyzed differently. Rather than comparing miniature experiments in the data analysis, researchers concentrate instead on the overall relationship between the variation of the independent variable and changes in behavior. The goal of the analysis is to determine the nature or the shape of this relationship. Suppose that the independent variable is the number of hours of food deprivation, and that we will be measuring the trials required to learn a difficult maze. How are we to describe the relationship? Presumably we will find an increase in performance as the animals become more hungry. But how will this increase in performance reveal itself? Will the increase occur steadily as the number of hours increases or will there be an absence of an effect at first followed by a steady increase? Specialized analyses are available that will permit us to distinguish between these two (and other) possibilities. I will discuss these procedures—called **trend analysis**—in Chapter 7. While it may not be obvious at this time, the analysis of trend requires a reasonable number of treatment conditions in order to give any underlying relationship between variations of the independent variable and changes in behavior an opportunity to be revealed.

A final reason why contemporary experiments contain more than two treatment conditions is the widespread use in psychology of designs in which two or more independent variables are manipulated simultaneously in the context of the same experiment. These designs, called **factorial designs**, require a minimum of four different treatment conditions and generally contain more. Factorial designs will be introduced in Part III.

Classification Variables. Experiments are frequently encountered that include the systematic variation of characteristics which are intrinsic to the subjects. The effect of intelligence on problem solving and the effect of sex on learning are examples of this type of study. Variables of this sort are variously referred to as **classification variables**, **subject variables**, **organismic variables**, and **individual-difference variables**. In the context of an experiment, classification variables are created by *selecting subjects* on the dimension to be included in the study. To "manipulate" intelligence, for example, we might segregate subjects into several groups on the basis of their IQ scores; these groups, then, would define the IQ variable for this experiment.

Manipulation of this sort does not constitute a true experiment, since the administration of the "treatments" is obviously not under the control of the experimenter. In an experiment, the independent variable is the only feature of the situation that is allowed to vary systematically from condition to condition. It is this characteristic of an experiment that permits us to infer that a particular manipulation caused systematic differences in the behavior observed among the different groups. But when a classification variable is involved, the subjects may also differ systematically from group to group with respect to characteristics other than the classification variable. Since such characteristics are not subject to a researcher's control, making an unambiguous statement about cause and effect is very difficult—if not impossible—where classification variables are under study.

In reality, this type of investigation is a *correlation* study, where the classification variable is simply another dimension that is observed and recorded in addition to the dependent variable. In fact, it is generally advisable to study the relationship between the classification variable and behavior *without* selecting and grouping subjects, and to use the actual scores on the classification variable in the analysis rather than lose this potentially valuable information by grouping.[1]

We frequently do see classification variables introduced in conjunction with independent variables that *are* manipulated by the experimenter. Such designs, which I will consider in Chapter 12, can produce a more sensitive context in which to study the effects of the independent variable. Moreover, these designs permit researchers to examine these effects separately for each classification group and to determine whether the effects change or remain the same for the different groups of subjects. Underwood and Shaughnessy (1975, pp. 94-104) show how this approach can be used to study processes presumably "tapped" by a classification variable.

Dependent Variables

Suppose we have completed the first step in an experimental investigation: the development of a meaningful hypothesis and the choice of a particular experimental design. It is now up to us to work out the specific and minute details of the study and to collect the data. We will have to make a decision concerning the particular aspect of the behavior we will observe and what measures of this behavior we will adopt. Each investigator will select measures that seem to "capture" the phenomenon being studied most accurately. Often these measures will overlap to some degree with those adopted by other investigators who have worked in this research area.

Even the behavior of a subject in an apparently simple experiment may be measured in a number of ways. Suppose we decide to study the effect of different types of food incentives on learning. Hungry rats will be used as the subjects, and their task will be to learn to approach a distinctive goal box which has been con-

---

[1]For a discussion of these alternatives, see Myers (1979, pp. 157–159). For a general discussion of the problems surrounding the interpretation of this sort of correlational data, see Underwood (1957, pp. 112-125).

sistently associated with food. Different groups of animals are given different types of food in the correct goal box. Since we are interested in learning *efficiency*, we would want to choose a dependent variable that reflects differences in time to learn. For example, we might record the total number of trials required for each animal to reach some predetermined level of performance—10 choices in a row of the correct goal box. We might also want to compare the different groups of subjects at more than one criterion of mastery. For instance, we might want to see if the groups differ early in learning, e.g., a criterion of 5 correct choices in a row, as well as late in learning. By requiring all of our subjects to attain the *highest* level of performance, 10 trials in a row, we are also able to compare the groups at levels of performance that reflect a lower degree of mastery. Alternatively, we might choose to give all animals a constant amount of training, 50 trials say, and to compare the different treatment conditions in the total number of correct choices over the 50 trials. Again, if we want, we can also look at performance at different stages of learning, e.g., the number of correct choices over the first 10 trials or over the second 10 trials. We can use any or all of these measures, just so long as all of the subjects have been tested on all 50 trials.

Up to this point, I have considered only measures which take into consideration the correctness of choice. Other aspects of behavior might be interesting to study. The time required by the rat to perform each trial is a commonly used measure. We could record the time for a rat to complete a given trial, from the opening of the start box to its entry into the goal box. More typically, we would probably choose to divide the total time period into subperiods and to record the duration of each subperiod separately. Common subperiods are (1) starting latency—time to leave the start box after the starting signal is given, (2) time spent within different segments of the approach to the discrimination choice point, (3) time spent at the choice point, and (4) time between the initiation of a choice and the entry into the goal box. In addition to time measures, we could record what the animal is doing during each trial. Does it stay oriented toward the patterns at the choice point at all times? What does it do at the choice point?

It is abundantly clear that any type of behavior which is singled out for study in an experiment may be indexed by a large number of response measures. With each measure, we can ask whether or not the independent variable was effective in producing differences among the treatment conditions. There is no simple rule to govern our actual selection of response measures. Some measures may provide redundant information, i.e., give exactly the same picture of the effect of the independent variable. We would not have to include all of these measures in our experiment, since any one of them would give the same information. Some measures may be explicitly specified by a theory that is being tested in the experiment. Some measures may be easier to record or less subject to error either in measurement or in recording. In any case, it is most economical to attempt to include in any experiment a sufficient variety of response measures to ensure as complete a description as possible of the phenomenon under study.

Control of Nuisance Variables ⁂

A major effort in designing experiments is to control what are often called **nuisance variables.** Nuisance variables are potential independent variables which if left uncontrolled could exert a systematic influence on the different treatment conditions. When this occurs the effects of the independent variable and the nuisance variables are intertwined and usually cannot be separated. Suppose, for instance, that we are interested in the effects of three drug dosages upon the learning of a maze by rats. We may find it convenient, perhaps, to run the three different dosage groups in the maze at different times of day, with one dosage group run in the morning, another in the afternoon, and the final dosage group in the evening. Or we might decide to have each of the dosage groups run by a different laboratory assistant.

In the first case, the three dosage groups each learn at a different time of day. If time of day influences performance on the learning task—as it very well might, considering the diurnal cycles of rats—we will be unable to reach an unambiguous conclusion concerning the influence of drug dosage on learning. There will always be the problem of determining how much of this effect is due to the different times of day and how much to the different dosages. In the second case, each assistant runs the rats in only one of the dosage groups. If the assistants treat their animals differently, and if these differences in treatment are related to the rats' performance, then again it will not be possible to attribute any differences in the behavior of the subjects in the three treatment groups to the experimental treatment. That is, how much of the treatment effect is due to the assistants and how much to the drug dosages?

We refer to either state of affairs as a ⌐confounding⌐ of the independent variable (drug dosage) with some other feature of the testing situation (here, time of day or laboratory assistants). As another example of confounding, consider the various treatment conditions listed in Table 1-1 (p. 7). In an earlier section, you saw that a valid experiment was formed when condition 1 was contrasted with any one of the other conditions (2, 2a, 2b, and so on). As an obvious example of confounding, suppose the second condition were the following:

a HUNGRY YOUNG HAMSTER given WATER reward for solving an EASY maze.

It is clear that no meaningful inferences can be drawn from an experiment that includes the original condition 1 and this one. Each critical feature of the experiment—drive, age, species, type of reward, and maze difficulty—is varied between the two conditions; any difference in learning observed between the two treatment conditions may be due to any one or to any combination of the changes between the two conditions. A less flagrant confounding, but a confounding nevertheless, is created by comparing condition 2 with condition 2a. A close examination of the critical features reveals two changes between the two conditions, namely, age and species: condition 2 specifies young rats while condition 2a specifies adult hamsters. In fact, no pair of the second conditions permits an unconfounded manipulation of a single independent variable. This only occurs when condition 1 is contrasted against one of the other conditions.

Confoundings in actual experiments are more subtle than the examples considered here. A significant amount of your training as a researcher will involve the development of an increased sensitivity to spot or identify potential confoundings. You can read about them in a variety of books, under the topic of **confounding of variables** or **internal validity** of experiments. See, for example, discussions of confounding in Neale and Liebert (1980, Chapter 7) and Underwood and Shaughnessy (1975). In addition, there are two useful undergraduate texts in paperback that are devoted entirely to the problem of internal validity (Huck and Sandler, 1979; Johnson and Solso, 1978). There is a more extensive and sophisticated discussion of these sorts of problems in books by Campbell and Stanley (1966), Cook and Campbell (1979), and Underwood (1957, Chapters 4 and 5), which you are encouraged to study early in your scientific training.

Confoundings are controlled either by holding nuisance variables at a constant value throughout an experiment, by introducing important nuisance variables as a fundamental part of the experimental design, or by transforming systematic variation into unsystematic variation through randomization procedures. I will consider randomization later in this chapter.

Subjects

The critical issues concerning the subjects tested in an experiment are their nature and their number. What sort of subjects should you use for your experiment? How many subjects should you include in each treatment condition? The first question is usually answered by the overall purpose of the research. The most obvious decision is between animal and human subjects. But what sorts of animals, of what ages, of what early training or experience? Similar issues are relevant in research with humans. Undoubtedly, theoretical considerations will generally have an important impact on the eventual selection of subjects. Your decision might also be influenced by the relative cost or availability of subjects—for example, choosing animals from a departmental breeding stock rather than from a commercial laboratory supplier or using student volunteers enrolled in introductory psychology classes rather than paid subjects.

The question concerning the number of subjects required is usually unanswerable, for the simple reason that many factors influence the answer and some of these factors are generally unknown. Sometimes control features of the experimental design set the ultimate number. For example, suppose that the basic task presented to all subjects requires a series of judgments of stimuli presented in succession. Most researchers would present the stimuli in different orders to different subjects in order to avoid serial-order biases. If nine orders were constructed, the number of subjects required per condition would be some multiple of 9—9, 18, 27—assuming that each order was used an equal number of times.

The primary factor, however, is the desired sensitivity of the experiment in providing an adequate test of the research hypotheses. Sensitivity, known technically as **power** and discussed in Chapter 4, refers to the ability of an experiment to detect differences between treatment conditions when they are present. One way to increase the sensitivity in an experiment is to increase the number of subjects assigned to each condition. I will consider the problem of estimating sample size and other ways of increasing the sensitivity of an experiment in subsequent chapters.

1.3 CONTROL IN EXPERIMENTATION

In the ideal experiment, we can treat the subjects in the different conditions exactly alike in every respect except for the necessary variation of the independent variable. Unfortunately, this ideal experiment is never performed in real life. That is, it is virtually impossible to conduct an experiment where the *only* difference among treatment groups is the experimental manipulation. Nonetheless, we are still able to conduct experiments and to draw meaningful conclusions from them.

Let us see how this is accomplished. First, certain features can in fact be held constant across the levels of the experiment. All of the testing can be done in the same experimental room, by the same experimenter, and with the same equipment and testing procedures. Second, control of other features of the experiment, though *not* absolute, is sufficiently close to be considered essentially constant. Consider, for example, the mechanical devices that are used to hold various features of the environment constant. A thermostat, for instance, does not achieve an absolute control of the temperature at some fixed value, but it *reduces* the variation of the room temperature. An uncontrolled room would be subjected to a wider range of temperatures during the course of an experiment than a controlled room, but a variation will still be present. This variation may be sufficiently small to allow us to view the temperature as constant. Even with these features controlled, however, many variables remain uncontrolled that might influence the behavior we are studying.

I have not mentioned yet a major source of uncontrolled variability present in any experiment, namely, the differences in performance among subjects. One obvious way to hold subject differences constant is to use the *same* subject in each treatment condition—a sort of biological analogue of absolute physical control. Unfortunately, even the same subject is not the same person each time he or she is tested. Moreover, there are potentially serious carry-over effects from one treatment to another, resulting from the successive administration of the different treatments to the same subjects. To avoid this problem, we could try to *match* sets of subjects on important characteristics and then assign one member of each matched set to a different treatment, but matching would never be exact. Thus, neither attempt to control for individual differences among subjects guarantees that the treatment groups will contain subjects of the same average ability.

Control by Randomization

These considerations lead us to an alternative method for dealing with the problem of control. Specifically, it consists of an elimination of *systematic* differences among the treatment conditions by means of **randomization**. Consider again the control of room temperature. What might we do about controlling the temperature if the room were *not* equipped with a thermostat? We could try to match sets of subjects arriving at different times for the experiment, but for whom the temperature of the room is the same, and then place one of the subjects in one group, one in another group, and so on. But this is an unrealistic and cumbersome procedure. Suppose, instead, that we decide which of the different treatments a subject will receive by some random means at the time of his or her arrival for the experiment and that we continue to use this method until we have obtained the number of subjects we planned to run in each of the treatment conditions. What happens to the different room temperatures in this case? In a sense, the different temperatures of the experimental room have an equally likely "chance" at the start of each testing session of being assigned to *any one of the treatment levels*. If we follow this procedure with enough subjects, statistical theory tells us that the *average* room temperatures for the treatment groups will be equal. Under these circumstances, then, we will have effected a control of room temperature.

That is fine for temperature, but what about other features of the testing environment which also change from session to session? It may not be immediately apparent, but once we have controlled *one* environmental feature by randomization, we have controlled *all* other environmental differences as well. Suppose we list some of the characteristics of the testing session present during the very first session in the experiment. The room will be at a certain temperature; there will be a certain humidity; the room illumination will be at a particular level; the noise from the outside filtering into the room will be of a certain intensity; the experiment will be given at a particular time of day, on a particular day, and by a particular experimenter; and so on.

When the experiment is about to begin, we choose a particular experimental treatment for the first subject in some random fashion. What this means is that at this point each of the treatment conditions has an equally likely chance of being the one chosen for the first experimental session. The implication is that the total composite of features which happens to be present at the time has an equally likely chance of being "assigned" to each of the experimental treatments. We come next to the second experimental session. The total composite of features present at the second session will be different from the one present at the first. The room will be at a different temperature, the noise level may not be the same, the session will be at a different time of day, and so on. Before the start of the session, we again choose randomly which treatment we will present. As with the first session, the composite of features present this time has an equally likely chance of being associated with each of the treatments.

Suppose this argument is continued until all of the subjects have been assigned to treatment conditions in the experiment. Then each and every feature of the experimental situation, which varies from session to session, has been assigned randomly to the different treatment conditions. There was no systematic bias leading to the running of one condition at the same time of day or only in warm rooms or only when the lights were bright, or whatever. The assignment of the testing sessions to the experimental conditions in a random fashion eliminates from the experiment the possibility of systematic biases involving any of these factors.

Subject differences are also "controlled" by randomization. The subjects who are chosen to participate in an experiment will differ widely on a host of characteristics. Some of these will affect the behavior being studied and, hence, must be controlled. Suppose we could give all of our subjects numbers that represent their general abilities to perform on the sort of task being studied. This number will be a composite score, reflecting the influence of intelligence, emotionality, attitude, background and training, and so on. Now suppose that we assign the subjects to the different treatment conditions randomly. Subjects with high composite scores are just as likely to be assigned to one of the treatments as to any of the others. The same is true for subjects with low and with medium composite scores. Thus, random assignment of subjects to treatments will ensure in the long run that there will be an equivalence of subjects across the different treatments.

Suppose we take one final step in this argument. Somehow we select the first subject who will be run in the experiment; this may be the first subject who shows up as a volunteer for the experiment or the rat in the first cage that we come to. When we randomly assign this subject to one of the treatment conditions, we are essentially assigning *jointly* the subject *and* the environmental factors. By assigning the subject randomly to the treatment conditions, then, we are assigning randomly *all* of the ability and environmental factors as well—whatever the combination of ability and environmental factors may be for this subject. Therefore, randomization of subjects in the assignment to conditions is an indispensable method of guaranteeing that in the long run the treatment conditions will be matched on all environmental factors and subject abilities.

A serious problem presented by this argument has undoubtedly occurred to you. Specifically, we *never* run a sufficiently large number of subjects in our experiment to qualify for the statistician's definition of the "long run." In practice, we are operating in the "short run," meaning that we have no guarantee that our groups will be equivalent with regard to differences in environmental features or to differences in the abilities of subjects. I will consider this problem in Chapter 2.

Methods of Randomization

Because of the fundamental importance of randomization to the design and analysis of experiments, I will consider in detail methods by which randomization may be accomplished. Whatever method we use, we must be able to argue that *all* factors not involved in the manipulation of the independent variable have been neutralized by randomization. As an example, suppose we conduct an experiment with three treatment conditions and we plan to run a total of 30 subjects in the experiment. For the first subject who shows up, we will determine which treatment he or she receives by some random process.[2] The treatment given to the second subject is determined in the same manner. This procedure is followed until all 30 subjects have served in the experiment. Note that *each subject* is randomly assigned to a treatment and *each testing session* is randomly assigned to a treatment. The critical features of the random assignment, then, are that each subject-session combination is *equally likely* to be assigned to any one of the three treatments and that the assignment of each subject is *independent* of that of the others. Following this procedure, then, we guarantee that each of the treatment conditions is equally likely to be assigned to a given subject and to whatever other uncontrolled factors might be present during any period of testing.[3]

In actual practice, we would probably place a *restriction* on this random procedure of assigning treatments to subjects in order to ensure an *equal number* of subjects in each treatment condition. (Reasons for this decision are considered in Chapter 5) When human subjects are appearing in the laboratory at their own convenience, i.e., at a time that they choose, a typical approach is to make the random assignments so that any given treatment selected is not run again until all of the other treatments are represented *once*. In effect, this is a procedure of sampling without replacement. In the example, we would decide randomly which of the three treatments to administer to the first subject. For the second subject, we would randomly select the treatment from the two remaining treatments. For the third subject, we must administer the final, remaining treatment, since there are only three treatments in the experiment. This completes a *block* of randomized treatments. The treatment given to the fourth subject is decided by selecting randomly from the *total pool* of treatments, i.e., three; the treatment given to the fifth subject is decided by selecting randomly from the remaining two treatments; and so on.

It is generally advisable to work with the smallest possible block, just as we did in the last paragraph. There is a good reason for following such a proce-

---

[2]If there were only two treatment conditions, the treatment selected could be determined by the flip of a coin. If more than two conditions are included in the experiment, we usually give each condition a different number and then refer to tables of random numbers, which provide a source of random sequences of digits. Such tables may be found in many statistics texts and in experimental psychology texts. There are also books of random numbers available, such as Moses and Oakford (1963) and a book published by the RAND Corporation (1955). The tables published in Moses and Oakford are especially useful, since they include random permutations of number sets of different sizes. For example, if there are 30 things that we want to randomize, it is far easier to use a random ordering of the numbers 1 to 50, say, and to select from that ordering the numbers 1 to 30, than it is to work through a random sequence of digits, two at a time, searching for the first occurrence of each one of these numbers.

[3]The importance of independent assignment is often overlooked. Consider, for example, deciding by some random method what to do with the entire first third of the subjects and assigning them en masse to the same condition, and continuing in this manner for the remaining subjects. Such a procedure will not satisfactorily control the nuisance variables operating in an experiment.

dure. We can think of two general classes of variables which must be controlled in any experiment: those which really do fluctuate randomly from session to session and those which do not. We do not have to worry about the first class of variables—even if we run all the subjects in one treatment first and all the subjects in another treatment second, the particular values of these variables at each testing session by definition occur randomly. Thus, we turn to randomization to control the second class of variables, variables which do not fluctuate haphazardly.

We are usually unable to specify ahead of time exactly what the cycles of fluctuation will be; however, we merely assume that they will be present. For example, subjects volunteering for an experiment do not represent a random flow of participants. There are undoubtedly different reasons why a subject volunteers early in the school term rather than late, and these reasons may reflect differences in abilities. The first subjects may be overly anxious or curious or smarter—who knows? The point is that we cannot assume that the flow of volunteers is random. Nor is the fluctuation of room temperature or of time of day or of noise level outside the testing room random. Randomizing in small blocks "helps" this control by ensuring that a block of three subjects, say, representing each treatment once, will not be placed in a room that is too different in temperature. Or three subjects appearing one after the other are more likely to have the same reason for volunteering at that time than would three subjects who do not appear in close sequence.

It is not sufficient, however, just to introduce some sort of randomization in the testing order. To make the randomization work, we must choose a method which guarantees that features of the experimental situation and differences in the abilities of the subjects are not allowed to exert a *systematic* influence in the experiment. Any factor which does not vary randomly in its "natural state" must be subjected to a process of **neutralization**, consisting in essence of the superimposition of a random process upon the assignment of testing sessions and subjects to the treatment conditions. That is, variables that fluctuate in a systematic fashion during the course of the experiment must be transformed into variables that now fluctuate *unsystematically* with respect to their association with the treatment conditions.

Random Assignment Versus Random Sampling

I should say a few words about the distinction between the **random assignment** of subjects to conditions and the **random sampling** of subjects from a known population.

Random sampling requires the specification of a population of subjects and then the assurance that each member of the population has an equally likely chance of being selected for the experiment. If these conditions are met, we will be able to *generalize* the results of our experiment to the population. It should be noted that even if we are able to obtain our subjects by randomly sampling from a population, we will still have to turn to randomization procedures in the assignment of treatments to subjects and to testing sessions. That is, even randomly selected subjects will come to the experiment one at a time and then be given one of the treatment conditions. Who receives which treatment must be determined by chance; otherwise, a systematic bias may result, and this bias will be damaging to any experiment whether the subjects are selected randomly from a population or not.

What about random sampling? Public opinion polls, voter preference polls, marketing research, and television ratings all depend upon random sampling from a known population. Any findings from the sample are then extended to the population. Only rarely will we see random sampling in an experiment, however. And when we do, the population from which the sample was drawn may be so restricted as to be uninteresting in itself, e.g., the rats in a laboratory animal colony, the students at a university taking a course in introductory psychology, or third-grade children in a particular school system. Almost invariably, our subjects are selected out of *convenience,* rather than at random. The failure to sample randomly from a known population means that we are not justified *statistically* in extending our results beyond the bounds of the experiment itself.

Since most researchers accept this "myopic" view of the results of an experiment, how can we ever discover results that *are* generalizable to a meaningful population of organisms? One answer is that past research in a number of laboratories with subjects chosen from different sources (e.g., different breeding stocks, different suppliers of laboratory animals, and human subjects from different schools in different sections of the country) have shown that these differences are relatively unimportant in the study of various phenomena. Knowing this, an investigator working in this field may feel safe in generalizing the results beyond the single experiment.

The distinction, then, is between a *statistical* generalization, which depends upon random sampling, and a *nonstatistical* generalization, which depends upon knowledge of a particular research area. Cornfield and Tukey (1956) make this point quite clear: "In almost any practical situation where analytical statistics is applied, the inference from the observations to the real conclusion has two parts, only the first of which is statistical. A genetic experiment on *Drosophila* will usually involve flies of a certain race of a certain species. The statistically based conclusions cannot extend beyond this race, yet the geneticist will usually, and often wisely, extend the conclusion to (a) the whole species, (b) all *Drosophila,* or (c) a larger group of insects. This wider extension may be implicit or explicit, but it is almost always present" (pp. 912-913). Edgington (1966) makes a similar point.

In short, the generalizability of a given set of results is influenced by statistical considerations, such as the question of random sampling. For most experimenters, however, the extension of a set of findings to a broader class of subjects (or conditions for that matter) is dictated primarily by subject-matter considerations, i.e., what is known in a particular field of research about the *appropriateness* of certain generalizations and the "length" of these generalizations. The availability of this information will depend on the state of development of the research area and the extent to which extrapolations beyond the particular subjects tested have been successful in the past.

1.4 BASIC EXPERIMENTAL DESIGNS

One useful feature of the procedures we will use to analyze experiments is the fact that the more complex designs are created from considerably simpler ones. In this book, I will cover the most common designs used in the behavioral sciences, taking advantage of the building-block nature of experimental design. In this final section, we will take a look at three basic designs as a preview of the remainder of this book. I will start by describing two designs in which a single independent variable is manipulated, the so-called **single-factor designs**. (*Factor* has the same meaning as *independent variable*.)

Completely Randomized Design

The **completely randomized design** is characterized by the fact that subjects are randomly assigned to serve in one of the treatment conditions. Although it is not necessary, equal numbers of subjects are usually assigned to each of the treatment conditions. Since any differences in behavior observed among the treatment conditions are based on different groups of subjects, this sort of experimental arrangement is also known as a **between-subjects design**. Completely randomized designs are simpler to understand conceptually, easier to design and to analyze, and relatively free from restrictive statistical assumptions. The main disadvantages are the large number of subjects required and a relative lack of sensitivity in detecting treatment effects when they are present.

Randomized Block Design

One type of **randomized block design** uses blocks of subjects who are matched closely on some relevant characteristic, e.g., body weight if the subjects are laboratory animals or IQ if the subjects are human. Blocks differ, however, on the values of the matching characteristic used to group subjects in different blocks. Once the blocks are formed, subjects within each block are assigned randomly to the treatment conditions. This type of design is not very common in psychology.

A more common form of randomized block design is one in which each subject (a "block") serves in all of the treatment conditions. This type of design is commonly referred to in psychology as a **repeated-measures design**. The design is also known as a **within-subjects design**, because any differences in behavior observed among the treatment conditions are based on the *same* set of subjects; that is, treatment effects are represented by differences *within* the single group of subjects serving in the experiment.

A within-subjects design requires fewer subjects and is more sensitive than a corresponding completely randomized design. Problems with the design center around relatively restrictive statistical assumptions and the fact that subjects can change during the repeated service in all of the treatment conditions. A randomized block design with matching does not suffer from either of these problems, of course. On the other hand, matching is rarely as effective in increasing sensitivity as is the use of the same subjects in all conditions, and it is often difficult to form well-matched blocks of subjects when an experiment consists of a large number of treatment conditions.

Factorial Design

Factorial designs permit the manipulation of more than one independent variable in the same experiment. The arrangement of the treatment conditions is such that information can be obtained about the influence of each of the independent variables considered *separately* and about how the variables *combine jointly* to influence behavior. Factorial designs are widely used in psychological research, and for good reason. The design permits investigators to move beyond a single-dimensional view of behavior—the view provided by experiments with single independent variables—to a richer and more revealing multidimensional view.

The two single-factor designs described earlier in this section provide the building blocks with which factorial designs are constructed. There are three general possibilities. At one extreme, there is the **completely randomized factorial design**, in which each subject is assigned randomly to only *one* of the treatment conditions making up the basic factorial design. At the other extreme is the **randomized block factorial design**—in its within-subjects version—with each subject receiving *all* of the required treatment conditions in a randomized order. Between these two extremes, we find designs that represent a "mixture" of the two basic single-factor designs, in which subjects receive *some,* but not all, of the treatment conditions defined by the basic factorial. This type of design is usually called a **mixed factorial design** or a **split-plot design**.

Other Designs

I have only touched the surface. There are many more types of designs, each with a specialized function. I will cover the most common of these designs in this book. Kirk (1968, pp. 11-21; 1972, pp. 241-260) provides a useful classification scheme that describes a great number of experimental designs and the building blocks used in their construction that you may find useful not only to broaden your horizons but also to introduce you to the variety of experimental designs that are available to researchers in the behavioral sciences.

SINGLE-FACTOR EXPERIMENTS

A two-group experiment was used in Chapter 1 to illustrate the experimental method. In the not too distant past, this type of experiment represented the *modal* design in the behavioral sciences. Today, in its place, we see experiments in which a single independent variable is represented by more than two different treatments, and we find many cases in which two or more independent variables are manipulated concurrently in the same experiment.

The major reason for this increase in the complexity of the research is that the basic two-group design can only indicate the presence or the absence of treatment effects, while an experiment with more than two treatment conditions provides for a more *detailed* description of the relationship between variations in the independent variable and changes in behavior. Additionally, as our knowledge increases and more facts are established, our theoretical explanations of this knowledge become increasingly complicated and more elaborate designs are needed to test them. That is, in order to identify the mechanisms and processes that lie behind any given phenomenon, an experimenter frequently must increase the number of treatments and the number of independent variables that he or she includes in a single experiment.

In Part II I will consider the analysis of experiments in which there is a single classification of the treatment conditions. By this I mean that the different treatments are classified only one way, either on the basis of *qualitative* differences or on the basis of *quantitative* differences among the treatment conditions. Qualitative and quantitative independent variables were discussed in Chapter 1 (pp. 7–8). I will usually refer to either type of manipulation as a **factor** and to the specific treatment conditions represented in an experiment as the **levels** of a factor. In this book, I will also use the terms **levels**, **treatments**, and **treatment levels** interchangeably.

The general purpose of the single-factor experiment may be illustrated by means of a simple example. Suppose that we wanted to compare the relative effectiveness of 10 different methods of teaching a foreign language in elementary school and that we had no particular reason to expect any one method to be better than any other. How might we analyze the results of this experiment? One procedure would be to treat each of the possible two-group comparisons as a different *two-group experiment.* That is, we would compare method 1 versus methods 2, 3, ..., 9, and 10; method 2 versus methods 3, 4, ..., 9, and 10; ...; method 8 versus methods 9 and 10; and, finally, method 9 versus method 10. There are 45 of these two-group comparisons. Obviously, this sort of analysis would require a considerable amount of calculation. Moreover, we should be concerned with the fact that we are using the same sets of data over and over again to make these comparisons. (Actually, we are using each group a total of nine times.) We cannot think of these comparisons as constituting 45 *independent* experiments; if one group is distorted for some reason or other, this distortion will be present in all nine of the comparisons in which it enters.

The single-factor analysis of variance allows us to consider all of the treatments in a *single* assessment. Without going into the details, this analysis sets in *perspective* any interpretations we may want to make concerning the differences we have observed. More specifically, the analysis will tell us whether or not it will be worthwhile to conduct any additional analyses comparing specific treatment groups.

I will first consider the logic behind the analysis of variance, and then worry about translating these intuitive notions into mathematical expressions and actual numbers.

2

Specifying Sources of Variability

As described in Chapter 1, the first step in testing a research hypothesis is to design an experiment in which the influence of known and of unknown variables is minimized. If uncontrolled, such variables could result in a systematic bias, that is, a confounding with the independent variable. While it is possible to control nuisance variables by holding them constant, the most common procedure is to spread their effects randomly over all the treatment conditions. Unfortunately, however, the use of randomization to control the operation of nuisance variables—which is nearly unavoidable in experimentation—creates a new problem: Differences observed among the treatment means are influenced jointly by the actual differences in the treatments administered to the different groups *and* by chance factors introduced by randomization. The decision confronting the experimenter is to decide whether the differences associated with the treatment conditions are *entirely* or just *partly* due to chance. I will now consider, in general terms, a statistical solution to this disturbing problem.

2.1 THE LOGIC OF HYPOTHESIS TESTING

Suppose we have just completed collecting the data from an experiment. As a first step in the analysis of the data, summary or descriptive statistics are calculated for each treatment condition—usually measures of "average" performance (the mean). Generally, we are not *primarily* interested merely in describing the performance of subjects in the different treatment conditions. Our main goal is to make *inferences* about the behavior of subjects who have not been tested in our experiment. Rarely will we choose to test all possible subjects in an experiment, such as all laboratory rats of a particular strain, or all college students enrolled in an introductory psychology class at a particular university. Instead, we select samples from these larger groups, administer the experimental conditions to these samples, and make inferences about the nature of the population on the basis of the experimental outcome. We refer to these large groups as **populations.** Members of any population are identified by a set of rules of membership. A **sample** consists of a smaller set of observations drawn from the population. In order to be able to generalize back to the population in a strict statistical sense, we must select the subjects constituting the sample randomly from the population. Summary descriptions calculated from the data of a sample are called **statistics,** while measures calculated from all of the observations within the population are called **parameters.** In most cases, I will use Roman letters to designate statistics and Greek letters to designate parameters.

At this point, we can view the subjects in the treatment conditions as representing samples drawn from different treatment populations. Statistics, calculated on the scores obtained from the different groups of subjects, provide us with estimates of one or more parameters for the different treatment populations. We are now ready to consider the formal process of hypothesis testing, where the research hypothesis is translated into a set of **statistical hypotheses,** which are then evaluated in light of the obtained data.

Statistical Hypotheses

A research hypothesis is a fairly general statement about the assumed nature of the world that gets translated into an experiment. (Typically, but not always, a research hypothesis asserts that the treatments *will* produce an effect. If it did not, we would probably not have performed the experiment in the first place!) Statistical hypotheses consist of a set of precise hypotheses about the parameters of the different treatment populations. Two statistical hypotheses are usually stated, and these are mutually exclusive or incompatible statements about the treatment parameters.

The statistical hypothesis which will be *tested* is called the **null hypothesis**, often symbolized as H_0. The function of the null hypothesis is to specify the values of a particular parameter (the mean, for example) in the different treatment populations (symbolized as μ_1, μ_2, μ_3, and so on). The null hypothesis typically chosen gives the *same* value to the different populations—i.e.,

$$H_0 : \mu_1 = \mu_2 = \mu_3 = \text{etc.}$$

This is tantamount to saying that *no* treatment effects are present in the population. If the parameter estimates obtained from the treatment groups are too deviant from those specified by the null hypothesis, H_0 is rejected in favor of the other statistical hypothesis, called the **alternative hypothesis**, H_1. The alternative hypothesis specifies values for the parameter that are *incompatible* with the null hypothesis. Usually, the alternative hypothesis states simply that the values of the parameter in the different treatment populations are *not* all equal. Specifically,

$$H_1 : \text{not all } \mu\text{'s are equal.}$$

A decision to reject H_0 implies an acceptance of H_1, which, in essence, constitutes support of our original *research* hypothesis. On the other hand, if the parameter estimates are reasonably close to those specified by the null hypothesis, H_0 is not rejected. This latter decision can be thought of as a failure of the experiment to support the research hypothesis. You will see in a later discussion that a decision to reject or not to reject the null hypothesis is not all that simple. Depending upon the true state of the world, i.e., the equality or inequality of the actual population means, we can make an error of inference with *either* decision, rejection or nonrejection. (More will be said about these errors in Chapter 3.)

Experimental Error

At the crux of the problem is the fact that we can always attribute some portion of the differences we observe among treatment means to chance factors. All uncontrolled sources of variability in our experiment are considered potential contributors to **experimental error**. In the behavioral sciences, the most important source of experimental error is that due to individual differences. In Chapter 1, I also mentioned variations in the various features of the testing environment as contributing to uncontrolled variability. Another source of experimental error is what may be called *measurement error.* A misreading of a dial, a misjudgment that a particular type of behavior has occurred, the variability in reaction time of an experimenter timing a given bit of behavior, and an error in transposing observations recorded in the laboratory to summary worksheets used in performing the statistical analyses are all included in this classification. While it is not obvious, a given experimental treatment is not exactly the same for each subject serving in that treatment condition; the experimental apparatus cannot be counted on to administer the same treatment for successive subjects. An experimenter cannot construct an identical testing environment (the reading of instructions, the experimenter-subject interaction, and so on) for all subjects in any treatment group. We describe all these different components of experimental error as *unsystematic,* stressing the fact that their influence is *independent* of the treatment effects.

Estimates of Experimental Error

Suppose we were able to estimate the extent to which the differences we observe among the group means are due to experimental error. We would then be in a position to begin to consider the evaluation of the hypothesis that the means of the treatment populations are equal. Consider the scores of subjects in any one of the treatment conditions. We certainly do not expect these scores to be equal. In the *ideal* experiment they would be. In an *actual* experiment, of course, all of the sources of uncontrolled variability will also contribute to a subject's score, resulting in a difference in performance for subjects who are administered the same treatment condition. The variability of subjects treated alike, i.e., within the same treatment level, provides an estimate of experimental error. By the same argument, the variability of subjects within each of the other treatment levels also offers estimates of experimental error. If we assume that experimental error is the same for the different treatment conditions, we can obtain a more stable estimate of this quantity by pooling and averaging these separate estimates.

Assume that we have drawn random samples from a population of subjects, administered the different treatments, recorded the performance of the subjects, and calculated the means of the treatment groups. Further, assume for the moment that the null hypothesis is *true*—that the population means associated with the treatment conditions are *equal.* Would we expect the *sample* means, the means calculated in the experiment, to be equal? Certainly not. From our discussion of the use of randomization to "control" unwanted factors in our experiment, it should be clear that the means will rarely be equal. If the sample means are not equal, the only reasonable explanation that we can offer for these differences is the operation of experimental error. All of the sources of unsystematic variability, which contribute to the differences among subjects within a given treatment condition, will also be operating to produce differences among the sample means.

Take, for instance, error that results from the random assignment of subjects to treatments. If the procedure is truly random, each subject will have an equal chance of being assigned to any one of the different treatments. But this in no way *guarantees* that the average ability of subjects assigned to these groups is equal. Similarly, for the other contributors to experimental error, there is no reason to expect these uncontrolled sources of error to balance out perfectly across the treatment conditions. In short, then, under these circumstances—an experiment conducted when the null hypothesis is true—differences among the sample means will also reflect the operation of experimental error.

Estimate of Treatment Effects

So far in this discussion I have considered only the case in which the null hypothesis is true. Certainly we hope that we will discover at least a few situations in which the null hypothesis is *false*! Under these circumstances, there are real differences among the means of the treatment populations. Assuming that the subjects in each treatment group are drawn randomly from corresponding treatment populations, the means of the different groups in the experiment should reflect the differences in the population means. The mere fact that the null hypothesis is false does *not* imply that experimental error has vanished, however. Not at all. The only change is that there is now an additional component contributing to the differences among the means, a systematic component as opposed to an unsystematic one, namely, **treatment effects**.

Thus, differences among treatment means may reflect *two different quantities*: When the population means are equal, the differences among the group means will reflect the operation of experimental error alone, but when the population means are not equal, the differences among the group means will reflect the operation of an unsystematic component and a systematic component, i.e., experimental error and treatment effects, respectively.

Evaluation of the Null Hypothesis

You have seen that when the null hypothesis is true, we will have two estimates of experimental error available from the experiment. If we form a *ratio* of these two estimates, we will find that we have produced a useful statistic. More specifically, consider the following ratio:

$$\frac{\text{differences among treatment means}}{\text{differences among subjects treated alike}}.$$

From this discussion, we can think of this ratio as contrasting an estimate of experimental error, which is based upon differences between groups with an estimate of experimental error, which is based upon pooled differences within groups.

That is, we have

$$\frac{\text{experimental error}}{\text{experimental error}}.$$

If we were to repeat this experiment a large number of times on new samples of subjects drawn from the same population, we would expect to find an average value of this ratio of approximately 1.0.

Consider now the same ratio when the null hypothesis is *false*. Under these circumstances, there is an additional component in the numerator, one which reflects the treatment effects. Explicitly, the ratio becomes

$$\frac{(\text{treatment effects}) + (\text{experimental error})}{\text{experimental error}}.$$

Given this situation, if we were to repeat the experiment a large number of times, we would expect to find an average value of this ratio that is *greater* than 1.0.

You can see, then, that the average value of this ratio, obtained from a large number of replications of the experiment, depends upon the values of the population means. If H_0 is true (i.e., the means are equal), the average value will approximate 1.0; while if H_1 is true (i.e., the means are not equal), the average value will approximate a number greater than 1.0. A problem remains, however, since in any one experiment, it is always possible to obtain a value that is *greater* than 1.0 when H_0 is *true* and one that is *equal* to or *less* than 1.0 when H_1 is *true*! Thus, merely checking to see whether the ratio is greater than 1.0 does not tell us which statistical hypothesis is correct.

What we will do about this is to make a decision concerning the acceptability of the null hypothesis which is based upon a consideration of the chance probability associated with the ratio we actually found in the experiment. If the probability of obtaining by chance a ratio of this size or larger is reasonably low, we will reject the null hypothesis. On the other hand, if this probability is high, we will not reject, or, in essence, we will accept the null hypothesis. (I will have more to say about the **decision rules** we follow in making this decision in Chapter 3.)

2.2 THE COMPONENT DEVIATIONS

In the remainder of this chapter, you will see the abstract notions of between-groups and within-groups variability become concrete arithmetic operations extracted from scores produced in single-factor experiments. The next chapter indicates how this information is used to provide a test of the null hypothesis.

Suppose we were interested in the effect on reading comprehension of three different instructions. One group of children is asked to attempt to memorize an essay; a second group is asked to concentrate on the ideas in the essay; and a third group is given no specific instructions. I will refer to the independent variable, types of instructions, as **factor** A and to the three levels of factor A (the three different instructional conditions) as levels a_1, a_2, and a_3. The subjects are drawn from a fourth-grade class, and we randomly assign $s = 5$ different subjects to each of the levels of factor A. All subjects are allowed to study the essay for 10 minutes, after which time they are given an objective test to determine their comprehension of the passage. The response measure, i.e., the score for each subject, is the number of test items correctly answered.

Our first step in the analysis would be to compute the means for the three sets of scores and to compare them. As explained previously, we cannot conclude that any differences among the group means represent the "real" effects of the different experimental treatments: the differences may have resulted from experimental error, the short-term siding of uncontrolled sources of variability with one treatment condition or another. You saw that the solution to this problem is to compare the differences among the group means against the differences obtained from subjects within each of the individual groups. Let us see how this is accomplished.

The three sets of scores are listed in the first column of Table 2-1. The means for the different treatment conditions are 15, 6, and 9 for conditions 1 to 3, respectively. The grand mean of all three conditions, obtained by summing all scores in the experiment and dividing by the total number of scores (15 in this case), is equal to 10. For the moment, I will focus on the worst score in condition a_2, which is two correct test responses on the objective test given following the presentation of the essay. I will represent this score as AS_{25}, where the first subscript specifies the level of factor A (a_2 in this case) and the second subscript indicates the subject's ordinal position in the original listing of the scores. This subject happens to be the fifth score in level a_2 as listed in Table 2-1. (I will discuss the notational system in the next section.)

Consider now the deviation of this score (AS_{25}) from the grand mean, symbolized as $\bar{T}$. This deviation ($AS_{25} - \bar{T}$) is represented geometrically at the bottom of Fig. 2-1 as the distance between the two vertical lines drawn from this score ($AS_{25} = 2$) on the left and the grand mean ($\bar{T} = 10$) on the right, respec-

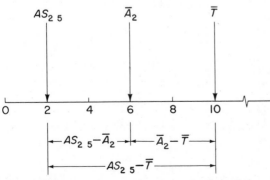

FIGURE 2-1.   Geometric representation of the component deviations.

tively. Consider next the vertical line drawn through the group mean for condition a_2 $(\bar{A}_2 = 6)$. From the figure, it is obvious that this deviation is made up of *two components*. One component consists of the deviation of the score from the mean of the group from which it was selected, that is, $AS_{25} - \bar{A}_2$, the component deviation on the left. The other component consists of the deviation of the group mean from the grand mean, that is, $\bar{A}_2 - \bar{T}$, the component deviation on the right. This relationship may be written as

$$AS_{25} - \bar{T} = (\bar{A}_2 - \bar{T}) + (AS_{25} - \bar{A}_2).$$

We can give each of the three deviations a name:

$AS_{25} - \bar{T}$ is called the **total deviation**.

$\bar{A}_2 - \bar{T}$ is called the **between-groups deviation**.

$AS_{25} - \bar{A}_2$ is called the **within-groups deviation**.

This subdividing of the total deviation—or **partitioning** as it is called—is illustrated with actual numbers in Table 2-1 under the heading, "Level a_2." To illustrate again for the fifth subject, AS_{25}, we have

$$AS_{25} - \bar{T} = (\bar{A}_2 - \bar{T}) + (AS_{25} - \bar{A}_2).$$

Table 2-1   Analysis of Component Deviation Scores

SCORE	Total $(AS_{ij} - \bar{T})$		Between $(\bar{A}_i - \bar{T})$	+	Within $(AS_{ij} - \bar{A}_i)$
			LEVEL a_1		
16	(6)	=	(5)	+	(1)
18	(8)	=	(5)	+	(3)
10	(0)	=	(5)	+	(−5)
12	(2)	=	(5)	+	(−3)
19	(9)	=	(5)	+	(4)
			LEVEL a_2		
4	(−6)	=	(−4)	+	(−2)
6	(−4)	=	(−4)	+	(0)
8	(−2)	=	(−4)	+	(2)
10	(0)	=	(−4)	+	(4)
2	(−8)	=	(−4)	+	(−4)
			LEVEL a_3		
2	(−8)	=	(−1)	+	(−7)
10	(0)	=	(−1)	+	(1)
9	(−1)	=	(−1)	+	(0)
13	(3)	=	(−1)	+	(4)
11	(1)	=	(−1)	+	(2)

Substituting numbers for symbols ($AS_{25} = 2, \bar{A}_2 = 6$, and $\bar{T} = 10$), we find

$$2 - 10 = (6 - 10) + (2 - 6),$$

and

$$-8 = (-4) + (-4).$$

Table 2-1 summarizes these calculations for each of the five subjects in this group. A similar partitioning can be conducted for each of the subjects in the other two groups. These are also summarized in the table.

Thus, you have seen that the score for each subject in an experiment can be expressed as a deviation from the grand mean and that this deviation can be partitioned into two components, a between-groups deviation and a within-groups deviation. These two component deviations are what we have been after, a quantity that will reflect treatment effects in the population (the between-groups deviation), in addition to experimental error, and a quantity that will reflect experimental error alone (within-groups deviation). In a moment, you will see how these deviations are translated into measures of variability.

2.3 NOTATION

Before presenting the different formulas, I should say a few words about the notational system adopted for this book. The basic job of any notational system is to express unambiguously the arithmetic operations in the most complex of designs as well as in the simplest. Unfortunately, most notational systems produce computational formulas that are difficult for students and researchers to read and to translate into action. The system used in this book is designed specifically for the analysis of experiments. Unfortunately, it will probably be different from notational systems you have encountered in introductory courses and in other books. Students report resenting the new system at first and resisting learning it—often translating the specified calculations into their old system—but invariably appreciate the system when they turn to more complex designs.

There are three major advantages of this system. First, the system uses different capital letters or different combinations of letters to designate basic quantities required in the analysis. The confusion generated by the usual notational system of subscripts, parentheses, and multiple summation signs with subscripts and superscripts is avoided, and the differences in the arithmetical operations are emphasized and made more distinct. Second, the system is designed to facilitate the reiterative computational sequences that are a part of the various calculations. As you will see in Chapter 10, the notational system works in conjunction with a general analysis scheme that can be applied to nearly all of the designs I will consider in this book. Finally, the system is similar to that used by Winer in his useful and authoritative *Statistical Principles in Experimental Design* (1971), a standard reference for researchers in psychology.[1]

A notational system is essentially a code. The symbols constitute a shorthand for specifying the operations to be performed on the data of an experiment. In the analysis of the completely randomized single-factor design, we need to designate only *three* basic quantities: the individual scores or observations (the *raw data*), the sum of these scores for each treatment condition (the *treatment sums* or *subtotals*), and the sum of all the scores or observations (the *grand sum* or *grand total*).

The Individual Scores

Each subject provides us with a single numerical value that reflects his or her performance on the response measure. This basic score is designated by a symbol consisting of two capital letters, AS. The use of the two letters emphasizes the fact that reference is being made to a quantity that is specified by *two* classifications, namely, a classification with respect both to the level of factor A (the A part of the symbol) and to an individual subject in that particular treatment condition (the S part of the symbol). Table 2-2 illustrates the use of the AS notation with numbers obtained from the numerical example of Table 2-1. I have used subscripts so that it is possible to specify each score uniquely. The first number designates the level of factor A and the second number designates the particular subject within that treatment condition. The order of these subscripts, treatment first and subject second, is identical to the order of the two capital letters, AS. To refer to a score without specifying any particular one, I use the two letters without a subscript, AS, or occasionally with letters as subscripts, AS_{ij}. Because the scores within the body of the total matrix of scores are each designated AS, I will refer to the display as an AS **matrix**.

The Treatment Sums

As a first step in the analysis, we will calculate the sums of the scores in each of the treatment groups. These subtotals, or treatment sums, are designated by a capital A to stand for the sums of the scores obtained under the levels of factor A. A numerical subscript permits the specification of the treatment sum for a particular treatment condition. The meaning of this symbol and the subscript are illustrated in Table 2-2. To designate a treatment sum without specifying any sum in particular, I will use A without a subscript, or occasionally with an i as a subscript: A_i. As a numerical example, the respective treatment sums for the three

---

[1]Appendix C-1 provides a direct comparison between standard notation and the present one. It was prepared to facilitate the transition from the more common system to the one we are about to consider and to assist you in reading other advanced texts after you have mastered the present system.

Table 2-2   A Summary of the Notational System

VALUE BEING DESIGNATED	FACTOR A		
	Level a_1	Level a_2	Level a_3
Basic scores or observations	$AS_{11} = 16$ $AS_{12} = 18$ $AS_{13} = 10$ $AS_{14} = 12$ $AS_{15} = 19$	$AS_{21} = 4$ $AS_{22} = 6$ $AS_{23} = 8$ $AS_{24} = 10$ $AS_{25} = 2$	$AS_{31} = 2$ $AS_{32} = 10$ $AS_{33} = 9$ $AS_{34} = 13$ $AS_{35} = 11$
Treatment sums	$A_1 = 75$	$A_2 = 30$	$A_3 = 45$
Grand sum	$T = \Sigma A = 75 + 30 + 45 = 150$		

groups at levels a_1, a_2, and a_3 are

$$A_1 = 16 + 18 + 10 + 12 + 19 = 75;$$

$$A_2 = 4 + 6 + 8 + 10 + 2 = 30;$$

and

$$A_3 = 2 + 10 + 9 + 13 + 11 = 45.$$

To obtain a numerical summary of the outcome of the experiment, we use the treatment sums to calculate the **treatment means**, $\bar{A}$, by dividing each treatment sum by the number of scores in each of the conditions. In this book, I use a lower-case s to designate **sample size**, i.e., the number of subjects in a treatment condition.[2] Thus, the formula for a treatment mean is

$$\bar{A} = \frac{A}{s}. \tag{2-1}$$

To refer to specific treatment means, I use the number subscript. From the data in Table 2-2,

$$\bar{A}_1 = \frac{A_1}{s} = \frac{75}{5} = 15.00;$$

$$\bar{A}_2 = \frac{A_2}{s} = \frac{30}{5} = 6.00;$$

and

$$\bar{A}_3 = \frac{A_3}{s} = \frac{45}{5} = 9.00.$$

[2]In most of the designs I will consider, equal sample sizes (s) are used in the treatment conditions. Although this represents a special case, it subsumes most of the experiments conducted in the behavioral sciences. The analysis of unequal sample sizes is presented in Chap. 15.

The Grand Sum

I designate the **grand sum** of the scores—i.e., the sum of all of the scores in the experiment—as T. Computationally, T may be calculated by summing the entire set of AS scores or by summing the treatment subtotals (A). Expressing these operations in symbols,

$$T = \Sigma \, AS = \Sigma \, A.$$

(The large Greek letter Σ, sigma, is read, "the sum of . . ." Thus, $\Sigma \, AS$ is read, "the sum of the AS scores," and $\Sigma \, A$ is read, "the sum of the A treatment totals.") When we translate this sum into a mean (the **grand mean**), the mean is designated $\bar{T}$. We calculate $\bar{T}$ as we would any arithmetic mean, by dividing the sum of the scores by the number of scores. This number can be calculated by multiplying the number of scores (s) in each treatment group by the number of treatment groups, which we will designate a. In symbols, the total number of scores is $a \times s$, or $(a)(s)$, and the grand mean is

$$\bar{T} = \frac{T}{(a)(s)}. \tag{2-2}$$

From the numbers in Table 2-2, where $T = 75 + 30 + 45 = 150$, $a = 3$ treatment groups, and $s = 5$ subjects per group,

$$\bar{T} = \frac{150}{(3)(5)} = 10.00.$$

Comments

You should study the notational system summarized and illustrated in Table 2-2 until you are comfortable with the meaning of the different symbols. It may be helpful to point out the following characteristics of the system:

1. Capital letters always refer to *data,* either individual scores or sums obtained from the scores. Thus, AS, A, and T represent different facets of the data, namely, the individual scores, the treatment-group sums, and the grand sum, respectively.
2. Capital letters listed *together* are part of the symbol and do *not* specify multiplication. The symbol AS represents a score of a subject in one of the treatment conditions; the symbol does *not* ask us to multiply A by S.
3. A single summation sign means that *all* such quantities are to be included in the summation. Additional notation will be required if I must specify the summation of a portion of the total set. I will point out these complications when we come to them.
4. Lower-case letters refer to numbers, either the number of levels of an independent variable ($a = 3$ in Table 2-2) or the number of subjects in a treatment condition ($s = 5$ in Table 2-2). Since these symbols *do* refer to numbers, they *can* be used to specify multiplication; to emphasize this property, I will use parentheses to make this point clear. Thus, $(a)(s)$ specifies

the total number of subjects in an experiment, which is obtained by multiplying the number of subjects in each group (s) by the number of groups (a). (In contrast, you will recall from above that capital letters do *not* multiply; AS refers to a basic score or observation, not to a product of two numbers. In addition, lower-case letters in subscripts of the form AS_{ij} do not multiply.)

2.4 SUMS OF SQUARES: DEFINING FORMULAS

In order to evaluate the null hypothesis, it is necessary to transform the between-groups and within-groups deviations into more useful quantities, namely, **variances**. For this reason the statistical analysis involving the comparison of variances—in this case between-groups and within-groups variances—reflecting different sources of variability is called the **analysis of variance**. A variance is defined as follows:

$$\text{variance} = \frac{\text{sum of the squared deviations from the mean}}{\text{degrees of freedom}}.$$

The quantity specified in the numerator, the **sum of the squared deviations from the mean**, usually shortened to **sum of squares** and abbreviated *SS*, reflects the degree to which the numbers in a set vary among themselves. When there is no variability, i.e., when the numbers are all the same, each deviation from the mean will be zero (because the mean is equal to each number in the set), and the sum of the squared deviations (as well as the variance) will equal zero. On the other hand, when the numbers in a set are *different*, they spread out from the mean and the sum of the squared deviations becomes a positive value. As the spread increases, the deviations from the mean increase and the *SS* increases as well.

The quantity in the denominator, **degrees of freedom** (*df*), is approximately equal to the number of numbers in the set. This means, therefore, that the variance is basically an *average* of the squared deviations. I will consider variances and the concept of degrees of freedom in the next chapter. Our concern now is the calculation of component sums of squares.

Let's return to the component deviations developed earlier in this chapter. You will recall that the deviation of each subject from the grand mean of the experiment can be divided into a between-group and a within-group portion. In symbols, the relationship becomes

$$AS_{ij} - \bar{T} = (\bar{A}_i - \bar{T}) + (AS_{ij} - \bar{A}_i).$$

A similar additive relationship holds if we square the three deviations for each subject and then sum the squares over all of the subjects in the experiment.[3] This important relationship may be stated as

$$SS_{\text{total}} = SS_{\text{between groups}} + SS_{\text{within groups}}. \tag{2-3}$$

---

[3]The algebraic proof of this statement can be found in Hays (1973, pp. 465–467) and Winer (1971, p. 155).

Translated into the numerical example from Table 2-1, Eq. (2-3) reads, "The sum of the squared deviations of all 15 subjects from $\bar{T}$ may be broken down into two components, one obtained by summing all of the squared deviations between individual group means and $\bar{T}$ and the other by summing all of the squared deviations of subjects from their respective group means." You will now see how these words are translated into formulas and numerical values.

Total Sum of Squares

The basic ingredients in the total sum of squares SS_T are the total deviations—i.e., the deviations of all the scores in the experiment from the grand mean, $\bar{T}$. The SS_T is formed by squaring the total deviation for each subject and summing the squares of the total deviations. In symbols,

$$SS_T = \Sigma\,(AS - \bar{T})^2. \qquad (2\text{-}4)$$

We can calculate SS_T for the numerical example we have been considering by squaring each of the total deviations presented in Table 2-1 (p. 30). More specifically,

$$SS_T = \Sigma\,(AS - \bar{T})^2$$
$$= (6)^2 + (8)^2 + \cdots + (3)^2 + (1)^2 = 380.$$

Between-Groups Sum of Squares

You saw in Fig. 2-1 that one of the components of a subject's total deviation is the deviation of the subject's group mean from the grand mean $(\bar{A} - \bar{T})$. If we square this component and sum the squares for all of the subjects in the experiment, we will obtain the between-groups SS. (I will refer to this quantity as the SS_A, indicating that this sum of squares is based on deviations involving the A means.) From the between-group deviations listed in Table 2-1,

$$SS_A = (5)^2 + (5)^2 + \cdots + (-1)^2 + (-1)^2 = 210.$$

An alternative way of expressing this formula takes note of the fact that the between-group deviation is the same for all subjects in any given group. In this example, the deviation is 5 for a_1, -4 for a_2, and -1 for a_3. We can obtain the same quantity by squaring these three between-groups deviations, multiplying the squared deviations by the number of subjects in each group (s), and then summing the three products. That is,

$$SS_A = s(\bar{A}_1 - \bar{T})^2 + s(\bar{A}_2 - \bar{T})^2 + s(\bar{A}_3 - \bar{T})^2.$$

In general, the equation becomes,

$$SS_A = \Sigma\,s(\bar{A} - \bar{T})^2, \qquad (2\text{-}5)$$

which may be simplified by placing s, the sample size, to the left of the summation sign; i.e., it is simpler to square and sum the deviations first and then to multiply by s. With this example,

$$SS_A = s \, \Sigma \, (\bar{A} - \bar{T})^2$$
$$= 5[(5)^2 + (-4)^2 + (-1)^2]$$
$$= 5(25 + 16 + 1) = 5(42) = 210.$$

Within-Groups Sum of Squares

The final sum of squares is the within-groups sum of squares, denoted by $SS_{S/A}$. The subscript S/A is read "S within A" and stresses the fact that we are dealing with the deviation of subjects from their own group means. As illustrated in Fig. 2-1, the basic deviation involved in the definition of the $SS_{S/A}$ is expressed by $AS - \bar{A}$. As a first step, we can obtain a sum of squares for *each group* by using these within-group deviations. From Table 2-1,

$$SS_{S/A_1} = (1)^2 + (3)^2 + (-5)^2 + (-3)^2 + (4)^2 = 60;$$
$$SS_{S/A_2} = (-2)^2 + (0)^2 + (2)^2 + (4)^2 + (-4)^2 = 40;$$

and

$$SS_{S/A_3} = (-7)^2 + (1)^2 + (0)^2 + (4)^2 + (2)^2 = 70.$$

In the analysis of variance, we will average the different within-group variances to obtain a more stable estimate of experimental error. As a first step, then, we will want to add together the separate within-group sums of squares, a process often referred to as **pooling**. In this example,

$$SS_{S/A} = \Sigma \, SS_{S/A_i}$$
$$= SS_{S/A_1} + SS_{S/A_2} + SS_{S/A_3}$$
$$= 60 + 40 + 70 = 170.$$

The equation for the pooled sum of squares may be expressed as follows:

$$SS_{S/A} = \Sigma \, (AS - \bar{A})^2, \tag{2-6}$$

where it is understood that the summation sign refers to *all* of the within-group deviations.[4]

---

[4]The formula for the within-group deviation for a particular group requires the use of subscripts to single out that set from the others. For level a_1, for example,

$$SS_{S/A_1} = \Sigma \, (AS_{1j} - \bar{A}_1)^2.$$

This expression indicates that we are interested in only one set of within-group deviations—those for level a_1. This is indicated by the subscript 1 added to AS and A. The use of the j subscript with AS indicates that *any* of the subjects in that group might be selected.

2.5 SUMS OF SQUARES: COMPUTATIONAL FORMULAS

While the defining formulas for the three sums of squares preserve the logic by which the component deviations are derived, we usually calculate the sums of squares with formulas that are equivalent algebraically, but much simpler computationally.

Basic Ratios

Each of the sums of squares is calculated by combining two quantities called **basic ratios**. All basic ratios follow the same construction rules, which should be memorized, as they will give you the ability to generate computational formulas for all of the designs considered in this book.

The *numerator term* for any basic ratio involves two steps:

1. **The initial *squaring* of a set of quantities**
2. ***Summing* the squared quantities if more than one is present**

There are three basic ratios, one involving the individual observations (AS), another involving the treatment sums (A), and the other involving the grand sum (T). To calculate the three required numerators, we simply conduct the two operations of squaring and then summing on each of these quantities, that is, $\Sigma (AS)^2$, ΣA^2, and T^2, respectively. To illustrate, the first quantity indicates that we are to sum the squared scores for all the subjects in the experiment; using the data from Table 2-2, (p. 33), we have

$$\Sigma (AS)^2 = (16)^2 + (18)^2 + \cdots + (13)^2 + (11)^2 = 1,880.$$

The second quantity specifies the sum of all of the squared treatment sums; using the subtotals from Table 2-2, we get

$$\Sigma A^2 = (75)^2 + (30)^2 + (45)^2$$
$$= 5,625 + 900 + 2,025 = 8,550.$$

The final quantity involves the grand total, which merely needs to be squared, since there is only one such quantity in an experiment. From Table 2-2,

$$T^2 = (150)^2 = 22,500.$$

The *denominator term* for any basic ratio is found by applying a simple rule that depends on the particular term appearing in the numerator:

Whatever the term, we divide by the number of scores that contributed to that term.

For example, if the term is T, we divide by $(a)(s)$, because this is the number of scores that are actually summed to produce T. If the term is A, we divide by s, because this is the number of scores that are summed to produce any one of the A

38

treatment sums. Finally, if the term is AS, we divide by one, because an AS score is based on a *single* observation; this is equivalent, of course, to not dividing at all.

We are now ready to consider the formulas for the three basic ratios. For convenience, each ratio is given a special symbol consisting of a pair of brackets enclosing the letter or letters appearing in the numerator. The formulas for the three basic ratios are

$$[T] = \frac{T^2}{(a)(s)} \; ; \tag{2-7}$$

$$[A] = \frac{\Sigma A^2}{s} \; ; \tag{2-8}$$

and

$$[AS] = \Sigma (AS)^2 \, . \tag{2-9}$$

Applying these new formulas to the partial answers we have already calculated, we find

$$[T] = \frac{22,500}{(3)(5)} = 1,500.00;$$

$$[A] = \frac{8,550}{5} = 1,710.00;$$

and

$$[AS] = 1,880.$$

Sums of Squares

All that remains is to specify how the three basic ratios are combined to produce the three required sums of squares, SS_T, SS_A, and $SS_{S/A}$. One approach is to derive each computational formula from the relevant defining formula.[5] Another approach is simply to note that each of the three deviations appearing in the defining formulas—that is, $AS - \bar{T}$, $\bar{A} - \bar{T}$, and $AS - \bar{A}$—separately indicates how the basic ratios are combined to form the appropriate computational formulas. To illustrate, the total sum of squares is based on the following deviation:

$$AS - \bar{T}.$$

The computational formula combines the two ratios identified by this deviation, $[AS]$ and $[T]$, as follows:

$$SS_T = [AS] - [T], \tag{2-10}$$

[5] Algebraic proofs of these deviations can be found in Hays (1973, pp. 473-474) and Kirk (1968, pp. 48-50).

or, more completely,

$$SS_T = \Sigma\,(AS)^2 - \frac{T^2}{(a)(s)}. \tag{2-10a}$$

Substituting the quantities we calculated in the last section, we find

$$SS_T = [AS] - [T]$$
$$= 1{,}880 - 1{,}500.00 = 380.00.$$

The treatment sum of squares, SS_A, is based on the deviation of the treatment means from the grand mean:

$$\bar{A} - \bar{T}.$$

The computational formula combines the two ratios identified by this deviation as follows:

$$SS_A = [A] - [T], \tag{2-11}$$

or, more fully,

$$SS_A = \frac{\Sigma\,A^2}{s} - \frac{T^2}{(a)(s)}; \tag{2-11a}$$

Substituting the quantities calculated previously, we find

$$SS_A = [A] - [T]$$
$$= 1{,}710.00 - 1{,}500.00 = 210.00.$$

Finally, the within-groups sum of squares is based on the deviation of individual observations from the relevant treatment mean, i.e.,

$$AS - \bar{A}.$$

The computational formula combines the two ratios identified by these deviations as follows:

$$SS_{S/A} = [AS] - [A], \tag{2-12}$$

or

$$SS_{S/A} = \Sigma\,(AS)^2 - \frac{\Sigma\,A^2}{s}. \tag{2-12a}$$

Substituting the quantities from the last section, we obtain

$$SS_{S/A} = [AS] - [A]$$
$$= 1{,}880 - 1{,}710.00 = 170.00.$$

As a computational check and as a demonstration of the relationship among these three sums of squares, we will apply Eq. (2-3) to these calculations:[6]

$$SS_T = SS_A + SS_{S/A} = 210.00 + 170.00 = 380.00.$$

Comment

You can verify for yourself that the computational formulas produced exactly the same answers as those obtained with the defining formulas previously. The only time different answers are found is when rounding errors are introduced in calculating the treatment means and the grand mean and these errors become magnified in squaring the deviations, but even then the differences will be small. While we will focus almost entirely on the computational versions of the formulas because they are easy to use and can be generated by means of a simple set of rules, you should keep in mind that they are equivalent to the defining versions, which reflect quite directly the logic behind the derivation of the sums of squares required for the analysis of variance.

2.6 SUMMARY

I considered first some of the logic underlying the process of hypothesis testing in a design where each subject serves in only one treatment condition. By way of summary, one can describe hypothesis testing as consisting of a contrast between two sets of differences. One of these sets is obtained from a comparison involving differences among the treatment means; these differences are often referred to as *between-groups* differences. The other set is obtained from a comparison involving differences among subjects receiving the same treatment within a treatment group; these differences are called *within-groups* differences. It was argued that the between-groups differences are the result of the combined effects of the experimental treatment and of experimental error, while the within-groups differences represent the influence of experimental error alone. You saw that the comparison ratio,

$$\frac{\text{between-groups differences}}{\text{within-groups differences}},$$

[6]A complete check of all our calculations may be obtained in a number of ways. One obvious method is to perform the analysis again, or, perhaps better still, to coax another person to go through the calculations independently. An alternative method is to add a constant, say, 1, to each AS score (i.e., to use $AS + 1$) and to repeat the complete analysis. For example, the original scores in level a_1 (16, 18, 10, 12, and 19) would thus become 17, 19, 11, 13, and 20, respectively. If you have made no error in either set of calculations, you should end up with *identical* sums of squares in the two analyses. The addition of a constant does not change the basic *deviations*, upon which the sums of squares are based, but it does change the actual numbers entering into the calculations when we use the computational formulas presented in this section.

provides a numerical index which is "sensitive" to the presence of treatment effects in the population. That is, with no treatment effects, the long-run expectation is that the ratio will approximate 1.0, since the treatment effects will be zero and we will be dividing one estimate of experimental error by the other. On the other hand, whenever there are treatment effects, the expectation is that the ratio will be greater than 1.0.

The statistical hypothesis we test, the null hypothesis, specifies the *absence* of treatment effects in the population. With the help of statistical tables and a set of decision rules, neither of which I have described yet, we can decide whether or not it is reasonable to reject the null hypothesis. If we reject the null hypothesis, we accept the alternative statistical hypothesis, which specifies the presence of treatment effects in the population. If we fail to reject the null hypothesis, essentially we conclude that the independent variable produced no systematic differences in the experiment.

The remainder of the chapter focused on the translation of these ideas into actual measures of variability based on the data of a single-factor experiment. You saw that between-groups and within-groups differences can be expressed as deviations from different means. I began by considering the deviation of AS scores from $\bar{T}$ and established the fact that for each observation this deviation may be divided into a between-group deviation $\bar{A} - \bar{T}$ and a within-groups deviation $AS - \bar{A}$. You saw that the defining formulas for the corresponding sums of squares were developed directly from these deviations. Our actual calculations, however, are performed with computational formulas, which are considerably easier to use and can be formed by using a set of simple rules. In the next chapter, I will complete the steps in the statistical evaluation of the null hypothesis.

2.7 EXERCISES[7]

1. In an experiment involving $a = 5$ treatment conditions, the following measures were obtained:

AS **MATRIX**

a_1	a_2	a_3	a_4	a_5
13	7	12	10	13
9	4	11	12	6
8	4	4	9	14
7	1	9	7	12
8	10	5	15	13
6	7	10	14	10
6	5	2	10	8
7	9	8	17	4
6	5	3	14	9
10	8	6	12	11

[7]The answers to this problem are found in Appendix B, beginning on p. 560.

(a) Calculate the sum of the scores and the sum of the squared scores for each of the treatment groups.
(b) Calculate the treatment means.
(c) Calculate the sums of squares for each of the sources of variability normally identified in the analysis of variance, that is, SS_A, $SS_{S/A}$, and SS_T. Reserve this information for Exercise 3 of Chapter 3.

3

Variance Estimates and the Evaluation of the F Ratio

We are ready to complete the analysis of variance. As you will see, the remaining calculations are quite simple and easy to follow, while the theoretical justification of the procedures is complicated and considerably more abstract. Consequently, I will present the calculations quickly and devote a major portion of this chapter to an explanation of these procedures and a discussion of the possible consequences stemming from the evaluation of the null hypothesis.

3.1   VARIANCE ESTIMATES (MEAN SQUARES)

The remainder of the analysis is outlined in Table 3-1 in an arrangement called a **summary table**. The first two columns list the sources of variability and their respective sums of squares. To be useful in the analysis, the two component sums of squares must be converted to variances, or **mean squares**, as variances are called in the analysis of variance. In this context, a variance is defined by the equation

$$\text{variance} = \frac{SS}{df},\qquad\qquad (3\text{-}1)$$

where SS refers to the component sum of squares and df represents the **degrees of freedom** associated with the SS.

Degrees of Freedom

The degrees of freedom, or df, associated with a sum of squares correspond to the number of scores with *independent information* which enter into the calculation of the sum of squares. Consider, for example, the use of a single sample mean to estimate the population mean. If we want to estimate the population variance as well, we must take account of the fact that we have used up some of the independent information already in estimating the population mean.

Consider a concrete example. Suppose that we have five observations in our experiment and that we determine the mean of the scores to be 7.0. This mean is used to estimate the population mean. With the number of observations set at five and the population mean set at 7.0, how much independent information remains for the estimate of the population variance? The answer is the number of observations which are *free* to vary—i.e., to take on any value whatsoever. The number in this example is *four,* one less than the total number of observations. The reason for this loss of "freedom" is that, while we are free to select any value for the first four scores, the final score is already determined. More specifically, the total sum of all five must equal 35, so that the mean of the sample will equal 7.0; as soon as four scores are selected, the fifth score is fixed and can be obtained by subtraction. In a sense, then, estimating the population mean places a restraint upon the values that the scores are free to take. The general rule for computing the *df* of any sum of squares is

$$df = \begin{pmatrix} \text{number of} \\ \text{independent} \\ \text{observations} \end{pmatrix} - \begin{pmatrix} \text{number of} \\ \text{restraints} \end{pmatrix} \tag{3-2}$$

or

$$df = \begin{pmatrix} \text{number of} \\ \text{independent} \\ \text{observations} \end{pmatrix} - \begin{pmatrix} \text{number of} \\ \text{population} \\ \text{estimates} \end{pmatrix} \tag{3-2a}$$

The *df* associated with each sum of squares in the analysis of variance are presented in the third column of Table 3-1. We can calculate the *df* for each sum of squares by applying Eq. (3-2). For the SS_A, there are *a* basic observations—that is, *a* different sample means. Since 1 *df* is lost as a result of estimating the overall population mean μ from the grand mean $\bar{T}$ of the experiment, $df_A = a - 1$. For the $SS_{S/A}$, the calculation of the *df* is more complicated. This sum of squares represents a pooling of separate estimates of experimental error obtained from the different treatment groups (see p. 63 for a demonstration of this point). If we consider any one of these groups—the *i*th group—there are *s* basic observations; we will lose 1 *df*, however, by estimating the mean of the treatment population (μ_i). Thus, there are $df = s - 1$ for each of the treatment groups. The total number of *df* for the $SS_{S/A}$ is found by pooling the *df* for each group, just as we pool the corresponding sums of squares. The formula given in Table 3-1,

$$df_{S/A} = a(s - 1),$$

simply has us multiply the *df* for any one of the groups $(s - 1)$ by the number of different groups (a). The *df* for the SS_T are obtained by subtracting 1 *df* from the total number of independent observations, $(a)(s)$. As a check, we can verify that the *df* associated with the component sums of squares sum to df_T. That is,

$$df_T = df_A + df_{S/A};$$

and

$$(a)(s) - 1 = (a - 1) + a(s - 1) = a - 1 + (a)(s) - a = (a)(s) - 1.$$

Mean Squares

The actual variance estimates, which, as I have already indicated, are called mean squares (MS), appear in the next column of Table 3-1. The mean squares for

Table 3-1   Summary Table for the One-Factor Analysis of Variance

SOURCE	SS	df	MEAN SQUARE (MS)	F RATIO
A	SS_A	$a - 1$	$\dfrac{SS_A}{df_A}$	$\dfrac{MS_A}{MS_{S/A}}$
S/A	$SS_{S/A}$	$a(s - 1)$	$\dfrac{SS_{S/A}}{df_{S/A}}$	
Total	SS_T	$(a)(s) - 1$		

the two component sources of variance are given by the formula

$$MS = \frac{SS}{df},$$ (3-3)

or, more specifically,

$$MS_A = \frac{SS_A}{df_A} \quad \text{and} \quad MS_{S/A} = \frac{SS_{S/A}}{df_{S/A}}.$$

The first mean square estimates the combined presence of treatment effects plus error variance, while the second mean square independently estimates error variance alone.

3.2 THE F RATIO

The final step in the calculations consists of the formation of the F ratio. The formula is listed in the last column of Table 3-1 and consists of the treatment mean square MS_A divided by the within-groups mean square $MS_{S/A}$. (The denominator of the F ratio, $MS_{S/A}$, is often called the **error term**, for obvious reasons.) From the arguments advanced in the last chapter, the average value of F, obtained by averaging an extremely large number of F's from imaginary experiments drawn repeatedly from the same theoretical treatment populations, is approximately 1.0 when the null hypothesis is true, and is greater than 1.0 when the null hypothesis is false. I will return to this argument in the next section following the completion of the numerical example we used in the last chapter to illustrate the calculation of the sums of squares.

The results of these earlier calculations are presented in Table 3-2. If you will recall, there were $a = 3$ treatment conditions and $s = 5$ subjects in this example; the original data may be found in Table 2-2 (p. 33).

The df for the three sources of variance are obtained by simple substitution into the formulas listed in Table 3-1. The results of these substitutions are pre-

Table 3-2   Summary Table

SOURCE	SS	df	MS	F
A	210.00	2	105.00	7.41
S/A	170.00	12	14.17	
Total	380.00	14		

sented in the summary table. Specifically,

$$df_A = a - 1 = 3 - 1 = 2;$$
$$df_{S/A} = a(s - 1) = 3(5 - 1) = (3)(4) = 12;$$

and

$$df_T = (a)(s) - 1 = (3)(5) - 1 = 15 - 1 = 14.$$

We can check our separate calculations by verifying that the df obtained for the component sums of squares equal the df obtained for the SS_T. That is,

$$df_T = df_A + df_{S/A} = 2 + 12 = 14.$$

The two variance estimates (mean squares) are found by dividing the SS by the appropriate df. In this example,

$$MS_A = \frac{210.00}{2} = 105.00 \quad \text{and} \quad MS_{S/A} = \frac{170.00}{12} = 14.17.$$

These numbers are entered in the MS column of the table. Last, the F ratio becomes

$$F = \frac{MS_A}{MS_{S/A}} = \frac{105.00}{14.17} = 7.41.$$

This value of F is larger than 1.0, bringing into question the correctness of the null hypothesis. On the other hand, we might have obtained a ratio this large (or larger) merely by virtue of the fact that the two mean squares are independent estimates of error variance when H_0 is true.

3.3 EVALUATING THE F RATIO

Sampling Distribution of F

In view of the minimal mathematical background assumed for the readers of this book, a reasonable approach to this topic is empirical rather than theoretical. Suppose that we had available a large population of scores and that we drew at random three sets of 15 scores each. We can think of the three sets as representing the results of an actual experiment, with $a = 3$ and $s = 15$, for which we *know* the null hypothesis is *true.* That is, the scores placed in each "treatment" condition were in fact drawn from the *same* population. Thus, $\mu_1 = \mu_2 = \mu_3 = \mu$. The two mean squares, MS_A and $MS_{S/A}$, are independent estimates of experimental error; we may estimate the operation of the same chance factors either by looking at the variability among the three sample means or by looking at the pooled variability of the scores within each of the samples.

Assume that we draw a very large number of such "experiments," each consisting of three groups of 15 scores each, and that we compute the value of F for each case. If we group the F's according to size, we can construct a graph relating F and frequency of occurrence. A frequency distribution of a statistic such as F is called a **sampling distribution** of the statistic.

This sort of empirical sampling study is called a *Monte Carlo* experiment. A sampling distribution of F, based on 1,000 experiments of the sort we have been discussing, is presented in Fig. 3-1. The sampling and calculations were performed on a high-speed computer.[1] The population consisted of 6,000 scores having a mean, μ, of 500. The histogram exhibits a regular trend, the frequency of cases tending to drop off rapidly with increasing values of F. The smoothed curve represents the *theoretical* sampling distribution of F. The approximation of the theoretical curve to the empirically obtained sampling distribution is extremely close. This correspondence provides a convincing intuitive meaning to the F distribution—namely, that it *is* the sampling distribution of F obtained when an infinitely large number of experiments, of the sort we have been discussing, are performed.

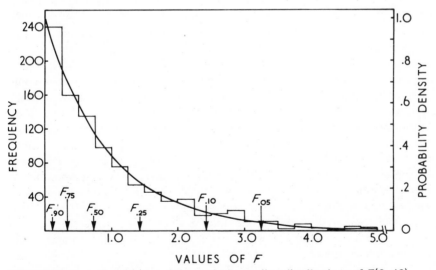

FIGURE 3-1.   Empirical and theoretical sampling distributions of $F(2, 42)$.

[1]The results of this sampling experiment were generously made available to me by Drs. Curtis D. Hardyck and Lewis F. Petrinovich.

In evaluating the null hypothesis, we could use information drawn from either the empirical or the theoretical sampling distributions. The great advantage of knowing the mathematical properties of the F distribution is that the sampling distribution can be determined for any experiment of any size—i.e., any number of groups and any number of subjects within these groups. Separate Monte Carlo experiments would have to be conducted for each new situation—an inefficient and costly procedure.

Let us return to Fig. 3-1 and see what useful information can be obtained from the F distribution. If we know the exact shape of the F distribution for a given experiment, we can make statements concerning how common or how rare an F observed in an actual experiment is. The F distribution is the sampling distribution of F when the population means are equal. If we consider a particular value of F, we can determine (with a working knowledge of the calculus) the probability of obtaining an F that large or larger by finding the percentage of the area under the curve which falls to the right of an ordinate erected at the value of F in question. Several values of F have been indicated in Fig. 3-1. The proportion of the curve falling to the right of F is indicated as a subscript. For example, only 10 percent of the time would we expect to obtain a value of F equal to or greater than 2.44 (symbolized $F \geq 2.44$). Stated another way, this probability represents the proportion of F's greater than or equal to 2.44 that will occur on the basis of chance factors alone.

The F Table. The F distribution is actually a family of curves. The exact shape of any one of the curves is determined by the number of df associated with the numerator and denominator mean squares in the F ratio. If we hold the numerator df (the number of treatment groups) constant and vary the denominator df (the number of subjects within groups), we will see relatively small changes in the shape of the curves. On the other hand, changing the number of treatment groups produces curves of quite different appearance. An example of another F distribution, with numerator and denominator df equal to 4 and 10, respectively, is sketched in Fig. 3-2. As a shorthand way of referring to a particular F distribution, we will use the expression $F(df_{num.}, df_{denom.})$, or, in this case, $F(4, 10)$.

For our experiment, we do not have to know the exact shape of the F distribution. The only information we need is the value of F, to the right of which certain proportions of the area under the curve fall. These values have been tabulated and are readily available. An F table is found in Table A-1 of Appendix A. A particular value of F in this table is specified by three factors: (1) the numerator df (represented by the columns of the table), (2) the denominator df (represented by the main rows of the table), and (3) the value of α (represented by the rows listed for each denominator df), where α refers to the proportion of area to the right of an ordinate drawn at F_α.

For example, the value of $F(4, 10)$ is 3.48 at $\alpha = .05$. This F is found by locating the intersection of the column at $df_{num.} = 4$ and the row at $df_{denom.} = 10$. The different values of $F(4, 10)$ in this location represent critical points for a number of different α levels. The one we want is at $\alpha = .05$. What this value of F means

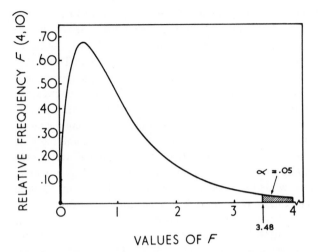

VALUES OF F

FIGURE 3-2. Theoretical sampling distribution of $F(4, 10)$.

is that an ordinate drawn at $F(4, 10) = 3.48$ will divide the sampling distribution of $F(4, 10)$ at a point where the proportion of the area under the curve to the right is .05. Said another way, $\alpha \times 100 = .05 \times 100$, which means that 5 percent of the area under the curve falls to the right of an ordinate drawn at $F(4, 10) = 3.48$. For $\alpha = .25$, $F(4, 10) = 1.59$ and for $\alpha = .01$, $F(4, 10) = 5.99$; 25 percent and 1 percent of the sampling distribution of $F(4, 10)$ fall to the right of these respective points.

Obviously, not all possible combinations of these three factors are listed in the table. The α levels, $\alpha = .25, .10, .05, .025, .01,$ and $.001$, are ones most commonly encountered. Additional levels of α can be found in the different editions of Fisher and Yates (e.g., 1953) and of Pearson and Hartley (e.g., 1970) or in the more convenient tables of Dixon and Massey (1957). The intervals between successive columns and rows increase with the larger numerator and denominator df's. For instance, the $df_{num.}$ include entries for consecutive values of df from 1 to 10; the next columns are $df_{num.} = 12, 15, 20, 24, 30, 40, 60,$ and ∞. The $df_{denom.}$ increase consecutively from 1 to 20, by two's from 20 to 30, and then by the sequence 40, 60, 120, and ∞. Fine gradations are not needed for the larger df values, since the numerical values of F do not change greatly from interval to interval.[2]

I have only considered the sampling distribution of F when the null hypothesis is *true*—i.e., when the population means are equal. Obviously, we do not intend

[2]When the critical value of F falls between two rows (or columns) of the table, most researchers follow the practice of choosing the row (or column) with the smaller number of degrees of freedom. This choice results in a critical value of F that is slightly larger than it should be. Other options are available if this procedure seems unreasonable, for example, linear interpolation (see Lindman, 1974, pp. 18–19) or the use of more extensive tables of F. This problem is not serious, however, and only becomes relevant when the obtained value of F lies very close to the critical value.

to conduct many experiments in which this is the case! We perform an experiment because we expect to find treatment effects. Suppose we assume that H_0 is false. What should happen to the F ratio? From previous discussions, I have argued that the average or **expected value** of the ratio should be greater than 1.0. This was because the MS_A contains two components, treatment effects and experimental error, while the $MS_{S/A}$ is the result of experimental error alone. The sampling distribution of the F ratio under these circumstances is no longer the F distribution. Instead, the theoretical distribution is called F' or **noncentral** F. It would be nice to be able to draw the F' distribution and to compare it with a corresponding F distribution. Unfortunately, however, this is difficult to do, since the F' distribution is a function of the *magnitude* of the treatment effects as well as of the numerator and denominator df's. Thus, while there is only one F distribution at any combination of numerator and denominator df's, there is a family of F' distributions, one distribution for each value that the treatment effects may take. On the other hand, we can say that the F' distribution will be shifted to the *right* of the F distribution and will be centered over numerically larger values of F'. This means, then, that whenever the null hypothesis is *false*, we will expect to find values of F that on the average are larger than 1.0, the value expected when the null hypothesis is *true*.

Test of the Null Hypothesis

We are now ready to piece together this information concerning the sampling distributions of F and F' to provide a test of the null hypothesis. We start our testing procedure by specifying H_0 and H_1, the null and alternative statistical hypotheses. To review briefly an earlier discussion, the two hypotheses are

$$H_0: \text{ all } \mu_i\text{'s are equal,}$$

and

$$H_1: \text{ not all } \mu_i\text{'s are equal.}$$

The hypothesis we will test, the null hypothesis, assumes that the means of the treatment populations are equal. The alternative hypothesis is a mutually exclusive statement which generally asserts simply that some of the population treatment means are not equal—i.e., that some treatment effects are present. We choose this particular null hypothesis because it is usually the only hypothesis that we can state *exactly*. There is no ambiguity in the assertion that the population means are equal; there is only one way in which this can happen. The alternative hypothesis is an *inexact* statement—an assertion that the population means are not all equal. Nothing is said about the *actual* differences which are present in the population. (If we had that sort of information, we would have no reason for conducting the experiment!) Another advantage of this particular null hypothesis is that the sampling distribution of F is known. Presumably the sampling distribution of F' can be worked out, but we will need a different distribution for treatment effects of different sizes. Just how we use the sampling distribution of F in evaluating the null hypothesis will be considered next.

Assume that we have conducted an experiment and that we have computed the value of F. What we have to decide is whether it is more likely that this value of F came from the F distribution or from the F' distribution. Logically, it could have come from only one, but which one? Since we are evaluating the null hypothesis, we will turn our attention to the F distribution. While some values of F are less likely to occur than are others, it is still possible theoretically to obtain *any* value of F in an experiment when the null hypothesis is true. From one point of view our situation is hopeless: if any value of F may have been the result of chance factors, then we can never be *certain* that the F we observe in an experiment was *not* drawn from the F distribution. Agreed. If we were to take this attitude, however, we would never be able to use the experimental method as a way of finding out about the world. That is, if we maintain that any difference among the sample means may be due to chance, there is no way that we can conclude that our experimental manipulations influenced behavior differentially. As Fisher (1951) puts it, ". . . an experiment would be useless of which no possible result would satisfy [us] " (p. 13). We will not take this attitude. We must be willing to make mistakes in rejecting the null hypothesis when H_0 is true; otherwise, we can never reject the null hypothesis.

Suppose we could agree upon a dividing line for any F distribution, where values of F falling above the line are considered to be unlikely and values of F falling below the line are considered to be likely. We would then see whether our observed F falls above or below this arbitrary dividing line. If the F falls above the line, we will conclude that the observed F is *incompatible* with the null hypothesis; that is, we will reject H_0 and conclude that the alternative hypothesis is true. If the F falls below the line, we will conclude that the observed F is *compatible* with the null hypothesis. Under these circumstances, then, we will not reject H_0. Following such a set of rules means that we *will* be able to conclude that our independent variable was effective, provided an F ratio is obtained which falls within the region of incompatibility. But it also means that we are willing to make a mistake by rejecting a true null hypothesis a certain proportion of the time.

Decision Rules

The crux of the problem, of course, is to find a way of objectively defining the regions of "compatibility" and "incompatibility." If the null hypothesis is true, we can determine the sampling distribution of F. Suppose we find a point on this distribution beyond which the probability of occurrence is very, very small. (The probability is represented by the proportion of the total area under the curve that appears beyond this particular point.) We will arbitrarily consider values of F falling within this region as *incompatible* with the *null hypothesis*. We must identify such a region in order to be able to reject the null hypothesis. Our decision rule, then, is to reject the null hypothesis when the observed F falls within the region of incompatibility. We do so, knowing full well that we may be making the wrong decision, which would be the case if the null hypothesis really were true.

Suppose, now, that we begin to enlarge the region of incompatibility, by moving the critical point of transition to the left—toward the larger portion of the curve—and cumulate the probabilities associated with these new portions of the curve. As we increase the size of this region, we also increase the chance of observing values from this region. Said another way, increasing the region of incompatibility results in the inclusion of F's which are becoming increasingly more *compatible* with the null hypothesis. Theoretically, an investigator may pick any cumulative probability, just as long as the decision is made before the start of the experiment. In practice, however, there is fairly common agreement upon a cumulative probability of $\alpha = 0.5$ to define the region of incompatibility for the F distribution. This probability is called the **significance level**.

We are now in a position to state more formally the decision rules that are followed after the calculation of the F ratio.[3] If the F value falls within the region of incompatibility, the null hypothesis is rejected and the alternative hypothesis is accepted. If the F value falls within the region of compatibility, the null hypothesis is not rejected. (These two regions are often called the regions of "rejection" and "nonrejection.") The decision to reject or not is made by comparing the observed value of F with the value of F located at the critical point of transition. Symbolically, the rules are stated:

$$\text{Reject } H_0 \text{ when } F_{\text{observed}} \geq F_{(\alpha)}(n, d); \text{ otherwise, do not reject } H_0. \quad (3\text{-}4)$$

In this statement, α refers to the significance level, and n and d to the df's associated with the numerator and denominator of the F ratio, respectively.

There is often some confusion concerning the exact wording of the decision rules, stemming largely from the fact that we cannot *prove* a hypothesis, only *disprove* it. When we say that a particular hypothesis is "accepted," we do *not* mean that it has been proved—just that it is consistent with the facts. Thus, if we reject H_0, this means that the results of the experiment are consistent with the alternative hypothesis that some of the treatment means are different; in this sense, then, we accept H_1. By the same token, if we do not reject H_0, this means that we consider the results of the experiment consistent with the hypothesis that the treatment means are equal. It is in this sense, too, that we are accepting the null hypothesis.

I will consider two examples of the use of the rejection rules. The first involves an evaluation of the F we calculated earlier in this chapter (see Table 3-2). In this example, $n = 2$ and $d = 12$. If we set $\alpha = .05$, the critical value of F which we find in the tabled values of the F distribution (Table A-1 of Appendix A) is 3.89. The rejection region consists of all values of F equal to or greater than 3.89. Substituting in Eq. (3-4), the decision rules become

$$\text{Reject } H_0 \text{ when } F_{\text{observed}} \geq 3.89; \text{ otherwise, do not reject } H_0.$$

[3]Hays (1973, pp. 332-375) provides a detailed discussion of this decision process.

Since the F obtained in this example exceeded this value ($F = 7.41$), we would conclude that treatment effects were present in this experiment.

For the second example, I will return to Fig. 3-1. If we set $\alpha = .05$, the critical value of F at $n = 2$ and $d = 42$ is approximately 3.23. (Table A-1 does not have a value for this combination of df's; the value I have given here is associated with $n = 2$ and $d = 40$.) The rejection region consists of all value of F equal to or greater than 3.23. Since the area under the curve to the right of an ordinate drawn at this value of F consists of 5 percent of the total area under the curve, the probability of obtaining an F at least as deviant as 3.23 is .05. When we substitute in Eq. (3-4), the decision rules become

Reject H_0 when $F_{observed} \geqslant 3.23$; otherwise, do not reject H_0.

The size of the rejection region each of us adopts is a personal choice. What probability we choose is often dictated by our concern for *failing* to reject the null hypothesis when a real difference among treatment means exists. (More about this in a moment.) In presenting the results of a statistical test, however, you should remember that not all researchers who will be reading the report will agree with your choice of significance level. Thus, in order to accommodate most of the researchers adopting different rejection regions, we indicate the *smallest* significance level within which the $F_{observed}$ will fall. For example, suppose we obtained an F of 6.33 in the second example we have just considered. An inspection of the F table indicates that the critical value of F at $\alpha = .01$ is approximately 5.18. One way to report the results of this test would be to make the following statement:

$$F(2, 42) = 6.33, p < .01,$$

which means that this value of F falls within a rejection region having an α level that is less than a probability (p) of .01. Such a statement would indicate that the null hypothesis would be rejected by all researchers adopting a significance level at least as small as 1 percent. Since few researchers will be more conservative than this, the smallest rejection region that we would need to report in a scientific journal is one at $\alpha = .01$. We must distinguish in this discussion between the transmission of information concerning the significance level of the $F_{observed}$ from our own decision to reject or not to reject the null hypothesis. In this example, our rejection region was $\alpha = .05$, but we reported the probability associated with the F as $p < .01$. Our decision to reject H_0 depends only upon the presence of $F_{observed}$ in *our* rejection region.

Summary

You have seen that a statistical test begins with the specification of the null and alternative hypotheses. We then conduct our experiment and calculate an F ratio. Next, we judge whether we have obtained an F which is incompatible with the hypothesis that the means of the treatment populations are equal. Incompatibility is defined arbitrarily ahead of time as an F which would occur on the basis of chance, assuming H_0 is true, a small proportion of the time, e.g., 1 time in 20 (5 percent). If the $F_{observed}$ falls within this region of incompatibility, we reject the null hypothesis; if it falls within the region of compatibility, we do not reject the null hypothesis.

3.4 ERRORS IN HYPOTHESIS TESTING

The procedures we follow in hypothesis testing do not guarantee that a correct inference will be drawn when we apply the decision rules enumerated in Eq. (3-4). On the contrary, whether or not we decide to reject the null hypothesis, we will be making either a correct decision or an incorrect decision, depending upon the state of affairs in the real world—i.e., the population. The two types of errors that we can commit are defined in Table 3-3. There are two states that "reality" can take: either the null hypothesis is true or it is false; and there are two decisions that we may make: either reject H_0 or do not. The four possible combinations of states of reality and types of decisions are enumerated in the table. Inspection reveals two situations in which we will make the *correct decision*, i.e., no error of inference: (1) if we reject H_0 when it is *false* and (2) if we accept H_0 when it is *true*. On the other hand, in two complementary situations we will make an *incorrect decision*, i.e., an error of inference: (1) if we reject H_0 when it is *true* and (2) if we accept H_0 when it is *false*. These errors of inference are called **type I and type II errors** or α and β **errors**, respectively. You should note that α and β are actually conditional probabilities, since α is the probability of error given (i.e., conditional) that H_0 is true and β is the probability of error given that H_1 is true.

To illustrate the two types of errors, we will consider a geometrical example. The upper panel in Fig. 3-3 represents the theoretical distribution of F when the null hypothesis is true—i.e., when there are no treatment effects. The region of rejection, which is specified by the shaded area to the right of the ordinate at F_α, represents the magnitude of the type I error. That is, an F which falls within this region will lead to a rejection of the null hypothesis and thus constitutes a type I error. The probability with which this will occur is α. The unshaded area to the left of F_α represents the probability of making a correct inference.

Table 3-3   Errors in Hypothesis Testing

	REALITY	
DECISION	H_0 *True,* H_1 *False*	H_0 *False,* H_1 *True*
Reject H_0, *Accept* H_1	Incorrect decision: type I error	Correct decision
Accept H_0, *Do not accept* H_1	Correct decision	Incorrect decision: type II error

The middle panel represents the theoretical distribution of F when the alternative hypothesis is true.[4] The region of rejection is again specified by the area to the right of F_α. It is clear that the critical value of F defining the beginning of the rejection region is the same in these two situations. The reason is that we set F_α with the null hypothesis in mind, and we are now considering the consequences of having set this rejection region when the alternative hypothesis is true. Consider, then, the rejection region—the area to the right of F_α. This area represents the probability of making a *correct inference* under these circumstances. The shaded area to the left of F_α (the region of nonrejection) represents the probability of making a type II error (β).

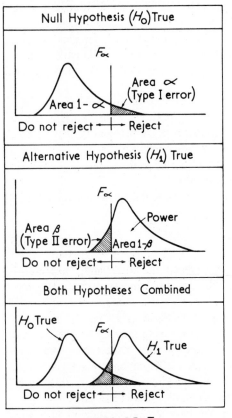

VALUES OF F

FIGURE 3-3. Sampling distribution of the F ratio when the null hypothesis is true (top panel) and when the alternative hypothesis is true (middle panel). The two sampling distributions are shown together in the bottom panel.

[4]I have taken liberties with the shape of this distribution. The noncentral F is not just a shifted-over version of the F distribution as depicted here. In reality, the distribution is usually more spread out and more symmetrical than the F distribution. In any case, the argument still holds.

The bottom panel brings together the two separate distributions. The reciprocity of the two types of errors is evident. Any change in the size of the rejection region (the area to the right of F_α) will produce changes in opposite directions for the two types of error. To be more specific, by moving the point of transition (F_α) to the right—i.e., lowering the α level—we decrease the type I error and increase the type II error. By moving F_α to the left—i.e., raising the α level—we increase the type I error and decrease the type II error.

It should be realized that a different display is needed for each particular alternative hypothesis we might consider. To make the point, however, it is sufficient to consider only one alternative hypothesis. The F distribution under the null hypothesis will not change with other alternative hypotheses. What does change is the location of the distribution of noncentral F. With an alternative hypothesis which specifies larger treatment effects than those depicted here, the noncentral F distribution will move to the right. Again, since F_α remains the same, this displacement of the distribution reduces the type II error. Similarly, a reduction in the treatment effects will move the distribution to the left and increase the type II error.

A quantitative index of the sensitivity of an experiment is its **power**. Power refers to the probability of *rejecting* the null hypothesis when an alternative hypothesis is *true*. Said another way, power represents the probability that a statistical test of the null hypothesis will result in the conclusion that the phenomenon under study exists. In this sense, power is interpreted as the probability of making a *correct* decision when the null hypothesis is false.

Power is usually defined in terms of the probability of making a type II error (β). Specifically,

$$\text{power} = 1 - \beta. \tag{3-5}$$

Thus, the smaller the type II error (β), the greater the power and, therefore, the greater the sensitivity of the test. I will discuss this important concept in more detail in the next chapter.

As long as we are committed to making decisions in the face of incomplete knowledge, as every scientist is, we cannot avoid making these errors. We can, however, try to minimize them. We directly control the size of the type I error in our selection of significance level. By setting a region of rejection, we are taking a calculated risk that a certain proportion of the time (for example, $\alpha = .05$), we will obtain F's that fall into this region when the null hypothesis is true.

How can we control type II error? We have already considered an obvious procedure: to *increase* the rejection region. Of course, we do so at the cost of an increase in type I errors! Every researcher must strike a balance between the two types of errors. If it is important to discover *new* facts, then we may be willing to accept more *type I* errors and thus *increase* the rejection region. On the other hand, if it is important not to clog up the literature with *false* facts, then we may be willing to accept more *type II* errors and *decrease* the rejection region. Arguments can be made for both sides of this type I/type II coin; I will discuss these arguments in Chapter 8. Other ways of reducing type II errors will be considered in Chapter 4 and subsequent chapters. For the time being, I will merely mention that type II errors may be decreased by adding to the number of observations in each treatment condition and by reducing error variance through the design of a more precisely controlled experiment.

3.5 A COMPLETE NUMERICAL EXAMPLE

Now that we have looked at each step of the one-factor analysis of variance, it is time to work through a numerical example from start to finish. Suppose a team of researchers is interested in the effect of sleep deprivation on the ability of subjects to perform a vigilance task, such as locating objects moving on a radar screen. They arrange to house the subjects in the laboratory so that they will have control over the sleeping habits of the subjects. There are $a = 4$ conditions, namely, 4, 12, 20, and 28 hours without sleep. There are $s = 4$ subjects randomly assigned to each of the different treatment conditions. The subjects have been well trained on the vigilance task before the start of the experiment. They are scored on the number of failures to spot objects on a radar screen during a 30-minute test period. The scores for each subject are presented in Table 3-4.

The analysis begins with the basic summing and squaring operation performed on the scores in each treatment condition. The results of these calculations are also listed in the table. For the subjects in level a_2, for example,

$$A_2 = \Sigma\, AS_{2j} = 36 + 45 + 47 + 23 = 151;$$

$$\overline{A}_2 = \frac{A_2}{s} = \frac{151}{4} = 37.75;$$

and

$$\Sigma\, (AS_{2j})^2 = (36)^2 + (45)^2 + (47)^2 + (23)^2 = 6,059.$$

The means are the primary descriptive statistic of an experiment and are examined closely for the presence of any interesting trend or outcome. An examination of the means in Table 3-4 indicates that the average number of failures increases steadily as the number of hours of sleep deprivation increases. The means would be reported in a journal article either in a table or, more likely, in a figure because a quantitative independent variable is involved. In addition to the mean, most researchers would calculate and report some measure of variability for each of the treatment conditions. The usual measure is the standard deviation, which can easily be calculated from the information in the table.

The first step in calculating the standard deviation is to obtain the sum of squares (*SS*) for each treatment group. For any given set of scores,

Table 3–4 Numerical Example: *AS* Matrix

	HOURS WITHOUT SLEEP (FACTOR A)			
	4 hr. a_1	*12 hr.* a_2	*20 hr.* a_3	*28 hr.* a_4
	37	36	43	76
	22	45	75	66
	22	47	66	43
	25	23	46	62
A_i:	106	151	230	247
$\bar{A}_i$:	26.50	37.75	57.50	61.75
$\sum_j^s (AS_{ij})^2$:	2,962	6,059	13,946	15,825
$\hat{\sigma}_i^2$:	51.00	119.58	240.33	190.92
$\hat{\sigma}_i$:	7.14	10.94	15.50	13.82

$$SS = (\text{sum of the squared scores}) - \frac{(\text{sum of the scores})^2}{s}. \tag{3-6}$$

As an example of the calculations, the sum of squares for the 4-hour group is equal to

$$SS = 2{,}962 - \frac{(106)^2}{4} = 153.00.$$

The formula for the variance ($\hat{\sigma}_i^2$) was given by Eq. (3–1).[5] Substituting the relevant data, we have

$$\hat{\sigma}_1^2 = \frac{SS}{df} = \frac{153.00}{4-1} = 51.00.$$

The variances for each treatment condition are presented in Table 3–4. Finally, the standard deviation of a set of scores ($\hat{\sigma}_i$) is defined as follows:

$$\text{standard deviation} = \sqrt{\text{variance}} = \hat{\sigma}_i. \tag{3-7}$$

For the 4-hour group,

$$\hat{\sigma}_1 = \sqrt{51.00} = 7.14.$$

[5]The mark above the lower-case Greek sigma signifies that the quantity calculated estimates a population characteristic (or parameter) from the data of a sample—in this case, an experiment.

The standard deviations for the different treatment conditions are also given in Table 3-4. The main reason for calculating measures of variability for each treatment condition is to determine whether the groups show comparable degrees of variability. While an inspection of the variances and standard deviations of the treatment conditions indicates some differences in variability from group to group, these are well within the range of values one would expect if chance factors alone were operating.[6]

The first step in the statistical analysis is the calculation of the three sums of squares. Starting with the three basic ratios which make up the sums of squares and the data in Table 3-4, we find

$$[T] = \frac{T^2}{(a)(s)}$$

$$= \frac{(106 + 151 + 230 + 247)^2}{(4)(4)}$$

$$= \frac{(734)^2}{16} = \frac{538,756}{16} = 33,672.25;$$

$$[A] = \frac{\Sigma A^2}{s}$$

$$= \frac{(106)^2 + (151)^2 + (230)^2 + (247)^2}{4}$$

$$= \frac{147,946}{4} = 36,986.50;$$

and

$$[AS] = \Sigma (AS)^2$$

$$= 2,962 + 6,059 + 13,946 + 15,825 = 38,792.$$

From the formulas presented in Chapter 2, we combine the basic ratios to obtain the sums of squares as follows:

$$SS_A = [A] - [T] = 36,986.50 - 33,672.25 = 3,314.25;$$

$$SS_{S/A} = [AS] - [A] = 38,792 - 36,986.50 = 1,805.50;$$

---

[6] I will discuss procedures for determining the significance of differences among treatment variances in Chap. 5.

and

$$SS_T = [AS] - [T] = 38,792 - 33,672.25 = 5,119.75.$$

As a check,

$$SS_A + SS_{S/A} = 3,314.25 + 1,805.50 = 5,119.75 = SS_T.$$

The remainder of the analysis is based upon the formulas listed in Table 3-1 (p. 47). The sums of squares we have just calculated are entered in Table 3-5. The df's associated with the different sums of squares are

$$df_A = a - 1 = 4 - 1 = 3;$$
$$df_{S/A} = a(s - 1) = 4(4 - 1) = 12;$$

and

$$df_T = (a)(s) - 1 = (4)(4) - 1 = 15.$$

As an arithmetic check,

$$df_A + df_{S/A} = 3 + 12 = 15 = df_T.$$

The between-groups and within-groups mean squares are formed by dividing the relevant sum of squares by the corresponding df. Specifically,

$$MS_A = \frac{SS_A}{a - 1} = \frac{3,314.25}{3} = 1,104.75$$

and

$$MS_{S/A} = \frac{SS_{S/A}}{a(s - 1)} = \frac{1,805.50}{12} = 150.46.$$

The F ratio is obtained by dividing the first mean square by the second:

$$F = \frac{MS_A}{MS_{S/A}} = \frac{1,104.75}{150.46} = 7.34.$$

The results of each of these steps are entered in the summary table. We will assume that the α level has been set at $p = .05$ before the start of the experiment. In order to evaluate the significance of the F, we locate the critical value of F at $\alpha = .05$ and $df_{num.} = 3$ and $df_{denom.} = 12$. From the F table (Table A-1 of Appendix A),

$$F(3, 12) = 3.49.$$

The decision rules given in Eq. (3-4) may be stated as follows:

Reject H_0 if $F_{observed} \geq 3.49$; otherwise, do not reject H_0.

Table 3-5   Summary of the Analysis

SOURCE	SS	df	MS	F
A	3,314.25	3	1,104.75	7.34*
S/A	1,805.50	12	150.46	
Total	5,119.75	15		

*$p < .01.$

Since $F_{observed}$ exceeds this value, we reject the null hypothesis and conclude that the independent variable has produced an effect.

The results of the statistical test are indicated by a footnote in the summary table. In this case, the entry $p < .01$ notes that the F we have observed is larger than the value of F marking off the 1 percent level of significance; i.e., $F_{(.01)} = 5.95$. As explained earlier, an indication that the obtained F falls within the 1 percent rejection region does not necessarily mean that we personally set α at $p = .01$. This particular statement of the outcome of our analysis is more informative, allowing individual researchers to use their own significance levels in evaluating our finding. Since we adopted the 5 percent level of significance, we would have rejected the null hypothesis in any case.

In Chapter 2 (p. 37), you saw that the within-groups sum of squares $SS_{S/A}$ is in effect the sum of the individual sums of squares for the treatment groups; that is, $SS_{S/A} = \Sigma \, SS_{S/A_i}$. The within-groups' mean square $MS_{S/A}$, which is based on $SS_{S/A}$, can also be viewed as a composite or pooled source of variance. More specifically, the error term for the analysis of variance is literally an *average* of the separate variances MS_{S/A_i} of the separate groups. In symbols,

$$MS_{S/A} = \frac{\Sigma \, MS_{S/A_i}}{a}. \qquad (3\text{-}8)$$

As an example, we can calculate the average within-groups variance with the variances presented in Table 3-4. More specifically,

$$MS_{S/A} = \frac{51.00 + 119.58 + 240.33 + 190.92}{4}$$

$$= \frac{601.83}{4} = 150.46,$$

which is identical to the value we calculated with the standard formulas. Viewing the error term as an average of the group variances emphasizes the point that each group produces an estimate of experimental error for each condition, and that these estimates are then averaged to provide a more stable estimate of experimental error for the entire experiment. I will discuss this point again in Chapter 5.

3.6 SUMMARY

In this chapter, I considered the final steps in the analysis of a single-factor experiment, namely, evaluating the F ratio. From the tabled values of the F statistic, which are based on theoretical sampling distributions of F, we are able to obtain the critical value of F. This value sets the lower boundary of the range of F's within which we will reject the null hypothesis. If the F we obtain from an analysis falls within this range—if it is equal to or greater than the critical value of F—we reject the null hypothesis and conclude that some treatment effects are present in the population. If the observed F is smaller than the critical value, we do not reject the null hypothesis.

Application of the decision rules will lead to errors of statistical inference at least part of the time. One such error, type I error, is that committed when the null hypothesis is falsely rejected. The magnitude of this error is called the significance level and is set by the researcher at a fairly low value (for example, $\alpha = .05$) before the start of the experiment. The other error, type II error (β), is that committed when the null hypothesis is not rejected and the alternative is true. The researcher controls this error indirectly by designing the experiment to be reasonably sensitive to the existence of treatment effects in the population.

3.7 EXERCISES[7]

1. Find the critical values of F for the following situations:
   (a) $F(4,30)$ at $\alpha = .05$. (b) $F(1, 120)$ at $\alpha = .001$.
   (c) $a = 7, s = 5, \alpha = .10$. (d) $a = 3, s = 9, \alpha = .25$.
2. Perform an analysis of variance on the following set of scores:

AS Matrix

a_1	a_2	a_3
8	9	2
0	4	0
9	8	5
4	1	7
2	8	7

Reserve your calculations for Exercise 3 of Chapter 5.
3. Complete the analysis of variance of the data presented in Exercise 1 of Chapter 2 (p. 42).
4. An experiment is conducted with $s = 5$ subjects in each of the $a = 6$ treatment conditions; the sums are given below in the first row of numbers and the sums of the squared AS scores are given in the second row of numbers.

---

[7]The answers to these problems are found in Appendix B, beginning on p. 561.

(a) Perform an analysis of variance in the usual manner. Reserve your calculations for Exercise 1 of Chapter 5.

(b) Calculate the $MS_{S/A}$ by the alternative method of obtaining the average of the variances for the six groups.

a_1	a_2	a_3	a_4	a_5	a_6
15	10	25	35	25	20
65	35	130	275	150	102

4

The Sensitivity of an Experiment

The error term for the completely randomized design is based on the variability of subjects given the same experimental treatment. These estimates for the different groups are combined to form the within-groups means square. The presence or absence of treatment effects is assessed by means of the F ratio. As I have noted several times, the expected value of the numerator of the F ratio is the sum of a treatment component and an error component, while the expected value of the denominator term contains only the error component. The logic behind the F test is that the F ratio will tend to be greater than 1.0 when treatment effects are present and approximately equal to 1.0 when they are not.

4.1 REDUCTION OF ERROR VARIANCE

Sensitivity and Error Variance

It is of interest to see how the sensitivity of an experiment is related to the size of the error component. With treatment effects of a given magnitude, any increase in the size of the error variance reduces the size of the F ratio and lessens our chances of rejecting the null hypothesis; any decrease in error increases these chances.

There are three major sources of error variance: random variation in the actual treatments, the presence of unanalyzed control factors, and individual differences ("permanent" or "temporary" factors affecting a subject's performance during the course of the experiment). All of these sources reflect themselves in a subject's score on the dependent variable and thus contribute to error variance. Certain steps can be taken to reduce the magnitude of these sources of experimental error, however, and I will mention them briefly.

Reduction of Treatment Variability

I have noted previously that no experimental treatment is *exactly* alike for every subject in a particular condition. The calibration of the equipment may change from session to session, the experimenter will not be perfectly consistent in the conduct of the experiment, and environmental factors such as noise level, illumination, and temperature will not be identical for each subject. To the extent that these different factors influence the behavior under study, their variation from subject to subject contributes to the estimate of experimental error. I should add to this list any errors of measurement and of recording that appear randomly in the data collection.

We can take certain steps to minimize these sources of variability. Carefully calibrated equipment, automation, well-trained experimenters, and special testing rooms help to accomplish this goal. In essence, this solution attempts to hold constant the specific conditions of testing in the experiment.

Unanalyzed Control Factors

Control factors are nuisance variables that are introduced into an experiment for a variety of reasons, but primarily for the removal of possible bias and for an increase in the generality of the results. For example, suppose an experimenter plans an experiment that requires far too many subjects for one assistant to test. If more than one assistant is employed, the researcher should make sure that each assistant runs an equal number of subjects in each of the treatment conditions. To do otherwise would introduce a potential confounding of assistants and treatments into the experiment.

Most researchers would disregard these control factors—different laboratory assistants, in this example—in the analysis of their experiments and simply analyze the results as a completely randomized single-factor design. Often this is a mistake because any variability associated with control factors contributes directly to error variance. That is, the variability of subjects within any group will now include differences associated with laboratory assistants, say, in addition to the usual factors contributing to experimental error. In short, a nonrandom source of variance, such as assistants, that is spread equally over all treatment conditions, as in this example, does not bias the treatment effects, but it does contribute to the size of the error term. The obvious solution to such a situation is to include control factors in the statistical analysis, using procedures that I will consider in later chapters of this book.

Reduction of Subject Variability

Undoubtedly the major source of error variance in the behavioral sciences is that contributed by individual differences. The fact that subjects differ widely in performance on laboratory tasks means that when they are assigned randomly to the treatment conditions, this variability becomes an important source of error variance. The most obvious way of reducing subject variability is to select subjects who are relatively similar on some important and relevant characteristic, for example, IQ in a learning test, visual acuity in a perception experiment, socioeconomic status in an attitude-change study, and so on. A second type of matching is accomplished in small sets that consist of subjects matched *within* a set while generally differing widely *between* sets. Neither procedure is widely used in psychology, however, perhaps because there are more effective methods of reducing subject variability. These preferred procedures include the use of the same subject in all of the treatment conditions and a statistical technique called the analysis of covariance, which adjusts estimates of error variance and of treatment effects on the basis of information obtained before the start of the study. Both of these procedures will be considered in subsequent chapters.

4.2 CONTROL OF TYPE I AND TYPE II ERRORS

As discussed in the last chapter, we are able to control the magnitude of type I error (false rejection of the null hypothesis) through our choice of a rejection region for the F distribution (the α level). The control of the type II error (failing to reject the null hypothesis when it is false) and of power unfortunately is not this simple. This is because power is dependent upon several factors including the size of the treatment effects, sample size, the degree of error variance, and the significance level. I described ways to decrease error variance in the preceding section and will consider the use of significance level in the control of power in this section. The estimation of power and the central role of sample size in controlling power directly will be discussed in subsequent sections. Estimating the size of treatment effects will be covered in the next chapter.

You have already seen the reciprocity between the two types of error in Fig. 3-3 (p. 57)–i.e., you know that any change in the size of the type I error will produce a change of opposite direction in the type II error. Given this reciprocity, then, one obvious way to decrease type II error (and to increase power) would be to increase the probability of a type I error. Unfortunately, however, we seem to be "stuck" with a rigidly set α level, since rarely will we see the α level set at any value greater than .05.

Why has type I error become fixed over the years? One answer is the absence of agreement concerning the relative seriousness of the two types of errors; in the absence of agreement, we *must* be arbitrary. It may be possible to establish a rational balancing of type I and type II errors in certain applied fields, however. In the medical sciences, for instance, we might be able to place a numerical value upon the consequences of failing to recognize a new wonder drug (a type II error) and contrast this with the value placed upon the consequences of switching to a new drug that is no better than the original one (a type I error). But in most research areas of the behavioral sciences we are without such guidance. How serious is it if a new hypothesis is not recognized or if an old one is incorrectly rejected? Without explicit values to guide us, we must proceed by conventions. Thus, we fix the type I error at a level that will be acceptable to most researchers–i.e., $\alpha = .05$ or lower–and allow the type II error (and power) to be what it has to be. We cannot answer the question of what is an acceptable level of power, since we are usually not in a position to be able to give weight to the relative consequences of the two types of error.

A second reason why we set the α level at some fixed value is that there are other ways by which the power of an experiment can be increased, as I pointed out at the beginning of this section. Of all these, the choice of *sample size* is the primary means by which power is controlled in an experiment. I will now discuss the factors that must be considered when sample size is used as a technique for controlling power.

4.3   DETERMINATION OF SAMPLE SIZE

Perhaps the question most frequently asked by students designing their first experiments concerns the number of subjects to assign to the different treatment conditions. The simplest answer is to indicate that they should use as many subjects as they can afford to! This apparent nonanswer is in fact good advice, since the greater the sample size, the greater the power and the more sensitive the experiment in detecting treatment differences in the population. There is a more complicated answer, however, which specifies a procedure that few researchers use, but which represents a rational solution to the problem.

In order to use this procedure, we must make some guesses about the probable outcome of the experiment and select a level of power with which we want to operate. The major stumbling block consists of being able to state *ahead of time* the nature of the treatment effects that are expected in the study. You can see why most investigators do not use this procedure to determine sample size. How can they specify the treatment effects when all that they can point to is a prediction that there will be a "significant" effect?[1] The other pieces of information we will require are an estimate of the size of the error term $MS_{S/A}$ and a decision on the level of power that will be acceptable to us. Error variance can be reasonably estimated from related research, but how do we decide on the amount of power we want in an experiment? Unfortunately, there are no established conventions for selecting a level of power as there are for selecting significance level.[2]

As a concrete example of the procedure followed in determining sample size, let's assume that we have decided to include four treatment conditions ($a = 4$) and estimate the expected minimum treatment effects, expressed as population treatment means μ_i, as follows:[3]

---

[1]Cohen (1977) enumerates a number of ways in which treatment effects can be expressed. Briefly, these range from an actual specification of the treatment means to a statement of the relative "size" of the treatment effects. For an elaboration of these procedures, see pp. 276–280 of Cohen's text.

[2]One authority on the topic recommends setting power at .80 (Cohen, 1977, pp. 53–56), but his reasons for selecting this particular value are not convincing in my opinion.

[3]In this example, we estimated each mean individually. It might make more sense in some applications to specify the minimum *distance* between pairs of means. For instance, we might say that we want the means to be separated by at least 4 units. The corresponding deviations would then be −6, −2, 2, and 6. It is not necessary, of course, to "space" the treatment means equally, as I have done. Any pattern which is most parsimonious with the expected outcome of the experiment can be used. Cohen (1977, pp. 276–280) proposes that researchers narrow their choice to a selection from among three patterns that differ in degree of variability represented. (See Exercise 2, p. 79, for an illustration of this procedure.)

TREATMENT MEANS	DEVIATIONS FROM μ
$\mu_1 = 16$	$\mu_1 - \mu = 16 - 20 = -4$
$\mu_2 = 21$	$\mu_2 - \mu = 21 - 20 = 1$
$\mu_3 = 23$	$\mu_3 - \mu = 23 - 20 = 3$
$\mu_4 = 20$	$\mu_4 - \mu = 20 - 20 = 0$

In addition, we will assume that an accurate estimate of the population variance ($\sigma^2_{S/A}$) is available, namely, $\sigma^2_{S/A} = 20$. We next substitute this information in the following formula:

$$\phi^2_A = \frac{s'[\,\Sigma\,(\mu_i - \mu)^2\,]/a}{\sigma^2_{S/A}}, \tag{4-1}$$

where the square root of ϕ^2_A is a quantity we will use in consulting special charts—called **power functions** of the F statistic—and s' is a possible sample size. (I have used s' rather than s to refer to sample size in order to emphasize the fact that different values of s' will be tried to determine the sample size needed to achieve a given level of power.) The other quantities in Eq. (4-1) should be familiar to you.

If we now solve for ϕ^2_A, we are then able to determine the effect of different sample sizes on power. To illustrate with this example,

$$\phi^2_A = \frac{s'[(-4)^2 + (1)^2 + (3)^2 + (0)^2]/4}{20}$$

$$= \frac{s'(26)/4}{20} = \frac{s'(6.5)}{20} = .325s'.$$

Solving for ϕ_A gives

$$\phi_A = \sqrt{\phi^2_A} = \sqrt{.325s'} = .57\sqrt{s'}.$$

With ϕ_A expressed in this form, we can vary sample size s', obtain a numerical value for ϕ_A, and determine from the power functions when we have attained the desired degree of power.

Let's see how this last step is accomplished. First, you should examine the power charts, which are provided in Table A-2 of Appendix A. There are eight different charts in this table. They differ with regard to the *numerator* degrees of freedom of the F ratio. (The charts are numbered consecutively, $df_{num.}$ equaling 1 to eight.) For any one chart, three factors are taken into consideration to find power. More specifically, there are two families of power functions for each chart, one for $\alpha = .05$ and the other for $\alpha = .01$. Except for the first chart, the functions for $\alpha = .05$ appear on the left and those for $\alpha = .01$ appear on the right. For a given α level, power functions are drawn for 11 different values of *denominator* degrees of freedom; $df_{denom.} = 6, 7, 8, 9, 10, 12, 15, 20, 30, 60$, and ∞. Intermediate values may be interpolated visually. The remaining factor is ϕ and appears on the baseline. Once all of these factors are coordinated on the chart—α, $df_{\text{denom.}}$, and ϕ—power is read directly off the ordinate.

Continuing with our example, let's see what happens when we use 5 as a trial sample size (that is, $s' = 5$). With this value,

$$\phi_A = .57 \sqrt{s'} = .57 \sqrt{5} = .57(2.24) = 1.28.$$

Turning to the third power chart in Table A-2 of Appendix A ($df_{\text{num.}} = 3$), we locate the function at $\alpha = .05$ for $df_{\text{denom.}} = a(s' - 1) = 4(5 - 1) = 16$. (We will use the function for $df = 15$.) We next move along this power function until we find the point at which $\phi = 1.28$ and then read off the power on the ordinate. In this case, power equals approximately .45. Presumably, this value is too low, which means that we must increase the sample size if we want power to approach a more acceptable level of .80 or higher. If we let $s' = 10$, for example,

$$\phi_A = .57 \sqrt{10} = .57(3.16) = 1.80.$$

To find out which power function to use this time, we will again have to calculate the $df_{\text{denom.}}$. In this case, $df = a(s' - 1) = 4(10 - 1) = 36$. Shifting to the function at $df = 30$, we find that the power associated with $\phi = 1.80$ is approximately .82. At this point, we might stop and use 10 as the sample size in the experiment, unless the estimated power is still too low, in which case we would try an even larger sample size.

In summary, then, estimating sample size involves what amounts to a trial-and-error operation. What we have to do is to fix the factors we can fix, such as the α level, the number of treatment levels, the estimate of the minimum treatment effects, and the estimate of error variance. We use this information to solve for ϕ_A expressed in terms of the trial sample size s'. We then estimate the power of the F test for any particular sample size by obtaining a numerical value for ϕ_A and entering this value appropriately in the relevant power chart. If the resultant power estimate is unsatisfactory (too low), we increase the sample size and repeat the operations.

Comments

The obvious difficulty in attempting to use power functions in the planning of an experiment is the problem of estimating the treatment effects and the population error variance. Authors of statistics texts can make up these values, since there is no experimental reality facing them! Researchers, in contrast, have to *do* the experiment and then suffer the consequences if they have overestimated or underestimated either of these values. In some instances, we can use past research to guide us in obtaining these estimates. Experiments conducted under relatively standard conditions, with subjects drawn from roughly the same population, offer a remarkably stable estimate of error variance.

The selection of the minimum treatment effects is the other stumbling block. Again, previous research may provide a hint as to what sorts of effects we might expect from a certain type of manipulation. In applied work, the situation is often clearer because actual dollar costs may be attached to the appearance of treatment differences of a certain magnitude. Frequently, however, an investigator is testing a theory, and the *size* of the treatment effects associated with the prediction is not very important—the experimenter wants to detect a difference but cannot specify its size. Obviously there will be a point at which an investigator will discard a theory if the prediction results in extremely small treatment effects. Nevertheless, if one theory predicts a particular outcome while alternative theories do not, the evaluation of this differential prediction may be of critical importance, and the size of the actual treatment effects of little interest per se.

An estimate of power, no matter how approximate, gives us some degree of control over type II error. If we are unable to make a reasonable guess concerning the size of the anticipated treatment differences or of the error variance, a practical procedure is to conduct a "pilot" study, a smaller version of the projected study, and to use the information obtained to provide the needed estimates. From this information, we can then make a rational decision concerning the sample size we will need in our experiment. The problem with this practical approach is that pilot studies tend to give unreliable results, largely due to the small numbers of subjects tested, and consequently, often provide information of questionable usefulness in designing a major study. In any case, a consideration of power—in spite of the uncertainties surrounding its determination—should be a necessary first step in the planning of any experiment.

It is interesting to note that researchers often implicitly take power into consideration when they design an experiment. This occurs when they have worked in a particular field for some time and have evolved a "feeling" for the general sensitivity of the experimental designs. Under these circumstances, they may take the position that most of the phenomena in which they are interested will be detected with a sample size of, say, $s = 16$. They will not be concerned with treatment effects that are not detected, given the level of sensitivity they expect in their research. Of course, when a manipulation is of *critical* interest, they will immediately drop this attitude and take whatever steps they can to assess the presence of treatment effects.

4.4 POWER AND INDEPENDENT REPLICATIONS

You have seen how power is affected directly by increases in sample size. There is a different approach to the question of power that in effect involves an increase in sample size, namely, independent replications—independent experiments testing the same or related research hypotheses. Suppose that the effects of a particular set of treatment conditions are small and the F is not significant. We have made a type II error because we have failed to reject the null hypothesis when the alternative hypothesis was true; stated another way, we simply lacked the statistical power with this experiment to permit the rejection of the null hypothesis. Suppose that we administer the same experiment a number of times and that each time the same thing happens—we fail to reject H_0—but each time we obtain the *same pattern* of results in each of these replications. The separate F tests, none of which is significant, fail to take into consideration the *consistency* of the data obtained in these independent experiments. Just how likely is it that we would obtain the same pattern each time on the basis of chance? As you will see, it is possible to combine the results of these separate experiments to determine whether or not the total set of findings still argues for the nonrejection of the null hypothesis.

A number of psychologists I know have expressed the opinion that the independent replication of a significant difference in *several* experiments is more convincing than a significant difference in a single experiment. Implicit in this statement is the belief that when a particular pattern of results is duplicated in spite of the many changes occurring from replication to replication, it must represent a relatively "robust" phenomenon. A significant finding in a single experiment may always be the result of a set of fortuitous circumstances, favoring some conditions over others, producing the particular pattern observed. We will never be sure of the falseness of the null hypothesis until we do replicate the finding one or more times. (Of course, it is still possible that the consistent results were the result of chance, but the probability that this will occur in several independent replications is quite small indeed.) Before the replications are conducted, we will still base our theories on the results of *single* experiments, knowing full well that the statistical machinery brought to play in the analysis of a single experiment is an attempt to assess the future replicability of a particular phenomenon. The ultimate test of any significant finding *is* its repeatability. As Fisher (1951) puts it, ". . . we may say that a phenomenon is experimentally demonstrable when we know how to conduct an experiment which will rarely fail to give us a statistically significant result" (p. 14).

There are other reasons why experiments are replicated. A common example is when researchers attempt to see if they can obtain the same set of findings when they repeat someone else's experiment. Alternatively, researchers may find that they have duplicated a number of treatment conditions in a series of experiments directed at entirely different problems. Or they may want to compare the results of experiments conducted in different laboratories. In these various cases, there are two or more treatment conditions that are present in several independent experiments, and the question of interest is whether the results are consistent or inconsistent from experiment to experiment.

A second type of replication is an integral part of the experimental design. Why would an experimenter choose to incorporate a number of replications into the experimental design? For one reason, it may only be possible to administer the experiment to a small number of subjects at a time. In animal-learning experiments, for example, each animal is given extensive training, often lasting for weeks. The same may be true for experiments in education, where the "treatments" consist of different methods of teaching applied over a school term. The length of these experiments may make it impossible to run more than a fraction of the subjects at a time. There may be other limitations in addition to time, such as limited space in which to house the animals during the experiment and limited equipment. The experimenter tries to include in each replication an equal number of subjects so that any general differences from one replication to the next will be spread equally over the treatment conditions. For another reason, the investigator might want to associate with replications such factors as the different experimenters conducting the study, the testing rooms, the "batch" of animals sent by the supplier, the time of day (or year), the school system, and so on. Any and all factors which can vary between replications are held constant for the subjects tested *within* the replication. The object in this arrangement of the testing is to make between-replication differences as great as possible and to hold these factors constant within the replications.

This type of experiment is more complicated than the single-factor design we are considering in this part of the book. Depending on the way in which the replications are arranged, the design is either a randomized block design (one subject per condition in each replication—now called a *block*) or a form of factorial design (more than one subject per condition in each replication or block). Both kinds of designs are covered in later chapters.

A Classification of Replications

Cooper and Rosenthal (1980) distinguish between replication and **extension** studies. For them, a replication study is one that provides an additional test of an already tested research hypothesis, while an extension study is one that is designed to move beyond the original hypothesis. Such an extension may take the form of changing potentially critical boundary conditions of an experiment—features that were held constant in the original study—in an attempt to establish the generality of the findings or in an attempt to gain support for any theoretical mechanisms offered to explain the earlier outcome.

Replications obviously can vary in the closeness with which they duplicate the original experimental procedures. Some researchers distinguish between **exact,** or **strict, replications,** where all assumed critical features between the two studies are duplicated and the others are permitted to change, and **inexact,** or **partial, replications,** where usually one critical feature is purposely changed in the new study.

All types of replications have their place in experimentation, but they differ in the sort of information they provide. An exact replication, if it successfully duplicates the original findings, adds little *new* information, but it does provide an important check on the possibility that the original finding was a type I error. Interesting and provocative new findings are especially good candidates for exact replications. If the replications are successful, they will help to establish the finding more firmly in the eyes of researchers in the field. On the other hand, if they are unsuccessful, they provide an early "warning" to others that the new phenomenon may not exist. In either case, a service has been provided to the field.

Partial replications produce useful information also, since a successful replication will permit researchers to extend or to generalize the phenomenon beyond the boundary conditions of the original study. An unsuccessful replication, however, provides ambiguous information about the original phenomenon: Was the first experiment a type I error or was the second experiment a type II error? Is it possible that the critical changes erased the original finding for some reason or other? There are examples of all these possibilities in the research literature. Thus, a strong risk is associated with replications that incorporate a major change in the boundary conditions, namely, that the reason (or reasons) for the failure to replicate often is (or are) not resolved by the second experiment. Additional work and additional replications generally are required.

Extension studies offer the highest risk of all replications if they are unsuccessful. In addition to the ambiguities associated with partial replications, failure to extend a phenomenon may mean that the theory was wrong in predicting a difference or that the derivation from the theory was in error or that the treatments chosen to test the theory were inappropriate, and so on.

The argument can be made for a blending of the different types of replication into a single experiment. That is, a researcher could include one set of treatments as an exact replication and the same set of treatments as either a partial replication or an extension study. This approach, which might be called a **systematic replication**, combines the values of the different kinds of replication. By including an exact replication, for example, the researcher has a check on the reliability of the original findings and a base against which to compare the other set of treatment conditions. Systematic replications of this sort are factorial designs and can be analyzed by the standard procedures covered in later chapters.

Statistical Analysis

Several statistical procedures are available to assess the consistency of outcome across a series of replications. Rosenthal (1978) provides a useful summary and illustration of these methods. All of these techniques focus on the difference between *two* means, however, which poses problems for experiments in which there are more than two conditions. In this latter situation, it is possible to treat the design as a factorial with the treatments as one factor and the independent replications as another. Winer discusses the analysis of this sort of design in detail (1971, pp. 391-394).[4]

As you will see in Chapters 6 and 7, it is possible to view a multilevel single-factor experiment as a number of smaller, two-group experiments in which portions of the larger experiment are selected for analysis. Under these circumstances the

---

[4]The first edition of this book presented an extended discussion and illustration of this statistical analysis (Keppel, 1973, pp. 542-546).

statistical analysis can follow the recommendations of Rosenthal by focusing on the outcome of these particular treatment differences and on how they hold up over the replications.

Statistical Summary of Research Findings

An important step in the development of an area of research is the transformation of findings reported in professional journals and publications into empirical generalizations and theory. Detailed and judicious summaries of research by knowledgeable reviewers, such as those appearing in the *Psychological Bulletin* and other journals, provide researchers with a critical sense of what has been established in the literature and what has not. Most reviewers use a type of "box-score" summary, segregating existing research on a particular topic or question into different categories representing degrees of support for a certain conclusion. This summary is usually based on the statistical tests reported in the original articles—significance or nonsignificance—with little or no attention paid to the patterns of the results or to the degree of support provided by the different experiments. As a consequence, potentially important information contained in the primary research literature is generally disregarded in the review process.

It may have occurred to you that the problem confronting the reviewer in sifting through a series of related studies is similar to that of a researcher assessing the success of a replication or a series of replications. In fact, the statistical procedures described by Rosenthal (1978), which I mentioned in the last section, can be easily adapted to provide a sound statistical basis for the review process. Rosenthal and Rubin (1979) have shown how one can compare statistical evidence reported in related studies in a quantitative and informative way. In a companion article, Cooper and Rosenthal (1980) reported a study comparing the conclusions drawn by a group of reviewers that used a statistical combining procedure with a group that used traditional methods to summarize an identical set of related papers (reports dealing with sex differences in persistence with tasks). They found sizable differences in the conclusions drawn by the individuals using the two different procedures and argue convincingly for adopting some form of statistical assessment into the review process.[5]

4.5 SUMMARY AND COMMENTS

The sensitivity of an experiment, formally expressed as power, should be of critical concern to anyone planning to conduct a research project. Most researchers take

---

[5]A similar point was made in an interesting paper by Tversky and Kahneman (1971), who found that intuitive judgments by psychologists concerning the replicability of hypothetical findings were often grossly in error. They argue that researchers should be urged to report power and confidence intervals in addition to the outcome of the F test in order to counteract this and other apparently strongly held biases.

appropriate steps to increase power through their choice of experimental design and by their attempts to reduce error variance. On the other hand, comparatively few take advantage of the procedures described in this chapter to estimate the *degree* of sensitivity before the experiment is conducted. In spite of the seeming impossibility of providing reasonable estimates of treatment effects and error variance and the absence of a power standard for the field such as we have for type I error, useful power estimates can be obtained either by using the simplifying procedures described by Cohen (1977) or by obtaining estimates from information appearing in earlier experiments.

What about the typical experiment conducted in psychology? Are not most experiments designed with sufficient power to detect the sorts of treatment effects that are of interest to researchers? Apparently not. Systematic reviews of the psychological literature have revealed an astonishingly low level of power in the published experiments surveyed (e.g., Cohen, 1962; Brewer, 1972). Although the interpretation of these findings is controversial, as a debate in the *American Educational Research Journal* reveals (see Cohen, 1973; Dayton, Schafer, and Rogers, 1973; Meyer, 1974b; Brewer, 1974; and Meyer, 1974a), the point remains that more attention should be given to power before an experiment is conducted and more energies should be directed in attempts to replicate newly reported findings. In this regard, Brown (1979) has shown that an apparent bias of journal editors (and investigators) to publish only significant results leads to an exaggeration of the probability of a successful replication, especially when sample size and treatment effects are small.

Power estimates obtained in the planning stage of an experiment force us to consider design sensitivity at a point where something can be done to increase the sensitivity of a study. Suppose a larger sample size is the only practical way for us to increase power. We would certainly begin to question the attractiveness of the experiment if we found that we needed an extremely large sample size to achieve acceptable power. Are the predicted treatment effects of sufficient importance to us—either empirically or theoretically—to commit this much time, money, and effort to go ahead with this research?[6] In working through this dilemma, we should keep in mind the meaning of a power estimate obtained at this point, namely, the probability that we will successfully reject the null hypothesis given the various assumptions we have made about the size and nature of the treatment effects, the sample size, the amount of error variance, and the significance level to use.

Power determinations also provide useful information *after* an experiment is conducted. The interpretation of nonsignificant findings is facilitated if we calculate power on the basis of our estimate of the size of the minimum treatment effects that would be of interest to us. If the power is low, we might want to pursue the same problem with a more sensitive experimental design, since the present one is obviously insensitive. On the other hand, if the power is relatively high, we might

---

[6]In this regard, Overall and Dalal (1965) show how a researcher can combine a power analysis with the demands of a limited research budget in order to choose the most sensitive experimental design from among the various alternatives.

be willing to conclude that the null hypothesis is more likely to be true—at least close enough to reality for us to treat the small differences as effectively zero.

4.6 EXERCISES[7]

1. Suppose an experimenter is planning an experiment with $a = 5$ different treatments. While it is difficult to specify expected outcomes in terms of actual means, it is sometimes possible to make predictions in terms of pairs of conditions. Suppose the experimenter is willing to assume the following population data: $\mu_1 = \mu_2$, $\mu_3 - \mu_2 = 4$, $\mu_4 - \mu_3 = 2$, and $\mu_4 - \mu_5 = 1$. On the basis of past research, the population error variance is estimated to be 15.
   (a) What sample size will be needed by the researcher to achieve power of .80 at $\alpha = .05$? (*Hint:* A set of means fitting this pattern can be constructed by assuming an arbitrary number for one of the means and solving for the others.)
   (b) What sample size will be needed if the researcher decides to work at $\alpha = .01$?
2. Cohen (1977) suggests considering the pattern of variability to be taken by the population treatment means in estimating treatment effects. He starts with the smallest and the largest means and then assigns values to the remaining means according to one of three possible patterns: *minimum variability* (the remaining means are placed at the midpoint between the two extremes), *intermediate variability* (the means are spaced equally between the two extremes), and *maximum variability* (half of the remaining means are given the minimum value and the other half are given the maximum value). Let's see how this procedure works. We will assume that $a = 8$, $s = 9$, population error variance $= 27.56$, the minimum population treatment mean $\mu_{min.} = 5$, and the maximum population treatment mean $\mu_{max.} = 12$. Assuming that we set $\alpha = .05$, what is the estimated power for the three patterns of variability suggested by Cohen?
3. Suppose we conducted a pilot study in order to estimate the sample size before undertaking an expensive and time-consuming investigation. There are two treatment conditions in the experiment. The means from the pilot study are 9.30 and 7.44; the within-groups variance is 2.48. Using these means as estimates of the population treatment means, and the within-groups variance as an estimate of the population variance, what sample size would be required in order to achieve a power estimate of approximately .90?

[7] The answers to these problems are found in Appendix B, beginning on p. 562.

5

Assumptions and Other Considerations

In this chapter, I consider a variety of important points and details that sur-round the use and interpretation of the analysis of variance. I begin with a brief discussion of the statistical model on which the F test is based, followed by a con-sideration of the consequences of violating some of the assumptions underlying the analysis of variance. I then examine supplemental indices that add useful informa-tion to the interpretation of a set of results. These will include interval estimates of the population treatment means, estimates of the relative size of treatment effects, and the use of within-group variances as a descriptive statistic. I will also discuss the difficulties associated with the inadvertent loss of subjects during the course of con-ducting an experiment.

5.1   THE STATISTICAL MODEL

The logic of the F test was discussed in Chapters 2 and 3 without reference to the statistical model underlying the analysis of variance. In this section and the next, I will describe certain critical features of this model, attempting to maintain a level of explanation that is in keeping with the purpose of this book. If you desire a more thorough description of this model and a specification of the steps involved in the statistical derivations based on the model, I recommend the discussion offered by Myers (1979, pp. 59–66).

Our discussion begins with the assumption of an infinitely large population of individuals. Let's assume that each of these individuals is randomly assigned to one of the treatment conditions. The set of scores obtained from subjects receiving the same treatment is called a **treatment population**. There is a different treatment pop-ulation for each condition of the experiment. The mean of a treatment population is μ_i, and the overall mean of the treatment populations is μ, obtained by averaging the μ_i's. For statistical purposes, an experiment is assumed to consist of samples of size s that are drawn randomly from the treatment populations. The null hypothesis represents one possible statement about the population treatment means, namely, that they are equal. The data from the experiment are used to test the reasonable-ness of this particular hypothesis.

The Linear Model

The linear model, which underlies the analysis of variance, is a mathematical statement expressing the score of any subject in any treatment condition as the linear sum of the parameters of the population. In the case of the completely ran-domized single-factor design, the model states

$$AS_{ij} = \mu + \alpha_i + \epsilon_{ij}, \tag{5-1}$$

where AS_{ij} = one of the observations in any one of the treatment groups;

μ = the grand mean of the treatment populations;

$\alpha_i = \mu_i - \mu$, known as the **treatment effect** for condition a_i; and

$\epsilon_{ij} = AS_{ij} - \mu_i$, assumed to reflect experimental error.

As discussed in the next section, certain assumptions are made concerning the distribution of the treatment populations, which I will mention only briefly here. These assumptions are usually expressed in terms of the ϵ_{ij}'s rather than in terms of the scores themselves. More specifically, there are three assumptions. First, it is assumed that the ϵ_{ij}'s are normally distributed, with a mean of zero, in each of the treatment populations. Second, it is assumed that the variance of each distribution of ϵ_{ij}'s is equal to σ_ϵ^2; that is,

$$\sigma_1^2 = \sigma_2^2 = \sigma_3^2 = \text{etc.} = \sigma_\epsilon^2.$$

This common variance σ_ϵ^2 is called **error variance**. Finally, it is assumed that the ϵ_{ij}'s are mutually independent, which means in essence that subjects are assigned randomly to the different treatments. Keeping these assumptions in mind, we can now consider the internal structure—known as the **expected values**—of the two mean squares we normally obtain in the analysis of variance.

Expected Mean Squares

Statistical theory provides us with information about the theoretical expectations, or contents, of statistics calculated from data. More specifically, the expected value of a statistic is the mean of the sampling distribution of that statistic obtained from repeated random sampling from the population. In the case of the two mean squares of interest to us, the expected values are the average values of MS_A and $MS_{S/A}$ calculated from an extremely large number of replicated experiments based on independent random sampling from the treatment populations. Let's look at the expected values of these two mean squares.

The within-groups mean square $MS_{S/A}$ provides an unbiased estimate of error variance σ_ϵ^2. That is, repeated random samplings would produce a sampling distribution of $MS_{S/A}$ with a mean equal to the variance in the population. Stated in symbols,

$$E(MS_{S/A}) = \sigma_\epsilon^2, \tag{5-2}$$

where $E(MS_{S/A})$ is read, "the expected value of the within-groups mean square."

The expected value of the treatment mean square, $E(MS_A)$, is not equal to the treatment component, but rather represents a combination of the treatment component and error variance. You can see this point quite vividly by considering the expected value for the treatment mean square, namely,

$$E(MS_A) = \sigma_\epsilon^2 + \frac{s \sum (\alpha_i)^2}{a-1}. \tag{5-3}$$

I will designate the second term on the right of the equal sign $s(\theta_A^2)$, where θ_A^2 is the treatment component, $\Sigma (\alpha_i)^2/(a - 1)$, and s is the number of observations contributing to the estimate of each treatment population mean. More compactly,

$$E(MS_A) = \sigma_\epsilon^2 + s(\theta_A^2). \tag{5-3a}$$

The symbol θ_A^2 is used to indicate that this particular quantity is based on an additional assumption that refers to the way in which the levels of the treatment variable have been selected for the experiment. That is, Eqs. (5-3) and (5-3a) reflect the **fixed-effects model**, which is appropriate when the levels of the treatment variable have been selected *arbitrarily*—as they are in most experiments. A different model, the **random-effects model**, applies when the treatment levels have been selected *randomly*. I will discuss random models and the effects of randomly chosen treatment levels on the analysis of variance in later chapters.

The essential logic of the analysis of variance lies in the construction of ratios having the form

$$\frac{MS_{\text{effect}}}{MS_{\text{error}}},$$

where the expected value of the MS_{error} matches the expected value of the MS_{effect} in all respects except for the component reflecting the effect. In the present case,

$$E(MS_A) = \sigma_\epsilon^2 + s(\theta_A^2);$$

and

$$E(MS_{S/A}) = \sigma_\epsilon^2.$$

Under the null hypothesis,

$$H_0: \mu_1 = \mu_2 = \mu_3 = \text{etc.} = \mu.$$

Since $\alpha_i = \mu_i - \mu$, the null hypothesis can also be stated as follows:

$$H_0: \alpha_1 = \alpha_2 = \alpha_3 = \text{etc.} = 0.$$

Either way, the "effect" component θ_A^2, or the **null-hypothesis component**, as it is often called, equals zero and the ratio

$$F = \frac{MS_A}{MS_{S/A}}$$

is distributed as $F(df_A, df_{S/A})$, provided the assumptions we will consider in detail shortly are satisfied. We can then relate the observed value of F to the tabled values of F and assess its significance through the application of the decision rules.

Additional Points

Sooner or later you will come upon two situations that will puzzle you: the meaning of an extremely small F and the substitution of a different test statistic, t, for the F statistic. I will consider both situations briefly.

Small F Ratios. An examination of the sampling distribution of F when the null hypothesis is true (see Fig. 3-1, p. 49) clearly indicates that F's less than 1 occur with great frequency. It may have occurred to you that we could establish a rejection region in the *left*-hand tail of the F distribution to determine whether an F is statistically *small*, i.e., falls within the 5 percent, say, smallest F ratios expected to occur by chance. The statistical test is easily accomplished simply by *inverting* the F ratio, $MS_{S/A}/MS_A$ or $1/F$, and comparing this value with the appropriate numerator and denominator degrees of freedom for this new statistic, $df_{num.} = df_{S/A}$ and $df_{denom.} = df_A$.

The occurrence of a statistically small F—an inverted F falling within this special rejection region—is quite difficult to interpret. If $\alpha = .05$, we would expect 5 percent of the F's to fall within the rejection region when the null hypothesis is true. Thus, one "explanation" is the normal operation of chance factors. But other explanations should at least be considered. Inexperienced researchers sometimes tamper with the random assignment of subjects to conditions by attempting to equate the groups if they seem too deviant on some common performance measure obtained before the introduction of the differential treatments, as in a practice session. This "compensation" for chance factors threatens the mathematical basis for the F test.

The Relationship Between F and t. Most experiments in psychology consist of more than two treatment conditions, although there was a time when the typical experiment contained only two different treatments. In those early years, however, researchers used a statistical test called the **Student t test**, or t **test**, to analyze the results of two-group studies. The interesting point is that the t test is a special case of the F test. That is, exactly the same information is derived from either test. We can translate from one statistic to the other by noting that when F is based on $df_{num.} = 1$ and $df_{denom.} = df_{S/A}$ and when t is based on $df_{S/A}$,

$$F = t^2 \quad \text{and} \quad t = \sqrt{F}.$$

Because of the algebraic equivalence between the two tests, you can simply remind yourself when you see a reference to a t test that the conclusions are interchangeable: if the t is significant, F is significant; if t is not significant, F is not significant.[1] The most frequent reference to t tests in the contemporary literature is in the comparison between two treatment means selected from a larger experiment. As you will see in the next chapter, the analysis of variance can easily be adapted to assess the significance of differences between pairs of means as well. I will not discuss the t test in this book.

---

[1] This equivalency holds only for **nondirectional** t tests, or **two-tailed tests,** as they are often called. I will discuss this matter in the next chapter.

5.2 VIOLATING THE ASSUMPTIONS OF THE ANALYSIS OF VARIANCE

As I indicated in the last section, certain assumptions concerning the distribution of scores within groups must be met if the analysis of variance is to work as described. The values listed in the F table are based on the theoretical F distribution. These values are appropriate for an analysis only when these distribution assumptions are satisfied. If they are not, then we have no simple way of determining whether or not $F_{observed}$ falls within the rejection region of the theoretical sampling distribution of this statistic—whatever it might be with a particular set of violations. The critical question for us, of course, is to see how our *conclusions* are affected by a failure of our experiment to meet these assumptions. Such a consideration is extremely important, since rarely will we find all of the assumptions met in the experiments we conduct. If even the slightest violation can result in a considerable change in the sampling distribution of the F statistic, then we are in trouble.

There has been an important development in the evaluation of the assumptions underlying the analysis of variance. It is a practical approach to the problem—in a sense, a "user's" approach. Monte Carlo experiments are performed with a computer, based on scores drawn at random from populations with characteristics *differing* from those assumed in the analysis. These populations are constructed to have the *same mean* but different shapes and different variances. The resultant sampling distribution of the F statistic, obtained from a large number of these random draws, is compared with the theoretical F distribution. Since the null hypothesis is true in these experiments (the population means are equal), the sampling distribution of the F statistic will equal the theoretical distribution of F only if the violations of the assumptions are *unimportant*. The degree to which the empirically derived sampling distribution deviates from the theoretical distribution provides an assessment of the practical consequences of these violations. As you will discover shortly, the sampling distribution of F is amazingly "robust"; i.e., it is insensitive to even flagrant violations of the assumptions.[2]

Normally Distributed Treatment Populations

The first assumption states that the individual treatment populations, from which the members of each treatment group are assumed to be randomly drawn, are normally distributed. As a rough test of this assumption, we could look at the distribution of the AS scores within each group and estimate the general shape of the distribution. Or we could check for normality by means of a rather elaborate but objective test (see, for example, Hays, 1973, pp. 725-727). Suppose that the sample distributions are of approximately the same *non*normal shape—or, even worse, that the distributions for the different groups appear to have been drawn

---

[2]For a comprehensive discussion of the consequences of violating these assumptions, see Glass, Peckham, and Sanders (1972).

from populations with qualitatively different distributions. What does this do to the sampling distribution of F? Apparently, very little, especially if the groups contain equal numbers of subjects. This has been known by statisticians for some time (see Box, 1953). Monte Carlo experiments have also been performed. We will consider one of these studies in some detail.

In the Monte Carlo experiments, attention is focused upon the rejection region of the F distribution. When the sampling is from populations meeting all of the assumptions, the percentage of F ratios which actually fall in the rejection region matches very closely the percentage expected on the basis of the theoretical distribution. An early Monte Carlo study performed by Norton (1952) is reported by Lindquist (1953, pp. 78–90). Norton drew samples from distributions which were normal, leptokurtic (highly peaked), rectangular, moderately and markedly skewed, and J-shaped. He also conducted Monte Carlo tests where the scores were drawn from distributions having the same shape and from distributions having different shapes. He found that with homogeneous distributions, there was a close matching of empirical and theoretical percentages. The match was not quite as good when the populations were of markedly different form. In this latter case, the discrepancies were of the order of a 2 to 3 percentage point overestimation of the 5 percent significance level and of a 1 to 2 percentage point overestimation of the 1 percent significance level. This means, for example, that when an experimenter chooses an $\alpha = .05$, the *actual* α level may be as large as $p = .08$.

In short, Norton's study indicates that if we used the 5 percent rejection region, even for the most deviant comparisons, the empirically determined rejection region (the type I error) would be no larger than $\alpha = .08$. (This overestimation would probably have been less if Norton had used larger sample sizes. His sample sizes were 3 or 5.) Norton's and later studies tell us, then, that it is safe to conclude that violations of the normality assumption do not constitute a serious problem, except if the violations are especially severe. Under these circumstances, we need only worry about F's that fall close to the critical value of F defining the start of the rejection region.

Homogeneity of Error Variance

The second assumption requires that the variances of the different treatment populations be equal. In terms of an experiment, the within-group mean squares for each group, which provide separate estimates of error variance, should be the same. A variety of statistical procedures is available to test this assumption, but the older and more well-known procedures share a common problem—a sensitivity to departures from *normality* as well as to the presence of heterogeneity. I will consider more modern alternatives to these earlier tests in Section 5.5.

The critical question before us is the effect of unequal within-group variances on the theoretical sampling distribution of F. As with deviations from normality, Monte Carlo studies show that even sizable differences among the variances do not appear to distort the F distribution seriously. (Violations are again more serious when unequal sample sizes are present.) Because of these findings, then, most researchers do not even bother to test the homogeneity assumption with their data.[3]

Independence of Error Components

The deviation of each score from the grand mean of the population $(AS_{ij} - \mu)$ is thought to contain two components, a between-group treatment effect α_i and a within-group deviation ϵ_{ij}, the latter forming the basis for our estimate of experimental error based on sample scores. A third assumption of the analysis of variance is that the error components are independent—independent within treatment groups as well as independent between treatment groups. Independence here means that each observation is in no way related to any other observation in the experiment. The random assignment of subjects to conditions is the procedure by which we obtain independence. Of course, this is just another way of saying that systematic biases must not be present in the assignment of subjects to conditions. This is not just a statistical assumption, but a basic requirement of experimental design as well. With nonindependence of error components between treatment groups, a confounding of variables is present, and we are unable to make unambiguous inferences concerning the independent influence of our independent variable on the behavior we are studying. This assumption, then, emphasizes the critical importance statistically, as well as experimentally, of ensuring the random assignment of subjects to the treatment groups.

5.3 ESTIMATING POPULATION TREATMENT MEANS

Estimation procedures usually associated with survey studies can be applied to the data of an experiment to provide interval estimates of the population treatment means. Interval estimates that are formed in consideration of the degree of risk are called **confidence intervals.** The degree of confidence is given by the expression

$$\text{confidence} = 100(1 - \alpha) \text{ percent.}$$

If we allow the proportion of erroneous interval estimates—intervals that do not include the population mean—we may ever make to be $\alpha = .05$, say, our interval

---

[3]Rogan and Keselman (1977) report that this general conclusion does not always hold, even with experiments containing relatively large and equal sample sizes. They found increases in type I error of 2 to 4 percentage points above the assumed, or nominal, significance level when the degree of heterogeneity was quite large. Although one could argue that these conditions probably exceed what is usually found in actual experimentation, a cautious researcher should perhaps become concerned about relatively extreme heterogeneity, e.g., a ratio of the largest to the smallest within-group variance of 10, say, especially if the observed F ratio falls close to the critical value of F established for the experiment.

estimates are referred to as

$$100(1 - .05) = 100(.95) = 95 \text{ percent confidence intervals.}$$

The formula for establishing the lower and upper limits of a confidence interval of a treatment population mean is

$$\bar{A}_i \pm (t)(\hat{\sigma}_M), \tag{5-4}$$

where $\bar{A}_i$ is the **point estimate** of the population mean, t is a standardized deviate from the t distribution, and $\hat{\sigma}_M$ is a point estimate of the standard deviation of the sampling distribution of the mean (also known as the **standard error of the mean**). We obtain the quantities specified in Eq. (5-4) as follows:

$\bar{A}_i$ is the mean of the treatment group.
t is found in Table A-3, to be explained in a moment.
$\hat{\sigma}_M$ is obtained by formula from the standard deviation of the treatment group $(\hat{\sigma}_i)$ given below.

More specifically,

$$\hat{\sigma}_M = \frac{\hat{\sigma}_i}{\sqrt{s}}. \tag{5-5}$$

The numerator of this fraction is an estimate of the treatment-population standard deviation, obtained from the individual observations in the treatment group, and s is the sample size.

As an example, we will calculate a confidence interval based on the data presented in Table 3-4 (p. 60). From the 4-hour condition (a_1), the mean is 26.50, the standard deviation is 7.14, and sample size is 4. From this information, we can obtain the three quantities specified in Eq. (5-4), $\bar{A}_i$, t, and $\hat{\sigma}_M$. The first quantity has already been calculated; i.e.,

$$\bar{A}_1 = 26.50.$$

The second quantity, t, depends upon the degrees of freedom associated with the within-group variance, namely, $df = s - 1$, and α. If we set $\alpha = .05$, we can find t in a table of the t distribution, Table A-3 of Appendix A. This is accomplished by locating the row where $df = s - 1 = 4 - 1 = 3$ and the column where $\alpha = .05$. This value is 3.18. For the final quantity, we substitute in Eq. (5-5) and find

$$\hat{\sigma}_M = \frac{\hat{\sigma}_i}{\sqrt{s}}$$

$$= \frac{7.14}{\sqrt{4}} = \frac{7.14}{2.00} = 3.57$$

From Eq. (5-4), we can obtain the two limits of the 95 percent confidence interval:

$$\bar{A}_i \pm (t)(\hat{\sigma}_M) = 26.50 \pm (3.18)(3.57)$$
$$= 26.50 \pm 11.35.$$

The value for the lower limit is

$$26.50 - 11.35 = 15.15,$$

and the value for the upper limit is

$$26.50 + 11.35 = 37.85.$$

The primary function of confidence intervals is to provide an index of the relative precision with which the treatment means are measured. A small confidence interval reflects greater precision than a larger one. Plots of treatment means with the upper and lower limits of confidence intervals displayed as vertical lines extending through the means are commonly found in research reports. This type of graph provides a useful picture of the degree of experimental error operating in an experiment.

5.4 ESTIMATING RELATIVE TREATMENT MAGNITUDE

Prediction is a primary goal of science. One index of our ability to predict behavior is the degree to which we can "force" it around with our experimental manipulations. Said another way, the importance of an experimental manipulation is demonstrated by the degree to which we can account for the total variability among subjects by isolating the experimental effects. It would be useful to have an index of the efficacy of experimental treatments. Such an index could guide us in our decision to follow or not to follow a certain direction in our research. It would point to manipulations that eventually must be included in any comprehensive theory of the behavior we are studying. In applied research, the importance of experimental treatments can be translated into dollars-and-cents language.

Many investigators already use one such index—the significance level associated with a given F test. Unfortunately, however, this index is simply not appropriate. All too frequently, we find researchers comparing an F test that is significant at $p < .00001$ with one that is significant at $p < .05$ and concluding that the first experiment represents an impressive degree of prediction while the second experiment commands only passing interest. The problem with such a comparison of F statistics is that the size of the F ratio is affected by other factors in addition to the size of the treatment effects, the most obvious of which is *sample size.* Thus, a large F may imply that treatment effects are large, or that sample size was large, or that both factors are contributing to the observed value of F.

Suppose we approach this important point from another direction. Consider two experiments, one with a sample size of 5 and the other with a sample size of 20, in which both experiments produce an F that is significant at $p = .05$. Which set of results would be most impressive, the one with the small sample size or the one with the large sample size? Rosenthal and Gaito (1963) report that many researchers will choose the experiment with the *larger* sample size, when in fact the experiment with the *smaller* sample size would be the correct choice. In view of the fact that power and sample size are positively correlated, we simply cannot use significance level alone as an index of the strength of an experimental effect. What we need is an index that is (1) responsive to the strength of the association between an experimental manipulation and changes in behavior and (2) independent of sample size.

A Measure of Relative Treatment Magnitude

Several measures of treatment magnitude are possible that are not directly influenced by sample size. The simplest measure available to us is provided by the population treatment means, or rather by the differences between the means, $\mu_i - \mu_{i'}$. Alternatively, we could express treatment magnitude in terms of the difference between a population treatment mean and the overall population mean; $\alpha_i = \mu_i - \mu$. As a measure of the average treatment effect, the α_i's can be transformed into a **population treatment variance** by summing the squared population treatment effects and dividing by the number of treatments, i.e.,

$$\frac{\Sigma\,(\alpha_i)^2}{a}.$$

This particular variance is related to the population treatment component θ_A^2 appearing in the expected value of the treatment mean square; see Eq. (5-3), p. 82. All of these measures offer convenient ways of representing the size of treatment effects in the population in absolute terms.[4]

Relative measures of treatment magnitude, where the population treatment variance is compared with additional sources of variability—e.g., error variance—are more widely used than the absolute measures mentioned in the last paragraph. Several measures of relative strength have been proposed, but the most popular is an index known as **omega squared** (ω^2).[5] When applied to the single-factor design, omega squared ω_A^2 consists of a ratio contrasting the population treatment variance with the total population variance obtained by summing the population treatment variance

$$\frac{\Sigma\,(\alpha_i)^2}{a}$$

[4]Myers (1979, pp. 84–85) shows how to estimate the absolute magnitude of θ_A^2 from the results of an experiment.

[5]Useful discussions of the history of the development of these measures, including comparisons between them, are provided by Dwyer (1974, pp. 732–734), Glass and Hakstian (1969, pp. 403–408), and Maxwell, Camp, and Arvey (1981).

and error variance σ_ϵ^2. In symbols,

$$\omega_A^2 = \frac{\dfrac{\Sigma\,(\alpha_i)^2}{a}}{\dfrac{\Sigma\,(\alpha_i)^2}{a} + \sigma_\epsilon^2}.$$

Defined this way, $\omega_A^2 = 0$ when population treatment effects are absent, and varies between 0 and 1.0 when they are present. Strength, as measured by ω_A^2, is clearly a *relative* measure, reflecting the proportional amount of the total population variance *accounted for* by the experimental treatments. This index is often referred to as the proportion of variation "explained" by the treatment manipulation in an experiment, or more simply as explained variance.

Estimating Omega Squared

Omega squared is estimated quite simply by using quantities already entered in the summary table of the analysis of variance.[6] That is,

$$\hat{\omega}_A^2 = \frac{SS_A - (a-1)(MS_{S/A})}{SS_T + MS_{S/A}}. \tag{5-6}$$

As an example, consider the results of the experiment that was analyzed in Chapter 3 and summarized in Table 3-5 (p. 63). For this experiment, $a = 4$, $SS_A = 3{,}314.25$, $MS_{S/A} = 150.46$, and $SS_T = 5{,}119.75$. Substituting in Eq. (5-6), we find

$$\hat{\omega}_A^2 = \frac{3{,}314.25 - (4-1)(150.46)}{5{,}119.75 + 150.46} = \frac{2{,}862.87}{5{,}270.21} = .543.$$

What this value indicates is that approximately 54 percent of the total variance is accounted for by the experimental treatments.

Other, algebraically equivalent formulas for estimating omega squared are available, but the one presented here requires considerably less computational effort when applied to more complex designs. (See Dodd and Schultz, 1973, for a comprehensive presentation of such formulas for a wide variety of experimental designs.) The disadvantage of Eq. (5-6) is that the formula obscures the logic of this particular index. The approach taken by Vaughan and Corballis (1969) does preserve this logic by using the information provided in the expected mean squares to estimate the variance of the population treatment effects,

$$\frac{\Sigma\,(\alpha_i)^2}{a},$$

---

[6]This discussion assumes the fixed-effects model, which describes most of the experimental designs in the psychological literature. The random-effects model, where the levels of the independent variable are selected randomly from a very large number of potential levels, requires a different formula. See Vaughan and Corballis (1969) and Dwyer (1974) for a treatment of random independent variables.

and the total population variance,

$$\sigma_\epsilon^2 + \frac{\Sigma (\alpha_i)^2}{a},$$

The formula for $\hat{\omega}_A^2$ is then a ratio of the first variance to the second.

Some Properties of $\hat{\omega}^2$

The index omega squared provides a relative measure of the strength of an independent variable. While logically the index can range from $\hat{\omega}_A^2 = .00$ to $\hat{\omega}_A^2 = 1.00$, there are certain realities that empirical data force upon the measure. For example, negative values will be obtained when $F < 1$.[7] In addition, it is highly unlikely that large values of $\hat{\omega}_A^2$ will be observed, because of the relatively large contribution of error variance found in most behavioral research. Thus, the size of the error component will effectively limit the ultimate size of $\hat{\omega}_A^2$. Cohen (e.g., 1977, pp. 284-288) suggests that a "large" effect in the behavioral and social sciences is an experiment that produces a value of .15 or greater. A "medium" effect is .06, and a "small" effect is .01. Although any admittedly arbitrary definition can be questioned, the rough "scale" offered by Cohen provides some perspective with which to interpret values of $\hat{\omega}_A^2$ reported in the literature.

The estimate of omega squared is not a test statistic, although in effect the "significance" of $\hat{\omega}_A^2$ is assessed by the regular F test. That is, a significant F implies that $\hat{\omega}_A^2$ is significantly greater than zero as well. On the other hand, $\hat{\omega}_A^2$ can provide useful information even when F is *not* significant. This is because $\hat{\omega}_A^2$ is unaffected by small sample sizes (and hence, low power) while the significance of the F test is affected by small sample sizes. The insensitivity of $\hat{\omega}_A^2$ to variations in sample size, which follows from its definition and is the critical reason for its use, has been demonstrated in several Monte Carlo sampling experiments (e.g., Carroll and Nordholm, 1975, p. 550; and Lane and Dunlap, 1978, p. 109).

Other Measures of Relative Treatment Magnitude

While $\hat{\omega}_A^2$ is the most commonly reported measure of relative treatment magnitude, other indices have been proposed. The most serious "competitor" is known as epsilon squared ($\hat{\epsilon}_A^2$). The formula for this index is

$$\hat{\epsilon}_A^2 = \frac{SS_A - (a-1)(MS_{S/A})}{SS_T}. \tag{5-7}$$

If you refer to Eq. (5-6), you will see the close similarity between the two indices. Since the denominator for $\hat{\omega}_A^2$ is larger than the denominator for $\hat{\epsilon}_A^2$ and the

---

[7] Since a negative ω_A^2 cannot occur in the population, some authors recommend setting $\omega_A^2 = 0$, which says that there is no estimated effect. Nevertheless, it still is advisable to report the negative value, if only in a footnote.

numerators are the same, $\hat{\epsilon}_A^2$ must always be either equal to or larger than $\hat{\omega}_A^2$. With the data from the last section,

$$\hat{\epsilon}_A^2 = \frac{3,314.25 - (4-1)(150.46)}{5,119.75} = \frac{2,862.87}{5,119.75} = .559.$$

By way of comparison, $\hat{\omega}_A^2 = .543$. As pointed out by Glass and Hakstian (1969, p. 408) and illustrated by Carroll and Nordholm (1975), the difference between these two indices will be quite small in most experiments.

Epsilon squared is a measure developed out of the multiple-regression tradition, while $\hat{\omega}_A^2$ apparently has no counterpart in multiple regression and correlation.[8] The most common index of strength in the multiple-regression literature is the squared multiple-correlation coefficient R^2. This index, which is also known as *eta squared* and as the *correlation ratio*, has been proposed as an index of relative strength for data from experiments. In the present context,

$$R^2 = \frac{SS_A}{SS_T} = \frac{3,314.25}{5,119.75} = .647.$$

The R^2 measure will always be larger than epsilon squared. In this sample, the difference is considerable.

Epsilon squared can be derived from R^2 by means of a correction formula; it is often called the "shrunken" R^2 (see Cohen and Cohen, 1975, pp. 106–107). It is important to be aware of the relationship between $\hat{\omega}_A^2$, $\hat{\epsilon}_A^2$ and R^2 because of the increasing trend among researchers to use analysis-of-variance and multiple-regression procedures interchangeably since they are derived from the same general model. Epsilon squared is a better estimate of strength in the population than is R^2. Thus, $\hat{\omega}_A^2$ and $\hat{\epsilon}_A^2$ are the two main options available to researchers. On balance, omega squared has the advantage that the index has been extended to more complex designs and models and is more well known to users of analysis of variance than is $\hat{\epsilon}_A^2$. Maxwell, Camp, and Arvey (1981) note some difficulties in using $\hat{\epsilon}_A^2$ in factorial experiments, and it is not clear whether $\hat{\epsilon}_A^2$ can be generalized for use with as many types of experimental designs as can $\hat{\omega}_A^2$. For these reasons, $\hat{\omega}_A^2$ appears to be the preferred index for researchers working with data from experiments.

Comments

A number of criticisms have been leveled against the unqualified use of $\hat{\omega}_A^2$ in drawing inferences from the results of experiments. The first concerns the interpretation of a relative-strength measure when it is applied to strictly correlational data, on the one hand, and to the results of an experiment, on the other. With correlational data, none of the variables under scrutiny is manipulated by the re-

---

[8]See Maxwell, Camp, and Arvey (1981) for a discussion of these two indices in the context of multiple regression.

searcher; the values observed with these variables are completely free to vary. With experimental data, the values of the independent variable—the actual treatment conditions—are usually under the direct control and manipulation of the investigator. As a result, the size of the relative-strength measure also is under at least the partial control of the experimenter. As an obvious example, the inclusion of an extreme group in an experiment, e.g., a nontreatment control condition or a particularly deviant point on a stimulus dimension, will greatly increase $\hat{\omega}_A^2$ over what it would be without that group.[9]

For this reason, then, Glass and Hakstian (1969) argue that $\hat{\epsilon}_A^2$, and $\hat{\omega}_A^2$, by implication, should not be applied to the fixed-effects model. Dooling and Danks (1975) echo this concern and offer some examples of inappropriate inferences drawn from the use of $\hat{\omega}_A^2$ in actual research. While several authors have noted that these various objections are true for any inferences based on the fixed-effects model—i.e., that conclusions are restricted to the specific treatment conditions included in the experiment (e.g., Keren and Lewis, 1979; Maxwell, Camp, and Arvey, 1981)—the concern is still valid. Researchers should be careful not to over-interpret the meaning of a particular value of $\hat{\omega}_A^2$ obtained in an experiment and should be cautious in comparing the sizes of indices of relative strength between different experiments and different research fields (see Friedman, 1968, p. 248, for a discussion of this point). A relative-strength index provides useful information, but it can mislead if accepted uncritically out of the context in which the investigation has been carried out, just as the outcome of a statistical test can be similarly misinterpreted.

A different sort of concern was expressed by Carroll and Nordholm (1975), who conducted a Monte Carlo experiment to study the sampling characteristics of $\hat{\omega}_A^2$ and $\hat{\epsilon}_A^2$. They found that the size of the standard error of the sampling distributions of both statistics was quite large, especially for small sample sizes ($s = 5$ or $s = 10$). What this means is that while the average value of either index is relatively uninfluenced by variations in sample size, one can still expect to find fairly large values when population effects are completely *absent*! For this reason, then, they expressed doubt that strength estimates will be useful when based on nonsignificant F tests, particularly when relatively small sample sizes are involved. They do feel that the calculation of strength indices following a significant F test with large sample sizes (e.g., $s = 20$) does have strong merit. Lane and Dunlap (1978), on the other hand, argue that relative-strength measures based only on significant F tests tend to *over*estimate the true strength of the effect in the population. This means, therefore, that researchers should probably not view a particular proportion or percentage as an unbiased estimate of population strength, which, of course, reduces the value of these measures as a consequence.

We can also question the general usefulness of $\hat{\omega}_A^2$. The index can be espe-

---

[9]Only when the levels of the independent variable are *randomly selected* from a larger population of potential levels—which is rare in the behavioral sciences—does the experimental situation converge on the correlational situation. This particular type of design corresponds to the random-effects model discussed in Chap. 21.

cially informative when an investigator begins work in a new and previously unanalyzed research area. A first strategy of research may be to search for independent variables that seem to produce large effects. It is exactly for this sort of enterprise that omega squared provides an important research tool for the investigator. In applied areas of research also, $\hat{\omega}_A^2$ can be used to isolate manipulations which produce economically interesting results. At other times, however, the size of $\hat{\omega}_A^2$ will be of little interest. Consider how this might come about. Initial explorations in a research area can often be characterized as reflecting relatively large treatment effects. In fact, it is usually the size of the new finding that draws researchers into these new fields. Subsequent research will usually not be concerned with the original finding, however, but with a refinement of the discovery into component parts, each being responsive to a different collection of experimental manipulations. As theories develop to account for these findings and for the interrelationships among the components, a researcher eventually finds that he or she is no longer working with large effects, but with small ones representing manipulations that are theoretically interesting. Under these circumstances, even small differences—as indexed by $\hat{\omega}_A^2$ —may provide a decision between two competing theoretical explanations. Thus, we could say that one indication of a "healthy" and productive area of research is a preponderance of experiments with relatively *small* values of $\hat{\omega}_A^2$!

Summary and Recommendations

The presence of a significant F test gives us some assurance that a *statistical association* (predictability between the treatment groupings and the scores on the dependent variable) exists. The size of the F itself does not reflect the degree of this statistical association unambiguously. The index omega squared provides this information and thus supplements any inference to be drawn from the outcome of the experiment. In addition, even with a nonsignificant F, it is still possible to obtain a sizable $\hat{\omega}_A^2$. This sort of situation would occur with an experiment of low power.

There is no question that both statistics, the significance level of an F test and $\hat{\omega}_A^2$, contribute to a complete understanding of the outcome of the statistical test. Moreover, it is clear that we should be looking for treatments that produce large estimates of statistical association. We have also seen that $\hat{\omega}_A^2$ may provide useful information when a statistical test is not significant. On the other hand, if we based *all* of our actions on the size of $\hat{\omega}_A^2$ alone, we would be making a mistake. Just as with power, we have the problem of deciding upon an *acceptable* level in this case of $\hat{\omega}_A^2$. Often a small statistical association may be sufficient to justify introduction of a change suggested by the treatment conditions.

You have also seen that strength measures have their own set of problems that you must be aware of and take into consideration when you are interpreting the results of a statistical analysis. We should use just as many different indices as we can to assist ourselves in this important task. Besides the results of statistical tests and of estimates of relative treatment strength, additional analyses are often conducted to shed some light on the meaning of particular outcomes of an experiment. These analyses may involve the original response measure or supplemental ones also obtained from the response protocols of the subjects. They may consist of the plotting of the means and other graphical devices, including the calculation of standard deviations and confidence intervals for each treatment condition. Of critical concern, of course, is your understanding of the implications of the different statistical indices, so that you can use them effectively to advance knowledge in your chosen field of research.

5.5 THE VARIANCE AS A DESCRIPTIVE STATISTIC

For most of us, our research hypotheses are couched in terms of differences that may be observed among the treatment means. Usually, we have little sustained interest in the within-group variances, except with regard to their role in the estimation of experimental error; we look at the variances only to test the homogeneity assumption of the statistical analysis. This does not always have to be the case. Important changes in behavior caused by the different treatments may not be revealed in average performance. Or, if we look for them, systematic differences among the treatment conditions might be reflected in average performance *and* in the variability of the subjects within these conditions.

Examples of the Variance Reflecting Treatment Effects

Suppose, for example, that subjects employ a number of different strategies in performing a particular task. If they are asked to study a prose passage for an eventual test of comprehension, some may try to extract basic idea units while others may attempt to commit the entire passage to memory. The variability of their performance will reflect any differential efficiency that may be associated with these strategies—extracting idea units may be more efficient in general than learning by rote—in addition to any difference in ability that may exist among subjects. Suppose that subjects in a standard, noninstructed condition are contrasted with subjects in a condition in which they are required to perform the task with a particular strategy. Conceivably, such a comparison would not show much of a difference between the means of the two treatment groups, and a statistical analysis might lead to the conclusion that no treatment effects were present. On the other hand, the subjects in the "restricted" or instructed condition might be *more variable* in performance than the subjects in the "free" or uninstructed condition. Subjects forced to abandon their usual strategy might experience great difficulty in switching to the new strategy, which, moreover, might even be incompatible with the old one. Any such negative transfer resulting from a forced switch in strategies would show up as an increase of within-group variability for the instructed condition.

Consider another experiment, focused on the effect of administering a mild electric shock to college students each time they make an error on a motor-tracking task. Suppose that the task consists of tracking a moving object with some sighting device. The score for each subject is the number of errors made during a 10-minute tracking period. There are two groups; one receives a shock each time a subject loses track of the object, and one does not. How might the experiment turn out? Subjects differ greatly in how they respond even to the threat of shock—some try harder while others "freeze" and perform poorly. If subjects reacted differentially in this experiment, there should be a marked increase in variance for the shock group, with some subjects reducing and others increasing their tracking errors. In fact, it is conceivable that the number of subjects responding "positively" to shock would be equal to the number of subjects responding "negatively," the result being no effect upon average tracking errors for the two conditions.

Thus, in some situations a comparison of variances may lead to some interesting speculations about individual differences and the way in which subjects within a group respond to the experimental treatments. These comparisons may reveal important clues to the processes responsible for whatever effects are observed among the treatment means.[10]

Statistical Analysis

The statistical hypotheses evaluated in comparing variances are similar to the ones we evaluate when comparing means. In effect, we are interested in determining whether the different treatment conditions affect the *variability* of the subjects differently. The null and alternative hypotheses are

$$H_0: \sigma_1 = \sigma_2 = \sigma_3 = \text{etc.};$$

$$H_1: \text{not all } \sigma_i\text{'s are equal.}$$

The problem now is to find a statistical procedure with which we can evaluate this null hypothesis.

Various statistical tests are available, ranging in simplicity from the **Hartley test**, where a ratio is formed by dividing the largest within-group variance by the smallest (known as F_{max}) and is evaluated by means of a special table, to the so-called **jackknife test**, where subsamples of variances are calculated for each treatment condition and treated in a relatively complex fashion. The difficulty in choosing from among the different procedures is that no one test is consistently "best" under all possible conditions. For example, it has been known for some time that the older tests (the Hartley, Cochran, and Bartlett tests) are affected by departures from normality as well as by the presence of heterogeneity of variance,

[10]Martin and Games (1977) offer several examples of studies from education testing hypotheses about variances. Birch and Lefford (1967) and Johnson and Baker (1973) represent interesting examples of the use of variance as a descriptive statistic in other areas of research.

which eliminates their use as a statistical test when the underlying shapes of the treatment-population distributions either are not known or are nonnormal.

Some useful Monte Carlo studies are available that compare a variety of procedures with data drawn from populations varying in a number of critical characteristics. The first question asked concerns the effect of nonnormality on type I error, i.e., the probability of rejecting the null hypothesis when the population variances are equal. As noted above, this is where the Hartley, Cochran, and Bartlett tests have difficulty; they tend to produce inflated type I error, rejecting the null hypothesis more frequently than specified by the significance level. The second question concerns the sensitivity of the different tests in detecting actual differences in the population variances. An ideally sensitive test should minimize the probability of type II errors—nonrejections of the null hypothesis—i.e., it should have high power. The results of these studies, then, give us the beginnings of an objective basis on which to select an ideal statistical test—one that keeps type I error close to the chosen α level while maintaining the largest amount of power.

I will summarize the combined findings from three independent Monte Carlo studies which examined the effects of different types of distributions and varying sample sizes on type I error and power for a number of popular tests (Games, Winkler, and Probert, 1972; Church and Wike, 1976; and Martin and Games, 1977).[11] You should understand that recommendations based on empirical determinations, i.e., Monte Carlo procedures, are limited by the particular features varied, e.g., the types and shapes of the distributions, the tests chosen for study, the sample sizes included, the equality or inequality of sample sizes, the degree and pattern of differences built into the different studies, and so on. In addition, there are few points of overlap between the different studies, which makes comparisons difficult but not impossible, because the points where there is overlap show fairly close agreement in outcome. The following recommendations seem justified.

1. When the underlying treatment populations are *normal,* one should use the Hartley test (F_{max}) because of its superior power and ease of computation (Games, Winkler, and Probert, 1972; Church and Wike, 1976).[12]
2. When the distributions are *asymmetrical,* one should use the Box text (Box, 1953) because it maintains type I error close to the stated α level and offers reasonable power.[13]

[11]Games, Keselman, and Clinch (1979) conducted a similar comparison in the context of a factorial design. They showed the useful application of certain statistical tests for analyzing the effects of two or more independent variables on the variability of subjects given different treatments.

[12]Martin and Games (1977) recommend the jackknife test, although they did not include the simpler Hartley test in their Monte Carlo study. The jackknife test does have the advantage over the Hartley test of being easily extended to factorial experiments, as illustrated by Games, Keselman, and Clinch (1979), and adapted for use in testing more specific hypotheses involving particular treatment conditions.

[13]Church and Wike (1976) recommend the jackknife test, although they did not include the Box test in their Monte Carlo study. Martin and Games (1977) included both and found greater power with the jackknife, but an inflated type I error.

In general, one should realize that power is a problem with tests of variances and that a researcher should consider using considerably larger sample sizes than would be employed in comparing means if the major interest in the study is to compare variances. Games, Winkler, and Probert (1972), for example, recommend the use of sample sizes above 2ᵒ under these circumstances.

The Hartley test is easy to conduct and is presented in a number of readily available sources, e.g., Kirk (1968, p. 62) and Winer (1971, pp. 206-208). The Box and jackknife tests are more complex, but they can be conducted with a hand calculator. Briefly, they involve the formation of subsamples of scores within each treatment condition and the calculation of variances for these subsamples. If there were 15 subjects in a group, we might form 5 randomly formed groups of 3 subjects, producing 5 subsample variances for each treatment condition. These subsample variances, after being transformed to logarithms, would become the "observations" in a single-factor analysis of variance. These tests are described and illustrated in a simple and comprehensive numerical example by Martin and Games (1977). In addition, Games, Winkler, and Probert (1972) offer useful advice on the optimal size of the subsamples (pp. 903-904). They also show that analyses of the sort we will consider in the next three chapters are readily adapted for use with these particular tests.[14]

5.6   LOSS OF SUBJECTS

Most experiments contain an equal number of subjects in each of the treatment conditions. The most obvious reason for this is to give equal weight in the statistical analysis to all of the conditions in the experiment. Additionally, the use of equal sample sizes minimizes the effects of violating the distributional assumptions of the analysis of variance, i.e., normality and homogeneity of variance. Finally, unequal sample sizes require different computational formulas for the sums of squares in the analysis of variance and can cause serious complications when they appear in factorial designs. I will discuss the analysis of experiments with unequal sample sizes in Chapte: 15.

In most cases, unequal sample sizes are not planned but are forced on us by the inadvertent loss of subjects during the course of the experiment. Why should subjects fail to complete an experiment? In animal studies, for example, subjects are frequently lost through death and sickness. In human studies, in which testing is to continue over several days, subjects are discarded when they fail to complete the experimental sequence. In a memory study, for instance, some of the subjects may fail to return for their terminal retention test a week later, perhaps because of illness or a conflicting appointment. Subjects also may be lost when studies require

[14]O'Brien (1981) suggests a simpler procedure that he offers as an alternative to the Box and jackknife tests.

them to reach a performance criterion, such as a certain level of mastery; those who fail to do so are eliminated from the experiment. A third class of situations occurs when some of the subjects fail to produce responses that meet the criteria established for the response measure. Suppose we are interested in the speed with which *correct responses* are made. If subjects fail to give a correct response, they cannot contribute to the analysis. Or suppose we want to analyze the percentage of times *errors* produced on some task are of a particular type. If subjects fail to make any errors, they cannot contribute to the analysis. In such situations, subjects are eliminated from the analysis because they fail to give scorable responses.

It is of *critical* importance to determine the *implication* of these losses. That is, we have assigned our subjects to the experimental conditions in such a way that any differences among the groups at the start of the experiment will be attributed to chance factors. It is this fundamental assumption which allows us to test the null hypothesis. We are not concerned with the loss of subjects per se, but with the question, Has the loss of subjects, for whatever reason, resulted in a loss of *randomness*? If it has, either we must find a way to restore randomness or simply junk the experiment. No form of statistical juggling will rectify this situation. If randomness may still be safely assumed or has been restored, we can proceed with the statistical analysis of the data.

In each situation, we have to determine whether the reason for the subject loss is in any way associated with particular experimental treatments. In animal research, for instance, certain experimental conditions (such as operations, drugs, high levels of food or water deprivation, exhausting training procedures) may actually be responsible for the loss of the subjects. If this were the case, only the strongest and healthiest animals would survive, and the result would be an obvious confounding of subject differences and treatment conditions: the difficult conditions would contain a larger proportion of healthy animals than the less trying conditions. Replacing the lost subjects with new animals drawn from the same population will not provide an adequate solution, since the replacement subjects will not "match" the ones who were lost. If it can be shown that the loss of subjects was approximately the same from all of the conditions or that the loss was not related to the experimental treatments, then we may be able to continue with the analysis.

The same considerations are relevant when human subjects fail to complete the experiment. In the memory study I mentioned, it is likely that more subjects will be lost with the longer retention intervals, where the subjects have a greater "opportunity" to get sick. It is not known whether or not the loss of these subjects affects randomness. A researcher could attempt to see if the subjects who were lost and the subjects who were retained were equivalent in learning, although equality at this point in the experiment does not necessarily mean that the two sets of subjects would have been equivalent at recall. In some experiments, an attempt is made to impose the same subject loss on *all* conditions. For example, suppose we require all subjects to return for the later retention test and we follow the rule of discarding any subject who fails to return. The subject who is tested at the long interval and does not return is dropped from the experiment by default. But so is the subject who is tested at a shorter interval and fails to return for the later appointment.

The loss of subjects through failure to reach a criterion of mastery poses similar problems. Clearly, subjects who fail to learn are by definition poorer learners. If one group suffers a greater loss, which may very well happen if the conditions differ in difficulty, the subjects "making" it in the difficult condition represent a greater proportion of fast learners than those completing the training in the easier conditions. The replacement of subjects lost in the difficult condition would not solve this problem, since the replacement subjects would not match in ability the subjects who were discarded. One possibility is to compare the different groups at a lower criterion—one that will allow *all* of the subjects to be included. In this way, *no* subjects will be lost. Such a solution will be adequate if the smaller sample of behavior provides sufficient information to suit the needs of the researcher.

Some experimenters solve this problem by artificially imposing a subject selection on the groups that suffer fewer or no losses. Thus, if it can be assumed that only the poorer subjects were dropped from the more difficult conditions for failure to reach the performance criterion, then it might be possible to drop an equal number of the *poorest* subjects from *all* of the treatment conditions. A similar procedure is sometimes followed when subjects fail to give scorable responses. Suppose, for example, that an investigator is studying the speed of correct response under a number of different treatment conditions. As I have pointed out, subjects may fail to give a correct response and thus not provide a speed score. Some researchers attempt to resolve this difficulty by excluding subjects with the poorest record from the other conditions in order to "restore" equivalence of the groups. In all of these situations, however, it is assumed that the subjects whose data are discarded in the manner described are subjects who would have failed to reach the criterion or to have given any correct responses *if they had been in the condition producing the failures*. This is often a questionable assumption, but it must be made before any meaningful inferences can be drawn from the data so adjusted.

Clearly, then, the loss of subjects is of paramount concern to the experimenter. You have seen that if the loss of subjects is related to the phenomenon under study, randomness is destroyed, and a systematic bias may be added to the differences among the means which cannot be disentangled from the influence of the treatment effects. This is a problem of experimental design which must be solved by the researcher. If the researcher can be convinced (and can convince others) that the subject loss could not have resulted in a bias, there are statistical procedures available that will allow his or her results to be analyzed. I will discuss these methods in Chapter 15.

1. (a) With the data from Exercise 4 of Chapter 3 (p. 64), calculate the 95 percent confidence intervals for the population treatment means.
   (b) What exactly does a confidence interval estimate?
2. Table 3–2 (p. 48) summarizes the analysis of a single-factor experiment.
   (a) Calculate $\hat{\omega}_A^2$ and $\hat{\epsilon}_A^2$ from these data.
   (b) What do these two quantities tell you about the outcome of this experiment?
3. (a) With the data presented in Exercise 2 of Chapter 3 (p. 64), calculate $\hat{\omega}_A^2$.
   (b) What does this quantity tell you about the outcome of this experiment?
4. Consider the analyses of variance obtained from two single-factor experiments summarized in the accompanying table.
   (a) Calculate $\hat{\omega}_A^2$ for these two studies.
   (b) What has this index told you about the relative outcomes of these two experiments?

Summary Tables for Two Experiments

SOURCE	SS	df	MS	F
A	233.33	2	116.66	6.52*
S/A	376.00	21	17.90	
Total	609.33	23		
A	233.33	2	116.66	6.52*
S/A	1,557.30	87	17.90	
Total	1,790.63	89		

*$p < .01$.

---

[15]The answers to these problems are found in Appendix B, beginning on p. 563.

6

Analytical Comparisons Among Treatment Means

For most researchers, the completion of the statistical analysis of the completely randomized single-factor experiment as outlined in the previous chapters is only a *first step* in the analysis of their data. The next three chapters will consider additional analyses we can use in the comprehensive examination of the data we have collected. In this chapter, I will concentrate on the analysis of experiments in which the independent variable consists of qualitative differences among the treatment conditions, where the interest is in isolating and assessing meaningful comparisons between specific treatment conditions. Chapter 7 focuses on the analysis of experiments in which a quantitative independent variable has been manipulated. In this case, the approach examines the mathematical nature of the relationship between variations in the amount of factor A and changes in behavior. While this may sound formidable, the analysis utilizes the same statistical procedures that I will discuss in the present chapter. Chapter 8 considers the complications resulting from the conduct of these additional analyses and offers some recommendations for a plan of analysis that will help to deal with them.

6.1 THE NEED FOR ANALYTICAL COMPARISONS

An **analytical comparison** will refer to a meaningful comparison between two or more treatment conditions that are components of a larger experimental design. In some circumstances, analytical comparisons are undertaken following a significant F test conducted on the entire experiment. In other circumstances, they are conducted *instead of* the overall F test, in which cases they are often referred to as **planned comparisons**.

The Composite Nature of SS_A

The between-groups sum of squares SS_A was defined in Chapter 2 in terms of the deviation of the group means from the grand mean:

$$SS_A = s \Sigma (\bar{A} - \bar{T})^2.$$

An alternative form of this equation shows that the SS_A reflects the degree to which the group means differ from one another:

$$SS_A = \frac{s \sum_{\text{pairs}} (\bar{A}_i - \bar{A}_{i'})^2}{a}, \tag{6-1}$$

where i and i' represent different levels of factor A and the summation refers to all *unique* pairs.

As an example, consider the data presented in Table 2-2. There were three levels of factor A, and $s = 5$ observations per group. The three means were as follows: $\bar{A}_1 = 15.00$, $\bar{A}_2 = 6.00$, and $\bar{A}_3 = 9.00$. Substituting in Eq. (6-1), we have

$$SS_A = \frac{5\,[(15.00 - 6.00)^2 + (15.00 - 9.00)^2 + (6.00 - 9.00)^2\,]}{3}$$

$$= \frac{5\,[(9.00)^2 + (6.00)^2 + (-3.00)^2\,]}{3} = 210.00.$$

This value is identical to the one obtained by the standard defining formula:

$$SS_A = s\,\Sigma\,(\bar{A} - \bar{T})^2$$

$$= 5\,[(15.00 - 10.00)^2 + (6.00 - 10.00)^2 + (9.00 - 10.00)^2\,]$$

$$= 5\,[(5.00)^2 + (-4.00)^2 + (-1.00)^2\,] = 210.00.$$

You have seen, then, that the between-groups sum of squares is really an *average* of the differences observed between the pairs of means and as such does not provide unambiguous information about the nature of the treatment effects. In fact, it may have occurred to you that the overall variation among the treatment means reflected in SS_A may be better understood by examining these contributing parts, namely, the comparisons between pairs of means. The composite nature of SS_A has led some authors to refer to an F ratio based on more than two treatment levels as the **omnibus** or **overall** F **test**.[1]

The Omnibus F Test. The analysis outlined in the preceding chapters provides a procedure to guide us in drawing inferences about differences that we observe among the treatment means. With a nonsignificant omnibus F, we are prepared to assert that there are no real differences among the treatment means and that the particular sample means we have observed show differences which are reasonably accounted for by experimental error. We will stop the analysis there. Why analyze any further when the differences can be presumed to be chance differences?

In contrast, a *significant* F allows, if not *demands*, a further analysis of the data. By accepting the alternative hypothesis, we are concluding that differences among the treatment means are present. But *which* differences are the real ones and which are not? As I have noted before, the alternative hypothesis is inexact and, consequently, so must be our conclusion. Suppose, for example, we are contrasting the following four means: 5.25, 4.90, 5.10, and 10.50, and that the F from the single-factor analysis is significant. What have we been told? Simply that the four population means are *not* equal to one another. Nothing is said about *particular* differences among the means. An inspection of the means in this example suggests that the treatment effects are not spread equally over the four means—one

---

[1]This composite nature of SS_A is also revealed when the total between-groups sum of squares is divided among a complete set of orthogonal comparisons, which I will consider later in this chapter.

group deviates from the other three, while these latter three do not deviate greatly from one another. The single-factor analysis does not locate the *source* (or sources) of the treatment effects. All that the analysis does is to indicate that there are real differences among the treatment means, somewhere. It is our job in this and the next two chapters to see how we can identify the sources contributing to the significant omnibus *F*.

Planned Comparisons

Most research begins with the formulation of one or more research hypotheses—statements about how behavior will be influenced if such and such treatment differences are manipulated. Experiments are designed specifically to test these particular research hypotheses. Most typically it is possible to design an experiment that will provide information relevant to *several* research hypotheses. Tests designed to shed light on these particular questions are planned before the start of an experiment and clearly represent the primary focus of analysis. A researcher is *not* interested in the omnibus *F* test—this test is more appropriate in the *absence* of specific hypotheses. Thus, most researchers form, or at least imply, an analysis plan when they specify their research hypotheses and design experiments to test them. This plan consists of a set of analytical comparisons chosen to extract information that is critical to the status of the research questions responsible for the initiation of the experiment in the first place. As you will see, analytical comparisons can be conducted directly on a set of data without reference to the significance or nonsignificance of the omnibus *F* test.

6.2 AN EXAMPLE OF PLANNED COMPARISONS

Consider a concrete example of an experiment designed with some explicit comparisons in mind. Suppose that subjects are given a list of 40 common English words to learn and that the method used allows them to recall these words in any order they want. The list is presented for six trials, each trial consisting of a study portion, in which the words are presented to the subjects, and a test portion, in which the subjects attempt to recall the words. Thus, each subject sees the list six times and is tested six times. Subjects are randomly assigned to five different conditions of training, which are summarized in Table 6-1.

For the first two groups, the words are presented all at once on a piece of paper for 2 minutes; different orderings of the 40 words are used on the six trials. The groups differ with regard to the arrangement of the words on the sheet of paper—for one group the words appear in a column and for the other group they are scattered around on the paper. The remaining three groups also study the list for a total of 2 minutes, but the words are presented one at a time, at a constant rate, on a mechanical device called a memory drum. For groups 3 and 4, each word is presented once for 3 seconds; the total presentation time for the whole list of words is 120 seconds (3 seconds × 40 words). The two groups differ with regard to the presentation of the words on successive trials. Group 3 receives the *same* presentation order on all six trials, while group 4 receives *different* presentation orders. The final group also receives the materials on the memory drum, but at a faster rate of presentation (1 second per word). However, in order to equate total study time per word, the words are presented three times before the recall test is administered. As with group 4, the presentation order is changed at the start of each study trial. In summary, there are five different conditions of training. What they all have in common is that the list of words is presented for a total of 2 minutes before recall is taken.

The hypothesis under test is the *total-time hypothesis.* This hypothesis states that learning will be the *same* for these different groups just so long as the total time for study is held constant. It does not matter how the words are presented, all at once or one at a time, at a fast rate or at a slow rate, in the same order on successive study trials or in different orders, scrambled on a page or in a neat column array. The expectation, then, is that the groups will not differ in performance over the six training trials.

We could test this hypothesis by comparing the five groups simultaneously in an overall analysis of variance. If this omnibus *F* were significant, we would know that the total-time hypothesis did not hold in this experiment. We would *not* know, however, which of the groups were responsible for its failure. The way in which the experiment was designed suggests a number of *meaningful* comparisons which represent more *analytical* tests of the total-time hypothesis.

Four such comparisons are indicated in Table 6-1. The first comparison contrasts the two groups receiving the words on a sheet of paper (groups 1 and 2) with two of the groups receiving the words on the memory drum (groups 4 and 5). The question asked here is whether or not performance will be affected by forcing subjects to study the words in a rigid pattern. The total-time hypothesis would say no. On the other hand, it would seem reasonable to expect that subjects who are free to distribute their study time among the 40 words as they wish may be able to organize the material in such a way as to aid recall; subjects who are studying the words one at a time for a fixed 3-second period may not be able to organize the material as effectively. Thus, an organizational theory of learning and memory would predict better performance by groups 1 and 2, relative to groups 4 and 5. (Groups 1 and 2 and groups 4 and 5 have been combined to provide more stable estimates of the paper and drum methods of presentation, respectively. The plus and minus signs denote the groups to be contrasted.) Group 3 was *not* included in this comparison, because the subjects in that group received the words in the same order on successive trials, while subjects in the other four groups received the words in different orders.

The second comparison focuses on the two "paper" groups and asks whether or not the *type of array* will affect performance. The total-time hypothesis would again say no. There is some suggestion in the literature that subjects will form more

Table 6-1   An Example of Planned Comparisons

	GROUP 1: PAPER, VARIED ORDER, COLUMN ARRAY	GROUP 2: PAPER, VARIED ORDER, SCATTERED ARRAY	GROUP 3: DRUM, SAME ORDER, 3-SEC. RATE	GROUP 4: DRUM, VARIED ORDER, 3-SEC. RATE	GROUP 5: DRUM, VARIED ORDER, 1-SEC. RATE
Comp. 1	+	+		−	−
Comp. 2	+	−			
Comp. 3				+	−
Comp. 4			+	−	

organizational groupings of the words in the scattered condition than in the column condition. An organizational theory maintains that the formation of these organizational groupings will aid performance. Thus, this latter theory would predict higher recall by the group receiving the scattered array.

The next comparison involves groups 4 and 5, groups differing in the rates at which the words are presented. This comparison asks whether or not performance will be affected when the exposure time is varied. The total-time hypothesis would say no. On the other hand, it is conceivable that subjects given a more leisurely study of each word (group 4) may have time to create organizational groupings, while subjects given a fast exposure (group 5) may not be able to do so, even though they are given the same total time to study each word. If this speculation is correct, an organizational theory would predict a difference in favor of the longer presentation rate.

The final comparison contrasts groups 3 and 4. The only difference between these two conditions is the use of the same or different orderings of the words on successive study trials. While the total-time hypothesis again would predict no difference in performance, there are other hypotheses that do. For example, some investigators have speculated that a constant presentation order provides the subject with stable serial-position cues which are not possible when the order varies from trial to trial. It is thought that this additional set of cues will aid the subject in recall. Thus, these researchers would predict better performance for group 3.

The object of this example was to illustrate that experiments are designed with meaningful comparisons in mind. The planned comparisons enumerated in Table 6-1 provide detailed information concerning the success or failure of the total-time hypothesis. If we knew only that the omnibus F was significant, we would not know *where* the hypothesis was deficient. The use of planned comparisons allows us to pinpoint the specific conditions under which the hypothesis does and does not hold.

6.3 COMPARISONS BETWEEN TREATMENT MEANS

You have seen in Eq. (6-1) that a sum of squares, which is based on the deviation of three or more treatment means from the overall mean, is equivalent to an average of all unique comparisons between *pairs* of means. In this and in subsequent sections I will be considering procedures for making contrasts which essentially reduce to comparisons between pairs of means. In some cases these comparisons will involve simple contrasts between pairs of treatment means; in others they will involve more complex contrasts. The means in these latter comparisons are based on combinations of two or more treatment means. All of these comparisons share the common feature that ultimately they can be reduced to a contrast between two means and, therefore, are based on a *single df*. Comparisons of this sort are referred to variously as **comparisons**, **contrasts**, or **single-*df* comparisons**.

Not all questions we will want to ask of our data reduce to comparisons between means, however. Occasionally, we will want to test the significance of subsets of three or more means, simply asking whether or not the means differ among themselves. For instance, suppose there are four treatment conditions, one a control condition and the others experimental treatments of some sort. It might make sense to ask two questions: (1) Do the *combined* experimental groups differ from the control condition—i.e., is there a general or an average experimental effect? (2) Do the experimental groups differ among themselves? In the first case we have a comparison between two means (the control mean versus an average of the three experimental means), while in the second case we have a comparison among the three experimental means. I will consider the former type of comparison in this section and the latter type in Section 6.5.

A Comparison as a Sum of Weighted Means

Suppose we have three treatment groups; group 1 is a control condition, and groups 2 and 3 receive different experimental treatments. One comparison that we might consider making is a contrast between the mean for the control group and the average of the means for the two experimental groups. The statistical hypotheses for this comparison are

$$H_0 : \mu_1 = \frac{\mu_2 + \mu_3}{2} ;$$

$$H_1 : \mu_1 \neq \frac{\mu_2 + \mu_3}{2} .$$

It is convenient to express this comparison as a difference between two means. In this case, the statistical hypotheses become

$$H_0 : \mu_1 - \frac{\mu_2 + \mu_3}{2} = 0;$$

109

$$H_1 : \mu_1 - \frac{\mu_2 + \mu_3}{2} \neq 0.$$

Either way, you can see that the rejection of the null hypothesis leads to the conclusion that this particular difference between the two means is significant.

In general, I will use the symbol ψ (read "sigh") to represent the difference between two means. In the present case,

$$\psi_1 = \mu_1 - \frac{\mu_2 + \mu_3}{2}.$$

Expressed slightly differently, this comparison becomes

$$\psi_1 = (1)(\mu_1) + (-\tfrac{1}{2})(\mu_2) + (-\tfrac{1}{2})(\mu_3).$$

The numbers multiplied by each mean are called **coefficients**. Any linear comparison between pairs of means can be represented in this manner: (1) the multiplication (or weighting) of the means by a set of coefficients, and (2) the algebraic summation of these weighted means. In other words, a comparison between two means can be expressed as a sum of weighted means. The reason for this particular formulation is not obvious at this time, but it will prove useful when we calculate the sum of squares for this sort of comparison.

A second comparison of interest in this experiment is a contrast between the two experimental groups. More specifically,

$$\psi_2 = \mu_2 - \mu_3.$$

This difference can also be written as a sum of weighted means as follows:

$$\psi_2 = (0)(\mu_1) + (1)(\mu_2) + (-1)(\mu_3).$$

In this case, the coefficient associated with the control group, which does not enter into this particular comparison, is equal to *zero*.

As a general formula, we can express any such comparison between two means as

$$\psi = (c_1)(\mu_1) + (c_2)(\mu_2) + (c_3)(\mu_3) + \cdots$$

or more compactly as

$$\psi = \Sigma\, c_i \mu_i, \tag{6-2}$$

where the c_i's represent the coefficients appropriate for a particular comparison. For a sum of weighted means to qualify as a comparison, at least two of the coefficients must be numbers other than zero and *the sum of the coefficients must equal zero*. That is,

$$\Sigma\, c_i = c_1 + c_2 + c_3 + \cdots = 0. \tag{6-3}$$

The reason for the first restriction is obvious: If fewer than two coefficients were nonzero, there would be no comparison. The reason for the second restriction is to ensure that a comparison is independent of the overall mean of the experiment. Hays (1973, pp. 594-595) discusses this point and explains why this independence is desirable, saying that "in most instances, we want to ask questions about combinations of population means that will be unrelated to any consideration of what the over-all mean of the combined populations is estimated to be" (p. 595). Both sets of coefficients in the preceding paragraph, $(1, -\frac{1}{2}, -\frac{1}{2})$ and $(0, 1, -1)$, sum to zero, which satisfies the requirements of Eq. (6-3), and they "perform" the comparisons that we intended—i.e., they result in the appropriate contrasts between means.

Usefulness of the Coefficients and Eq. (6-2)

These examples illustrate the fact that comparisons involving a set of treatment means may be specified by different sets of coefficients. You also saw that by using these coefficients to weight the corresponding treatment means, we could produce the comparison represented by the coefficients. There are several reasons why it is useful to express comparisons in terms of a sum of weighted means—i.e., in terms of Eq. (6-2); these points will be illustrated later with actual examples. I will simply list them at this time in order to justify the amount of attention I will give to this particular procedure in the sections that follow.

First, the procedure is *general*; it may be used to compare the means of two groups as well as for complicated comparisons between combined means in experiments with any number of levels. Second, special sets of coefficients are available for the analytical analysis of experiments in which *quantitative* independent variables are present—i.e., where the levels of the independent variables differ in *amount*. Third, the statistical evaluation of these different comparisons is easily accomplished by using the coefficients to compute the sums of squares associated with the comparisons. Fourth, you will see that the independence of two or more comparisons is readily determined by comparing the sets of coefficients. Thus, it will be possible to ascertain whether several planned comparisons are mutually independent by comparing the coefficients associated with the comparisons we plan to make. Finally, sets of coefficients may be used to represent sources of variance in designs with two or more independent variables. Not only is this an interesting way of thinking about the analyses of multifactor experiments, but sets of coefficients may be used to illustrate the independence of sources of variance in these designs. (This point is explored further in Appendix C-2.)

Constructing Coefficients

An appropriate set of coefficients can be obtained simply by using the denominators appearing in the formal statement of a comparison as a difference between two means. As an example, consider an experiment with five treatment conditions. Suppose we wanted to compare the average mean for groups 2 and 4 with the average mean for groups 1, 3, and 5. Expressed as a difference, this comparison becomes

$$\psi = \frac{\mu_2 + \mu_4}{2} - \frac{\mu_1 + \mu_3 + \mu_5}{3}.$$

The coefficient for the two means to the left of the minus sign is $\frac{1}{2}$; and the coefficient for the three means to the right of the minus sign is $-\frac{1}{3}$. Thus, coefficients representing this comparison are the set $(-\frac{1}{3}, \frac{1}{2}, -\frac{1}{3}, \frac{1}{2}, -\frac{1}{3})$. The coefficient is 1 when a single mean is involved and 0 when a mean is not involved in a comparison. A comparison such as

$$\psi = \mu_1 - \frac{\mu_3 + \mu_5}{2}$$

is expressed by the following set of coefficients: $(1, 0, -\frac{1}{2}, 0, -\frac{1}{2})$.

This method of selecting coefficients produces what I will call a *standard set*. Standard sets express the differences between means directly and are used to calculate confidence intervals for these comparisons (see Myers, 1979, pp. 305-306). In calculating the sum of squares for a comparison, however, fractional coefficients introduce rounding errors as well as frequent arithmetical errors. Since the computational formula for a comparison sum of squares may be used with *any* set of coefficients, provided that the *relative weights* of the groups remain the same, we can eliminate fractional coefficients altogether by multiplying the set of coefficients by the lowest common denominator. In the first example, the lowest common denominator is 6 and the resulting coefficients are $(-2, 3, -2, 3, -2)$; in the second, it is 2 and the coefficients are $(2, 0, -1, 0, -1)$.

Sums of Squares for Comparisons Between Treatment Means

The data of the experiment are used to evaluate the significance of a comparison. The comparison itself is given by the formula

$$\hat{\psi} = \Sigma\,(c_i)(\bar{A}_i). \qquad (6\text{-}4)$$

The formula for the sum of squares for a comparison is not too many steps removed from Eq. (6-4). Specifically,

$$SS_{A_{\text{comp.}}} = \frac{s\,(\hat{\psi})^2}{\Sigma\,(c_i)^2}, \qquad (6\text{-}5)$$

where the squared quantity in the numerator is the sum of the weighted means, i.e., $\hat{\psi} = \Sigma\,(c_i)(\bar{A}_i)$, s is the sample size, and the quantity in the denominator is the sum of the squared coefficients. You should note that Eq. (6-5) assumes an equal number of subjects in each treatment condition. The analysis of experiments with unequal sample sizes is discussed in Chapter 15.

The computational formula is often written in terms of treatment sums rather than means. In this case, Eq. (6-5) becomes

$$SS_{A\,comp.} = \frac{[\,\Sigma\,(c_i)(A_i)]^2}{s[\,\Sigma\,(c_i)^2\,]}. \qquad (6\text{-}6)$$

The correspondence between the two formulas is apparent—the only differences are in the use of sums and in the location of s in the denominator rather than in the numerator. Either formula can be used to calculate the sum of squares. The formula written in terms of the treatment means has the advantage of dealing directly with the actual difference under consideration, while the formula written in terms of sums produces less rounding error.

As an example of these calculations, I will use the data originally listed in Table 2-2. In this example, $a = 3$ and $s = 5$. For illustrative purposes, let's assume that level a_1 represents a control condition and levels a_2 and a_3 represent experimental groups receiving two different drugs. Two obvious comparisons are suggested by this design, namely, a comparison between the control group and the average of the two drug groups and a comparison between the two drug groups. The means for the three groups are presented again in Table 6-2, along with the coefficients representing these two comparisons.

The first comparison shows a sizable difference in favor of the control condition. More specifically,

$$\hat{\psi}_1 = \Sigma\,(c_i)(\bar{A}_i)$$
$$= (1)(15.00) + (-\tfrac{1}{2})(6.00) + (-\tfrac{1}{2})(9.00)$$
$$= 15.00 - 3.00 - 4.50 = 7.50$$

The sum of squares associated with this difference between the two means, 7.50, is found by substituting in Eq. (6-5):

$$SS_{A\,comp.\,1} = \frac{s\,(\hat{\psi})^2}{\Sigma\,(c_i)^2}$$
$$= \frac{5(7.50)^2}{(1)^2 + (-\tfrac{1}{2})^2 + (-\tfrac{1}{2})^2}$$
$$= \frac{5(56.25)}{1 + .25 + .25} = \frac{281.25}{1.50}$$
$$= 187.50$$

The second comparison reveals a smaller difference in favor of the second drug condition. That is,

$$\hat{\psi}_2 = (0)(15.00) + (1)(6.00) + (-1)(9.00) = -3.00.$$

Table 6-2 Numerical Example of Two Comparisons

	TREATMENT LEVELS		
	a_1	a_2	a_3
Means	15.00	6.00	9.00
Comparison 1	1	$-\frac{1}{2}$	$-\frac{1}{2}$
Comparison 2	0	1	-1

For the sum of squares associated with this difference,

$$
SS_{A_{\text{comp. 2}}} = \frac{5(-3.00)^2}{(0)^2 + (1)^2 + (-1)^2}
$$

$$
= \frac{5(9.00)}{0 + 1 + 1} = \frac{45.00}{2}
$$

$$
= 22.50.
$$

Evaluating Comparisons

The two sums of squares we have just calculated have been entered in a new summary table, Table 6-3. If the comparisons listed in Table 6-2 were *planned* comparisons, we might not even bother to perform the omnibus F test. Table 6-3 also presents the SS_A calculated in Chapter 3 (see Table 3-2, p. 48). You should note that the two comparisons we have just computed completely account for or "use up" the total between-groups sum of squares. That is,

$$
SS_{A_{\text{comp. 1}}} + SS_{A_{\text{comp. 2}}} = 187.50 + 22.50 = 210.00 = SS_A.
$$

This will happen only when we have calculated a complete set of **orthogonal comparisons**. (Just how we determine orthogonality will be discussed in Section 6.4.)

Table 6-3 Analysis of Variance

SOURCE	SS	df	MS	F
Treatment (A)	(210.00)	(2)		
Comp. 1	187.50	1	187.50	13.23 **
Comp. 2	22.50	1	22.50	1.59 *
Within (S/A)	170.00	12	14.17	
Total	380.00	14		

** $p < .01.$
* $p > .10.$

The *df* for each of the comparisons is 1. The mean square is calculated in the usual way *(SS/df)*, and the *F* ratio is formed as follows:

$$F_{comp.} = \frac{MS_{A_{comp.}}}{MS_{S/A}} \tag{6-7}$$

and is evaluated by means of the *F* table under the appropriate entry for the *df* associated with the numerator *(df = 1)* and with the denominator $[df = a(s-1)]$.

While it can be shown that these two comparisons use independent information in their construction, it should be mentioned that the two *F* ratios are not, strictly speaking, *statistically* independent. The reason for this state of affairs is that the $MS_{S/A}$ is used to test both of the comparisons. In appears, however, that this lack of statistical independence of the tests does not present a practical problem as long as the *df* for the denominator of the *F* ratio are reasonably large (see, for example, Hays, 1973, pp. 589-590; Kirk, 1968, p. 74).

The within-groups mean square for these data, previously calculated in Chapter 3, is presented in Table 6-3. The results of the two *F* tests are indicated in the table. Specifically, they show that variability among the treatment means is produced primarily by the difference between the mean of group 1 (the control in our example) and the mean of groups 2 and 3 combined (the experimental groups in our example). The great advantage of this analysis is in the additional information that it provides. If we had looked at the overall *F* ratio, as we did in Chapter 3, we would have rejected the null hypothesis and concluded that the three treatment means are not all the same. With the present analysis, we are able to *pinpoint* the locus of the differences contributing to the significant omnibus *F*.

Directional Alternative Hypotheses. The alternative hypotheses I have considered so far have been *nondirectional* in the sense that differences between two means in either the positive or negative direction are considered incompatible with the null hypothesis. That is, with $H_0: \mu_1 = \mu_2$ and $H_1: \mu_1 \neq \mu_2$, the null hypothesis will be rejected whenever $F_{comp.}$ falls within the rejection region, which obviously can happen if $\mu_1 > \mu_2$ or if $\mu_2 > \mu_1$. Thus, rejecting the null hypothesis in this case permits the conclusion that the observed difference between the two means—in whatever direction it may be—is significant. This type of alternative hypothesis, which is most common in psychology, is called a **nondirectional hypothesis**.

It is possible to choose an alternative hypothesis that specifies a particular direction of the difference, that is, $H_1: \mu_1 > \mu_2$ or $H_1: \mu_2 > \mu_1$. This type of alternative hypothesis is called a **directional hypothesis**.[2] The advantage of a directional hypothesis is that a larger rejection region is permitted. More specifically,

----

[2]Directional and nondirectional hypotheses are also known as "one-tailed" and "two-tailed" tests, respectively. The "tail" refers to the rejection regions of the *t* distribution, where a nondirectional test would have rejection regions in both the positive and negative tails while a directional test would have a single rejection region, as specified by the alternative hypothesis.

a directional test is evaluated at $p = 2(\alpha)$, where α is a researcher's usual rejection probability. Rather than evaluating the significance of $F_{comp.}$ at $\alpha = .05$, say, we would use $\alpha = 2(.05) = .10$ instead. In the numerical example, the critical value of F would be $F(1, 12) = 3.18$ for a directional test, $p = .05$, as compared with $F(1, 12) = 4.75$ for a nondirectional one at the same significance level.[3]

The disadvantages are several. First, a strict interpretation of a directional test means that a true difference in the *opposite* direction must be ignored. In some fields a new therapy or drug or teaching method is compared with an older, established one, with an eye toward adopting the new approach only if it improves upon the one currently in use. In this case, a researcher may not be concerned that *negative effects* of the new approach will not be tested statistically by a directional test. But this restriction is considered too much of a price to pay by researchers working in areas of basic research. By far the main disadvantage, however, is the widespread nonacceptance of directional tests by researchers and journal editors in the behavioral sciences. The basic reason is the belief that researchers will not turn their backs on strong results in the opposite direction—nor, perhaps, should they—and thus will not follow exactly the requirements of a directional test. Since I am in sympathy with this position, you can assume the use of nondirectional tests in this book unless otherwise specified. For those interested in the controversy surrounding directional and nondirectional tests, Kirk (1972) has reprinted some of the papers (pp. 276–290) and provides an extensive listing (p. 324) of others contributing to the critical discussion of this issue in the literature.

Unequal Variances. The use of the within-groups mean square to evaluate the significance of a single-*df* comparison assumes homegeneity of variance. You will recall that this same assumption underlies the evaluation of the omnibus F, although it does not appear to be critical except under certain special circumstances. This relative insensitivity of F to violations of the homogeneity assumption does *not* extend to comparisons, however. More specifically, a problem is present whenever the *absolute values* of the coefficients (the values of the coefficients with the sign disregarded) are not the same. This occurs, for example, when we compare pairs of means where the coefficients are in the form $(1, -1, 0, 0, \text{etc.})$, producing unequal absolute values $(1, 1, 0, 0, \text{etc.})$, and when we combine different numbers of means to form certain complex comparisons, such as $(2, -1, -1)$, where the absolute values of the coefficients also are not the same $(2, 1, 1)$. Comparisons such as $(1, 1, -1, -1)$, which have equal absolute values, do not seem to pose a problem for the analysis and are analyzed in the usual fashion.

Different ways of coping with the problem of unequal variances have been studied by Games and Howell (1976) for comparisons between pairs of means and by Kohr and Games (1977) for more complex comparisons. The solution includes using for each comparison a different error term, which is based on what amounts

---

[3]The doubling of α for the F distribution is equivalent to locating the entire α level, e.g., .05, in the tail of the t distribution specified by the directional hypothesis. Since the sampling distribution of F includes differences between means in *both* directions, the doubling of α adjusts for this difference between the F and t distributions and focuses attention on F's reflecting the direction specified by the directional alternative hypothesis.

to an averaging of the variances of the groups included in the comparison. The formula for the new error term is

$$MS_{error} = \frac{\Sigma \, (c_i^2)(\hat{\sigma}_i^2)}{\Sigma \, c_i^2}, \tag{6-8}$$

where c_i refers to the coefficients of a single-*df* comparison and $\hat{\sigma}_i^2$ refers to the corresponding group variances.[4] When the comparison involves the difference between two treatment means, Eq. (6-8) produces an error term that literally is an average of the two within-group variances. Suppose there were three conditions and the comparison involved the difference between the means of the first two groups $(1, -1, 0)$. The error term for this comparison would be

$$MS_{error} = \frac{(1)^2(\hat{\sigma}_1^2) + (-1)^2(\hat{\sigma}_2^2) + (0)^2(\hat{\sigma}_3^2)}{(1)^2 + (-1)^2 + (0)^2}$$

$$= \frac{\hat{\sigma}_1^2 + \hat{\sigma}_2^2}{2}.$$

The error term for a complex comparison, e.g., $(1, 1, -2)$, would be

$$MS_{error} = \frac{(1)^2(\hat{\sigma}_1^2) + (1)^2(\hat{\sigma}_2^2) + (-2)^2(\hat{\sigma}_3^2)}{(1)^2 + (1)^2 + (-2)^2}$$

$$= \frac{\hat{\sigma}_1^2 + \hat{\sigma}_2^2 + 4(\hat{\sigma}_3^2)}{6}.$$

The F ratio in either case is formed by substituting in the formula

$$F_{comp.} = \frac{MS_{A \, comp.}}{MS_{error}}. \tag{6-9}$$

The degrees of freedom for the numerator remain unchanged $(df_{num.} = 1)$, while the degrees of freedom for the denominator require special computation. For comparisons between two treatment means, the degrees of freedom are obtained simply by summing the degrees of freedom associated with the two relevant treatment-group variances. That is, $df_{denom.} = (s - 1) + (s - 1) = 2(s - 1)$. For complex comparisons, the denominator df must be calculated by a relatively complex formula developed by Welch (1947) and presented by Games (1978a, p. 664). Games also provides a numerical example (pp. 670-671), in which he calculates the required degrees of freedom for the denominator of $F_{comp.}$ (called DF_E by Games). (In particular, see columns 6 and 7 of Table 7, p. 671.)

---

[4]The formulas presented by Games and Howell (1976) and by Kohr and Games (1977) are written in terms of the t statistic and unequal sample sizes. I have adapted the formulas to provide F ratios instead; these new formulas assume equal sample sizes. See Lindman (1974, pp. 60-63) for a related procedure.

Power of a Comparison

Considerations of power can be applied to comparisons during the planning stage of an experiment. Power estimates for comparisons force us to specify the smallest difference between two means we are willing to detect and to estimate the sample size necessary to achieve acceptable power to detect this minimum difference.

The calculations required to determine the necessary sample size are quite similar to those presented in Chapter 4 for the omnibus test (see pp. 70-72). We start by calculating the quantity

$$\phi^2_{comp.} = \frac{s'(\psi)^2}{(\sigma^2_{S/A})(\Sigma c_i^2)} , \tag{6-10}$$

where s' is the trial sample size, ψ is the numerical value of the minimum difference for a particular comparison, $\sigma^2_{S/A}$ is the estimate of error variance based on previous research, and Σc_i^2 is the sum of the squared coefficients specifying the comparison. The value of $\phi_{comp.}$ is used in searching Table A-2 of Appendix A to obtain an estimate of the power expected for this comparison as planned. If the power is too low, the usual solution is to increase sample size. This is checked out by entering a new value for s' in Eq. (6-10) and computing the power associated with this new experimental situation.

Power estimates for comparisons are usually not conducted by researchers, although they most certainly should be. Calculation of the power of the omnibus F test is simply not relevant for specific comparisons. The most rational strategy would be to base sample size on the comparison that is expected to produce the smallest difference between means. If acceptable power is achieved for the smallest comparison of interest, it will be achieved for all of the other comparisons planned for the experiment.

6.4 ORTHOGONAL COMPARISONS

Meaning of Orthogonality

The valuable property of orthogonal comparisons is the independence of information provided by them. To illustrate, let's work with the two orthogonal comparisons I have been discussing throughout this chapter, namely, a comparison between a control and the two combined drug conditions, and a comparison between the two drug conditions.

Suppose the two means in the first comparison are equal, e.g., the mean for the control group is 5 and the mean for the combined drug groups is 5. I want to show that this fact tells us absolutely nothing about the outcome of the second comparison. That is, the two drug groups may be *identical* with means of 5 and 5;

or the mean for the first drug group may be *greater* than the mean for the second group, e.g., 7 versus 3 (or any two numbers that average to 5); or the mean for the first group may be *smaller* that the mean for the second, e.g., 4 versus 6 (or again any two numbers that average to 5). In each of these possible ways for the second comparison to come out, the *same* outcome is observed for the first comparison. The information provided by the two comparisons is independent.

The same point can be made if we assume that the first comparison shows a difference, e.g., a mean of 6 for the control group and a mean of 4 for the combined drug groups. Again, this fact gives us no hint of how the second comparison will turn out: the two drug groups may be *equal,* e.g., 4 and 4; the first drug group may be *better* than the second, e.g., 6 versus 2; or the first drug group may be *worse* than the second, e.g., 1 versus 7. It is clear, then, that orthogonality means independence of information.

Definition

A numerical test of the orthogonality of any two comparisons is provided by the following relationship between the two sets of coefficients:

$$\Sigma (c_i)(c_i') = 0, \tag{6-11}$$

where c_i and c_i' are corresponding coefficients in the two comparisons. As an illustration of Eq. (6-11), consider the two comparisons from the last section, $(1, -\frac{1}{2}, -\frac{1}{2})$ and $(0, 1, -1)$. To test for orthogonality, we substitute corresponding coefficients into Eq. (6-11) and determine the sum of these products. In this example,

$$\Sigma (c_i)(c_i') = (c_1)(c_1') + (c_2)(c_2') + (c_3)(c_3')$$
$$= (1)(0) + (-\frac{1}{2})(1) + (-\frac{1}{2})(-1)$$
$$= 0 - \frac{1}{2} + \frac{1}{2} = 0.$$

In contrast, consider two comparisons that are not orthogonal, such as $(1, -1, 0)$ and $(1, 0, -1)$. Both sets of coefficients obviously satisfy Eq. (6-3), that is, $\Sigma c_i = 0$, and so represent single-*df* comparisons, but they fail the test for orthogonality:

$$\Sigma (c_i)(c_i') = (1)(1) + (-1)(0) + (0)(-1)$$
$$= 1 + 0 + 0 = 1.$$

Orthogonality and the Analysis of Variance

Just so many questions reflecting independent bits of information can be asked of any given set of data. The number of such comparisons is equal to the *df* for the SS_A —that is, $a - 1$. Formally, we can say that

with *a* treatment means, the total number of comparisons which are orthogonal to each other and to $\overline{T}$ is equal to $a - 1$.

If we have three means, for example, it is only possible to construct two orthogonal comparisons.

An important point that should be mentioned is that the sums of squares produced by a complete set of orthogonal comparisons account for the SS_A completely. That is, if we calculate the sums of squares associated with $a - 1$ mutually orthogonal comparisons, we exhaust all of the independent information in our data. In symbols,

$$SS_A = \Sigma\, SS_{A\,\text{comp.}}, \qquad\qquad (6\text{-}12)$$

where $\Sigma\, SS_{A\,\text{comp.}}$ represents the sum of a complete set of orthogonal comparisons.

I have already demonstrated that Eq. (6-12) holds for the analysis summarized in Table 6-3 by showing that

$$SS_{A\,\text{comp. 1}} + SS_{A\,\text{comp. 2}} = SS_A.$$

Suppose we apply two *non*orthogonal comparisons to the same set of data, where $a = 3$ and $s = 5$. Specifically,

	a_1	a_2	a_3	
Mean:	15.00	6.00	9.00	$\hat{\psi}$
Comp. 1:	1	-1	0	9.00
Comp. 2:	1	0	-1	6.00

The two comparisons are not orthogonal; i.e.,

$$\Sigma\,(c_i)(c_i') = (1)(1) + (-1)(0) + (0)(-1) = 1 + 0 + 0 = 1.$$

From the formula for a single-*df* comparison, Eq. (6-5),

$$SS_{A\,\text{comp.}} = \frac{s(\hat{\psi})^2}{\Sigma\,(c_i)^2},$$

we find

$$SS_{A\,\text{comp. 1}} = \frac{5(9.00)^2}{(1)^2 + (-1)^2 + (0)^2} = 202.50;$$

and

$$SS_{A\,\text{comp. 2}} = \frac{5(6.00)^2}{(1)^2 + (0)^2 + (-1)^2} = 90.00.$$

The sum of these two comparisons, $202.50 + 90.00 = 292.50$, greatly exceeds the total for the SS_A given in Table 6-3 ($SS_A = 210.00$).

Only orthogonal comparisons possess the equality stated in Eq. (6-12). What is being said is that the sum of squares obtained from a set of a treatment means is a *composite* of the sums of squares associated with a set of $a - 1$ mutually orthogonal comparisons. This fact and the related property of complete *nonredundancy,* or *independence,* makes them especially attractive to researchers. A detailed analysis involving a properly constructed set of orthogonal comparisons represents an efficient way to examine the results of an experiment. But efficiency is not everything, and we will form incomplete sets of orthogonal comparisons and sets of nonorthogonal comparisons when they are dictated by the nature of the questions we want to ask of our data. I will pursue this point in the next section.

This property of orthogonal comparisons can be extended to the entire analysis of variance. That is, each one of the degrees of freedom in an experiment, $df_T = (a)(s) - 1$, can be used to represent an independent facet of the total sum of squares. This point adds a new meaning to the concept of degrees of freedom: The degrees of freedom associated with an experiment specify the maximum number of independent pieces of information that can be derived from the particular set of data. This important property of the analysis of variance is illustrated in Appendix C–2.

Orthogonality and Planned Comparisons

As noted earlier in this chapter, planned comparisons are a desirable alternative to the omnibus F test. What is not clear, however, is whether any restrictions are placed on the nature or the number of those comparisons we may plan to test. Authors of statistical sourcebooks for psychologists are not in agreement on this issue. Some maintain that planned comparisons must be independent in the sense that they should provide nonredundant information. At one point in his discussion, Hays (1973), for example, refers to this property of independence as a *requirement* (p. 606). In contrast, Winer (1971) states that "in practice the comparisons that are constructed are those having some meaning in terms of the experimental variables; whether these comparisons are orthogonal or not makes little or no difference" (p. 175).

Consider again the comparisons I outlined earlier for a study contrasting methods of presentation in a learning experiment. These comparisons, which were originally summarized in Table 6-1, are listed again in the upper portion of Table 6-4. As I have noted previously, the absolute values of the coefficients are not critical. What has to be present is the desired relative weights. Comparison 1, for example, could be written as $(-1, -1, 0, 1, 1)$ or as $(\frac{1}{2}, \frac{1}{2}, 0, -\frac{1}{2}, -\frac{1}{2})$ and still produce the same sum of squares. Each of the four comparisons qualifies as a contrast—i.e., the coefficients sum to zero, as shown in the last column on the right. The six different tests of independence are enumerated in the bottom half of the table. Each test involves a different pair of comparisons. As an example of the calculations, consider the test of comparisons 1 and 3:

$$\Sigma\, (c_i)(c_i') = (1)(0) + (1)(0) + (0)(0) + (-1)(1) + (-1)(-1).$$

Table 6-4   Example of a Test for Mutual Orthogonality

	GROUP 1: PAPER, VARIED ORDER, COLUMN ARRAY	GROUP 2: PAPER, VARIED ORDER, SCATTERED ARRAY	GROUP 3: DRUM, SAME ORDER, 3-SEC. RATE	GROUP 4: DRUM, VARIED ORDER, 3-SEC. RATE	GROUP 5: DRUM, VARIED ORDER, 1-SEC. RATE	SUM
			Comparisons			
Comp. 1:	1	1	0	−1	−1 =	0
Comp. 2:	1	−1	0	0	0 =	0
Comp. 3:	0	0	0	1	−1 =	0
Comp. 4:	0	0	1	−1	0 =	0
			Tests for Orthogonality[a]			
Comp. X Comp.						
1 X 2:	1	−1	0	0	0 =	0
1 X 3:	0	0	0	−1	1 =	0
1 X 4:	0	0	0	1	0 =	1
2 X 3:	0	0	0	0	0 =	0
2 X 4:	0	0	0	0	0 =	0
3 X 4:	0	0	0	−1	0 =	−1

[a]Test for orthogonality: $\Sigma\, (c_i)(c_i') = 0$.

These products are listed in the row labeled "1 X 3," and the sum of these products, zero, is indicated in the last column of the table. An inspection of the sums for the different pairs of contrasts reveals that comparison 4 is not orthogonal either to comparison 1 or to comparison 3. The remaining comparisons, however, are all orthogonal (1 X 2, 1 X 3, 2 X 3, and 2 X 4). If we just consider comparisons 1, 2, and 3, we can say that they are *mutually* orthogonal, since each possible pair of comparisons is orthogonal.

A fourth comparison (4') which would be orthogonal to the first three is one that compares group 3 with the average of the remaining groups. In terms of coefficients, the set is (−1, −1, 4, −1, −1) or, with fractions, (−¼, −¼, 1, −¼, −¼). To test for orthogonality,

$$1 \times 4': \Sigma\,(c_i)(c_i') = (1)(-1) + (1)(-1) + (0)(4) + (-1)(-1) + (-1)(-1)$$
$$= -1 - 1 + 0 + 1 + 1 = 0,$$

$$2 \times 4': \Sigma\,(c_i)(c_i') = (1)(-1) + (-1)(-1) + (0)(4) + (0)(-1) + (0)(-1)$$
$$= -1 + 1 + 0 + 0 + 0 = 0.$$

$$3 \times 4': \Sigma\,(c_i)(c_i') = (0)(-1) + (0)(-1) + (0)(4) + (1)(-1) + (-1)(-1)$$
$$= 0 + 0 + 0 - 1 + 1 = 0.$$

Thus, we have constructed a set of mutually orthogonal comparisons. But what usable information do we obtain from this new comparison? One difference in treatment between group 3 and the others is the order of the words on successive trials—the *same* order is used for group 3 and *different* orders are used for the other groups. There are other treatment differences as well, however. Group 3 receives the words on a memory drum; two of the remaining groups receive the words on the drum and two on a piece of paper. Group 3 receives the material at a 3-second rate of exposure per word; the same rate is used for group 4, but group 5 receives the words at a 1-second rate and groups 1 and 2 receive the words all at once. Since more than one treatment difference is reflected in this new contrast, any difference in behavior that is observed cannot be unequivocally attributed to *one* of the differences in treatment. The comparison is useless.

This demonstration with comparison 4' stresses the fact that the *meaningfulness* of a comparison is of critical importance in the analysis of an experiment and not its inclusion in an orthogonal set of comparisons. But what about the issue of including nonorthogonal comparisons among a set of planned comparisons? There are just so many meaningful comparisons that we can plan before the start of an experiment; most of these will provide independent information. Occasionally, we will think of comparisons which are *partially* redundant—such as comparison 4 in this example—but which provide important information that is not completely obtainable from the other orthogonal comparisons. Each of the four comparisons in Table 6-4 asks an important and interesting question, however, even though the comparisons themselves are not mutually orthogonal. The "ideal" experiment is one that is designed so that interesting questions can be easily interpreted. To this end, researchers must exercise judgment in the planning stages to guarantee that the important questions studied in an investigation can be answered unambiguously by the proposed experimental design. This is true for orthogonal as well as nonorthogonal comparisons. Nonorthogonal comparisons require special care to avoid logical ambiguities that can arise when information is shared between partially redundant questions.

6.5 COMPARING THREE OR MORE MEANS

Occasionally an analysis plan will include the examination of a subset of three or more means that represent a part of a larger experimental design. Studies with control or baseline conditions are common examples. Suppose we were interested in the effects of different incentives on the solving of problems by fifth-grade students. Groups receiving three forms of incentives—verbal praise (a_1), monetary reward (a_2), and extra credit (a_3)—are included, in addition to a control group (a_4) receiving no incentives. An obvious plan would be to compare the three incentive groups among themselves to see if the different rewards differ in effectiveness. Depending on the outcome of this analysis, we would then conduct additional comparisons to analyze the results of this experiment fully.

The simplest way to compare the three incentive conditions is to treat them as an independent experiment, where $a = 3$, in this case, rather than the 4 in the original design, and then to use the standard formula for the between-groups sum of squares from Chapter 3.[5] More specifically, there would be three conditions in this analysis (levels a_1, a_2, and a_3—omitting a_4, of course). The treatment sums are A_1, A_2, and A_3, and the new grand sum is $T = A_1 + A_2 + A_3$. For this analysis, $a = 3$, but sample size continues to be s. The computational formula for the sum of squares representing variation among these three conditions is

$$SS_{A \text{ set}} = \frac{A_1^2 + A_2^2 + A_3^2}{s} - \frac{T^2}{(a)(s)},$$

where the subscript "set" refers to the set of means included in this analysis. The degrees of freedom are 1 less than the number of means being compared; that is, $df_{A \text{ set}} = 3 - 1 = 2$. The mean square is formed in the usual way; i.e.,

$$MS_{A \text{ set}} = \frac{SS_{A \text{ set}}}{df_{A \text{ set}}}.$$

The F ratio is formed by dividing the mean square by the error term obtained from the overall analysis based on all the treatment conditions. That is,

$$F_{\text{set}} = \frac{MS_{A \text{ set}}}{MS_{S/A}}.$$

The statistical hypotheses for this test are as follows:

$$H_0 : \mu_1 = \mu_2 = \mu_3,$$

and

$$H_1 : \text{Not all } \mu_i\text{'s are equal.}$$

The critical value of F is found in Table A-1 under the appropriate numerator and denominator degrees of freedom and significance level. The df associated with this mean square are 2. The df associated with the error term come from the *larger* analysis, where there are *four* groups, rather than three groups, contributing to this source of variance. Thus, if $s = 6$, then $df_{S/A} = 4(6 - 1) = 20$ in this particular example.

This type of analysis is generally limited to experiments where the formation of subgroups makes logical sense and where the outcome of the statistical test may influence subsequent analyses. Suppose, for example, that the F_{set} is *not* significant. We would probably then average the three incentive conditions and compare this combined mean with the mean for the single control condition. On the other hand, if F_{set} *is* significant, we have to probe further to determine in what ways the incentive conditions differ among themselves and also probably compare each of the incentive means with the control mean individually.

[5]Alternatively, we can take advantage of the property of orthogonal comparisons, as specified by Eq. (6-12), and obtain the desired quantity by calculating the sums of squares for two *orthogonal* single-*df* comparisons involving the incentive conditions alone, e.g., $(2, -1, -1, 0)$ and $(0, 1, -1, 0)$, and adding them together.

6.6 EXERCISES[6]

1. An experimenter is investigating the effects of two drugs on the activity of rats. Drug A is a depressant, and drug B, a stimulant. Half of the subjects receiving either drug are given a low dosage, and half, a high dosage. The experimenter also runs a control group that is given an injection of an inert substance, such as a saline solution. Five different groups are represented in the experiment, each containing $s = 4$ rats assigned randomly from the stock of laboratory rats on hand. The animals are injected and then their activity is observed for a fixed period of time. The treatment sums for each group of four rats are given below:

	DRUG A		DRUG B	
Control a_1	Low a_2	High a_3	Low a_4	High a_5
60	55	32	66	92

The within-groups mean square $MS_{S/A}$ is found to be 37.00.
(a) Perform a one-way analysis of variance on these data.
(b) Construct a set of coefficients that will provide the following comparisons:
  (1) Control versus combined experimental groups.
  (2) Drug A versus drug B.
  (3) Low versus high dosage for drug A.
  (4) Low versus high dosage for drug B.
(c) Show that these four comparisons are mutually orthogonal.
(d) Extract the sums of squares associated with these comparisons and test their significance.
(e) Verify that the sum of the comparison sums of squares equals the SS_A.

2. Consider an experiment with $a = 5$ levels. This means, of course, that the SS_A is associated with $a - 1 = 4$ df and that this sum of squares may be divided into four independent comparisons. Listed below are four "starts" at constructing a set of orthogonal comparisons. Complete each of these sets, retaining the comparisons that have been specified already.

		(a)						(b)		
a_1	a_2	a_3	a_4	a_5		a_1	a_2	a_3	a_4	a_5
Comp. 1:	4	-1	-1	-1	-1	Comp. 1:	3	0	-1	-1	-1
Comp. 2:	0	-1	-1	3	-1	Comp. 2:	0	0	1	-1	0

		(c)						(d)		
a_1	a_2	a_3	a_4	a_5		a_1	a_2	a_3	a_4	a_5
Comp. 1:	1	0	0	0	-1	Comp. 1:	3	3	-2	-2	-2
Comp. 2:	0	0	1	-1	0	Comp. 2:	0	0	-1	2	-1

3. In Section 6.2, I described a memory experiment and a set of planned comparisons that could be used to analyze the data. Let's assume that the experiment

---

[6]The answers to these problems are found in Appendix B, beginning on p. 554.

was conducted with $s = 5$ subjects in each of the five treatment conditions. The treatment sums obtained on the response measure were as follows:

a_1	a_2	a_3	a_4	a_5
63	84	47	48	42

We will assume that $MS_{S/A} = 13.50$.

(a) Conduct the four planned comparisons indicated in Table 6-1 (p. 108). What conclusions do you draw from this analysis?

(b) The comparisons in this set are not mutually orthogonal (see Table 6-4, p. 122). Show that the sum of the comparison sums of squares does *not* equal the SS_A.

4. The experiment described in Section 6.5 was concerned with the effects of different incentives on the solving of problems by fifth-grade students. There were three incentive groups, verbal praise (a_1), monetary reward (a_2), and extra credit (a_3), and a no-incentive control group (a_4). The experiment was conducted with $s = 10$ children. The response measure consisted of the number of problems solved in 20 minutes. The following treatment sums were obtained:

a_1	a_2	a_3	a_4
48	53	47	32

Assume that $MS_{S/A} = 4.11$.

(a) Determine whether the three incentives were differentially effective in influencing the number of problems solved.

(b) Conduct a single-*df* comparison between the control condition and the combined incentive conditions.

(c) Is the omnibus F significant? Is this finding compatible with the conclusions you drew from the other two analyses? Explain.

7

Analysis of Trend

The procedures covered in the last chapter are quite general and can be applied to the analysis of any single-factor experiment. When a qualitative independent variable is manipulated, the analysis usually consists of a systematic examination of differences between treatment means. The analyses summarized in Table 6–4 (p. 122) of an experiment comparing five different methods of presentation is a good example of a multilevel study analyzed as a set of component two-group experiments. When a *quantitative* independent variable is manipulated, however, what is typically employed is a specialized form of single-*df* comparison called **trend analysis**—the topic of this chapter.

7.1 THE ANALYTICAL NATURE OF TREND ANALYSIS

With a quantitative independent variable, the treatment levels represent different *amounts* of a single common variable. The levels can be ordered or spaced along the stimulus dimension in terms of the amount of the variable. Examples of quantitative or scaled independent variables are the number of hours of food deprivation, different dosage levels of a particular drug, rates of stimulus presentation, and the intensity of the unconditioned stimulus in a conditioning experiment.

In analyzing this sort of experiment, we are often interested in the *shape* or the *form* of the function relating the independent and dependent variables. Moreover, we are generally *not* interested in making orthogonal comparisons of the sort we discussed in the preceding chapter. That is, if we have selected for inclusion in our study more than two levels of a quantitative independent variable, we are probably not concerned with differences between groups representing contiguous points on the independent variable. If we believe that there are no abrupt breaks in nature— i.e., that a function will be continuous over the extent of the independent variable studied—then it is unimportant to test the separation of contiguous means, because we are really interested in the overall relationship between the independent and dependent variables.

An analysis of the shape of a function is dictated when we find ourselves asking questions that focus on the "ups and downs" of a function. We might, for example, find ourselves asking whether it is accurate to describe the outcome of an experiment as representing a **linear** function (a steady rise or fall in the treatment means as the independent variable is increased) or a **nonlinear** function of some sort. If the actual trend reflected in the data is important for our understanding of the experimental outcome, then a trend analysis is most appropriate.

7.2 PURPOSES OF TREND ANALYSIS

Tests for trend are motivated by two sorts of concern, one based on theoretical predictions and one which is purely empirical or descriptive in nature. In the first case, we may only want to know whether or not the function exhibits a particular shape that is critical for our theory. Theories of stimulus generalization, for example, sometimes make specific statements concerning the shape of the function relating performance to different points on a stimulus dimension.[1] Under these circumstances we would probably focus our attention on comparisons that are sensitive to this question. In the second case, our interest in trend is *post hoc*—we are looking for the *simplest* function that will describe our results adequately.

Let's see how a trend analysis can help in the description of a set of data. Suppose that we have conducted a memory experiment in which retention tests were administered to different groups of subjects at seven different intervals following the termination of learning. The results of this hypothetical experiment are presented in Fig. 7-1. How might we describe these data? We would probably *not* be satisfied with a description that said the following: "The retention function first rises, dips, rises again, falls precipitously this time, rises slightly, and then dips once more." This statement quite accurately describes the picture we obtain when we connect successive points on the independent variable; however, our job is not just to report functional relationships, but to make speculations concerning the basic processes underlying these relationships. I will develop this point in some detail.

Suppose we felt that the function in Fig. 7-1 was the result of different memory processes operating over these time intervals. It would be unreasonable to postulate that a *single* process was responsible for this function. What sort of hypothetical process would follow the ups and downs of the function depicted in Fig. 7-1? A more likely theoretical explanation would postulate *several* memory processes, each following a different course with time. One process could be thought to

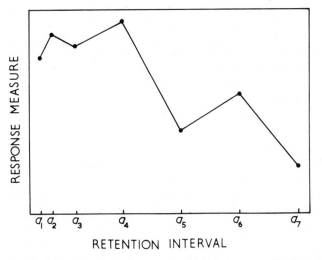

FIGURE 7-1.   Recall as a function of the retention interval.

[1] Grant's classic paper (1956) introducing trend analysis to psychologists is an excellent example of the theoretical use of these procedures. Grant identified two processes operating in his study and used trend analysis to detect their presence in the data. For more information about this study, see Exercise 1 at the end of this chapter.

increase and decrease *early* during the retention interval, while a second process reaches a peak at the fourth retention interval. Then something would have to be postulated to explain the rapid drop in the curve following this high point. And so on—an extremely complicated theory.

Most of us would hope that nature is not *that* complicated! Thus, we find ourselves looking for an *idealized* relationship—one which still reasonably describes the data but requires the assumption of the *smallest number* of processes. This goal is accomplished by trend analysis, which researchers turn to in order to ask three general questions about the function relating the independent and dependent variables. First, they would like to know whether the data show an overall tendency to rise or to fall over the range of treatment levels included in an experiment. Second, they are interested in the possibility of a general bending of the function in an upward or a downward direction. Most of the analyses conducted by experimenters involve the assessment of these two trends. Third, researchers ask questions about the presence of more complex trends, but such trends are rare in psychology.

In short, trend analysis consists of a set of procedures which permits the assessment of the "strength" of the important fluctuations observed in the data plot and which tells us the generalized form that the underlying function might take. Both of these goals—a test of theoretical predictions and data description—are achieved by means of an analysis of the trend into a set of orthogonal components, a procedure I will consider shortly.

7.3 COMPONENTS OF TREND

As mentioned previously, we are often searching for the simplest function to describe our data. A linear function is the least complex and would normally be the first one that we consider. To say that a function is linear means that the curve either rises or drops at the same rate along the extent of the independent variable; a straight line may be used to describe the data. The data plotted in Fig. 7-1 can be described fairly adequately by a linear function. That is, a straight line with a downward slope reflects the variation among the data points fairly well. If the linear function actually represents the trend among the population means, we can devise a relatively simple explanation of the forgetting; a theory in which there is a *single* process changing at a constant rate with time is sufficient.

Of course, the linear function does not fit the data of Fig. 7-1 all that well. A closer inspection of the curve seems to suggest that there is a consistent rise over the shorter retention intervals and *then* a linear drop over the longer intervals. A function that shows *concavity*—a single bend either upward or downward—is one containing a **quadratic** component. Assuming that the concave shape in Fig. 7-1 is a correct description of the real world, we will find it necessary to complicate our earlier one-process theory. One way to explain the quadratic component is to postulate an additional process with a different time course whose influence is superimposed on the first. For instance, we could hypothesize a consolidation process, in which memory traces grow in strength for a short time following learning, as being responsible for the initial rise in the retention curve. We could then add another process, decay or interference with the memory trace, for example, that we consider fully responsible for forgetting after the consolidation process ceases to function. Presumably, both processes are operating during the shorter retention intervals.

Consider the four curves plotted in Fig. 7-2. Each curve represents a "pure" example of a different component of trend observed in the context of an experiment containing five equally spaced intervals on some quantitative independent variable. The first two curves reflect linear and quadratic components, respectively. The next two curves are more complex, the third reflecting a **cubic** trend component and the fourth a **quartic** trend component. In actual situations, however, the outcomes are generally not this clear. Chance factors, for example, can be expected to distort the picture to some extent. In addition, a set of data might contain more than one of these trend components, which will complicate the picture as well. Trend analysis provides an objective method for assessing the separate contributions of each of these pure components by using a technique called the **analysis of orthogonal polynomials**. The analysis helps to cut through the "noise" present in all empirical investigations and to focus on detecting the presence of different trends.

Most existing theories in psychology make predictions about linear and quad-

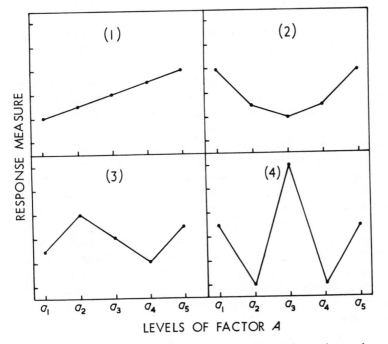

FIGURE 7-2.   Examples of linear, quadratic, cubic, and quartic trend components.

ratic components only, although there are some notable exceptions.[2] The most obvious reason for the postulation of linear and quadratic trends is their relative theoretical simplicity. Consider either right-hand curve in Fig. 7-3—a common curve in psychology. This function can be analyzed as two components: (1) the net downward slope (the linear component) and (2) the upward concavity (the quadratic component). A theoretical explanation of this outcome would focus on these two components, namely, a general downward trend and the flattening out of this trend at the higher values of the independent variable.

With higher-order trends, the complexity of the theoretical interpretions increases considerably. Our discussion of trend analysis will concentrate primarily on the analysis of the linear and quadratic components, although the method of analysis is easily extended to allow an assessment of the higher-order components.

Choice of Intervals

Suppose we conduct an experiment in which we include five points on some stimulus dimension. We probably will include two groups at the extremes of the dimension to ensure that we "capture" the full range of effectiveness of the independent variable. How should we locate the other three groups?

Our first reaction might be to place them at equally spaced intervals. While many factors influence the choice of the specific intervals, the overriding consideration is the selection of levels that will "pick up" important changes in the response measure. Only if the function relating the independent and dependent variables is *linear* will equally spaced intervals be the most efficient choice. This may be seen in Fig. 7-3. The function plotted in the two left-hand graphs is linear. Equally spaced intervals (upper graph) result in equal changes between successive intervals, while unequal intervals (lower graph) result in small changes where the intervals are closely spaced and large changes where they are spread out. In a sense, then, no interval is "wasted" in the first situation, while two of the intervals are wasted in the second. But what happens when the function is not linear? One possible outcome is depicted in the two graphs on the right. Here, the situation is reversed. An equal spacing of intervals (upper graph) results in three intervals which show very little change and one interval which brackets around the point in the function where the maximum change is occurring. Unequal spacing (lower graph) does not waste any of the intervals, since the intervals are closely spaced where there is a precipitous change and widely spaced where only small changes occur.

The "trick" in designing an experiment, of course, is to know the shape of the function ahead of time so that we can make an efficient choice of our intervals. In most research applications, we usually do have enough information to provide a basis for a rational choice in the spacing. Without such information, however, it is better to use equal intervals.

---

[2]See Hayes-Roth (1977) for an interesting example of the theoretical prediction of higher-order trends.

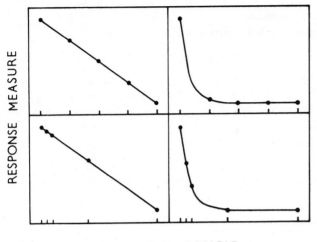

RESPONSE MEASURE

INDEPENDENT VARIABLE

FIGURE 7-3. Spacing of points along a stimulus dimension.

7.4 METHOD OF ORTHOGONAL POLYNOMIALS

The purpose of trend analysis is to find a mathematical expression to relate changes in the treatment means (the dependent variable) to changes in the treatment variable (the independent variable). A useful mathematical function in psychology is the **polynomial**, which I will describe in some detail in this section.

The Polynomial

A polynomial is an algebraic expression having two or more terms. There are different orders of polynomials, depending on the nature of the terms in the equation. The simplest polynomial is the straight line, which represents a **first-order polynomial** or **linear equation**. For example, the first-order equation can be expressed as

$$Y = b_0 + b_1 X,$$

where Y refers to values of the dependent variable, b_0 and b_1 are constants, and X refers to values of the independent variable. A more familiar form of the linear equation can be obtained if we substitute a_Y for b_0 and b_Y for b_1 to produce:

$$Y = a_Y + b_Y X.$$

You may recall from an algebra or introductory statistics course that a_Y is the Y

intercept, the value of Y when $X = 0$, and that b_Y is the slope, an index reflecting the degree of "tilt" of the straight line.

The **quadratic, or second-order, equation** is given in the form

$$Y = b_0 + b_1 X + b_2 X^2,$$

where the b's are a different set of constants and X and Y refer to values of the independent and dependent variables, respectively. The second-order equation is characterized by the third term on the right of the equals sign, $b_2 X^2$, the squared values of the independent variable X being responsible for the quadratic shape.

In general, the highest degree of polynomial that may be used to describe a set of a means is $a - 1$. The equation at the $a - 1$ order takes the following form:

$$Y = b_0 + b_1 X + b_2 X^2 + \cdots + b_{a-1} X^{a-1}. \tag{7-1}$$

Orthogonal Polynomials

The method of orthogonal polynomials dissects a set of data into a number of orthogonal comparisons, one for each of the b's in Eq. (7-1) except b_0. Each comparison represents the pure form of a different order of polynomial, one for the linear order, one for the quadratic order, and so on. Associated with each comparison is variation that in addition to experimental error reflects the degree to which that particular trend component is present in the data. The components are then tested for significance. The statistical hypotheses evaluated in trend analysis are similar to those formed for analytical comparisons in general. If we let ψ_{trend} equal the linear, quadratic, and so on, trend components based on population treatment means, we can state the statistical hypotheses as follows:

$$H_0: \psi_{\text{trend}} = 0$$

and

$$H_1: \psi_{\text{trend}} \neq 0.$$

Depending on which components are significant, Eq. (7-1) is revised and simplified, the nonsignificant components being dropped from the equation.

This, in essence, is trend analysis. The method of orthogonal polynomials provides an objective way of assessing the presence or absence of particular trend components in a set of data. If theory predicts the emergence of a particular trend component (or components), this method tests the validity of the prediction. If a researcher is interested in just how well the lower-order components describe the data, this method helps with this decision as well. The only new idea introduced by the method of orthogonal polynomials is that the observed relationship between the independent and dependent variables may be divided into components of trend; otherwise, the method is like any other analysis involving orthogonal single-*df* comparisons.

Coefficients and Computational Formulas

Trend analysis requires a different set of special coefficients for each of the orthogonal trend components to be extracted from the data. As long as the levels of an independent variable are spaced equally on some continuum, we can look up the sets of coefficients in Table A-4 of Appendix A. Examples of equally spaced intervals are exposure intervals of 50, 250, and 450 milliseconds; noise levels of 20, 50, and 80 decibels; and drug dosages of 1, 2, and 3 grains. The coefficients provided in Table A-4 list appropriate sets for all trend components up to the *quintic* (fifth-order polynomial) for experiments in which the number of treatment conditions ranges from 3 to 10. More extensive tables are available in Fisher and Yates (e.g., 1953) and Pearson and Hartley (e.g., 1970).

You might take a moment to examine the coefficients presented in Table A-4. First, you should note that all sets of coefficients sum to zero; hence, they satisfy the basic requirement for a single-df comparison that $\Sigma\, c_i = 0$. Second, you may wish to verify that the sets of coefficients for any given size of experiment are all mutually orthogonal, i.e., that $\Sigma\, (c_i)(c_i') = 0$. Third, each set of coefficients reflects a perfect example of the relevant trend component. That is, if you were to plot each set of linear coefficients on a graph, you would find that each set describes a perfectly straight line. Similarly, a plot of each set of quadratic coefficients would produce a symmetrical concave curve—a "pure" example of a quadratic function. In short, the coefficients possess the very trend components they are designed to detect. Finally, you will note that the slopes for all of the linear coefficients are positive, i.e., increase from left to right. While not obvious, this set will work perfectly well for detecting the presence of either positive or *negative* linear trend.[3] The same thing is true for the positive or negative orientation of the coefficients for the other trend components as well.

What if the levels of the independent variable are unequally spaced, as, for example, are the retention intervals in Fig. 7-1 (p. 129)? Under these circumstances, you *cannot* use the coefficients listed in Table A-4 and must construct your own sets of coefficients for the particular spacings of the levels represented in your experiment. A detailed explanation of how this can be accomplished may be found in Appendix C-3.

The sum of squares for any given trend component is calculated by substituting relevant information into the general formula for single-df comparisons that we originally discussed in Chapter 6. That is,

$$SS_{A\,\text{trend}} = \frac{s(\hat{\psi}_{\text{trend}})^2}{\Sigma\, (c_i)^2}. \tag{7-2}$$

---

[3]You may recall from Chap. 6 that multiplying all coefficients for a comparison by a constant has no effect on the sum of squares for the comparison. Multiplying a set of linear coefficients by the constant -1 will change the signs of the coefficients but leave the sum of squares unchanged.

The mean square for a trend component is obtained by dividing the sum of squares by $df = 1$. The F ratio is formed by dividing this mean square by the error term from the overall analysis, $MS_{S/A}$, which is evaluated at $df_{num.} = 1$ and $df_{denom.} = df_{S/A}$.

A Numerical Example

As an example of an analysis using the method of orthogonal polynomials, consider an experiment designed to test the proposition that subjects learn better when the training is distributed over a period of time than when the training is massed all at once. If we wanted to, we could investigate this question with just two groups, one group receiving massed training and another group receiving distributed training of some sort. But a more comprehensive investigation would include a number of different conditions of distributed training.

Assume the following experiment: Subjects are given some material to learn for 10 trials, with the independent variable, *intertrial interval* (the interval between successive trials), being manipulated at intervals of 0 seconds (the massed condition) and 20, 40, and 60 seconds (the distributed conditions). This means that one group of subjects receives no spacing between successive trials, another group receives 20 seconds between trials, another group 40 seconds, and a final group 60 seconds. Suppose that $s = 20$ subjects are included in each of the four independent groups. The results of this hypothetical experiment, expressed in terms of the number of correct responses over the 10 learning trials, are given in the upper half of Table 7-1.

Table 7-1   Numerical Example: Overall Analysis

	BASIC DATA				
	Intertrial Interval (A)				
	0 sec. a_1	20 sec. a_2	40 sec. a_3	60 sec. a_4	SUM
A_i:	309	429	452	401	1,591
s:	20	20	20	20	80
$\bar{A}_i$:	15.45	21.45	22.60	20.05	
$\sum_i^s (AS_{ij})^2$:	5,175	9,461	10,550	8,529	33,715

	SUMMARY OF THE ANALYSIS			
Source	*SS*	*df*	*MS*	*F*
A	590.34	3	196.78	10.08*
S/A	1,483.65	76	19.52	
Total	2,073.99	79		

*$p < .01$.

As an initial step, it is generally a good idea to perform the overall analysis of variance, even though you may not be particularly interested in the omnibus F. You do need to calculate $MS_{S/A}$ in any case, and this is a convenient way to do so. First, we will calculate the three basic ratios:

$$[T] = \frac{T^2}{(a)(s)}$$

$$= \frac{(1,591)^2}{(4)(20)} = 31,641.01;$$

$$[A] = \frac{\Sigma A^2}{s}$$

$$= \frac{(309)^2 + (429)^2 + (452)^2 + (401)^2}{20} = 32,231.35;$$

and

$$[AS] = \Sigma (AS)^2$$

$$= 5,175 + 9,461 + 10,550 + 8,529 = 33,715.$$

The sums of squares are next, i.e.,

$$SS_A = [A] - [T] = 590.34;$$

$$SS_{S/A} = [AS] - [A] = 1,483.65;$$

and

$$SS_T = [AS] - [T] = 2,073.99.$$

These values are entered in the lower half of Table 7-1, where the remainder of the statistical analysis is summarized.

An inspection of the means in Table 7-1 suggests that a spacing interval between learning trials has an increasing beneficial effect up to a certain point (somewhere between 40 and 60 seconds), after which performance tends to decline. Given this outcome, we would expect to find both a linear component (resulting from the general upward rise of the function) and a quadratic component (due to the slight downward concavity) emerging from the trend analysis. In this analysis, we will assume that we planned to conduct a component analysis of trend before the data were collected. In fact, there is even a theory that predicts exactly this finding (Underwood, 1961).

Whatever the case, it is of interest to find out more about the form of the relationship between the length of the intertrial interval and learning. Since the four levels are evenly spaced on the independent variable, we can use the orthogonal polynomial coefficients that are listed in Table A-4 of Appendix A. Also listed in the table are the sums of the squared coefficients, which are needed for the analysis. The coefficients and sums for the three possible components (linear, quadratic, and cubic) are presented in the upper half of Table 7-2. A numerical subscript has been

Table 7-2   Numerical Example: Trend Analysis

	INTERTRIAL INTERVAL (A)				
	0 sec. a_1	20 sec. a_2	40 sec. a_3	60 sec. a_4	
$\bar{A}_i$:	15.45	21.45	22.60	20.05	
	COEFFICIENTS				$\Sigma\,(c_i)^2$
Linear (c_{1i}):	−3	−1	1	3	20
Quadratic (c_{2i}):	1	−1	−1	1	4
Cubic (c_{3i}):	−1	3	−3	1	20
	COMPUTATIONS				Sum
$(c_{1i})(\bar{A}_i)$:	−46.35	−21.45	22.60	60.15	14.95
$(c_{2i})(\bar{A}_i)$:	15.45	−21.45	−22.60	20.05	−8.55
$(c_{3i})(\bar{A}_i)$:	−15.45	64.35	−67.80	20.05	1.15

added to the designation of each set of coefficients to distinguish between the different sets. That is, c_{1i} refers to the linear coefficients, c_{2i} to the quadratic coefficients, and c_{3i} to the cubic coefficients. For convenience, the treatment means $\bar{A}_i$ are also included in the table.

The formula for the $SS_{A\,\text{trend}}$ is given by Eq. (7-2):

$$SS_{A\,\text{trend}} = \frac{s(\hat{\psi}_{\text{trend}})^2}{\Sigma\,(c_i)^2}.$$

For the sum of the weighted treatment means, $\Sigma\,(c_i)(\bar{A}_i)$, we have

$$\hat{\psi}_{\text{linear}} = \Sigma\,(c_{1i})(\bar{A}_i) = (-3)(15.45) + (-1)(21.45) + (1)(22.60) + (3)(20.05);$$

$$\hat{\psi}_{\text{quadratic}} = \Sigma\,(c_{2i})(\bar{A}_i) = (1)(15.45) + (-1)(21.45) + (-1)(22.60) + (1)(20.05);$$

and

$$\hat{\psi}_{\text{cubic}} = \Sigma\,(c_{3i})(\bar{A}_i) = (-1)(15.45) + (3)(21.45) + (-3)(22.60) + (1)(20.05).$$

These calculations are completed in the bottom half of Table 7-2. The next step is to substitute these last three sums into Eq. (7-2). We have, for the three components,

$$SS_{A\,\text{linear}} = \frac{20(14.95)^2}{20} = 223.50;$$

$$SS_{A\,\text{quadratic}} = \frac{20(-8.55)^2}{4} = 365.51;$$

Table 7-3 Summary of the Trend Analysis

SOURCE	SS	df	MS	F
Intertrial interval (A)	(590.34)	(3)		
Linear	223.50	1	223.50	11.45*
Quadratic	365.51	1	365.51	18.72*
Cubic	1.32	1	1.32	<1
S/A	1,483.65	76	19.52	
Total	2,073.99	79		

*$p < .01$.

and

$$SS_{A \text{ cubic}} = \frac{20(1.15)^2}{20} = 1.32.$$

These three component sums of squares are presented together in a summary table in Table 7-3. Except for rounding errors, the three orthogonal components sum to the SS_A we obtained earlier:

$$\Sigma SS_{A \text{ comp.}} = 223.50 + 365.51 + 1.32 = 590.33.$$

The F ratios are formed by dividing the component mean squares by the overall error term, the $MS_{S/A}$. As indicated in the table, the linear and quadratic components are significant.

Order of Testing Components

I have indicated already that it is possible to extract $a - 1$ orthogonal trend components from a set of a treatment means. Usually, we will not be directly interested in the presence or absence of trends beyond the linear and quadratic components. Of course, if a theory made a specific prediction concerning a higher-order component, we would certainly test that prediction by isolating the variance due to that particular form of trend. We might only look at the variability associated with a single trend component, if, for theoretical reasons, this component were singled out. These comparisons are planned and are conducted as I have outlined.

A different way of proceeding is often followed when there is no specific theory to guide the analysis and we are simply interested in discovering the trend components that will jointly describe the outcome of the experiment fairly accurately. Following a significant omnibus F, the first step is to calculate the linear sum of squares and to test the significance of this component. In order to decide whether to continue searching for other significant components, we perform another "omnibus" F test based on the sums of squares remaining after the linear component has been removed. That is, we will test the significance of

$$SS_{A\,\text{residual}} = SS_A - SS_{A\,\text{linear}}.$$

The "residual" sum of squares has

$$df = df_A - df_{A\,\text{linear}} = (a - 1) - 1,$$

and the corresponding mean square is evaluated against the $MS_{S/A}$. If this F is significant, then we can extract the next higher component, the quadratic in this case. If the F is not significant, we stop. (We subject the residual sum of squares to a test of significance for the same reason that we perform an omnibus F test—in the absence of any particular hypotheses, to see whether there is any variation among the means to worry about.)

If we continued with the analysis and extracted the quadratic component, we would test the significance of this component and then test the new residual sum of squares:

$$SS_{A\,\text{residual}} = SS_A - SS_{A\,\text{linear}} - SS_{A\,\text{quadratic}},$$

which is associated with

$$df = df_A - df_{A\,\text{linear}} - df_{A\,\text{quadratic}}$$
$$= (a - 1) - 1 - 1.$$

If this F is not significant, we stop extracting components; if it is, we continue with the process.

It should be pointed out again, however, that little is gained by way of behavioral insight when we find significant higher-order components. The main purpose of this sort of analysis is to see just how well fairly simple polynomials (linear and quadratic) fit the data as a first approximation. One index of the success of this approach is the degree to which these simpler functions account for the overall treatment variability observed in the experiment. The ratio of component sum of squares $SS_{A\,\text{trend}}$ to treatment sum of squares SS_A can be used to provide this information. In the present example, the linear component accounts for $223.50/590.34 \times 100 = 37.9$ percent of the between-groups variation, and the quadratic component accounts for $365.51/590.34 \times 100 = 61.9$ percent of the between-groups variation.

7.5   LIMITATIONS OF TREND ANALYSIS

I should mention several limitations of the analysis of trend. First, we must continually remind ourselves that our only knowledge about the underlying function for the population comes from the limited number of points we have selected for the experiment. We assess the importance of different orthogonal trend components on the basis of the means we *do* have. How do we know that the same underlying trend would be suggested if other points had been selected for the experiment? Is it accurate to draw a continuous function between the points that we do have—would values of the independent variable falling between the ones included in the experiment fall on the revised polynomial? In our example, we are asking whether we can safely predict the treatment means for such values on the independent variable as an intertrial interval of 10 seconds, say, or of 50 seconds. In most cases, such predictions are reasonably accurate.

A related and more serious question concerns the extrapolation of the function *outside* the two extreme values on the independent variable included in the experiment. Translated to our experiment, we are asking about the shape of the function beyond the shortest and the longest intervals included in the study. Consider the function depicted in Fig. 7-4. We will assume that it represents the function in the population. Our experiment has focused on one portion of the continuum, the band between 0 and 60 seconds. On the basis of a trend analysis, we concluded that there is a linear and a quadratic component. But the underlying function is *primarily quadratic.* We would have seen this clearly had we included a 2-minute intertrial interval, for instance. All that we can say about this function is what we have found within the band we selected for the experiment. We did have a clue in this experiment that a quadratic trend was present from the reversal of trend between 40 and 60 seconds. On the other hand, the reversal of trend does not necessarily mean that performance will continue to drop as we increase the intertrial interval; perhaps it will level off. We cannot tell from this experiment.

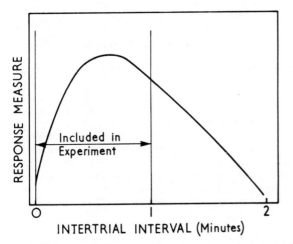

FIGURE 7-4.   Hypothetical function relating the length of the intertrial interval to some measure of learning.

Other limitations are not as serious as the one we have just considered. One is that the orthogonal polynomial coefficients in Table A-4 of Appendix A assume equal spacings on the independent variable. We are able to solve this difficulty by calculating sets of orthogonal polynomial coefficients that are appropriate to the actual spacings represented in an experiment (see Appendix C-3.).A trend analysis also assumes an equal number of subjects in each of the treatment conditions. Trend analyses of experiments with unequal sample sizes are discussed in Chapter 15. Finally, the analysis is based upon the assumption that the polynomial is the appropriate mathematical function to describe a set of data. In some areas of psychology, certain phenomena are better described by an exponential function or by a logarithmic function. Nevertheless, the method of orthogonal polynomials still can approximate these alternative functions fairly well.

7.6 EXERCISES[4]

1. Grant (1956) analyzed data from an experiment examining the gradient of stimulus generalization. Subjects were first trained to respond to a 12-inch visual stimulus. Following training, seven different groups of subjects were extinguished on stimuli of different sizes (9, 10, 11, 12, 13, 14, and 15 inches). He measured the degree of responding on the first extinction trial, expecting to find two factors: (1) a general tendency for responding to increase with the size of the stimulus (an upward-sloping linear trend component) and (2) a concave-downward generalization gradient, with responding tapering off in both directions from the 12-inch training stimulus. There were $s = 14$ subjects in each group. The means for the $a = 7$ groups are as follows:

9 IN.	10 IN.	11 IN.	12 IN.	13 IN.	14 IN.	15 IN.
1.52	2.64	4.28	3.86	3.86	2.79	3.70

   (a) Plot the data and examine the nature of the trend observed in this experiment.
   (b) Conduct an analysis of the linear and quadratic trends. (The within-groups mean square was 5.84.)
2. Hullian theory postulated a complicated relationship between anxiety level and performance on a complex task. Basically, the theory predicted that an inverted U-shaped function (concave downward) should result, with performance best at medium levels of anxiety and relatively poor at low and at high levels of anxiety. To test this prediction, an investigator attempted to measure the backward memory span (a rather difficult task) of subjects, who on the basis of performance on a pencil-and-paper test of anxiety were placed in one of six categories (levels a_1 to a_6), where a_1 = low anxiety and a_6 = high anxiety. There were five subjects in each of the anxiety levels. The span lengths obtained were as follows:

---

[4]The answers to these problems are found in Appendix B, beginning on p. 567.

a_1	a_2	a_3	a_4	a_5	a_6
1	2	3	3	4	3
0	1	4	5	3	2
1	1	2	2	2	3
1	2	5	5	4	4
1	2	3	3	3	2

(a) Perform an overall analysis of variance on these data.
(b) Conduct a trend analysis, assuming that the levels of the anxiety variable are equally spaced.
(c) What can you conclude from this experiment?

8

Correction for Multiple Comparisons

One of the most complex and perhaps most confused topics in statistical inference concerns an unfortunate by-product of the conscientious and detailed analysis of an experiment, namely, an increased vulnerability to type I error. That is, type I errors *cumulate* with each statistical test performed in a predictable and unavoidable fashion—unavoidable, unless steps are taken to correct this process. This chapter examines this problem and solutions designed to solve it. My coverage will be selective, focusing on particular recommendations rather than presenting a comprehensive description of the topic. If you wish to study the problem in more depth, you might read first two early discussions (Ryan, 1959; Wilson, 1962) and then three informative and useful papers by Games (1971b, 1978a, and 1978b).[1]

8.1 PROBLEMS ASSOCIATED WITH ANALYTICAL COMPARISONS

Increase in Type I Error

The major problem resulting from the performance of a series of analytical comparisons on a set of data is the unpleasant fact that the more comparisons we conduct, the more type I errors we will make when the null hypothesis is true. In talking about this relationship, the distinction is often made between the type I error **per comparison (PC)** and the error rate **familywise (FW)**.[2] The *PC* error rate, which we will continue to call α, uses the *comparison* as the conceptual unit for the error rate. If we evaluated several comparisons in an experiment, each at $\alpha = .05$, we would be using a *PC* error rate; our probability of making a type I error would be .05 for each of the separate comparisons. In contrast, the type I *FW* error rate, α_{FW}, considers the probability of making *one or more* type I errors in the *set of comparisons* under scrutiny.

The relationship between the two error rates is expressed by the formula

$$\alpha_{FW} = 1 - (1 - \alpha)^c, \qquad (8\text{-}1)$$

where c represents the number of orthogonal comparisons that are conducted. With the *PC* error rate set at $\alpha = .05$ and with $c = 3$ comparisons contemplated, the *FW* type I error rate is

$$\alpha_{FW} = 1 - (1 - .05)^3 = 1 - (.95)^3 = 1 - .857 = .143.$$

If we were working at the 1 percent significance level,

$$\alpha_{FW} = 1 - (1 - .01)^3 = 1 - (.99)^3 = 1 - .970 = .030.$$

---

[1] The 1971 paper should be read in conjunction with Games (1971a), which corrects a number of typographical errors in the original article.

[2] Following the recommendation of others, I have adopted the term *familywise* to replace the earlier term *experimentwise*. Both terms refer to the same concept in the context of the single-factor design. The distinction between the two terms becomes critical in factorial designs.

The familywise error rate is approximated by

$$\tilde{\alpha}_{FW} = c(\alpha), \tag{8-2}$$

but the approximation $\tilde{\alpha}_{FW}$ will always overestimate α_{FW}, though less for small values of α and for small numbers of comparisons. In the present example, with $\alpha = .05$,

$$\tilde{\alpha}_{FW} = 3(.05) = .15,$$

as compared with the $\alpha_{FW} = .143$ obtained with Eq. (8-1). For the smaller α level, $p = .01$, the two values are identical when carried to two decimal places.

When several comparisons are involved in the analysis of an experiment, researchers have different attitudes about which conceptual unit for the error rate is most appropriate. The point to be emphasized now is that when we conduct a number of comparisons on a set of means, there is an *FW* error rate with which we must contend and this error rate increases directly with the number of comparisons tested.

The relationship between *FW* error rate and the number of analytical comparisons is not an exclusive property of orthogonal comparisons, however, but holds for nonorthogonal comparisons as well. While the calculation of *FW* rate when nonorthogonal comparisons are involved in an analysis plan is not simple, it is still accurate to say that the *FW* error rate increases with the number of comparisons conducted regardless of orthogonality (see Harter, 1957, for a discussion of the problem).

Planned Comparisons

Experiments are usually designed with specific hypotheses in mind, and most researchers conduct analyses relevant to these hypotheses directly without reference to the outcome of the omnibus F test. Although the omnibus test may be computed, its significance or nonsignificance does not modify this particular course of action. Unplanned comparisons, in contrast, refer to the analysis of *unexpected* findings, outcomes that are revealed only after the data have been collected and partially analyzed. These **post hoc comparisons**, as they are also called, can sometimes be critically important in the development of a field of research.

While both planned and post hoc comparisons lead to an increase in *FW* error, they are usually treated differently in any attempt to reduce or to control the *FW* error rate. The most widely used strategy is to evaluate planned comparisons in the normal way—at the usual *PC*, or α, rate—and to exercise control of the *FW* rate for post hoc comparisons through special evaluation procedures designed to cope with the problem.[3]

---

[3]Not all commentators on the problem of *FW* error agree that planned comparisons should be left uncorrected, however. The correction they usually recommend for planned comparisons is the Bonferroni, or Dunn, test, which applies a less severe correction than those associated with tests developed for use with post hoc comparisons. The Bonferroni test is discussed in detail by Kirk (1968, pp. 79–81) and Myers (1979, pp. 298–300).

Planned comparisons are specified in the initial planning of an experiment. Collectively, they represent the answers an investigator hopes to obtain to the research questions that generated the experiment in the first place. Although the definition of planned comparisons is clear, the restrictions suggested by various authors are not. The two major areas of concern are the orthogonality of the set of planned comparisons and the number of comparisons to be included in the set. I will consider both issues in some detail.

The Issue of Orthogonality. I have already discussed this issue in Chapter 6 (pp. 121-123). Consensus seems to favor a set of meaningful comparisons which more often than not contains some nonorthogonal comparisons, i.e., a set of comparisons that are not mutually orthogonal. As you saw in Chapter 6, complete orthogonal sets do not necessarily contain comparisons that are all psychologically meaningful, on the one hand, nor do they completely enumerate the total set of meaningful comparisons associated with an experiment, on the other. The value of orthogonal comparisons lies in the independence of *inferences,* which, of course, is a desirable quality to achieve. That is, orthogonal comparisons are such that any decision concerning the null hypothesis representing one comparison is uninfluenced by the decision concerning the null hypothesis representing any other orthogonal comparison (see pp. 118-119).

The potential difficulty with nonorthogonal comparisons, then, is in interpreting the different outcomes. If we reject the null hypotheses for two nonorthogonal comparisons, which comparison represents the "true" reason for the observed differences? If we reject one null hypothesis and not the other, what can we make of the results? I do not mean to say that such ambiguities always arise when nonorthogonal comparisons are involved or that they are unresolvable when they do, but simply to suggest that nonorthogonal comparisons be interpreted with particular care in order to avoid this sort of problem.

The Number of Planned Comparisons. While everyone seems to agree that planned comparisons should be limited in number, there is no agreement on what this number should be. One obvious possibility is to restrict the number of comparisons to the number of degrees of freedom associated with the treatment source of variance ($df_A = a - 1$). But this suggestion, or any other recommendation for that matter, is an *arbitrary* restriction. On the other hand, the point I wish to make is simply that many researchers do limit the number of planned comparisons and, depending on the research hypotheses and on the complexity of the experiment, the number of planned comparisons will range slightly above or below df_A. A conscientious researcher will realize that the number of comparisons affects the *FW* rate, however, and will reach a threshold of concern for this fact somewhere near the "natural" limit set by the number of degrees of freedom.

The Modified Bonferroni Test. One possible solution to this problem is to assume that most researchers are willing to test up to $a - 1$ planned comparisons *without correcting* for *FW* error. Suppose we use this number—the *df* associated with the between-groups mean square—to set the *FW* standard for planned comparisons and to introduce corrections only when the number of comparisons *exceeds*

df_A. This can be accomplished easily by calculating the α_{FW} associated with $a - 1$ orthogonal comparisons and then dividing this probability by the *actual* number of planned comparisons included in the analysis plan.[4] The resulting probability is a new *PC* rate to be used in assessing these comparisons that maintains α_{FW} at this presumably acceptable standard. In symbols, we use Eq. (8-2) to calculate the maximum *FW* error for planned comparisons,

$$\tilde{\alpha}_{FW\,\text{planned}} = (df_A)(\alpha),\qquad\qquad(8\text{-}3)$$

and divide this value by the number of comparisons *actually planned* (c):

$$\tilde{\alpha}_{\text{planned}} = \frac{\tilde{\alpha}_{FW\,\text{planned}}}{c}.\qquad\qquad(8\text{-}4)$$

This method of adjusting the *PC* rate is related to a procedure known as the **Bonferroni test**, which I mentioned in footnote 3 (p. 146). In the Bonferroni test, the numerator in Eq. (8-4) is the overall *FW* rate adopted by a researcher for the experiment—*not* the $\tilde{\alpha}_{FW\text{planned}}$ I have suggested as a method for controlling *FW* error with planned comparisons. I will refer to the present technique as the **modified Bonferroni test**.

As an example, consider an experiment with $a = 5$ conditions. Assuming that the maximum number of planned comparisons that will be conducted without correction is equal to $df_A = 4$, and adopting the standard significance level $\alpha = .05$, we obtain an approximate probability for this "acceptable" *FW* rate by substituting in Eq. (8-3). That is,

$$\tilde{\alpha}_{FW\,\text{planned}} = 4(.05) = .20.$$

This *FW* rate of .20, then, represents the assumed risk that researchers are generally willing to take when planned comparisons are at stake.

Suppose we wanted to conduct $c = 5$ planned comparisons. We find from Eq. (8-4) that

$$\tilde{\alpha}_{\text{planned}} = \frac{.20}{5} = .04$$

is the adjusted significance level that will be used to evaluate the significance of *all five* planned comparisons. A quick calculation will indicate that this new rejection probability results in an *FW* rate of $c(\tilde{\alpha}_{\text{planned}}) = 5(.04) = .20$, which is the *FW* rate we adopted in this example for the entire set of planned comparisons.

Table 8-1 summarizes the calculations of $\tilde{\alpha}_{\text{planned}}$ for several values of c, using $a = 5$. You will note that when $c \leqslant df_A$, no correction is applied and the *FW* varies with the number of comparisons. On the other hand, when $c > df_A$, the *FW* rate remains constant at $\tilde{\alpha}_{FW\,\text{planned}} = .20$ and the significance level used to evaluate the comparisons is systematically lowered as a consequence.

---

[4]These calculations are based on orthogonal comparisons, which will tend to cause overestimation of the *FW* error when nonorthogonal comparisons are involved, but this "overcorrection" makes little practical difference in an actual research application.

Table 8-1   The Modified Bonferroni Test for Planned Comparisons

NUMBER OF COMPARISONS (c)	REJECTION PROBABILITY ($\tilde{\alpha}_{planned}$)	APPROXIMATE FAMILYWISE ERROR ($\tilde{\alpha}_{FW}$)
1	.05	.05
2	.05	.10
3	.05	.15
4	.05	.20
5	.040	.20
6	.033	.20
7	.029	.20
8	.025	.20
9	.022	.20
10	.020	.20

One difficulty with the Bonferroni test is the need to determine the critical value of F when $\tilde{\alpha}_{planned}$ falls between the probabilitites provided in the standard F tables. Since the F's associated with most planned comparisons will involve 1 df in the numerator, it is possible to use the unit normal distribution and approximate the value of t, which, when squared, will give us the corresponding critical value of F. The value of t at an α level of significance is found by the formula

$$t(df_{S/A}) = z + \frac{z^3 + z}{4(df_{S/A} - 2)}, \tag{8-5}$$

where z represents the point on the unit normal distribution above which [$\frac{1}{2}(\alpha) \times 100$] percent of the curve falls.[5]

As an example, I will work with a calculation we can verify in the F table. From Table 8-1, you can see that $c = 8$ planned comparisons offers such a choice ($\tilde{\alpha}_{planned} = .025$). From a table of the unit normal curve, available in most introductory texts, the value of z above which $\frac{1}{2}(.025) \times 100 = 1.25$ percent of the area of the curve falls is 2.24. Substituting in Eq. (8-5) and assuming $df_{S/A} = 40$,

$$t(40) = 2.24 + \frac{(2.24)^3 + 2.24}{4(40 - 2)}$$

$$= 2.24 + \frac{11.24 + 2.24}{152} = 2.33.$$

To verify the goodness of the approximation, we square this value to give us

$$F(1, 40) = [t(40)]^2 = (2.33)^2 = 5.43.$$

The value of $F(1, 40)$ from Table A-1 in Appendix A at $\alpha = .025$ is 5.42.

---

[5] Dividing α by 2 provides a critical value of z that locates one half of the rejection region in the positive tail and the other one half of the rejection region in the negative tail of the unit normal distribution.

Summary. The decision to restrict the number of planned comparisons or to introduce some correction in the decision process depends on our attitude concerning type I and type II errors and the sort of balancing that we want to achieve between them. You must work this problem out for yourself and then deal with the additional problem of convincing others that your findings will hold up on replication. In short, part of your planning should include a concern for planned comparisons and your attitude toward them, as well as a concern for the logic of the experimental design, and a realistic estimate of power for the experiment in general and for the planned comparisons in particular. The implicit standard adopted by most researchers of conducting up to $a - 1$ planned comparisons without special correction seems reasonable except, perhaps, when the number of treatment conditions is particularly large and the FW error for planned comparisons becomes sizable as a consequence. Planned comparisons *are* special and should be evaluated with a sensitive statistical test. The modified Bonferroni test described in the preceding paragraphs offers a way of maintaining this standard in situations where the number of comparisons exceeds this assumed limit.

Post Hoc Comparisons

Post hoc comparisons often take the form of an intensive "milking" of a set of results—e.g., the comparison of all possible pairs of treatment means. The motivation, of course, is to extract the maximum amount of information from any given study. Another reason for conducting post hoc comparisons is that the results of such tests often lead to future experiments. An interesting comparison, significant or not, may form the basis for a new experiment. In the next study, for example, we might choose to manipulate more extensively the different treatments contributing to the comparison we have isolated.

The total number of possible single-df comparisons, which includes differences between pairs of means and complex comparisons between means, is staggering, even for a "modest" experimental design. For $a = 3$, there are 6 such comparisons, possible; for $a = 4$, there are 25; for $a = 5$, there are 90; and for $a = 6$, there are 301.[6] You can appreciate the concern for the FW rate when the pool of potential comparisons is as large as these!

There are several approaches designed to deal directly with this problem. All such techniques employ the same basic solution, namely, to reduce the size of the critical region—i.e., to lower the significance level. In fact, Games (1971b; 1978b) points out that the different procedures all involve the same underlying test statistic and differ only in the ways by which this reduction in the PC rate is achieved. The logic is straightforward: If we make it more difficult to reject the null hypothesis for each comparison tested, which must happen when the size of the rejection region is reduced, fewer type I errors will be committed and the FW error rate will thus be lowered. Just how much of an "adjustment" is made depends on a number

---

[6]The total number of comparisons is $1 + (3^a - 1)/2 - 2^a$.

of factors, such as our willingness to make type I errors in general, the number of post hoc comparisons actually conducted, and the pool of comparisons from which comparisons are specifically chosen. As you will see when you enter the research arena, there is no general agreement among researchers or even among authors of statistical texts and articles concerning these points.

In the next two sections, I will consider a number of procedures that have been developed to cope with the increased FW error rate associated with post hoc comparisons. Section 8.2 describes a technique that can be used to control the FW rate for any type of comparison between means. Section 8.3 focuses on techniques that have been designed specifically for comparisons between pairs of treatment means. I will not cover all of the tests that have been proposed or are even currently in use but will concentrate on those that for various reasons seem best suited to our needs. I have been assisted in this selection of tests by the analysis and recommendations of Games (1978b).[7]

8.2 FAMILYWISE CORRECTIONS FOR ALL COMPARISONS: THE SCHEFFÉ TEST

The **Scheffé test** is a technique that allows a researcher to maintain the FW rate at a particular value regardless of the number of comparisons actually conducted. For this reason, then, the Scheffé test is flexible in its application to the analysis of an experiment.

The Scheffé test requires no special tables, since it is based on the values of the F statistic appearing in standard F tables. The procedure is simple. We calculate $F_{\text{comp.}}$ in the usual fashion but evaluate the significance of the obtained F with a special critical value, F_S. This quantity is defined as follows:

$$F_S = (a - 1)F(df_A, df_{S/A}),\qquad(8\text{-}6)$$

where $F(df_A, df_{S/A})$ is the critical value of F for the *omnibus* analysis of variance and is found in Table A-1 under the desired α level. (Be sure to note that the value of $df_{\text{num.}}$ is equal to $a - 1$ and *not* to $df_{\text{comp.}}$—a common mistake made by students in my classes.) The choice of significance level at this point sets the maximum value that familywise error α_{FW} may take regardless of the number of comparisons conducted. Thus, an F chosen from Table A-1 at the .05 level of significance and entered into Eq. (8-6) will create a cricital value of F (F_S) that sets a maximum limit on the FW rate at .05. Using critical values of F at other α levels sets the limit at these probabilities correspondingly.

As an example, suppose we performed an experiment with $a = 5$ treatment conditions and $s = 9$ subjects assigned randomly to each group. We will assume that the $MS_{S/A}$, which is based on $a(s - 1) = 5(9 - 1) = 40$ degrees of freedom, is

---

[7]For a comprehensive summary and comparison of these and other techniques, see Kirk (1968, pp. 87–98) and Winer (1971, pp. 185–204).

13.22. The sums and the means for the treatment groups are presented in Table 8-2. Suppose we decided to compare the average of two of the groups (a_1 and a_5) with the average of the other three (a_2, a_3, and a_4). The first average is $(12.78 + 11.44)/2 = 12.11$, and the second average is $(7.89 + 7.11 + 8.78)/3 = 7.93$, indicating a sizable difference between the two means $(12.11 - 7.93 = 4.18)$. A convenient set of coefficients with which to calculate the comparison sum of squares is $(3, -2, -2, -2, 3)$. Substituting the necessary values in Eq. (6-5), we have

$$SS_{A \text{ comp.}} = \frac{s(\hat{\psi})^2}{\Sigma (c_i)^2}$$

$$= \frac{9[(3)(12.78) + (-2)(7.89) + (-2)(7.11) + (-2)(8.78) + (3)(11.44)]^2}{(3)^2 + (-2)^2 + (-2)^2 + (-2)^2 + (3)^2}$$

$$= 189.00.$$

The next operation is to form an F ratio. Since we are still contrasting only two means in this comparison, the number of df for the $SS_{A \text{ comp.}}$ is 1 and the $MS_{A \text{ comp.}} = 189.00/1 = 189.00$. The F ratio is specified in Eq. (6-7) and consists simply of dividing the $MS_{A \text{ comp.}}$ by the $MS_{S/A}$. In this case,

$$F_{\text{comp.}} = \frac{189.00}{13.22} = 14.30.$$

Normally this F would be compared with the critical value of $F(1, 40)$, which at $\alpha = .05$ is 4.08. For the Scheffé test, however, we determine the critical value F_S by substituting in Eq. (8-6), for which we will need the critical value for the omnibus F, which in this case is $F(4, 40) = 2.61$ at $\alpha = .05$. Substituting in Eq. (8-6), we find

$$F_S = (a - 1)F(df_A, df_{S/A})$$
$$= (5 - 1)(2.61) = 10.44.$$

Since the obtained $F_{\text{comp.}}$ of 14.30 exceeds this critical value demanded by the Scheffé test (10.44), we can reject the null hypothesis.

Perhaps you noticed the severity of the Scheffé correction, which is reflected in the difference between the two critical values, 4.08 versus 10.44. Translated to a *PC* rate, the Scheffé correction is equivalent to a significance level of about $\alpha =$

Table 8-2   Numerical Example: Treatment Sums and Means

	LEVELS				
	a_1	a_2	a_3	a_4	a_5
Sums	115	71	64	79	103
Means	12.78	7.89	7.11	8.78	11.44

.0025. This marked reduction in the *PC* rate (from $\alpha = .05$ to $\alpha = .0025$) is necessary to set the *FW* error at a value no greater than $\alpha_{FW} = .05$. When the frame of reference consists of all possible comparisons, however, which in this case is 90, the correction needs to be severe.

8.3 COMPARISONS BETWEEN PAIRS OF MEANS

There are times when a researcher may be interested in evaluating the significance of all possible differences between pairs of treatment means. The number of such **pairwise comparisons**, as they are frequently called, may be determined by solving the following simple formula: $a(a - 1)/2$. Applied research is often of this type— different books are compared in a classroom setting to determine which book is best; a consumer testing agency evaluates a number of similar products and attempts to order and to group the products in terms of effectiveness; and so on. In these cases, the intent is clearly to compare each treatment condition—each book or product, for example—with all other treatment conditions. Presumably there would be little or no interest in more complex comparisons unless there were good reasons for combining certain conditions, e.g., products from the same manufacturer or books by the same author. Theoretically motivated research, on the other hand, produces experimental designs that generate a limited number of meaningful comparisons that generally will *not* include all possible pairwise comparisons, but rather a smaller number of pairwise comparisons combined with a couple of more complex comparisons.

Many alternative tests have been developed to control *FW* error under the circumstances where a researcher wishes to conduct pairwise comparisons. The Scheffé test is *not* recommended for this situation, since it is less powerful than the more specialized techniques I consider in this section. I will cover three such tests in detail: the **Dunnett test**, which is used when the pairwise comparisons consist of differences between one condition (usually a control or baseline condition) and several others (usually experimental conditions); the **Tukey test**, which provides *FW* control when all of the pairwise comparisons are to be conducted; and the **Fisher test**, which offers *FW* control by means of an initial criterion that must be met before the comparisons can be conducted.

The Dunnett Test

When we include a control condition in an experiment, we are often interested in a number of different comparisons. As a first step in the analysis, we might compare the control group with the average score for the experimental groups combined—a sort of overall control-experimental contrast. Additionally, we might evaluate the significance of any differences observed among the experimental groups alone—a sort of omnibus *F* for the experimental groups. Finally, we would probably consider multiple comparisons involving a contrast of each of the experimental groups with the single control group. Because of the necessary increase in the number of comparisons when a single control group is compared with several experimental groups, we might want to exercise some control over the FW error rate.

The Dunnett test is a specialized FW correction technique that compensates for the increased number of type I errors but is not as "corrective" as are other post hoc tests, because it takes into consideration only a limited number of comparisons—the control-experimental contrasts. The simplest way to conduct the Dunnett test is to calculate the control-experimental mean differences and to compare them against a critical mean difference $(\bar{d}_D)$ that must be exceeded to be significant at the chosen FW level. The formula for calculating this critical difference is

$$\bar{d}_D = \frac{q_D \sqrt{2(MS_{S/A})}}{\sqrt{s}}, \tag{8-7}$$

where q_D refers to an entry in Table A-5 of Appendix A, $MS_{S/A}$ is the error term from the overall analysis of variance, and s is the sample size for each group. The value of q_D is determined by the total number of conditions k involved in the analysis, the degrees of freedom associated with the error term $(df_{S/A})$, and the value chosen for FW error (α_{FW}). If you choose to work with the F test, you can use

$$F_D = (q_D)^2 \tag{8-7a}$$

as the critical value with which to evaluate $F_{\text{comp.}}$.

As an example, I will use the data from Table 8-2. To set the example in context, let's assume that these data were drawn from an experiment comparing the amounts of memory loss for several different experimental conditions. There are four experimental groups $(a_2, a_3, a_4,$ and $a_5)$, each differing in the types of interfering activities they received between learning and recall. A control group (a_1) received a neutral task during the period in which the experimental subjects were experiencing interference.

While other questions might be asked of the data (e.g., questions about meaningful comparisons among the *experimental* groups), it is of interest to determine whether each of the experimental groups showed a significant loss relative to the control group. In order to calculate the critical C-E difference, we need to obtain q_D. Although the argument could be made that only differences in favor of the control group make any sense, most researchers would prefer to choose what is termed a **nondirectional** alternative hypothesis. What this means is that we want to be alert to positive as well as negative differences in the experiment. If we set our significance level at $q_{FW} = .05$, we will set aside half of the rejection region for positive deviations and the other half for negative deviations. Such a procedure is often called a **two-tailed test**.

To find the value of q_D, we locate the part of Table A-5 labeled "two-tailed comparisons" and look for the entry at $k = 5$, $df_{error} = df_{S/A} = 40$, and $\alpha_{FW} = .05$. (A directional test would be conducted with the values given in the part of Table A-5 labeled "one-tailed comparisons.") For this combination, $q_D = 2.54$. Substituting in Eq. (8-7) gives as the critical difference between the control and an experimental mean

$$\bar{d}_D = \frac{(2.54)\sqrt{2(13.22)}}{\sqrt{9}} = 4.35.$$

This is the difference that must be exceeded in order to allow the rejection of the null hypothesis that the control group and a particular experimental group are equal. From Table 8-2 (p. 152), the observed differences are

$$\bar{A}_1 - \bar{A}_2 = 12.78 - 7.89 = 4.89; \qquad \bar{A}_1 - \bar{A}_3 = 12.78 - 7.11 = 5.67;$$
$$\bar{A}_1 - \bar{A}_4 = 12.78 - 8.78 = 4.00; \qquad \bar{A}_1 - \bar{A}_5 = 12.78 - 11.44 = 1.34.$$

Since the first two differences (involving a_2 and a_3) exceed the critical value of 4.35, we can conclude that the specific interfering activities represented by these two conditions produced a significant memory deficit. The other two experimental treatments (a_4 and a_5) did not result in a significant loss of memory.

The Tukey Test

The Tukey test is designed to maintain the *FW* rate at the chosen value of α_{FW} for the entire set of pairwise comparisons.[8] The test is performed easily by arranging the treatment means in ascending order of magnitude on the dependent variable, as illustrated in Table 8-3. Entries within the body of this table represent the differences between any two treatment means. In the first row, for example,

$$\bar{A}_2 - \bar{A}_3 = 7.89 - 7.11 = .78; \bar{A}_4 - \bar{A}_3 = 8.78 - 7.11 = 1.67; \text{and so on.}$$

Differences are not entered for comparisons below the main diagonal of the table, since the listing would be an exact mirror image of the differences appearing above the diagonal.

The next step is to calculate the *minimum* pairwise difference between means that must be exceeded to be significant with the Tukey test. This value ($\bar{d}_T$) is given by the formula

$$\bar{d}_T = \frac{q_T \sqrt{MS_{S/A}}}{\sqrt{s}}, \qquad (8\text{-}8)$$

where q_T refers to an entry in the table of the **studentized range statistic** (Table A-6 in Appendix A), $MS_{S/A}$ is the error term from the overall analysis of variance,

---

[8]This test, like the Scheffé test, was designed to cover all comparisons, but it is more powerful than the Scheffé for pairwise tests and less powerful than the Scheffé for complex contrasts.

Table 8-3 An Example of Pairwise Comparisons

	LEVELS				
	(ORDERED BY SIZE OF TREATMENT MEANS)				
	a_3	a_2	a_4	a_5	a_1
MEANS	7.11	7.89	8.78	11.44	12.78
$\bar{A}_3 = 7.11$	—	.78	1.67	4.33	5.67
$\bar{A}_2 = 7.89$		—	.89	3.55	4.89
$\bar{A}_4 = 8.78$			—	2.66	4.00
$\bar{A}_5 = 11.44$				—	1.34
$\bar{A}_1 = 12.78$					—

and s is the sample size for each group. If you look at Table A-6, you will see that three quantities enter into the determination of q_T: df_{error} (the df associated with the $MS_{S/A}$), r (the number of treatment means—a in this design), and α_{FW} (the FW error rate chosen for the Tukey test).[9] For this example, $df_{error} = df_{S/A} = 40$, $r = a = 5$, and $\alpha_{FW} = .05$; the value of q_T is 4.04. Substituting in Eq. (8-8), we find

$$\bar{d}_T = \frac{(4.04)\sqrt{13.22}}{\sqrt{9}} = 4.90.$$

An inspection of the differences in Table 8-3 reveals that only the largest difference $(\bar{A}_1 - \bar{A}_3 = 12.78 - 7.11 = 5.67)$ exceeds the critical value for the Tukey test and would be declared significant.

The Tukey test can be used in conjunction with the F test, although calculating $F_{comp.}$ for each pair is not as convenient as calculating mean differences. In any case, the critical value of F (F_T) against which $F_{comp.}$ is compared is given by the following formula:

$$F_T = \frac{(q_T)^2}{2}. \tag{8-8a}$$

Sequential tests. Two popular alternatives to the Tukey test are the **Duncan** and the **Newman-Keuls tests.** These tests are distinguished by the fact that significance testing follows a series of sequential tests, each with a different critical value to establish the significance between pairs of means. The computational details of these tests may be found in Kirk (1968, pp. 91-94) and Winer (1971, pp. 191-201). All three tests have been compared in Monte Carlo experiments designed to reveal how well they control FW error and what their power characteristics are, i.e., how well they detect treatment differences when they are present. The study most well known to psychologists was conducted by Petrinovich and Hardyck (1969); other relevant studies have been reported by Carmer and Swanson (1973)

---

[9]Table A-6 is also used with the Newman-Keuls test, described briefly in the next section, in which case r takes on different values depending on the particular pairwise difference under consideration.

and by Einot and Gabriel (1975). The collective evidence seems to support the conclusion that the Tukey test is preferred over the other two tests.[10]

The Fisher Test

A different sort of correction procedure is the **protected least significant difference test**, which I will call the **Fisher test**. The test consists of two steps: the test of the omnibus F, followed by the unrestricted testing of all pairwise differences if the overall F is significant. If the omnibus F is not significant, no additional tests are conducted. A formula for the critical value of the Fisher test ($\bar{d}_F$) is

$$\bar{d}_F = \frac{t\sqrt{2(MS_{S/A})}}{\sqrt{s}}, \tag{8-9}$$

where t is found in Table A-3 of Appendix A under the chosen value of α and the degrees of freedom associated with $MS_{S/A}$. (The F table can be used by taking the square root of the critical value of F under $df_{num.} = 1$ and $df_{denom.} = df_{S/A}$.) This critical value is equivalent to the criterion for an uncorrected *planned comparison* expressed in terms of the difference between two means. Transformed to an F,

$$F_F = F(1, df_{S/A}). \tag{8-9a}$$

To illustrate the calculations, I will again use the data from Table 8-2. The first step is to evaluate the overall F. From the treatment totals in Table 8-2 (p. 152), we find

$$[A] = \frac{\Sigma A^2}{s} = 4{,}356.89;$$

$$[T] = \frac{T^2}{(a)(s)} = 4{,}147.20;$$

$$SS_A = [A] - [T] = 209.69;$$

and

$$MS_A = \frac{SS_A}{df_A} = \frac{209.69}{5-1} = 52.42.$$

The F ratio,

$$F = \frac{MS_A}{MS_{S/A}} = \frac{52.42}{13.22} = 3.97,$$

[10]Einot and Gabriel rejected the standard Newman-Keuls test because of its inadequate control of FW error and studied instead a modified Newman-Keuls test that is too complicated for general use by researchers. They recommend the Tukey test for its simplicity when compared with this modified Newman-Keuls test, and its favorable power characteristics relative to the other sequential procedures compared in their study.

is significant, exceeding the critical value of $F(4, 40) = 2.61$ at $\alpha = .05$. With this outcome, the Fisher test permits us to evaluate all pairwise differences against the following critical difference:

$$\bar{d}_F = \frac{t\sqrt{2(MS_{S/A})}}{\sqrt{s}}$$

$$= \frac{(2.02)\sqrt{2(13.22)}}{\sqrt{9}} = 3.46.$$

Using this value to assess the differences presented in Table 8-3, we find five of the comparisons to be significant. (In contrast, the Tukey test, with a critical value of $\bar{d}_T = 4.90$, declared only one difference, $\bar{A}_1 - \bar{A}_3 = 5.67$, to be significant.)

You should note that the Fisher test involves no special corrections once the overall F is found to be significant. Familywise error is controlled in effect by conditionalizing one's decision to conduct pairwise comparisons on the significance of the omnibus F test. That is, type I errors can be committed only when this F is *significant*; and when the overall null hypothesis is true, this will happen only a small proportion of the time, namely, the proportion specified by α. Thus, *FW* error is kept under control on the average by reducing greatly the proportion of times when a researcher conducts pairwise comparisons and the overall null hypothesis is true.

Carmer and Swanson (1973) compared 10 post hoc correction techniques using Monte Carlo procedures and concluded that the Fisher test offers the sort of balance between type I error and power that most researchers would find attractive and acceptable. Cohen and Cohen (1975), for example, recommend the Fisher test as a general strategy for analyzing the outcome of a complex study (see pp. 162–165 of that text). What is captured by the Fisher test is the attitude that a significant ombibus F usually means that population treatment effects are probably present and that additional tests are used to identify them; a certain number of type I errors will occur in this second stage, but they are far outweighed by a need to detect the true differences.

A serious problem with the Fisher test is its apparent incompatibility with a planned-comparison approach. The primary function of post hoc test procedures is to protect against reporting too many "accidents," i.e., type I errors. The Fisher test performs this function by stopping the researcher 95 percent of the time when the null hypothesis is completely true, i.e., when there are no differences in the population. But consider a case in which a single "deviant" mean is added to a set of equal means. The Fisher test no longer offers the same sort of protection for these equal means that it provided originally. This is because the omnibus F will now be significant *more* than 5 percent of the time—on account of the presence of this single deviant mean—and there will be an increased "opportunity" to make type I errors on comparisons involving the original set of treatments. Since experiments with planned comparisons are designed to detect at least one difference that will be significant, a researcher is generally assured a significant omnibus F and, as a result, the "license" provided by the Fisher test to conduct uncorrected post hoc tests. For this reason, then, it seems inappropriate to use the Fisher test when either planned comparisons are involved in the design or "dependable" treatment differences, e.g., control-experimental effects, have been incorporated into the experiment.

Two other problems with the Fisher test should be mentioned. First, the test was designed for pairwise comparisons, but not all interesting research questions fit this particular mold. It is probably safe to assume, however, that the Fisher test "works" even when complex comparisons are included in the analysis since the test holds the type I errors to the chosen level of significance regardless of what one does later. Second, the Fisher test seems to run into serious difficulties when unequal variances are paired with unequal sample sizes in an experiment (Keselman, Games, and Rogan, 1979).

In summary, we need to know more about the properties of the Fisher test before it gains the widespread use advocated by Cohen and Cohen (1975). If my analysis of the incompatibility of the planned-comparison approach and the Fisher test is correct, the test can be recommended only for situations in which no specific differences are predicted by the researcher.

8.4   PRACTICAL POINTS TO CONSIDER

You can now appreciate the serious dilemma faced by all researchers. On the one hand, you attempt to design experiments that are analytically rich and lead to a number of interesting comparisons and analyses, while on the other hand, you fully realize that familywise type I error is present whenever two or more statistical tests are performed in the analysis of a single experiment. At one extreme you could take the position that all possible findings are important and resist either restricting the number of comparisons undertaken or employing some procedure to control the increase in *FW* error. At the other extreme, you could maintain that accidental findings are to be avoided and adopt strong corrective methods to prevent the cumulation of type I error resulting from the assessment of two or more comparisons. In the first case, you would evaluate all comparisons at the same *PC* rate (e.g., $\alpha = .05$); in the second case, you would subject all comparisons to the Scheffé correction (e.g., $\alpha_{FW} = .05$). The extreme positions are clear, but few individuals subscribe to either point of view. What most of us do is to strike some balance between these two extremes in an attempt to detect the presence of the most important findings while still maintaining a reasonable control of *FW* error.

In this section, I will discuss a number of ways to resolve the unavoidable conflict between type I and type II errors. I will begin by considering a way to reduce a relatively large number of planned comparisons to a smaller and more focused set by permitting the outcome of certain key comparisons to guide the rest of the analysis. Next, I will mention a different sort of strategy that allows a researcher to achieve a tight control over *FW* error and avoids loss of power as well. Finally, I will offer some general recommendations for dealing with the evaluation of multiple comparisons.

Conditionalized Planned Comparisons

An important stage in the design of any experiment is to consider the nature and quality of the information obtainable from the study as planned. At this point, we can verify that the study will permit answers to our original research questions. This listing also provides a form of early warning that the number of planned comparisons approaches or exceeds the number beyond which a researcher will begin to become concerned about familywise type I error. If this number is not exceeded, we will assume that the researcher will test these comparisons directly once the data are collected and make no adjustment for the theoretical size of the *FW* error. But what if the number of planned comparisons exceeds this value? One might decide to do nothing and to live with the estimated *FW* error. Alternatively, one could reduce the length of the list to include only comparisons of primary concern, in which case the "secondary" comparisons might be subjected to some form of *FW* control while the more important comparisons are not.

There is another way of dealing with this problem, which is best described by a concrete example. Suppose an experiment is conducted that compares the performance of subjects following the administration of two drugs, A and B. Suppose further that two different control conditions were deemed necessary and that two batches of drug A were available to the experimenter. The experiment can be viewed as a single-factor design with $a = 5$ treatment conditions. The design and 20 single-*df* comparisons that ask potentially meaningful questions of this experiment are presented in Table 8-4.

Although this set of meaningful comparisons falls far short of including the 90 single-*df* comparisons possible when $a = 5$, the number of comparisons probably exceeds the threshold beyond which most experimenters become concerned with *FW* error. Suppose, however, we test comparison 1 first and conditionalize the remaining 19 comparisons on the outcome of this single test. This particular comparison assesses the equivalence of the two control conditions. If the comparison is *not* significant, we will probably consider combining the two groups in any further comparisons and omit from consideration comparisons that involve the two control conditions separately. On the other hand, if the comparison is *significant,* we will be forced to evaluate drug effects with each control separately and probably omit from consideration comparisons where the two control conditions are combined.

This conditionalizing of subsequent comparisons on the outcome of comparison 1 is summarized in the upper portion of Table 8-5. Comparisons listed on the left are the ones conducted if the observed difference between the two control means is not significant, while comparisons listed on the right are the ones conducted if the difference is significant. In the first case, the total number of comparisons tested is 10, including the initial comparison; in the second case, the total

Table 8-4 A Set of Meaningful Comparisons

MEANINGFUL COMPARISONS	CONTROL 1	CONTROL 2	DRUG A_1	DRUG A_2	DRUG B
1	+1	−1	0	0	0
2	+3	+3	−2	−2	−2
3	+1	+1	0	0	−2
4	+1	+1	−1	−1	0
5	+3	0	−1	−1	−1
6	+1	0	0	0	−1
7	+2	0	−1	−1	0
8	0	+3	−1	−1	−1
9	0	+1	0	0	−1
10	0	+2	−1	−1	0
11	+1	+1	−2	0	0
12	+1	+1	0	−2	0
13	+1	0	−1	0	0
14	+1	0	0	−1	0
15	0	+1	−1	0	0
16	0	+1	0	−1	0
17	0	0	+1	−1	0
18	0	0	+1	+1	−2
19	0	0	+1	0	−1
20	0	0	0	+1	−1

number is 15. In either case, however, the total number of comparisons tested has been reduced from the original number of 20.

Comparison 17 can be used in a similar fashion to narrow down the number of planned comparisons actually tested in the analysis of this experiment. In this case, the comparison involves an assessment of the equivalency of the two batches of drug A. If the two batches produce equivalent results, we would probably combine the two groups in all further analyses involving drug A. The comparisons we test under these circumstances are listed on the left in the middle section of Table 8-5. If the two batches are *not* equivalent, we are forced to conduct separate analyses for the two batches and omit comparisons where they are combined. These comparisons are listed on the right in the table. The total number of comparisons tested including the initial one is 12 when comparison 17 is not significant and 13 when comparison 17 is significant. Again, there is a reduction in the number of comparisons tested when we use this conditionalized, or branching, technique.

If we conditionalize on *both* of these initial comparisons, we can reduce the number tested still further, as is illustrated in the fourfold table presented in the bottom section of Table 8-5. The largest number of comparisons tested in this arrangement if we include the first two is 10, when both comparisons are significant, and the smallest number is 6, when neither comparison is significant.

This plan for reducing the number of planned comparisons would probably not evoke any controversy. Most researchers would agree that one should combine the two control conditions or the two batch conditions, since there is no com-

Table 8-5 An Example of Conditionalizing Planned Comparisons

TEST OF COMPARISON 1	
Not Significant	*Significant*
Test: comp. 2, 3, 4, 11, 12, 17, 18, 19, and 20.	Test: comp. 5, 6, 7, 8, 9, 10, 13, 14, 15, 16, 17, 18, 19, and 20.

TEST OF COMPARISON 17	
Not Significant	*Significant*
Test: comp. 1, 2, 3, 4, 5, 6, 7, 8, 9, 10, and 18.	Test: comp. 1, 3, 6, 9, 11, 12, 13, 14, 15, 16, 19, and 20.

	TEST OF COMPARISON 1	
TEST OF COMPARISON 17	*Not Significant*	*Significant*
Not Significant	Test: comp. 2, 3, 4, and 18.	Test: comp. 5, 6, 7, 8, 9, 10, and 18.
Significant	Test: comp. 3, 11, 12, 19, and 20.	Test: comp. 6, 9, 13, 14, 15, 16, 19, and 20.

pelling *theoretical reason* for not doing so. That is, the question is in essence *empirical*, rather than theoretical. Thus, the decision to combine or not to combine conditions can be reasonably decided by the outcome of the two statistical tests. The only question that might be raised concerns the presumed acceptance of the null hypothesis when the nonsignificant conditions are combined. One way to deal with this difficulty is to test the significance of these branching comparisons at a *higher* than normal probability level (e.g., $\alpha = .10$ or $.25$) in order to increase power and one's confidence in "accepting" the null hypothesis by combining nonsignificant conditions.

A Decision to Suspend Judgment

The major obstacle in the way of recommending a general plan for dealing with multiple comparisons that will satisfy most researchers is the differences in attitudes toward type I and type II errors held by different investigators. This stumbling block can be *circumvented* rather than removed simply by adding a *third decision category* to the evaluation process when the two concerns responsible for the problem—*FW* and power—are in conflict. This conflict occurs, of course, whenever $F_{comp.}$ is significant as a planned comparison evaluated at an uncorrected α level of significance, but it is not significant when the α level is corrected for familywise type I error. Instead of deciding to reject or not to reject the null hypothesis in such ambiguous cases, I propose that we recognize this ambiguity by deciding to **suspend judgment** concerning the status of the null hypothesis. By taking no formal action in this situation, we avoid committing either a type I or a type II error. As a consequence, the decision contributes nothing to familywise error, since the null hypothesis has not been formally rejected. Suspending judgment calls attention to a potential true difference and avoids creating the obscurity often associated with a difference that is labeled "nonsignificant." The idea of suspending judgment is not new, but was suggested by Hays (1973, pp. 350-353) to deal with a similar problem in the evaluation of the overall *F* test. Applied to multiple comparisons, the use of a third decision category of suspending judgment introduces flexibility and clarity into a situation in which arbitrariness and ambiguity instead have been the rule.

How might this new procedure work out in practice? The first step is to determine the critical value of the test statistic at the *uncorrected* level of significance (α). This value, which I will call CV_α, is used to define the lower boundary of the rejection region for planned comparisons. The second step is to set a more stringent criterion for rejection that reflects one's concern for familywise type I error. This value, which I will call CV_{FW}, refers to the rejection region for the correction technique considered most appropriate for the analysis. I can now state the decision rules as follows:

If the test statistic equals or exceeds CV_{FW}, reject H_0.

If the test statistic falls between CV_α and CV_{FW}, suspend judgment.

If the test statistic is less than CV_α, do not reject H_0.

As an illustration, let's return to the experiment used as a numerical example of the Scheffé test (pp. 151-152). For that particular experiment, the critical value for the Scheffé test was $F_S = 10.44$, while the critical value for planned comparisons was $F_\alpha = 4.08$. The test statistic calculated from the data was an *F* ratio ($F_{comp.}$). The decision rules for this case become:

If $F_{comp.} \geqslant 10.44$, reject H_0.

If $F_{comp.}$ falls between 4.08 and 10.44, suspend judgment.

If $F_{comp.} < 4.08$, do not reject H_0.

The value for $F_{comp.}$ in this example was 14.30 and H_0 is rejected.

As another illustration, consider the example presented in conjunction with the Tukey test (pp. 155-156). In this case, the test statistic is expressed as the difference between two means, symbolized as $\hat{\psi}$. For the Tukey test, the critical value is $\bar{d}_T = 4.90$. The corresponding value for planned comparisons, calculated from Eq. (8-9) on p. 158, is 3.46. The decision rules are:

If $\hat{\psi} \geqslant 4.90$, reject H_0.

If $\hat{\psi}$ falls between **3.46** and **4.90**, suspend judgment.

If $\hat{\psi} < 3.46$, do not reject H_0.

If you refer to Table 8-3 (p. 156), where all possible pairwise differences are enumerated, you can see that one of the comparisons exceeds 4.90 and leads to the rejection of H_0 (5.67), four fall between 3.46 and 4.90 and lead to the suspension of judgment (4.89, 4.33, 4.00, and 3.55), and the remaining five are less than 3.46 and lead to the nonrejection of H_0 (2.66, 1.67, 1.34, .89, and .78).

The three-decision system recognizes the ambiguity that exists when a comparison is significant under one criterion (as a planned comparison) but not significant under a more severe criterion (as a corrected post hoc comparison). By suspending judgment, we avoid committing either type of error, and simply conclude that the evidence is not sufficiently strong to justify either one of the usual conclusions. Since we have not rejected the null hypothesis, no type I error is committed, and the *FW* error is left unaffected by this decision. Since we have suspended judgment, no type II error is committed, and interesting and unexpected findings, often overlooked when a Scheffé test or other correction technique is used, can be assimilated into the interpretation of the experiment and perhaps earmarked for future replication and study.

Recommendations and Guidelines

You are now in a position to make up your own mind concerning the evaluation of analytical comparisons. The fact that there is little agreement among commentators writing in statistical books and articles concerning specific courses of action to be followed with multiple comparisons simply means that the issues *are* complex, and that no single solution can be offered to meet adequately the varied needs of researchers. Consequently, you should view the situation not with despair and frustration, but rather with a realization that you can and *must* work the problem out for yourself. The first step is to understand the basic issue—which is simple, really—that analytical comparisons, which are conducted in virtually every experiment we will consider in psychology, increase type I error in a predictable and inevitable fashion. Does this bother you? Your *degree* of concern, which is based on your attitude toward the relative importance of type I and type II errors for you and for your research field, will contribute greatly to your decision. Whatever plan you may adopt, however, you should make some attempt to estimate the degree of power under which you will be operating for comparisons of primary interest to you. I will now offer some recommendations and guidelines that may assist you in deciding how to evaluate the analytical comparisons derived from your research.

Planned Comparisons. Planned comparisons are usually the motivating force behind an experiment. These comparisons are targeted from the start of the investigation and represent an interest in particular combinations of conditions—not in the overall experiment. Planned comparisons are examples of what Tukey (1977) calls **confirmatory statistical analysis,** where specific questions that can be confirmed or disconfirmed are tested in an experiment. In keeping with the special status accorded planned comparisons, I recommend using the uncorrected *PC* rate, α, to evaluate the relevant test statistics. If the number of planned comparisons exceeds the number of degrees of freedom associated with the overall treatment mean square, I suggest the use of the modified Bonferroni test (pp. 147-149) to maintain the *FW* error for planned comparisons at the level dictated by df_A, namely, $(a - 1)(\alpha)$. Planned comparisons need not be orthogonal, although orthogonal comparisons do provide an unambiguous allocation of the treatment variation.

Post Hoc Comparisons. In post hoc data analysis, the type of question asked shifts from "Is *this* difference significant?" which characterizes planned comparisons, to "*Which* differences are significant?" which characterizes post hoc comparisons. The concern is with the whole set of treatments, rather than particular combinations of conditions. The probability of finding significant differences by chance depends on the number of treatment conditions; hence, it makes sense to worry about the *FW* rate under these circumstances.

It is my opinion that post hoc comparisons should be subjected to a more stringent standard to guard against committing an unacceptably large number of type I errors. Just which correction technique you choose depends on the nature of the comparisons examined in the post hoc analysis. If the comparisons consist only of differences between a control condition and several experimental conditions, the Dunnett test (pp. 153-155) is appropriate. If various simple pairwise differences are considered, the Tukey test (pp. 155-156) is recommended. Finally, if more complex comparisons are involved, the Scheffé test (pp. 151-153) is the best choice.

To counteract any loss of power when post hoc corrections are applied, I recommend the use of the decision category to suspend judgment (pp. 162-164). By suspending judgment on post hoc differences that would be significant as planned comparisons but are not sufficiently large to be significant with a post hoc test, we can minimize the danger of missing small but interesting findings discovered during the course of systematically combing through the data. The question of power can then be dealt with later—by conducting future experiments that are specifically designed to study these post hoc findings for which judgment was suspended. In short, what Tukey (1977) calls **exploratory data analysis,** the unearthing of interesting and unexpected findings, often generates the planned comparisons studied and examined in subsequent experiments.

8.5 EXERCISES[11]

1. Table 8-4 (p. 161) lists 20 potentially meaningful single-df comparisons for a particular experiment. Translate the sets of coefficients defining these comparisons into a verbal statement describing the question asked by each comparison.

2. The bottom portion of Table 8-5 (p. 162) summarizes an analysis plan that depends on the joint outcome of two preliminary statistical tests.
   (a) Using the modified Bonferroni test, determine the values of $\alpha_{planned}$ to be used in each of the four alternative plans. Use $\alpha = .05$ as your starting point. (Be sure to include the two preliminary comparisons in your calculations.)
   (b) What is the critical value of F in each of these situations? Assume $s = 10$.

3. Assume that we have a control group and seven experimental groups, with $s = 16$ subjects for each group. The $MS_{S/A} = 28.75$. The totals for each group are given below:

C	E_1	E_2	E_3	E_4	E_5	E_6	E_7
289	270	241	279	191	213	205	198

   (a) Is the overall F significant?
   (b) Use Dunnett's test to determine which of the treatment means is significantly different from the mean of the control group. Use a two-tailed test at $\alpha = .05$.
   (c) Make the same set of comparisons with the Scheffé procedure, $\alpha = .05$. Do your conclusions change?

4. Suppose we have an experiment with independent groups of $s = 7$ subjects randomly assigned to each of 8 treatment conditions. The error term $MS_{S/A} = 58.65$. The treatment sums are given below:

a_1	a_2	a_3	a_4	a_5	a_6	a_7	a_8
316	333	307	373	398	227	123	436

   (a) Conduct the Fisher test on all pairwise differences, using $\alpha = .05$.
   (b) Evaluate the same pairwise differences with the Tukey test, $\alpha = .05$.
   (c) How would you modify your conclusions in part (b) if you adopted the three-decision procedure described in Section 8.4 (pp. 162–164)?

[11]The answers to these problems are found in Appendix B, beginning on p. 568.

FACTORIAL EXPERIMENTS WITH TWO FACTORS

In this part, I will consider experiments where treatment conditions are classified with respect to the levels represented on *two* independent variables. In Part IV I will go on to discuss experiments involving the joint manipulation of three or more independent variables. In all of these discussions, I will be assuming that subjects serve in only one of the treatment conditions, that they provide only a single score or observation, and that they are randomly assigned to one of the conditions. Formally, we refer to these sorts of experiments as **completely randomized factorial designs**.

The most common means by which two or more independent variables are manipulated in an experiment is a *factorial arrangement of the treatments,* or, more simply, a **factorial experiment or design**. I will use these terms interchangeably. In a factorial design, the experiment includes every possible combination of the levels of the independent variables. Suppose, for example, that two variables are manipulated concurrently in a study—the magnitude of the food reward given to a hungry rat for completing a run through a maze and the difficulty of the maze the rat will be given to learn. Let's assume there are three levels of food magnitude (small, n· lium, and large) and two levels of maze difficulty (easy and hard). The fa orial arrangement of the treatment conditions is specified by the six cells in the table below. I will often call such an arrangement a **factorial matrix** or simply a **matrix**. The cells in the matrix represent the following treatment combinations: small-easy, small-hard, medium-easy, medium-hard, large-easy, and large-hard. Each magnitude of reward (represented by the columns) is combined with each type of maze (represented by the rows). Factorial designs are sometimes referred to as experiments in which the independent variables are completely **crossed**. We can think of the crossing in terms of a *multiplication* of the levels of the different independent variables. In the present example, the treatment combinations may be enumerated by multiplying (small + medium + large) by (easy + hard) to produce the six treatment combinations of the design.

An Example of a Two-Variable Factorial Experiment

TYPE OF MAZE	REWARD MAGNITUDE		
	Small	Medium	Large
Easy			
Hard			

Chapter 9 considers the important characteristics of factorial designs. In Chapter 10, I will cover the standard analysis of the two-factor experiment. Chapter 11 presents analytical comparisons that are particularly useful in the detailed analysis of this type of experimental design. Finally, Chapter 12 will be concerned with additional points and complications that often arise when two independent variables are manipulated in the same experiment.

9

Introduction to
the Factorial Design

A great deal of the research in the behavioral sciences consists of the identification of variables contributing to a given phenomenon. Quite typically, an experiment may be designed to focus attention on a single factor. A main characteristic of this type of investigation is that it represents an assessment of how a variable operates under "ideal" conditions—with all other important variables held constant, or permitted to vary randomly, across the different conditions. An alternative approach is to study the influence of one independent variable in conjunction with variations in one or more additional independent variables. Here the primary question is whether a particular variable studied concurrently with other variables will show the same effect as it would when studied in isolation.

Both types of experiments certainly have their place in the behavioral sciences. The manipulation of a single variable in an experiment is most useful when its combination with other independent variables is relatively simple. When the combination is complex, the results of single-factor experiments will give an inaccurate picture of the effect of the variable under study.

9.1   ADVANTAGES OF THE FACTORIAL EXPERIMENT

The factorial experiment is probably most effective at the *reconstructive* stage of a science, where investigators begin to approximate the "real" world by manipulating a number of independent variables simultaneously. Of course, the type of experiment chosen by a researcher depends upon the complexity with which the phenomenon under study is determined. But it is clear that the factorial experiment has advantages of economy, control, and generality.

Economy

Suppose we are putting together a reading series for use in elementary schools and that we have reason to believe that the format of the books will influence reading speed. Two independent variables that might be of interest are the length of the printed lines and the contrast between the printed letters and the paper. Assume that we choose three line lengths (3, 5, and 7 inches) and three different levels of contrast (low, medium, and high). If we were to manipulate the variables in two separate single-factor experiments, the designs might look like those presented in the upper part of Table 9–1. In the experiment on the left, there is a total of 90 subjects (Ss), with $s = 30$ subjects assigned to each of the three length conditions. In the experiment on the right, the same number of subjects ($s = 30$) would be randomly assigned to each of the three levels of contrast. Other than differences in line length, on the one hand, and print-paper contrast, on the other, all of the subjects are treated alike. At the completion of the two experiments, we are able to analyze the data with the techniques discussed in Part II and make statements concerning the influence of line length and contrast on speed of reading.

Compare these two single-factor experiments with the factorial design presented in the bottom half of Table 9-1, in which the same two variables are manipulated simultaneously. In this experiment the two independent variables are completely crossed, meaning that all possible combinations of the three levels of the two variables are represented. Since each variable has three levels in this example, there is a total of 3 X 3 = 9 unique treatment groups. This design is called a 3 X 3 factorial (read "three by three"). It should be noted that the sample size in each of the groups is $s = 10$. This number was chosen to provide a comparison with the two single-factor experiments. That is, we start this experiment by obtaining 90 school children; we then randomly assign 10 subjects to serve in each of the 9 treatment combinations.

After the experiment is completed, we will have 10 reading scores in each cell of the matrix. What if we want to obtain an estimate of the average effects of line length on reading speed? This information is obtained easily enough by collapsing across the levels of the other variable (contrast) and dividing by the appropriate number of scores. That is, the mean for the 3-inch condition is found by summing the 30 reading scores in the first column of the matrix (10 scores each from the low-, medium-, and high-contrast conditions) and dividing by 30. The average performance of the subjects receiving 5- and 7-inch lines is obtained in a similar fashion. Turn now to a determination of the average effects of the other independent variable. The average effects of the low-, medium-, and high-contrast conditions are calculated by collapsing across the length classification—i.e., adding together the scores from the three levels of line length for each of the contrast conditions and dividing by 30.

Table 9-1   Comparison of One- and Two-Factor Designs

SEPARATE SINGLE-FACTOR EXPERIMENTS

Line Length (in.)			Print-Paper Contrast		
3	5	7	Low	Medium	High
30 Ss[a]	30 Ss	30 Ss	30 Ss	30 Ss	30 Ss

FACTORIAL ARRANGEMENT

Print-Paper Contrast	Line Length (in.)		
	3	5	7
Low	10 Ss	10 Ss	10 Ss
Medium	10 Ss	10 Ss	10 Ss
High	10 Ss	10 Ss	10 Ss

[a] S = subject.

These average estimates of the influence of line length and of contrast are based upon the *same* number of subjects (30) as were the estimates provided by the two single-factor experiments. But note: The factorial experiment produces these estimates much more economically, with only half the number of subjects. The economy of the factorial design represents a distinct advantage over separate single-factor studies.

Experimental Control

In the preceding example, both of the independent variables were of scientific interest to us. That is, we were interested in the influence of each of the variables on reading speed. (This was implied when we considered conducting two single-factor experiments.) There will be times when we turn to a factorial experiment, not so much to obtain information on the two variables, but as a way of controlling important but unwanted sources of variability. (I will discuss this use of the factorial design more thoroughly in Chapter 15.)

The most common example of the use of a factorial experiment to control variability is with **individual-difference** or **subject variables**. Suppose we wanted to study the length variable in a single-factor experiment but we knew that differences in the intelligence of the subjects would contribute to an especially large within-groups mean square. Under these circumstances, we would need a fairly strong between-groups effect to produce a significant F ratio. One way to solve this problem would be to select a group of subjects which is relatively homogeneous in intelligence (e.g., restrict IQ to the range 100–110) and to assign subjects at random to the three length conditions. The within-groups mean square will be smaller in this case, since the variability of subjects treated alike will be smaller with the restricted groups of subjects than with the unrestricted ones.

One drawback with this procedure is that the results of our experiment will be limited in generality; that is, we can only generalize our results to people in the range 100–110. It is exactly in this situation that the factorial experiment is ideal. In this case the two factors are line length and IQ. More specifically, if we form a number of levels of IQ and randomly assign the subjects within these levels to the three length conditions, we will receive the benefit of a reduced error term. I will not now consider in detail how this comes about, except to say that our estimate of error variance, the within-groups mean square, is still based upon the variability of subjects treated alike and that the variability within each length-IQ condition is less than would be the case if subjects were unselected. (I will discuss this type of design in Chapter 12.)

Generality of Results

In the single-factor experiment, all variables except the one being manipulated are maintained at the same level in all the different treatment groups. Such a procedure is necessary, of course, to "guarantee" that the differences observed among the treatment conditions are due solely to the operation of the independent variable. One consequence of this control is a certain lack of generality of the results; that is, the particular pattern of results may be unique to the specific values of other relevant stimulus variables maintained at a constant level throughout the course of the experiment.

The factorial experiment provides one solution to this limitation by allowing the effect of an independent variable to be averaged over several different levels of another relevant variable. As I noted in discussing the factorial arrangement in Table 9-1, the importance of line length for reading speed is assessed by comparing the scores of all of the 3-, 5-, and 7-inch subjects, one third of whom were tested at each of the three contrast levels included in the experiment. Thus, in the factorial experiment, the effect of line length represents a more general effect, averaged over three levels of contrast, than in the case of the single-factor experiment, where only *one* print-paper contrast would be used. We refer to the overall effect of one independent variable, obtained by combining the scores over the different levels of the second variable, as its **main effect**. Similarly, the main effect of contrast is found by collapsing across the groups of subjects differing in lengths of line. This second main effect also represents a more general effect than would be obtained in the corresponding single-factor experiment. In a sense, main effects result from "converting" a factorial design, by averaging, into a single-factor one.

The comparison between a single-factor experiment and a factorial experiment is accurate, however, only up to a point. The factorial experiment will provide the same type of information as its single-factor counterpart only when there is no **interaction** between the two independent variables. What this means is that when the effects of one of the independent variables (line length, say) are the *same* at each of the levels of the other variable (contrast)—i.e., there is *no* interaction—the main effect of line length will be the *same* as the treatment effects of line length in the single-factor experiment. On the other hand, when the effects of line length are different at the different levels of contrast (i.e., there *is* an interaction), the information provided by the main effect will *not* be the same. This is not as bad as it may sound, since the researcher will have discovered something that is *not* obtainable from the single-factor experiment, namely, the unique manner in which the two independent variables combine jointly to influence behavior. When an interaction is present, an investigator will not be interested in the main effects anyway—anything that might be said about the effects of one independent variable must be qualified by a consideration of the levels of the other. I will consider the concept of interaction next.

9.2 INTERACTION

Interaction is the one new concept that is introduced by the factorial experiment. Main effects have essentially the same meaning as in the single-factor analysis of variance and they are calculated in exactly the same way. Moreover, as you will see in later chapters, factorials with three or more variables involve no additional principles. Thus, it was important to understand the single-factor analysis of variance, since many of the principles and procedures found in this simplest of experimental designs, such as partitioning of sums of squares, the logic of hypothesis testing, and planned and post hoc comparisons, are also found in the more complicated designs. By the same token, the two-factor analysis of variance forms a building block for designs involving three or more variables, with the concept of interaction linking them all together.

An Example of No Interaction

One way to understand what an interaction means is to take a concrete example in which an interaction is either present or absent. Table 9-2 presents some hypothetical results for the experiment on reading speed I have been discussing. Assume that an equal number of subjects are included in each of the nine conditions and that the values presented in the table represent the mean reading scores obtained in the experiment. The main effect of line length (factor A) is obtained by summing (or collapsing across) the three cell means for the different contrasts and then averaging these sums. The last row of the table gives these means for the three length conditions. These averages are called the column **marginal** means of the matrix. Thus, the average reading speed for subjects in the 3-inch condition is found by combining the means from the three contrast conditions and obtaining an average. In this case, we have

$$\bar{A}_1 = \frac{.89 + 3.89 + 4.22}{3} = \frac{9.00}{3} = 3.00.$$

This mean represents the average performance of *all* the subjects in the experiment who received the 3-inch lines; the specific conditions of factor B, the three print-paper contrasts, are unimportant at this point. We can obtain similar averages for the subjects reading the 5- and 7-inch materials. These are given in the other two columns.

In like fashion, the *row* marginal averages give us information concerning the general effect of different print-paper contrasts. That is, the average reading speed

TABLE 9-2   Example of No Interaction

| CONTRAST (FACTOR B) | LINE LENGTH (FACTOR A) | | | |
	3 in. (a_1)	5 in. (a_2)	7 in. (a_3)	Mean
Low (b_1)	.89	2.22	2.89	2.00
Medium (b_2)	3.89	5.22	5.89	5.00
High (b_3)	4.22	5.55	6.22	5.33
Mean	3.00	4.33	5.00	4.11

for subjects in the low-contrast condition is given by an average of the means for the three length conditions. Thus,

$$\bar{B}_1 = \frac{.89 + 2.22 + 2.89}{3} = \frac{6.00}{3} = 2.00.$$

This averaging for the other contrast conditions appears in the final column of the table. Each of these marginal means represents the average performance of *all* the subjects who received the specified contrast condition, disregarding the particular condition of factor A—i.e., which line length—these subjects also received.

Let's look at the two sets of marginal averages. They have been plotted in the upper two graphs of Fig. 9-1. (For the purposes of this example, I have assumed that the levels of the contrast variable are equally spaced.) In both cases you can see that the independent variables influence reading scores positively, performance increasing with increases in either line length or print-paper contrast. These plots can be thought of as general descriptions of the overall effects of the two independent variables.

Now, would you say that these overall relationships are *representative* of the

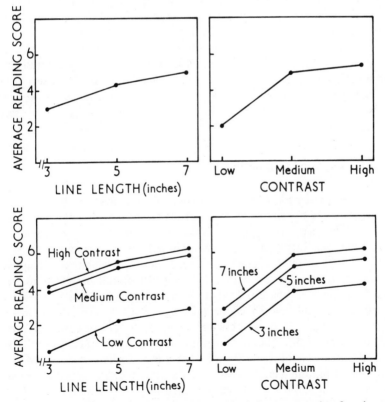

FIGURE 9-1.   Plot of data presented in Table 9-2; an example of no interaction.

results obtained in the "single-factor" experiments found *within* the body of Table 9-2? There are two sets of these experiments—those reflected by the means in different rows and those reflected by the means in different columns. In the first case, we are looking at the effect of varying line length (factor *A*) at the three different levels of contrast (factor *B*), while in the second case we are considering the effect of varying contrast (factor *B*) at the three different levels of line length (factor *A*). I will refer to the first set of "single-factor" experiments (the cells in the individual rows) as the **simple effects of factor *A*** and to the second set (the cells in the individual columns) as the **simple effects of factor *B***. It is important to distinguish carefully between simple effects and main effects. Simple effects refer to the *detailed*, or *specific*, effects of an independent variable; these effects are revealed by examining the treatment means within the body of the matrix *row by row* or *column by column*. Main effects, on the other hand, reflect the *general*, or *average*, effects of an independent variable; these effects are revealed by the *marginal* means. The word *main* does not refer to *importance*. A less confusing designation would be *average*—the average effect of factor *A* or of factor *B*—rather than *main*.

Returning to our original question, are the simple effects of either factor representative of the corresponding *main* effect? Consider the data within the body of the table. These means are presented in two double-classification plots in the lower portion of Fig. 9-1. The classification is accomplished by marking off one of the independent variables along the baseline—line length in the graph on the left and contrast in the graph on the right—and connecting the means produced by groups receiving the same level of the other independent variable—contrast on the left and line length on the right. In either plotting of the results, the sets of function are *parallel*, which means that the exact pattern of differences obtained with one of the independent variables is *exactly the same* at each level of the second independent variable.

An Example of Interaction

Table 9-3 presents a second set of hypothetical results using the same experimental design. Note that the same main effects are present; i.e., the means in the marginal row and marginal column of Table 9-3 are identical to the corresponding means in Table 9-2. There is a big difference, however, when we look at the simple, or specific, effects of the two independent variables. To facilitate the comparisons of the simple effects, the data within the body of the table have been plotted in Fig. 9-2. In either plot, you can see that the pattern of differences depicted by the simple effects is *not* the same as that depicted by either the row or the column marginal means (the main, or average, effects). In short, then, an interaction is present.

To be more specific, consider the simple effects of line length at level b_1—the means in the first row of Table 9-3. This row is a "single-factor" experiment in which subjects from three levels of line length are tested, but *all* with a low print-paper contrast. These three means are presented in the left-hand graph of Fig. 9-2. An inspection of the figure indicates that the relationship is positive and even linear.

TABLE 9-3   Example of Interaction

| CONTRAST (FACTOR B) | LINE LENGTH (FACTOR A) | | | |
	3 in. (a_1)	5 in. (a_2)	7 in. (a_3)	Mean
Low (b_1)	1.00	2.00	3.00	2.00
Medium (b_2)	3.00	5.00	7.00	5.00
High (b_3)	5.00	6.00	5.00	5.33
Mean	3.00	4.33	5.00	4.11

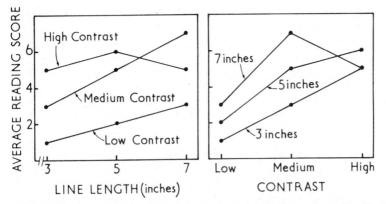

FIGURE 9-2.   Plot of data presented in Table 9-3; an example of interaction.

The simple effect at b_2 (the second row) also shows a positive linear trend for the subjects receiving the medium materials, but it is steeper than for the low-contrast case. But see what happens to the subjects tested with the high-contrast materials. In this third "single-factor" experiment the relationship is curvilinear: the reading scores first increase and then decrease with line length.

You can see the same sort of deviation of the simple effects when we look at the means in each of the three data *columns*. Here we are considering "single-factor" experiments in which contrast is varied but length is held constant. For the simple effect of contrast for 3-inch lines (the first column) you can see that the relationship is linear. For the simple effect for 5-inch lines (the second column) the relationship is not as sharply defined, with the function starting to "bend over" from the linear trend. In the third column (7-inch lines) we have an actual reversal of the trend—i.e., a curvilinear relationship, maximum performance being found with a medium contrast.

With either plot of the data, we can determine at a glance that the particular form of the relationship between the independent variable plotted on the baseline (line length or contrast) and the scores—i.e., the shape of the curve drawn between successive points on the baseline—is not the same at the three different levels of the

177

other independent variable. A simple way to describe this situation is to say that the three curves are *not parallel.* When we find that an interaction is present, it is usually a good idea to plot the results of the experiment just as I have done in Fig. 9-2. The shape or form of the interaction will become readily apparent. We do not typically plot the data both ways, but choose for the baseline the independent variable that makes the most sense for the research hypotheses under consideration. Whichever way the data are plotted, an interaction will be revealed by nonparallel curves for the conditions plotted within the body of the figure.

Definitions of Interaction

The presence of interaction indicates that conclusions based on main effects *alone* will not fully describe the data. Instead, the effects of each of the independent variables must be interpreted with the levels of the other independent variable in mind. I will now consider several definitions that specify this important concept succinctly and precisely.

One definition is stated in terms of the two independent variables:

An interaction is present when the effects of one independent variable on behavior change at different levels of the second independent variable.

This definition contains a critical point often missed by beginning students, namely, the focus on the *behavioral effects* of the independent variables. A common mistake is to think of two independent variables influencing one another. *Interaction* refers to the particular manner in which the two independent variables combine to influence behavior, not one another. What this definition is saying, then, is that an interaction is present when the particular pattern of differences observed with one of the independent variables—the effects of this independent variable on behavior—is different, i.e., changes, when we examine the results systematically for each level— row by row or column by column—of the other independent variable.

A more formal definition of interaction is in terms of the simple effects, since a simple effect *is* the effect of one independent variable at a specific level of the other independent variable:

An interaction is present when the simple effects of one independent variable are not the same at different levels of the second independent variable.

A related definition focuses on the main, or average, effects:

An interaction is present when the main effect of an independent variable is not representative of the simple effects of that variable.

In the first example (Fig. 9-1), the simple effects of either independent variable are identical and therefore equal to the corresponding main effects. This means that the row and column marginal means are *perfectly representative* of the treatment differences revealed by the means in the body of Table 9-2 and reflected by the separate plots in Fig. 9-1. As you will see, the absence of statistically significant interaction usually means that any subsequent analyses will generally focus on the marginal means rather than on the individual treatment means. Stated another way, we can describe and analyze the effects of one of the independent variables without considering the specific levels of the other independent variable.

In the second example, the simple effects of line length (the function relating line length and reading speed) are not the same at all levels of print-paper contrast. Stated in terms of the other variable, the simple effects of print-paper contrast (the function relating contrast and reading speed) are not the same at all levels of line length. Either way, the data presented in Table 9-3 and plotted in Fig. 9-2 fit the definition of interaction. The presence of an interaction indicates that conclusions based on the two main effects will not fully describe the data. Each of the variables must be interpreted with the levels of the other variable in mind. To this end, any analyses conducted after the establishment of a significant interaction will tend to concentrate on the individual treatment means rather than on the overall marginal means.

Often the term **additive** is used to describe the joint effects of two noninteracting variables. What this means is that the effect of one variable simply adds to the effect of the second variable. When an interaction is present, the combination is **nonadditive**—i.e., an additional effect must be added to specify the joint effects of the two variables. This effect, of course, is the interaction.

Other definitions of interaction are possible, of course. In the first edition of this book (1973), for example, I presented a simple arithmetic definition that expressed interaction in terms of differences between means (pp. 179–181). It is also possible to represent interaction as a set of interaction contrasts.[1] I will consider interaction contrasts as a useful tool in the analysis of a factorial experiment in Chapter 11.

Implications of Interaction for Theory

The presence of an interaction often requires more complexity in our theoretical explanations of data than would be the case if no interaction were present. Consider the two different outcomes we have been discussing. Both examples indicate the importance of the two independent variables. In the first case, where there is no interaction, the effect of one of the independent variables adds to the effect of the other variable. The combination is simple. In the second case, on the other hand, the combination is complex—it will take a considerable amount of theoretical ingenuity to explain why the relationship between line length and average reading score is different with the three types of print-paper contrast or why the relationship between contrast and average reading score is different for the different line lengths.

---

[1] This definition of interaction is illustrated in Appendix C-2. Cohen and Cohen (1975) offer the same definition in terms of "products of variables" (p. 291). They also use the term "conditionalized" to express interaction. That is, interaction is present when the effects of one of the independent variables are "conditionally related" to the other independent variable.

The discussion above has focused on the complexity of post hoc explanations of a set of data when an interaction is found. In an increasing number of experiments being reported in the literature, interactions not only are predicted but represent the major interest of the studies. Consider, for example, research in developmental psychology. Gollin (1965) indicates that it is not particularly revealing of developmental processes simply to compare a number of different age groups on a given task. Instead, he suggests that more interesting information is obtained from the discovery of *interactions* involving some manipulated independent variables and the age dimension. To show that two age groups differ on one task but not on another allows us to speculate about different developmental processes present in the two groups and required of the two tasks. To find a main effect of age or of task suggests very little about the processes involved in the phenomena under study. As Gollin puts it, "The uncovering of both the similarity *and* the difference in performance obviously gives us an order of information about the two groups which is quite different than if we had simply demonstrated that they did or did not differ on one or the other task" (p. 166).

The discovery or the prediction of interactions may lead to a greater understanding of the behavior under study. Lashley's classic study of the effect of the amount of brain damage on maze learning by rats is an excellent example. Lashley varied the amount of cortical tissue destroyed from a small amount (1 to 10 percent) to a large amount (over 50 percent) and tested these animals on three mazes differing in difficulty. He found very slight differences among the operated groups on the easiest maze, but extremely dramatic differences on the most difficult maze. If Lashley had run his animals on only one of the mazes, he would have missed this important finding: that the destruction of cortical materials affects primarily the acquisition of complex learning tasks. That is, there is no uniform *overall* learning deficit. The effect of brain damage depends on the complexity of the material being acquired.

In short, then, if behavior is complexly determined, we will need factorial experiments to isolate and to tease out these complexities. The factorial allows us to manipulate two or more independent variables concurrently and to obtain some idea of how the variables combine to produce the behavior. An assessment of the interaction provides a hint to the rules of combination.

Further Examples of Interaction and Lack of Interaction

In order to broaden (and to test) your understanding of the two-variable or $A \times B$ interaction and to get some practice in extracting information from double-classification tables and plots, consider the hypothetical outcomes of a 4 $\times$ 3 factorial experiment in which factor A is represented at four levels and factor B at three. The means for each set of 12 treatment combinations are presented in Table 9-4 (p. 182).

You have seen that the means in the margins of a two-factor matrix reflect the main effects of the two independent variables and that the means within the body of the matrix reflect the presence or absence of an interaction. In this discussion I will assume that if any differences are present among the column marginal means or among the row marginal means, a corresponding main effect is present, and that if the effect of one independent variable changes at the different levels of the other independent variable, an interaction is present. (As you will see, the *significance* of main effects and of interaction effects is assessed by means of an F ratio.) We will look at eight examples, representing each of the possible combinations of the presence or absence of the two main effects and the interaction effect.

Consider the first example in Table 9-4. This example represents a completely negative study; none of the three effects is present. This state of affairs is illustrated by the identical 12 means in the body of the matrix. The column marginal means are equal, indicating the absence of a main effect of factor A; similarly, the equal row marginal means indicate an absence of a main effect of factor B. A plot of the 12 means in panel 1 of Fig. 9-3 indicates that no $A \times B$ interaction is present in the data. The second example illustrates a case in which only factor A affects performance. You can see this by inspecting the column means, which are not equal, and the row means, which are equal. There is also no interaction, as may be seen in panel 2 of the figure—the three curves at b_1, b_2, and b_3 have an identical shape. In the next example, the marginal means show that there is a main effect of factor B but no effect of factor A. Again, no interaction is present, since the three curves at the different levels of factor B are parallel. The outcome in example 4 indicates that a main effect of both independent variables is present. This may be seen in the two sets of marginal means. The plot in Fig. 9-3 shows that the effects of factor A are/the same at each of the levels of factor B—i.e., there is no interaction.

The last four examples contain $A \times B$ interactions. Look at the marginal means for example 5. There are no differences among the column means and no differences among the row means; hence, there are no main effects of factors A and B, respectively. On the basis of the main effects, then, we might conclude that our manipulations were ineffective. But look at the cell means within the body of the matrix. The two independent variables produce quite striking effects. The simple effect of factor A is positive at b_1, absent at b_2, and negative at b_3. The $A \times B$ interaction is so severe that the simple effects of the two variables have been canceled. This example stresses the point that the main effects reflect treatment *averages* and as such do not necessarily reflect the constituent parts.

The next two examples show situations in which there is an interaction and one main effect. The main effect in example 6 is revealed in the column means—i.e., a main effect of factor A—while the interaction is readily apparent in the plot of the cell means in panel 6 of Fig. 9-3. In this case, the effect of factor A is quite substantial at b_1 and nonexistent at b_3. In example 7 the situation is reversed; the row means indicate a main effect of factor B and the nonparallel lines in panel 7 indicate an interaction of the two variables. The final experiment (example 8) provides an instance in which all three effects are present. Not only is there a main effect for

Table 9–4 Eight Different Outcomes of the Same Two-Factor Experiment

(1)

LEVELS OF FACTOR B	— LEVELS OF FACTOR A				
	a_1	a_2	a_3	a_4	Mean
b_1	4	4	4	4	4.0
b_2	4	4	4	4	4.0
b_3	4	4	4	4	4.0
Mean	4.0	4.0	4.0	4.0	

(2)

LEVELS OF FACTOR B	— LEVELS OF FACTOR A				
	a_1	a_2	a_3	a_4	Mean
b_1	2	4	6	8	5.0
b_2	2	4	6	8	5.0
b_3	2	4	6	8	5.0
Mean	2.0	4.0	6.0	8.0	

(3)

	a_1	a_2	a_3	a_4	Mean
b_1	7	7	7	7	7.0
b_2	6	6	6	6	6.0
b_3	3	3	3	3	3.0
Mean	5.3	5.3	5.3	5.3	

(4)

	a_1	a_2	a_3	a_4	Mean
b_1	5	6	7	8	6.5
b_2	4	5	6	7	5.5
b_3	2	3	4	5	3.5
Mean	3.7	4.7	5.7	6.7	

(5)

	a_1	a_2	a_3	a_4	Mean
b_1	1	3	5	7	4.0
b_2	4	4	4	4	4.0
b_3	7	5	3	1	4.0
Mean	4.0	4.0	4.0	4.0	

(6)

	a_1	a_2	a_3	a_4	Mean
b_1	1	3	5	7	4.0
b_2	2	3.3	4.7	6	4.0
b_3	4	4	4	4	4.0
Mean	2.3	3.4	4.6	5.7	

(7)

	a_1	a_2	a_3	a_4	Mean
b_1	4	5	6	7	5.5
b_2	4	4	4	4	4.0
b_3	4	3	2	1	2.5
Mean	4.0	4.0	4.0	4.0	

(8)

	a_1	a_2	a_3	a_4	Mean
b_1	1	3	5	7	4.0
b_2	1	2	3	4	2.5
b_3	1	1	1	1	1.0
Mean	1.0	2.0	3.0	4.0	

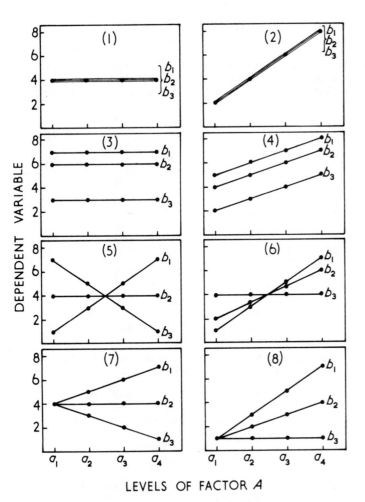

LEVELS OF FACTOR A

FIGURE 9-3.   Plot of data presented in Table 9-4.

each of the two variables (see the column and row means), but the form of the function relating factor A to the dependent variable is different at each level of factor B, indicating the presence of an $A \times B$ interaction.

You have seen that it is possible to obtain eight different combinations of the presence or absence of the two main effects and of the interaction effects. Obviously, there is an infinite number of ways in which the actual means may turn out to reflect one of these combinations. The presence of main effects is revealed by the variation among the marginal means of the two-way matrix, and the presence of an $A \times B$ interaction is revealed by the appearance of nonparallel lines in a double-classification plot of the means within the body of the data matrix. You are now ready to see how you can obtain variances which will reflect these three effects and how you can test their significance.

9.3 EXERCISES[2]

1. The individual AB cell means for a 4 × 2 factorial experiment are given below in a set of six examples. Indicate for each example which factorial effects are present. (Assume that the means are population values and, thus, are error-free.)

(a)

	a_1	a_2	a_3	a_4
b_1	10	12	14	16
b_2	8	10	12	14

(b)

	a_1	a_2	a_3	a_4
b_1	10	14	12	16
b_2	7	11	9	13

(c)

	a_1	a_2	a_3	a_4
b_1	10	14	12	16
b_2	12	10	8	14

(d)

	a_1	a_2	a_3	a_4
b_1	10	12	14	16
b_2	14	12	10	8

(e)

	a_1	a_2	a_3	a_4
b_1	10	12	14	16
b_2	8	9	10	11

(f)

	a_1	a_2	a_3	a_4
b_1	12	12	8	12
b_2	8	8	12	8

2. Assume the following are population treatment means associated with the treatment conditions defined by a 3 × 2 factorial design:

	a_1	a_2	a_3
b_1	37	43	49
b_2			

Specify what you would expect the population treatment means to be for level b_2 under the following sets of circumstances:

(a) Only a main effect of factor A is present.

(b) Both main effects are present, but no interaction.

(c) Only an A × B interaction is present.

(d) A main effect of factor A and an A × B interaction are present, but no main effect of factor B.

---

[2]The answers to these problems are found in Appendix B, beginning on p. 571.

10

Rationale and Rules for Calculating the Major Effects

You saw in Chapter 2 how the total sum of squares could be partitioned into two parts: (1) a part reflecting the deviation of the treatment groups from the overall mean (the between-groups sum of squares—SS_{bg}) and (2) a part reflecting the variability of subjects treated alike (the within-groups sum of squares—SS_{wg}). I then discussed how we could test the null hypothesis. In subsequent chapters of Part II you saw that we could ask more refined questions of the data by dividing the SS_{bg} into component sums of squares. The analysis of the factorial experiment follows a similar pattern, except that the SS_{bg} is *not* of systematic interest. That is, we are primarily interested in the *further division* of the SS_{bg} into three orthogonal components: (1) a sum of squares reflecting the main effect of factor A (SS_A), (2) a sum of squares reflecting the main effect of factor B (SS_B), and (3) a sum of squares representing the $A \times B$ interaction ($SS_{A \times B}$). In this chapter I will consider only the most common case, that having the same number of subjects in each of the treatment conditions. The analysis of experiments with unequal sample sizes is discussed in Chapter 15.

10.1 PARTITIONING THE TOTAL SUM OF SQUARES

Design and Notation

I will pause at this point to expand the notational system so that I can make explicit the operations needed for the analysis of the two-way factorial. The system I will use is summarized in Table 10-1.[1] The factorial arrangement of the two independent variables, illustrated with $a = 2$ and $b = 3$, is enumerated in the upper portion of the table. I have indicated that there is a total of $(a)(b) = (2)(3) = 6$ treatment conditions, each with a sample of s different subjects who have been randomly assigned to the different conditions.

A basic observation or score in this design is denoted ABS_{ijk} to indicate that it represents the score of a single subject in a particular combination of the levels of factors A and B. These scores are arranged in the **ABS matrix**, which appears in the middle portion of the table. If it is necessary to specify a particular score in one of the treatment conditions, I will use all three subscripts—one for the level of factor A (the i subscript), one for the level of factor B (the j subscript), and one for the score within the treatment cell (the k subscript). With these subscripts, $i = 1, 2, \ldots, a; j = 1, 2, \ldots, b;$ and $k = 1, 2, \ldots, s$. As in the single-factor case, however, I will drop the subscripts whenever there is no ambiguity about what arithmetic operations are being specified.

An AB matrix, where the remainder of the notational system is illustrated, is presented in the bottom portion of Table 10-1. The basic entry within the body of this matrix (often called the **cells** of the matrix) is the quantity AB_{ij}. This quantity

---

[1]Appendix C-1 offers an overview of the notational system used in this book. See pp. 613–617 for a comparison of the notational systems adopted by various authors to designate the arithmetical operations required in the two-factor design.

Table 10-1   Design and Notation for the Two-Factor Design

EXPERIMENTAL DESIGN

	Factor A	
Factor B	a_1	a_2
b_1	$s = 4$	$s = 4$
b_2	$s = 4$	$s = 4$
b_3	$s = 4$	$s = 4$

ABS MATRIX

Treatment Combinations

a_1b_1	a_1b_2	a_1b_3	a_2b_1	a_2b_2	a_2b_3
ABS_{111}	ABS_{121}	ABS_{131}	ABS_{211}	ABS_{221}	ABS_{231}
ABS_{112}	ABS_{122}	ABS_{132}	ABS_{212}	ABS_{222}	ABS_{232}
ABS_{113}	ABS_{123}	ABS_{133}	ABS_{213}	ABS_{223}	ABS_{233}
ABS_{114}	ABS_{124}	ABS_{134}	ABS_{214}	ABS_{224}	ABS_{234}

AB MATRIX[a]

Levels of Factor B	Levels of Factor A		Marginal Sum
	a_1	a_2	
		Sum →	
b_1	AB_{11}	AB_{21}	B_1
b_2 Sum	AB_{12}	AB_{22}	B_2 Sum
b_3	AB_{13}	AB_{23}	B_3
Marginal Sum	A_1	A_2	T
		Sum →	

[a]Note: $AB_{ij} = \displaystyle\sum_{k=1}^{s} ABS_{ijk}$.

represents the sum of the *ABS* scores at a particular combination of levels of the two factors. These are the totals that we would obtain if we summed the $s = 4$ individual scores in any one column of the *ABS* matrix. For example,

$$\Sigma ABS_{21k} = ABS_{211} + ABS_{212} + ABS_{213} + ABS_{214} = AB_{21}.$$

More formally,

$$\sum_{k=1}^{s} ABS_{ijk} = AB_{ij}.$$

187

(The notation added to the summation sign specifies that the summation includes all *ABS* scores in the group receiving level a_i in conjunction with level b_j, beginning with the first score ($k = 1$) and ending with the last score ($k = s$). This notation indicates which of the three subscripts is "active"—k in this case—and formally specifies the limits of the summation.) I will also refer to these sums as the **treatment sums** or **totals**. They form the basic ingredient in the determination of the sums of squares associated with different experimental treatments.

In order to calculate the two main effects, we will have to obtain the column and row totals shown in the margins of the *AB* matrix and hereafter referred to as the column and row marginal totals, respectively. These sums are found by collapsing across (i.e., summing over) the other subscript. More specifically, column marginal totals are formed by summing the cell totals in all of the rows for each of the *a* columns. These totals are denoted A_i. For example,

$$\Sigma AB_{1j} = AB_{11} + AB_{12} + AB_{13} = A_1,$$

or more completely,

$$\sum_{j=1}^{b} AB_{ij} = A_i.$$

The row marginal totals are calculated in an analogous manner, by summing the cell total in all of the columns for each of the *b* rows. These are referred to as B_j. That is,

$$\sum_{i=1}^{a} AB_{ij} = B_j.$$

Finally, the grand total is obtained by summing either set of marginal totals:

$$T = \Sigma A = \Sigma B.$$

(Where there is no ambiguity in the summation, as is the case here, the summation sign requires no additional notation.)

For purposes of examining results and reporting data, we will want to convert the various treatment sums listed in the *AB* matrix into means. This is accomplished, of course, by dividing each sum by the appropriate number of observations. The symbol for a mean is a bar placed over the symbol identifying the nature of the sum. That is,

$$\overline{AB} = \frac{AB}{s} \; ; \; \overline{A} = \frac{A}{(b)(s)} \; ; \; \overline{B} = \frac{B}{(a)(s)} \; ;$$

and

$$\overline{T} = \frac{T}{(a)(b)(s)}.$$

Component Deviations

Suppose factor A were manipulated at $a = 2$ levels and factor B at $b = 3$ levels, so that we had a total of $(a)(b) = (2)(3) = 6$ different treatment groups, each containing s subjects. As a first step, it is useful to think of the six treatment means as coming from a single-factor experiment. According to the formulas given in Chapter 2, the variability of the $(a)(b)(s)$ subjects can then be broken down into

$$SS_T = SS_{bg} + SS_{wg}.$$

Up to this point, then, there is nothing new to the analysis. We will now refine the SS_{bg}.

The SS_{bg} is based on the deviation of each individual treatment mean from the total mean—that is, $\overline{AB}_{ij} - \overline{T}$. Consider the deviation produced by a group of subjects receiving a particular treatment combination represented by the combination of level a_i and level b_j $(a_i b_j)$. This deviation can be influenced by three sources of variability:

$$\overline{AB}_{ij} - \overline{T} = (A_i \text{ effect}) + (B_j \text{ effect}) + (A_i \times B_j \text{ interaction effect}).$$

Each of these effects can be expressed as a deviation involving familiar quantities:

$$\overline{AB}_{ij} - \overline{T} = (\overline{A}_i - \overline{T}) + (\overline{B}_j - \overline{T}) + (\overline{AB}_{ij} - \overline{A}_i - \overline{B}_j + \overline{T}). \quad (10\text{-}1)$$

Suppose we try to understand Eq. (10-1) a little better. First, we can verify that the equation is correct by performing the indicated additions and subtractions. To be more specific, there is only one $\overline{AB}_{ij}$ on the right-hand side of Eq. (10-1) and so it will stay, but $\overline{A}_i$ and $\overline{B}_j$ will both drop out, since each appears once as a positive quantity and once as a negative quantity. The final term, $\overline{T}$, appears three times on the right—twice as a negative quantity and once as a positive quantity. Thus, we are left with the same expression, $\overline{AB}_{ij} - \overline{T}$, on both sides of the equation.

The second point concerns the specification of the interaction effect. To show that the third quantity on the right of Eq. (10-1) reflects an interaction, we can redefine an interaction as a *residual* deviation. That is, the interaction effect represents whatever is left of the deviation of the individual treatment mean from $\overline{T}$ that cannot be accounted for by the two relevant main effects. In symbols,

$$\text{interaction effect} = (\text{deviation from } \overline{T}) - (A_i \text{ effect}) - (B_j \text{ effect})$$

$$= (\overline{AB}_{ij} - \overline{T}) - (\overline{A}_i - \overline{T}) - (\overline{B}_j - \overline{T}).$$

Performing some simple algebra, we obtain

$$\text{interaction effect} = \overline{AB}_{ij} - \overline{T} - \overline{A}_i + \overline{T} - \overline{B}_j + \overline{T}$$

$$= \overline{AB}_{ij} - \overline{A}_i - \overline{B}_j + \overline{T}.$$

We are now ready to include the individual subjects from the different treatment groups in this specification of component deviations. We can easily expand Eq. (10-1) to accommodate the deviation of any given subject (ABS_{ijk}) from the mean of all of the subjects $(\overline{T})$. A complete subdivision of the total deviation

189

$(ABS_{ijk} - \bar{T})$ is given by the formula

$$ABS_{ijk} - \bar{T} = (\bar{A}_i - \bar{T}) + (\bar{B}_j - \bar{T}) + (\overline{AB}_{ij} - \bar{A}_i - \bar{B}_j + \bar{T})$$
$$+ (ABS_{ijk} - \overline{AB}_{ij}). \tag{10-2}$$

In words, the deviation of a subject from the grand mean can be broken down into four separate components: (1) the treatment effect at level a_i, (2) the treatment effect at level b_j, (3) the interaction effect at the combination of levels a_i and b_j, and (4) the deviation of the subject from his or her individual treatment mean.

Now that the component deviations have been enumerated for each subject, they can be squared and summed to produce the corresponding sums of squares for the analysis. Expressing these operations with symbols produces what are called *defining formulas.* Rather than looking at these defining formulas, which preserve the "meaning" of Eq. (10-2), I will move directly to the corresponding computational formulas, which are much easier to use in calculating sums of squares.

10.2   A SYSTEM FOR GENERATING COMPUTATIONAL FORMULAS

In this section, I will consider a system for generating the computational formulas for sums of squares. The system is introduced here in the context of the two-factor design but can be applied to a large variety of experimental designs, as you will see in later chapters. The method is based on an isomorphic relationship between the *df* statement for a given source of variance and the corresponding formula for the sum of squares. The main purpose of this section is to introduce you to this useful system. In the next section, I will summarize the complete analysis and discuss in more detail the meaning behind some of the operations.

The system consists of three steps. First, we identify the sources of variance normally extracted in an analysis of variance. Second, we use the *df* statement for each of these sources to specify the basic ratios required and how they are combined to form each corresponding sum of squares. Finally, we construct the formulas for the basic ratios from a set of simple rules.

Identifying the Sources of Variance

There is a simple rule for specifying the sources of variance. I have already discussed what these sources would be in the present case, but it is useful to see how the rule applies in a situation with which we are familiar. This rule "works" with completely balanced designs of the sort covered through Chapter 15 of this book. The rule will be modified to accommodate the analysis of the more complex designs presented in Part V.

1. **List all factors, including the within-groups factor.**

2. **Form all possible interactions with these factors, omitting the within-groups factor.**

For the two-factor design, step 1 results in a listing of

$$A, B, \text{ and } S/AB.$$

The within-groups factor S/AB (read "subjects within AB") represents the variability due to subjects treated alike; that is, this source consists of the variability of subjects in each of the $(a)(b)$ groups, pooled or summed over these different groups. Step 2 results in the listing of a single interaction:

$$A \times B.$$

Using the *df* Statement

I will discuss the meaning of degrees of freedom in the next section. For the present I will just consider formulas that specify the df's for the different sources of variance. For the two main effects, the df's are simply the number of levels for each factor less 1:

$$df_A = a - 1 \quad \text{and} \quad df_B = b - 1.$$

For the $A \times B$ interaction, the degrees of freedom are the product of the df's associated with factors A and B. More specifically,

$$df_{A \times B} = (df_A)(df_B) = (a - 1)(b - 1). \tag{10-3}$$

The calculation of the df for the within-groups source S/AB is more complicated. The variability for this source is due to a subject factor (factor S), and for this factor, $df_S = s - 1$. However, since this factor is present in each of the $(a)(b)$ treatment conditions, the df for S/AB is found by multiplying df_S by the total number of these groups, $(a)(b)$:

$$df_{S/AB} = (a)(b)(df_S) = (a)(b)(s - 1).$$

Finally, the value of the df for the total sum of squares consists of the total number of observations $(a)(b)(s)$ less 1:

$$df_T = (a)(b)(s) - 1.$$

Table 10-2 summarizes the steps followed in generating the computational formulas for the different sums of squares. The sources of variance and their corresponding df's are listed in the first two columns. In column 3 the different df's are multiplied out in an expanded form, with the sets of letters arranged by decreasing numbers of letters. When present, the number 1 is listed last. As you will see, the expanded df statement represents the backbone of the overall computational scheme.

Each term in these expanded df statements—single letters, combinations of letters, or 1—denotes a different basic ratio needed to calculate any given sum of

Table 10-2   Generating the Computational Formulas

(1) SOURCE	(2) *df*	(3) EXPANDED *df*	(4) COMPUTATIONAL FORMULA[a]
A	$a - 1$	$a - 1$	$[A] - [T]$
B	$b - 1$	$b - 1$	$[B] - [T]$
$A \times B$	$(a - 1)(b - 1)$	$(a)(b) - a - b + 1$	$[AB] - [A] - [B] + [T]$
S/AB	$(a)(b)(s - 1)$	$(a)(b)(s) - (a)(b)$	$[ABS] - [AB]$
Total	$(a)(b)(s) - 1$	$(a)(b)(s) - 1$	$[ABS] - [T]$

[a]Letters inside brackets represent basic ratios. See text and Table 10-3 for an explanation.

squares. In addition, the expanded df statements themselves indicate how these basic ratios are to be combined to produce the different sums of squares. This point is made explicit in column 4, where each computational formula is written in terms of the basic ratios. The pair of brackets symbolizes a basic ratio; the letter or letters inside the brackets specifies (or specify) quantities from either the ABS or the AB matrix that are used in calculating that particular ratio. You will note that the letter T has been substituted for the numeral 1 in the move from column 3 to column 4, but other than that, the translation from the expanded df statement to the computational formula is simple and direct. You should also note the correspondence between these formulas and the respective deviations specified in Eq. (10-2). All that remains is to summarize the operations required to define each basic ratio.

Forming the Basic Ratios

You will recall from Chapter 2 that basic ratios follow a consistent computational scheme, namely, the squaring and then summing of a set of quantities followed by a division specified by the number of observations contributing to any one of the quantities in the set. Table 10-3 summarizes these operations for each of the basic ratios required for the analysis of variance.

Column 1 lists the basic quantities entering into the calculations, namely, the two sets of marginal totals (A and B), the individual treatment sums from the body of the AB matrix (AB), the individual observations (ABS), and the grand total (T). Column 2 indicates the squaring the summing operations performed on the entire set of relevant sums (in the case of A, B, AB, and T) or the entire set of scores (in the case of ABS). The appropriate denominator for each basic ratio is specified in column 3. You should verify that each denominator represents the number of observations contributing to any one of the squared terms; that is, an A sum is based on $(b)(s)$ observations, a B sum is based on $(a)(s)$ observations, an AB sum is based on s observations, an ABS score is based on 1 observation (not indicated in the table), and the grand sum T is based on $(a)(b)(s)$ observations. Finally, each basic ratio is uniquely coded in order to simplify computational formulas for the different sums of squares.

Table 10-3   Development of the Basic Ratios

(1) BASIC QUANTITY	(2) SQUARE AND SUM	(3) COMPLETE RATIO	(4) LETTER CODE
A	ΣA^2	$\dfrac{\Sigma A^2}{(b)(s)}$	$[A]$
B	ΣB^2	$\dfrac{\Sigma B^2}{(a)(s)}$	$[B]$
AB	$\Sigma (AB)^2$	$\dfrac{\Sigma (AB)^2}{s}$	$[AB]$
ABS	$\Sigma (ABS)^2$	$\Sigma (ABS)^2$	$[ABS]$
T	T^2	$\dfrac{T^2}{(a)(b)(s)}$	$[T]$

Summary

This system is general and may be applied to all of the designs I will consider in this book. The system elaborated here ensures that you will never "forget" the computational formulas, since you can very easily *reconstruct* them. Some of the steps will drop out with practice. You should not lose touch with the basic system, however, as it will prove extremely useful in generating formulas for the more complex designs considered in Parts IV and V.

In the next section I will consider the computational formulas again, but this time in conjunction with the remaining steps in the analysis of variance.

10.3 SUMMARY OF THE ANALYSIS OF VARIANCE

Sums of Squares

The computational formulas for the component sums of squares are presented in Table 10-4. For convenience, each term in the computational formulas is expressed in its complete form only once—when it first appears in the analysis. Thereafter, each term is designated by the letter code in which a particular term is identified by the letter or letters appearing in the numerator. The totals required for the SS_A are the column marginal totals in the AB matrix presented in Table 10-1 (p. 187). The totals required for the SS_B come from the row marginal totals in the AB matrix. The totals for the first term in the computational formula for the $SS_{A \times B}$ are the individual cell totals found within the body of the AB

193

matrix. Finally, the scores for the first term in the formula for the $SS_{S/AB}$ appear in the *ABS* matrix.

The within-groups sums of squares ($SS_{S/AB}$) reflects the variability of subjects treated alike. That is, it consists of the variability of subjects receiving the same treatment combination, pooled over all of the $(a)(b)$ treatment groups. While the correspondence between the computational formula and the deviation $(ABS_{ijk} - \overline{AB}_{ij})$ is apparent, the fact that this sum of squares represents a pooling of the separate within-groups sums of squares for the different $(a)(b)$ groups is not.

Degrees of Freedom

The *df* for any source of variance must satisfy the statement given in Eq. (3-2): The *df* equal the number of different observations on which each sum of squares is based less the number of restraints operating on these observations. For the two main effects, the observations involved are the marginal sums (or means) for the rows and columns. For the SS_A the number of observations is a; since the column marginal totals A_i must sum to the grand total T, there is one restraint. Thus,

$$df_A = a - 1.$$

This restraint is symbolized in Table 10-5 by an **X** placed in the margin at a_4. (This level was arbitrarily picked; any of the *a* levels would do.) For the SS_B the number of observations is b; since the marginal row totals B_j must also sum to T, one restraint is placed on the independence of these observations. Thus,

$$df_B = b - 1.$$

Table 10-4   Computational Formulas: Two-Factor Analysis of Variance

SOURCE	COMPUTATIONAL FORMULA[a]	df	MS	F
A	$\dfrac{\Sigma A^2}{(b)(s)} - \dfrac{T^2}{(a)(b)(s)}$	$a - 1$	$\dfrac{SS_A}{df_A}$	$\dfrac{MS_A}{MS_{S/AB}}$
B	$\dfrac{\Sigma B^2}{(a)(s)} - [T]$	$b - 1$	$\dfrac{SS_B}{df_B}$	$\dfrac{MS_B}{MS_{S/AB}}$
$A \times B$	$\dfrac{\Sigma (AB)^2}{s} - [A] - [B] + [T]$	$(a-1)(b-1)$	$\dfrac{SS_{A \times B}}{df_{A \times B}}$	$\dfrac{MS_{A \times B}}{MS_{S/AB}}$
Within (S/AB)	$\Sigma (ABS)^2 - [AB]$	$(a)(b)(s-1)$	$\dfrac{SS_{S/AB}}{df_{S/AB}}$	
Total	$[ABS] - [T]$	$(a)(b)(s) - 1$		

[a]Bracketed letters represent complete terms in the computational formulas; a particular term is identified by the letter(s) appearing in the numerator.

This restraint is symbolized by an **X** placed in the margin at b_3.

The df for the $SS_{A \times B}$ are obtained from Eq. (10-3):

$$df_{A \times B} = (a - 1)(b - 1),$$

the product of the df associated with the two main effects. You can understand this formula by considering the cells within the AB matrix presented in Table 10-5. The question basically is how many of the AB totals are *free* to vary once certain restrictions of the matrix are met. You have already seen that the marginal sums for the columns and rows must satisfy the requirement that

$$\Sigma A = \Sigma B = T.$$

What about the AB_{ij} sums within the body of the matrix? For any one of the columns, the sum of the cell totals must equal the corresponding *marginal total*. This places one restriction on each of the columns; these restrictions are represented by X's in the row at level b_3. (This row was again picked arbitrarily.) A similar restriction is placed on the rows: The sum of the cell totals in any one of the rows must equal the corresponding marginal totals. These restrictions are indicated by X's in the column at level a_4. The unmarked cells, then, represent the df for the $A \times B$ interaction. This rectangle is bounded on one side by $a - 1$ columns and on the other side by $b - 1$ rows, and the total number of "free" cells without X's is the quantity $(a - 1)(b - 1)$.

The df for the within-groups sum of squares $SS_{S/AB}$ follow the same general rule for the determination of the number of df. Since this sum of squares consists of a within-group sum of squares that is pooled over the $(a)(b)$ groups, we can start by finding the df for each individual cell in the matrix:

$$df_{S/AB_{ij}} = s - 1.$$

One df is lost because of the restriction that the s different ABS scores must sum to the cell total AB_{ij}. Now, if we sum the df's over the $(a)(b)$ cells, we obtain

$$df_{S/AB} = \Sigma \, df_{S/AB_{ij}} = (a)(b)(s - 1).$$

Table 10-5 Representation of df Associated with the SS_A, SS_B, and $SS_{A \times B}$

FACTOR B	FACTOR A				Sum
	a_1	a_2	a_3	a_4	
b_1				X	B_1
b_2				X	B_2
b_3	X	X	X	X	X
Sum	A_1	A_2	A_3	X	T

Mean Squares and F Ratios

The mean squares are found by dividing each sum of squares by its corresponding df:

$$MS = \frac{SS}{df}.$$

These are enumerated in the fourth column of Table 10-4. The F ratios are formed in each case by dividing the mean squares by the $MS_{S/AB}$:

$$F_A = \frac{MS_A}{MS_{S/AB}}, \quad F_B = \frac{MS_B}{MS_{S/AB}}, \quad F_{A \times B} = \frac{MS_{A \times B}}{MS_{S/AB}}.$$

These F ratios are evaluated in the F table under the appropriate numerator and denominator df's.

The logic behind the construction of these ratios is the same as that offered in the single-factor case. Briefly, each mean square in the numerator of the F ratio is assumed to provide a population estimate of the particular effect plus error variance. The denominator in the F ratio $(MS_{S/AB})$ provides an estimate of error variance alone. The null hypothesis in each case is that the population treatment effects (the effects due to factor A, to factor B, and to the interaction of the two factors) are zero. The within-groups mean square $(MS_{S/AB})$ is the appropriate error term for the three mean squares because the numerator mean squares $(MS_A, MS_B,$ and $MS_{A \times B})$ and the denominator mean square $(MS_{S/AB})$ are independent estimates of error variance when the null hypothesis is true. Under these circumstances, the expected values of the three F ratios will be approximately 1.0. A significant F indicates that the null hypothesis is untenable, and we then accept the alternative hypothesis that there are treatment effects present.

Orthogonality of the Two-Way Analysis

It is possible to show that the SS_A, SS_B, and $SS_{A \times B}$ are mutually orthogonal—i.e., that they provide independent information about the outcome of the experiment. (See Appendix C-2, pp. 625-628, for a proof of this statement.) As I noted in Chapter 6, these tests are not *statistically* independent, since the same error term is used to form each F ratio. This, however, does not appear to present a problem for our interpretation of the results of an experiment. The three sources of variance extracted in the analysis I have been discussing represent an efficient way of dividing up the df associated with the total between-groups sum of squares. It would certainly be possible to divide this sum of squares into a *different* set of orthogonal comparisons. Nevertheless, investigators present most factorial experiments in a way that makes obvious their intention to extract and to evaluate the sources of variance listed in Table 10-4. In actuality, then, we can think of the analysis of a two-way factorial experiment as consisting of a set of *planned orthogonal comparisons*. But we are not restricted to these comparisons alone. Often we will want to isolate the locus of a significant main effect or of an interaction. Procedures for accomplishing these comparisons will be discussed in Chapter 11.

10.4 A NUMERICAL EXAMPLE

We are now ready for a numerical example showing all of the steps required for the analysis of a two-way factorial experiment. The example consists of a hypothetical investigation of the role of drive level and magnitude of reward on the learning of a discrimination problem by monkeys. The animals are given five trials a day for four days on a set of 20 "oddity" problems. In this task, three objects (two the same, one different) are presented to the monkeys, and the subject's task is to learn to select the nonduplicated (odd) object. A food reward is placed in a well underneath the correct object. A trial consists of the presentation of the three objects and the monkey's selection of one of them. The response measure is the number of correct selections in the 20 training trials. One of the independent variables (factor A) is the magnitude of the food reward, either 1, 3, or 5 grapes, while the other variable (factor B) is the drive level of the animals, either 1 hour of food deprivation or 24 hours of food deprivation. Four monkeys are randomly assigned to each treatment combination. Thus, the design is a 3 $\times$ 2 factorial with $s = 4$ subjects. The individual ABS scores appear in Table 10-6.

Table 10-6   Numerical Example: Preliminary Analysis

	1 Grape, 1 hr. $a_1 b_1$	3 Grapes, 1 hr. $a_2 b_1$	5 Grapes, 1 hr. $a_3 b_1$	1 Grape, 24 hr. $a_1 b_2$	3 Grapes, 24 hr. $a_2 b_2$	5 Grapes, 24 hr. $a_3 b_2$
	1	13	9	15	6	14
	4	5	16	6	18	7
	0	7	18	10	9	6
	7	15	13	13	15	13
AB_{ij}:	12	40	56	44	48	40
$\sum_{k=1}^{s} (ABS_{ijk})^2$:	66	468	830	530	666	450
$\overline{AB}_{ij}$:	3.00	10.00	14.00	11.00	12.00	10.00
$\hat{\sigma}_{ij}$:	3.16	4.76	3.92	3.92	5.48	4.08

Preliminary Analysis

The first step in any analysis is to perform some initial calculations on the ABS scores to facilitate the later calculations and to provide a first glimpse at the results. For each treatment combination, we obtain the sum of the scores and the sum of the squared scores. For the group at $a_1 b_1$,

$$AB_{11} = \Sigma ABS_{11k} = 1 + 4 + 0 + 7 = 12;$$

and

$$\Sigma (ABS_{11k})^2 = (1)^2 + (4)^2 + (0)^2 + (7)^2 = 66.$$

From these sums, we can calculate the treatment means $\overline{AB}_{ij}$ and standard deviations $\hat{\sigma}_{ij}$. For the same group,

$$\overline{AB}_{11} = \frac{AB_{11}}{s} = \frac{12}{4} = 3.00;$$

and

$$\hat{\sigma}_{11} = \sqrt{\frac{\Sigma (ABS_{11k})^2 - (AB_{11})^2/s}{s - 1}}$$

$$= \sqrt{\frac{66 - (12)^2/4}{4 - 1}}$$

$$= \sqrt{\frac{66 - 36}{3}} = \sqrt{\frac{30}{3}} = 3.16.$$

The means and standard deviations for all of the treatment groups are presented in the last two rows of Table 10-6.

It is usually a good idea to plot the treatment means so that you can see more readily whether an interaction is present. This has been done in Fig. 10-1. The figure shows a rather sizable interaction of the two variables. It appears that magnitude (factor A) has little differential effect on correct responding by hungry monkeys and an increasing positive effect with less hungry monkeys. In other words, hungry animals are not affected by the differences in the size of the food reward, while less hungry animals are. Now that we have a "feel" for the way the experiment came out (and what the analysis should reveal), we can proceed with the calculations.

Analysis of Variance

The first step is to arrange the AB' sums from Table 10-6 in an AB matrix to facilitate the calculations of the different sums of squares. This has been done in Table 10-7. In order to avoid time-consuming errors, it is a good idea to verify that the sum of the row marginal totals equals the sum of the column marginal totals.

198

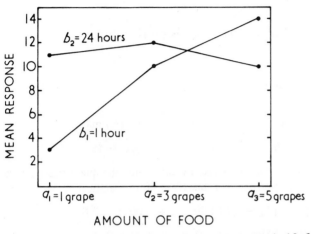

FIGURE 10-1.   Plot of the data presented in Table 10-6.

Table 10-7   *AB* Matrix

| DRIVE (FACTOR *B*) | AMOUNT OF FOOD (FACTOR A) | | | Sum |
	1 GRAPE (a_1)	3 GRAPES (a_2)	5 GRAPES (a_3)	
1 hr. (b_1)	12	40	56	108
24 hr. (b_2)	44	48	40	132
Sum	56	88	96	240

Next, we substitute the information available in the *AB* and *ABS* matrices into the computational formulas for the sums of squares given in Table 10-4. We perform these operations in two steps: (1) the calculation of the basic ratios and (2) the addition and subtraction of these terms in the actual determination of the various sums of squares. We will now solve for these basic quantities and identify each by means of the letter code. Working first with the *AB* matrix, we obtain

$$[T] = \frac{T^2}{(a)(b)(s)} = \frac{(240)^2}{(3)(2)(4)} = \frac{57,600}{24} = 2,400.00;$$

$$[A] = \frac{\Sigma A^2}{(b)(s)} = \frac{(56)^2 + (88)^2 + (96)^2}{(2)(4)} = \frac{20,096}{8} = 2,512.00;$$

$$[B] = \frac{\Sigma B^2}{(a)(s)} = \frac{(108)^2 + (132)^2}{(3)(4)} = \frac{29,088}{12} = 2,424.00;$$

199

and

$$[AB] = \frac{\Sigma (AB)^2}{s} = \frac{(12)^2 + (44)^2 + \cdots + (56)^2 + (40)^2}{4}$$

$$= \frac{10,720}{4} = 2,680.00.$$

The final calculation requires the subtotals presented in the *ABS* matrix:

$$[ABS] = \Sigma (ABS)^2 = 66 + 468 + 830 + 530 + 666 + 450 = 3,010.$$

We can now obtain the sums of squares by combining the quantities we have just calculated in the patterns specified in Table 10-4. More specifically,

$$SS_A = [A] - [T] = 2,512.00 - 2,400.00 = 112.00;$$

$$SS_B = [B] - [T] = 2,424.00 - 2,400.00 = 24.00;$$

$$SS_{A \times B} = [AB] - [A] - [B] + [T]$$

$$= 2,680.00 - 2,512.00 - 2,424.00 + 2,400.00 = 144.00;$$

$$SS_{S/AB} = [ABS] - [AB] = 3,010 - 2,680.00 = 330.00;$$

and

$$SS_T = [ABS] - [T] = 3,010 - 2,400.00 = 610.00.$$

These sums of squares have been entered in Table 10-8 as an example of a standard analysis-of-variance summary table. We should check for computational errors in our calculations by summing the component sums of squares to verify that the total equals the SS_T.

The numerical values of the degrees of freedom are found by simple substitution in the formulas appearing in Table 10-4:

$$df_A = a - 1 = 3 - 1 = 2;$$

$$df_B = b - 1 = 2 - 1 = 1;$$

Table 10-8   Summary of the Analysis

SOURCE	SS	df	MS	F
A	112.00	2	56.00	3.06
B	24.00	1	24.00	1.31
A X B	144.00	2	72.00	3.93*
S/AB	330.00	18	18.33	
Total	610.00	23		

*$p < .05$.

$$df_{A \times B} = (a - 1)(b - 1) = (3 - 1)(2 - 1) = 2;$$
$$df_{S/AB} = (a)(b)(s - 1) = (3)(2)(4 - 1) = 18;$$

and

$$df_T = (a)(b)(s) - 1 = (3)(2)(4) - 1 = 24 - 1 = 23.$$

As a check, we should verify that the sum of the component degrees of freedom equals df_T.

The mean squares are obtained by dividing each sum of squares by the appropriate df. Finally, each mean square reflecting in part the contribution of a different component of interest is tested against the mean square representing experimental error—i.e., the within-groups mean square $MS_{S/AB}$.[2] The observed F ratios are compared with the critical values of F listed in Table A-1 in Appendix A. In this example, only the interaction source of variance reaches an acceptable level of significance.

10.5   THE STATISTICAL MODEL

The linear model underlying the present analysis begins with a statement of the components contributing to any score in the experiment (ABS_{ijk}). That is,

$$ABS_{ijk} = \mu + \alpha_i + \beta_j + \alpha\beta_{ij} + \epsilon_{ijk}$$

where

μ is the overall mean of the population;
α_i is the average treatment effect at level a_i ($\alpha_i = \mu_i - \mu$);
β_j is the average treatment effect at level b_j ($\beta_j = \mu_j - \mu$);
$\alpha\beta_{ij}$ is the interaction effect at cell $a_i b_j$ ($\alpha\beta_{ij} = \mu_{ij} - \mu_i - \mu_j + \mu$); and
ϵ_{ijk} is the experimental error associated with each score
  ($\epsilon_{ijk} = ABS_{ijk} - \mu_{ij}$).

The statistical hypotheses for the main effects and the interaction can be stated in terms of these parameters. That is,

$$A \text{ main effect: } H_0: \text{ All } \alpha_i = 0.$$

$$H_1: \text{ Not all } \alpha_i = 0.$$

---

[2]The $MS_{S/AB}$ is literally an average of the separate group variances. To illustrate, we can use the standard deviations in Table 10-6 (p. 197) to calculate $MS_{S/AB}$. That is,

$$MS_{S/AB} = \frac{\Sigma \hat{\sigma}_{ij}^2}{(a)(b)} = \frac{(3.16)^2 + (4.76)^2 + \cdots + (5.48)^2 + (4.08)^2}{(3)(2)}$$

$$= \frac{110.05}{6} = 18.34,$$

which is identical to the value in Table 10-8 except for the inevitable rounding error.

$$B \text{ main effect: } H_0: \text{ All } \beta_j = 0.$$
$$H_1: \text{ Not all } \beta_j = 0.$$
$$A \times B \text{ interaction: } H_0: \text{ All } \alpha\beta_{ij} = 0.$$
$$H_1: \text{ Not all } \alpha\beta_{ij} = 0.$$

The expected values of the mean squares that we calculate in the analysis of variance, $E(MS)$, refer to the factors contributing to the average value of each mean square obtained with repeated samplings from a given set of treatment populations. For the present design,

$$E(MS_A) = \sigma_\epsilon^2 + (b)(s)(\theta_A^2);$$
$$E(MS_B) = \sigma_\epsilon^2 + (a)(s)(\theta_B^2);$$

and

$$E(MS_{A \times B}) = \sigma_\epsilon^2 + (s)(\theta_{A \times B}^2).$$

In the fixed-effects model, which is the model treated here and which is appropriate for most research applications, the three values of θ^2 are defined as follows:[3]

$$\theta_A^2 = \frac{\Sigma \,(\alpha_i)^2}{a-1} \;;\; \theta_B^2 = \frac{\Sigma \,(\beta_j)^2}{b-1} \;;\; \text{ and } \theta_{A \times B}^2 = \frac{\Sigma \,(\alpha\beta_{ij})^2}{(a-1)(b-1)} \;.$$

To round out the picture,

$$E(MS_{S/AB}) = \sigma_\epsilon^2.$$

The essential logic behind the analysis of variance lies in the construction of ratios having the form

$$\frac{MS_{\text{effect}}}{MS_{\text{error}}},$$

where the expected value of the MS_{error} matches the expected value of the MS_{effect} in all respects except for the variance component reflecting the effect. Symbolically,

$$E(MS_{\text{effect}}) = \text{error } + \text{ effect}$$

and

$$E(MS_{\text{error}}) = \text{error}.$$

Under the null hypothesis, the variance component reflecting the effect will be zero, the "effect" component (or **null-hypothesis component**, as it is often called)

[3]Structural models are discussed in Chap. 21.

drops out, and

$$E(MS_{\text{effect}}) = E(MS_{\text{error}}).$$

Under these circumstances, then, the ratio

$$\frac{MS_{\text{effect}}}{MS_{\text{error}}}$$

will be distributed as $F(df_{\text{effect}}, df_{\text{error}})$, provided the usual assumptions of normality, homogeneity of variance, and independence are satisfied (see pp. 85–87). We can then relate the observed ratio to the tabled values of F and assess its significance through the application of the standard decision rules.

For this design, I have already noted that

$$E(MS_{S/AB}) = \sigma_\epsilon^2.$$

Consequently, this mean square is the appropriate error term for all three of the mean squares reflecting factorial effects—because in each case, when the null hypothesis is true, the null-hypothesis component drops out and we are dividing one estimate of error variance by another, independent estimate of error variance.

10.6 ESTIMATION PROCEDURES

Estimating Population Treatment Means

Confidence-bounded intervals can be constructed for the population treatment means μ_{ij} and the population means defining main effects (μ_i = the average of the μ_{ij}'s at a particular level of factor A; μ_j = the average of the μ_{ij}'s at a particular level of factor B). A general formula specifying the upper and lower limits of confidence intervals is

$$\text{(population estimate)} \pm t(\hat{\sigma}_M), \qquad (10\text{-}4)$$

where the population estimate comes from the appropriate observed mean ($\overline{AB}_{ij}$, $\overline{A}_i$, or $\overline{B}_j$), t is obtained from Table A-3 in Appendix A (at $df = df_{S/AB}$ and the chosen level of α), and $\hat{\sigma}_M$ is the estimate of the appropriate standard error of the mean. A general formula for this last quantity is as follows:

$$\hat{\sigma}_M = \frac{\hat{\sigma}}{\sqrt{\text{(number of observations)}}}, \qquad (10\text{-}5)$$

where $\hat{\sigma} = \sqrt{MS_{S/AB}}$ and the number of observations refers to the number of scores contributing to the mean from the experiment upon which the population estimate is based—s, $(b)(s)$, and $(a)(s)$ for $\overline{AB}_{ij}$, $\overline{A}_i$, and $\overline{B}_j$, respectively.

Estimating Treatment Magnitude (Omega Squared)

Estimates of treatment magnitude, which was discussed in Chapter 5 (pp. 89-96), can be obtained from factorial designs.[4] The general definition of such estimates, $\hat{\omega}^2_{effect}$, can be expressed in the following way:

$$\hat{\omega}^2_{effect} = \frac{SS_{effect} - (df_{effect})(MS_{wg})}{SS_T + MS_{wg}}.$$ (10-6)

Using Eq. (10-6) to estimate $\hat{\omega}^2_{A \times B}$ in a two-factor experiment, for example, we have

$$\hat{\omega}^2_{A \times B} = \frac{SS_{A \times B} - (a - 1)(b - 1)(MS_{S/AB})}{SS_T + MS_{S/AB}}.$$ (10-7)

Substituting the information from the earlier numerical example (see Table 10-8, p. 200) in Eq. (10-7), we find

$$\hat{\omega}^2_{A \times B} = \frac{144.00 - (3 - 1)(2 - 1)(18.33)}{610.00 + 18.33}$$

$$= \frac{144.00 - 36.66}{628.33} = \frac{107.34}{628.33} = .171.$$

In this example, the interaction accounts for 17.1 percent of the total variance.[5]

10.7 DETERMINING SAMPLE SIZE

We considered power and design sensitivity in Chapter 4, where you were shown how power determinations can be used to choose an adequate sample size. (See pp. 70-73 for a review of these procedures.) Power estimates can be used to serve the same important function in factorial designs as well.[6]

In order to estimate sample size, we have to specify the nature of the population treatment effects we are interested in detecting and to guess at the magnitude of error variance we expect to be operating in the experiment. These and other values, including a trial sample size s', are entered in a formula producing a value for ϕ^2_{effect}; the square root of this value, ϕ_{effect}, is referred to power charts to provide

---

[4]Computational formulas for omega squared for a wide variety of factorial designs are found in Dodd and Schultz (1973), Dwyer (1974), and Vaughan and Corballis (1969).

[5]An objection has been raised concerning the appropriateness of the general formula for estimating omega squared. See Keren and Lewis (1979) for a discussion of this problem. They present a revised index, called a **partial omega squared,** and relate this new index to a partial correlation coefficient (p. 123).

[6]Extensions of power estimates to factorial designs are given comprehensive treatment by Cohen (1977, pp. 364-379) and by Guenther (1964, e.g., pp. 47-49, 107-108, and 128-129).

an estimate of power associated with the particular circumstances. If power is inadequate, the most straightforward solution is to increase sample size, although other solutions are possible (see pp. 67-69). A new trial sample size is used to calculate ϕ^2_{effect} again to determine the level of power achieved by this increase in sample size. This trial-and-error procedure is repeated until the desired level of power is attained.

A general formula for ϕ^2_{effect} is given by

$$\phi^2_{\text{effect}} = \frac{(\text{no. obsn.}) \, [\, \Sigma \, (\text{dev.})^2 \,]}{(df_{\text{effect}} + 1)(\sigma^2_{\text{error}})} \tag{10-8}$$

where

(no. obsn.) refers to the number of observations that will contribute to each basic deviation;

$\Sigma \, (\text{dev.})^2$ represents the basic population deviations constituting the treatment effects in question, that is, α_i, β_j, or $\alpha\beta_{ij}$;

df_{effect} refers to the df associated with the treatment effects based on sample values; and

σ^2_{error} is the population error variance.

Table 10-9 illustrates how Eq. (10-8) is adapted for use with the $A \times B$ factorial design. The basic deviations for each factorial effect are listed in the second column of the table. These deviations come from the formal statement of the structural model (see Section 10-5, p. 201). In the third column appear the numbers of observations on which estimates of these deviations would be based in the actual experiment. For the main effect of factor A, $(b)(s')$ observations are available to estimate the deviation for any given mean; for the main effect of factor B, $(a)(s')$ observations are available; and for the interaction, s' observations are available. The formulas for ϕ^2_{effect} are completed in the final column of the table.

Consider the three completed formulas. In determining the sample size to be

Table 10-9   Values of ϕ^2_{effect} in the $A \times B$ Design

SOURCE	DEVIATION	NUMBER OF OBSERVATIONS	ϕ^2_{effect}
A	α_i	$(b)(s')$	$\dfrac{(b)(s')[\Sigma \, (\alpha_i)^2 \,]}{(a)(\sigma^2_{S/AB})}$
B	β_j	$(a)(s')$	$\dfrac{(a)(s')[\, \Sigma \, (\beta_j)^2 \,]}{(b)(\sigma^2_{S/AB})}$
$A \times B$	$\alpha\beta_{ij}$	s'	$\dfrac{s' \, [\, \Sigma \, (\alpha\beta_{ij})^2 \,]}{[(a-1)(b-1)+1](\sigma^2_{S/AB})}$

Note: $\alpha_i = \mu_i - \mu$; $\beta_j = \mu_j - \mu$; and $\alpha\beta_{ij} = \mu_{ij} - \mu_i - \mu_j + \mu$.

used in any given experiment, we will vary s', since the levels of factors A and B (a and b, respectively) are determined by the nature of the experimental questions we want to ask and thus are presumably fixed at this stage of the planning. If we are interested in achieving a certain power for all three factorial effects, the final sample size will be determined by the *largest* estimate of s'. Generally, the largest estimate will come from the *interaction*. The reason is that power is in part a function of the actual number of observations contributing to the different means; because of the nature of the factorial design, fewer observations contribute to the cell means (i.e., the interaction) than to either set of marginal means (i.e., the main effects). Thus, if we are interested primarily in interaction, which often we will be with a factorial design, then we only need to work with the corresponding relevant formula in our estimation of sample size. (See Exercise 4 at the end of this chapter for a numerical example of determining sample size with these formulas.)

10.8   EXERCISES[7]

1. A two-variable factorial experiment is designed in which factor A consists of $a = 5$ equally spaced levels of shock intensity and factor B consists of $b = 3$ discrimination tasks of different difficulty (b_1 = easy, b_2 = medium, and b_3 = hard). There are $s = 5$ rats assigned to each of the $(a)(b) = (5)(3) = 15$ treatment conditions. The task for the animals is to learn to avoid the shock by solving the discrimination task within a 10-second period. The response measure consists of the number of learning trials needed to reach the criterion of an avoidance of the shock on three consecutive trials. The data given in the accompanying ABS matrix.

ABS MATRIX

Treatment Conditions

a_1 b_1	a_1 b_2	a_1 b_3	a_2 b_1	a_2 b_2	a_2 b_3	a_3 b_1	a_3 b_2	a_3 b_3	a_4 b_1	a_4 b_2	a_4 b_3	a_5 b_1	a_5 b_2	a_5 b_3
6	14	15	5	12	14	8	11	16	13	14	16	15	15	17
7	18	18	11	10	17	11	10	20	12	19	18	19	12	15
3	12	14	6	15	15	13	15	17	10	17	19	13	16	19
4	13	13	5	14	11	9	17	13	14	12	11	17	18	14
9	11	15	7	11	14	7	12	16	9	13	14	12	13	16

(a) Conduct an analysis of variance on these data.

(b) Estimate omega squared for each of the factorial effects.

2. Consider the factorial design displayed in the accompanying ABS matrix and the scores produced by the $s = 3$ subjects in each of the treatment conditions.

[7]The answers to these problems are found in Appendix B, beginning on p. 572.

ABS MATRIX

Treatment Conditions

a_1 b_1	a_1 b_2	a_1 b_3	a_1 b_4	a_1 b_5	a_2 b_1	a_2 b_2	a_2 b_3	a_2 b_4	a_2 b_5	a_3 b_1	a_3 b_2	a_3 b_3	a_3 b_4	a_3 b_5
10	11	9	12	9	11	15	19	8	11	8	12	11	10	11
9	8	7	7	9	8	12	16	9	12	11	9	7	9	9
7	8	9	6	11	6	16	20	7	8	10	8	7	7	8

(a) Conduct an analysis of variance on these data.

(b) Estimate omega squared for each of the factorial effects.

3. In order to conserve space, most psychology journals do not publish analysis-of-variance summary tables, except where the analysis is complicated and where there are many significant sources of variance. Thus, the most that we can expect to find is a table of means and a report of the obtained values of F. At times, however, we will wish that the researcher had extracted a certain comparison which is of particular interest to us or had conducted a multiple comparison between pairs of means. We can perform these analyses *ourselves* even though the researcher has not provided us with a detailed summary of the analysis. Suppose we have been given the following table of means:

	a_1	a_2	a_3
b_1	11	12	10
b_2	3	10	14

and we have been told that only the $A \times B$ interaction is significant, $F = 3.93$, $p < .05$. Assuming that there are $s = 4$ subjects in each treatment condition, reconstruct the entire summary table, the SS's the df's, and the F's.

4. The AB matrix from a 3×2 factorial experiment with $s = 5$ subjects is given below:

	a_1	a_2	a_3
b_1	22	30	36
b_2	11	15	30

(a) Perform an analysis of variance. (Assume $MS_{S/AB} = 10.50$.)

(b) On the basis of this experiment, what sample size would you need to achieve a significant main effect of factor B, setting $\alpha = .05$ and power $= .80$? Use the $MS_{S/AB}$ to estimate σ^2_{error} and the means from the experiment to estimate population effects (β_j).

11

Detailed Analysis
of Main Effects
and Interaction

Not only does the factorial design represent an efficient way of studying the separate and joint effects of two or more independent variables on behavior, but the design is also a rich source of analytical comparisons that can be used to pinpoint the specific treatment conditions responsible for a significant main effect or a significant interaction. A test for interaction usually represents a logical first step in the analysis of a two-factor experiment in the sense that the outcome of this test generally will influence the nature of the analyses that follow. That is, if the interaction *is* significant, less attention will be paid to the two main effects, and the analysis will focus on a search for the specific conditions contributing to the significant interaction. On the other hand, if the interaction is *not* significant, attention is generally directed to the detailed analysis of the two main effects. Thus, the analysis of interaction concentrates on the individual treatment means and the joint variation of the two independent variables, while the analysis of the main effects concentrates on the marginal means and the variation of each independent variable averaged over the levels of the other.

In Part II, I considered the varieties of analytical comparisons we might choose to make either in lieu of the omnibus F test (planned comparisons) or following a significant omnibus F. All of the procedures presented in the earlier chapters are applicable and easily adapted to factorial experiments. Since the basic ideas are the same, we need not pursue these procedures as deeply as we did in Chapters 6, 7, and 8. I will begin with the analysis of main effects, where the parallel with the single-factor experiments will be obvious, and then turn to the analysis of interaction, which is more complicated.

11.1 COMPARISONS INVOLVING THE MARGINAL MEANS

The marginal means for any one variable are obtained by collapsing across, or in essence eliminating, the classification of the other variable. We have two sets of marginal means, one for each of the two independent variables. You can actually think of each set of means as coming from two single-factor studies. As you will see, the only change in the computational formulas is an adjustment for the number of observations actually involved in the comparisons being made.

The significance of comparisons is also evaluated by a within-groups mean square, which is $MS_{S/AB}$ in the two factor case. At first glance, one might have thought that an estimate more analogous to the single-factor analysis would be one based upon subjects receiving the same level of factor A or factor B, forgetting about the B classification or the A classification, respectively. We can see that such a variance would not represent an estimate of "pure" experimental error, but the additional contribution of the other variable at each level of the variable of interest. Only the error term for the two-factor analysis provides the sort of estimate we need—one that assesses the *unsystematic* variability produced in our particular experiment.

Computational Formulas

If we are interested in comparisons involving the $\bar{A}_i$ means, we can use the familiar formula for single-df comparisons from Chapter 6, which, in the factorial case, is

$$SS_{A\,comp.} = \frac{(b)(s)(\hat{\psi}_A)^2}{\Sigma(c_i)^2},$$ (11-1)

where $(b)(s)$ is the number of observations contributing to each mean, $\hat{\psi}_A$ represents the comparison between the $\bar{A}_i$ means, and the c_i terms are the coefficients representing the comparison being conducted. In terms of the $\bar{A}_i$ marginal means,

$$\hat{\psi}_A = \Sigma(c_i)(\bar{A}_i).$$ (11-1a)

It is not really necessary to present the formula in terms of factor B also, since the identification of a particular factor as A or B in an actual experiment is purely arbitrary. I will consider the corresponding formula in this initial discussion, however. If we are comparing the $\bar{B}_j$ means, the number of observations is $(a)(s)$—s observations in each cell of the AB matrix and a levels of factor A over which the averaging takes place. The formula becomes

$$SS_{B\,comp.} = \frac{(a)(s)(\hat{\psi}_B)^2}{\Sigma(c_j)^2},$$ (11-2)

where $(a)(s)$ is the number of observations, $\hat{\psi}_B$ is the comparison between the $\bar{B}_j$ means, and the c_j terms are the coefficients. In terms of the $\bar{B}_j$ marginal means,

$$\hat{\psi}_B = \Sigma(c_j)(\bar{B}_j).$$ (11-2a)

After this point, the procedure is identical to that outlined for the single-factor case. The F ratios for comparisons of either type are

$$F_{A\,comp.} = \frac{MS_{A\,comp.}}{MS_{S/AB}} \quad \text{and} \quad F_{B\,comp.} = \frac{MS_{B\,comp.}}{MS_{S/AB}},$$

where the denominator is the estimate of error variance calculated for the two-factor analysis of variance—i.e., the pooled within-groups variance.[1] The df for the numerator and denominator for both F ratios are $df_{num.} = 1$ and $df_{denom.} = (a)(b)(s-1)$.

A Numerical Example

As an example, consider the data in Table 10-6 (p. 197) and suppose that we wanted to compare two means, $\bar{A}_1$ and $\bar{A}_3$ (1 grape versus 5 grapes). For this

---

[1]The use of the $MS_{S/AB}$ as the error term assumes homogeneity of variance. If this assumption is not met, the analysis becomes complicated (see Kirk, 1968, pp. 97–98).

comparison, the coefficients would be 1, 0, and -1 for levels a_1, a_2, and a_3, respectively. For this comparison, then, we have the following:

	a_1	a_2	a_3
Coefficients (c_i)	1	0	-1
Marginal means $(\bar{A}_i)$	7.00	11.00	12.00

We then substitute in Eq. (11-1a) to calculate the mean difference,

$$\hat{\psi}_A = \Sigma \, (c_i)(\bar{A}_i) = (1)(7.00) + (0)(11.00) + (-1)(12.00) = -5.00,$$

and in Eq. (11-1) to calculate the comparison sum of squares,

$$SS_{A_{comp.}} = \frac{(b)(s)(\hat{\psi}_A)^2}{\Sigma \, (c_i)^2} = \frac{(2)(4)(-5.00)^2}{(1)^2 + (0)^2 + (-1)^2} = \frac{200.00}{2} = 100.00.$$

The mean square and F ratio are as follows:

$$MS_{A_{comp.}} = \frac{100.00}{1} = 100.00 \quad \text{and} \quad F = \frac{100.00}{18.33} = 5.46.$$

(The value for the $MS_{S/AB}$, 18.33, was taken from Table 10-8.) Since the critical value of $F(1, 18) = 4.41$ at $\alpha = .05$, the null hypothesis is rejected, and we can conclude that the difference between the two means ($\hat{\psi}_A = -5.00$) is significant.

Interpreting Main Effects

In general, the interpretation of any main effect depends on the presence or absence of significant interaction effects. If there is no interaction, or if the interaction is significant but trivial, the outcome of the F tests involving the main effects can be interpreted without qualification. With a sizable and significant interaction, on the other hand, the meaning of these F tests must be interpreted with caution.

To illustrate, consider the example presented in Fig. 11-1. On the left, the two curves do not cross within the limits of the factor A selected for the experiment. In spite of the interaction showing that the largest difference between b_1 and b_2 is found at a_2, it is also true that b_1 is *consistently* above b_2. This is an example of an **ordinal interaction**, where the relative ranking of the levels of factor B in this case does *not* change at the different levels of factor A. In this situation, it would be appropriate to conclude that in general the treatment represented by level b_1 results in performance that is higher than the treatment at level b_2. If we replot (on the right), with factor B on the baseline, we see what is called a **disordinal interaction**. In this view of the experiment, the rank order of the levels of factor A *changes* at the different levels of factor B. No general conclusion may be reached concerning the influence of factor A.

The example shows that before significant main effects are interpreted and an

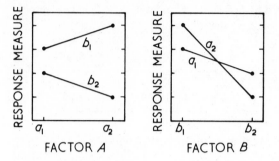

FIGURE 11-1. Example of an ordinal interaction (left panel) and of a disordinal interaction (right panel).

interaction is present, it is wise to plot the data both ways (or to look at the values within the *AB* matrix with regard to both the rows and the columns) to see whether ordinality exists. If it does, the main effect may be interpreted as a main effect. If it does not, the main effect cannot be interpreted independently of the interaction.

11.2 ANALYSIS OF INTERACTION

As with the omnibus *F* test in a single-factor design, a significant interaction in a two-factor design is not very informative by itself. The presence of an interaction merely indicates that the main effects of the two variables do not predict perfectly the individual cell means—that some variability among the cell means is not fully attributable to the two independent variables. While an interaction may take any number of forms, only a few of these will be "tolerable" to the researcher. Most investigators do not wish just for an interaction—any interaction—when they design a factorial experiment. They are expecting a *certain pattern* of results. In a real sense, many comparisons that they conduct involving the cell means represent an attempt to assess the veracity of their predictions.

Interaction can be analyzed by means of two useful procedures. The first divides the factorial design into a set of single-factor experiments, as illustrated in the upper portion of Table 11-1. Each row of the design represents a single-factor experiment in which factor *A* has been manipulated and can be analyzed in any meaningful fashion to reveal the nature of the results. Each experiment differs with regard to the specific *B* treatment held constant for any given row. This approach to examining interaction is called an **analysis of the simple effects of factor *A*.** Interaction is defined as differences between the simple effects; the analysis of simple effects is designed to establish the differential patterns of these single-factor outcomes. The simple effects of either factor *A* or factor *B*, or even both factors, can be examined in an analysis. Only the simple effects of factor *A* have been shown in Table 11-1, to simplify the exposition.

Table 11-1 The Analysis of Interaction

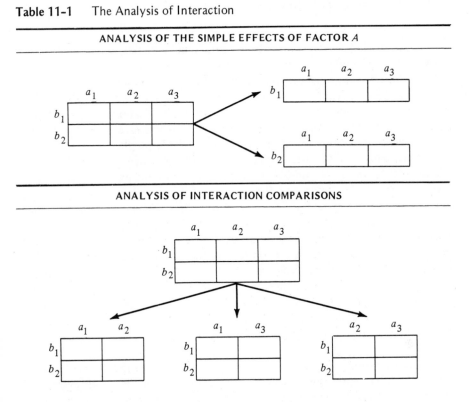

ANALYSIS OF THE SIMPLE EFFECTS OF FACTOR A

ANALYSIS OF INTERACTION COMPARISONS

The second general method of analyzing interaction transforms the factorial design into a set of smaller factorials, as illustrated in the lower portion of Table 11-1. The first design, on the left, for example, consists of a factorial experiment in which factor A consists of two, rather than three, levels, namely, a_1 and a_2. The second design involves levels a_1 and a_3, and the third design involves levels a_2 and a_3. Tests for interaction in these and other "miniature" factorial designs created from the original factorial manipulation also help to isolate the particular features of the two independent variables responsible for the overall interaction. I will call this second approach used to analyze interaction the **analysis of interaction comparisons.**

Both types of analyses decompose the factorial design into smaller components. The analysis of simple effects concentrates on the component single-factor experiments created by the factorial design, while the analysis of interaction comparisons concentrates on the smaller component factorial experiments which collectively make up the larger factorial design. I will consider both approaches to the analysis of interaction in this chapter.

11.3 ANALYSIS OF SIMPLE EFFECTS

An analysis of simple effects turns to the data found in the body of the AB matrix and examines the outcome of the experiment row by row or column by column (or at times both ways). A significant interaction means quite literally that the simple effects of either independent variable are not the same. An examination of the simple effects is undertaken to establish statistically the nature of these different patterns of results. Consider the data from the numerical example of the last chapter, which are presented again in Fig. 11-2. We know that the interaction is significant, and our eyes tell us that the interaction is due to a strong positive relationship between the amount of food (factor A) and the mean number of correct responses for the animals that are only slightly hungry ($b_1 = 1$ hour without food) and the apparent absence of an effect when the animals are quite hungry ($b_2 = 24$ hours without food). An analysis of the simple effects of factor A could provide statistical evidence in support of this observation. As you will see in a moment, the analysis concentrates on one of the sets of three groups—the animals tested after 1 hour or those tested after 24 hours—and treats the data as if they had come from a *single-factor* experiment conducted at that particular level of factor B. Each set is analyzed separately and yields the sort of information available from any single-factor design. In this example, we would expect to find a significant simple effect for the 1-hour groups and no significant simple effect for the 24-hour groups.

The same sorts of questions can be asked of the other independent variable, amount of food deprivation (factor B). An examination of Fig. 11-2 suggests that the interaction can be described also as resulting from a sizable superiority of the more hungry animals given a reward of 1 grape and a marked reduction and even a

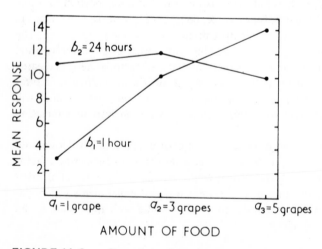

FIGURE 11-2.   Plot of the data presented in Table 10-6.

214

reversal of this effect for the animals given 3 and 5 grapes, respectively. An analysis of the simple effects would test each of these three differences separately and provide statistical evidence for this particular observation.

Computational Formulas

Table 11-2 makes explicit the relationship between the simple effects of factor A and the main effect of factor A. The main effect is based on the deviation of the marginal means $(\bar{A}_1, \bar{A}_2,$ and $\bar{A}_3)$ from the grand mean $(\bar{T})$. The simple effects of factor A are based on analogous deviations, except that the individual means are the cell means in a particular row of the AB matrix and the "grand mean" is the average of *those particular* means. Consider the simple effect of factor A at level b_1, which represents the variability of the three cell means at $a_1, a_2,$ and a_3 about the overall *marginal mean* $\bar{B}_1$. Table 11-2 illustrates the nature of this source of variance.

Table 11-2 Means Involved in the Simple Effects of Factor A

	FACTOR A				
FACTOR B	a_1	a_2	a_3	Marginal Mean	Effect
b_1	$\overline{AB}_{11}$	$\overline{AB}_{21}$	$\overline{AB}_{31}$	$\bar{B}_1$	$\longrightarrow A$ at b_1
b_2	$\overline{AB}_{12}$	$\overline{AB}_{22}$	$\overline{AB}_{32}$	$\bar{B}_2$	$\longrightarrow A$ at b_2
Marginal Mean	$\bar{A}_1$	$\bar{A}_2$	$\bar{A}_3$	$\bar{T}$	$\longrightarrow A$ Main effect

The simplest way to view this analysis is to convert each row of the AB matrix into a single-factor design and then obtain the desired sums of squares by means of the computational formulas appropriate for an *actual* single-factor design. To assist in this translation, we can change the notation system from the factorial representation to one appropriate for a single-factor experiment. Continuing with this example, we isolate the relevant row in the AB matrix of sums, upon which the analysis will be conducted, and transform the notation in the following manner:

	a_1	a_2	a_3	Sum
Factorial symbols	AB_{11}	AB_{21}	AB_{31}	B_1
Single-factor symbols	"A_1"	"A_2"	"A_3"	"T"

(The quotation marks around the single-factor symbols are intended to remind you that these are special symbols designed for this analysis.) The necessary formula for the sum of squares, which we will refer to as "A at b_1," can now be written as follows:

$$SS_{A \text{ at } b_1} = \frac{\Sigma \, (\text{``}A\text{''})^2}{s} - \frac{(\text{``}T\text{''})^2}{(a)(s)}. \qquad (11\text{-}3)$$

You can see, then, that a simple effect is quite literally the between-groups variation of a single-factor experiment extracted from the larger factorial design. Translated back to the factorial notation, Eq. (11-3) becomes

$$SS_{A \text{ at } b_1} = \frac{\Sigma \, (AB_{i1})^2}{s} - \frac{B_1^2}{(a)(s)}. \qquad (11\text{-}3a)$$

The degrees of freedom for each simple effect equal one less than the number of cell sums; i.e.,

$$df_{A \text{ at } b_j} = a - 1. \qquad (11\text{-}4)$$

The mean squares for simple effects are obtained as usual, by dividing each sum of squares by the appropriate df. The error term for each of these mean squares is the within-groups mean square from the original analysis, $MS_{S/AB}$. That is,

$$F = \frac{MS_{A \text{ at } b_j}}{MS_{S/AB}}, \qquad (11\text{-}5)$$

unless there is heterogeneity of within-group variances. If heterogeneity is present, one solution is to use an error term which is based on the within-group variability of only those observations involved in the calculation of that particular simple main effect, rather than one which pools all observations in the experiment. The result is simply a one-way analysis of variance, both effect and error term calculated on the scores at level b_j.

An analogous analysis can be conducted on the simple effects of factor B—i.e., the effect of the B manipulation at the different levels of factor A. The nature of this analysis is illustrated in Table 11-3. Consider the simple effect within the box. The deviation of these cell means ($\overline{AB}_{11}$ and $\overline{AB}_{12}$) from the overall marginal mean $\overline{A}_1$ represents the simple effect of factor B at level a_1. The computational formula for the sum of squares, written in factorial notation, is

$$SS_{B \text{ at } a_1} = \frac{\Sigma \, (AB_{1j})^2}{s} - \frac{A_1^2}{(b)(s)}. \qquad (11\text{-}6)$$

The degrees of freedom for any simple effect are 1 less than the number of cell means; in the case of B simple effects,

$$df_{B \text{ at } a_i} = b - 1. \qquad (11\text{-}7)$$

Table 11-3 Means Involved in the Simple Effects of Factor B

FACTOR B	FACTOR A			Marginal Mean
	a_1	a_2	a_3	
b_1	$\overline{AB}_{11}$	$\overline{AB}_{21}$	$\overline{AB}_{31}$	$\overline{B}_1$
b_2	$\overline{AB}_{12}$	AB_{22}	AB_{32}	$\overline{B}_2$
Marginal Mean	$\overline{A}_1$	$\overline{A}_2$	$\overline{A}_3$	$\overline{T}$
	↓	↓	↓	↓
Effect	B at a_1	B at a_2	B at a_3	B Main effect

The mean squares and F ratios are formed in the usual way:

$$MS_{B \text{ at } a_i} = \frac{SS_{B \text{ at } a_i}}{df_{B \text{ at } a_i}};$$

(11-8)

and

$$F = \frac{MS_{B \text{ at } a_i}}{MS_{S/AB}}.$$

(11-9)

A Numerical Example

I will illustrate the analysis of simple effects with the data summarized in Fig. 11-2. The AB matrix for this example is presented again in Table 11-4. I will calculate the simple effects of the food variable (factor A) at the two levels of drive (1 hour and 24 hours). The effects of varying the amount of food reward with nearly satiated animals are reflected in the cell sums in the first row of the AB

Table 11-4 AB Matrix from Chapter 10

DRIVE (FACTOR B)	AMOUNT OF FOOD (FACTOR A)			Sum
	1 Grape (a_1)	3 Grapes (a_2)	5 Grapes (a_3)	
1 hr. (b_1)	12	40	56	108
24 hr. (b_2)	44	48	40	132
Sum	56	88	96	240

matrix. Applying Eq. (11-3a) to these data, we find

$$SS_{A \text{ at } b_1} = \frac{\Sigma (AB_{i1})^2}{s} - \frac{B_1^2}{(a)(s)}$$

$$= \frac{(12)^2 + (40)^2 + (56)^2}{4} - \frac{(108)^2}{(3)(4)}$$

$$= 248.00.$$

The effects of the food manipulation with hungry animals (simple effect of A at level b_2) are reflected in the cell sums appearing in the second row of the AB matrix. Substituting in Eq. (11-3a), we have

$$SS_{A \text{ at } b_2} = \frac{\Sigma (AB_{i2})^2}{s} - \frac{B_2^2}{(a)(s)}$$

$$= \frac{(44)^2 + (48)^2 + (40)^2}{4} - \frac{(132)^2}{(3)(4)}$$

$$= 8.00.$$

These two sums of squares are entered in Table 11-5.

It may not be evident, but each simple effect contains *two* treatment effects: (1) a portion of the $A \times B$ interaction *and* (2) a portion of the *main effect* of factor A. That is, while the $SS_{A \times B}$ is independent of (i.e., orthogonal to) the SS_A, the simple effects of factor A are not orthogonal to either SS_A or $SS_{A \times B}$. What this means, then, is that a significant simple effect does *not* represent significant interaction effects at the particular level of the other independent variable but, rather, the variability of the interaction and main effects combined. We may see this by summing the complete set of simple effects and finding that

$$\Sigma SS_{A \text{ at } b_j} = SS_{A \times B} + SS_A. \tag{11-10a}$$

In words, the sum of the simple effects of factor A equals the total of the sums of squares associated with factor A and the $A \times B$ interaction. What Eq. (11-10 a) tells us is that an analysis of simple effects is *not* a breakdown of the $SS_{A \times B}$ into a complete set of orthogonal comparisons.[2]

One useful application of Eq. (11-10a) is to provide a check on our arithmetic. That is, if the sum of the simple effects does not equal the sum of the $SS_{A \times B}$ and the SS_A, then we know that we have made an error in our calculations. From the original overall analysis (Table 10-8, p. 200), $SS_{A \times B} = 144.00$ and $SS_A = 112.00$. Substituting in Eq. (11-10a),

$$248.00 + 8.00 \stackrel{?}{=} 144.00 + 112.00$$

$$256.00 = 256.00.$$

[2]Marascuilo and Levin (1970) make this point quite clearly and offer a procedure by which the significance of interaction effects alone may be evaluated.

Table 11-5   Analysis of the Simple Effects of Factor A

Source	SS	df	MS	F
A at b_1	248.00	2	124.00	6.76*
A at b_2	8.00	2	4.00	<1
S/AB		18	18.33	

*$p < .01$.

An analogous relationship exists for the other set of simple effects. In this case, the sum of the simple effects equals the sum of the sums of squares associated with factor B and the $A \times B$ interaction. In symbols,

$$\Sigma \, SS_{B \text{ at } a_i} = SS_{A \times B} + SS_B. \tag{11-10b}$$

(You can verify this relationship by completing Exercise 3 at the end of this chapter, where the data of Table 11-4 are used to illustrate the calculation of the simple effects of factor B.)

The remainder of the analysis is summarized in Table 11-5. The df's, mean squares, and F ratios are obtained through straightforward substitution in the relevant formulas. The resulting F's substantiate statistically what we observed in our earlier perusal of Fig. 11-2, namely, that the amount of food is effective only when the animals are relatively satiated.

Additional Analyses (Simple Comparisons)

Given the analogy between the analysis of simple effects and the analysis of a corresponding single-factor design, you would certainly expect to conduct additional comparisons involving the means producing significant overall F's. A significant simple effect does not establish the locus of the effect if three or more treatment conditions are involved. The most common strategy used to examine a significant simple effect is to conduct a number of single-df comparisons involving the relevant means, chosen to shed light on the reason or reasons for the significant effect. I will call such analyses **simple comparisons**—*comparisons* to be continuous with the single-factor design and *simple* to indicate that the comparisons represent a detailed analysis of simple effects.

Again, an easy way to conceptualize the analysis is to think of a set of row or column means as the products of a single-factor design and then to apply the computational formulas of Chapter 6 to obtain the desired sums of squares. As an example, suppose we wanted to compare the 1- and 3-grape conditions for the relatively satiated animals. The relevant data and coefficients are as follows:

	a_1	a_2	a_3
$\overline{AB}$ means	3.00	10.00	14.00
Coefficients	1	-1	0

The formula for a single-df comparison conducted with data from a single-factor design is given by Eq. (6–5); i.e.,

$$SS_{A_{comp.}} = \frac{s(\hat{\psi})^2}{\Sigma\,(c_i)^2}.$$

Simply substituting the $\overline{AB}$ cell means for the $\overline{A}$ treatment means in the single-factor design, we obtain

$$SS_{A_{comp.\ at\ b_1}} = \frac{s(\hat{\psi}_{A\ at\ b_1})^2}{\Sigma\,(c_i)^2}, \tag{11-11}$$

where $\hat{\psi}_{A\ at\ b_1}$ refers to the difference between the two means specified by this comparison. That is,

$$\hat{\psi}_{A\ at\ b_1} = \Sigma\,(c_i)(\overline{AB}_{i1}). \tag{11-11a}$$

Entering the relevant quantities in these two equations, we find

$$\hat{\psi}_{A\ at\ b_1} = (1)(3.00) + (-1)(10.00) + (0)(14.00) = -7.00;$$

and

$$SS_{A_{comp.\ at\ b_1}} = \frac{4(-7.00)^2}{(1)^2 + (-1)^2 + (0)^2} = \frac{196.00}{2} = 98.00.$$

The number of df for this comparison is 1. The F ratio is formed by dividing the mean square for the comparison by the overall error term from the original analysis, $MS_{S/AB}$. We calculate

$$F_{A_{comp.\ at\ b_1}} = \frac{98.00}{18.33} = 5.35,$$

which is significant at $p < .05$ ($df_{num.} = 1$ and $df_{denom.} = df_{S/AB} = 18$).

Simple comparisons are amazingly versatile. Any meaningful comparison involving one of the independent variables with the other independent variable held constant can be conducted. Such comparisons might include pairwise comparisons such as the one illustrated in the last paragraph, more complex comparisons which involve the averaging of conditions, and trend analysis. In all of these cases, the focus is on the means in a particular row or column of the AB matrix, which, as you have seen, can be transformed into an equivalent single-factor design in order to facilitate the specific calculations.

Comments

The analysis of simple effects is especially useful when theory predicts the nature of an interaction. Testing the significance of simple effects under these circumstances often helps to establish the details of the theoretical prediction. The interaction test tells us whether the simple effects are the same (no interaction) or different (interaction). An analysis of simple effects probes more deeply into the interaction to determine the specific portions of the original AB matrix that are largely responsible for its statistical significance.

One limitation of the analysis of simple effects is the influence of significant main effects. You saw with Eqs. (11-10a) and (11-10b) that simple effects reflect interaction and a main effect. If the main effect is large, little new information may be learned from an analysis of the simple effects. Under these circumstances analyses described in the next section may prove more useful.[3]

Occasionally you will see simple effects tested with no mention of the statistical test of the interaction. The typical pattern of results will consist of two simple effects—one that is significant and one that is not—and the inference drawn by the researcher that interaction is present. The trouble with this argument is that the formal test of interaction assesses the *differences* in simple effects. An inference of interaction that is based on the test of simple effects *alone* does not provide this necessary assessment. What if the difference between two levels of factor A is 10 at level b_1 (and significant) and the same difference is 7 at level b_2 (and not significant)? It is entirely possible that the test of interaction which consists of a comparison between these two differences (10 versus 7) is not significant. The point is that the interaction test is the appropriate way to assess the presence or absence of interaction; a comparison of the statistical decisions concerning simple effects is not.

Finally, you must be on guard to avoid a similar mistake when interpreting simple comparisons. A simple comparison interpreted in the context of a particular treatment level poses no problem. When the same simple comparison is compared *between levels,* however, it is necessary to conduct an additional analysis that compares the set of simple comparisons *directly.* This analysis assesses the significance of the interaction between the comparison, on the one hand—level a_1 versus level a_2 in our example—with the second independent variable (factor B = drive level), on the other. If significant, this interaction will permit the conclusion that the comparison between groups of animals given 1 or 3 grapes has a statistically different outcome depending on the drive level under which the animals are tested. I will discuss this type of test in the next section.

11.4 INTERACTION COMPARISONS

Interaction comparisons represent a different approach to the analysis of interaction that does an analysis of simple effects. Return to Table 11-1 (p. 213) for a moment. The lower display illustrates the basic nature of interaction comparisons, namely, a focus on a meaningful component of the original factorial design. Suppose a_1 represents a control condition, while a_2 and a_3 represent two drug conditions. A component factorial formed by isolating levels a_1 and a_2 provides information about the interaction of *these two treatment conditions* with the

---

[3]See, also, the analysis described by Marascuilo and Levin (1970).

other independent variable. The overall $A \times B$ interaction does not provide this specific information directly, because in essence it is a composite of other interaction comparisons. You will recall a similar argument applied to the omnibus F test in the single-factor design. This omnibus nature of the $A \times B$ interaction is present whenever either independent variable consists of more than two levels.

Interaction comparisons are created whenever particular levels of an independent variable are singled out for analysis. The interaction comparisons pictured in Table 11-1 consist of pairwise comparisons between two levels of factor A. Interaction comparisons can also be formed by combining levels. In this example, we might be interested in comparing the control condition a_1 with the combined drug conditions $a_2 + a_3$ in order to see whether this comparison, i.e., the difference between the control and average drug conditions, interacts with the other variable (factor B). It should be obvious that either independent variable can supply the comparison examined in an interaction comparison. In this example, factor B consists of only two levels, which means that the only analytical comparison involving this factor is the difference between b_1 and b_2; but with additional levels of factor B, interaction comparisons involving this independent variable are now possible. I will designate interaction comparisons by the following notation:

$A_{comp.} \times B$ refers to an interaction comparison in which factor A supplies the comparison while the levels of factor B remain intact.
$A \times B_{comp.}$ refers to an interaction comparison in which factor B supplies the comparison while the levels of factor A remain intact.

Boik (1979) refers to the interaction obtained from either type of interaction comparison as a **partial interaction**.[4] It is also possible to form interaction comparisons by applying single-df comparisons to *both* independent variables *simultaneously*. I will use the expression $A_{comp.} \times B_{comp.}$ to designate this sort of interaction comparison. (Boik refers to the interaction obtained from this particular type of comparison as an **interaction contrast**.) I will consider the analysis of partial interactions first, followed by the analysis of interaction contrasts.

Analysis of Partial Interactions

Computational Formulas. Let's consider a concrete example where the analysis of partial interactions makes obvious sense. Suppose we are interested in the amnesic effects of certain drugs on different types of material learned in the laboratory. Factor A, the drug manipulation, consists of a nondrug control condition (a_1) and two different anesthetics commonly used for minor surgical opera-

---

[4]Boik presents a detailed illustration of interaction comparisons in a useful and readable article. While his emphasis is upon the post hoc analysis of significant factorial effects, which lead to corrections for familywise type I error, the use of interaction comparisons to ask pointed and meaningful questions of the data is clearly demonstrated nevertheless. I will discuss the issues surrounding familywise error in Sec. 11.7.

tions (a_2 and a_3). The question of interest is whether the memory for material learned under the two drugs will be impaired in any way when tested the next day. Since drug-induced memory deficits may vary, depending on the nature of the learning material, it makes sense to include three different types of learning material as a second independent variable. The characteristics of the learning material are not of concern at the moment. The design is a 3 X 3 factorial; $s = 5$ subjects are randomly assigned to each of the treatment combinations.

Given the nature of this experimental design, most researchers would not be interested in testing the overall A X B interaction, since it does not bear directly on the interesting research questions examined by this experiment. Two of these research questions are expressed as partial factorials in Table 11-6. The partial factorial on the left focuses on the two drug conditions a_2 and a_3; the control condition a_1 has been omitted entirely. An analysis of the interaction for this partial factorial will answer the question of whether the two drugs produce similar or different effects with the three types of learning materials (factor B). The partial factorial on the right compares the control condition a_1 with an average of the two drug conditions. The interaction in this case will answer the question of whether the difference between the control and combined drug conditions varies with the type of material learned. Both interaction comparisons ask meaningful questions of the data; the overall A X B interaction quite literally is a combination of these two partial interactions.[5]

The sums of squares for these two partial interactions, $SS_{A \text{ comp.} \times B}$, may be calculated from either treatment means or treatment sums. I will use treatment

Table 11-6   Examples of Two Partial Factorials

	Drug X a_2	Drug Y a_3		Control a_1	Combined Drugs $a_2 + a_3$
b_1			b_1		
b_2			b_2		
b_3			b_3		

[5]If the comparisons used to define partial factorials are mutually orthogonal and use up all of the degrees of freedom associated with the relevant manipulated variable ($df_A = 2$ in this case), as they do in Table 11-6, then the sum of the interaction sums of squares will equal $SS_{A \times B}$. This fact emphasizes the omnibus quality of the overall A X B interaction.

means to be consistent with the formulas used to calculate single-df sums of squares in Chapter 6. Some hypothetical means for this experiment are presented in Table 11-7. I will illustrate the calculations first with the interaction comparison comparing the two drug conditions. The analysis begins by calculating $\hat{\psi}_A$ at b_j for each level of factor B, using as coefficients the set $(0, 1, -1)$. These operations produce:

$$\hat{\psi}_{A \text{ at } b_1} = \Sigma \, (c_i)(\overline{AB}_{i1}) = (0)(8.3) + (1)(7.8) + (-1)(8.0) = -.2;$$

$$\hat{\psi}_{A \text{ at } b_2} = \Sigma \, (c_i)(\overline{AB}_{i2}) = (0)(8.8) + (1)(8.0) + (-1)(7.6) = .4;$$

and

$$\hat{\psi}_{A \text{ at } b_3} = \Sigma \, (c_i)(\overline{AB}_{i3}) = (0)(8.1) + (1)(4.5) + (-1)(3.8) = .7.$$

Each of the three differences, $-.2$, $.4$, and $.7$, results from a simple comparison involving factor A at the three levels of factor B. The test for interaction consists of an assessment of the differences among these three simple comparisons. If the null hypothesis that the three simple comparisons are the same is rejected, we can conclude that a partial interaction is present.

    A relatively simple way to calculate the sum of squares for a partial interaction is to take advantage of the relationship between the simple effects of a factor, the main effect of that factor, and the interaction, that we considered in Section 11.3 (pp. 218-219). In terms of factor A, this relationship is expressed as follows:

$$\Sigma \, SS_{A \text{ at } b_j} = SS_{A \times B} + SS_A.$$

Extended to simple comparisons, we have

$$\Sigma \, SS_{A \text{comp. at } b_j} = SS_{A \text{comp.} \times B} + SS_{A \text{comp.}}$$

Since you already know how to calculate sums of squares for simple comparisons and comparison main effects, we can calculate the third quantity by *subtraction*. To be more explicit,

$$SS_{A \text{comp.} \times B} = \Sigma \, SS_{A \text{comp. at } b_j} - SS_{A \text{comp.}} \qquad (11\text{-}12)$$

Table 11-7   Treatment Means for the Numerical Example

	CONTROL a_1	DRUG X a_2	DRUG Y a_3
b_1	8.3	7.8	8.0
b_2	8.8	8.0	7.6
b_3	8.1	4.5	3.8
Mean	8.40	6.77	6.47

As a first step, let's calculate the simple comparisons. From Eq. (11-11), we can write a general formula,

$$SS_{A_{\text{comp. at } b_j}} = \frac{s(\hat{\psi}_{A \text{ at } b_j})^2}{\Sigma (c_i)^2}. \qquad (11\text{-}13)$$

Calculating first

$$\Sigma (c_i)^2 = (0)^2 + (1)^2 + (-1)^2 = 2$$

and substituting in the equation for simple comparisons, we find

$$SS_{A_{\text{comp. at } b_1}} = \frac{5(-.2)^2}{2} = .10;$$

$$SS_{A_{\text{comp. at } b_2}} = \frac{5(.4)^2}{2} = .40;$$

and

$$SS_{A_{\text{comp. at } b_3}} = \frac{5(.7)^2}{2} = 1.23.$$

The sum of these sums of squares gives us the first quantity required by Eq. (11-12),

$$\Sigma SS_{A_{\text{comp. at } b_j}} = .10 + .40 + 1.23 = 1.73.$$

Next we calculate the comparison main effect. From Eq. (11-1a) we calculate $\hat{\psi}_A$ using the $\bar{A}_i$ means provided in Table 11-7:

$$\hat{\psi}_A = \Sigma (c_i)(\bar{A}_i) = (0)(8.40) + (1)(6.77) + (-1)(6.47) = .30.$$

Substituting in Eq. (11-1), we find

$$SS_{A_{\text{comp.}}} = \frac{(b)(s)(\hat{\psi}_A)^2}{\Sigma (c_i)^2} = \frac{(3)(5)(.30)^2}{2} = .68.$$

Finally, we calculate the interaction sum of squares by means of Eq. (11-12) and find

$$SS_{A_{\text{comp.}} \times B} = \Sigma SS_{A_{\text{comp. at } b_j}} - SS_{A_{\text{comp.}}} = 1.73 - .68 = 1.05.$$

The number of degrees of freedom for a partial interaction is given by the formula

$$df_{A_{\text{comp.}} \times B} = (df_{A_{\text{comp.}}})(df_B). \qquad (11\text{-}14)$$

In this example, $df_{A \text{ comp.} \times B} = 1(3 - 1) = 2$. The mean square is obtained by dividing the sum of squares by the degrees of freedom:

$$MS_{A \text{ comp.} \times B} = \frac{1.05}{2} = .53.$$

The F ratio is formed by dividing this mean square by the within-groups mean square from the overall analysis of variance $MS_{S/AB}$. That is,

$$F = \frac{MS_{A \text{ comp.} \times B}}{MS_{S/AB}}. \tag{11-15}$$

If we assume that $MS_{S/AB} = 1.75$,

$$F = \frac{.53}{1.75} = .30,$$

which is not significant, since $F < 1$. If the F table had been necessary, the critical value of F would be found at $df_{\text{num.}} = 2$ and $df_{\text{denom.}} = df_{S/AB} = 36$.

A Second Numerical Example.   I will now calculate the second partial interaction proposed earlier, between the control and the combined drug conditions and factor B. Coefficients for this comparison are the set $(1, -\frac{1}{2}, -\frac{1}{2})$. Table 11-8 provides the sets of means reflecting this comparison at each level of factor B. At b_1, for example, the control mean comes from Table 11-7 directly, and the combined mean is obtained by averaging the treatment means for the two drug conditions, that is, $(7.8 + 8.0)/2 = 7.90$. The simple comparisons $\hat{\psi}_{A \text{ at } b_j}$, expressed as differences between the control and combined drug means, are presented in the column on the far right. An inspection of these differences suggests the possibility that this partial interaction may be significant.

Starting with the simple comparisons, we calculate

$$\Sigma (c_i)^2 = (1)^2 + (-\tfrac{1}{2})^2 + (-\tfrac{1}{2})^2 = 1.50;$$

and then from Eq. (11-13), we find

$$SS_{A \text{ comp. at } b_1} = \frac{5(.40)^2}{1.50} = .53;$$

$$SS_{A \text{ comp. at } b_2} = \frac{5(1.00)^2}{1.50} = 3.33;$$

and

$$SS_{A \text{ comp. at } b_3} = \frac{5(3.95)^2}{1.50} = 52.01.$$

The sum of these sums of squares is

$$\Sigma SS_{A \text{ comp. at } b_j} = .53 + 3.33 + 52.01 = 55.87.$$

Table 11-8   Numerical Example of a Partial Factorial

	CONTROL CONDITION	COMBINED DRUG CONDITIONS	$\hat{\psi}_A$ at b_j
b_1	8.30	7.90	.40
b_2	8.80	7.80	1.00
b_3	8.10	4.15	3.95
Mean	8.40	6.62	

The sum of squares for the comparison main effect is obtained by substituting in Eqs. (11-1a) and then (11-1) as follows:

$$\hat{\psi}_A = 8.40 - 6.62 = 1.78;$$

and

$$SS_{A\,\text{comp.}} = \frac{(3)(5)(1.78)^2}{1.50} = 31.68.$$

From Eq. (11-12),

$$SS_{A\,\text{comp.} \times B} = 55.87 - 31.68 = 24.19.$$

The number of df for this partial interaction is $df_{A\,\text{comp.} \times B} = (df_{A\,\text{comp.}})(df_B) = 1(2) = 2$, and the mean square is $24.19/2 = 12.10$. The F is

$$F = \frac{MS_{A\,\text{comp.} \times B}}{MS_{S/AB}} = \frac{12.10}{1.75} = 6.91,$$

which is significant, $p < .01$.

Interaction Contrasts

An interaction contrast offers an even more focused view of interaction by examining the data through the joint application of *two* single-df comparisons, one involving the levels of factor A and the other involving the levels of factor B. The result is a 2 × 2 matrix where the interaction represents a highly specific analysis of the overall interaction. Continuing with the example from the last section, suppose the three different types of learning material constituting factor B consisted of the following:

b_1 = low-frequency words with average emotional content.
b_2 = high-frequency words with average emotional content.
b_3 = high-frequency words with high emotional content.

The partial interactions we tested in the last section did not differentiate among these different conditions, but just compared the simple comparisons at the three levels of factor B and essentially averaged the differences. In some cases, this level of analysis is sufficient since there is little interest in analyzing the B manipulation any further. But in many cases, such as this example, the other independent variable provides analytical ways of viewing this manipulation as well. What I want to suggest is that any variability attributed to factor B in general, which is what the partial interactions provide information about, can often be better understood by organizing the data more analytically, taking into consideration meaningful comparisons involving factor B.

Examples. Two comparisons that might be of interest and will serve as illustrations of interaction contrasts are a comparison between the low- and high-frequency words with average emotional content (b_1 versus b_2) and a comparison between the two sets of high-frequency words varying in emotionality (b_2 versus b_3). Let's see how these two comparisons help to pinpoint the locus of the significant partial interaction obtained in the last section.

Table 11-9 illustrates the nature of these two interaction contrasts. The 2 × 2 matrix in the upper half of the table focuses on the interaction between the control versus combined-drug comparison from factor A and the low- versus high-frequency comparison from factor B. Level b_3 (words of high emotional content) is omitted in this analysis. A comparison of the differences between the control and combined drug means, listed to the right of the matrix, gives us a convenient look at the interaction.[6] That is, these differences are simple comparisons involving factor A, and interaction is defined in terms of differences in simple effects. The simple comparison for low-frequency words is .40, while the simple comparison for high-frequency words is 1.00. Do these two differences differ significantly? A test of the interaction contained in this 2 × 2 matrix provides an answer to this question

Th. ; same interaction can be examined in terms of the simple effects of the other ind pendent variable (factor B). More specifically, the high-frequency words are better recalled under the control condition, while this difference is reversed slightly under the combined drug conditions. A test for interaction would indicate whether the low-high difference observed with the control condition ($8.30 - 8.80 = -.50$) is significantly different from the low-high difference observed with the combined drug conditions ($7.90 - 7.80 = .10$).

The second matrix, in the lower half of the table, examines a different facet of the partial interaction, namely, the interaction between the control versus combined-drug comparison from factor A and the emotionality comparison from factor B. In this case, the partial-interaction matrix has been refined by deleting level b_1 (low-frequency words) to permit a concentration on the effects of the emotional tone of the material being learned under the different A treatments. Is there interaction reflected by the data entered in this matrix? A comparison of the

[6]You might find it useful to plot the data from the matrix and examine the interaction visually.

Table 11-9 Two Examples of Interaction Contrasts

INTERACTION BETWEEN CONTROL VS. COMBINED-DRUG AND LOW VS. HIGH FREQUENCY

	Control Condition	Combined Drug Conditions	$\hat{\psi}_A$ at b_j
Low Frequency (b_1)	8.30	7.90	.40
High Frequency (b_2)	8.80	7.80	1.00

INTERACTION BETWEEN CONTROL VS. COMBINED-DRUG AND AVERAGE VS. HIGH EMOTIONALITY

	Control Condition	Combined Drug Conditions	$\hat{\psi}_A$ at b_j
Average emotionality (b_2)	8.80	7.80	1.00
High emotionality (b_3)	8.10	4.15	3.95

differences between the control and combined drug means indicates that the effect of the drugs in depressing recall is smaller when the words are of average emotional content (a difference of 1.00) than when the words are of high emotional content (a difference of 3.95). Interaction is present. A test of the difference between these two simple comparisons (1.00 versus 3.95) will provide the statistical evidence needed to evaluate the significance of this interaction. Interaction is also evident when we consider the differences in terms of the B comparison. Under the control condition, the high-emotionality words are recalled more poorly than average words ($8.80 - 8.10 = .70$), but under the combined drug condition, this difference is exaggerated ($7.80 - 4.15 = 3.65$).

Computational Formulas. Translating an interaction contrast into a sum of squares is a surprisingly simple matter. The key to the calculations is the estimate of the interaction under consideration, which I will designate $\hat{\psi}_{A \times B}$. One way to obtain an estimate of the interaction is from the means in the 2 $\times$ 2 matrix directly. This can be accomplished by calculating the two simple comparisons for either factor and subtracting one from the other. For the upper example in Table 11-9,

$$\hat{\psi}_{A \times B} = .40 - 1.00 = -.60;$$

and for the lower example,

$$\hat{\psi}_{A \times B} = 1.00 - 3.95 = -2.95.$$

These estimated interaction effects are then entered into the following formula to obtain the desired sum of squares:

$$SS_{A_{comp.} \times B_{comp.}} = \frac{s(\hat{\psi}_{A \times B})^2}{[\Sigma (c_i)^2][\Sigma (c_j)^2]}, \qquad (11-16)$$

where the c_i's are the coefficients defining $A_{comp.}$ and the c_j's are the coefficients defining $B_{comp.}$.[7] For the first example, $\Sigma (c_i)^2 = (1)^2 + (-\frac{1}{2})^2 + (-\frac{1}{2})^2 = 1.5$, and $\Sigma (c_j)^2 = (1)^2 + (-1)^2 + (0)^2 = 2$. Substituting in Eq. (11-16) gives us

$$SS_{A_{comp.} \times B_{comp.}} = \frac{5(-.60)^2}{(1.5)(2)} = \frac{1.80}{3} = .60.$$

For the second example, $\Sigma (c_i)^2$ remains the same, and $\Sigma (c_j)^2 = (0)^2 + (1)^2 + (-1)^2 = 2$. From Eq. (11-16),

$$SS_{A_{comp.} \times B_{comp.}} = \frac{5(-2.95)^2}{(1.5)(2)} = \frac{43.51}{3} = 14.50.$$

An equivalent method for defining the estimated interaction effect is frequently used, which defines the interaction effect as a sum of the weighted treatment means rather than in terms of simple comparisons. The starting point is the AB matrix of treatment means and a listing of the two sets of coefficients defining the interaction contrast along the appropriate sides of the matrix. Table 11-10 illustrates the placement of the coefficients for both examples we have been considering. The weights applied to each treatment mean are specialized coefficients (d_{ij}) which are simply the *products* of the pairs of coefficients—one from $A_{comp.}$ and the other from $B_{comp.}$—associated with each treatment mean. In the matrix on the left, for example, the coefficient for $\overline{AB}_{11}, d_{11}$, is found by multiplying the coefficient at level a_1 (1) by the coefficient at level b_1 (1); that is, $d_{11} = (1)(1) = 1$. The coefficient for $\overline{AB}_{23}, d_{23}$, is found by multiplying the coefficient at level a_2 $(-\frac{1}{2})$ by the coefficient at level b_3 (0); that is, $d_{23} = (-\frac{1}{2})(0) = 0$. The d_{ij}'s for both interaction contrasts are enumerated within the body of the two AB matrices. The interaction effect is calculated by weighting each treatment mean by the appropriate d_{ij} and summing the weighted treatment means. That is,

$$\hat{\psi}_{A \times B} = \Sigma (d_{ij})(\overline{AB}_{ij}). \tag{11-17}$$

Table 11-10   Coefficients for the Interaction Contrasts

		c_i					c_i	
	(a_1)	(a_2)	(a_3)		(a_1)	(a_2)	(a_3)
c_j	1	$-\frac{1}{2}$	$-\frac{1}{2}$	c_j	1	$-\frac{1}{2}$	$-\frac{1}{2}$
(b_1) 1	1	$-\frac{1}{2}$	$-\frac{1}{2}$	(b_1) 0	0	0	0
(b_2) -1	-1	$\frac{1}{2}$	$\frac{1}{2}$	(b_2) 1	1	$-\frac{1}{2}$	$-\frac{1}{2}$
(b_3) 0	0	0	0	(b_3) -1	-1	$\frac{1}{2}$	$\frac{1}{2}$

[7]This notation can be confusing, in that the specific coefficient c_2, say, is ambiguous—does it refer to level a_2 or to level b_2? Usually the experimental context resolves this ambiguity. A more complete notation would include a distinguishing symbol, for example, c_{A2} and c_{B2}.

If you will refer back to the *AB* matrix of means appearing in Table 11-7 (p. 224), the interaction effect for the contrast on the left becomes

$$\hat{\psi}_{A \times B} = (1)(8.3) + (-\tfrac{1}{2})(7.8) + (-\tfrac{1}{2})(8.0)$$
$$+ (-1)(8.8) + (\tfrac{1}{2})(8.0) + (\tfrac{1}{2})(7.6)$$
$$+ (0)(8.1) + (0)(4.5) + (0)(3.8) = -.60$$

and the interaction effect for the contrast on the right becomes

$$\hat{\psi}_{A \times B} = (0)(8.3) + (0)(7.8) + (0)(8.0)$$
$$+ (1)(8.8) + (-\tfrac{1}{2})(8.0) + (-\tfrac{1}{2})(7.6)$$
$$+ (-1)(8.1) + (\tfrac{1}{2})(4.5) + (\tfrac{1}{2})(3.8) = -2.95.$$

These estimates are identical to those obtained by the other method.

Each method serves a function in the analysis of interaction contrasts. The method dealing with the 2 × 2 matrix directly has the advantage of making the nature of the interaction explicit. The method that uses special coefficients and the total *AB* matrix of means is a step removed from the 2 × 2 matrix but represents an efficient way of calculating the interaction effect when a large number of interaction contrasts is involved. Whichever method you use, however, you should make a practice of examining the 2 × 2 matrix or a graph of these data, especially when an interaction contrast is significant. It is this display of means, defined entirely in terms of two single-*df* comparisons, that must be interpreted when significant interaction is obtained.

Evaluation of Interaction Contrasts. Each interaction contrast is associated with 1 *df*. The *F* ratio is formed by dividing an interaction mean square by the error term from the overall analysis of variance. That is,

$$F = \frac{MS_{A_{\text{comp.}} \times B_{\text{comp.}}}}{MS_{S/AB}}, \tag{11-18}$$

which is evaluated against a critical value of *F* with $df_{\text{num.}} = 1$ and $df_{\text{denom.}} = df_{S/AB}$. The first example examining the interaction of the control and combined drug comparison with learning materials of high and low frequency gives

$$F = \frac{.60}{1.75} = .34,$$

which is not significant. The second example involving the same $A_{\text{comp.}}$ with materials varying in emotionality gives

$$F = \frac{14.50}{1.75} = 8.29,$$

which is significant, $p < .01$. Table 11-9 (p. 229) shows the nature of this interaction. There is a relatively small deficit observed in recall when words of average emotional content are learned under these drugs, but a significantly larger deficit when learning material consists of highly emotional words.

Simple Comparisons

I discussed simple comparisons previously when I considered the analysis of simple effects. In the case of simple effects, we often turn to simple comparisons in order to determine the factors responsible for a significant simple effect. Similarly, in the case of interaction comparisons—partial interactions and interaction contrasts—we will frequently turn to an analysis of simple comparisons in order to identify unambiguously the factors responsible for the significant interaction. In the example from the last section, the significant interaction contrast of control versus drug and emotionality could be analyzed further into a test of the difference between the control and combined drug conditions with words of average emotional content and a test of the same comparison but with words of high emotional content. You would find, if we conducted these two tests, that the first comparison is not significant and the second comparison is, thus establishing statistically the specific nature of the results. (For a presentation and illustration of the procedures involved in conducting simple comparisons, see pp. 219–220.)

Trend Analysis

When the levels of one (or both) of the independent variables of a factorial represent points along a quantitative dimension or scale, it is usually fruitful to examine trend components in some systematic fashion. Chapter 7 showed how linear and higher-order trend components can be extracted from a single-factor experiment. The general purpose of trend analysis is to search for underlying trends that are relatively simple in form—i.e., functions that contain trends no more complicated than quadratic or cubic. When applied to main effects, trend analysis is essentially identical to the single-factor case. When applied to interaction, trend analysis uses the same computational formulas required for interaction comparisons, but attempts to describe interaction in terms of relatively simple trend components.

Suppose we performed a 5×3 factorial experiment where the $a = 5$ levels are equally spaced on some quantitative scale. Two possible outcomes of this experiment are presented in Fig. 11-3. If we consider the functions at each level of factor B, they are all primarily linear in shape; i.e., a straight line drawn through each set of five means would provide a relatively accurate description of the data. The graph on the left depicts a case where the slopes of the three curves at b_1, b_2, and b_3 are approximately equal; hence, a linear component of the interaction does *not* appear to be present. In contrast, the graph on the right represents an interaction which is almost entirely located in the linear component. That is, straight lines drawn through the means at b_1, b_2, and b_3, which accurately describe the three functions, have different slopes.

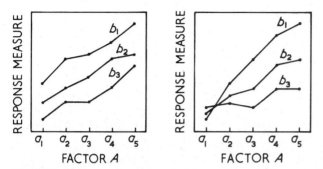

FIGURE 11-3. Example of the presence (right panel) and the absence (left panel) of a $A_{\text{linear}} \times B$ interaction.

To say that the linear component of the interaction is significant, then, is to indicate that the best-fitting *linear* function for factor A is not the same for the different levels of factor B. Said another way, the simple linear components—the particular set of simple comparisons which focus on linear trend—are not the same. In essence, we are comparing the slopes of best-fitting functions drawn through the cell means at the different levels of factor B. If we find that the $SS_{A \times B}$ is due largely to the interaction of these linear functions—i.e., to the differences in slope—we will have pinpointed the source of the interaction to a particular mathematical component of the function relating variations in the independent variable (factor A in this case) to the behavior under study. An equivalent way to think of this interaction is in terms of changes in the effects of factor B as factor A systematically varies in amount. More specifically, the differences among the three B treatments increase *linearly*—are steadily increasing—as factor A increases. However one views it, the linear component of this particular interaction provides a succinct and accurate summary of the overall $A \times B$ interaction depicted in Fig. 11-3.

Consider next the example presented in Fig. 11-4, in which factor A again is a quantitative independent variable. Clearly, an interaction is present. Let's try to describe the interaction in terms of trend components. At level b_1, the means rise and fall as factor A increases, describing a reasonable quadratic trend. A quadratic trend is also present at level b_2, but it is roughly of opposite curvature. What we see, then, is a rather sizable *quadratic component* of the $A \times B$ interaction. Interpreted another way, the presence of a quadratic component of the interaction means that the effects of factor B—in this case the difference between b_1 and b_2—are described by a quadratic function: the differences are small at a_1, increase at a_2 and a_3, and again become small at a_4. Whether anything can be made out of this particular finding, of course, depends on existing theory and the ingenuity of the investigator.

The analysis of interaction trend components follows identically the procedures outlined earlier in this section. All that is necessary to perform a trend analysis is to look up the trend coefficients in Table A-4 in Appendix A and to substitute the necessary quantities in the computational formulas. I will not illustrate

233

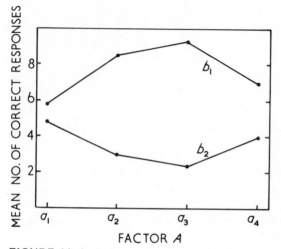

FIGURE 11-4. An example of a quadratic trend component of an $A \times B$ interaction.

trend analysis here, although you can obtain practice with these procedures in Exercise 6 at the end of this chapter, which illustrates the analysis of trend with the data presented in Fig. 11-4.[8]

Orthogonality and Interaction Comparisons

Interaction comparisons are defined by the particular single-df comparisons chosen by a researcher to be examined in the context of the factorial design. Partial interactions, for instance, represent interaction comparisons in which a single-df comparison is applied to the levels of one of the independent variables (either factor A or factor B) and the interest becomes the interaction of this comparison with the other independent variable—i.e., either $A_{comp.} \times B$ or $A \times B_{comp.}$. Interaction contrasts, on the other hand, consist of interaction comparisons in which single-df comparisons are applied to both independent variables simultaneously to permit the determination and assessment of highly focused interaction contrasts. When we are considering a set of interaction comparisons, it is possible to determine which comparisons are mutually orthogonal and which are not. This is accomplished easily by testing for orthogonality among the $A_{comp.}$'s as a set and among the $B_{comp.}$'s as a set. You will recall that two comparisons are orthogonal if the products of corresponding coefficients sum to zero. For comparisons involving factor A, this test is $\Sigma \, (c_i)(c_i') = 0$ for the two sets of coefficients defining any two comparisons c_i and c_i', and for comparisons involving factor B, the test is $\Sigma \, (c_j)(c_j') =$

[8]Worked examples of trend analysis are available in numerous sources, including Kirk (1968, pp. 189-198), Lindman (1974, pp. 250-255), Myers (1979, pp. 445-452), Winer (1971, pp. 478-484), and the earlier edition of this book (pp. 225-234).

0 for the two sets of coefficients defining any two comparisons c_j and c'_j. If the comparisons used to create different interaction comparisons are orthogonal by this simple test, the interaction comparisons themselves will be orthogonal as well.

In Chapter 6, I considered an important property of orthogonal comparisons, namely, the relationship between the number of degrees of freedom associated with the treatment sum of squares in the single-factor design (SS_A) and the maximum number of mutually orthogonal comparisons that can be based on the treatment means. This same relationship holds for the factorial design. More specifically, the maximum number of orthogonal *interaction comparisons* that can be extracted from any given interaction sum of squares $SS_{A \times B}$ is equal to the degrees of freedom associated with this source of variability; that is, $df_{A \times B} = (a - 1)(b - 1)$. An example of this particular relationship is presented in Appendix C-2 (pp. 626-627).

What about orthogonality and the selection of analytical comparisons in the systematic analysis of interaction? My response to this question is identical to my response to the same question asked of analytical comparisons in the single-factor design. That is, single-df comparisons, whether appearing in the analysis of a single-factor experiment or in the analysis of a multifactor one, need not be mutually orthogonal. Instead, the set of comparisons selected by a researcher is usually dictated by the logic of the experimental design and the research hypotheses rather than by an overriding concern for mutual orthogonality.

11.5 A SUMMARY OF THE ANALYSIS OF INTERACTION

It should be clear by now that a factorial experiment provides a wealth of information beyond that found with the overall analysis of variance. Not all analyses are relevant to all factorial experiments, since the nature of the experimental design and your research questions will lead you to a particular collection of tests. It is important to maintain a general understanding of the analyses—what they measure and what information they yield—so that you can incorporate them into your thinking as you plan an experiment. In this section, I will summarize the important techniques for analyzing interaction. You should try to see how the isolation of different facets of the original AB matrix of treatment means helps to analyze the nature of any given interaction.

Analysis of Simple Effects

An analysis of simple effects usually flows directly from the original rationale for a factorial experiment, namely, an extension of an independent variable studied in a single-factor design to a factorial design in which the variable is manipulated in conjunction with a second independent variable. Does the first independent variable "behave" the same under different levels of the second independent variable?

This question focuses directly on the simple effects. If the interaction is significant, the simple effects are not the same and analyses are undertaken to identify the pattern of these differences. An analysis of simple effects consists of slicing the *AB* matrix unidimensionally into a set of single-factor experiments—either a set of experiments reflecting the variation of factor *A* with factor *B* held constant, or a set reflecting the variation of factor *B* with factor *A* held constant. Usually, we do not need to conduct both.

The nature of the analysis of simple effects is illustrated in Table 11-11. The original factorial design appears in the top left side of the table. The X's appearing in each of the cells of the *AB* matrix indicate that the entire set of *AB* treatment means is under examination, as would be the case for testing the significance of the overall *A* × *B* interaction. Let's assume that the interaction is significant and that simple effects are the next logical step in the analysis. If factor *A* represents the manipulation of interest in this analysis, we look systematically at each row of the *AB* matrix and then at specific simple comparisons if the within-row differences (simple effects) are significant. The stages in this particular analysis are diagramed with the matrices on the right using X's to indicate the cell means relevant to the analysis. For simplicity, I have indicated only one simple comparison following the discovery of a significant simple effect. There may be others that will be relevant, of course, and they do not necessarily have to be the same for each row of the matrix. Depending on the outcome of this analysis, however, it may be necessary to conduct further tests to determine whether a significant comparison at one level of factor *B* is statistically different from the outcome observed with the same comparison at the other levels of factor *B*. (See pp. 220–221 for a discussion of this point.)

The analysis of the other set of simple effects, diagramed beneath the original factorial, is indicated to complete the picture. In this case, the *AB* matrix is divided into single-factor experiments involving the other independent variable (factor *B*). Again, we would probably follow a significant simple effect with additional comparisons in an attempt to isolate the factors responsible for the significant effect.

Analysis of Interaction Comparisons

Interaction comparisons are planned comparisons which can be conducted instead of a test of the overall *A* × *B* interaction. Rather than working with the total *AB* matrix at the outset, we conceive of the design as a series of smaller, more analytically focused factorial designs. A particularly meaningful single-*df* comparison involving either (or both) of the two independent variables guides us to a new factorial created by the comparison (or comparisons). This transformed factorial provides a refined look at the overall *A* × *B* interaction, one that focuses on particularly meaningful ways of viewing the original manipulation.

If the interaction comparison is created by transforming one of the independent variables into a single-*df* comparison, we have a partial factorial design. Two

Table 11-11   Schematic Diagram of the Analysis of Simple Effects

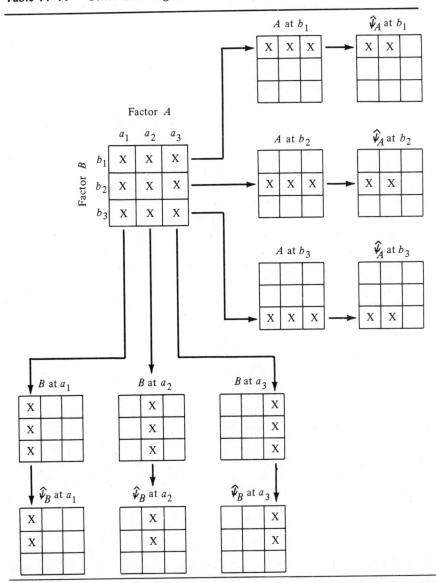

partial factorials, one formed by crossing a comparison involving factor A with factor B ($A_{comp.} \times B$) and the other formed by crossing a comparison involving factor B with factor A ($A \times B_{comp.}$), are diagramed in Table 11-12. Along the top of the table, you can see the formation of a partial factorial from an $A_{comp.}$ and then an additional analysis of the simple comparisons if the interaction is significant. (Only one simple comparison is shown, to simplify the display.) Along the left

237

Table 11-12 Schematic Diagram of the Analysis of Interaction Comparisons

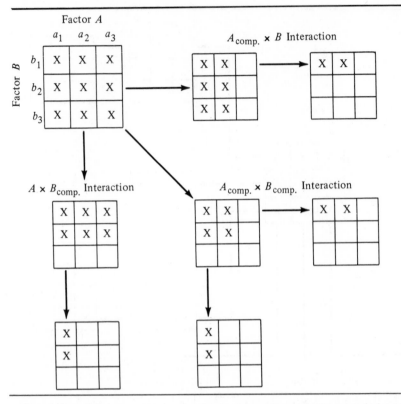

side of the table, you can see the same systematic analysis extended to the other independent variable. Finally, on the diagonal extending from the AB matrix, we have the most refined of the interaction comparisons—the interaction contrast—formed by crossing a comparison involving factor A with a comparison involving factor B. Again, simple comparisons are indicated in the table to follow if the $A_{comp.} \times B_{comp.}$ interaction is significant.

Comments

This summary of the detailed analysis of interaction is not intended to imply that the analysis of a factorial experiment is characterized by the mechanical application of these analysis techniques to the results of an experiment. I consider a research plan theoretically motivated and inspired where the researcher attempts to follow up significant findings in an illuminating manner. It takes practice to use these analyses productively, but the time spent mastering these basic analyses will greatly increase the usefulness of the factorial design as a device for discovering new relationships between independent variables and behavior.

11.6 OTHER PARTIAL FACTORIALS

Interaction comparisons are usually based on single-df contrasts applied to either one of the two independent variables (in the case of partial factorials) or to both independent variables simultaneously (in the case of interaction contrasts). Occasionally, a particular manipulation may suggest an analysis involving more than one degree of freedom. I considered the analysis of this sort of comparison in Chapter 6 (pp. 123-124), with an example consisting of a variation in types of incentives—verbal praise, monetary reward, and extra credit—and the inclusion of a control condition in which no specific incentives were received. A natural subdivision of this particular independent variable is a comparison among the three incentive conditions ($df_{set} = 2$) and a comparison between the combined incentive conditions and the control ($df_{comp.} = 1$). When this sort of independent variable is included as part of a factorial design, the same logic justifying these two comparisons can be extended to the analysis of the factorial.

To illustrate, suppose factor B consisted of three types of problems so that the design became a 4 $\times$ 3 factorial (4 incentive conditions $\times$ 3 types of problems). From this experiment, we could form two partial factorial designs, one forming a 3 $\times$ 3 factorial to isolate the three incentive conditions, and the other forming a 2 $\times$ 3 factorial to combine the three incentive conditions for a comparison with the control condition. The analysis of the 2 $\times$ 3 partial factorial follows the procedures outlined in Section 11.4 (pp. 222-227). The analysis of the 3 $\times$ 3 partial factorial requires a different approach.

This latter statistical analysis is most easily accomplished by extracting that part of the AB matrix that is relevant to the 3 $\times$ 3 partial factorial and conducting a normal analysis of variance based only on the sums appearing in this new matrix. All of the analyses appropriate for a factorial design in general can be conducted on this partial factorial; the formulas are easily adapted by redefining the notation to reflect the changes in the new matrix. The error term for this analysis is the pooled within-groups mean square from the *total* design ($MS_{S/AB}$), and the degrees of freedom associated with this error term remain unchanged. A numerical example of this type of partial factorial can be found in Exercise 5 at the end of this chapter.

11.7 CORRECTIONS FOR FAMILYWISE ERROR

Familywise type I error becomes relevant the instant a researcher conducts more than one statistical test in the analysis of an experiment. Familywise error (FW), you will recall from Chapter 8, refers to the probability of making at least one type I error in a set of statistical tests. Any increase in the number of statistical tests conducted, therefore, results in an increase in FW error as well. Familywise error is the inevitable penalty associated with conducting additional comparisons. On the other hand, inhibiting this exploration of a set of data, or making it more difficult to reject the null hypothesis, incurs a different sort of penalty, namely, an increase in type II error. Any solution to this problem requires finding some way to come to terms with the two types of errors of statistical inference. I will discuss the problem and offer suggestions that take into consideration the judicious balancing of the two types of error.

Planned Comparisons

Planned comparisons of some sort are usually found in the analysis of factorial experiments. Certainly the tests of the standard factorial effects, i.e., the two main effects and the interaction, qualify as planned comparisons. That is, the very nature of the design implies that these three tests were planned before the data were collected. It is common practice in psychology to disregard the increase in *FW* error associated with these three tests.

Planned comparisons in the form of simple effects and interaction comparisons are still not common in psychology. One reason for the relative infrequency of such planned comparisons undoubtedly is psychologists' general lack of familiarity with the statistical techniques and procedures—especially in the case of interaction comparisons. In my opinion, the planning of simple effects and interaction comparisons should be as common in designing a factorial experiment as are single-*df* comparisons in the designing of a single-factor experiment.

What about *FW* correction procedures for these sorts of planned comparisons? A logical extension of the arguments I offered in Chapter 8 concerning planned comparisons and the single-factor design would be to test planned comparisons with the factorial design at the usual *PC* rate (α), without correction. If desired, a modified Bonferroni test (pp. 147–149) can be employed in order to hold the familywise error at a level determined by the degrees of freedom associated with the particular factorial effect under consideration (df_A or df_B when the analyses involve the marginal means and $df_{A \times B}$ when the analyses involve the interaction).

Familywise Correction for Post Hoc Comparisons

Definition of a Family. The early discussions of this topic, e.g., Ryan (1959), used the term "experimentwise" error to refer to what I am calling familywise error. Experimentwise error refers to the cumulative type I error potentially operating in the complete analysis of an experiment. The two terms refer to the same statistical concept when the design is a single-factor experiment. They refer to different concepts, however, when the design is a factorial. The reason for the later name change was to distinguish between a correction for cumulative type I error based on the *entire* factorial experiment (experimentwise correction) and a correction separately based on the standard factorial effects—main effects and interaction—traditionally extracted from the factorial (familywise correction). The familywise approach appears to be the most popular in contemporary research. What this means, then, is that investigators who choose to correct for cumulative type I error use as the point of reference the three major subdivisions (or families) of the factorial and permit *experimentwise error* to increase as a result. A reasonable defense of this procedure is that the main effects and interaction, which are orthogonal to one another, lead to distinctly different sets of analyses and ask entirely different sorts of questions.

Main Effects. The procedures discussed in Chapter 8 for the single-factor design are easily adapted to the detailed analysis of the two main effects. All that is necessary is to substitute the factorial error term $MS_{S/AB}$ for $MS_{S/A}$ in the single-factor formulas and remember to use $df_{S/AB}$ rather than $df_{S/A}$ when the degrees of freedom of the error term are relevant. The other change is to adjust for the increase in *sample size* when marginal means are involved. That is, the formulas in Chapter 8 assume that each treatment mean is based on a sample size of s. Marginal means are based on a larger number of observations—$(b)(s)$ for the $\bar{A}_i$'s and $(a)(s)$ for the $\bar{B}_j$'s—and the correction formulas are adjusted accordingly. In all other respects, the procedures are identical.

Interaction. The analysis of interaction can take many directions, as you have seen in this chapter. Since these directions will vary depending on the nature of the two independent variables and the sorts of comparisons that are meaningful and of interest to a researcher, it is impossible to offer a general plan that will work satisfactorily in all research situations. One could take an extreme position and apply the Scheffé test as a maximum safeguard against type I errors. Under this plan, which is probably appropriate only in a "data-snooping" expedition in which all possible single-*df* comparisons are of potential interest, the obtained F ratios are evaluated against

$$F_S = [(a)(b) - 1]\, F(df_{num.}, df_{denom.}), \qquad (11\text{-}19)$$

where the F refers to the critical value of F obtained from the F table with $df_{num.} = (a)(b) - 1$ and $df_{denom.} = df_{S/AB}$. The significance level chosen sets the maximum value that α_{FW} will take if all possible comparisons are conducted. This is not a realistic correction, however, for research that is characterized by a limited number of meaningful and theoretically interesting comparisons.

Cicchetti (1972) describes an adaptation of the Tukey test for comparisons between *pairs of cell means*. His procedure eliminates from consideration all pairwise differences formed by crossing either a row or a column boundary, for example, $\overline{AB}_{11}$ versus $\overline{AB}_{23}$, since such comparisons are generally uninterpretable because of the simultaneous change of the levels of *both* independent variables. His correction is based instead on all pairwise comparisons that stay within either set of boundaries. As a result, the correction is considerably smaller than one based on the entire set of pairwise differences that can be formed from the $(a)(b)$ cell means. The Scheffé test can be modified in a similar fashion (Keppel, 1973, pp. 244-246).

A procedure designed for interaction comparisons has been proposed and illustrated by Boik (1979). What he proposes is to evaluate partial interactions and interaction contrasts using a Scheffé-like correction. The example chosen by Boik to illustrate the analyses and the corrections is one that leads to a thoughtful analysis of the significant overall interaction but, I should point out, could have just as easily been conducted as a theoretically motivated set of *planned* comparisons. More specifically, his factor A consisted of two forms of therapy (a_2 and a_3) and a baseline condition with no therapy (a_1), and his factor B consisted of the systematic variation in the dose level of some antianxiety medication (b_1 received a placebo, b_4 received the maximum dose, and the other two levels were given intermediate doses). The planned comparisons of interest in this example should be obvious to you by now.

Comments

You are certainly more on your own when the topic of familywise error is raised in the planning and analysis of a factorial experiment than was the case with the single-factor experiment. In either situation, you will have to set your own criteria and worry about the consequences stemming from your decision. But there has been considerably less discussion of the problem with the factorial design. Current practice in psychological research favors the use of planned comparisons without correction for *FW* rate. Certainly, more discussion of the problem of *FW* error is needed so that researchers can see clearly the issues at stake and the long-term consequences of alternative solutions to the problem.

If corrections for *FW* are viewed as desirable in a given piece of research, I suggest the use of the procedure introduced in Chapter 8, which specifies three possible decisions following the calculation of the test statistic. If we let CV_{FW} represent the critical value associated with the rejection region established by an *FW* correction technique and CV_α, the critical value associated with the rejection region for planned comparisons, we can state the three decision rules as follows:

If the test statistic $\geqslant CV_{FW}$, reject H_0.

If the test statistic falls between CV_α and CV_{FW}, suspend judgment.

If the test statistic $< CV_\alpha$, do not reject H_0.

For further information on this three-tier decision process, see the discussion in Section 8.4 (pp. 162–164).

11.8 EXERCISES[9]

1. An experimenter is interested in the effects of alcohol on aggressive behavior in fish. There are to be four treatment conditions: no alcohol, laboratory alcohol, and two commercial brands of whiskey known to contain large amounts of

[9]The answers to these problems are found in Appendix B, beginning on p. 574.

various impurities valued for their distinctive contribution to the taste and smell of the two whiskeys. A fish is placed in a tank containing the appropriate substance and after a period of time is exposed to another fish introduced into the tank in a clear plastic tube. Aggression is measured by the number of bites directed toward the other fish during a 5-minute testing period. A second independent variable, the length of exposure to the water in the testing tank, is combined factorially with the alcohol variable. This variable will consist of five levels, namely, lapses of 2, 4, 6, 8, and 10 minutes before the second fish is introduced into the tank.

(a) What meaningful questions can the experimenter consider in analyzing the main effects of the alcohol variable?

(b) What information is provided by a trend analysis of the main effects of the exposure variable?

(c) How can these two sets of comparisons be combined to study the interaction of these two variables analytically? What will each analysis tell you?

2. Suppose an experiment is conducted in which three strains of rats are to be compared. One strain was obtained by selectively breeding rats that performed exceptionally well in a maze-learning task (the "bright" rats); a second strain was obtained by selectively breeding rats that performed quite poorly in the same task (the "dull" rats); and a third strain consisted of rats that were bred without regard for maze-learning performance (the "mixed" rats). One group from each strain was raised under "enriched" conditions, and a second group was raised under "impoverished" conditions. Following 6 months of exposure to one of the two environments, all of the rats were tested in a standard laboratory maze. There were eight rats randomly assigned to each of the environments from each of the three strains. The response measure consisted of the trials needed to perform the maze without error. The following treatment means were obtained:

ENVIRONMENT (FACTOR B)	STRAIN (FACTOR A)		
	Bright	Mixed	Dull
Enriched	3.50	4.00	7.50
Impoverished	3.75	7.75	11.00

Assume that the statistical analysis indicates that the interaction is significant, leading us to concentrate on the individual treatment means rather than on the marginal means. For each of the following questions, identify the specific means to be compared; indicate whether the test is a simple effect, an interaction comparison, or a simple comparison; and calculate the mean square:

(a) Do the three groups of rats differ in learning performance when they have been reared in the enriched environment?

(b) Do the bright and mixed strains reared in the enriched environment differ in learning performance?

(c) What are the effects of the different environments on each of the three strains of rats?

(d) Are bright and mixed rats affected equally by the two different environments?

3. From the data appearing in Table 11–4 (p. 217),

(a) Test the significance of the simple effects of factor B.

(b) Show that the total sum of squares associated with the simple effects equals the sum of SS_B and $SS_{A \times B}$.

4. Below are listed the treatment means for three 2×2 factorial designs.

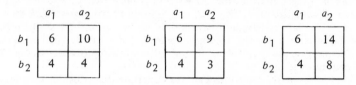

(a) In each case, how would an analysis of the simple effects of factor A help to pinpoint the nature of the interaction?

(b) What could you say about the significance of the interaction in the middle case if you were told that both simple effects of A are significant?

(c) What could you say about the significance of the interaction in the case on the right if you were told that both simple effects of A are significant? What could you say if only the simple effect at b_1 were significant?

5. In Section 6.5 we considered an experiment on the effects of different incentives on the solving of problems by fifth-grade students. We will consider the same experiment in the context of a factorial manipulation. Factor A consists of four levels (verbal praise, monetary reward, extra course credit, and no specific incentive), and factor B consists of two levels of problem complexity (simple and complex). There are $s = 5$ children randomly assigned to the eight treatment conditions. The response measure is the number of problems solved in 20 minutes. The sums for the different treatment groups are given below:

INCENTIVE CONDITIONS (A)

TASKS (B)	Verbal	Monetary	Course Credit	None
Simple	72	65	69	70
Complex	48	53	47	32

For this example, $\Sigma\,(ABS)^2 = 5,582$.

(a) Conduct an analysis of variance on these data.

(b) Given the nature of this experimental design, it is unlikely that a researcher would be interested in the analysis you conducted in part (a). Instead, certain partial factorials would be more desirable alternatives. An obvious analysis is to examine the partial factorial formed by crossing the three incentive conditions with the complexity variable. Test the significance of this interaction. What does this test reveal?

(c) On the basis of the results you obtained in part (b), you would probably consider next (or more likely have planned ahead of time) a partial factorial formed by crossing the comparison between the combined incentive conditions and the control conditions with the complexity variable. Test the significance of this interaction. What does this test reveal?

(d) Given the outcome of the test you conducted in part (c), evaluate the significance of the simple comparison involving the combined incentive and control conditions at both levels of factor B.

(e) On the basis of these various analyses, what conclusions can you draw from this study?

6. Consider an experiment in which performance on a task is studied as a function of pretraining experience. One independent variable consists of the amount of pretraining—3, 6, 9, and 12 trials (factor A)—and the other variable consists of the nature of the pretraining—facilitating or interfering (factor B). The outcome of this experiment is presented in Fig. 11-4 (p. 234). The treatment sums and the AB matrix are presented below:

	a_1	a_2	a_3	a_4	Sum
b_1	29	42	46	35	152
b_2	24	15	12	20	71
Sum	53	57	58	55	223

There were $s = 5$ subjects in each of the treatment conditions.

(a) Conduct an overall analysis of variance. Assume that $\Sigma\,(ABS)^2 = 1,613$.

(b) Since the $A \times B$ interaction is significant and factor A represents a quantitative manipulation, it is a natural next step to examine the trend components of the interaction. What does this analysis reveal?

(c) In part (b) you discovered that the quadratic component of the interaction is significant. An inspection of Fig. 11-4 suggests that this interaction results from the presence of a concave-downward trend at b_1 and a concave-upward trend at b_2. Are either of these simple quadratic trends significant?

7. Suppose we have a 2 × 2 factorial design with $s = 10$ subjects in each treatment condition and that we obtain the following cell sums:

	a_1	a_2
b_1	30	80
b_2	40	20

(a) Calculate the SS_A, SS_B, and $SS_{A \times B}$.

(b) See if you can work out a way of calculating these same quantities by constructing a set of three single-df comparisons.

12

Other Types of Two-Factor Designs

This chapter deals with the analysis of completely randomized experiments involving two independent variables that, for various reasons, do not fit the standard factorial design we have been considering in the last three chapters. I will begin with a discussion of a factorial design in which one of the independent variables consists of an individual-difference, or subject, variable. Next, I will discuss factorial experiments that include a control condition outside the factorial manipulation and, consequently, do not fit the standard factorial analysis. As a third topic, I will consider the usefulness of redefining the levels of the independent variables in a factorial experiment in order to shift the focus of attention from the interaction to the main effects. Finally, I will examine an entirely different type of two-factor experiment in which the two independent variables do not cross, but are combined in an entirely different arrangement called **nesting**.

12.1 TREATMENTS X BLOCKS DESIGN

For the designs discussed so far in this book, individual differences are essentially allowed to remain unchecked. We assign subjects to the experimental treatments in a random fashion, so that a good subject is just as likely to be assigned to a particular condition as is a poor one. Obviously, we do not expect groups of subjects assigned this way to be equivalent on all critical subject characteristics. Some groups will be favored with the better subjects, some will not. There is no *bias*, however, since each treatment condition has equal probability of having high- and low-ability subjects.

One way to help the system "work" is to select subjects from the most *homogeneous population* possible. If, in a hypothetical situation, we were able to obtain a pool of perfectly matched subjects and then assigned these subjects randomly to the different conditions, we would feel quite confident that the groups were nearly equivalent at the outset. (There are still other factors that would be responsible for variability in the scores of subjects treated alike, such as variations in the testing environment, in the actual treatments, in the subjects themselves, and so on.) If we could assign subjects to the treatments from a homogeneous pool, there would be another related benefit: a marked reduction in the within-groups mean square. I will pursue this point in some detail, since the latter possibility holds great interest for the researcher.

The first step in accomplishing a reduction in error variance is to find some basis for the selection of subjects for our experiment. That is, we must identify those characteristics of subjects which are known to influence the behavior of interest and which may be measured *before* the start of the experiment. We can find examples of such characteristics in most areas of the behavioral sciences. In problem-solving experiments, for instance, we might turn to scores on intelligence tests or to grade-point averages. In psychophysical experiments, differences in sensory acuity might be considered an important matching variable. In educational research, social-class differences are a possibility, while in social psychology, differences in certain attitudes may be used by the investigator.

If we are able to identify important sources of individual differences before the start of the experiment, we can select a homogeneous group of subjects to serve in the study. We would randomly assign these selected subjects to the different treatment conditions. This type of procedure would reduce the within-groups variance by restricting the variation due to a particular subject characteristic that otherwise would be left unchecked in an experiment. We must be concerned, of course, about the potentially limited generalizability such a set of results would offer. That is, the treatment effects obtained with subjects of "average" intelligence or with subjects from middle-income-families might not be representative of the effects that would be obtained with subjects from other portions of the general population. To be more specific, there might be an *interaction* between the treatments and the subject characteristic that formed the basis for the selection. Fortunately, it is possible to avoid this difficulty and at the same time to maintain the advantage of homogeneous groupings of subjects.

The Treatments × Blocks design provides a solution to this problem of generalization by including more than one block of homogeneous subjects in the experiment. Rather than drawing a single group of subjects from one ability level, the blocks design includes groups of homogeneous subjects drawn from two or more ability levels. There are several different names for this sort of design, e.g., the **randomized blocks design**, the **Treatments × Levels design**, and the **stratified design**, but I will use the **Treatments × Blocks** designation, since it is particularly descriptive of the nature of the experimental design.

The Design and Analysis

Suppose we have a pool of 60 subjects available for an experiment and that there are $a = 4$ levels of the treatment factor (factor A). If we were conducting a completely randomized single-factor experiment, we would randomly assign $s = 15$ subjects to each of the four experimental conditions. On the basis of information available to us before the start of the experiment, let's assume that we can classify the 60 subjects into three blocks, each containing 20 subjects who are relatively homogeneous on the classification factor. The Treatments × Blocks design is formed by assigning the subjects within each block to the four experimental conditions, as diagramed in the upper portion of Table 12-1. (The Treatments × Blocks design appears on the right and the corresponding single-factor design appears on the left.)

We can view the Treatments × Blocks design as consisting of three independent experiments, one containing subjects of high ability, say, a second containing subjects of medium ability, and a third containing subjects of low ability. In each case, the subjects within each of these blocks are assigned randomly to the four treatment conditions. Note that the design was constructed in two steps: first an initial grouping of subjects into blocks, and then the random assignment of subjects within each block to the different treatments. In essence, the original single-factor

Table 12-1 Comparison of Blocked and Unblocked Single-Factor Experiments

COMPLETELY RANDOMIZED DESIGN					TREATMENTS X BLOCKS DESIGN			
Levels of Factor A					*Levels of Factor A*			
a_1	a_2	a_3	a_4	*Blocks*	a_1	a_2	a_3	a_4
$s = 15$	$s = 15$	$s = 15$	$s = 15$	b_1	$s = 5$	$s = 5$	$s = 5$	$s = 5$
				b_2	$s = 5$	$s = 5$	$s = 5$	$s = 5$
				b_3	$s = 5$	$s = 5$	$s = 5$	$s = 5$

SOURCES OF VARIANCE AND *df*'s

Source	df	Source	df
A	$a - 1 = 3$	A	$a - 1 = 3$
S/A	$a(s - 1) = 56$	B	$b - 1 = 2$
		$A \times B$	$(a - 1)(b - 1) = 6$
Total	$(a)(s) - 1 = 59$	S/AB	$(a)(b)(s - 1) = 48$
		Total	$(a)(b)(s) - 1 = 59$

experiment has become a two-factor design, factor A being completely crossed with the blocking factor (factor B in this example).

The sources of variance and corresponding *df*'s for the two designs are given in the lower portion of the table. As you can see, the analysis of this design requires no new computational procedures. We simply apply the formulas for the analysis of the completely randomized two-factor experiment. The sums of squares are extracted in the usual way and the error term is based upon a pooling of subjects within specific treatment-block combinations. This general type of design, in which blocking is introduced as an independent variable, may be extended to multifactor designs. All that the presence of blocks does is to increase by 1 the number of factors represented in the experiment.

The use of a blocking factor often results in an experiment that is more sensitive than the corresponding experiment without blocks. The error term in the completely randomized experiment of Table 12-1, $MS_{S/A}$, reflects the variability of subjects from populations in which the blocking factor is allowed to vary unchecked. In contrast, the error term for the Treatments X Blocks design, $MS_{S/AB}$, reflects the variability of subjects from populations in which variation in the blocking factor is greatly restricted. Additionally, any Treatments X Blocks interaction, which remains undetected in the completely randomized experiment (except for differences in within-group variances), is isolated and removed from the error term in the Treatments X Blocks design.

Designing Experiments with Blocking

Selecting the Blocking Factor. The primary criterion for selecting a subject characteristic that will form the basis for the blocking or grouping into homogeneous groups is a substantial correlation with the response measure (the dependent variable) in the experiment itself. The degree of error-term reduction is directly related to the size of this correlation. Other considerations may come into play, however. For example, there is the ease with which the information about the subjects can be obtained. Some measures may be readily accessible from school records, while others may require the administration of a test or an interview before they are available to the experimenter. Another consideration is theoretical. Some blocking factors may arouse theoretical interest in the prediction of certain interactions of the treatments and the blocking factor, while others may not. Still, if the researcher's main concern is the refinement of the error term, he or she will pay greatest attention to the first criterion—the correlation between the blocking factor and the behavior under study.

Methods of Blocking. We will assume that a blocking factor has been selected and that the scores are available before the start of the experiment. Two questions of immediate concern are (1) the number of blocks into which subjects will be classified and (2) the number of subjects in each block. We can have as many levels of the blocking factor as we wish, provided there are sufficient numbers of subjects in each block to assign *two* to each treatment condition. (We can have *one* subject per condition, but the analysis becomes more complicated.) As you will see subsequently, however, it is possible to make a rational choice concerning the optimal number of blocking levels in any given experiment.

With regard to the second question, most typically we will see equal numbers of subjects assigned to each blocking level and to each treatment condition within these blocks. Suppose we have four treatments in our experiment and we have 60 subjects available for testing. On the basis of IQ scores, say, we could divide these subjects into a number of different categories. Suppose we choose three categories formed by ranking the subjects in terms of IQ and designating the 20 subjects with the highest scores "high," the 20 with the next highest scores "medium," and the remaining 20 subjects "low." The subjects within each block would then be randomly assigned to the four treatments, with the restriction that there would be $s = 5$ subjects in each treatment condition.

There are variants of this procedure, of course.[1] If the blocks contain unequal numbers of subjects, as would be the case if the researcher wanted to preserve the underlying distribution in the population of the blocking factor, the assignment of subjects to conditions would still require equal numbers of subjects in each treatment condition within the blocks. While it may make sense to allow block size to vary, there is usually no reason to weight one treatment more heavily than another by assigning to it a greater proportion of the subjects.

---

[1]Lindquist (1953, pp. 127–132) presents a detailed discussion of alternative methods of constituting the levels of the blocking factor.

Optimal Number of Blocks. I have already asserted that the degree to which blocking results in a reduction of the error term, relative to the completely randomized design, depends on the magnitude of the correlation between the scores forming the basis of the blocking and the scores on the dependent variable. Not so obvious is the relationship between the efficiency of the design and a number of other factors—(1) the total number of subjects, (2) the number of treatment levels, and (3) the number of ability blocks. Although the interrelationships among these various factors are complex, it is possible to summarize them in such a way as to assist us in designing an experiment.

First, you should realize that in a large number of applications, most of these factors are effectively *constant* and cannot be changed. For example, we may have to "live" with the facts that there is a certain correlation between the pretest scores and the dependent variable, that our pool of available subjects may be limited and cannot be increased, and that the number of treatment levels is dictated to a large extent by the purpose of our experiment. What we *can* vary is the *number of blocking levels* that we include in the experiment. Given these restrictions, we want to select the number of levels that will achieve maximum precision.

Feldt (1958) has provided this information in a useful summary table, which is duplicated in Table 12-2. For different correlations between the scores on the blocking factor and scores on the dependent variable (.2, .4, .6, and .8), for two numbers of levels of factor A (2 and 5), and for various total sample sizes (20 to 150), the *optimal* numbers of blocks are tabulated. (The values in Table 12-2 have been rounded to the nearest integer.) For example, suppose we have 50 subjects available for our study and that we have five different treatment conditions. Under these circumstances, the optimal numbers of ability levels will be 2, 4, 5, and 5 for correlations of .2, .4, .6, and .8, respectively.

It will be noted that for some entries in the table it is not possible to obtain equal numbers of subjects for each treatment-block combination. If we have 50 subjects available, for instance, and a correlation of .4 and will include five treatment levels in the experiment, Table 12-2 indicates that four blocks will be optimal. Following this advice, we would have a total of 4(5) = 20 treatment-block combinations. But since there are only 50 subjects to apportion among these combinations, we will have to decide whether to use this optimal block size or not. If we decided in favor of the optimal block size, namely, $b = 5$, we would then set $s = 2$ and use only 40 subjects. On the other hand, in the interests of *power*, it may be better to use all subjects, with less than the optimal number of levels. Under these circumstances, then, we would have five blocks with $s = 2$ and would use all 50 subjects.

Feldt indicates that we can reasonably approximate combinations not presented in the table by means of linear interpolation for the number of treatment levels and the total number of available subjects. In order to obtain approximations for correlations not presented in the table, we should make the interpolation in terms of the squared correlation coefficient.[2]

----

[2] See Myers (1979, p. 155) for a detailed explanation of this procedure.

Table 12-2 Optimal Number of Blocks for Selected Experimental Conditions, Assuming Blocks Defined by Equal Proportions of the Population (from Feldt, 1958)[a]

CORRELATION[b]	TREATMENT LEVELS	TOTAL NUMBER OF SUBJECTS AVAILABLE					
		20	30	50	70	100	150
.2	2	2	3	4	5	7	9
	5	1	2	2	3	4	6
.4	2	3	4	6	9	13	17
	5	2	3	4	5	7	10
.6	2	4	6	9	13	17	25
	5	2	3	5	7	9	14
.8	2	5	7	12	17	23	25
	5	2	3	5	7	10	15

[a]By permission of the author and the editor of *Psychometrika*.
[b]Correlation between the pretest and the dependent variable.

Comments

The advantages of the Treatments X Blocks design are considerable. We may make an experiment more precise by eliminating from the error term sources of variance associated with the blocking factor. Additionally, the design allows an assessment of possible interactions between treatment effects and blocks. If such an interaction is significant, then we will know that the effects of the treatments do not generalize across the abilities or classification of subjects represented in the experiment. If these interactions are not significant, then we have achieved a certain degree of generalizability of the results.

Certain disadvantages of blocking must be mentioned also. First, there is the cost of introducing the blocking factor. Second, it may be difficult to find blocking factors that are highly correlated with the dependent variable used in the experiment. Finally, we must be concerned with the possible loss of power when the blocking factor is poorly correlated with the dependent variable. Suppose, for example, that there is no correlation between the pretest and the dependent variable. Under these circumstances, the error term will be based on sets of scores that are just as "heterogeneous" as those in a completely randomized experiment without blocking, and we will suffer a loss in power because there are fewer df associated with the error term in the block design than in the one without blocking. This discrepancy in error term df's increases with the number of blocks, the number of treatment levels, and the number of treatment factors. In this regard, Feldt (1958) concludes that it is more efficient to use the *unblocked* design when the correlation between the blocking factor and the dependent variable is *less than .2*. Again, if the assessment of Treatments X Blocks interactions is the primary purpose of the study, then a low correlation will not affect the decision to use randomized blocks in an experiment.

12.2 FACTORIAL DESIGNS WITH A SINGLE CONTROL CONDITION

Occasionally, a factorial experiment will be conducted in which a single control or baseline condition is included as a reference point against which the different factorial conditions will be compared. As an example, consider a problem-solving study in which factor A consists of two types of information (relevant or irrelevant) presented either by an authority figure or by a stranger (factor B) while a control group receives no information. We have, then, a 2 X 2 factorial with a single, or "outside," control group for a total of five treatment conditions. Let's see how we might analyze the results of this particular study.

We would begin the analysis with the factorial portion of the experimental design, extracting whatever information is necessary to describe the data fully. As a second step, we would perform single-df comparisons that include the control condition. At this point, it is useful to treat the experiment as a single-factor design and to use computational formulas that are appropriate for the now $a = 5$ treatment conditions. For a comparison between the control mean and the mean for the four combined factorial groups, for example, we could use $+1$ as the coefficient for the control mean and $-\frac{1}{4}$ as the coefficient for each of the four factorial groups. For a comparison between the control and a single factorial group, we could use $+1$ for the control, -1 for the factorial group, and 0 for the remaining three groups. If we designate the obtained mean difference for any comparison $\hat{\psi}$, the formula for the sum of squares associated with this comparison will be

$$SS_{\text{comp.}} = \frac{s(\hat{\psi})^2}{\Sigma (c_i)^2},$$

where s is the sample size and c_i refers to the coefficients for the comparison. (Remember that there are $a = 5$ coefficients in this part of the analysis.)

The error term for all of the analyses is a within-groups mean square that combines the within-group variance based on the control subjects with the within-group variance based on the subjects in each of the cells of the factorial. Again it is convenient to view the analysis in terms of a single-factor design. In this way, the standard formulas for the within-groups mean square would be used to calculate the error term. There will be $a = 5$ groups, each with $s - 1$ degrees of freedom, and the error term will have $5(s - 1)$ df.

As another example, consider an experiment in which several types of drugs (factor A) are combined with a number of dosage levels (factor B) to form a factorial design, while a single no-drug, or placebo, group serves as a reference condition against which all drug effects are compared. This situation, in which the factorial design includes a *quantitative* manipulation (dose) and the control represents zero dose, poses a special problem and requires a different sort of analysis from the one described initially in this section.

Suppose we include two drugs in this experiment with the intent to compare the drug-response curves and we plan to conduct a trend analysis in which the control condition represents the zero point on the dosage dimension. The problem for the analysis is that while the research question implies a factorial design that includes two control conditions with zero dosage, there is in fact only one. To be more specific, suppose drug dosage were varied as follows: 0 (control), .5, 1.0, and 1.5 milligrams. The dosage manipulation (factor B), then, would consist of $b = 4$ levels. With two drugs (factor A), the implied design is a 2 X 4 factorial, but the actual design is a 2 X 3 (dosages) plus a *single* control condition (zero dosage). The problem, then, is that one cell is missing from the AB matrix.

Several solutions are possible. For example, one could exclude the control condition from the trend analysis and base the determination of trend components on groups actually receiving the drug. The control would then be used for specific comparisons with the drug conditions. The analysis would resemble the one described for the first example. Another solution, suggested by Winer (1962, p. 264), uses the same control data twice to fill in the missing cell. Himmelfarb (1975) discusses these and other ways to analyze this sort of design.

12.3 REORGANIZATION OF INDEPENDENT VARIABLES

There are times when the clarity of an experimental design can be increased by "reorganizing" the independent variables. Consider an experiment studying the effects of environmental contexts on memory. Subjects learn material in one of two different contexts (X and Y) and then are tested later in one or the other context. The experimental design can be described as a 2 X 2 in which factor A consists of two learning contexts and factor B consists of two testing contexts. The design can be diagramed as follows:

TESTING CONTEXT (FACTOR B)	LEARNING CONTEXT (FACTOR A)	
	X (a_1)	Y (a_2)
X (b_1)	X–X	Y–X
Y (b_2)	X–Y	Y–Y

The theory under consideration is that performance will be better when learning-testing contexts are the same than when they are different. The expectation, then, is that the difference between a_1 and a_2 at b_1 will be in favor of a_1, where the learning-testing context is the same (X-X), while the difference between a_1 and a_2 at b_2 will be in favor of a_2, where the learning-testing context is also the same (Y-Y). The simple effect of factor A at b_1 is different from the simple effect of factor A at b_2, which means that the theory predicts an interaction between the two independent variables.

Many individuals have difficulty seeing or thinking in terms of an interaction. Suppose we changed the levels of one of the independent variables to "same context" and "different context." We would then have one of two arrangements:

TESTING CONTEXT (B)	LEARNING CONTEXT (A)	
	X (a_1)	Y (a_2)
Same (b_1)	X-X	Y-Y
Different (b_2)	X-Y	Y-X

TESTING CONTEXT (B)	LEARNING CONTEXT (A)	
	Same (a_1)	Different (a_2)
X (b_1)	X-X	Y-X
Y (b_2)	Y-Y	X-Y

The rearrangement on the left changes the levels of factor B to include under level b_1 the two treatment conditions in which the testing context is the *same* as the learning context—X-X for a_1 and Y-Y for a_2—and under level b_2 the two treatment conditions in which the testing context is different from the learning context—X-Y for a_1 and Y-X for a_2. The rearrangement on the right reorganizes factor A along similar lines. Under level a_1 are the two treatment conditions in which learning and testing contexts are the same, while under level a_2 are the two treatment conditions in which the two contexts are different. It is important to note that this type of rearrangement of the independent variables does not change the specific treatments given to the individual groups—in each of these 2 X 2 designs the same four combinations of learning and testing contexts are present, namely, X-X, Y-Y, X-Y, and Y-X. What has changed is the way the manipulations are *described*. In the original design, the question of interest was examined by the $A \times B$ interaction. In the reorganized design on the left, the same question is expressed as the main effect of factor B (same versus different testing context); in the reorganized design on the right, the question is expressed as the main effect of factor A (same versus different learning context).

Reorganizing independent variables in this manner does not change the statistical outcome of a particular theoretical question. As you have seen, what does change is the factorial effect that expresses it. The advantage of the reorganization is to increase communication with others in bridging the gap between the research question and the relevant statistical test.

Examples of designs that might benefit from reorganizing independent variables are found in many fields of research. The learning-memory field provides numerous instances. We have examined one. Another example from this field includes experiments concerned with the effects of memory cues that either correspond or do not correspond to the cues present during learning. In the drug literature, experiments on state-dependent memory are often treated as reorganized designs. For example, subjects learn some task in either a sober or an intoxicated state and are tested on that task some time later under one or the other state of intoxication. In these studies the interest lies in determining whether performance is better when the two drug states during learning and subsequent testing are the same (sober-sober and intoxicated-intoxicated) than when they are changed (sober-intoxicated and intoxicated-sober).[3]

12.4   NESTED INDEPENDENT VARIABLES

When a researcher manipulates more than one independent variable in an experiment, a factorial design is generally employed. As you know, factorial designs are characterized by including all possible combinations of the levels of the independent variables manipulated in the experiment. Another type of multifactor design is one in which an independent variable is **nested** within the levels of another independent variable. For an example, consider a concept-attainment task in which conjunctive and disjunctive problems (factor A) are to be compared. Most experimenters would probably represent each problem type with a number of different instances, which I will designate factor B. Factor A and factor B are not combined factorially in this design, since the set of instances representing either problem type is *uniquely defined* by the characteristics of that particular type. For all practical purposes, therefore, the set of conjunctive problems is independent of the set of disjunctive problems. This same sort of independence is not present in the factorial design, however, since each factor is *consistently defined* at all levels of the other factor in the experiment. In this example, then, instances are nested within problem types; we will use the symbol B/A (read "B within A" or "B nested in A"), where the letter to the *left* of the diagonal designates the *nested* factor while the letter to the *right* of the diagonal designates the factor within which the nesting occurs.[4]

It may have occurred to you that we have already seen an example of a nested factor—namely, the within-groups factor. In a single-factor design, for example, we can isolate variability due to factor A and to the pooled variability of subjects treated alike. While this latter source does not represent an independent variable of the sort we have considered, "subjects" can be thought of as a factor

---

[3]Shaffer (1977) discusses the reorganization of independent variables in detail and offers a relatively simple rule that can be used to accomplish the translation easily.

[4]In some references, this nested factor would be represented as $B(A)$.

consisting of *s* different levels (i.e., *s* different subjects). "Subjects" does *not* cross with the levels of factor *A*—there is a different collection of *s* subjects in each of the *a* levels of the independent variable. Since the definition or meaning of "subjects" as a factor is different at each level of factor *A*, it qualifies as a nested factor. (This is why one refers to this source of variance as *S/A*, the variability of subjects nested within factor *A*.) One way that subjects could be made to cross with factor *A* is to have each of *s* subjects serve in *all* of the *a* treatment conditions. With this sort of arrangement, we would have an *A × S* (*S* for subjects) factorial, with each subject represented at all levels of factor *A*. I will discuss this type of design in Chapter 17.

We will examine the analysis of the two most common forms of nesting found in the behavioral sciences, the nesting of control, or generalization, factors and the nesting of subject groupings. Quite complicated forms of nesting are occasionally found in contemporary research, but the procedures followed in the analysis of the simpler forms of nesting can be readily generalized to the more complex forms. General rules for this extension are provided in Appendix C-4 (pp. 635–642). Also, you will find complex examples of nesting discussed in a number of readily available sources, e.g., Glass and Stanley (1970, pp. 474–482), Kirk (1968, pp. 229–236), Lindman (1974, Chapter 8), Myers (1979, Chapter 9), and Winer (1971, pp. 359–366, 464–468).[5]

Nesting of Control (or Generalization) Factors

Control (or generalization) factors are independent variables that are introduced either to afford a necessary balancing of stimulus materials within an experiment or to provide an increase in the generalizability—also known as the *external validity*—of the results of the study. This class of independent variables holds little systematic interest for the researcher. A control factor becomes nested when the levels of that factor are uniquely defined at the levels of another factor, usually the independent variable of primary interest. The experiment that I considered earlier contrasting two types of conceptual tasks, is an example of this type of nesting. There, the introduction of a number of examples of each type of problem represented the nested control factor.

The Statistical Analysis. I will consider the statistical analysis of this type of nesting in the context of a numerical example, which is based on an experiment reported by Underwood and Richardson (1956).[6] The part of the experiment we will examine involves determining the relative learning difficulty of four different lists of nonsense syllables that are to be learned in a fixed serial order. These different lists constitute factor *A*. For reasons connected with other purposes of the experiment, Underwood and Richardson included a control factor, namely, the serial order of the nonsense syllables within the different lists. There were 10 orders of

---

[5]You will sometimes find nested designs discussed under the classification of "hierarchical" or "hierarchal" designs, which represent a particular form of nesting.
[6]The data for this example were kindly furnished by Dr. Benton J. Underwood.

each basic list. Since the syllables in one list were unrelated to the syllables in the other lists, the serial orders of the syllables are nested within each of the four lists. I will designate the control factor B/A.

The design of the experiment is diagramed in Table 12-3. You will note that factor B consists of the same number of levels ($b = 10$) at each of the $a = 4$ levels of factor A, which was necessary in this particular experiment—for reasons I cannot go into—but also is desirable in general, since the analysis would be more complicated if this balancing were not present. I have introduced a slightly different notation to designate levels of the nested factor. The first subscript refers to a particular level of factor B, in this case one of the 10 serial orders of a particular list. The subscript in parentheses refers to the particular condition of factor A that has been scrambled serially 10 times. Thus, $b_{9(1)}$ refers to the ninth serial list associated with level a_1, and $b_{3(4)}$ refers to the third serial list associated with level a_4. The parentheses serve the same function as the diagonal line I introduced earlier, i.e., to signify the exact nature of the nesting.

The results of the experiment are summarized in the table. The response measure consists of the number of trials needed to attain one perfect recitation of the serial list. Each entry in a cell of this matrix represents a *sum* of the learning scores for $s = 10$ subjects receiving a particular list and list order. The treatment total for any level of factor A is A_i, which is based on $(b)(s) = (10)(10) = 100$ observations. The grand sum T is based on the scores of all the subjects, which in this case is $(a)(b)(s) = (4)(10)(10) = 400$. The sum of all the individual scores, which are not presented, is $\Sigma (ABS)^2 = 445{,}317$.

Table 12-3   Nesting of a Control Factor

EXPERIMENTAL TREATMENTS (FACTOR A)							
a_1		a_2		a_3		a_4	
List (b/a_1)	Sum	List (b/a_2)	Sum	List (b/a_3)	Sum	List (b/a_4)	Sum
$b_{1(1)}$	277	$b_{1(2)}$	207	$b_{1(3)}$	520	$b_{1(4)}$	277
$b_{2(1)}$	270	$b_{2(2)}$	187	$b_{2(3)}$	413	$b_{2(4)}$	295
$b_{3(1)}$	269	$b_{3(2)}$	206	$b_{3(3)}$	503	$b_{3(4)}$	197
$b_{4(1)}$	331	$b_{4(2)}$	178	$b_{4(3)}$	461	$b_{4(4)}$	223
$b_{5(1)}$	305	$b_{5(2)}$	172	$b_{5(3)}$	385	$b_{5(4)}$	232
$b_{6(1)}$	273	$b_{6(2)}$	204	$b_{6(3)}$	361	$b_{6(4)}$	195
$b_{7(1)}$	383	$b_{7(2)}$	222	$b_{7(3)}$	330	$b_{7(4)}$	280
$b_{8(1)}$	372	$b_{8(2)}$	167	$b_{8(3)}$	446	$b_{8(4)}$	260
$b_{9(1)}$	233	$b_{9(2)}$	167	$b_{9(3)}$	419	$b_{9(4)}$	297
$b_{10(1)}$	205	$b_{10(2)}$	217	$b_{10(3)}$	419	$b_{10(4)}$	330
Sum	2,918	Sum	1,927	Sum	4,257	Sum	2,586
Mean	29.18	Mean	19.27	Mean	42.57	Mean	25.86

We calculate first the treatment sum of squares SS_A as follows:

$$SS_A = \frac{\Sigma A^2}{(b)(s)} - \frac{T^2}{(a)(b)(s)} \tag{12-1}$$

$$= \frac{(2,918)^2 + (1,927)^2 + (4,257)^2 + (2,586)^2}{(10)(10)}$$

$$- \frac{(2,918 + 1,927 + 4,257 + 2,586)^2}{(4)(10)(10)}$$

$$= 370,374.98 - 341,523.36 = 28,851.62.$$

The next sum of squares reflects the variability of the nested factor. This source is made up of four parts, one for each level of factor A. At level a_1, for example, the nested factor (B/A_1) consists of the variability of each of the ten $\overline{AB}_{j(1)}$ means from their mean, i.e., the column or treatment mean $\overline{A}_1$. (You may have noticed that this quantity is identical to the *simple effect of B* at a_1 in an equivalent 4×10 factorial design.) The computational formula for the sum of squares, based on sums rather than means, is as follows:

$$SS_{B/A_1} = \frac{\Sigma (AB_{j(1)})^2}{s} - \frac{A_1^2}{(b)(s)}. \tag{12-2}$$

You will recognize a familiar set of operations. The first basic ratio on the right of the equals sign focuses on the 10 cell totals at level a_1, which are squared, summed, and divided by s, the numer of observations contributing to any one of the cell sums. The second basic ratio involves the column sum A_1, which is squared and divided by the number of observations contributing to the sum, namely, $(b)(s)$. As with the analysis of simple effects, you can think of this sum of squares as being based on a single-factor experiment involving factor B with factor A held constant at a_1. If you used the computational formula for the treatment source of variance from Chapter 2, you would obtain exactly the same numerical quantity as we will with this formula.

I will now substitute the relevant sums from Table 12-3 into the computational formula for this nested sum of squares. More specifically,

$$SS_{B/A_1} = \frac{(277)^2 + (270)^2 + \cdots + (233)^2 + (205)^2}{10} - \frac{(2,918)^2}{(10)(10)}$$

$$= 88,049.20 - 85,147.24 = 2,901.96.$$

The computational formulas for the remaining three nested factors are obtained in the same way. At level a_2, the nested factor B/A_2 consists of the variability of each of the ten $\overline{AB}_{j(2)}$ means from the $\overline{A}_2$ treatment mean. The nested factors at levels a_3 and a_4 represent the same sort of variability. Again you will note that each of these nested factors refers to the simple effects of B at levels a_2, a_3, and a_4, respectively, in an equivalent factorial design. Continuing with the calculations, we find

$$SS_{B/A_2} = \frac{\Sigma (AB_{j(2)})^2}{s} - \frac{A_2^2}{(b)(s)}$$

$$= \frac{(207)^2 + (187)^2 + \cdots + (167)^2 + (217)^2}{10} - \frac{(1{,}927)^2}{(10)(10)}$$

$$= 37{,}528.90 - 37{,}133.29 = 395.61;$$

$$SS_{B/A_3} = \frac{\Sigma (AB_{j(3)})^2}{s} - \frac{A_3^2}{(b)(s)}$$

$$= \frac{(520)^2 + (413)^2 + \cdots + (419)^2 + (419)^2}{10} - \frac{(4{,}257)^2}{(10)(10)}$$

$$= 184{,}398.30 - 181{,}220.49 = 3{,}177.81;$$

and

$$SS_{B/A_4} = \frac{\Sigma (AB_{j(4)})^2}{s} - \frac{A_4^2}{(b)(s)}$$

$$= \frac{(277)^2 + (295)^2 + \cdots + (297)^2 + (330)^2}{10} - \frac{(2{,}586)^2}{(10)(10)}$$

$$= 68{,}725.00 - 66{,}873.96 = 1{,}851.04.$$

The overall nested factor B/A is simply a sum of the $a = 4$ nested sums of squares we have just obtained. Thus,

$$SS_{B/A} = \Sigma SS_{B/A_i}$$

$$= 2{,}901.96 + 395.61 + 3{,}177.81 + 1{,}851.04 = 8{,}326.42.$$

The within-groups sums of squares for this nested design is identical to the within-groups sum of squares for an equivalent $A \times B$ factorial. That is, in both designs, this sum of squares is based on the variability of subjects treated alike; in this particular design, the source consists of the variability of the $s = 10$ subjects contributing to each of the $(a)(b)$ cells in the design matrix. The calculation is straightforward, based on the deviation of each ABS score from the appropriate cell mean. Rather than calculate a within-cell sum of squares for each cell in the matrix, we can use the computationally simpler formula that we used to obtain the within-groups sum of squares in the factorial design. More specifically,

$$SS_{S/AB} = \Sigma (ABS)^2 - \frac{\Sigma (AB)^2}{s}, \tag{12-3}$$

which is identical to the corresponding formula for the factorial design, which you can verify by turning back to Table 10-4 (p. 194). The first quantity specified by Eq. (12-3) was provided earlier; that is, $\Sigma (ABS)^2 = 445{,}317$. The second quantity requires the squaring and summing of the cell totals. Substituting in Eq. (12-3), we find

$$SS_{S/AB} = 445{,}317 - \frac{(277)^2 + (270)^2 + \cdots + (297)^2 + (330)^2}{10}$$

$$= 445{,}317 - 378{,}701.40 = 66{,}615.60.$$

Finally, the total sum of squares, which is based on the deviation of each ABS score from the grand mean $\bar{T}$, is obtained in the normal way, namely,

$$SS_T = \Sigma (ABS)^2 - \frac{(T)^2}{(a)(b)(s)} \tag{12-4}$$

Since we have numerical values for both basic ratios specified by Eq. (12-4), we can calculate SS_T quite simply:

$$SS_T = 445{,}317 - 341{,}523.36$$

$$= 103{,}793.64.$$

The various sums of squares we have calculated are entered for summary purposes in Table 12-4.

The degrees of freedom for all sources of variance except the nested source are calculated in the normal way, i.e.,

$$df_A = a - 1; \quad df_{S/AB} = (a)(b)(s - 1);$$

and

$$df_T = (a)(b)(s) - 1.$$

The degrees of freedom associated with the nested factor B/A are equal to the sum of the degrees of freedom associated with the nested factor at each level of factor

Table 12-4   Summary of the Analysis

Source	SS	df	MS	Error Term	F
Treatments (A)	28,851.62	3	9,617.21	B/A	41.58*
Order/Treatments (B/A)	8,326.42	36	231.29	S/AB	1.25
S/AB	66,615.60	360	185.04	None	
Total	103,793.64	399			

*$p < .01$.

A. For any level of factor *A*, the degrees of freedom are equal to the number of levels of the nested factor *B* less 1. Summing this value over the *a* levels of factor *A* give us

$$df_{B/A} = (a)(b-1) . \qquad (12\text{-}5)$$

Substituting in these formulas, we obtain the numerical values presented in Table 12-4. The mean squares, calculated in the standard fashion, are also entered in the table.

Error Terms for the F Ratios. The error term for any *F* ratio in the analysis of variance depends on the assumptions of the statistical model upon which the analysis is based. We have been operating with the simplest model, namely, the fixed-effects model associated with the completely randomized factorial design. This model assumes that the levels of the independent variables are selected arbitrarily and systematically, which is generally the case in most—but not all—experimental research. With the assumption of fixed effects, and the distributional assumptions also specified by the model, the within-groups mean square is the appropriate error term for all of the analyses we have covered. If we adopted the fixed-effects model in this particular example of nesting, we would use the $MS_{S/AB}$ as the error term with which to evaluate the significance of the treatment source *A* and the nested source *B/A*.

However, this model is probably not appropriate for this type of design. Let's see why. The nested factor consists of $b = 10$ serial orders of a particular list of nonsense syllables at a given level of factor *A*. These 10 orders constitute only a small proportion of all possible orderings of this list. Some of these orderings will be more difficult to learn than others. Since we have included in this experiment what amounts to a small sample of all possible orderings, it is possible that this set of 10 lists may be easier (or harder) than the average based on all possible lists. We have no way of knowing. The same situation exists for each of the four basic lists constituting the levels of factor *A*.

What this means, therefore, is that some unknown portion of the variability attributed to factor *A* is influenced by chance factors associated with the selection of the 10 orderings for each level of factor *A*. If the average difficulty of the 10 lists at a_1, say, is greater than the average based on the total population of lists, $\overline{A}_1$ will be influenced adversely; on the other hand, if the average difficulty is less than the population average, $\overline{A}_1$ will be influenced positively. The same argument holds for each of the other *A* treatment means. You will note that this argument is similar to the one we considered when you were first introduced to the consequences of randomly assigning *subjects* to the different treatment conditions. In that case, it was argued that the groups would not be matched perfectly by this procedure, but that this inequality could be taken into consideration by the use of an error term that estimated uncontrolled chance factors directly. Here, however, the argument is a bit more complicated.

The treatment mean square MS_A is potentially influenced by *three*, rather than two, factors in this example of a nested design. More specifically, we have the null-hypothesis component—potential population treatment effects--and experimental error stemming from the same sources of chance factors I have discussed previously. But in addition, there is a third factor, representing the possible influence of the nested factor—in this case, differences in the inherent difficulty of the particular sets of serial orders selected independently for each treatment condition. In symbols,

$$E(MS_A) = \sigma_\epsilon^2 + s(\sigma_{B/A}^2) + b(s)(\theta_A^2).$$ (12-6)

Since the expected value of the within-groups mean square is

$$E(MS_{S/AB}) = \sigma_\epsilon^2,$$

you can see the problem, namely, that the usual error term is *too small,* since it does not include the effects of the nested factor. This makes sense as soon as you remind yourself that the within-groups mean square is based on the within-cell variability where subjects are all given the *same* list to learn. While this mean square adequately "captures" the usual experimental error σ_ϵ^2, it is uninfluenced by the differences in the difficulty of the different lists nested within factor A.

Fortunately, there is a simple way out of this problem—to use the nested mean square $MS_{B/A}$ as the error term. This mean square is potentially influenced by *two* sources of variability, experimental error *and* differences among lists of the same type. That is, $MS_{B/A}$ is also influenced by differences in the difficulty of lists drawn from the same basic pool, which in turn influence MS_A. In symbols,

$$E(MS_{B/A}) = \sigma_\epsilon^2 + s(\sigma_{B/A}^2).$$ (12-7)

Given this argument, then, the appropriate error term with which to evaluate the effects of factor A is the $MS_{B/A}$, since the expected value of the F ratio will be approximately 1 if the null hypothesis is false. Thus,

$$F = \frac{MS_A}{MS_{B/A}}.$$ (12-8)

In this example,

$$F = \frac{9,617.21}{231.29} = 41.58,$$

which is significant ($p < .01$). (The critical value of F is found with $df_{num.} = df_A = 3$ and $df_{denom.} = df_{B/A} = 36$.)

Comments. In this analysis, we viewed the nested factor as a *random* independent variable, an independent variable which is appropriately viewed as a random sample of levels selected from a larger population of potential levels. This random selection may not describe the actual procedures followed by Underwood and Richardson in constructing their serial orders, but the consequences of list construction fit this conceptualization reasonably well. In any case, the argument that the treatment mean square may reflect in part differences stemming from imperfect matching of list difficulty across the levels of factor A compels us to turn to an error term that takes this possibility into consideration. In short, Eq. (12-8) should be used whenever the nested factor can be thought of as a subset selected from a much larger set of possible levels.

It is also possible to evaluate the significance of the *nested* factor. In this case,

$$F = \frac{MS_{B/A}}{MS_{S/AB}} . \tag{12-9}$$

With these data,

$$F = \frac{231.29}{185.04} = 1.25,$$

which is not significant, $p > .10$. (In this case, $df_{num.} = df_{B/A} = 36$ and $df_{denom.} = df_{S/AB} = 360$.) We would conclude that the serial order of the lists, which is represented by the nested factor, does not constitute a significant source of variability in this particular experiment.

I should point out that this type of design requires that careful consideration about the nature of the independent variables be given before the start of the experiment. With random independent variables present in any type of experiment, the error terms will often have many fewer degrees of freedom that does the within-groups mean square. In this example, there were 36 degrees of freedom associated with $MS_{B/A}$ and 360 degrees of freedom associated with $MS_{S/AB}$. In most experiments, however, the degrees of freedom for the nested factor are considerably smaller than 36. This brings up the issue of power and what to do about the loss of power when the appropriate error term is $MS_{B/A}$ rather than $MS_{S/AB}$. In the planning stage, a useful approach is to increase the number of levels of the *nested* factor, even at the expense of the within-groups error term. For example, Underwood and Richardson could have used 20 lists at each level of factor A and 5 subjects per list. The degrees of freedom for the nested error term would have been $df_{B/A} = (a)(b - 1) = (4)(20 - 1) = 76$, while for the within-groups error term they would have been $df_{S/AB} = (a)(b)(s - 1) = (4)(20)(5 - 1) = 320$. The cost of preparing the additional materials necessitated by increasing the number of lists would have to be weighed against the potentially valuable increase in power that also results from this course of action. It is also possible to increase power by pooling the nested and within-groups sums of squares if the former source is not significant. The problem with this method of increasing power is that the implications of this sort of pooling are not fully understood by statisticians and cannot be counted on until *after* the data are collected. I will discuss this course of action later in this chapter (see pp. 269–270).

Finally, the issue of the statistical model and the appropriate error term has received considerable attention in certain areas of psychology where the nesting of control factors is commonly employed, e.g., psycholinguistics. While the arguments are similar to those discussed here, they are set in the context of within-subjects designs, where subjects serve in more than one of the conditions of the experiment, which greatly complicates the statistical model and the analysis of variance. I will consider this particular analysis in Chapter 21.

Nesting of Subject Groupings

In some experiments, it is convenient and even desirable to include independent subgroupings of subjects within the different treatment conditions. There are situations, for example, in which it makes better sense to administer the experiment to subgroups of subjects rather than to individual subjects. Usually, the group procedure provides efficiency over the running of the subjects individually. If two or more such groups are randomly assigned to each experimental condition, we have an example of the nesting of groups within treatments. Each of the groups is represented only once in one of the conditions of the experiment—they are *unique* to a single treatment condition.

We often see this sort of design employed when there is some attempt to sample groups from a much larger population, such as classes from a large school system or patients from different hospitals in a large city or in a state. It is not necessary that the subjects be tested in a group with group procedures, however. In the case of medical research, for instance, individual patients from several hospitals may be administered a particular treatment while patients from other hospitals are given different treatments. The fact that patients from any given hospital receive only one of the treatments, rather than being represented in all of the treatment combinations, signifies a nested design. In this case, hospitals are nested within treatment conditions.

Unfortunately, a serious design problem is often associated with this type of nesting, namely, the potential confounding of group differences and the experimental treatments. Suppose that an educator decides to compare a number of methods of teaching arithmetic (factor A) to children at a particular grade level. Let's assume that it is more convenient to administer one of the methods to the students in an entire classroom than to administer the different methods to an equal number of students in any given classroom. Suppose that this person locates three classes for the study and assigns them randomly each to a different method of teaching. A moment's reflection will lead to the realization that methods and classrooms are *completely confounded.*[7] That is, any differences observed at the end of the experiment might have resulted either from the differential effectiveness of the three methods, from differences in the arithmetic abilities of students in the three classes, or from both sources of differences. The situation begins to be corrected when more than one classroom is assigned to a particular method.

[7]Technically, this arrangement violates the assumption of the independence of observations required of the design.

One obvious reason for the existence of this problem lies in the fact that the formation of groups of subjects—classrooms, in this example—is usually not accomplished randomly, but rather more or less systematically. The criteria for particular group membership might very well have direct relevance to the performance under investigation. For instance, it is quite possible that the arithmetic skills of the children were one of the bases for assignment to a particular class. Another reason is the possibility that other factors might also affect performance. In this example, there are different teachers, different classroom experiences, even differences in the scheduling of training sessions that might have some influence on arithmetic performance. These kinds of problems are discussed in detail by Campbell and Stanley (e.g., 1966). A final source of difficulty, which may be quite serious when only one group is assigned to each treatment and all of the group members in each group are tested at the same time, is the effect of an unplanned event that affects groups differentially. An unannounced fire drill or an emotional outburst during testing could conceivably influence the performance of the subjects in one group and not those in the other groups. Glass and Stanley (1970, pp. 501–508) provide a useful discussion of this and other problems associated with the testing of intact groups.

Statistical Analysis. As an example of the nesting of groups within treatments, I will consider the results from an actual experiment.[8] In this study, subjects were given training on a list of unrelated words, followed by either 0, 2, 4, or 6 trials on a different set of words; then they were asked to recall all of the words they had learned in the experiment. The response measure of interest was the number of first-list words recalled. The independent variable, trials, will be called factor A. Subjects were run in groups of $s = 5$ subjects each. These groups consisted of volunteers who had agreed "independently" to serve in the experiment at the same time and date. The subjects within any group were treated identically. Twenty-four groups so formed were assigned in equal numbers to each of the four experimental conditions in a random fashion, six groups per condition. Since the different groups were independent of one another, *groups* is a factor (factor B) that is nested within each treatment condition; that is, B/A.

The results of this experiment are presented within the body of the AB matrix of Table 12-5. The entries in the matrix are the total numbers of words recalled by the 5 subjects within each subgroup. For these data, $\Sigma (ABS)^2 = 15,292$. An inspection of the totals for the four treatment conditions indicates that there was a progressive decline in first-list recall as the number of trials on the second list increased. That is, learning a second list has an increasingly deleterious effect on the memory for the first list.

The sources of variance obtained from this analysis are similar to those in the last section, namely, the treatment source (A), the subject-grouping factor B/A, and the variability of the subjects within each subgroup (S/AB).[9] Starting with the

---

[8]Postman and Keppel (1967).

[9]Some authors would designate this factor $S/B/A$ to emphasize the fact that subjects are nested within subgroups, which in turn are nested within treatments.

Table 12-5 Nesting of Subject Groupings

EXPERIMENTAL TREATMENTS (FACTOR A)							
0 Trials (a_1)		2 Trials (a_2)		4 Trials (a_3)		6 Trials (a_4)	
Groups (b/a_1)	Sum	Groups (b/a_2)	Sum	Groups (b/a_3)	Sum	Groups (b/a_4)	Sum
$b_{1(1)}$	85	$b_{1(2)}$	57	$b_{1(3)}$	45	$b_{1(4)}$	28
$b_{2(1)}$	66	$b_{2(2)}$	56	$b_{2(3)}$	41	$b_{2(4)}$	49
$b_{3(1)}$	58	$b_{3(2)}$	58	$b_{3(3)}$	45	$b_{3(4)}$	40
$b_{4(1)}$	80	$b_{4(2)}$	48	$b_{4(3)}$	32	$b_{4(4)}$	30
$b_{5(1)}$	74	$b_{5(2)}$	48	$b_{5(3)}$	49	$b_{5(4)}$	42
$b_{6(1)}$	77	$b_{6(2)}$	54	$b_{6(3)}$	33	$b_{6(4)}$	53
Sum	440	Sum	321	Sum	245	Sum	242
Mean	14.67	Mean	10.70	Mean	8.17	Mean	8.07

treatment source,

$$SS_A = \frac{\Sigma A^2}{(b)(s)} - \frac{T^2}{(a)(b)(s)}$$

$$= \frac{(440)^2 + (321)^2 + (245)^2 + (242)^2}{(6)(5)} - \frac{(440 + 321 + 245 + 242)^2}{(4)(6)(5)}$$

$$= 13{,}841.00 - 12{,}979.20 = 861.80.$$

This time I will calculate the nested factor B/A all at once, instead of calculating first the separate sums of squares and then summing them as in the first example of nesting we considered. More specifically,

$$SS_{B/A} = \frac{\Sigma (AB)^2}{s} - \frac{\Sigma A^2}{(b)(s)} \qquad (12\text{-}10)$$

$$= \frac{(85)^2 + (66)^2 + \cdots + (42)^2 + (53)^2}{5}$$

$$- \frac{(440)^2 + (321)^2 + (245)^2 + (242)^2}{6(5)}$$

$$= 14{,}105.20 - 13{,}841.00 = 264.20.$$

The within-groups sum of squares is calculated from Eq. (12-3):

$$SS_{S/AB} = \Sigma (ABS)^2 - \frac{\Sigma (AB)^2}{s}$$

$$= 15{,}292 - \frac{(85)^2 + (66)^2 + \cdots + (42)^2 + (53)^2}{5}$$

$$= 15{,}292 - 14{,}105.20 = 1{,}186.80.$$

From the calculations obtained previously, we can easily obtain the total sum of squares. That is,

$$SS_T = \Sigma\,(ABS)^2 - \frac{T^2}{(a)(b)(s)}$$

$$= 15{,}292 - 12{,}979.20 = 2{,}312.80.$$

These sums of squares are entered in Table 12-6 for a convenient summary of the analysis.

Tests of Significance. The degrees of freedom and mean squares are calculated with the same formulas as in the previous example. Again, we have the question concerning the appropriate error term with which to evaluate the treatment source of variance. Perhaps in this form of nesting you can see more easily that the nested factor is random and understand why this factor is the appropriate error term with which to test the significance of MS_A. Let's go over the argument again.

In the usual completely randomized single-factor design, MS_A is assumed to reflect the potential operation of two sources of variability, treatment effects and error variance. With this nested design, however, there is the possibility of a *third* component, the presence of an effect of the *nested* factor. In this experiment, the testing groups were not matched on any relevant factors; rather, groups were constituted by whatever factors were responsible for volunteers' signing up at the same time and date for a psychology experiment. There is every reason to believe, therefore, that real differences did exist among the 24 subgroups before the start of the experiment. We rely on the random assignment of the groups to conditions to spread these differences "evenly" (i.e., without bias) among the four treatment conditions. However, just as we do not expect the assignment of *subjects* to conditions in a completely randomized single-factor experiment to result in perfectly equivalent groups, we must not expect the assignment of *groups* to conditions to

Table 12-6   Summary of the Analysis

Source	SS	df	MS	Error Term	F
Trials (A)	861.80	3	287.27	B/A	21.75*
Groups/Trials (B/A)	264.20	20	13.21	S/AB	1.07
S/AB	1,186.80	96	12.36	None	
Total	2,312.80	119			

*$p < .01.$

accomplish this either. Thus, the MS_A may reflect in part group differences, in addition to any systematic treatment effects and error variance.

Given this argument, then, if we use the $MS_{S/AB}$ as the error term with which to evaluate the MS_A, there may be a *bias* in favor of rejecting the null hypothesis. That is, the MS_A can be thought to contain three components (treatment effects, group effects, and error variance) and the $MS_{S/AB}$ to contain one (error variance). When the null hypothesis is true, the treatment component drops out and we have a quantity in the numerator of the F ratio which is *not* an unbiased, independent estimate of error variance—it includes variance due to differences among the different groups as well. This bias is a *positive* bias, since it will result in the false rejection of the null hypothesis at a rate greater than that specified by α.

We can avoid this bias by finding an error term which contains *all* of the components present in the MS_A *except* the treatment component. Such a source is the $MS_{B/A}$, which reflects the group component *and* error variance. Thus, when the null hypothesis is *true*, the ratio

$$\frac{MS_A}{MS_{B/A}}$$

is distributed as F, with $df_{num.} = df_A$ and $df_{denom.} = df_{B/A}$. In the present example,

$$F = \frac{287.27}{13.21} = 21.75.$$

An inspection of the critical value of $F(3, 20)$ indicates that the null hypothesis is rejected handily.

The error term for the other mean square, the pooled nested effect, is the within-groups mean square $MS_{S/AB}$. The formation of this ratio tests the hypothesis that there are no systematic group differences. That is, when the null hypothesis is *true*, we have one estimate of error variance divided by another independent estimate of error variance, the result of which is distributed as $F(df_{B/A}, df_{S/AB})$. As indicated in Table 12-6, the hypothesis is not rejected.

Comment. I simply want to underscore the difficulty discussed earlier in the use of the nested factor as the error term in this sort of analysis, namely, the relatively small number of degrees of freedom associated with this source of variance. In the numerical example, this was not a serious problem, since there were six levels of the nested factor per treatment condition. But there would be a considerable loss of power if only two groups, e.g., classrooms or subgroups, were assigned to each of the different treatment conditions. The best solution to the problem is to reduce the size of the subgroups and to increase the number of groups to be assigned to the treatments. This tactic will increase power directly without requiring an increase in the total number of subjects tested. A post hoc procedure, which I mentioned earlier, is to consider pooling the two error terms following a preliminary testing of the statistical model underlying the analysis I have been discussing. Briefly, such a test consists of the evaluation of the significance of the *nested* factor

B/A at a less stringent significance level, for example, $\alpha = .10$ or $.25$. This action is taken to attempt to avoid making a type II error, i.e., failing to detect group differences when they are present. If the F is significant, then the nested factor is used to evaluate the significance of factor A; if the F is not significant, the nested factor and the within-groups factor are pooled to provide a more stable error term with which to evaluate the treatment effects. For a detailed description of the testing of statistical models and the pooling of sources of variance, see Kirk (1968, pp. 214-217), Myers (1979, pp. 233-234), and Winer (1971, pp. 378-384). Since the issues here are somewhat complicated, however, you should consider seeking advice if you are thinking of using this pooled mean square as your error term for evaluating the effects of the treatments.

12.5   EXERCISES[10]

1. As an example of a Treatments × Blocks design, consider the data presented in Exercise 1 of Chapter 2 (p. 42), in which there were $a = 5$ treatment conditions and $s = 10$ subjects randomly assigned to each condition. Suppose that 5 assistants had collected these data, each running a total of 10 subjects, 2 per condition. Experimenters can be treated as "blocks" and the data analyzed as a Treatments × Blocks design. The data, arranged by the $b = 5$ blocks, are presented in the following table:

EXPERIMENTERS (B) (BLOCKS)	TREATMENTS (A)				
	a_1	a_2	a_3	a_4	a_5
b_1	13	7	12	10	13
	9	4	11	12	6
b_2	8	4	4	9	14
	7	1	9	7	12
b_3	8	10	5	15	13
	6	7	10	14	10
b_4	6	5	2	10	8
	7	9	8	17	4
b_5	6	5	3	14	9
	10	8	6	12	11

   (a) Analyze the data as a Treatments × Blocks design.
   (b) Compare the results of this analysis with the single-factor analysis you completed in Exercise 3 of Chapter 3 (p. 64). What have you gained from this new analysis? What have you lost?
2. Suppose that an educator decides to compare three methods of teaching arithmetic (factor A) to children at a particular grade level. Six classes are available. For convenience, it was decided to use a nested design in which two

---

[10]The answers to these problems are found in Appendix B, beginning on p. 581.

classes are randomly assigned to each of the three methods. Let's assume that there are $s = 21$ students in each of these classes.

(a) Construct an analysis-of-variance summary table indicating the sources of variance, degrees of freedom, and error terms appropriate for the analysis.

(b) What major disadvantage do you see with this particular design? What advice would you offer to help remedy this problem?

3. A researcher is interested in comparing two different concept-formation tasks, one involving a disjunctive concept and the other involving a conjunctive concept. In order to increase the generalizability of the experiment, the researcher includes five different examples of each of the two types of task. The sums entered in the AB matrix presented below represent the number of trials required to reach a performance criterion; each sum is based on $s = 2$ subjects. For this example, $\Sigma (ABS)^2 = 511$.

DISJUNCTIVE CONCEPT (a_1)		CONJUNCTIVE CONCEPT (a_2)	
Problems (b/a_1)	AB Sums	Problems (b/a_2)	AB Sums
$b_{1(1)}$	2	$b_{1(2)}$	6
$b_{2(1)}$	5	$b_{2(2)}$	7
$b_{3(1)}$	2	$b_{3(2)}$	6
$b_{4(1)}$	8	$b_{4(2)}$	12
$b_{5(1)}$	14	$b_{5(2)}$	20

(a) Perform an analysis of variance on these data.

(b) What changes would you make in the design of this experiment if you wanted to pursue the topic?

4. The experiment summarized in Table 12-3 (p. 258) consisted of four treatment conditions, with 10 lists of nonsense syllables nested in each of the conditions. In actual fact, the four conditions formed a 2×2 factorial consisting of two levels of similarity among the nonsense syllables (low and high) crossed with two degrees of meaningfulness (low and high). More specifically,

Level a_1 = low similarity, low meaningfulness.
Level a_2 = low similarity, high meaningfulness.
Level a_3 = high similarity, low meaningfulness.
Level a_4 = high similarity, high meaningfulness.

See if you can figure out the analysis of this experiment. (*Hint:* The only new calculations involve the analysis of the factorial part of the design.)

IV

HIGHER-ORDER FACTORIAL EXPERIMENTS

The analysis of experiments involving three or more independent variables introduces no new concepts or procedures. Our task in Part IV is to see how the basic analyses of one- and two-factor experiments are extended to these multifactor designs. As in the preceding discussions, we will assume a completely randomized design in which subjects are randomly assigned to a single treatment condition. Designs in which subjects serve in two or more treatment conditions are considered in Part V.

In Chapters 13 and 14, I will discuss in detail the analysis of the relatively common three-factor design in which three independent variables are arranged in a completely crossed fashion. As before, this means that each possible combination of the levels associated with each independent variable is represented in the design. The two-way factorial was represented by a rectangle, the levels of factor A defining one dimension and the levels of factor B defining the other dimension. Continuing with this geometrical representation, one can picture the three-way factorial as a rectangular solid in which the levels of factors A and B mark off the width and height, respectively, and the levels of the third factor, C, mark off the depth. This may be seen in the figure appearing on the next page, where each of the separate blocks making up the display represents a different combination of the levels of the three factors.

Chapter 13 presents an overview of the three-way design and the standard analysis that is normally applied to it. Chapter 14 is concerned with the detailed analysis of the three-factor design—that is, the use of simple effects and of interaction comparisons to provide an analytical picture of the results of this type of factorial experiment. The development of the statistical analyses in these two chapters will provide an illustration of how the basic procedures developed in Part III for the simplest form of factorial experiment, the two-factor design, can be extended and generalized to the meaningful analysis of the three-factor design. In Chapter 15, I will consider the general case—the analysis of factorial experiments with any number of independent variables—including procedures that

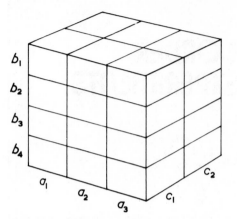

Geometric Display of a 3 X 4 X 2 Factorial Design

allow the construction of computational formulas for the two types of analytical comparisons often conducted instead of or in conjunction with the standard analysis, namely, analyses of simple effects and of interaction comparisons.

13

The Three-Factor Design: The Basic Analysis

This chapter examines closely the single new statistical quantity introduced by adding a third independent variable to a two-way factorial design—the three-way interaction. Following this discussion, I will turn to the computational formulas for the standard analysis of variance of data obtained from a three-factor experiment and end the chapter with a numerical example. Chapter 14 illustrates the rich detail of information that can be extracted in addition to the usual factorial effects of main effects and interactions.

13.1 FACTORIAL COMPONENTS OF THE THREE-WAY DESIGN

It is instructive to think about the ingredients that go into a three-factor design. Consider the display presented in Table 13-1. In the top section of the table, each of the independent variables is represented in a different single-factor experiment. You have seen in Chapter 9 that the two-way factorial is in essence constructed from two single-factor experiments. Three such two-way factorial experiments are possible with three independent variables: a crossing of factors *A* and *B*, a crossing of factors *A* and *C*, and a crossing of factors *B* and *C*. These experiments are enumerated in the middle section of the table. Finally, a three-way factorial can be viewed as a *two-way factorial crossed with a third factor*. Three of these crossings are possible, and they are listed in the bottom section of the table. Each one of these instances of a three-way factorial specifies the same set of treatment combinations.

Any one of the three ways of displaying the three-factor design can be used to organize the data from an experiment. I will refer to these displays as *ABC* **matrices.** At a glance, you can see that all possible $(a)(b)(c) = (3)(4)(2) = 24$ combinations of the three independent variables are enumerated as individual cells in the *ABC* matrix. This particular design would be referred to as a 3 × 4 × 2 factorial.

Suppose we consider Table 13-1 in reverse. We start with the three-way factorials at the bottom. By collapsing across any one of the three independent variables and combining the scores contained therein, we will obtain a two-dimensional data matrix: an *AB* matrix when we collapse across the levels of factor *C*, an *AC* matrix when we collapse across the levels of factor *B*, and a *BC* matrix when we collapse across the levels of factor *A*. From these three matrices we can obtain information concerning the respective two-way interactions, which represent interactions averaged over the levels of the remaining independent variable. Because of the collapsing, these interactions will not necessarily be the same as those obtained from a standard two-way factorial.[1]

From the two-way matrices, we can obtain information concerning respective main effects for each of the three independent variables. These main effects are

---

[1] These interactions will be identical only when there is no three-way interaction, a concept I will discuss in the next section.

Table 13-1 Relationship Between the Three-Way Factorial and Lower-Order Designs

SINGLE-FACTOR EXPERIMENTS

Factor A

a_1	a_2	a_3

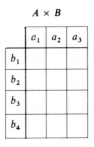

Factor B

b_1	b_2	b_3	b_4

Factor C

c_1	c_2

TWO-WAY FACTORIALS

$A \times B$

	a_1	a_2	a_3
b_1			
b_2			
b_3			
b_4			

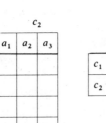

$A \times C$

	a_1	a_2	a_3
c_1			
c_2			

$B \times C$

	b_1	b_2	b_3	b_4
c_1				
c_2				

THREE-WAY FACTORIALS

$(A \times B) \times C$

c_1

	a_1	a_2	a_3
b_1			
b_2			
b_3			
b_4			

c_2

	a_1	a_2	a_3
b_1			
b_2			
b_3			
b_4			

$(A \times C) \times B$

b_1

	a_1	a_2	a_3
c_1			
c_2			

b_2

	a_1	a_2	a_3
c_1			
c_2			

b_3

	a_1	a_2	a_3
c_1			
c_2			

b_4

	a_1	a_2	a_3
c_1			
c_2			

$(B \times C) \times A$

a_1

	b_1	b_2	b_3	b_4
c_1				
c_2				

a_2

	b_1	b_2	b_3	b_4
c_1				
c_2				

a_3

	b_1	b_2	b_3	b_4
c_1				
c_2				

estimates of the effects of one of the independent variables averaged over the levels of the other two independent variables. In addition to the main effects and two-way interactions, which may be investigated with appropriate two-way factorial experiments, we obtain from the *ABC* matrix information about the manner in which the three variables combine to affect the behavior we are studying. That is, we are able to determine the presence or absence of a *three-way interaction.*

13.2   THREE-WAY INTERACTION

The three-way interaction is called by a number of names, such as the **three-way,** the **second-order,** the **triple,** or the *A* × *B* × *C* **interaction.** I will use these labels interchangeably. One way to understand the meaning of this higher-order inter-action is to look at a concrete example. This illustration comes from an experiment reported by Wallace and Underwood (1964), in which the main purpose was an assessment of the triple interaction. To understand why this was the case, we must consider some of the reasoning behind this experiment.

An Example of a Three-Way Interaction

Briefly, Wallace and Underwood began with the assumption that the presenta-tion of a common word will elicit from the subject an implicit associative response; e.g., a subject may think of the word *table* upon the presentation of the word *chair,* or of *apple* upon the presentation of the word *orange.* These associations are thought to be the result of experience with a language. Linguistic associations are assumed to facilitate learning when they correspond to the requirements of the learning task and to interfere with learning when they do not. One implication of this theory was tested in the experiment by including, as two of the independent variables, the *strength* of the linguistic associations and the *type* of learning task.

The degree of strength (factor *A*) was varied by constructing learning materials from two pools of words. One pool contained groups of words from the same con-ceptual class, such as FRUITS: *apple, peach, pear*; or COLORS: *green, blue, red*; or PARTS OF THE BODY: *leg, head, arm.* The other pool contained no words from the same conceptual class—e.g., *fly, saw, snow, car, sun,* and so on. It was assumed that words from the same category are highly associated, while words from different categories are not. Two types of learning tasks (factor *B*) were compared: a free-recall task in which subjects could recall a series of words in any order they wished, and a paired-associate task in which they were required to learn specific word pairs. A crossing of these two factors resulted in two free-recall lists and two paired-associate lists. In each case, one of the lists contained words of a low degree of association and another contained words of a high degree of association. The free-recall lists were constructed by randomly ordering the words from a given pool, while the paired-associate lists were constructed by randomly forming *pairs* of words from the pool.

It was predicted that there would be an interaction between these two independent variables. More specifically, it was anticipated that the presence of strong interword associations would *facilitate* free-recall learning in that the high interconnections among the words within a group would facilitate the recall of the separate words. Thus, the high list would be learned more quickly than the low list. In direct contrast, it was predicted that strong interword associations would *retard* paired-associate learning, since the interconnections among the words would be in conflict with the arbitrary pairs that the subjects were required to learn. Thus, the high list would be learned more slowly than the low list. In short, then, they predicted an interaction between factors A and B—namely, that associative strength (factor A) would have opposite effects on the two learning tasks (factor B).

For the third independent variable, Wallace and Underwood compared the learning of these tasks and materials by college students and by mental retardates. This final variable was introduced with the thought that the degree of linguistic development was being "manipulated." It was assumed that college students have stronger and more extensive linguistic habits than do mental retardates. Therefore, it was predicted that associative strength would have *less* effect upon the performance of retarded subjects than it would on the performance of college students. That is, the negative and positive effects of associative strength (the $A \times B$ interaction), which I described in the last paragraph, should be found with college students, but should be greatly diminished or even absent with retardates.

The complete design is specified in Table 13-2. Each of the three independent variables (strength, task, and type of subject) is represented by two levels. Thus, there are $(a)(b)(c) = (2)(2)(2) = 8$ treatment combinations in the experiment. The results of the study are reproduced in Fig. 13-1. It will be noted that the expected strength $\times$ task $(A \times B)$ interaction was obtained with the college students but was virtually nonexistent with the mental retardates. This pattern of results represents an interaction of *three* independent variables. For Wallace and Underwood, the outcome provided strong support for their theoretical speculations. That is, they found that assumed linguistic associations could facilitate as well as interfere with learning and that the magnitude of these opposed effects seemed to depend upon the degree of linguistic development of the subjects.

Table 13-2 Experimental Design of Wallace and Underwood (1964)

College Students			Mental Retardates		
	Degree of Association			Degree of Association	
TASK	Low	High	TASK	Low	High
Free recall			Free recall		
Paired associate			Paired associate		

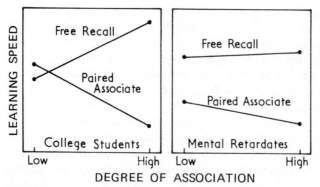

FIGURE 13-1   From Wallace, W. P., and Underwood, B. J. Speed of learning as a function of learning task, degree of association, and type of subject. *Journal of Educational Psychology*, 1964, *55*, 362–370. Copyright 1964 by the American Psychological Association. Reprinted by permission.

Defining the Three-Way Interaction

In developing a definition of the three-way interaction, let's return to Chapter 9 and the definitions of the *two*-way interaction. In that context, I defined an interaction as a situation in which the effects of one of the independent variables change at different levels of the second independent variable. We can define a three-way interaction by modifying this relatively simple definition to accommodate the increased complexity of the higher-order interaction. More specifically, we say that

> **Three variables interact when the *interaction* of two of the variables changes at different levels of the *third* variable.**

You can see that this definition is satisfied by the data summarized in Fig. 13-1. More specifically, the two-way interaction of strength and task is *different* for college students (one level of the third variable) than it is for mental retardates (the other level of the third variable).

When considering interactions, many students have difficulty making the transition from two to three independent variables. Suppose we go back to an interaction of two variables. Recall from the discussion in Chapter 9 that a two-way interaction is present when the *simple effects* of one of the variables are not the same at the different levels of the other variable. By analogy,

> **A three-way interaction is present when the *simple interaction* effects of two variables are not the same at different levels of the third variable.**

Three sets of simple interactions are possible in this type of design: the $A \times B$ interaction effects at the different levels of factor C ($A \times B$ at c_k), the $A \times C$ interaction effects the different levels of factor B ($A \times C$ at b_j), and the $B \times C$ interaction effects at the different levels of factor A ($B \times C$ at a_i). When there is a three-way interaction, the simple interaction effects for any one of the sets will not be the same at the different levels of the corresponding third variable.

It is important to note that the simple interaction effects merely need to be different—they do not need to represent significant two-way interactions themselves. This is why Fig. 13-1 is such a good example. If we had conducted the experiment only with retardates as subjects, we would *not* have observed the two-way interaction; under these circumstances we would have concluded that associative strength produces no effect with either type of learning task. However, if we had conducted this experiment only with college students, we would have concluded that there is a severe interaction of the two variables. In short, when you consider the results of these separate "two-factor" experiments together in a three-factor design, you can see that no one summary statement is possible—we *must* indicate that the two independent variables, associative strength and learning task, produce a different pattern of results with the two types of subjects. Said another way, the presence of an $A \times B \times C$ interaction signals the fact that the interpretation of the two-way interactions, which we obtain by collapsing across the levels of one of the variables, must be made with caution, just as an $A \times B$ interaction in the two-factor case means that the interpretation of the main effects must be made with caution. Translated to our example, you can see that a general statement describing the interaction of associative strength and learning task cannot be made without a specification of the type of subject being tested.

Additional Illustrations of Interaction and Noninteraction

Additional examples of interaction and noninteraction are found in Exercises 1 and 2 at the end of this chapter. These problems are designed to test your understanding of the definition of the triple interaction, as well as of two-way interactions and of main effects. Another example is provided by the numerical example used to illustrate the analyses discussed in this chapter. This example contains a three-way interaction (see Fig. 13-2, p. 291). Exercises 3 and 4 provide additional numerical examples, one with a significant higher-order interaction and one without.

It is much easier to grasp the meaning of a three-way interaction when the experiment is your own and you have gone through the agonizing steps in planning the experiment than when it is an example in a statistics text, where the independent variables are represented by theoretically neutral letters. A researcher does not turn to a three-way factorial unless he or she has thought about the real possibilities of the higher-order interaction—of what it will mean if it does materialize as predicted and what it will mean if it does not. Wallace and Underwood, for example, already knew that associative strength would show opposite results with the free-recall and paired-associate tasks. Their intent was to test their theoretical interpretation of this interaction by manipulating a *third* independent variable that would reduce or eliminate this interaction. This variable, represented by a contrast of college students and mental retardates, was assumed to be a way of reducing the strength of linguistic associations without changing the nature of the materials. Their prediction of a three-way interaction followed directly from their original theoretical explanation and their assumption of the effects of comparing college students and mental retardates.

The point is that we usually build up to a three-way interaction by the logic of our own research. You should understand precisely what is meant by a higher-order interaction, so that you will know when you are predicting its occurrence or nonoccurrence in a three-way factorial. To this end, the "neutral" examples in the exercises for this chapter will prove useful.

13.3   COMPUTATIONAL FORMULAS AND ANALYSIS SUMMARY

Design and Notation

Before turning to the actual analysis, I will discuss the notation needed to specify the various calculations. The notational system is illustrated in Tables 13-3 and 13-4. The basic design is summarized in the upper portion of Table 13-3. Inspection indicates that the design is a $3 \times 2 \times 2$ factorial, with factor A represented with $a = 3$ levels, factor B with $b = 2$ levels, and factor C with $c = 2$ levels. I have also indicated that $s = 3$ subjects would be randomly assigned to each of the $(a)(b)(c) = (3)(2)(2) = 12$ treatment combinations.

A basic score or individual observation becomes $ABCS_{ijkl}$ in the notational system for the three-factor design. The four capital letters are needed to designate

Table 13-3   Design and Notation for the Three-Factor Design

EXPERIMENTAL DESIGN

		Factor C				
	c_1			c_2		
	Factor A			Factor A		
Factor B	a_1	a_2	a_3	a_1	a_2	a_3
b_1	$s = 3$	$s = 3$	$s = 3$	$s = 3$	$s = 3$	$s = 3$
b_2	$s = 3$	$s = 3$	$s = 3$	$s = 3$	$s = 3$	$s = 3$

ABCS MATRIX

Treatment Combinations

$a_1b_1c_1$	$a_1b_2c_1$	$\cdots$	$a_3b_1c_2$	$a_3b_2c_2$
$ABCS_{1111}$	$ABCS_{1211}$	$\cdots$	$ABCS_{3121}$	$ABCS_{3221}$
$ABCS_{1112}$	$ABCS_{1212}$	$\cdots$	$ABCS_{3122}$	$ABCS_{3222}$
$ABCS_{1113}$	$ABCS_{1213}$	$\cdots$	$ABCS_{3123}$	$ABCS_{3223}$

the score of a single subject in a particular combination of the levels of the factors *A*, *B*, and *C*. These *ABCS* scores are enumerated in the **ABCS matrix** in the lower half of Table 13-3. When it is necessary to specify a particular observation in one of the *abc* treatment conditions, I will do so by using four subscripts, namely, an *i* to refer to the level of factor *A*, a *j* to refer to the level of factor *B*, a *k* to refer to the level of factor *C*, and an *l* to refer to the specific subject in the *ijk*th cell. With these subscripts, $i = 1, 2, \ldots, a; j = 1, 2, \ldots, b; k = 1, 2, \ldots, c;$ and $l = 1, 2, \ldots, s$. I will use notational subscripts only when necessary to avoid ambiguity in the calculations.

Table 13-4 presents the four matrices from which we will calculate the different treatment effects. The first is the **ABC matrix**. This matrix contains the totals for each of the $(a)(b)(c)$ treatment conditions; they are denoted as ABC_{ijk}. The ABC_{ijk} sums are obtained by adding up the individual $ABCS_{ijkl}$ scores in each of the $(a)(b)(c)$ cells or groups. You have seen that there are *s* of these scores in each group. More formally, then, a cell sum is defined as

$$ABC_{ijk} = \sum_{l=1}^{s} ABCS_{ijkl}.$$

For an example of the summation,

$$ABC_{312} = ABCS_{3121} + ABCS_{3122} + ABCS_{3123}.$$

The other three matrices presented in Table 13-4 are two-factor matrices formed when the levels of a third factor are disregarded—i.e., summed across or collapsed over. Thus, the **AB matrix** superimposes the left-hand and right-hand portions of the *ABC* matrix, eliminating the *C* classification. Any sum listed within the body of the *AB* matrix is obtained by combining corresponding treatment sums from the different levels of factor *C*. For example,

$$AB_{11} = ABC_{111} + ABC_{112} \qquad \text{and} \qquad AB_{32} = ABC_{321} + ABC_{322}$$

The marginal totals in the *AB* matrix represent familiar ground: the column marginal totals are the A_i sums, the row marginal totals are the B_j sums, and the sum of either the row marginal totals or the column marginal totals is the grand sum *T*.

The *AC* and *BC* matrices are formed in a similar way. The totals within the body of the **AC matrix** are obtained by summing corresponding totals from the different levels of factor *B*. For example,

$$AC_{22} = ABC_{212} + ABC_{222} \qquad \text{and} \qquad AC_{31} = ABC_{311} + ABC_{321}.$$

The marginal totals of the *AC* matrix provide the A_i sums (column marginal totals), the C_k sums (row marginal totals), and *T* (the sum of either the row or column marginal totals).

Turning finally to the **BC matrix**, we see that the totals within the body of this matrix are found by collapsing across the levels of factor *A*. For the sum at

Table 13-4   Summary Matrices for the Three-Factor Design

ABC Matrix

	c_1			c_2		
	a_1	a_2	a_3	a_1	a_2	a_3
b_1	ABC_{111}	ABC_{211}	ABC_{311}	ABC_{112}	ABC_{212}	ABC_{312}
b_2	ABC_{121}	ABC_{221}	ABC_{321}	ABC_{122}	ABC_{222}	ABC_{322}

AB Matrix

	a_1	a_2	a_3	Sum
b_1	AB_{11}	AB_{21}	AB_{31}	B_1
b_2	AB_{12}	AB_{22}	AB_{32}	B_2
Sum	A_1	A_2	A_3	T

AC Matrix

	a_1	a_2	a_3	Sum
c_1	AC_{11}	AC_{21}	AC_{31}	C_1
c_2	AC_{12}	AC_{22}	AC_{32}	C_2
Sum	A_1	A_2	A_3	T

BC Matrix

	c_1	c_2	Sum
b_1	BC_{11}	BC_{12}	B_1
b_2	BC_{21}	BC_{22}	B_2
Sum	C_1	C_2	T

$b_1 c_2$, for example,

$$BC_{12} = ABC_{112} + ABC_{212} + ABC_{312}.$$

You may have noticed that marginal totals in any two-way matrix (AB, AC, or BC) are duplicated in the other matrices. This redundancy is useful in an actual analysis as a check on one's arithmetic in forming a two-way matrix from the ABC, or three-way, matrix.

Partitioning the Total Sum of Squares

In the three-way factorial presented in Table 13-3, there are $s = 3$ subjects in each cell of the ABC matrix and, thus, $(a)(b)(c)(s) = 36$ subjects in the entire experiment. As with any completely randomized experiment, the variability of the individual scores from the overall mean (the SS_T) can be partitioned into a between-groups sum of squares (SS_{bg}—the variability of the $\overline{ABC}$ treatment means from $\overline{T}$) and a within-groups sum of squares (SS_{wg}—the variability of subjects treated alike, pooled over the specific treatment conditions). As with the two-factor analysis described in Chapter 10, we can subdivide the SS_{bg} into a set of useful components.

I have already hinted at the nature of these sources of variance. That is, the SS_{bg} can be partitioned into a set of three main effects (one for each independent variable), a set of three two-way interactions ($A \times B$, $A \times C$, and $B \times C$), and the three-way interaction. In symbols,

$$SS_{bg} = SS_A + SS_B + SS_C + SS_{A \times B} + SS_{A \times C} + SS_{B \times C} + SS_{A \times B \times C} . \quad (13\text{-}1)$$

It is a simple step to include in Eq. (13-1) the variability of the individual subjects:

$$
\begin{aligned}
SS_T &= SS_{bg} + SS_{wg} \\
&= SS_A + SS_B + SS_C + SS_{A \times B} + SS_{A \times C} + SS_{B \times C} \\
&\quad + SS_{A \times B \times C} + SS_{S/ABC}
\end{aligned}
\quad (13\text{-}2)
$$

The last source of variance, the $SS_{S/ABC}$, is the within-groups sum of squares and refers to the pooled sums of squares of subjects within each of the different $(a)(b)(c)$ treatment conditions. I will now construct the computational formulas for these component sums of squares.

Generating the Computational Formulas

In Chapter 10 I presented a procedure by which the computational formulas for the sums of squares are constructed from the corresponding df statements. I will apply the same set of rules to the present analysis. The development of the formulas takes place in three basic steps, through which I will work quickly. If further guidance is required, refer back to the earlier discussion (pp. 190–193).

Identifying the Sources of Variance. This step has been completed by Eq. (13-2), but I will still apply the rules given in Chapter 10 as an additional demonstration of how they work. Specifically,

1. **List factors:** A, B, C, and S/ABC, and
2. **Form interactions:** $A \times B$, $A \times C$, $B \times C$, and $A \times B \times C$.

These sources of variance are presented in column 1 of Table 13-5.

Using the df Statements. The df associated with each source of variance are listed in column 2 of Table 13-5. The df for the main effects equal the number of treatment levels less 1. The df for the interaction sums of squares are found by multiplying the df's associated with the factors specified by the interaction:

$$df_{A \times B} = (df_A)(df_B) = (a - 1)(b - 1),$$
$$df_{A \times C} = (df_A)(df_C) = (a - 1)(c - 1),$$
$$df_{B \times C} = (df_B)(df_C) = (b - 1)(c - 1),$$
$$df_{A \times B \times C} = (df_A)(df_B)(df_C) = (a - 1)(b - 1)(c - 1).$$

In each case, the *df* reflect the number of cells in the corresponding data matrices that are free to vary (see pp. 194-195).

The *df* for the $SS_{S/ABC}$ are calculated by pooling the *df* associated with factor *S*, that is, $s - 1$, over the $(a)(b)(c)$ treatment groups:

$$df_{S/ABC} = (a)(b)(c)(df_S) = (a)(b)(c)(s - 1).$$

The *df* for the SS_T are 1 less than the total number of observations in the experiment; i.e.,

$$df_T = (a)(b)(c)(s) - 1.$$

Column 3 of Table 13-5 lists the different sets of *df* statements in expanded form. This arrangement forms the backbone of the generating system. The individual terms in these expressions—the letters and combinations of letters—indicate the nature of the basic ratios, which I will consider next, and the specific way in which these ratios are combined to form the various sums of squares required for the analysis of variance.

Forming the Basic Ratios.   The construction of basic ratios, you will recall, follows a consistent pattern of operations, i.e., the squaring and then summing of a set of quantities (scores or sums of scores) followed by a division specified by the number of observations contributing to any one of the quantities in the set. Column 4 of Table 13-5 lists the basic ratio for the first term in each formula except in the last row, where the basic ratio associated with the numeral 1 in the expanded *df* statements, $[T]$, is listed to complete the enumeration. You should verify for yourself the systematic way each basic ratio is constructed.

Summary of the Analysis of Variance

Sums of Squares and Degrees of Freedom.   The formulas for the sums of squares and the respective degrees of freedom are presented in Table 13-5 in columns 5 and 2, respectively.

Mean Squares and F Ratios.   The mean squares are obtained by dividing each component sum of squares by its corresponding *df*, as indicated in Table 13-5, column 6. Each of these mean squares, except the $MS_{S/ABC}$, provides an estimate of the population treatment effects (main effects or interaction) plus error variance.[2] The $MS_{S/ABC}$ provides an independent estimate of error variance. The null hypothesis in each case specifies the absence of population treatment effects, while the alternative hypothesis specifies their presence. When the null hypothesis is true, ratios formed by dividing these mean squares by the $MS_{S/ABC}$ are distributed as *F* (with appropriate numerator and denominator *df*'s). Obtained *F* ratios which exceed theoretical values at some significance level (α) lead to the rejection of the null hypothesis and the acceptance of the alternative hypothesis.

---

[2]This statement is correct only for the fixed-effects model, which is appropriate for most research applications. See Chapter 21 (pp. 519-524) for a discussion of the different models and how the analysis is changed under the alternative ones (in particular, see Table 21-3, p. 529).

Table 13-5   Constructing the Computational Formulas from the Expanded df Statements

(1) SOURCE	(2) df	(3) df EXPANDED	(4) BASIC RATIO	(5) SUM OF SQUARES	(6) MS	(7) F
A	$a - 1$	$a - 1$	$[A] = \dfrac{\Sigma A^2}{(b)(c)(s)}$	$[A] - [T]$	$\dfrac{SS_A}{df_A}$	$\dfrac{MS_A}{MS_{S/ABC}}$
B	$b - 1$	$b - 1$	$[B] = \dfrac{\Sigma B^2}{(a)(c)(s)}$	$[B] - [T]$	$\dfrac{SS_B}{df_B}$	$\dfrac{MS_B}{MS_{S/ABC}}$
C	$c - 1$	$c - 1$	$[C] = \dfrac{\Sigma C^2}{(a)(b)(s)}$	$[C] - [T]$	$\dfrac{SS_C}{df_C}$	$\dfrac{MS_C}{MS_{S/ABC}}$
$A \times B$	$(a-1)(b-1)$	$ab - a - b + 1$	$[AB] = \dfrac{\Sigma (AB)^2}{(c)(s)}$	$[AB] - [A] - [B] + [T]$	$\dfrac{SS_{A \times B}}{df_{A \times B}}$	$\dfrac{MS_{A \times B}}{MS_{S/ABC}}$
$A \times C$	$(a-1)(c-1)$	$ac - a - c + 1$	$[AC] = \dfrac{\Sigma (AC)^2}{(b)(s)}$	$[AC] - [A] - [C] + [T]$	$\dfrac{SS_{A \times C}}{df_{A \times C}}$	$\dfrac{MS_{A \times C}}{MS_{S/ABC}}$
$B \times C$	$(b-1)(c-1)$	$bc - b - c + 1$	$[BC] = \dfrac{\Sigma (BC)^2}{(a)(s)}$	$[BC] - [B] - [C] + [T]$	$\dfrac{SS_{B \times C}}{df_{B \times C}}$	$\dfrac{MS_{B \times C}}{MS_{S/ABC}}$
$A \times B \times C$	$(a-1)(b-1)(c-1)$	$abc - ab - ac - bc$ $+ a + b + c - 1$	$[ABC] = \dfrac{\Sigma (ABC)^2}{s}$	$[ABC] - [AB] - [AC] - [BC]$ $+ [A] + [B] + [C] - [T]$	$\dfrac{SS_{A \times B \times C}}{df_{A \times B \times C}}$	$\dfrac{MS_{A \times B \times C}}{MS_{S/ABC}}$
S/ABC	$(a)(b)(c)(s-1)$	$abcs - abc$	$[ABCS] = \Sigma (ABCS)^2$	$[ABCS] - [ABC]$	$\dfrac{SS_{S/ABC}}{df_{S/ABC}}$	
Total	$(a)(b)(c)(s) - 1$	$abcs - 1$	$[T] = \dfrac{T^2}{(a)(b)(c)(s)}$	$[ABCS] - [T]$		

287

Statistical Model and Assumptions. The linear model for the three-factor design contains a listing of the different population effects potentially contributing to a single observation in the experiment. That is,

$$ABCS_{ijkl} = \mu + \alpha_i + \beta_j + \gamma_k + \alpha\beta_{ij} + \alpha\gamma_{ik} + \beta\gamma_{jk}$$

$$+ \alpha\beta\gamma_{ijk} + \epsilon_{ijkl}, \tag{13-3}$$

where μ is the overall mean of the population,

> α_i, β_j, and γ_k are the average treatment effects at levels a_i, b_j, and c_k, respectively,

> $\alpha\beta_{ij}$, $\alpha\gamma_{ik}$, and $\beta\gamma_{jk}$ are the average interaction effects at $a_i b_j$, $a_i c_k$, and $b_j c_k$, respectively,

> $\alpha\beta\gamma_{ijk}$ is the three-way interaction effect at cell $a_i b_j c_k$, and

> ϵ_{ijkl} is experimental error unique to subject l in group $a_i b_j c_k$.

From this model and the assumptions concerning the underlying treatment populations—normality, homogeneity of variance, and independence—expected mean squares can be formed which specify the factor (or factors) contributing to each mean square entering into the formation of the F ratios. Under the fixed-effects assumption (see footnote 2, p. 286), each numerator term has an expected value involving the α, β, and γ terms in question and the random variability of the ϵ_{ijkl}. Thus, for example, the expected value of the $MS_{A \times B}$ is

$$E(MS_{A \times B}) = \frac{(c)(s) \, \Sigma \, (\alpha\beta_{ij})^2}{(a-1)(b-1)} + \sigma_\epsilon^2.$$

The expected value of the denominator, $MS_{S/ABC}$, has only the random component; i.e.,

$$E(MS_{S/ABC}) = \sigma_\epsilon^2.$$

Consequently, when the null hypothesis is true, the null-hypothesis component is zero and we have a ratio consisting of two independent estimates of experimental error, which permits us to use the F distribution to evaluate the reasonableness of the null hypothesis.

13.4 A NUMERICAL EXAMPLE

Background

A numerical example of the basic analyses is drawn from a reasonable, but hypothetical, study in human memory. In a typical study of memory, different groups of subjects are given a test on a list of verbal materials at different periods of time following the learning of the list. These intervals between training and testing are called *retention intervals*. Any decrement in performance observed over the retention intervals is called forgetting. A common explanation of forgetting is that interference from linguistic sources is responsible for any losses detected in the experiment. It has been assumed that this interference comes from linguistic habits that conflict with the material being learned. I will focus on one source of this interference, namely, conflicting linguistic habits that the subject encounters during the retention interval—after the learning is completed but before the memory test is administered.

Suppose we manipulate the *amount* of linguistic activity that a subject experiences during the interval by confining subjects to the laboratory and exposing them to an activity that *minimizes* linguistic experience or to one that *maximizes* it. What I am proposing, then, is a factorial design with two independent variables, length of the retention interval and type of interval activity, and I am predicting an interaction, namely, greater forgetting for the "maximum" condition than for the "minimum" condition. In order to establish the critical nature of the linguistic activity, we will also compare the effect of these different activities upon the forgetting of different kinds of verbal materials—materials that have a low, medium, or high correspondence to the language. The expectation is that linguistic activity will interfere greatly with the materials of low correspondence and only slightly with the materials of high correspondence.

If we piece together all these speculations, you see that we are predicting an interaction of the three independent variables. Specifically, we are predicting (1) that with increased linguistic activity, we will observe small amounts of forgetting with the high material and large amounts of forgetting with the low material over the different retention intervals and (2) that with reduced activity, we will observe approximately the same small amounts of forgetting with the different types of material. The first expectation specifies a two-way interaction of the type of material and the length of the retention interval at one level of the third variable— increased linguistic activity—and the second expectation specifies the *absence* of an interaction of these two variables at the other level of the third variable— reduced linguistic activity. In short, a triple interaction is predicted because the interaction of two variables is expected to be different at the two levels of the third variable.

The Design

The factorial design is summarized by the ABC matrix presented in Table 13-6. There are three retention intervals (1, 4, and 7 hours), three types of materials that will be learned (low, medium, and high), and two types of linguistic activity (minimum and maximum)—a $3 \times 3 \times 2$ factorial. These independent variables have been arbitrarily designated factors A, B, and C, respectively. Each treatment cell of the ABC matrix contains $s = 15$ subjects. Although the individual $ABCS$ scores are not given, a sufficient amount of information is provided to allow the completion of the analysis, namely, the values of the cell sums (ABC_{ijk}) and the quantity

Table 13-6   Design and Results of a Three-Way Factorial (ABC Matrix)

MATERIAL (FACTOR B)	INTERVAL ACTIVITY (FACTOR C)					
	Minimum (c_1)			Maximum (c_2)		
	Retention Interval (Factor A)			Retention Interval (Factor A)		
	1 hr. (a_1)	4 hr. (a_2)	7 hr. (a_3)	1 hr. (a_1)	4 hr. (a_2)	7 hr. (a_3)
Low (b_1)	205	198	182	209	178	146
Medium (b_2)	210	193	177	203	182	169
High (b_3)	208	197	179	211	197	182

$$\Sigma\,(ABCS)^2 = 44{,}187$$

$\Sigma\,(ABCS)^2$. The cell totals are entered in the ABC matrix, and the sum of the squared $ABCS$ scores is given at the bottom of the table.

A reasonable first step is to plot the means calculated from the sums in the ABC matrix to give us some indication of how the experiment came out. This has been done in Fig. 13-2. You will note that the retention functions for the condition in which subjects are given minimum linguistic activity show a small amount of forgetting and roughly parallel curves; i.e., the forgetting is the same for all three types of material. The display on the right, where the interval activity maximizes linguistic involvement, shows an increase in forgetting as the material deviates more and more from that found in the language; in short, there appears to be a higher-order interaction. We now have to assess the significance of this effect.

The Analysis

We begin by preparing the necessary two-way matrices; these are presented in Table 13-7. The marginal totals of the two-way matrices provide the sums needed to calculate the three main effects. The totals within the body of the matrices provide the additional sums needed to calculate the three two-way interactions. The cell totals in the ABC matrix are used in the calculation of the three-way interaction and the within-groups sums of squares. In order to guard against computational errors in the formation of these matrices, it is a good idea to verify for each two-way matrix that the sum of the row and column marginal totals equals the grand sum T.

We are now ready to calculate the basic terms entering into the computational formulas for the sums of squares. From any of the two-way matrices,

$$[T] = \frac{T^2}{(a)(b)(c)(s)} = \frac{(3{,}426)^2}{(3)(3)(2)(15)} = 43{,}472.13.$$

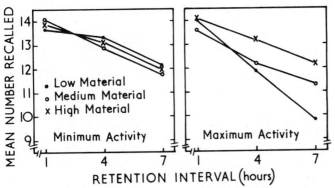

FIGURE 13-2. Mean recall as a function of retention interval (factor A), type of material (factor B), and interval activity (factor C).

From the margins of either the AB or the AC matrix, we have

$$[A] = \frac{\Sigma A^2}{(b)(c)(s)} = \frac{(1,246)^2 + (1,145)^2 + (1,035)^2}{(3)(2)(15)} = 43,719.62.$$

From either the AB or BC matrix,

$$[B] = \frac{\Sigma B^2}{(a)(c)(s)} = \frac{(1,118)^2 + (1,134)^2 + (1,174)^2}{(3)(2)(15)} = 43,490.62;$$

Table 13-7   Two-Way Matrices

AB MATRIX

	a_1	a_2	a_3	Sum
b_1	414	376	328	1,118
b_2	413	375	346	1,134
b_3	419	394	361	1,174
Sum	1,246	1,145	1,035	3,426

AC MATRIX

	a_1	a_2	a_3	Sum
c_1	623	588	538	1,749
c_2	623	557	497	1,677
Sum	1,246	1,145	1,035	3,426

BC MATRIX

	c_1	c_2	Sum
b_1	585	533	1,118
b_2	580	554	1,134
b_3	584	590	1,174
Sum	1,749	1,677	3,426

and from either the AC or BC matrix,

$$[C] = \frac{\Sigma C^2}{(a)(b)(s)} = \frac{(1,749)^2 + (1,677)^2}{(3)(3)(15)} = 43,491.33.$$

Our next task is the computation of the first terms entering into the determination of the SS's for the two-way interactions. From the AB matrix,

$$[AB] = \frac{\Sigma (AB)^2}{(c)(s)} = \frac{(414)^2 + (413)^2 + \cdots + (346)^2 + (361)^2}{(2)(15)}$$

$$= \frac{1,312,384}{30} = 43,746.13,$$

from the AC matrix,

$$[AC] = \frac{\Sigma (AC)^2}{(b)(s)} = \frac{(623)^2 + (623)^2 + \cdots + (538)^2 + (497)^2}{(3)(15)}$$

$$= \frac{1,968,704}{45} = 43,748.98,$$

and from the BC matrix,

$$[BC] = \frac{\Sigma (BC)^2}{(a)(s)} = \frac{(585)^2 + (580)^2 + \cdots + (554)^2 + (590)^2}{(3)(15)}$$

$$= \frac{1,958,786}{45} = 43,528.58.$$

We next obtain the first term of the $SS_{A \times B \times C}$. The totals needed for this sum of squares are found in the ABC matrix:

$$[ABC] = \frac{\Sigma (ABC)^2}{s} = \frac{(205)^2 + (210)^2 + \cdots + (169)^2 + (182)^2}{15}$$

$$= \frac{657,174}{15} = 43,811.60.$$

The final quantity needed for the $SS_{S/ABC}$ and the SS_T is

$$[ABC] = \Sigma (ABCS)^2 = 44,187.$$

These basic quantities and the patterns in which we combine them to calculate the sums of squares are entered in the second column of Table 13–8. The final steps in the analysis are summarized in the remaining columns of the table. The results of the F tests are given in the final column of the table. All factors are significant, except the $A \times B$ interaction. The important challenge now is to be able to assess the "meaning" of these various statistical comparisons.

Table 13-8 Summary of the Analysis of Variance

SOURCE	BASIC RATIO[a]	SUM OF SQUARES	df	MS	F
Retention Interval (A)	$[A] = 43,719.62$	$[A] - [T] = 247.49$	2	123.75	83.05***
Material (B)	$[B] = 43,490.62$	$[B] - [T] = 18.49$	2	9.25	6.21***
Interval Activity (C)	$[C] = 43,491.33$	$[C] - [T] = 19.20$	1	19.20	12.89***
$A \times B$	$[AB] = 43,746.13$	$[AB] - [A] - [B] + [T] = 8.02$	4	2.01	1.35
$A \times C$	$[AC] = 43,748.98$	$[AC] - [A] - [C] + [T] = 10.16$	2	5.08	3.41*
$B \times C$	$[BC] = 43,528.58$	$[BC] - [B] - [C] + [T] = 18.76$	2	9.38	6.30***
$A \times B \times C$	$[ABC] = 43,811.60$	$[ABC] - [AB] - [AC] - [BC]$ $+ [A] + [B] + [C] - [T] = 17.35$	4	4.34	2.91**
S/ABC	$[ABCS] = 44,187$	$[ABCS] - [ABC] = 375.40$	252	1.49	
Total	$[T] = 43,472.13$	$[ABCS] - [T] = 714.87$	269		

[a]Bracketed letters represent complete terms in computational formulas; a particular term is identified by the letter(s) appearing in the numerator.

*$p < .05$.
**$p < .025$.
***$p < .01$.

13.5 ADDITIONAL ANALYSES

I started this example with a discussion of what we were hoping to find with the experiment and why. More specifically, I predicted that the type of material learned would be an important determiner of forgetting, but only when the retention interval was filled with a large amount of linguistic activity. An inspection of Fig. 13-2 indicates that such an outcome was obtained. Moreover, you have seen that the corresponding three-way interaction is significant. There are several factors that should be considered at this point.

Simple Interaction Effects

One obvious analysis would be to attempt to identify the source or locus of the significant triple interaction. To conclude that a three-way interaction is present simply means that the variation among the treatment means cannot be entirely accounted for by the main effects and the two-way interactions; the test for interaction is an *omnibus F* test. You are familiar with this problem, of course, as the same thing was true when we found a significant main effect or interaction in the one-way and two-way cases.

We have spent a good deal of time considering analyses that are intended to isolate the components or factors contributing to a significant main effect or interaction. I discussed in Chapter 11 an analysis specifically designed to analyze a significant $A \times B$ interaction: an analysis of the *simple effects* of the two independent variables. You saw that this analysis was a direct and useful way of extracting information from a significant two-way interaction. The same sort of analysis may be adapted for use with the higher-order interactions. For the triple interaction, the analysis becomes an isolation of the **simple interaction effects.**

It is important to emphasize that it is the *meaning* of the experiment that dictates what to examine (i.e., which simple interactions are the ones to examine), and not some abstract statistical principle that one can reliably follow. In the present example, the analysis is obvious. That is, I predicted that there would be no interaction between the type of learning material and the length of the retention interval for the subjects given minimal linguistic activity, while I specified a particular type of interaction between the two variables for the subjects given the maximal linguistic activity. In this case, then, an analysis of the simple interaction effects of the three-way interaction would consist of separate analyses of the Interval X Material interaction at the two levels of the activity variable. I will discuss how this is accomplished in the next chapter.

Interaction Comparisons

A second major way of studying interaction is in terms of partial factorials created by isolating or combining different levels of the independent variables. The most common way to form partial factorials is by using single-*df* comparisons to define one or more of the independent variables and to express the three-way inter-action in terms of comparisons and "intact" independent variables. In the present example, the most obvious comparisons are the trend components associated with the forgetting curves. More specifically, we could ask whether the three-way inter-action is reflected primarily in the differences in the slopes of the best-fitting straight lines or whether differences in higher-order trend are also involved. An examination of Fig. 13-2 (p. 291) suggests that the interaction is due to differences in slope rather than to differences in curvature. That is, each of the six forgetting curves can be fitted fairly well by straight lines. For the curves on the left—those obtained under minimal linguistic activity—the slopes are roughly the same, while for the curves on the right—those obtained under maximal linguistic activity—the slopes are distinctly different.

The usefulness of interaction comparisons is more readily seen when qualita-tive independent variables are involved. I will present such an example in Chapter 14 when I consider the analysis of interaction comparisons in the three-factor design.

Interpreting Lower-Order Effects

A second point we should consider also stems from the fact that the three-way interaction is significant. Specifically, there is little reason for us to be greatly interested in the outcomes of the other F tests. The reason is that in every one of these comparisons we must remind ourselves of the fact that the higher-order interaction is significant. Consider the two-way interactions, for example. We found in our analysis a significant interaction of retention interval and activity (see Table 13-8). To see what this interaction looks like, we can inspect the relevant sums in Table 13-7 or, better, we can plot the data. This has been done in the left-hand panel of Fig. 13-3. The nature of this interaction is clear from the plot: The forget-ting curve is steeper for the maximum condition than for the minimum condition. Knowing what we now know, however, we would say that this summary of the results, which disregards the *type* of learning material, is too crude for our purposes, since it "hides" the important three-way interaction. Look back at Fig. 13-2. The retention functions are essentially identical for the high material under the two activity conditions. With this information known to us, we certainly would *not* want to offer a general conclusion that greater forgetting is always associated with greater linguistic activity; we would want to qualify this statement with a specifica-tion of the nature of the material being learned.

We see a similar difficulty in the plot of the Material $\times$ Activity interaction in the right panel of Fig. 13-3. (The three levels of the learning material have been arbitrarily spaced equally on the baseline of the figure.) You can see here that the type of material produces no effect under the minimum condition and a large effect under the maximum condition. Again, inspection of Fig. 13-2 indicates that this is *not true* at the shortest retention interval, where all of the scores are approximately the same; it is only at the longer intervals that this interaction shows itself strongly.

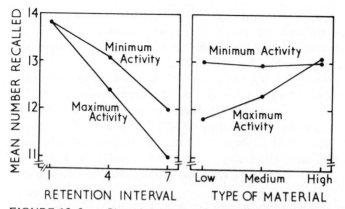

FIGURE 13-3.   Plot of the $A \times C$ (or Interval $\times$ Activity) interaction (left panel) and the $B \times C$ (or Material $\times$ Activity) interaction (right panel).

Thus, with either of the significant two-way interactions, we find it necessary to recognize the presence of the significant three-way interaction. We are not satisfied with these simplified statements, because they do not accurately reflect the characteristics of the phenomenon as we know it now.

What conclusions can we draw from the three significant *main effects*? Clearly, we have found a sizable amount of forgetting, but we must qualify this statement, since the exact amount depends upon the type of activity filling the retention interval and the type of material that was learned. Consider the main effect of material. In general, the material that corresponds to linguistic habits is recalled better than material that does not. But again we must qualify this conclusion, because we also know that this effect is most pronounced at the longer intervals and under the condition of maximal linguistic activity. Looking at the final main effect, we see that less is recalled by subjects in the maximum condition than in the minimum condition. However, it is also clear that the effect of the two types of activity does not show itself until 4 hours have passed, and that this is true primarily for the material of low correspondence to language.

In summary, then, any statements concerning the main effects and two-way interactions in our example are *not accurate descriptions* of how the three independent variables have affected behavior. It is convenient to remember that the order in which we *interpret* the outcomes of an analysis of variance is exactly the *reverse* of the order in which we extract the component sums of sqaures. In the present example, we have seen that the significant triple interaction reduces our interest in any of the lower-order effects. If the higher-order interaction had *not* been significant, then we would have immediately shifted our attention to the next level of effects—the two-way interactions. The reason for looking at these interactions before considering the main effects is the same: A significant two-way interaction limits our interest in the main effects of the two variables entering into the interaction. (I discussed this point previously in the context of the two-way factorial.)

If an independent variable does *not* interact with a second independent variable, then its main effect may be interpreted unambiguously. Otherwise, we will give most of our attention to an interpretation of any significant interactions that might appear in our analysis.

It is possible, in the higher-order designs, to have one or more variables which do not interact with the other variables. Under these circumstances, the main effects of any *noninteracting* variables may be interpreted without qualification. For example, suppose the following sources of variance are significant: *A, C,* and *A* × *B*. The main effect of factor *C* may be interpreted without qualification, while any interpretation of the main effect of factor *A* must be tempered by a consideration of the *A* × *B* interaction. (Exercise 3 at the end of this chapter illustrates such a situation.)

Of course, you should not be dismayed by the reduced interest in the lower-level sources of variance when the higher-level sources are significant. It was exactly for the possibility of an interaction that we included the different variables in a factorial experiment. We suspected that the influence of any one of the variables would depend upon the levels of the other critical variables, and this is what we discovered from this analysis. If the interaction had not been significant, we could have developed a relatively simple explanation of the behavior we have been studying. Since it is significant, we must attempt to construct an explanation that will account for the complicated way in which the different variables combined to influence behavior.

Supplementary Analyses

So far in this discussion, I have mentioned analyses that we might consider conducting on a single set of data, such as the set presented in Table 13-6. These data represent one measure of memory: the number of words correctly recalled. Other sorts of data from the same experiment may provide additional information concerning the most reasonable interpretation of the basic results. The main interest here was in memory for correct words. Perhaps the errors that the subject made during learning and during the retention test may provide useful supplementary information. For instance, the errors that subjects made with the low material might reflect the intrusion of relatively strong linguistic habits. Such a finding would lend support to the assumption that linguistic habits are an important source of interference in learning and forgetting. Similarly, an analysis of the actual verbal activity undertaken by each subject in the maximum condition may prove to be revealing. It might be shown, for example, that the subjects who are the most active linguistically during the retention interval will show a greater interaction of material and retention interval than those who are less active.

The statistical analysis of the results obtained from supplementary measures may be patterned after the main analysis, or it may focus upon a particular interaction or a comparison between selected groups. Often these supplementary analyses occur to investigators *after* they have conducted the main analyses and are trying to interpret the meaning of the different outcomes. Given that we have found a significant three-way interaction, for example, what kinds of differences might we expect to find with the supplementary response measures? In view of the post hoc nature of these questions, we might consider a post hoc correction of some sort. If we take to heart the exploratory nature of these analyses, however, we can avoid this problem by omitting a formal statistical analysis. That is, we might simply indicate that certain comparisons are *suggestive* of a particular interpretation and forego the formal analysis. Too often researchers use statistical analyses at this point as a sort of stamp of approval or disapproval. The blind use of a statistical test on measures or comparisons which were not originally incorporated into the design of the experiment will tend to suppress potentially interesting findings. We usually expect an experiment not only to answer the questions that we put to it but also to suggest new avenues of approach to a problem. We must be careful not to stifle these unexpected findings by the use of the same relatively stringent statistical standards we reserve for the main analysis.

I cannot cover the subject of supplementary analyses in any systematic fashion, because they will usually be unique to a particular research problem or even to a particular experiment. I just wish to point out that very few researchers stop with a single analysis. Instead, they comb their data and press their ingenuity to extract additional information concerning the nature of the phenomenon being studied. If one of the supplementary measures presents a different picture, this finding may become the basis for a new explanation of the outcome of the experiment or the jumping-off point for a new experiment. We must pay as much attention to supplementary analyses as to the analysis of the main response measure. We need to be aware, however, that any increase in the number of comparisons we conduct, whether with the main response measure or with supplementary measures, will increase our *familywise* error rate. Just what you do about this problem is fundamentally your own decision.

13.6 EXERCISES[3]

1. Below are presented the outcomes of 10 three-way factorial experiments. The design in each example is the same—a 2 X 2 X 2 factorial. The main intent of this exercise is to test your ability to identify three-way interactions when they are present in a set of data. Indicate the presence or absence of a triple interaction for each example. (We will assume for this problem that these means are "error-free.") When the three-way interaction is *not* present, indicate which, if any, of the two-way interactions are present. Finally, are there any main effects that may be interpreted unambiguously in any of these examples?

---

[3]The answers to these problems are found in Appendix B, beginning on p. 583.

EXAMPLES	a_1 b_1 c_1	a_1 b_1 c_2	a_1 b_2 c_1	a_1 b_2 c_2	a_2 b_1 c_1	a_2 b_1 c_2	a_2 b_2 c_1	a_2 b_2 c_2
1	1	1	1	1	3	3	3	3
2	2	2	1	1	3	3	2	2
3	3	2	2	1	4	3	3	2
4	1	1	3	3	3	3	1	1
5	1	2	2	3	2	3	1	2
6	2	0	1	1	4	2	3	3
7	2	4	1	3	0	3	1	4
8	2	3	1	4	0	4	1	3
9	2	2	1	1	4	4	3	4
10	1	0	2	3	2	3	1	0

2. In each part of this exercise you will be given an ABC matrix for a $2 \times 2 \times 2$ factorial design. Some of the cell sums are filled in and some are left blank. Your task is to fill in the blank cells with numbers that will result in the presence of the sources of variance that are specified and no others. This means that the specified sources are to produce sums of squares that are *greater* than zero and the nonspecified sources are to produce sums of squares that are *equal* to zero. Be sure to convince yourself that you have accomplished this. One tedious, but infallible, way is to assume some cell frequency, such as $s = 10$, and solve for the different sums of squares.

(a) Source present: SS_A.

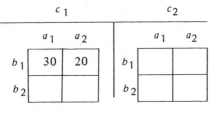

(b) Sources present: SS_A, SS_B, and SS_C.

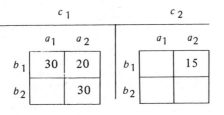

(c) Source present: $SS_{A \times B}$.

	c_1				c_2	
	a_1	a_2			a_1	a_2
b_1	30	20		b_1		
b_2	20	30		b_2		

(d) Sources present: SS_C and $SS_{A \times B}$.

	c_1				c_2	
	a_1	a_2			a_1	a_2
b_1	30	20		b_1		
b_2	20	30		b_2	30	

(e) Source present: $SS_{A \times B \times C}$.

	c_1				c_2	
	a_1	a_2			a_1	a_2
b_1	30	20		b_1		
b_2	20	30		b_2	30	

(f) Sources present: SS_C and $SS_{A \times B \times C}$.

	c_1				c_2	
	a_1	a_2			a_1	a_2
b_1	30	20		b_1		20
b_2	20	30		b_2		

3. Consider the results of a 3 × 3 × 2 factorial experiment, presented below in an *ABCS* matrix, in which there are $s = 4$ subjects in each treatment condition.

ABCS **MATRIX**

Treatment Conditions

a_1 b_1 c_1	a_1 b_1 c_2	a_1 b_2 c_1	a_1 b_2 c_2	a_1 b_3 c_1	a_1 b_3 c_2	a_2 b_1 c_1	a_2 b_1 c_2	a_2 b_2 c_1	a_2 b_2 c_2	a_2 b_3 c_1	a_2 b_3 c_2	a_3 b_1 c_1	a_3 b_1 c_2	a_3 b_2 c_1	a_3 b_2 c_2	a_3 b_3 c_1	a_3 b_3 c_2
7	7	2	2	4	1	10	6	4	1	7	1	13	12	9	7	8	7
4	5	4	3	3	3	7	5	6	3	4	3	10	13	8	6	5	7
5	5	3	4	0	2	6	5	3	4	5	3	13	11	9	7	6	4
6	6	3	1	3	2	8	6	5	5	5	0	8	12	10	6	6	6

(a) Conduct an analysis of variance on these data. Save your calculations for Exercise 1 at the end of Chapter 14.
(b) Given the outcome of the analysis, to what sources of variance would you now give close attention?
4. Suppose a $4 \times 3 \times 2$ factorial experiment is conducted and the following results are obtained:

	c_1					c_2			
	a_1	a_2	a_3	a_4		a_1	a_2	a_3	a_4
b_1	35	46	49	55	b_1	37	49	56	65
b_2	42	51	55	62	b_2	40	38	44	42
b_3	29	40	45	49	b_3	27	23	19	14

(a) Conduct an analysis of variance on these data. For this problem assume that $s = 5$ and $\Sigma (ABCS)^2 = 9{,}490$. Save your calculations for Exercise 2 at the end of Chapter 14.
(b) Given the outcome of the analysis, to what sources of variance would you now give close attention?

14

The Three-Factor Design: Simple Effects and Interaction Comparisons

In Chapter 11 I argued that an investigator would probably not be interested in making a large number of multiple comparisons with a two-way factorial. The reason is that the researcher, who knows enough about the phenomenon under study to manipulate two variables that he or she feels are relevant and may interact, does not intend to sift through the data in an indiscriminate fashion, searching for significant differences. Such a procedure is *unanalytical,* since comparisons between cells which do not occupy the same row or column in the *AB* matrix will be difficult, if not impossible, to interpret. The same argument holds for the higher-order factorials. Our main interest, therefore, will be in analyses that can ask *analytical* questions of our data.

I will consider two such analyses in this chapter. The first approach, the analysis of simple effects, attempts to isolate the source or sources of a higher-order interaction in terms of simple effects. The second approach, the analysis of comparisons, accomplishes the same goal by assessing the contribution of specific single-*df* comparisons to interactions observed with the three-factor design.

14.1 ANALYSIS OF SIMPLE EFFECTS: AN OVERVIEW

You will recall that a significant interaction in a two-factor design means that the simple effects of either independent variable are not the same at all levels of the other independent variable. For that reason, the statistical assessment of simple effects, which will indicate which of these simple effects are significant when considered in isolation and which are not, represents an important analytical tool for examining the nature of a significant $A \times B$ interaction. The analysis of simple effects serves the same function in the three-factor design, except that there are more analytical questions possible resulting from the complexity of the three-way interaction and from the fact that there are three *two*-way interactions that also may enter the picture.

The Critical Nature of the Three-Way Interaction

The specific types of analyses undertaken by a researcher depend on any theoretical predictions made before the start of an experiment, of course, and on the significance of the three-way interaction. Just as the $A \times B$ interaction served a critical role in the analysis of a two-factor design—suggesting whether to analyze in detail the interaction or to focus instead on the two main effects—the $A \times B \times C$ interaction serves an identical role in the analysis of a three-way design. One definition of a three-way interaction is in terms of simple interaction effects. More specifically, a three-way interaction is present when the interaction of two of the independent variables is not the same at all levels of the third variable. These two-way interactions are simple interactions, interactions observed in the context of the ABC matrix. Consider again the bottom portion of Table 13-1 (p. 277), in which the three-way factorial is viewed as several two-factor experiments performed at each of the levels of a third independent variable. There were three possibilities: two $A \times B$ experiments conducted at levels c_1 and c_2; four $A \times C$ experiments conducted at levels b_1, b_2, b_3, and b_4; and three $B \times C$ experiments conducted at levels a_1, a_2, and a_3. I will focus on the first arrangement, although the same points can be made with any one of the three displays.

Table 14-1 illustrates schematically the analysis of the simple effects of an $A \times B \times C$ interaction. The matrix at the upper left depicts the original ABC matrix. I have placed **X**'s in each cell of the matrix to indicate that all of the cells are involved in assessing the significance of the three-way interaction. Let's assume that this interaction is significant. The next step is to assess the $A \times B$ interactions at levels c_1 and c_2. The one at c_1 is illustrated in the table, the **X**'s again indicating the ABC cells involved in this statistical analysis. If this simple interaction is not significant, the analysis stops; on the other hand, if the interaction is significant, it moves to the next analytical step, namely, an analysis of the simple effects of factor A (or factor B) at the different levels of the other factor. Just one of these is illustrated in Table 14-1, the simple effect of factor A at b_1c_1. The **X**'s indicate the cells involved in the analysis. If any of these simple effects is significant, the final step is to search for significant simple comparisons, as we would in any two-factor design. One such comparison, a_1 versus a_2, is illustrated in the table.

In summary, a significant higher-order interaction can be analyzed systematically into a set of increasingly focused statistical tests. A significant $A \times B$ interaction at c_1 can be examined more closely to detect the sources of the significance of *this* particular simple interaction. A significant simple interaction at this stage of the analysis can be analyzed further to isolate significant comparisons at this particular row or column of the ABC matrix. What we see, then, is a systematic "slicing" of the ABC matrix in order to locate the factor (or factors) responsible for the significant three-way interaction.

A Nonsignificant Three-Way Interaction

The lack of a significant three-way interaction means that the results of the experiment can be safely described in terms of *two-dimensional* designs—an $A \times B$ design (collapsing over factor C), an $A \times C$ design (collapsing over factor B), or a $B \times C$ design (collapsing over factor A). In a sense, the three-way design is collapsed into less complex two-way designs for analysis and interpretive purposes, the same way we focused on main effects in a two-factor design when the $A \times B$ interaction was not significant. These particular two-way designs are represented by corresponding AB, AC, and BC matrices.

At this level of discourse, the logic applied to the analysis is that appropriate to a standard two-factor design. Assuming that the three-way interaction is not significant, the next step might be to test the significance of the two-way interactions. I will focus on the $A \times B$ interaction, which is represented in Table 14-1 by

Table 14-1   Systematic Analysis of Simple Effects

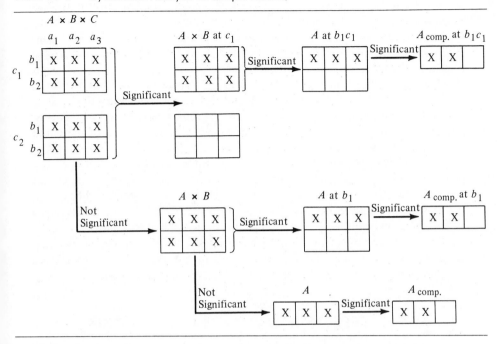

the AB matrix placed below and to the right of the ABC matrix. The X's in this matrix indicate that all of the cells are involved in the assessment of the $A \times B$ interaction. If this interaction is significant, the next step is to test significant simple effects—the simple effects of factor A at the two levels of factor B or the simple effects of factor B at the three levels of factor A. In Table 14-1, only the simple effect of factor A at b_1 is displayed in the row extending to the right of the matrix. Assuming a significant outcome of this test, simple comparisons would next be conducted. A simple comparison between levels a_1 and a_2 is shown in the table on the far right of this row.

The final stage in this process occurs when a two-way interaction is not significant. Under these circumstances, main effects become the object of study and significant main effects are then followed by tests of comparisons. If the main effect of factor A were significant, for example, we might next consider testing the significance of the comparison between levels a_1 and a_2 as illustrated in Table 14-1 or any other comparison that made sense in terms of the experiment.

Comments

Labels used to designate these different analyses can be confusing. I use the term **simple effects** in a generic sense to refer to an analysis based on a subset drawn from any multidimensional table. All of the analyses enumerated in Table 14-1

305

represent simple effects in this sense—except the bottommost analyses, which involve the A main effect—since each is based on a subset of cells drawn from either a two-way or a three-way matrix. When a simple effect examines the influence of a *single* independent variable, I will refer to the analysis as a **simple main effect**. Two such analyses are indicated in Table 14-1, one derived from the ABC matrix (A at $b_1 c_1$) and the other derived from the AB matrix (A at b_1). In both cases, a single independent variable is manipulated (factor A). To distinguish between the simple main effects conducted on the two different matrices, I will specify the level (or levels) held constant in the analysis. In the first case, then, the analysis is of the **simple main effect of A at $b_1 c_1$**, and the second case is the analysis of the **simple main effect of A at b_1**.[1]

The analyses presented in Table 14-1 are not intended to represent a general blueprint or obligatory plan for the analysis of three-factor experiments. On the contrary, statistical analyses are the *servants* of the researcher and should be chosen to focus on the comparisons that are relevant to the research questions developed in the initial planning stages of an experiment. The table does provide a useful summary and overview of a variety of statistical tests, however, showing how analyses of simple effects are related to the standard three-way analysis of variance. I will now consider how these different analyses are actually conducted.

14.2 SIMPLE EFFECTS BASED ON THE *ABC* MATRIX

As I have noted already, analyses of simple effects based on the individual cells of the ABC matrix are undertaken when the three-way interaction is significant. The analysis begins with an analysis of simple interaction effects, which is nothing more than an analysis of the interaction of two of the independent variables at each of the levels of the third. I also noted that this breakdown may be made three different ways: We can look at the simple $A \times B$ interactions at the c levels of factor C, at the simple $A \times C$ interactions at the b levels of factor B, or at the simple $B \times C$ interactions at the a levels of factor A. The particular breakdown chosen for the analysis depends on the most meaningful way for a researcher to think about the three-way interaction.

Analysis of Simple Interactions

The analysis of simple interactions quite literally consists of a two-way analysis of variance conducted separately at the different levels of the third independent variable. The only change is that the error term for the analysis comes from the three-way design, i.e., the error term is $MS_{S/ABC}$. Otherwise, the analysis is the same. I mention this fact since computational formulas written in terms of the ABC matrix are frequently difficult for students to comprehend. I will attempt to avoid

---

[1] Kirk (1968, p. 222) and Winer (1971, p. 457) refer to the simple main effect of A at b_1 as a **simple main effect** and to the simple main effect of A at $b_1 c_1$ as a **simple, simple main effect**.

this confusion by transforming the three-way notation into a two-way notation to stress the identity between the analysis of simple interactions and a two-way analysis of variance, and, as a result, by building a complex analysis on a simpler set of operations with which you are already familiar. (I adopted a similar strategy in my presentation of simple effects in the two-factor design; see pp. 215-216.) I will focus on the simple $A \times B$ interactions for pure convenience, although you should have no difficulty generalizing the principal features of the analysis to the other two sets of simple interactions.

Table 14-2 Special Notation for Analyzing Simple Effects

	ABC MATRIX AT LEVEL c_k				TRANSFORMED MATRIX			
	a_1	a_2	a_3	Sum	a_1	a_2	a_3	Sum
b_1	ABC_{11k}	ABC_{21k}	ABC_{31k}	BC_{1k} b_1	"AB_{11}"	"AB_{21}"	"AB_{31}"	"B_1"
b_2	ABC_{12k}	ABC_{22k}	ABC_{32k}	BC_{2k} b_2	"AB_{12}"	"AB_{22}"	"AB_{32}"	"B_2"
Sum	AC_{1k}	AC_{2k}	AC_{3k}	C_k Sum	"A_1"	"A_2"	"A_3"	"T"

Computational Formulas. I will begin by transforming the three-way matrix into a two-way matrix. Table 14-2 displays the three-factor notation for one of the $A \times B$ interactions—at level c_k—on the left. The transformed matrix is shown on the right. (Please note that quotation marks are used to distinguish this special notation from the one used in an actual $A \times B$ design.) As you can see, the transformed notation exactly duplicates that used for the two-way design. This means, therefore, that the computational formula for the simple-interaction sum of squares will be equivalent to the $SS_{A \times B}$ in the two-factor analysis of variance. More specifically,

$$SS_{A \times B \text{ at } c_k} = \frac{\Sigma (\text{"}AB\text{"})^2}{s} - \frac{\Sigma (\text{"}A\text{"})^2}{(b)(s)} - \frac{\Sigma (\text{"}B\text{"})^2}{(a)(s)} + \frac{(\text{"}T\text{"})^2}{(a)(b)(s)}. \quad (14\text{-}1)$$

Except for the quotation marks, Eq. (14-1) is identical to the formula for the $SS_{A \times B}$ presented in Table 10-4 (p. 194). The degrees of freedom are the same also, namely,

$$df_{A \times B \text{ at } c_k} = (a - 1)(b - 1). \quad (14\text{-}2)$$

The mean square is obtained by dividing the sum of squares by the appropriate number of degrees of freedom. The F ratio is given by the formula

$$F = \frac{MS_{A \times B \text{ at } c_k}}{MS_{S/ABC}}, \quad (14\text{-}3)$$

unless there is heterogeneity of within-groups variance.[2]

---

[2]Under these circumstances, separate error terms based on the pooled within-group mean squares should be calculated for each of the AB matrices at the different levels of factor C. In this case, the analysis is exactly a two-way analysis, including the error term.

A Numerical Example. I will return to the numerical example from Chapter 13. You will recall that the triple interaction was significant (see Table 13-8, p. 293). From Fig. 13-2 (p. 291) you saw that the interaction appeared to result from the fact that the forgetting curves for subjects recalling the different types of materials were the same when the retention interval was filled with a minimum amount of linguistic activity (c_1) but were different when the interval was filled with a large amount of linguistic activity (c_2). An analysis of the simple interaction effects might provide statistical support for these observations.

For convenience, the *ABC* matrix from Chapter 13 is presented again as two "transformed" *AB* matrices in the upper half of Table 14-3. Applying Eq. (14-1) to the data appearing in the *AB* matrix at c_1 (minimum activity), we find

$$SS_{A \times B \text{ at } c_1} = \frac{(205)^2 + (210)^2 + \cdots + (177)^2 + (179)^2}{15}$$

$$- \frac{(623)^2 + (588)^2 + (538)^2}{(3)(15)} - \frac{(585)^2 + (580)^2 + (584)^2}{(3)(15)}$$

$$+ \frac{(1,749)^2}{(3)(3)(15)}$$

$$= 22{,}743.00 - 22{,}740.38 - 22{,}659.58 + 22{,}659.27 = 2.31,$$

and applying it to the data appearing in the *AB* matrix at c_2 (maximum activity), we have

$$SS_{A \times B \text{ at } c_2} = \frac{(209)^2 + (203)^2 + \cdots + (169)^2 + (182)^2}{15}$$

$$- \frac{(623)^2 + (557)^2 + (497)^2}{(3)(15)} - \frac{(533)^2 + (554)^2 + (590)^2}{(3)(15)}$$

$$+ \frac{(1,677)^2}{(3)(3)(15)}$$

$$= 21{,}068.60 - 21{,}008.60 - 20{,}869.00 + 20{,}832.07 = 23.07.$$

Like the simple effects of the two-way interaction, the sum of the simple interaction effects of the three-way interaction contains two sources of variance, the three-way interaction and the *two-way interaction* we have been considering. In symbols,

$$\Sigma SS_{A \times B \text{ at } c_k} = SS_{A \times B \times C} + SS_{A \times B}. \tag{14-4}$$

In our example, the values for the left-hand sums of squares come from Table 14-3 and those for the right-hand sums of squares from Table 13-8 (p. 293). Substituting in Eq. (14-4), we get

$$2.31 + 23.07 \overset{?}{=} 17.35 + 8.02$$

$$25.38 \approx 25.37.$$

Table 14–3   Numerical Example: Simple Interaction Effects

	"AB" MATRIX AT c_1 (MINIMUM ACTIVITY)					"AB" MATRIX AT c_2 (MAXIMUM ACTIVITY)			
	1 hr. (a_1)	4 hr. (a_2)	7 hr. (a_3)	Sum		1 hr. (a_1)	4 hr. (a_2)	7 hr. (a_3)	Sum
Low (b_1)	205	198	182	585	Low (b_1)	209	178	146	533
Medium (b_2)	210	193	177	580	Medium (b_2)	203	182	169	554
High (b_3)	208	197	179	584	High (b_3)	211	197	182	590
Sum	623	588	538	1,749	Sum	623	557	497	1,677

SUMMARY OF THE ANALYSIS

Source	SS	df	MS	F
$A \times B$ at c_1	2.31	4	.58	<1
$A \times B$ at c_2	23.07	4	5.77	3.87*
S/ABC		252	1.49	

*$p < .01$.

The remainder of the analysis is completed in the lower half of the table. The results of the F tests indicate that the interaction of retention interval and materials is not significant when the interval is filled with minimum linguistic activity and is significant when it contains maximum linguistic activity.

Analysis of Simple Main Effects

The significance of the $A \times B$ interaction under maximum linguistic activity suggests further analysis, which in this case would consist of looking at the variation among the cells in any given row or any given column. In this example, the analysis could focus on factor A (retention interval) or on factor B (materials). In the first case, we would ask whether significant forgetting is found for each type of material; this analysis examines the simple main effects of factor A—the influence of the A manipulation—at levels b_1c_2 (low-maximum), b_2c_2 (medium-maximum), and b_3c_2 (high-maximum). In the second case, we would ask whether the different materials are equally well recalled at the different time delays; this analysis examines the simple main effects of factor B at levels a_1c_2 (1 hour-maximum), a_2c_2 (4 hours-maximum), and a_3c_2 (7 hours-maximum).

Computational Formulas. We are going over familiar ground, namely, the

309

analysis of simple effects based on a two-way matrix. It does not matter that the data come from a three-factor design; as we have seen with the simple $A \times B$ interaction, the formulas correspond to those appropriate for a two-way data matrix. In this analysis, we are isolating a row (or a column) from the two-way matrix and viewing the analysis as a *single*-factor manipulation. When I considered this type of analysis in Chapter 11, I transformed the notation from a two-way matrix to one appropriate for a single-factor design to simplify the resulting formula and to emphasize the nature of the analysis. I will assume that you no longer need this instructional aid for a two-way matrix and will work directly with the sums appearing in the "AB" matrix of Table 14-3. To illustrate, consider the simple main effect of factor A at level b_1. This analysis focuses on the cells appearing in the first row of the "AB" matrix and the deviation of these particular cell means from the mean for that row. In symbols,

$$SS_{A \text{ at } b_1 c_k} = \frac{\Sigma \, (\text{``}AB_{i1}\text{''})^2}{s} - \frac{(\text{``}B_1\text{''})^2}{(a)(s)}. \tag{14-5}$$

The degrees of freedom associated with this simple effect are

$$df_{A \text{ at } b_1 c_k} = a - 1. \tag{14-6}$$

The error term for all of these analyses is $MS_{S/ABC}$, unless heterogeneity of variance is present (see footnote 2, p. 307).

The formulas for the other set of simple main effects follow the same sort of pattern. As an example, let's consider the formula for the simple main effect of factor B at level a_3. This analysis focuses on the cells appearing in the third column of the "AB" matrix and the deviations of these particular cell means from the mean for that column. That is,

$$SS_{B \text{ at } a_3 c_k} = \frac{\Sigma \, (\text{``}AB_{3j}\text{''})^2}{s} - \frac{(\text{``}A_3\text{''})^2}{(b)(s)}. \tag{14-7}$$

The degrees of freedom are

$$df_{B \text{ at } a_3 c_k} = b - 1. \tag{14-8}$$

A Numerical Example. As an example, I will compute the simple main effect of factor A at a particular combination of factors B and C, namely, $b_1 c_2$. In terms of Table 14-3 (p. 309), where the treatment sums are presented, we focus our attention on the first row (level b_1) in the "AB" matrix on the right (level c_2). Substituting in Eq. (14-5), we find

$$SS_{A \text{ at } b_1 c_2} = \frac{(209)^2 + (178)^2 + (146)^2}{15} - \frac{(533)^2}{(3)(15)}$$

$$= 6,445.40 - 6,313.09 = 132.31.$$

The resulting F,

$$F = \frac{132.31/2}{1.49} = \frac{66.16}{1.49} = 44.40,$$

is significant, $p < .01$.

Comment. Just how we decide to analyze a three-way interaction depends on the experimental questions we want to ask. In some cases, our hypothesis implies an interest in the simple interaction effects. That is, we are interested in how the interaction of two independent variables will change when a third variable is introduced. Wallace and Underwood (see Fig. 13-1, p. 280), for example, were looking at the form of the *interaction* of tasks and degree of association for college students and mental retardates. They were not interested in the simple main effects, such as the effect of associative strength for college students learning paired associates or the effect of associative strength for college students learning by free recall. On the other hand, there may be situations in which such a breakdown of the three-way interaction provides useful information. This will happen when we are really interested in the presence or absence of an effect of one of the independent variables in the "separate experiments" formed at the combination of levels of the other two variables.

Another way to evaluate the usefulness of an analysis of simple main effects is to consider the different sources of variance contributing to the sum of the simple main effects of the triple interaction. That is,

$$\Sigma \, SS_{A \text{ at } b_j c_k} = SS_{A \times B \times C} + SS_{A \times B} + SS_{A \times C} + SS_A . \tag{14-9}$$

Consider what Eq. (14-9) implies: an analysis of simple main effects is relatively useless when sources other than the triple interaction contribute greatly to the variability of the means involved. In the present example, the *main* effect of factor A is an important source of variability. If we had completed the analysis of the simple main effects we began in the numerical example, we would have found them *all* to be significant. What would we have learned from this analysis? Very little, except that significant forgetting was obtained for all combinations of materials and activity. In short, then, the analysis of the simple main effects of the triple interaction does not serve a useful *analytical* function in this example because of the presence of a large main effect relative to the other components specified in Eq. (14-9). The most appropriate analysis of this experiment is the analysis of the simple *interaction* effects, since the comparisons reflect a direct test of the hypothesis being considered.

Analysis of Simple Comparisons

As you saw in the context of a two-factor design, the discovery of a significant simple effect will often initiate a search for meaningful comparisons that are responsible for the significant F. It is an easy matter to extend the analysis to a three-factor design. Suppose we wanted to see whether there was significant forgetting between 1 and 4 hours (a_1 versus a_2) for the simple main effect we examined in the last section. The coefficients for this comparison are 1, −1, and 0. Adapting the formula from Chapter 11, Eq. (11-11), p. 220, we obtain

$$SS_{A \text{ comp. at } b_1 c_2} = \frac{s(\hat{\psi}_{A \text{ at } b_1 c_2})^2}{\Sigma (c_i)^2}, \tag{14-10}$$

where s is the number of observations, $\hat{\psi}_{A \text{ at } b_1 c_2}$ is the mean difference obtained with this comparison, and c_i represents the coefficients involving the levels of factor A. The data for the analysis are found in the first row on the right in Table 14-3. Translating these cell sums ($s = 15$) to means, we obtain 13.93, 11.87, and 9.73 for levels a_1, a_2, and a_3, respectively. The mean difference is

$$\hat{\psi}_{A \text{ at } b_1 c_2} = (1)(13.93) + (-1)(11.87) + (0)(9.73) = 2.06.$$

Substituting in Eq. (14-10), we obtain

$$SS_{A \text{ comp. at } b_1 c_2} = \frac{15(2.06)^2}{(1)^2 + (-1)^2 + (0)^2} = 31.83.$$

This comparison has 1 df. The F,

$$F = \frac{MS_{A \text{ comp. at } b_1 c_2}}{MS_{S/ABC}} = \frac{31.83}{1.49} = 21.36,$$

is significant, $p < .01$. The conclusion is that significant forgetting was observed (an average loss of 2.06 responses) over the 3-hour period assessed by this comparison.

14.3   SIMPLE MAIN EFFECTS BASED ON TWO-WAY MATRICES

As I argued in the last chapter, we will probably undertake a detailed analysis of a significant two-way interaction only when the three-way interaction is *not* significant. With a significant triple interaction, anything that we may say about two-way interactions and main effects will be colored by the presence of the higher-order interaction. But if the $A \times B \times C$ interaction is not significant, then we can consider the two-way interactions directly, without ambiguity. One useful analysis of a significant two-way interaction is a determination of the simple main effects of the interaction. It should be clear that although we are working with data from a three-factor design, the analysis will now focus on the two-way matrices formed by collapsing the sums in the ABC matrix across one of the three factors.

Analysis of Simple Main Effects

Our orientation now is in respect to the two-way matrices, which come under close scrutiny when the $A \times B \times C$ interaction is not significant. Under these circumstances, we first test the two-way interactions. If one is significant, we begin to "slice" the relevant two-way matrix row by row or column by column in an attempt to determine the nature of the interaction. Suppose the $A \times B$ interaction were significant. The analysis at this point would be equivalent to an analysis of a significant interaction in a *two*-factor design. That is, we would examine the simple main effects of factor A at the different levels of factor B or the simple main effects of factor B at the different levels of factor A. Similar analyses may, of course, be conducted with significant $A \times C$ and $B \times C$ interactions. As before, our goal in these analyses is to pinpoint the source of a particular significant interaction. I will refer to these analyses as **simple main effects,** to be consistent with the terminology I used in the last section.

Computational Formulas. The meaning of this analysis and the procedures to be followed are exactly as those outlined in Chapter 11 (see pp. 214-217). Briefly, we locate the particular two-way matrix that contains the cell sums in which we are interested: the AB matrix for the $A \times B$ interaction, the AC matrix for the $A \times C$ interaction, or the BC matrix for the $B \times C$ interaction. Then we calculate a set of sums of squares representing the variability of one of the variables at the different levels of the other variable. For any one of these interactions, the two variables can serve either function. That is, we could look at the $B \times C$ interaction in terms of the variability due to factor B at the different levels of factor C or the variability due to factor C at the different levels of factor B. The particular way that we choose to perform the analysis depends upon the most meaningful way to examine the data.

Suppose we were looking at the interaction of retention interval and material from the numerical example in the last chapter. It makes more sense to determine the magnitude of the effect attributable to the increasing retention interval (i.e., forgetting) for the different types of learning materials than to consider the variation due to material at each retention interval. We are interested in the course of forgetting and not in the recall of different lists at 1 hour or at 4 hours or at 7 hours.

The computational formulas presented in Chapter 11 need only an adjustment for the number of observations. To be more specific, suppose we wanted to determine the simple main effects of factor A at level b_1. The computational formula presented in Chapter 11 took the form:

$$SS_{A \text{ at } b_1} = \frac{\Sigma (AB_{i1})^2}{s} - \frac{B_1^2}{(a)(s)}.$$

The only change needed for the three-way factorial is in the denominators, to accommodate the fact that each AB sum contains $(c)(s)$ observations—instead of s—and the B_1 sum contains $(a)(c)(s)$ observations—instead of $(a)(s)$. Specifically,

$$SS_{A \text{ at } b_1} = \frac{\Sigma (AB_{i1})^2}{(c)(s)} - \frac{B_1^2}{(a)(c)(s)}. \tag{14-11}$$

The new denominators, of course, reflect the operation of a familiar rule: We divide by the number of observations contributing to the basic total.

Computational formulas for other simple main effects follow this pattern. Consider, for example, the simple main effect of factor C at level b_1. For this analysis, we would be concentrating on the BC matrix and the deviation of the means in the body of the matrix at b_1 from the marginal mean $\bar{B}_1$. The sum of squares for this simple main effect is given by the formula

$$SS_{C \text{ at } b_1} = \frac{\Sigma (BC_{1k})^2}{(a)(s)} - \frac{B_1^2}{(a)(c)(s)}. \tag{14-12}$$

The numerators reflect the attention being paid to the variability due to factor C with factor B held constant at b_1, and the denominators reflect the application of the computational rule.

The df for simple main effects are simply the df associated with the corresponding main effects: $a - 1$ for simple effects of factor A; $b - 1$ for simple effects of factor B; and $c - 1$ for simple effects of factor C. Each mean square is tested against the overall within-groups error term $MS_{S/ABC}$, unless there is heterogeneity of variance (see footnote 2, p. 307), and the resulting F is evaluated at the appropriate numerator and denominator df's.

A Numerical Example. I will not formally work out a numerical example here. Except for the change in the denominators, the calculations are identical to those followed in the two-factor case. (A worked example of this analysis is found in Chapter 11, pp. 217-219.) You will find an example of this sort of analysis applied to the three-factor case in Exercise 1 at the end of this chapter.

Analysis of Simple Comparisons

Significant simple main effects may be followed up with tests of simple comparisons. Again, the discussion of this analysis in Chapter 11 (pp. 219-220) is relevant here. The only change in the computational formulas is for the number of observations contributing to each of the means being compared in the analysis. Otherwise, the formulas presented there are perfectly valid here.

Analysis of Main Effects

As discussed in Chapter 13 (pp. 296-297), main effects become particularly interesting in the analysis of a three-factor design when one (or more) of the independent variables fails (or fail) to interact with any of the others. Suppose none of the two-way interactions is significant; assuming that the three-way interaction is not significant as well, we will be vitally interested in the outcome of all three *main* effects. If one of the two-way interactions is significant, we may have difficulties interpreting either main effect of the two interacting factors, but we can analyze and safely interpret the noninteracting main effect. If two of the interactions are significant, there may be little systematic interest in any of the three main effects.

Let's assume that a main effect is significant and interpretable. As in a two-factor design, we would be interested in identifying the comparisons contributing to this significant effect. The computational formulas for this type of analysis can be easily adapted from the corresponding two-factor case simply by adjusting for the increased number of observations—due to the presence of factor C—in the three-factor design. For these formulas and an illustration of the procedures, see Chapter 11 (pp. 210–211). Exercise 1(b) at the end of this chapter provides an illustration of this type of analysis.

14.4 INTERACTION COMPARISONS: AN OVERVIEW

The formation of interaction comparisons represents a different approach to the analysis of interaction than does the analysis of simple effects. Theoretical or other considerations often suggest a number of partial factorials—a set of smaller, more focused factorial designs—that I will refer to collectively as **interaction comparisons.** Your first introduction to interaction comparisons occurred in Chapter 11, in the context of the two-factor design. The potential for interaction comparisons in the three-factor design is considerably greater than in the two-factor case, as you will see in a moment.

A Classification of Interaction Comparisons

Consider the three-factor design depicted in Table 14–4—a $3 \times 3 \times 3$ factorial. At the top of the table, I have placed **X**'s in all of the cells of the ABC matrix to emphasize the fact that all treatment conditions contribute equally to the overall three-way interaction extracted by the standard analysis of variance and contribute to the undifferentiated character of this interaction.

The first level at which the triple interaction is refined occurs when one of the independent variables is viewed in terms of one or more single-df comparisons. I have chosen factor A and a comparison between levels a_1 and a_2 to illustrate this case. Under these circumstances, level a_3 is entirely disregarded in the calculation of the resulting $A_{\text{comp.}} \times B \times C$ interaction, with the result that an ABC matrix is produced in which only part of the information available for the three-way interaction is examined. This situation is illustrated by the absence of **X**'s in the cells associated with level a_3 in the second ABC matrix presented in Table 14–4. In this case, any three-way interaction will reflect the interaction of $A_{\text{comp.}}$ with the other two independent variables—a more focused picture of the overall $A \times B \times C$ interaction.

The next level of refinement occurs when *two* of the independent variables are simultaneously viewed as single-df comparisons, a situation illustrated in the third ABC matrix in the table. In this case, factor B is represented by a comparison between levels b_2 and b_3, while Factor A continues to be represented by the original

Table 14-4   Systematic Representation of Interaction Comparisons

$A \times B \times C$ Interaction

	c_1			c_2			c_3		
	a_1	a_2	a_3	a_1	a_2	a_3	a_1	a_2	a_3
b_1	X	X	X	X	X	X	X	X	X
b_2	X	X	X	X	X	X	X	X	X
b_3	X	X	X	X	X	X	X	X	X

$A_{\text{comp.}} \times B \times C$ Interaction

	c_1			c_2			c_3		
	1	−1	0	1	−1	0	1	−1	0
	X	X		X	X		X	X	
	X	X		X	X		X	X	
	X	X		X	X		X	X	

$A_{\text{comp.}} \times B_{\text{comp.}} \times C$ Interaction

	c_1			c_2			c_3		
	1	−1	0	1	−1	0	1	−1	0
0									
1	X	X		X	X		X	X	
−1	X	X		X	X		X	X	

$A_{\text{comp.}} \times B_{\text{comp.}} \times C_{\text{comp.}}$ Interaction

	c_1 (1)			c_2 (0)			c_3 (−1)		
	1	−1	0	1	−1	0	1	−1	0
0									
1	X	X					X	X	
−1	X	X					X	X	

comparison (a_1 versus a_2). The cells involved in this comparison are again indicated by **X**'s. The focus of this partial factorial is reflected by the fact that only 12 of the 27 cells are involved in the determination of the three-way interaction, which is a considerable reduction from the 18 cells in the first partial factorial and the 27 cells in the undifferentiated three-way factorial. This level of interaction comparison produces an $A_{\text{comp.}} \times B_{\text{comp.}} \times C$ interaction.

The highest level of refinement occurs when all three factors are expressed as comparisons to produce an $A_{\text{comp.}} \times B_{\text{comp.}} \times C_{\text{comp.}}$ interaction, which is reflected in the last ABC matrix in the table. Here, factor C is represented by a comparison between levels c_1 and c_3 and the other two comparisons remain as before. The focus of this interaction comparison is maximal with the three-way interaction expressed in its simplest and most analytical state, as shown by the eight **X**'s, namely, a $2 \times 2 \times 2$ factorial design. This fundamental component of the overall three-way interaction will be called an **interaction contrast of the three-way interac-**

316

tion and given a special symbol, $\hat{\psi}_{A \times B \times C}$. This symbol emphasizes the fact that an interaction contrast can be expressed numerically as the difference between pairs of means—which you will see in the next section—and as such represents a facet (or component) of interaction that can be subdivided no further, since the *df* for an interaction contrast is 1.

An Example

The selection of single-*df* comparisons in an actual experiment will be dictated by the nature of the independent variables and the sorts of questions a researcher wants to ask. Thus, the particular level of interaction comparison appropriate for any given investigation will vary depending on the logic of the experimental situation. The experiment I will present as an example was originally considered as a two-factor design in Chapter 11. The experiment studied the amnesic effects of two anesthetics normally administered before minor operations. Factor *A* consisted of three levels, a no-drug condition and two different anesthetics. Factor *B* consisted of three types of learning material, low-frequency words with average emotional content, high-frequency words with average emotional content, and high-frequency words with high emotional content. At this point, the design duplicates the example considered in Chapter 11. Suppose a third factor is introduced to create a three-way factorial consisting of three groups of individuals with different language backgrounds. One group learned English as a sole language. The other two groups are bilingual, one having learned English first before learning a second language and the other the reverse. The nature of these different independent variables is summarized in the upper portion of Table 14–5. A set of fictitious means is presented in the lower portion of the table.

Each independent variable in this example can be rearranged into a number of meaningful single-*df* comparisons. Factor *A*, for example, yields a comparison between the two drug conditions (a_2 versus a_3) and a comparison between the control and the average of the two combined drug conditions as well as comparisons between the control and each drug condition separately. Factor *B* provides a comparison between low- and high-frequency words (b_1 versus b_2) and a comparison between average- and high-emotionality words (b_2 versus b_3). Finally, factor *C* can be rearranged into several comparisons, including a contrast between the two bilingual groups (c_2 versus c_3), a comparison between the monolingual group (c_1) and the average of the two combined bilingual groups, and contrasts between the monolingual group and each of the bilingual groups considered separately. The obvious level of analysis of the three-way interaction in this example is an *interaction contrast* ($A_{comp.} \times B_{comp.} \times C_{comp.}$ or $\hat{\psi}_{A \times B \times C}$) since each factor lends itself to the specification of a set of meaningful single-*df* comparisons. I will choose one of them from each set to illustrate the nature of this type of analysis. Less focused partial factorials are usually called for when one or even two of the independent variables cannot be rearranged profitably to form single-*df* comparisons. In these cases, partial factorials of the form $A_{comp.} \times B \times C$ and $A_{comp.} \times B_{comp.} \times C$, for example, will result.

Table 14-5   A Three-Factor Design

LEVELS OF THE INDEPENDENT VARIABLES

Factor A	Factor B	Factor C
a_1 = No drug	b_1 = Low frequency, average emotionality	c_1 = English only
a_2 = Drug X	b_2 = High frequency, average emotionality	c_2 = English first
a_3 = Drug Y	b_3 = High frequency, high emotionality	c_3 = English second

NUMERICAL EXAMPLE

	c_1				c_2				c_3		
	a_1	a_2	a_3		a_1	a_2	a_3		a_1	a_2	a_3
b_1	9	8	8	b_1	9	4	4	b_1	9	4	4
b_2	9	8	8	b_2	9	8	8	b_2	9	8	8
b_3	9	4	4	b_3	9	8	8	b_3	9	8	8

The interaction contrast I will discuss examines the partial factorial formed by crossing the control versus combined-drug comparison ($A_{\text{comp.}}$) with the low-high frequency comparison ($B_{\text{comp.}}$) and the monolingual versus combined bilingual comparison ($C_{\text{comp.}}$). Let's derive this interaction by successively applying the three defining comparisons to the original ABC matrix of cell means and in this way see how the interaction contrast is formed.

As a first step, I will impose the comparison between the control condition and the combined drug conditions ($A_{\text{comp.}}$) on the means in Table 14-5 to produce a new ABC matrix in which factor A is redefined in terms of this comparison. This has been accomplished in the topmost matrix in Table 14-6 by averaging the two drug conditions. From this particular matrix, we can determine whether the control vs. combined-drug comparison interacts with the other two independent variables. Next, I will impose the $B_{\text{comp.}}$ (low-frequency words versus high-frequency words) on this matrix simply by dropping the data appearing at level b_3 from the analysis (the high-emotionality words). The resulting matrix is presented in the middle of Table 14-6. Finally, the single-df comparison involving factor C—a contrast between individuals who have learned only English and an average of the two bilingual groups—is imposed on the middle matrix to create the interaction contrast, which is presented in the bottom portion of the table.

Is there a three-way interaction in this final matrix of means? To see if there is, we could plot the means and examine the graph for the presence of a triple interaction or study the simple interaction effects created by crossing two of the factors, for example, $A_{\text{comp.}} \times B_{\text{comp.}}$, at the two levels of the third factor, $C_{\text{comp.}}$. If the two simple interactions are the *same*, there is *no* three-way interaction; if

Table 14-6 Defining an Interaction Contrast

$$A_{comp.} \times B \times C$$

	Level c_1		Level c_2		Level c_3	
	Control	Combined Drugs	Control	Combined Drugs	Control	Combined Drugs
b_1	9	8	9	4	9	4
b_2	9	8	9	8	9	8
b_3	9	4	9	8	9	8

$$A_{comp.} \times B_{comp.} \times C$$

	Level c_1		Level c_2		Level c_3	
	Control	Combined Drugs	Control	Combined Drugs	Control	Combined Drugs
Low Frequency	9	8	9	4	9	4
High Frequency	9	8	9	8	9	8

$$A_{comp.} \times B_{comp.} \times C_{comp.}$$

	Single Language		Combined Bilingual	
	Control	Combined Drugs	Control	Combined Drugs
Low Frequency	9	8	9	4
High Frequency	9	8	9	8

they are *different,* a three-way interaction *is* present. The numerical value for the $A_{comp.} \times B_{comp.}$ interaction can be obtained by comparing the effect of $A_{comp.}$, say, at the two levels of $B_{comp.}$ separately for the two levels of $C_{comp.}$. To illustrate, from the matrix for the English-only group (one level of $C_{comp.}$), we find a difference between the control and combined drug conditions of $9 - 8 = 1$ for the low-frequency condition and a difference of $9 - 8 = 1$ for the high-frequency condition. For this particular $A_{comp.} \times B_{comp.}$, then, there is no interaction, because the effects of $A_{comp.}$ are the same at both levels of $B_{comp.}$; i.e., $1 - 1 = 0$. From the matrix for the combined bilinguals (the other level of $C_{comp.}$), the difference associated with $A_{comp.}$ is $9 - 4 = 5$ for the low-frequency condition and is $9 - 8 = 1$ for the high-frequency condition. The numerical value for the simple interaction is obtained by subtracting these two differences; i.e., $5 - 1 = 4$; a simple interaction is present. Since the two simple interactions I have just calculated, 0 and 4, are different, the answer to the original question is yes, an interaction contrast is present in these particular data. The numerical value of $\hat{\psi}_{A \times B \times C}$ is obtained simply by taking the difference between these two simple interactions; $\hat{\psi}_{A \times B \times C} = 0 - 4 = -4$. (You should verify this conclusion by plotting the data in a graph.)

Comment

Partial interactions possess a great deal of analytical power, especially when compared with the overall three-way interactions from which they are derived. It is important for you to see how useful single-*df* comparisons can be in pinpointing the locus of a higher-order interaction so that partial interactions can become a functional part of the planned comparisons you specify when you are designing an experiment. The analysis procedures I will present in the next section maintain the logic of the interaction comparisons by working directly with the partial factorial matrix reflecting the interaction of particular interest.

14.5 ANALYSIS OF INTERACTION COMPARISONS

The computational procedure I will present in this section is based on an ordinary three-way analysis of variance. The system is general and can be applied to all three types of partial factorials and to the more complex factorial designs as well. The system is particularly well suited to the analysis of the within-subjects designs considered in Part V. I have resisted presenting special-case formulas, as they tend to obscure the logic and simplicity of this overall plan.

An Overview of the Computational System

We begin by constructing what I will call an *ABC* **comparison matrix**—a matrix that represents the particular interaction comparison in which we are interested.

Table 14-6 provides numerical examples of the *ABC* comparison matrices associated with three different partial factorials possible with the three-way factorial design. Since we will be using the computational formulas from Chapter 13, however, we will base our actual calculations on *sums* rather than means.

Forming the Comparison Matrix. In most cases, you will have no difficulty in forming the comparison matrix: you simply isolate or combine *ABC* sums appropriately to represent the partial factorial of interest. All that you must remember is each set of coefficients underlying the rearrangement of cells. (We will need this information later in the analysis.) For the examples in Table 14-6, the coefficients were $c_i = 1, -\frac{1}{2}, -\frac{1}{2}$ for $A_{\text{comp.}}$, $c_j = 1, -1, 0$ for $B_{\text{comp.}}$, and $c_k = 1, -\frac{1}{2}, -\frac{1}{2}$ for $C_{\text{comp.}}$.

A systematic procedure you may want to use when the coefficients are complex, as we find to be the case with trend analysis, starts with the original *ABC* matrix of sums and the coefficients for one of the factors, e.g., the c_i's associated with $A_{\text{comp.}}$. An *ABC* comparison matrix is constructed with two levels reserved for factor *A*, which now has become $A_{\text{comp.}}$. Each sum in the original *ABC* matrix is multiplied by the relevant coefficient and compiled in the comparison matrix on the basis of *sign*, the positive terms are placed in the first cell reserved for $A_{\text{comp.}}$, which I will label level $a_{(+)}$, and the negative terms are placed in the other cell reserved for $A_{\text{comp.}}$, which I will label level $a_{(-)}$. If there is more than one positive or negative term, the terms are combined and the *sum* is placed in the new matrix. At this point, the signs are dropped, since they have served their function of identifying which levels are relevant for the comparison.

If more than one factor is to be expressed as a single-*df* comparison, we repeat the process described in the last paragraph except that we use the coefficients for a second factor, for example, c_j for $B_{\text{comp.}}$, to weight the terms in the comparison matrix we just formed with the coefficients for $A_{\text{comp.}}$. The sums in the original *ABC* matrix are *not* used. This new matrix will now have two levels for factor *B*, one labeled $b_{(+)}$ for the positive terms and the other labeled $b_{(-)}$ for the negative terms. If the third factor is also a comparison ($C_{\text{comp.}}$), the same process is followed: The c_k's are used to weight the terms in the second comparison matrix and a new and final matrix is formed with two levels of factor *C*, one labeled $c_{(+)}$ for the positive terms and the other labeled $c_{(-)}$ for the negative terms.

This procedure sounds more complicated than it is in practice, as you will see when I present a numerical example. Many times a comparison will consist of a contrast between two treatment levels, in which case the construction of a comparison matrix is obvious. Moreover, many three-factor designs will contain one or more independent variables represented by only *two* levels, which will also reduce the complexity of the analysis. A $3 \times 2 \times 2$ design, for example, permits partial factorials to be created from rearrangements of the levels of the first factor only. In any case, I will assume you are now able to construct the *ABC* comparison matrix appropriately and have kept track of the set or sets of coefficients underlying the construction of the matrix.

The Analysis of Variance. The sums of squares for the analysis are calculated with the formulas presented in Chapter 13 for an ordinary analysis of variance, omitting the calculation of the error term $MS_{S/ABC}$, which is obtained from the original analysis. You must remember to define the levels of each factor appropriately to reflect the number of levels in the *comparison* matrix. For the topmost partial factorial in Table 14–6 (p. 319), where $A_{comp.}$ replaces factor A and the other two independent variables are the same, only the number of levels of factor A changes from 3 in the original design to 2 in this partial factorial. I will use a prime to represent the levels associated with a comparison; thus, we have $a' = 2$, $b = 3$, and $c = 3$. Sample size s remains unchanged regardless of the form of the partial factorial.

The analysis will extract the usual factorial sources of variance, namely, three main effects, three two-way interactions, and the three-way interaction. We will be interested only in the sources involving the redefined factors. If we continue with the $A_{comp.} \times B \times C$ example, the sources of interest will be those involving the "new" factor A, which I will designate A' to keep it distinct from A in the original analysis. From this particular analysis of variance, then, we will be interested in

$$SS_{A'} = SS_{A\,comp.} \; ;$$

$$SS_{A' \times B} = SS_{A\,comp. \times B} \; ;$$

$$SS_{A' \times C} = SS_{A\,comp. \times C} \; ;$$

and

$$SS_{A' \times B \times C} = SS_{A\,comp. \times B \times C} \cdot$$

The remaining sums of squares (SS_B, SS_C, and $SS_{B \times C}$) are of no special interest to us, but simply a "by-product" of this analysis procedure. In fact, you should be careful not to confuse these sums of squares with their counterparts in the *original* analysis—they are usually different, since they are not based on the entire set of data. This particular analysis is being conducted only to calculate the sums of squares involving $A_{comp.}$.

At this point, a special correction is applied to the critical sums of squares to adjust for the particular coefficients chosen to represent each comparison.[3] This "normalizing" adjustment is accomplished quite easily by dividing each sum of squares of interest in the analysis by a quantity that has the following form:

$$\frac{\text{the sum of the squared coefficients}}{2} \cdot$$

In the case of the $A_{comp.} \times B \times C$ partial factorial, the coefficients consisted of the set $(1, -\frac{1}{2}, -\frac{1}{2})$. The correction term for this analysis is

---

[3]With the procedures presented previously, sums of squares for comparisons did not depend on the actual values of the coefficients but on their *relative* values. Thus, a set of coefficients (1, −2, 1) will give the same numerical outcome as will other sets of coefficients that also reflect this comparison, e.g., ($\frac{1}{2}$, −1, $\frac{1}{2}$). This is because the coefficients appear both in the numerator and in the denominator of the computational formula for a comparison sum of squares and in effect the coefficients are cancelled. The procedure outlined here corrects for the use of coefficients as a separate step.

$$\frac{\Sigma (c_i)^2}{2} = \frac{(1)^2 + (-\frac{1}{2})^2 + (-\frac{1}{2})^2}{2} = \frac{1.50}{2} = .75.$$

Each sum of squares would be divided by the factor .75 before the analysis was continued. The correction factors for the other two comparisons, if they had been included in the analysis, would be calculated similarly. For $B_{comp.}$, where the coefficients are 1, -1, and 0 and $\Sigma (c_j)^2 = (1)^2 + (-1)^2 + (0)^2 = 2$, the correction term would be

$$\frac{\Sigma (c_j)^2}{2} = \frac{2}{2} = 1,$$

while for $C_{comp.}$, where the coefficients are 1, $-\frac{1}{2}$, and $-\frac{1}{2}$ and $\Sigma (c_k)^2 = (1)^2 + (-\frac{1}{2})^2 + (-\frac{1}{2})^2 = 1.50$, the correction term would be

$$\frac{\Sigma (c_k)^2}{2} = \frac{1.50}{2} = .75.$$

When a partial factorial is defined by two or more single-*df* comparisons, the correction term consists of the *product* of the correction factors for the various sets of coefficients. In the case of the $A_{comp.} \times B_{comp.} \times C$ presented in Table 14–6, for example, the correction term is

$$\left[\frac{\Sigma (c_i)^2}{2}\right] \left[\frac{\Sigma (c_j)^2}{2}\right] = (.75)(1) = .75.$$

Each of the sums of squares in this analysis that are of interest would be divided by .75. For the interaction contrast presented in Table 14–6, the correction term is

$$\left[\frac{\Sigma (c_i)^2}{2}\right] \left[\frac{\Sigma (c_j)^2}{2}\right] \left[\frac{\Sigma (c_k)^2}{2}\right] = (.75)(1)(.75) \doteq .5625.$$

All of the sums of squares in this analysis would be divided by .5625, since they are all of potential interest.

The degrees of freedom and the mean squares are defined in the usual manner. The within-groups mean square $MS_{S/ABC}$ is the error term for all sources obtained with this analysis. If there is reason to suspect heterogeneity of variance, the error term is based on a pooling of the within-group variances of the particular conditions involved in constructing the comparison matrix.

A Numerical Example

As an example of the calculations, let's consider the partial factorial in which factor A alone is redefined as a single-*df* comparison consisting of a contrast between the control and the combined drug conditions. (The analysis of interaction contrasts, which would probably be the partial factorials in which we would be most interested, appears as Exercise 3 at the end of this chapter.) I will assume that $s = 5$ in this example. The *ABC* matrix of treatment sums from the complete experiment is presented in the upper portion of Table 14–7. This matrix would be the starting point for the construction of any partial factorial. (Please note that the entries in this matrix are *sums* rather than means.)

The first step consists of the construction of the *ABC* comparison matrix, which is derived from the original matrix by multiplying the *ABC* sums by the relevant c_i coefficients. For this comparison, we have been using the set $(1, -\frac{1}{2}, -\frac{1}{2})$, although we could have used a more convenient set, e.g., $(2, -1, -1)$, and have avoided fractional coefficients and potential rounding error. The *ABC* comparison matrix appears in the middle portion of Table 14–7. The entries under $a_{(+)}$ come from level a_1, and those under $a_{(-)}$ are obtained by combining the weighted sums from levels a_2 and a_3. The three two-way matrices based on the *ABC* comparison matrix, which are also needed for the three-way analysis of variance, are presented in the bottom portion of the table. We are ready to calculate the uncorrected sums of squares.

Following the ordinary procedures summarized in Chapter 13 (see Table 13–5, p. 387), we calculate first the basic ratios, remembering that $a' = 2$ in this partial factorial. That is,

$$[T] = \frac{T^2}{(a')(b)(c)(s)} = \frac{(705)^2}{(2)(3)(3)(5)} = 5{,}522.50;$$

$$[A] = \frac{\Sigma A^2}{(b)(c)(s)} = \frac{(405)^2 + (300)^2}{(3)(3)(5)} = 5{,}645.00;$$

$$[B] = \frac{\Sigma B^2}{(a')(c)(s)} = \frac{(215)^2 + (255)^2 + (235)^2}{(2)(3)(5)} = 5{,}549.17;$$

$$[C] = \frac{\Sigma C^2}{(a')(b)(s)} = \frac{(235)^2 + (235)^2 + (235)^2}{(2)(3)(5)} = 5{,}522.50;$$

$$[AB] = \frac{\Sigma (AB)^2}{(c)(s)} = \frac{(135)^2 + (135)^2 + \cdots + (120)^2 + (100)^2}{(3)(5)} = 5{,}698.33;$$

$$[AC] = \frac{\Sigma (AC)^2}{(b)(s)} = \frac{(135)^2 + (135)^2 + \cdots + (100)^2 + (100)^2}{(3)(5)} = 5{,}645.00;$$

$$[BC] = \frac{\Sigma (BC)^2}{(a')(s)} = \frac{(85)^2 + (65)^2 + \cdots + (85)^2 + (85)^2}{(2)(5)} = 5{,}602.50;$$

and

$$[ABC] = \frac{\Sigma (ABC)^2}{s} = \frac{(45)^2 + (45)^2 + \cdots + (40)^2 + (40)^2}{5} = 5{,}805.00.$$

The sums of squares are calculated as follows:

$$SS_{A'} = [A] - [T] = 122.50;$$

$$SS_B = [B] - [T] = 26.67;$$
$$SS_C = [C] - [T] = 0.00;$$
$$SS_{A' \times B} = [AB] - [A] - [B] + [T] = 26.66;$$
$$SS_{A' \times C} = [AC] - [A] - [C] + [T] = 0.00;$$
$$SS_{B \times C} = [BC] - [B] - [C] + [T] = 53.33;$$

and

$$SS_{A' \times B \times C} = [ABC] - [AB] - [AC] - [BC] + [A] + [B] + [C] - [T]$$
$$= 53.34.$$

Table 14-7 Numerical Example of a Partial Factorial

ABC MATRIX

	c_1				c_2				c_3		
	a_1	a_2	a_3		a_1	a_2	a_3		a_1	a_2	a_3
b_1	45	40	40	b_1	45	20	20	b_1	45	20	20
b_2	45	40	40	b_2	45	40	40	b_2	45	40	40
b_3	45	20	20	b_3	45	40	40	b_3	45	40	40

ABC COMPARISON MATRIX

	c_1			c_2			c_3	
	$a(+)$	$a(-)$		$a(+)$	$a(-)$		$a(+)$	$a(-)$
b_1	45	40	b_1	45	20	b_1	45	20
b_2	45	40	b_2	45	40	b_2	45	40
b_3	45	20	b_3	45	40	b_3	45	40

AB COMPARISON MATRIX

	$a(+)$	$a(-)$	Sum
b_1	135	80	215
b_2	135	120	255
b_3	135	100	235
Sum	405	300	705

AC COMPARISON MATRIX

	$a(+)$	$a(-)$	Sum
c_1	135	100	235
c_2	135	100	235
c_3	135	100	235
Sum	405	300	705

BC COMPARISON MATRIX

	b_1	b_2	b_3	Sum
c_1	85	85	65	235
c_2	65	85	85	235
c_3	65	85	85	235
Sum	215	255	235	705

As a computational check, we should verify that the between-groups sum of squares,

$$SS_{bg} = [ABC] - [T] = 282.50,$$

equals the sum of the factorial sums of squares. To illustrate,

$$SS_{bg} = SS_{A'} + SS_B + SS_C + SS_{A' \times B} + SS_{A' \times C} + SS_{B \times C} + SS_{A' \times B \times C}$$
$$282.50 = 122.50 + 26.67 + 0.00 + 26.66 + 0.00 + 53.33 + 53.34$$

$$= 282.50.$$

It is now necessary to normalize the sums of squares of interest to us (the sums of squares involving $A_{comp.}$) by dividing each SS by the factor

$$\frac{\Sigma (c_i)^2}{2} = \frac{(1)^2 + (-\frac{1}{2})^2 + (-\frac{1}{2})^2}{2} = \frac{1.50}{2} = .75.$$

These normalized sums of squares are presented in Table 14–8. As an example of the correction,

$$SS_{A\ comp.} = \frac{122.50}{.75} = 163.33.$$

The degrees of freedom for the critical sums of squares are also presented in Table 14–8. The remainder of the analysis, which is not shown, involves the calculation of the mean squares—obtained by dividing the SS's by the relevant df's—and the F ratios, obtained by dividing each mean square by the within-groups mean square from the original analysis. Each F is evaluated in the F tables under $df_{num.}$ $= df_{effect}$ and $df_{denom.} = df_{S/ABC}$.

Follow-Up Comparisons

Earlier in this chapter you saw that a significant three-way interaction is usually followed by an analysis of simple interaction effects. This is a natural step, since a significant triple interaction means that the simple interactions between two of the independent variables are not the same at all levels of the third. Exactly the same strategy can be followed after discovering a significant three-way interaction involving an interaction comparison. The general form of the analysis starts with

Table 14–8   Normalized Sums of Squares

SOURCE	SS	df
$A_{comp.}$	163.33	1
$A_{comp.} \times B$	35.55	2
$A_{comp.} \times C$	0.00	2
$A_{comp.} \times B \times C$	71.13	4

simple interactions—presumably one involving single-df comparisons. Consider the examples presented in Table 14-6 (p. 319). For the first interaction comparison $(A_{comp.} \times B \times C)$, we would probably examine the $A_{comp.} \times B$ interactions at the three levels of factor C or the $A_{comp.} \times C$ interactions at the three levels of factor B. For the $A_{comp.} \times B_{comp.} \times C$ interaction comparison, we would probably focus on the simple interactions formed by the two comparisons, i.e., the $A_{comp.} \times B_{comp.}$ interactions at the three levels of factor C. For the interaction contrast, the focus would be a simple interaction between two of the single-df comparisons and the two categories of conditions defining the third single-df comparison.

As an example, I will consider the $A_{comp.} \times B \times C$ interaction I calculated in the preceding section. The computational efforts focus on a subpart of the ABC comparison matrix. Suppose we are interested in the simple $A_{comp.} \times B$ interactions. There are three of them, one associated with each level of factor C. If you look back at the comparison matrix in Table 14-7 (p. 325), you will see that a simple interaction is present at each level of factor C and that the form of this interaction is not the same at all three levels. I will illustrate the calculations with the data appearing at level c_1.

We begin by isolating that portion of the ABC comparison matrix that is of interest to us, in this case, the ABC cell sums at c_1. These data are presented in Table 14-9. The next step is to calculate the interaction sum of squares, which, as you can see, is equivalent to an $A \times B$ interaction in a two-factor design at this point. Calculating the interaction sum of squares, we find

$$SS_{A' \times B \text{ at } c_1} = \frac{(45)^2 + (45)^2 + \cdots + (40)^2 + (20)^2}{5}$$

$$- \frac{(135)^2 + (100)^2}{(3)(5)} - \frac{(85)^2 + (85)^2 + (65)^2}{(2)(5)}$$

$$+ \frac{(235)^2}{(2)(3)(5)}$$

$$= 1{,}935.00 - 1{,}881.67 - 1{,}867.50 + 1{,}840.83$$

$$= 26.66.$$

Table 14-9   Simple Interaction of a Partial Factorial $(A_{comp.} \times B$ at Level $c_1)$

	$a(+)$	$a(-)$	Sum
b_1	45	40	85
b_2	45	40	85
b_3	45	20	65
Sum	135	100	235

To normalize the sum of squares, we divide 26.66 by .75, the correction factor for A_{comp}. That is,

$$SS_{A_{comp.} \times B \text{ at } c_1} = \frac{26.66}{.75} = 35.55.$$

This sum of squares is based on

$$df_{A_{comp.} \times B \text{ at } c_1} = (df_{A_{comp.}})(b-1) = (1)(3-1) = 2.$$

The mean square and F ratio are calculated as before in the analysis of the partial factorial.

Extending the Analysis to Lower-Order Effects

If the three-way interaction of a partial factorial is not significant, attention is directed to the lower-order effects—in this case, the two-way interactions and the main effects. At this point, the statistical analysis becomes equivalent to those appropriate for a two-factor design. The only change required is for the number of observations. In the AB matrix, for example, the cell sums will be based on $(c)(s)$ observations, rather than on s observations in an actual two-factor design; computational formulas from Chapter 10 can be used with the three-factor design simply by substituting $(c)(s)$ for s. Similarly, the formulas for the analysis of main effects in the two-factor design are adjusted for the differences in the number of observations on which the marginal means are based—$(b)(c)(s)$ instead of $(b)(s)$ for the A sums and $(a)(c)(s)$ instead of $(a)(s)$ for the B sums. In all cases, you must remember to normalize the sums of squares obtained with the method we have been using to calculate interaction comparisons which is accomplished by dividing each sum of squares by the appropriate correction factor.

Continuing with the same example, let's assume that the $A_{comp.} \times B \times C$ interaction is not significant, which means that we might want to turn to the two-way interactions and main effects. To illustrate, consider the AB comparison matrix appearing in Table 14–7 (p. 325). (This analysis was conducted previously, pp. 324–326, but is repeated here for convenience.) Basic ratios from this matrix are

$$[T] = \frac{T^2}{(a')(b)(c)(s)} = \frac{(705)^2}{(2)(3)(3)(5)} = 5,522.50;$$

$$[A] = \frac{\Sigma A^2}{(b)(c)(s)} = \frac{(405)^2 + (300)^2}{(3)(3)(5)} = 5,645.00;$$

$$[B] = \frac{\Sigma B^2}{(a')(c)(s)} = \frac{(215)^2 + (255)^2 + (235)^2}{(2)(3)(5)} = 5,549.17;$$

and

$$[AB] = \frac{\Sigma (AB)^2}{(c)(s)} = \frac{(135)^2 + (135)^2 + \cdots + (120)^2 + (100)^2}{(3)(5)} = 5,698.33.$$

The sum of squares for this analysis are

$$SS_{A'} = [A] - [T] = 122.50;$$

$$SS_B = [B] - [T] = 26.67;$$

and

$$SS_{A' \times B} = [AB] - [A] - [B] + [T] = 26.66.$$

Normalizing the two sums of squares involving $A_{\text{comp.}}$, we find

$$SS_{A \text{ comp.}} = \frac{122.50}{.75} = 163.33 \quad \text{and} \quad SS_{A \text{ comp.} \times B} = \frac{26.66}{.75} = 35.55.$$

The degrees of freedom are

$$df_{A \text{ comp.}} = 1 \quad \text{and} \quad df_{A \text{ comp.} \times B} = (df_{A \text{ comp.}})(b - 1) = (1)(3 - 1) = 2.$$

The $MS_{S/ABC}$ is used as the error term for the F ratio.

Analysis of Trend

With a quantitative independent variable, the most likely analytical comparisons that will be examined are trend components. Consider again the numerical example from Chapter 13, the results of which are presented again as Fig. 14-1 on p. 330. Factor A (length of the retention interval) is a quantitative independent variable consisting of equally spaced levels on the time dimension (1, 4, and 7 hours). As you have seen in previous discussions, the A manipulation can be decomposed into $df_A = 2$ trend components, namely, linear and quadratic. An inspection of Fig. 14-1 suggests that the different forgetting curves all appear to be linear. Thus, we would expect to find that most of the factorial effects associated with factor A are reflected in the linear component of trend—i.e., that they are differences in slope—rather than in the quadratic component. More specifically, the three-way interaction appears to be largely the result of one sort of patterning of the *linear* component for the three types of material under the condition of minimum linguistic activity (i.e., parallel lines of downward slope) and of a different patterning under the conditions of maximum linguistic activity (i.e., diverging lines of downward slope). An analysis of linear trend would provide statistical support for this observation.

The procedures we have worked through in this section can be used for any single-df comparison, and this includes trend components. As an example, consider the ABC matrix of sums presented in the top half of Table 14-10. From Table A-4 in Appendix A, we find the sets of coefficients to be $(-1, 0, 1)$ for the linear component and $(1, -2, 1)$ for the quadratic component. Following the procedure outlined earlier, we construct an ABC comparison matrix by redefining the levels of factor A into two categories: one in which the positive weighted sums are compiled and the other in which the negative weighted sums are compiled. (The actual signs

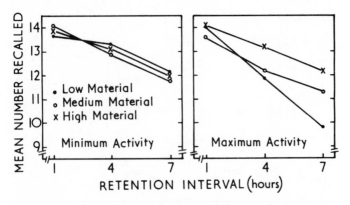

FIGURE 14-1.   Plot of Data from Chapter 13 (Fig. 13-2).

are dropped at this point.) The *ABC* matrix for the linear component is shown at the bottom of Table 14-10 on the left. You will notice that the sums at level a_3 (for which the coefficient is positive) are listed under $a_{(+)}$ in the comparison matrix and the sums at level a_1 (for which the coefficient is negative) are listed under $a_{(-)}$ in the comparison matrix. The *ABC* matrix for the quadratic component is shown on the right. In this case, the *sums* of the weighted cell totals from levels a_1 and a_3 are listed under $a_{(+)}$, since the coefficients for these levels are both positive, and the cell totals from level a_2 multiplied by -2 are listed under $a_{(-)}$.

From this point on, the analysis is identical to the one we considered previously involving a qualitative independent variable (control and two combined drug conditions). To summarize, we conduct an ordinary three-way analysis of variance on the sums in the comparison matrix, remembering that $a' = 2$ in this analysis. The sums of squares involving $A_{comp.}$, which are the only ones we want to examine in this analysis, are normalized by dividing each *SS* by the correction factor. For the linear component, the correction factor is

$$\frac{\Sigma (c_i)^2}{2} = \frac{(-1)^2 + (0)^2 + (1)^2}{2} = \frac{2}{2} = 1;$$

and for the quadratic component, the correction factor is

$$\frac{\Sigma (c_i)^2}{2} = \frac{(1)^2 + (-2)^2 + (1)^2}{2} = \frac{6}{2} = 3.$$

The df's, MS's, and F's are formed in exactly the same manner described in the preceding section.

As I noted earlier, a visual inspection of the data presented in Fig. 14-1 suggests that the three-way interaction can be described in terms of differences in slope. (Statistical analysis of these data—see Exercise 4—will substantiate this observation.) While a trend analysis can be extremely useful in pinpointing the *form* of a given relationship between independent and dependent variables, you should realize that for this sort of analysis to have any importance it should have implications for

Table 14-10   *ABC* Matrices for Trend Analysis

ABC MATRIX

	c_1				c_2		
	a_1 (1 hr.)	a_2 (4 hr.)	a_3 (7 hr.)		a_1 (1 hr.)	a_2 (4 hr.)	a_3 (7 hr.)
b_1	205	198	182	b_1	209	178	146
b_2	210	193	177	b_2	203	182	169
b_3	208	197	179	b_3	211	197	182

ABC LINEAR MATRIX

	c_1			c_2	
	$a_{(+)}$	$a_{(-)}$		$a_{(+)}$	$a_{(-)}$
b_1	182	205	b_1	146	209
b_2	177	210	b_2	169	203
b_3	179	208	b_3	182	211

ABC QUADRATIC MATRIX

	c_1			c_2	
	$a_{(+)}$	$a_{(-)}$		$a_{(+)}$	$a_{(-)}$
b_1	387	396	b_1	355	356
b_2	387	386	b_2	372	364
b_3	387	394	b_3	393	394

theory. In the present example, what difference does it make if the higher-order interaction is located primarily in the interaction of the linear component of the retention functions? The theory, as it was presented in Chapter 13, merely predicted an interaction of a particular type—it did not specify the orthogonal trend component(s) that would be involved. (If it had done so, of course, the theory would be very precise indeed.) In some research areas there is speculation concerning the shapes of the functions relating the independent and dependent variables. In discrimination learning, for example, there have been different theoretical statements concerning the shape of the gradient of stimulus generalization; in the area of motivation, there have been theories that predict an inverted U-shaped function (a quadratic component) relating performance and drive level. Under these circumstances the analysis of the trend components of the interactions may carry with it comparisons of important theoretical interest.

14.6 SUMMARY AND COMMENTS

Factorial designs contain a great deal of information, but it is up to you to take full advantage of this valuable research tool. To be able to manipulate several independent variables simultaneously and to determine how they jointly influence behavior expands our ability to examine phenomena more realistically and more comprehensively. But mastering the skills necessary to conduct an ordinary analysis of variance or even just learning to read and to comprehend an analysis-of-variance summary table is only a first step in the total process. Far more challenging and far more critical is learning to utilize the factorial design to its maximum potential and to design experiments that capitalize on the analytical methods and techniques available to the sophisticated research analyst.

You should pay special attention to Chapter 11, which first introduces you to these analytical techniques—analysis of simple effects and of interaction comparisons—in the context of the two-factor design. Make certain that you understand what the analysis of simple effects can tell you about the nature of interaction and how partial factorials can provide an analytical way to view the manipulation of complex independent variables. Simple effects are central to the definition of interaction. A significant two-way interaction means that the simple main effects of one factor are not the same at all levels of the other factor, and an analysis of these simple effects provides a useful and logical method for determining the ways in which these simple main effects are different. The use of partial factorials recognizes the fact that certain manipulations are too global to be of much interest and are better studied in terms of more analytical and more focused contrasts. Partial factorials provide a way of studying these analytically useful manipulations in the context of the factorial design.

This chapter provides your first glimpse at generalizing these techniques to higher-order factorial designs. You should expect to move back and forth between these two chapters, however, since the more complex analyses presented in this chapter are critically dependent on a mastery and an understanding of the simpler analyses presented in Chapter 11. Both ways of assessing interaction find relevant application in most factorial experiments. If single-df comparisons are not planned or obvious, then analyses of simple effects will dominate the data analysis. On the other hand, if these comparisons provide useful ways of thinking about the manipulated variables, then partial factorials and the analysis of interaction comparisons will receive more emphasis.

14.7 EXERCISES[4]

1. The analysis in Exercise 3 in Chapter 13 (p. 301) revealed that the three-way interaction was not significant. This would mean, of course, that we would probably look next at the two-way interactions rather than at simple interaction effects. In this problem, the $A \times C$ interaction is the only significant two-way interaction in the analysis.

    (a) In order to identify the locus of this interaction, test the significance of the simple main effects of factor C at the different levels of factor A.

    (b) You will note that all three main effects are significant. Two of the main effects (A and C) are not of much interest, because any interpretation will have to be tempered with a consideration of the interaction of these two

---

[4]The answers to these problems are found in Appendix B, beginning on p. 586.

independent variables. The one main effect that we might consider giving further attention is the main effect of factor B. This independent variable does not enter into any interactions with the other factors. Let's assume you are interested in making the following orthogonal comparisons involving the $\bar{B}_j$ means: (1) condition b_2 versus the combined effects of the other two conditions, and (2) condition b_1 versus condition b_3. Test the significance of these comparisons.

2. The analysis in Exercise 4 in Chapter 13 (p. 301) produced a significant three-way interaction. Any interpretation of two-way interactions as well as of main effects must be made in light of the way in which the three independent variables interact to produce the significant triple interaction. An inspection of the treatment sums in the ABC matrix suggests that one way of describing the interaction is to focus on the simple $A \times B$ interaction effects at the two levels of factor C. (We could have just as well looked at the other two sets of simple interaction effects—the simple $A \times C$ interactions at the different levels of factor B and the simple $B \times C$ interactions at the different levels of factor A. Which set we consider in an actual experiment depends on the independent variables we have manipulated and any hypotheses we may have about the outcome.) For this problem, then, test the significance of the simple $A \times B$ interaction effects.

3. With the data appearing in the ABC matrix in Table 14-7 (p. 325), conduct an analysis of the interaction contrast specified in the bottom portion of Table 14-6 (p. 319). (Assume that $s = 5$.).

4. Table 14-10 (p. 331) presents the data from the numerical example of Chapter 13 arranged to facilitate the examination of linear and quadratic trends. Conduct a trend analysis on these data. (The error term for this analysis can be found in Table 13-8, p. 293.)

15

Analysis of
the General Case

I have discussed in detail the analysis of completely randomized experiments—from experiments in which a single independent variable is manipulated to factorial experiments in which two or three independent variables are manipulated concurrently. These designs represent a large proportion of the experiments conducted in the behavioral sciences. Occasionally, we will encounter experiments in which more than three independent variables are included in the design. As you will see, it is relatively easy to extend the analyses we have considered so far to these higher-order factorial experiments. Before I discuss the analysis of the general case, however, I will consider again and in more detail the uses of multifactor experiments in the behavioral sciences.

15.1 USE OF MULTIFACTOR EXPERIMENTS IN THE BEHAVIORAL SCIENCES

Advantages and Disadvantages

Advantages. The advantages listed in Chapter 9 for the two-way factorial are even more compelling for the higher-order factorials. Of these, perhaps the most important is the closer approximation to the "real" world—the greater **external validity** that is afforded by the controlled multifactor experiment. With the inclusion of additional relevant independent variables, we begin to reach the point where in effect we "understand" the behavior under study. Presumably our theoretical explanations will keep abreast of the elaboration of our designs and they will begin to take on the flavor of a comprehensive, general theory of behavior. At the present time, factorials with more than three independent variables of experimental interest are still rare in the literature, a fact that probably reflects the level of development in the behavioral sciences. However, we can say that when a theoretical explanation is "ready" for predictions involving a number of independent variables, the factorial experiment provides an analytical and useful tool for the testing of these predictions.

Other advantages of the higher-order factorials should also be mentioned. They are efficient, providing information about the influence of an increased number of independent variables at very little increase in cost (i.e., subjects, time, and energy). Further, the multifactor experiment allows the determination of the way in which the different variables *combine* to influence behavior jointly. I am referring, of course, to the assessment of interactions. The three-way factorial, for example, produces 4 interactions, the four-way factorial contains 11 interactions, and the five-way factorial contains 26. The point is that higher-order factorials are satisfyingly analytical and rich with factual information.

Disadvantages. We pay a price for this "luxury," however, and this is the possibility of *too much* complexity. This may sound like a direct contradiction of the preceding paragraphs, and in a sense it is. The inclusion of a large number of independent variables in an experiment carries with it the *potential* of a significant higher-order interaction involving *all* of the manipulated variables. Such an interaction would require an extremely complicated statement just to describe the outcome. With the two-way factorial, an interaction indicates that any description of the influence of one of the factors demands a consideration of the specific levels represented by the other factor. With a three-way factorial, a significant higher-order interaction implies that any description of one of the two-way *interactions* must be made with reference to the specific levels selected for a third factor. Interactions involving four or more variables require even more complicated descriptions. Now, if it is difficult merely to *summarize* the pattern of a particular interaction, imagine the problem we will have in *explaining* these results. Obviously, if a significant higher-order interaction exerts an important influence on the phenomenon we are studying, we cannot ignore its presence. On the other hand, we might make faster progress by attempting to understand the results of the simpler designs before attempting to tackle the more complex. I will return to this issue presently.

Another point concerns economy. As we add variables to a factorial, the number of different treatment groups expands greatly. A 3×3 design requires a total of 9 treatment combinations, while a $3 \times 3 \times 3$ needs 27 and a $3 \times 3 \times 3 \times 3$ needs 81. If we hold constant the total number of subjects we will use in the experiment, the number of subjects in each specific treatment group—s—must get smaller and smaller as we increase the number of treatment groups. Suppose (picking a large round number) we had available a pool of 200 subjects. With this pool of subjects, we could include as the maximum number of subjects in each treatment condition, and still maintain equal sample size, $s = 22$ subjects in the 3×3 design, $s = 7$ subjects in the $3 \times 3 \times 3$ design, and $s = 2$ in the $3 \times 3 \times 3 \times 3$ design. The gain in economy breaks down at some point, since we are also concerned about the *reliability* associated with each of the basic treatment means. In human learning, for example, the minimum sample size acceptable to researchers ranges from 8 to 12 subjects.[1] If we set this minimum at $s = 10$, say, we will need only 90 subjects in the two-factor experiment, 270 subjects in the three-factor experiment, and 810 subjects in the four-factor experiment.

This important concern for the reliability or stability of the *individual* treatment means clearly reduces some of the apparent efficiency of the factorial experiment. Additionally, an ambitious factorial experiment, when adjusted to a reasonable sample size, may require many more subjects than are available. In the

---

[1] This number depends upon the size of the within-groups variance. The larger the variability of subjects treated alike, the more subjects that will be required to reach a given criterion of stability. Stability generally refers to the size of the *confidence interval* drawn around the sample means. The size of this interval depends upon the α level acceptable to an experimenter, the sample size (s), and the size of the within-groups mean square. For any given α level, a constant interval may be achieved by applying the following formula: $(MS_{wg})/\sqrt{s}$. Any increase in the MS_{wg} requires a corresponding increase in the sample size in order to ensure the maintenance of a constant confidence interval.

present example, for instance, the demand for subjects in the three-factor and four-factor experiments far exceeds the 200 subjects that are available for testing.

There are several solutions to this problem. One that we often see is the selection of a "minimal" factorial design, each variable being represented by only two levels—a 2^v design, where v equals the number of independent variables. The drawback to this procedure is that we may lose important information by failing to provide for a more representative sampling of the different variables. The selection of the levels for each variable is arbitrary but, if it is done in some realistic fashion, the chance of missing some important behavioral change associated with any variable is reduced as the number of levels is increased. A second solution is the use of a **confounded factorial design**, a form of which—the **Latin square design**—I will discuss in Section 15.6.[2] Third, we could use a **repeated-measures design**, in which if each subject served in two conditions, for example, the total number of subjects might be half those required if independent groups were used. We will consider this type of design in Part V. Of course, some phenomena are best studied with independent groups, so that the repeated-measures design does not provide a general solution to this problem. Finally, if we are able to obtain additional information about the subjects before the start of the experiment, it may be possible to use a Treatments $\times$ Blocks design or the **analysis of covariance**, both of which require fewer subjects to achieve a given degree of precision. The Treatments $\times$ Blocks design was discussed in Chapter 12 (pp. 247–253), and the analysis of covariance will be discussed in Chapter 20.

Predicting Higher-Order Interactions. Complex designs allow the analytical study of behavior under conditions approximating the functional stimulating environment. A question often asked, however, concerns the *interpretation* of significant higher-order interactions when and if they appear. Can anyone conceive of a four-way factorial in which a significant four-way interaction is predicted? Not too long ago, the same question was asked about three-way designs—and probably before that about two-way designs; yet these latter types of designs are now relatively commonplace in certain areas of the behavioral sciences (e.g., experimental psychology).

The answer to this very reasonable question is that complex factorial experiments seem to *evolve* from less complex ones. That is, if a particular two-way interaction has cropped up in a number of different experiments, the effect will be "accepted" by the scientific community as a "fact." Eventually, theories will be developed to attempt to explain this fact. At this point, it is usually not too difficult to think of a *third* independent variable that will interact with the other two. By the same token, as we begin to assimilate the meaning of a particular three-way interaction, we will be able to think of a *fourth* independent variable whose interaction with the other three variables provides an interesting test of the current theoretical interpretations of the earlier finding. Suppose we consider an example based on a three-factor experiment with which we are already familiar.

---

[2] For a thorough discussion of the confounded factorial design, see Kirk (1968, pp. 319–454) and Winer (1971, pp. 604–684).

In the Wallace and Underwood study (see pp. 278–280), three independent variables were manipulated in a factorial arrangement: associative strength, type of learning task, and presumed linguistic development (college students versus retardates). A significant triple interaction was found, with associative strength having a positive effect in free-recall learning and a negative effect in paired-associate learning, but *only* with college students. The investigators assumed that the critical mechanism involved was the *implicit associative response,* the strength of which may be governed in a number of ways. In their experiment, strength was varied two ways, specifically, the nature of the materials and the degree of linguistic development. Suppose we add another independent factor that also taps this process—one that involves what we may call associative pretraining. What if we added a factor (factor D) consisting of two levels: pretraining with the clusters of words that will subsequently be used in the main phase of the experiment (level d_1) and no pretraining (level d_2)? The experiment now could be described as the crossing of strength, task, linguistic development, and pretraining. Further, suppose we assume this pretraining to be such that it will strengthen the weak linguistic habits of the retardates and leave the habits of the college students, which are probably near some maximum strength already, unchanged. If this assumption is correct, we should again find the three-way interaction of Wallace and Underwood (strength $\times$ task $\times$ development) with the subjects at d_2 (no pretraining) and the elimination or the reduction of the same interaction with the subjects at d_1 (pretraining). Note that this latter expectation can be made even more explicit—the positive and negative effects of associative strength observed with the two learning tasks should be present now with *both types* of subjects, college students and retardates.

Whether this four-way factorial is feasible to run or even of theoretical interest is not the point here. What you have seen is that a higher-order factorial can *evolve* from a significant three-way interaction. If we can explain an interaction at one level of complexity, as Wallace and Underwood did in their interpretation of the interaction of strength, task, and type of subject, we will probably be able to conjure up an interesting test of this explanation by predicting an interaction of an even higher order. It may be for this reason that we see so few higher-order designs in the behavioral sciences—the theoretical development in many research areas has not yet reached a point where higher-order designs are useful (i.e., would be interpretable if higher-order interactions were significant). The factorial experiment is not adapted to the "shotgun" approach that is simply looking for relevant variables. The results of such an attempt are likely to be wholly uninterpretable. It is, rather, a device for advancing a field which has reached an appropriate stage of theoretical development.

I have been arguing for an analytical evolution of factorial experiments. We should know how a variable "reacts" in relative isolation, and often this requires an extensive analysis of the function relating variations in the independent variable to behavior. Armed with this knowledge and perhaps an idea concerning the processes that may be responsible for this functional relationship, we can then increase the complexity of our design.

Internal Validity and Experimental Control

In the design of any experiment, we attempt to hold constant as many factors as we can that may influence the behavior we are studying. We test all animals in the same apparatus, perhaps with the same experimenter, and often under a high degree of control of the experimental environment (temperature, illumination, background noise, and so on). Ideally, we would like to be able to hold physically constant all important variables except the ones under systematic study. Factors which we are unable to control in this fashion, or which are not sufficiently important to control, we allow to vary randomly across the treatment conditions. Thus, randomization of these so-called nuisance factors is the major way in which we obtain **internal validity**—i.e., the elimination of biases which, if present, might invalidate any conclusions drawn concerning the manipulations in the experiment.

Another way of achieving internal validity is through the **counterbalancing** of materials across conditions. A simple experiment on transfer of training provides a good example. In a transfer study, an experimenter is interested in a comparison of a subject's performance on two tasks (A and B) that are learned in succession. To be able to compare the two tasks and to attribute any differences to transfer, we must guarantee that they are equal in difficulty. We could determine this through a preliminary comparison of the two tasks, but a far easier method is simply to balance the order in which the tasks are presented. For half of the subjects the tasks are learned in the order A–B; for the other half, the tasks are learned in the reverse order, B–A. The order in which the tasks are presented thus becomes a control factor. It also is an experimental necessity—the problem of differential difficulty of the two tasks must be solved before any meaning can be attached to differences observed in the experiment.

There is an important difference between these two methods of achieving internal validity. The first method (randomization) spreads the influence of uncontrolled variables over the treatment groups equally. These variables do not systematically affect the treatment means, and so any bias is removed. They do, however, influence the *sensitivity* of the experiment, because any variability due to nuisance variables becomes "deposited" in the error term—i.e., results in an increase in the variability of subjects treated alike. With a larger error term, our ability to detect the presence of real treatment effects is reduced. In contrast, the second method achieves control without affecting the size of the within-groups mean square; instead, lists or stimulus orders or balancing procedures are introduced into the design as *independent variables,* and any variance due to control factors may be isolated and kept distinctly apart from the within-groups variance.

External Validity and Multifactor Designs

You have seen that in order to achieve an acceptable degree of internal validity, we must greatly restrict the conditions under which we study a given phenomenon. This implies, then, that most of our research is of limited generality.

The degree to which we *can* generalize our findings beyond the present conditions of testing has been called the **external validity** of an experiment. Frequently, a researcher will introduce a factor into an experiment solely in the hope of increasing the external validity of the experiment. Where one set of stimulus materials is sufficient, two or three will be used; where one experimenter could conduct the experiment, several are employed; where one arrangement of a list of words will suffice, a number of orderings is constructed. In most cases these factors can be thought of as independent variables added to the main experimental design; thus, they effectively transform a two-factor or a three-factor experiment into an experiment of greater complexity.

These factors are certainly not introduced into an experiment because of their inherent interest. Moreover, it is clear that the resultant increase in external validity is really not very great in any far-reaching sense. In spite of these qualifications, control factors still serve an important function in establishing the generalizability of a phenomenon. To be more specific, suppose we are interested in the effect of different stimulants on reading comprehension. Since different groups of subjects receive different stimulants, we could test all of the subjects on the *same* passage of prose material. There is no compelling reason to include two or more passages, as there can be no confounding of the passage with the stimulants. Most experimenters, however, would feel more comfortable with the experiment if additional passages *were* introduced. The reason is the possibility that the outcome of the experiment may be due to some unknown peculiarity of the single passage used in the experiment. For an unknown reason, drug A produces better performance than drug B, but only with a particular passage. This may sound farfetched to the beginning student, but it is observed all too frequently in actual research situations.

If an independent variable by definition requires different sets of materials, one also feels a little uneasy with only one set per condition. Consider an experiment concerned with the perception of words varying in three degrees of pleasantness. Obviously, we would need three different lists of words, one containing pleasant words, one containing neutral words, and one containing unpleasant words. Suppose we constructed these three lists and conducted the experiment—one list per condition. How could we be sure that these lists were *representative* of the pools of words from which they were drawn? Certainly, we would feel "safer" if more than one list per condition were prepared.

Now that you have seen why we introduce control factors into an experiment, either for the sake of internal validity or for an increase in external validity, the question is, What do we do about it? Some researchers ignore the control factors altogether in any statistical treatment of the data, and thus fail to take advantage of the potentially useful information about the interaction of control factors and independent variables of experimental interest, or of the possible refinement of the error term resulting from the removal of sources of variability associated with the control factors from the estimate of experimental error. The statistical analysis, on the other hand, is sometimes difficult, especially when a control factor is viewed as a random-effects variable. I will consider this and other problems in Chapter 21.

15.2 THE STANDARD ANALYSIS OF FACTORIAL EXPERIMENTS

Granting that higher-order designs have an important role to play in the developing behavioral sciences, we must ask if there are general ways of treating such designs, no matter what their particular form. You have seen how a simple set of rules can be used to generate the computational formulas for two- and three-factor experiments. Fortunately, this system can be easily extended to factorial experiments with more than three independent variables.

Rules for Generating Computational Formulas

You would probably find little difficulty in applying the rules from Chapter 10 to generate the computational formulas for, say, a four-way design. As you become experienced with the pattern underlying the analysis of variance, you will be able to delete a number of the steps needed to construct the computational formulas. The shorthand formulas I will consider in this section do not specify detailed operations required to calculate a given sum of squares; they do give enough information to complete the analysis once one is experienced with them.

The sources of variances are specified by the rule stated in Chapter 10 (pp. 190-191). Once the sources have been identified, the next question concerns the computational formulas for the corresponding sums of squares. The general formula for any term in the computational formula, which I have called a basic ratio, is

$$\frac{\Sigma \, (\text{relevant sum})^2}{(\text{appropriate divisor})}. \qquad (15\text{-}1)$$

That is, we identify the relevant sum, square it, combine all of the quantities in the particular set of squares, and divide this total by the number of observations summed prior to the squaring operation. When the quantity identified is a single score rather than a sum, the basic ratio is simply $\Sigma \, (\text{score})^2$.

The next step in constructing the formulas for the sums of squares consists of a systematic reiterative process in which we add and subtract basic ratios in accord with the pattern specified by the expanded df statement. This statement identifies the basic ratios involved by means of the letter code I have been using and indicates how they are combined to form the sum of squares. If a source consists entirely of crossed factors, for example, $A \times B \times C$, the df statement consists of the product of the df's associated with the factors involved in the interaction. If a source contains a nested factor, such as factor S in completely randomized designs—for example, S/ABC—or actual independent variables in nested designs (see pp. 637-638), the df statement is formed by multiplying two quantities, one of which consists of the df associated with the nested factor (or the product of the df's if more than one nested factor is involved) and the other of which consists of the number of *levels* associated with the factor in which the nesting occurs (or the product of the levels if more than one such factor is involved). Thus,

$$df_{S/ABC} = (df_S)[(a)(b)(c)] = (a)(b)(c)(s - 1).$$

In general, the identifying letters to the left of the diagonal refer to the nested factor (factor S here) and those to the right of the diagonal refer to the factors in which the nesting occurs (the factorial combination of factors A, B, and C).

Statistical Models

The linear model underlying any analysis of variance begins with a single observation and specifies the potential components contributing to it. With the completely randomized design, where subjects are assigned randomly to only one of the treatment conditions, these components flow directly from the sources of variability usually extracted in a standard analysis of variance—that is, components for main effects, interactions, and experimental error.[3] As a reminder, the three-factor design yields three main effects (A, B, and C), three two-way interactions ($A \times B$, $A \times C$, and $B \times C$), a three-way interaction ($A \times B \times C$), and a within-groups source of variance (S/ABC). The corresponding linear model reflects these sources, in addition to the grand mean, as follows:

$$ABCS_{ijkl} = \mu + \alpha_i + \beta_j + \gamma_k + \alpha\beta_{ij} + \alpha\gamma_{ik} + \beta\gamma_{jk}$$
$$+ \alpha\beta\gamma_{ijk} + \epsilon_{ijkl} \,.$$

From this model, and certain assumptions, expected values can be derived for each of the mean squares extracted from the analysis, and F ratios formed in such a way that the expectation of the numerator mean square exactly matches the expectation of the denominator mean square except for the so-called null-hypothesis component—the component that becomes zero under the null hypothesis.

Complications do arise when one or more of the independent variables are assumed to correspond more appropriately to a random-effects model than to a fixed-effects model. An independent variable is considered random when the levels are chosen randomly from some larger pool of potential levels. (You saw some examples of random independent variables when I considered nested designs in Chapter 12.) Such independent variables are usually easy to identify from the procedures followed in the selection of the levels for the experiment. Fixed-effects factors are independent variables for which the levels are chosen deliberately and arbitrarily. Most experimental research describes this latter type of manipulation. The presence of random factors in an experiment introduces additional components into the expectations of some of the mean squares and so usually requires the selection of an alternative error term to replace the within-groups mean square,

---

[3]In designs with repeated measures, where subjects serve in more than one of the treatment conditions, additional components become possible, but I will not discuss this complication at this time.

which is the appropriate error term when all of the factors are fixed. I will discuss these topics in Chapter 21 and in Appendix C-4.

15.3 ANALYSIS OF SIMPLE EFFECTS

Simple effects are central to our understanding of interaction, since the concept itself is defined in terms of *differences* among simple effects. An $A \times B$ interaction is defined in terms of differences between the simple effects of factor A, say, at the different levels of factor B (and conversely in terms of the simple effects of factor B and the levels of factor A). An $A \times B \times C$ interaction is defined in terms of differences between simple two-way interactions at the different levels of the third variable. By extension, a four-way interaction is defined in terms of differences between simple three-way interactions at the different levels of the fourth factor. And so on.

The Pattern of Analysis

A significant interaction, therefore, signals the presence of possible differences in simple effects, and a natural plan of analysis is to examine these simple effects in detail to determine which represent significant variation and which do not. As you saw in Chapter 14 (Table 14-1, p. 305), the analysis of a three-way interaction actually represents a successive slicing of the ABC matrix, starting with the simple interactions, such as, $A \times B$ at c_k, and continuing with simple main effects, such as, A at $b_j c_k$, and simple comparisons, such as, $A_{comp.}$ at $b_j c_k$, when any of these successively sliced simple effects is significant. A significant four-way interaction, which involves the $ABCD$ matrix, would be sliced in an analogous fashion, namely, simple three-way interactions, followed by simple two-way interactions, and simple main effects. (For a discussion of this procedure, see pp. 304–305.)

If the highest-order interaction is *not* significant, attention then shifts to the next lower sources of variance, where the data are collapsed over one of the independent variables. A nonsignificant $A \times B$ interaction in a two-way design would force attention on the two main effects; a nonsignificant $A \times B \times C$ interaction in the three-way design would move to the three two-way matrices; a nonsignificant $A \times B \times C \times D$ interaction in the four-way design would move to the four three-way matrices; and so on. The process of collapsing a higher-order matrix to produce lower-order ones which are then analyzed themselves is continued until a significant source of variance is found, at which time detailed analyses of simple effects will be conducted on the data of the matrix producing the significant interaction. That is, the slicing of the relevant matrix then begins. If the significant source is a main effect, the additional analyses will generally take the form of single-*df* comparisons.

In short, the pattern of analysis is usually dictated by the outcome of systematically chosen statistical tests that are arranged in a hierarchy starting with the highest-order interaction at the top and the main effects at the bottom. The significance of the highest-order interaction generally determines whether simple interactions will be examined next (when the interaction is significant) or whether the interactions appearing at the next lower level in the hierarchy will be tested instead (when the interaction is not significant).

The Statistical Analysis

A workable strategy for analyzing the simple effects was illustrated in previous chapters, namely, to treat the "sliced" matrix as if it were a data matrix from a lower-level design. In Chapter 14, for example, you saw how the simple $A \times B$ interaction could be analyzed by thinking of the isolated data matrix as a *two-factor* design. The same general principle is applicable to all factorial designs. In the four-way design, for example, the simple $A \times B \times C$ interaction at any one of the levels of factor D can be analyzed easily by treating the isolated data matrix as a three-factor design, recoding the cells as "ABC," if necessary, and applying the standard formulas to the analysis. The analyses of "collapsed" matrices are treated the same way, except that attention must be paid to the number of observations contributing to each treatment sum in the matrix so that the computational formulas will produce sums of squares that have been weighted appropriately. (See pp. 312–314 for an example of this procedure in the context of a three-factor design.)

The computational plan outlined in Section 15.2 and illustrated and elaborated on in various other sections of this books shows you how to generalize the standard analysis of variance to multifactor designs of any complexity. The plan for analyzing simple effects described in this section capitalizes on this overall scheme as well by treating all analyses as if they were based on data generated by a lower-level design. The advantage of this particular approach is that you can apply what you have learned concerning the analysis of these less complex designs directly to the analysis of simple effects. You do not need to master specialized formulas, but rather you simply need to understand the nature of the simple effects you are examining—which you must know in any case—and to transform the data matrix to a design which you already know how to analyze.

15.4 ANALYSIS OF INTERACTION COMPARISONS

Interaction can also be analyzed by expressing higher-order interactions in terms of meaningful single-df comparisons. Such a redefinition of independent variables creates what I have called interaction comparisons—factorial designs redefined in terms of a meaningful arrangement of treatment levels to reflect focused, analytical comparisons. The logic of interaction comparisons is easily extended to higher-order factorial designs. The trick is to express interactions in terms of specific comparisons—as if they in fact constituted two levels of an independent variable. Control versus combined drug conditions, monolingual versus bilingual, low frequency versus high frequency are all examples of this sort of transformation of an "omnibus" manipulation into focused contrasts involving meaningful ways of regrouping the original levels of an experiment.

The Nature of the Analysis

Each independent variable is regrouped, if applicable, into a single-*df* comparison and combined factorially with the other independent variables—regrouped or not—into the original factorial manipulation to form a partial factorial design. The interest is in the statistical outcome of an analysis of variance performed on this partial factorial design. Interactions and main effects are now expressed in terms of the different single-*df* comparisons. We have examined examples of this type of analysis in the context of two-factor (Chapter 11) and three-factor (Chapter 14) designs. The basic rationale of this approach to analyzing interaction, as outlined in these earlier chapters, is equally applicable to the higher-order designs.

The Statistical Analysis

A method by which the analysis of interaction comparisons can be extended to higher-order factorial designs was illustrated in Chapter 14 for the three-factor design. The procedure begins with the particular matrix on which the analysis will be conducted. Usually this matrix will be the highest one possible, e.g., the *AB* matrix in the two-factor design, the *ABC* matrix in the three-factor design, the *ABCD* matrix in the four-factor design, and so on. This matrix is then transformed systematically into a comparison matrix. This is accomplished by applying one of the comparisons to the original matrix to create a comparison matrix in which positive sums are assigned to one "level" of the comparison factor and negative sums are assigned to the other "level" of the comparison factor. (See pp. 317–320 for an example of this procedure applied to the three-factor design.) Comparisons involving other independent variables are imposed, one by one, on the most recently derived comparison matrix until the desired matrix is obtained. This final comparison matrix provides the basic information on which the desired sums of squares will be based.

The next step is to calculate the sums of squares appropriate to the comparison matrix, using the formulas for an ordinary analysis of variance, and remembering to adjust the levels for the factors appearing as comparisons in the analysis. Finally, the critical sums of squares—those involving the comparisons of interest in the analysis—are normalized by dividing by the following correction factor:

$$\left[\frac{\Sigma (c_i)^2}{2}\right] \left[\frac{\Sigma (c_j)^2}{2}\right] \left[\frac{\Sigma (c_k)^2}{2}\right] \dots , \tag{15-2}$$

where each term in Eq. (15-2) represents a correction factor for a particular comparison represented in the comparison matrix. So-called intact factors, which are not redefined in the analysis, do not contribute to the correction. After this point, the analysis proceeds as usual, with df's, MS's, and F's calculated in the usual manner for the standard analysis of variance. The error term consists of the within-groups mean square from the original analysis of variance.

In short, the analysis of interaction comparisons is no more complicated than the original analysis of variance. Since this analysis follows relatively simple computational rules, as I have demonstrated on many occasions, the analysis of these partial factorials should involve no mystery and no special computational effort. Again, as with simple effects, the critical task before you is to understand what the interaction comparisons tell you about the outcome of your experiment. Your intellectual effort should be devoted to understanding your research outcome; the computational procedures are primarily mechanical at this point.

15.5 ANALYSIS OF EXPERIMENTS WITH UNEQUAL SAMPLE SIZES

So far, I have considered only cases in which equal numbers of subjects are placed in each basic treatment condition. This approach was justified, since most experiments are conducted with equal sample sizes. Also, the specialized formulas needed for the analysis of experiments with unequal sample sizes might have diminished your comprehension of the computational simplicities of the formulas required for the case with equal sample sizes. I have already discussed some of the reasons we encounter experiments with unequal sample sizes. (It may be beneficial to review the discussion at this time—see pp. 99–101.)

There are really two problems associated with the analysis of the data from experiments with unequal numbers of subjects in the different treatment conditions. The first is of utmost importance: The unequal sample sizes must *not* have resulted from the systematic operation of psychological sources. In other words, the reason for the differential numbers of subjects must be *unrelated* to the experimental treatments. Otherwise, the benefit derived from a random assignment of subjects to conditions—a "guarantee" of equivalent groups of subjects in each treatment condition—is lost. If this in fact happens, the scientific value of the experimental results is greatly reduced unless some procedure is found that will restore the equivalency.

In the discussion that follows, we will assume that unequal sample sizes have occurred for reasons independent of the experimental conditions. A common reason for unequal sizes is the use of different intact groups of subjects, such as students in different classrooms, for the different treatment conditions. Since classes will rarely have the same numbers of students in attendance, unequal sample sizes will result. (With this sort of experiment, it is absolutely necessary to convince ourselves and others that the groups of subjects in these intact groups—e.g., classes—are equivalent with regard to abilities that are important for the task being studied. Subjects are not assigned to classes randomly and hence are not assigned to the treatments randomly even if the *classes* are.) Some common reasons for the loss of subjects are sickness or death or the failure to complete the experiment for reasons unrelated to the task itself.

The second problem is practical: How do we analyze the data? One method for dealing with unequal sample sizes is the random discarding of data so that the same number of subjects is represented in each of the treatment conditions. This method is rejected by most researchers, however, since perfectly good data are eliminated from the analysis and power is lost. I will concentrate on a statistical solution to the problem called the **analysis of unweighted means**. This analysis focuses on the treatment *means* and treats them equally in the calculation of systematic sources of variability; differences in sample sizes do not influence these estimates. Other statistical methods are available, which I will consider later in this section, but the analysis of unweighted means is most appropriate when equal sample sizes have been planned and fate unfortunately has entered to produce inequalities.

The Method of Unweighted Means

Let's see how the method of unweighted means is used to calculate the treatment sum of squares in a single-factor experiment (SS_A) when unequal sample sizes are present. The formulas for the method of unweighted means are very similar to those appropriate for equal group sizes. In essence, the analysis assumes that the experiment has been run with groups of equal size where the size is an *average* of the group sizes actually present in the experiment.

The defining formula for SS_A with equal sample size s is expressed as follows:

$$SS_A = s[\, \Sigma \, (\bar{A} - \bar{T})^2 \,].$$ (15-3)

The corresponding defining formula for unweighted means is quite similar:

$$SS_A = s_h[\, \Sigma \, (\bar{A} - \bar{T}')^2 \,].$$ (15-4)

Consider first the quantity within the brackets; we are squaring and then summing the deviation of the *group means* from the *average mean* $\bar{T}'$. This latter quantity represents an *average* of the a treatment means. That is,

$$\bar{T}' = \frac{\Sigma \bar{A}}{s}.$$

(The prime is used to distinguish this unweighted average from the mean we use in the analysis of weighted means. This latter mean, $\bar{T}$, takes into consideration the numbers of subjects in each of the groups. With equal sample sizes, $\bar{T}' = \bar{T}$.) The final step in the calculations is the multiplication of the quantity within the brackets by an *average* sample size. The appropriate average, s_h, is called the

harmonic mean. In the context of the present analysis,

$$s_h = \frac{a}{1/s_1 + 1/s_2 + \cdots + 1/s_a} = \frac{a}{\Sigma\,(1/s_i)}. \tag{15-5}$$

In words, we divide the total number of treatment means, a, by the sum of the reciprocals of the various sample sizes, s_i.

The error term for the analysis is a within-groups mean square based on an average of the individual within-group variances weighted by the corresponding degrees of freedom. That is,

$$MS_{S/A} = \frac{(s_1 - 1)(\hat{\sigma}_1^2) + (s_2 - 1)(\hat{\sigma}_2^2) + \cdots}{(s_1 - 1) + (s_2 - 1) + \cdots} \tag{15-6}$$

$$= \frac{\Sigma\,SS_{S/A_i}}{\Sigma\,df_{S/A_i}}, \tag{15-6a}$$

where

$$SS_{S/A_i} = \sum_{j=1}^{s_i} (AS_{ij})^2 - \frac{A_i^2}{s_i}, \tag{15-7}$$

the sum of squares for an individual group. A computational example of this analysis is provided by Exercise 1 at the end of this chapter.

Consider Example 1 presented in Table 15-1 and the data for a single-factor experiment with unequal sample sizes. For the unweighted-means analysis, we will need to calculate the harmonic mean s_h and the unweighted average of the a treatment means $(\overline{T}')$ before we can substitute in Eq. (15-4). For the harmonic mean of the sample size, we follow the operations specified in Eq. (15-5):

$$s_h = \frac{3}{1/5 + 1/10 + 1/35} = \frac{3}{.20 + .10 + .03} = \frac{3}{.33} = 9.09$$

For the unweighted overall mean,

$$\overline{T}' = \frac{\Sigma\,\overline{A}}{a} = \frac{1.00 + 2.00 + 3.00}{3} = \frac{6.00}{3} = 2.00.$$

Substituting in Eq. (15-4), we have

$$SS_A = s_h\,[\,\Sigma\,(\overline{A} - \overline{T}')^2\,]$$

$$= (9.09)[(1.00 - 2.00)^2 + (2.00 - 2.00)^2 + (3.00 - 2.00)^2]$$

$$= (9.09)[(-1.00)^2 + (0.00)^2 + (1.00)^2]$$

$$= (9.09)(2.00) = 18.18.$$

Table 15-1   The Results of Two Experiments with Unequal Sample Sizes

	Example 1				Example 2		
	a_1	a_2	a_3		a_1	a_2	a_3
A_j:	5	20	105	A_j:	10	70	15
s_j:	5	10	35	s_j:	10	35	5
$\bar{A}_j$:	1.00	2.00	3.00	$\bar{A}_j$:	1.00	2.00	3.00

To understand how this analysis works, consider the second example presented in Table 15-1. For the unweighted-means analysis, we need

$$s_h = \frac{3}{\frac{1}{10} + \frac{1}{35} + \frac{1}{5}} = \frac{3}{.10 + .03 + .20} = \frac{3}{.33} = 9.09$$

and

$$\bar{T}' = \frac{1.00 + 2.00 + 3.00}{3} = \frac{6.00}{3} = 2.00.$$

Completing the substitution in Eq. (15-4), we have

$$SS_A = (9.09)[(1.00 - 2.00)^2 + (2.00 - 2.00)^2 + (3.00 - 2.00)^2]$$
$$= (9.09)[(-1.00)^2 + (0.00)^2 + (1.00)^2]$$
$$= (9.09)(2.00) = 18.18.$$

You will note that the *same* treatment means are present in the two examples and that the *same* sample sizes are also present. All that has been changed is the allocation of the three sample sizes to the treatment conditions. This change in the distribution of the numbers of subjects has left unchanged the analysis performed on the unweighted means. Given that we are able to accept a set of data as being free of bias in spite of unequal numbers of subjects in the different treatment conditions, we are implying that the *means* reflect the potential outcome *had equal numbers of subjects been present*. Therefore, our conclusions must be influenced by the differences among the *unadjusted* (i.e., unweighted) treatment means and not influenced in addition by the unequal sample sizes. I will now consider the analysis of a two-factor design with unequal sample sizes. The procedure we will use is general and can be extended easily to other factorial experiments. (An example of the analysis of a single-factor design is provided by Exercise 1 at the end of the chapter.)

Analysis of Two-Factor Designs with Unequal Sample Sizes

In Chapter 5, I considered a variety of reasons why unequal sample sizes might be found in an experiment where equal numbers of subjects had been planned. These were the result of some sort of subject loss—subjects' failing to achieve a performance criterion or failing to return for a second testing session, equipment breakdown, experimenter error, and so on. In any given case, we must determine whether the loss is unrelated to the treatment conditions. If it is, the analysis may proceed; if it is not, other action is called for, such as artificially dropping subjects from particular conditions or even scrapping the experiment.

We should add to our worries another problem that might occur when subject losses are incurred. In most experiments, several control factors are present in the design in addition to the independent variables. These factors are usually equally represented in the different treatment conditions in the complete design. A loss of subjects may upset this balancing, and a possible confounding of the control factors and the experimental treatments may occur. In short, then, unequal sample sizes produced by subject loss represent an extremely serious experimental problem.[4]

If, in spite of all these considerations, we are still convinced that a meaningful analysis of the data is possible, we will find it necessary to use a new set of formulas. The analysis may be used in situations where the differences among the sample sizes are not great. In this analysis, the means for each treatment combination are taken to represent the means that would have been observed if equal sample sizes had been present. In essence, the analysis is conducted on the *individual means,* each cell mean being treated as if it had been obtained from a group with the common sample size.

Computational Procedures. The simplest way to conduct an analysis of unweighted means is to start with the treatment means ($\overline{AB}$ in this case) and for analysis purposes to transform them into *sums* by multiplying each mean by s_h, the harmonic mean of the sample sizes. That is,

$$AB' = s_h(\overline{AB}),$$

where AB' represents the transformed treatment sum. These transformed sums are then entered in a standard AB matrix (AB' matrix to be exact), and we continue with the analysis as we would normally with equal sample sizes. The only change in the formulas for the sums of squares is the substitution of the harmonic mean of the sample sizes s_h for s in the computational formulas for equal sample sizes. You will see how this works in a moment. The harmonic means is

$$s_h = \frac{(a)(b)}{1/s_{11} + 1/s_{12} + \cdots} = \frac{(a)(b)}{\Sigma\,(1/s_{ij})}. \tag{15-8}$$

That is, we divide the total number of treatment cells, $(a)(b)$, by the sum of the reciprocals of each sample size, s_{ij}.

The within-groups sum of squares $SS_{S/AB}$ is *not* adjusted by s_h but represents as usual a pooling of the sums of squares of subjects who have been treated alike.

---

[4]When imbalances are produced as the result of subject loss, it is usually not possible to perform an analysis including the control factors. The reason is that the different combinations of treatments and control factors are not completely balanced because of the loss of subjects.

For any one treatment condition,

$$SS_{S/AB_{ij}} = \sum_{k=1}^{s_{ij}} (ABS_{ijk} - \overline{AB}_{ij})^2$$

$$= \sum_{k=1}^{s_{ij}} (ABS_{ijk})^2 - \frac{(AB_{ij})^2}{s_{ij}}. \tag{15-9}$$

You will note that the squared cell sum AB_{ij} is divided by the actual number of observations on which it is based, s_{ij}, and *not* by the harmonic mean s_h. The within-groups sum of squares is obtained by summing these individual within-group sums of squares. That is,

$$SS_{S/AB} = \Sigma\, SS_{S/AB_{ij}}$$

$$= \Sigma\, (ABS)^2 - \Sigma \frac{(AB_{ij})^2}{s_{ij}}. \tag{15-10}$$

The degrees of freedom are computed in the normal fashion: $df_A = a - 1$, $df_B = b - 1$, and $df_{A \times B} = (a - 1)(b - 1)$, except for $df_{S/AB}$. In this case,

$$df_{S/AB} = \Sigma\, (s_{ij} - 1),$$

a pooling of the df associated with each treatment cell. This formula may be rewritten as

$$df_{S/AB} = \Sigma\, s_{ij} - (a)(b).$$

The calculation of the mean squares and the F ratios follows the formulas for equal sample size (see Table 10-4, p. 194).[5]

In summary, then, we use the cell means as estimates of what the outcome of the experiment would be were equal sample sizes present. We calculate sums of squares on these means, using standard computational formulas adjusted by the average (harmonic) number of subjects per treatment group. After this point, the analysis parallels the equal-sample case.

A Numerical Example. I will consider an experiment in which unequal cell frequencies occur as the result of subdividing subjects within the different treatment conditions *after* the conduct of the experiment. This frequently happens when individual-difference variables are investigated and it is difficult to ensure an equal number of males and females, or of low- and high-anxiety subjects, or of

---

[5] An alternative way of deriving $MS_{S/AB}$ is to obtain an average of the within-group variances weighted by the appropriate degrees of freedom. That is,

$$MS_{S/AB} = \frac{\Sigma\, (s_{ij} - 1)(\hat{\sigma}_{ij}^2)}{df_{S/AB}}.$$

slow and fast learners, for example, in each condition. The subjects are assigned randomly to all of the treatment conditions, and the assumption is that on the average the subjects of a particular type will be represented without bias in each of the conditions. The numbers of subjects in each subgroup will obviously not be equal. (If such a subdivision were possible before the start of the experiment, a Treatments × Blocks design would probably be used—see pp. 247-253.)

As a hypothetical example, suppose an experimenter decided to compare male and female subjects after the data had been collected on a number of different problem-solving tasks. The original plan was to compare three types of tasks (factor A), with $s = 20$ subjects solving each type. The dependent variable is the number of problems solved in 5 minutes. After the experiment, the subjects in each group are divided into males and females and scored separately (factor B). These subtotals and the sample sizes are presented in the upper half of Table 15-2. Let's assume that $\Sigma (ABS)^2 = 2,970$. The corresponding cell means are listed in the AB matrix in the lower half of the table. Inspection of this latter matrix reveals that the problems differ in difficulty and that sex differences are not consistent for all tasks; i.e., there is a Task × Sex interaction. Since the subjects were assigned to the three types of tasks at random, there is no reason to believe that the assignment of males and females to the tasks was biased. Thus, an analysis of the unweighted means is appropriate.

The first step in the analysis is to calculate the harmonic mean of the sample

Table 15-2   Numerical Example: Unweighted-Means Analysis

AB MATRIX (SUMS)				
			Tasks (A)	
Sex (B)		a_1	a_2	a_3
Male (b_1)	Sum:	96	57	54
	s_{i1}:	13	11	8
Female (b_2)	Sum:	72	44	49
	s_{i2}:	7	9	12

AB MATRIX (MEANS)				
	a_1	a_2	a_3	Average
b_1	7.38	5.18	6.75	6.44
b_2	10.29	4.89	4.08	6.42
Average	8.84	5.04	5.42	

sizes. Substituting the relevant information in Eq. (15-8), we find

$$s_h = \frac{(a)(b)}{\Sigma (1/s_{ij})}$$

$$= \frac{(3)(2)}{\dfrac{1}{13} + \dfrac{1}{11} + \dfrac{1}{8} + \dfrac{1}{7} + \dfrac{1}{9} + \dfrac{1}{12}}$$

$$= \frac{6}{.08 + .09 + .12 + .14 + .11 + .08}$$

$$= \frac{6}{.62} = 9.68.$$

The next step is to multiply the harmonic mean by each of the cell means to create a transformed AB' matrix from which we can extract the factorial sums of squares. This matrix is presented in Table 15-3. To illustrate the calculation of AB' sums, consider the value listed in cell $a_2 b_1$. It is based on the corresponding cell mean, $\overline{AB}_{21} = 5.18$. Multiplying by $s_h = 9.68$ gives

$$AB'_{21} = s_h(\overline{AB}_{21}) = 9.68(5.18) = 50.14.$$

We now use the standard computational formulas for the sums of squares, remembering to substitute s_h for s. Starting with the basic ratios, we find

$$[T'] = \frac{(T')^2}{(a)(b)(s_h)} = \frac{(373.36)^2}{(3)(2)(9.68)} = 2,400.10;$$

$$[A'] = \frac{\Sigma (A')^2}{(b)(s_h)} = \frac{(171.05)^2 + (97.48)^2 + (104.83)^2}{(2)(9.68)} = 2,569.72;$$

$$[B'] = \frac{\Sigma (B')^2}{(a)(s_h)} = \frac{(186.92)^2 + (186.44)^2}{(3)(9.68)} = 2,400.10;$$

Table 15-3 AB' Matrix

	a_1	a_2	a_3	Sum
b_1	71.44	50.14	65.34	186.92
b_2	99.61	47.34	39.49	186.44
Sum	171.05	97.48	104.83	373.36

Table 15-4   Summary of the Analysis

SOURCE	CALCULATIONS		SS	df	MS	F
A		$[A'] - [T'] =$	169.62	2	84.81	10.28**
B		$[B'] - [T'] =$	0.00	1	0.00	<1
$A \times B$	$[AB'] - [A'] -$	$[B'] + [T'] =$	75.91	2	37.96	4.60*
S/AB		$2{,}970 - 2{,}524.54 =$	445.46	54	8.25	

*$p < .025$
**$p < .01$.

and

$$[AB'] = \frac{\Sigma (AB')^2}{s_h} = \frac{(71.44)^2 + (99.61)^2 + \cdots + (65.34)^2 + (39.49)^2}{9.68}$$

$$= 2{,}645.63.$$

The arithmetical operations required to transform the basic ratios into sums of squares are listed in Table 15-4.

The calculation of the $SS_{S/AB}$ requires the use of the treatment *sums* (AB), which we can find in the upper portion of Table 15-2. Performing the operations specified by Eq. (15-10), we find

$$SS_{S/AB} = \Sigma (ABS)^2 - \sum \frac{(AB_{ij})^2}{s_{ij}}$$

$$= 2{,}970 - \left[\frac{(96)^2}{13} + \frac{(72)^2}{7} + \cdots + \frac{(54)^2}{8} + \frac{(49)^2}{12} \right]$$

The remaining steps in the analysis are summarized in Table 15-4. You can see that the problem-solving tasks differed in difficulty and that there was a Task × Sex interaction.[6]

Analytical Comparisons. Any of the additional analyses discussed for use with the two-way factorial design in Chapter 11 may be conducted with the unweighted-means analysis. The formulas that are written in terms of treatment *sums* will use the transformed information in the AB' matrix. The formulas that are written in terms of treatment means will use the means directly.[7] The only

[6]The interpretation of data obtained from an experiment in which characteristics of subjects are "manipulated" (sex, in this example) poses special problems for the researcher. Underwood (1957, pp. 112-125) provides a detailed discussion of these problems of inference.

[7]The means used to extract comparisons involving main effects are obtained by averaging the specific cell means $(\overline{AB})$ as illustrated in Table 15-2. With equal sample sizes, marginal means can be obtained by dividing marginal sums by the number of observations; with unequal sample sizes, this is not done, in order to give all means equal weight in the statistical analysis.

change that must be made is to substitute s_h for s whenever the latter quantity appears in a computational formula. Otherwise, the methods and procedures are identical to those outlined for equal sample sizes.

Heterogeneity of Variance

As noted in earlier chapters, the F statistic is relatively insensitive to departures from the assumption of equal within-group variances. Problems are created, however, when single-df comparisons are performed and marked heterogeneity is present (see pp. 116–117). The presence of unequal sample sizes complicates matters still further in the sense that overall F tests as well as single-df comparisons require special attention. Games (1978a) discusses these problems in detail and provides worked examples for omnibus F tests and single-df comparisons, which he refers to as the $df_u F$ statistic and the t_0 statistic, respectively.

The combination of heterogeneity of variance and corrections for familywise type I error introduces additional complications.[8] Games (1978a) and others have addressed themselves to this particular problem, e.g., Games and Howell (1976) and Keselman and Rogan (1977). Keselman, Games, and Rogan (1979) note serious problems with the Fisher two-stage strategy of following a significant omnibus F test with uncorrected pairwise comparisons, since the initial filtering, afforded by the omnibus F test, does not work effectively with unequal sample sizes and variances. They show that this problem can be corrected through the use of special F tests that take into consideration the differences in sample sizes and the heterogeneity of variances.

Summary and Comments

The analysis of data based on unequal sample sizes may be extended to other experimental designs. The necessary formulas are adapted in a manner analogous to those we examined for the two-way factorial experiment. As I have noted before, the analysis of unweighted means is the appropriate analysis for experiments where equal sample size was assumed as part of the original research plan but where subjects were lost for reasons unrelated to the independent variables. If this critical assumption cannot be maintained, additional steps must be taken to remove any biases that may be introduced by the differential loss of subjects from the treatment conditions. Sometimes it is possible to drop subjects from groups in order to compensate for a seriously unbalanced loss of subjects (see p. 101), but such compensatory dropping of subjects must be fully justified by the researcher. That is, it is necessary to show that any destruction of the equivalence of groups, which is afforded by the random assignment of subjects to conditions, has been eliminated

---

[8] For a general discussion of familywise correction techniques, see pp. 145–151.

by the subsequent dropping of subjects from the unaffected or partially affected groups; otherwise, the analysis may be meaningless.

Occasionally unequal sample sizes are *planned.* This might happen when an investigator is studying an individual-difference variable and wants to use sample sizes for the different categories of individuals that are proportional to the representation of these categories in some relevant population. Suppose, for example, that we want to see whether subjects differing in IQ have different sensory thresholds. Suppose further that we use three IQ levels, low (81 to 100), medium (101 to 120), and high (121 to 140). Since we would not expect equal proportions of subjects to fall into these three categories in the population, we might want to maintain this proportionality in the experiment by using unequal sample sizes. Under these circumstances, one could use the **analysis of weighted means,** but certain restrictions are placed on the nature of these inequalities.[9]

An alternative procedure is the **method of least squares,** which, although it involves complex computations, is beginning to replace the analysis of weighted means because of the widespread availability of computer programs designed to apply this method to experiments with unequal sample sizes. An attractive feature of the method is that it can accommodate disproportionality.[10] For this reason it is widely used with field data, where unequal sample sizes are generally the rule rather than the exception. The interpretation of such analyses—referred to in the psychological literature as **nonorthogonal designs**—is quite complicated and the subject of considerable debate (see, for example, Appelbaum and Cramer, 1974; Carlson and Timm, 1974; Overall and Spiegel, 1969; and Overall, Spiegel, and Cohen, 1975). It is important to realize that the *interpretation* of nonorthogonal designs can be different from that of orthogonal designs, and that some of the principles that apply to experiments with equal sample sizes do not apply to experiments with unequal sample sizes.

Coming back to the analysis of experiments, where equal sample sizes are the rule rather than the exception, the unweighted-means analysis is the most reasonable solution to the problem of unequal sample sizes created by factors unrelated to the experimental variables. Nonorthogonal designs are becoming increasingly common in the behavioral sciences and must be analyzed by special (and still controversial) procedures and interpreted with great care. General textbooks on multiple regression and correlation provide useful discussions of these complications. Of particular use to researchers with a background in analysis of variance are the books by Cohen and Cohen (1975) and by Kerlinger and Pedhazur (1973).

---

[9]This restriction consists of the requirement that the sample sizes within any particular row (or column) of the *AB* matrix, say, must be in the same *proportion* as the sample sizes in all other rows (or columns). Myers (1979, pp. 109–111) discusses this restriction and the consequences for the analysis if disproportionality is present. Winer (1971, pp. 419–422) provides a useful discussion of this type of experiment, and Glass and Stanley (1970, pp. 432–439) work through a numerical example of the procedures.

[10]For worked examples, see Kirk (1968, pp. 204–208) and Winer (1971, pp. 498–503).

15.6 LATIN SQUARE DESIGNS

In this section, I will consider an additional type of multifactor design known as **Latin square designs.** Latin square designs are factorial designs in which only a fraction of the potential treatment combinations are included in an experiment, providing some useful information about additional independent variables but not as much as one obtains from a completely balanced factorial experiment.

Suppose a researcher is interested in comparing four treatments (factor A) and would like to include two additional factors in the design (factors B and C). Depending on the number of levels chosen for factors B and C, the resulting number of required treatment conditions could easily become unmanageable. The minimum number of conditions, assuming that $a = 4$ and both factors B and C are represented by two levels each, would be 16, the number required for a $4 \times 2 \times 2$ factorial. Any increase in the number of levels for either one of these additional factors will have marked effects on the total number of conditions required by the new design. This fact highlights the point made earlier in this chapter that factorial designs can quickly become economically infeasible with modest increases in either the numbers of levels of the factors or the number of factors included in a factorial design.

The Basic Design

The Latin square design represents one solution to this frustrating problem. The logic of the design is to include only a fraction of the treatment conditions in the experiment. Consider the following arrangement:

	b_1	b_2	b_3	b_4
c_1	a_1	a_2	a_3	a_4
c_2	a_2	a_4	a_1	a_3
c_3	a_3	a_1	a_4	a_2
c_4	a_4	a_3	a_2	a_1

The original treatment conditions (levels of factor A) are arranged inside a square formed by the two other factors, each represented by $b = c = 4$ levels. The combinations of levels of the three factors indicated by this square constitute the actual treatment conditions to be included in the experiment. Rather than $(a)(b)(c) = (4)(4)(4) = 64$ combinations, only 16 are specified. Note carefully how these combinations were created—each level of factor A occurs only *once* in any given column or row of the table. Since each column or row represents a level of either factor B or factor C, this arrangement means that any combination of these two factors is associated with only *one* level of factor A rather than all four levels, as would be the case in an actual factorial design. Many different squares are possible with this example. It is critical that the particular square used not be constructed systematically, however, but rather be selected by some random process.[11]

Classically, the Latin square design was used as a way of controlling so-called nuisance factors. The conditions within the square represented the treatment conditions of interest (factor A in this example) and the two sides of the square represented the nuisance variables (factors B and C). Suppose factor B consisted of four different times of day when the experiment could be conducted and factor C referred to four different experimenters hired to conduct the experiment. Contrast this arrangement with a single-factor experiment in which neither time nor experimenter is specifically controlled in the random assignment of subjects to the conditions, experimenters, and times of day. While *bias* can be avoided by having each experimenter test an equal number of subjects under the four conditions and by testing the four conditions with the same frequency at the four times, any influence of these two factors would contribute to the *within-groups mean square*. A factorial arrangement of either factor (Treatments X Experimenters or Treatments X Time) would represent a partial solution to this problem; a *three-way* factorial would solve the problem completely by removing the influence of these two nuisance factors from the error term. The Latin square design performs the same service as the three-way factorial, but with fewer groups.

Any sort of nuisance factor that a researcher feels should be controlled in this manner is a candidate for a Latin square arrangement. In addition, the Latin square can be adapted for use with a factorial manipulation (see Myers, 1979, pp. 264–266). It is even possible to include independent variables of systematic interest to an experimenter, although this use of the Latin square is quite rare in the behavioral sciences.[12] The most common use of the Latin square in psychology is to remove practice effects from error terms in designs where subjects serve in more than one treatment condition. (This use of the Latin square will be discussed in Part V.)

There are clear advantages to Latin square designs: an expansion of the number of variables manipulated with no increase in the number of groups, the increased generality of the results obtained under varied conditions of testing, and the possibility of increasing power through the control of sources of variability that are left unchecked in a standard experimental design. Unfortunately, however, there are serious disadvantages as well. The designs are complex, difficult for many to comprehend and to analyze. This may be one reason why they are not more widely used by researchers in psychology and related fields.[13] A second limitation is the

---

[11] Details concerning the construction of Latin squares can be found in Kirk (1968, pp. 151–155), Myers (1979, pp. 252–255), and Winer (1971, pp. 685–691).

[12] Kirk (1968) provides an extensive coverage of these sorts of designs in Chap. 9, 10, and 11.

[13] Useful and comprehensible discussions of Latin square designs in which subjects are assigned randomly to the different treatment conditions are provided by Kirk (1968, Chap. 6) and by Myers (1979, pp. 259–270).

requirement that all three factors used to form the Latin square have the same number of levels, although there are more complicated forms of Latin square designs that relax this particular restriction. A far more serious problem associated with this sort of design, however, is the confounding of main effects by the presence of interactions between the three factors forming the Latin square.

One way to understand this latter difficulty is to consider the degrees of freedom available to estimate factorial effects in the Latin square design. In the example I have been considering (p. 357), there are 16 different groups; the total between-cells variability, which is based on the deviation of each $\overline{ABC}$ mean from the grand mean $\overline{T}$, has $16 - 1 = 15$ degrees of freedom. Each of the main effects uses 3 df, leaving $15 - 9 = 6$ df for the three two-way interactions and the three-way interaction. Each two-way interaction is associated with $(3)(3) = 9$ df, for a total of 27 df; the triple interaction has $(3)(3)(3) = 27$ df. The discrepancy between the number of degrees of freedom available (15) and those required by the standard analysis of variance (63) highlights the fact that there is insufficient information available in a Latin square design to estimate independently the different factorial effects normally associated with a three-way design. The Latin square design is not a complete factorial, of course, but these interactions can still influence the treatment means. Only in the complete design are things balanced to maintain orthogonality (independence) between the different sources of systematic variability. What this means is that some amount of the variability attributed to the main effects is contributed by interactions that may be present in the experimental situation.

To see this problem most vividly, consider the following Latin square:

	b_1	b_2
c_1	a_1	a_2
c_2	a_2	a_1

The main effect of factor A is based on a comparison between the two a_1 means, $\overline{ABC}_{111}$ and $\overline{ABC}_{122}$, and the two a_2 means, $\overline{ABC}_{221}$ and $\overline{ABC}_{212}$. Expressed as a difference, the main effect is represented by

$$\overline{ABC}_{111} + \overline{ABC}_{122} - \overline{ABC}_{221} - \overline{ABC}_{212}.$$

Consider now the $B \times C$ interaction. This source compares the simple effects of factor B at the two levels of factor C. Expressed as differences between the cell means, the interaction is equal to

$$(\overline{ABC}_{111} - \overline{ABC}_{221}) - (\overline{ABC}_{212} - \overline{ABC}_{122}).$$

Removing parentheses and placing the positive means on the left and the negative means on the right, we have

$$\overline{ABC}_{111} + \overline{ABC}_{122} - \overline{ABC}_{221} - \overline{ABC}_{212},$$

which is *identical* to the A main effect. In short, the A main effect and the $B \times C$ interaction are *completely confounded*. The same situation holds for the other two main effects: B is confounded with $A \times C$, and C is confounded with $A \times B$. A similar argument can be made for larger Latin squares except that the confounding is partial rather than complete.[14]

What can be done about this problem? If interaction effects are *absent* or are assumed to be minimal, the interpretation of main effects is unambiguous. The critical interaction for the treatment main effect (factor A) is between the two nuisance factors (B and C). In our example, these were the time of day and the experimenter. Well-trained and carefully supervised experimenters should eliminate any $B \times C$ interaction in this example and leave the treatment main effect unconfounded. A Latin square is best used when you have a moderate number of levels you wish to study and two (or more) minor variables (1) for which the number of levels can be chosen to agree with those of the treatment factor, (2) for which you anticipate large main effects, and (3) which you are fairly certain will produce no interactions.

Statistical Analysis

I will consider the analysis of the simplest type of Latin square. We will continue with the example presented at the beginning of this section, namely, a single-factor experiment with $a = 4$ treatment conditions arranged in a Latin square with two nuisance factors (B and C). The design and some hypothetical treatment sums are presented in the upper half of Table 15-5. (The individual scores contributing to each treatment sum are not presented in this example; let's assume that $s = 5$ subjects were assigned randomly to each of the treatment conditions indicated in the table.) While this data matrix resembles a BC matrix—since levels of factor B define the columns and levels of factor C define the rows—and we will treat it as such in calculating main effects, it is in reality an ABC matrix, because factor A is arranged within the body of the Latin square and contributes to the designation of a particular group.

We will start the analysis of the Latin square by calculating the total between-groups sum of squares, which is based on the deviation of each cell mean $\overline{ABC}$ from $\overline{T}$. The computational formula for the sum of squares is

$$SS_{bg} = \frac{\Sigma (ABC)^2}{s} - \frac{T^2}{(b)(c)(s)}. \tag{15-11}$$

While familiar quantities are involved in Eq. (15-11), you should examine closely the denominator for the second term on the right of the equals sign. In a three-way factorial design, the denominator would actually be $(a)(b)(c)(s)$—the total number of observations contributing to the grand sum T. In the Latin square design, this

---

[14]Myers (1979, pp. 256–259) illustrates this point with a detailed numerical example.

Table 15-5   Numerical Example: Latin Square

BC MATRIX

	b_1	b_2	b_3	b_4	Sum
c_1	a_1 15	a_2 8	a_3 27	a_4 24	$C_1 = 74$
c_2	a_2 13	a_4 18	a_1 18	a_3 30	$C_2 = 79$
c_3	a_3 20	a_1 10	a_4 16	a_2 10	$C_3 = 56$
c_4	a_4 20	a_3 25	a_2 5	a_1 16	$C_4 = 66$
Sum	$B_1 = 68$	$B_2 = 61$	$B_3 = 66$	$B_4 = 80$	$T = 275$

AC MATRIX

	a_1	a_2	a_3	a_4	Sum
c_1	15	8	27	24	74
c_2	18	13	30	18	79
c_3	10	10	20	16	56
c_4	16	5	25	20	66
Sum	59	36	102	78	275

number is $(b)(c)(s)$, which is sometimes written as $(a)^2(s)$, since in the Latin square $a = b = c$. I have used $(b)(c)$ simply because the product reflects the nature of the ABC matrix as it is arranged in Table 15-5. Substituting in Eq. (15-11), we find

$$SS_{bg} = \frac{(15)^2 + (13)^2 + \cdots + (10)^2 + (16)^2}{5} - \frac{(275)^2}{(4)(4)(5)}$$

$$= 1{,}094.60 - 945.31 = 149.29.$$

This sum of squares represents the total variability due to systematic, i.e., manipulated, sources of variability and will be used to calculate a special sum of squares unique to Latin square designs: a pooling of the sums of squares reflecting the partial information available about interactions.

    The next step is to obtain the sums of squares for the three main effects. The B and C main effects can be obtained from the marginal sums in the upper matrix. The A main effect can be calculated from the marginal sums in the lower matrix in Table 15-5, in which the ABC sums have been aligned with the levels of factors A and C rather than with factors B and C as in the upper matrix. (I could have used factors A and B in order to reveal the A treatment sums as well.) While the necessary information could have been obtained directly from the upper matrix by isolating the relevant ABC sums at each level of factor A, the rearrangement of the entire matrix helps to avoid transcription errors that easily creep in during the process. The formulas for the three main effects should be quite familiar to you, except that again you must pay attention to the denominator terms, which may not be exactly what you would expect, although they all follow the general computational rule, namely, that we divide by the number of observations contributing to each of the sums squared in the numerator. More specifically,

$$SS_A = \frac{\Sigma A^2}{(c)(s)} - \frac{T^2}{(b)(c)(s)} \qquad (15\text{-}12\text{a})$$

$$= \frac{(59)^2 + (36)^2 + (102)^2 + (78)^2}{(4)(5)} - \frac{(275)^2}{(4)(4)(5)}$$

$$= 1{,}063.25 - 945.31 = 117.94;$$

$$SS_B = \frac{\Sigma B^2}{(c)(s)} - \frac{T^2}{(b)(c)(s)} \qquad (15\text{-}12\text{b})$$

$$= \frac{(68)^2 + (61)^2 + (66)^2 + (80)^2}{(4)(5)} - \frac{(275)^2}{(4)(4)(5)}$$

$$= 955.05 - 945.31 = 9.74;$$

and

$$SS_C = \frac{\Sigma C^2}{(b)(s)} - \frac{T^2}{(b)(c)(s)} \qquad (15\text{-}12\text{c})$$

$$= \frac{(74)^2 + (79)^2 + (56)^2 + (66)^2}{(4)(5)} - \frac{(275)^2}{(4)(4)(5)}$$

$$= 960.45 - 945.31 = 15.14.$$

These sums of squares are entered in Table 15-6.

The sum of squares reflecting the partially confounded interactions, $SS_{bg(\text{residual})}$, is obtained by subtracting the sums of squares for the three main effects from the total between-groups sum of squares. That is,

$$SS_{bg(\text{residual})} = SS_{bg} - SS_A - SS_B - SS_C \qquad (15\text{-}13)$$

$$= 149.29 - 117.94 - 9.74 - 15.14 = 6.47.$$

The within-groups sum of squares is based on the deviation of each $ABCS$ score from the relevant treatment mean and then pooled over the entire set. Computationally, this quantity is calculated as follows:

$$SS_{S/ABC} = \Sigma (ABCS)^2 - \frac{\Sigma (ABC)^2}{s}. \qquad (15\text{-}14)$$

Table 15-6 Summary of the Analysis

SOURCE	SS	df	MS
Between Groups	(149.29)	(15)	—
A	117.94	3	39.31
B	9.74	3	3.25
C	15.14	3	5.05
Between Groups (residual)	6.47	6	1.08
S/ABC	Not given	64	Not given
Total	Not given	79	

Since I have not provided individual scores for this example, we are unable to perform these calculations.

To complete the analysis, we calculate the total sum of squares in the usual manner,

$$SS_T = \Sigma\,(ABCS)^2 - \frac{T^2}{(b)(c)(s)}.$$ (15-15)

The degrees of freedom for the residual between-groups source are obtained by subtraction. Specifically,

$$df_{bg(\text{residual})} = df_{bg} - df_A - df_B - df_C$$ (15-16)

$$= [(4)(4) - 1] - (4 - 1) - (4 - 1) - (4 - 1)$$

$$= 16 - 1 - 4 + 1 - 4 + 1 - 4 + 1 = 6.$$

The formula for the $df_{S/ABC}$ is

$$df_{S/ABC} = (b)(c)(s - 1)$$ (15-17)

$$= (4)(4)(5 - 1) = 64.$$

Finally, we have

$$df_T = (b)(c)(s) - 1$$ (15-18)

$$= (4)(4)(5) - 1 = 79.$$

Again I should point out that you will often see formulas for Latin square designs written in such a way as to capitalize on the fact that the levels of the three factors are equal. Thus, you might see Eq. (15-18) written in terms of factor A; that is,

$$df_T = (a)^2(s) - 1,$$

which, of course, will give an identical answer.

The mean squares are calculated by dividing each sum of squares by the appropriate number of degrees of freedom. The F ratios are formed by dividing each systematic source of variance by the within-groups mean square.

I indicated earlier that the entire analysis of variance rests on the assumption that interactions are not present in the experiment. One way to assess the validity of this assumption is to test the significance of the residual between-groups mean square. While this mean square contains only partial information about interaction, this may be sufficient to provide a useful test of this critical assumption. On the other hand, a significant interaction does not necessarily mean that the *A* main effect is affected, since only certain interactions are partially confounded with this effect. In any case, Latin square designs find useful application in a variety of experimental settings and are worthy of consideration if the conditions mentioned earlier are met (p. 360).

15.7 EXERCISES[15]

1. Consider the following scores in a completely randomized single-factor experiment:

AS Matrix

a_1				a_2			a_3		a_4	
7	8	7	16	6	2	3	5	6	9	9
3	3	6	11	2	3	3	6	5	4	6
2	11	6	5	3	5	6	2	9	5	11
8	9	9	3	4	4	2	8	3	8	5
14	8	8	6	5	2	2	5	10	8	2
				0			7	14		

Analyze the results using unweighted means.

2. The following experiment, a 3 X 3 factorial, is conducted with unequal sample sizes:

ABS **MATRIX**

	a_1	a_2	a_3
b_1	8, 10, 9, 12, 14, 7, 9, 13, 12, 12.	18, 12, 14, 12, 16, 17, 13, 16, 13, 15, 16, 14.	12, 12, 10, 14, 13, 10, 9, 10.
b_2	10, 6, 10, 11, 9, 6, 9, 6, 7, 7, 6, 12, 7, 8, 8.	16, 13, 14, 14, 15, 12, 18, 12, 15, 17, 20, 13, 13, 16, 15, 12, 14, 14.	22, 19, 20, 21, 18, 16, 18, 17, 19, 20, 19, 18.
b_3	10, 12, 8, 9, 12.	13, 8, 12, 13, 9, 9.	10, 9, 12, 12.

(a) Perform an analysis of the unweighted means.
(b) Suppose you wanted to obtain the simple effects of factor *B*. How would you do it; i.e., what formula would you use? Assuming that you have an answer, extract these sums of squares and test their significance.

[15]The answers to these problems are found in Appendix B, beginning on p. 591.

WITHIN-SUBJECTS DESIGNS

All of the experimental designs I have considered in the preceding chapters have been based on the assumption that subjects are assigned randomly to the different conditions in the experiment and are given only one of the treatments. I have referred to such experiments as completely randomized designs. They are also known as **between-subjects designs**, because all of the sources of variability extracted in the analysis of variance represent differences *between* subjects. In contrast, it is possible to represent each of these designs in a different arrangement, where subjects serve in all or in a particular subset of the treatment conditions. Under these circumstances, some of the sources of variance isolated in the analysis will reflect differences *within* each subject, and for this reason, such designs are called **within-subjects designs**. Another common way to describe within-subjects designs is to refer to designs with repeated measures. Both terms—*within-subjects* and *repeated-measures*—stress the nature of this type of design, namely, that repeated measurements are taken and treatment effects are associated with differences observed within subjects.

Within-subjects designs constitute a very large proportion of the experiments conducted in the behavioral sciences. On the one hand, within-subjects designs are the obvious choice to study such behavioral changes as learning, transfer of training, forgetting, attitude change, and so on, while on the other hand, they are particularly efficient and sensitive, especially in comparison with an equivalent between-subjects design. In this part of the text, I will examine in detail the most common examples of within-subjects designs. What you will find is that the computational formulas for the sources of variation due to the experimental factors—i.e., the main effects and interactions—remain unchanged. The only new procedures introduced by within-subjects designs involve the selection and calculation of the appropriate error term for a particular source of variance or comparison.

Essentially any between-subjects design can be converted to a within-subjects design, but this conversion requires the implementation of a number of special procedures that attempt to eliminate potential problems associated with this type of design. Chapter 16 will consider these problems and their solution. The remaining chapters in Part V will be concerned with the more specific details of the statistical analysis of the most common within-subjects designs found in the behaviorial sciences.

16

Introduction to Within-Subjects Designs

The number of possible ways in which within-subjects designs can be constructed increases greatly with the number of independent variables included in an experiment. I will begin our discussion with the possibilities available with the two-factor design. The remainder of the chapter will be concerned with the special problems created when a within-subjects manipulation is introduced into an experimental design and with the usual ways by which these problems are solved.

16.1   EXAMPLES OF WITHIN-SUBJECTS DESIGNS

The simplest form of within-subjects design is considered in Chapter 17 and involves a single independent variable all levels of which are administered to the same subjects. When two independent variables are combined factorially, two types of within-subjects designs are possible. The design either will be entirely a "pure" within-subjects design, with all subjects serving in all $(a)(b)$ treatment combinations, or will involve repeated measures for one factor and independent measures (i.e., independent groups) for the other. This latter design is frequently referred to by psychologists as a **mixed design** and by statisticians as a **split-plot design**. The term *mixed* is particularly apt in that there are sources of variance that are produced by between-subjects differences and by within-subjects differences—both types of differences contribute to the statistical analysis. I will distinguish between the two designs by placing the within-subject's (or repeated) factor within parentheses. Thus, the completely repeated case will be designated the $(A \times B \times S)$ design and the mixed case as the $A \times (B \times S)$ design. The factor B within the parentheses involves the repeated measures. To round out the picture, the completely randomized two-factor design is designated as usual without the parentheses and without the specification of S; i.e., it is designated $A \times B$.

The distinction between the three types of designs may be readily seen in Table 16-1. For this display, the same 2×3 design, each factorial containing a total of $(a)(b)(s) = 18$ observations, is represented in the table. The upper display indicates that each of $s = 3$ subjects serves in all six of the treatment combinations. The middle display depicts the $A \times (B \times S)$ design. Here the same six treatment combinations are present, but any given subject serves in only three of them. Moreover, the particular set of three is explicitly specified, namely, that the same set of subjects (s_1, s_2, and s_3) serves in all three levels of factor B, but only in combination with the a_1 level of factor A, while a different set of subjects (s_4, s_5, and s_6) receives the three levels of factor B in combination with the a_2 level of factor A. In the bottom panel of Table 16-1, the $A \times B$ design is depicted. In this case there are $s = 3$ *different* subjects in each of the six treatment combinations; no subject serves in more than one condition of the experiment.

The complexity of higher-order within-subjects designs increases dramatically with the number of independent variables. As you will see in Chapter 19, however, a fairly simple rule can be stated to guide us through the appropriate statistical

Table 16–1   Comparison of Two-Factor Designs

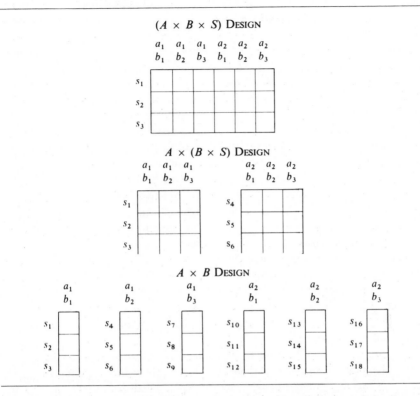

analysis. Again, the primary complication is not in the calculation of the factorial effects, but in the error terms with which they are evaluated statistically.

Advantages of Within-Subjects Designs

The main advantage of within-subjects designs is the control of subject heterogeneity—i.e., individual differences. Take as an example a single-factor experiment. When independent groups of subjects are present in the different conditions, it is likely that the groups will differ somewhat on any single attribute we wish to measure. These between-group differences, which are the natural outcome of the random assignment of subjects to conditions, will be superimposed over whatever treatment effects we may have been fortunate enough to produce by our experimental manipulations. But suppose we select only *one group* of subjects as opposed to the a different groups and have the subjects in this single group serve in all of the treatment conditions. On the face of it, such a procedure seems to guarantee treatment conditions with subjects of identical ability and implies that any differences observed among the treatment conditions reflect the effects of the treatments alone.

A moment's reflection, however, will indicate that this is an oversimplification. For this ideal outcome to result, a subject would have to perform *identically* when serving in different conditions for which treatment effects were in fact *zero*. Such an expectation is unrealistic, since we do not expect identical scores even when a subject is repeatedly tested in the *same* condition of the experiment. Individuals will respond differently on each test for a host of reasons: changes in attention and motivation, learning about the task, and so on. Not only is a subject not the "same" individual on successive tests, but we also expect other uncontrolled sources of variability, such as variations in the physical environment or in the testing apparatus, to show themselves by producing differences between the treatment means. In short, then, the variance attributed to factor *A* will still contain an error component even when the same subjects are tested in all of the treatments.

On the other hand, these sorts of changes will probably *not* be as great as the differences produced through the random assignment of subjects to the different experimental conditions. The error component associated with factor *A,* therefore, should be *smaller* in the case of repeated measures than that expected in an experiment with independent groups of subjects. This reduction in error variance represents a direct increase in economy and power. There are also other ways in which the repeated-measures design is economical. The running time per observation, for example, may be cut drastically by the omission of detailed instructions that overlap the different treatment conditions. With animals as subjects, a great deal of time can be saved in the pretraining needed to "prepare" the animals for the experimental treatments.

In addition to an increase in efficiency, the repeated-measures design has become the most common experimental design with which to study such phenomena as learning, transfer, and practice effects of all sorts. In these research areas, the interest is in the changes in performance that result from successive experience with a task. In a learning experiment, for example, the experience consists of repeated exposures of the same learning task—number of trials becomes the independent variable. In a transfer experiment, the interest may be in the development of learning skills through experience with other tasks and materials. In these studies each subject receives each level of the independent variable, which in this case consists of the various numbers of previous trials or tasks.

Disadvantages of Within-Subjects Designs

Three major disadvantages are associated with repeated-measures designs, and they are all interrelated. The first concerns the fact that subjects will change systematically during the course of multiple testing. I will refer to any such overall change as a **practice effect**. Subjects may show a general improvement during the course of testing, in which case the practice effect is positive; alternatively, fatigue may build up on the successive tests to produce a negative practice effect. In some research areas, we can effectively disregard these positive practice effects when we have reason to believe that performance has effectively reached an asymptote so that additional practice on the task does not produce any further improvement. For instance, if we are studying sensory functioning or performance on motor tasks which are highly learned, we ordinarily assume that a general practice effect is not present. On the other hand, if fatigue or boredom is the major source of change in performance with multiple testing, it may be possible to eliminate these factors by introducing a rest of sufficient length between successive tasks or by using highly motivating instructions and incentives. In most cases, however, researchers generally assume that practice effects will be present. The question, then, is, What's the problem?

Since practice effects are a real possibility, it follows that the *current performance* of a subject will reflect in part the effect of the particular treatment being administered—the direct effect of the treatment—as well as any practice effect that may be present—indirect effects from prior experience in the experiment. Only the treatment administered *first* is immune to the effects of practice. A problem arises if we use the same order in administering the treatments to all subjects, since we will be unable to disentangle the contribution of the treatment effect from the contribution of the practice effect. In this case, practice effects and treatment effects are confounded. A common solution to this problem is to employ enough testing orders to ensure the equal occurrence of each experimental treatment at each stage of practice in the experiment. This is usually accomplished through counterbalancing; the resulting experimental design becomes a form of Latin square. I will consider counterbalancing in the next section.

A second difficulty with within-subjects designs is the possibility of **differential carry-over effects**, which counterbalancing will not control. In contrast with general practice effects, which affect all treatment conditions equally, differential carry-over effects are quite *specific,* the earlier administration of one treatment affecting a subject's performance on a later condition one way and on a different condition another way. Consider, for example, an experiment with $a = 3$ conditions. Will two of the conditions—a_1 and a_2—equally affect the subsequent administration of the third, a_3? Suppose the three treatment conditions differ greatly in difficulty. Will subjects receiving the most difficult condition first behave exactly the same way under the conditions of medium difficulty, say, as subjects receiving the easiest condition first? Or will subjects receiving a control condition first display the same level of performance on one experimental treatment as do subjects receiving instead another experimental treatment first? In either case, if the answer is no, we have an instance of differential carry-over effects. I will discuss this problem in Section 16.3.

A final problem of the repeated-measures designs is statistical. The statistical model justifying the analyses is highly restrictive in the sense that the individual scores are supposed to exhibit certain mathematical properties. I will consider these assumptions in Chapter 19. For the moment, however, it is sufficient to observe that even when carry-over effects can be shown to be symmetrical and to have caused no distortion of the effects of the independent variable, the data still may not fit the assumptions of the model, producing complications in the statistical analyses.

16.2 CONTROL OF PRACTICE EFFECTS

The possibility of general practice effects in most applications of within-subjects designs in psychology requires steps to be taken to avoid the confounding of practice effects with treatment effects that would occur if the treatments were applied to all subjects in the same order. While this confounding could be eliminated by using a different random ordering of the treatments for each subject, most researchers use some form of systematic counterbalancing instead.

Counterbalancing

You were already introduced to counterbalancing when I considered Latin square designs in Chapter 15. In that case, the levels of two factors (B and C) defined the columns and rows of a square matrix and the treatment factor (A) was placed within the body of the square. This particular arrangement places any given treatment once in any given row or column. The two factors defining the rows and columns of a Latin square in within-subjects designs are usually two "nuisance" factors, testing position (first, second, third, etc.) and subjects (or sequences of treatments).

Consider the counterbalancing arrangement presented in the upper portion of Table 16-2. There are $a = 4$ treatment conditions and each subject is to receive each condition once. The order in which the conditions are presented is represented by the columns of the square (testing positions) and the particular sequence of treatments is indicated by the entries in the rows of the square. To complete the Latin square, four sequences are needed. In an actual experiment, a sequence would also represent either a single subject if only one subject received any given sequence or, more commonly, a group of subjects all of whom receive the same sequence. In either case, it is generally recommended to assign an equal number of subjects to each of the sequences of the Latin square.

In the first sequence, for example, the subjects receive the treatments in the order a_1, a_2, a_3, a_4, while in the other three sequences, subjects receive the different treatments in the orders specified in the table. If you examine the entries in the first column of the table, you will note that each level of factor A is presented *once* as the first task that different subjects receive. Similarly, in the other columns, the treatments appear once as the second, third, and fourth tasks that different subjects receive. The purpose of this arrangement is to balance any practice effects over the four treatment conditions equally.

Examining Practice Effects. Consider the data presented in the body of this matrix. Let's assume that these data reflect the scores of four subjects obtained by following the counterbalancing scheme indicated in the matrix. The matrix given below rearranges these scores according to the relevant treatment conditions. The column marginal means for this data matrix indicate the treatment effects found when we average over the four subjects (sequences). Suppose we had presented the

Table 16-2   An Example of Counterbalancing

SUBJECT (OR SEQUENCE)	TESTING POSITION (P)			
	P_1	P_2	P_3	P_4
s_1	a_1 1	a_2 8	a_3 13	a_4 15
s_2	a_3 6	a_1 5	a_4 14	a_2 12
s_3	a_2 4	a_4 11	a_1 8	a_3 14
s_4	a_4 7	a_3 10	a_2 11	a_1 9

SUBJECT (OR SEQUENCE)	TREATMENT CONDITION (A)			
	a_1	a_2	a_3	a_4
s_1	1	8	13	15
s_2	5	12	6	14
s_3	8	4	14	11
s_4	9	11	10	7
Sum	23	35	43	47
Mean	5.75	8.75	10.75	11.75

conditions in only *one* of these orders, the fourth sequence, say. If the scores in this row are any indication, a different outcome of the results would have been observed from the one we find with the marginal means. In fact, if you examine the results obtained with each of the other sequences, you will discover that each has produced a different outcome as well. These differences in outcome have occurred because the differences observed reflect both the effects of the treatments and the effects of practice. The counterbalancing scheme, however, where all four sequences are included and averaged, as has been done in the table, allows us to spread the practice effect equally over the four conditions and to observe the treatment effects unadulterated or colored by the effects of practice.

To see how this occurs, it is convenient to plot the scores as a function of condition and of testing positions. That is, we examine the treatment conditions one at a time and locate the relevant data in the Latin square matrix where testing-order information is available. For example, consider the treatment at a_2. Table 16-2 reveals that this condition was presented first in sequence 3, second in sequence 1, third in sequence 4, and fourth in sequence 2. The four scores associated with the different testing positions—4, 8, 11, and 12—are then plotted on a graph according to the position of testing. This has been done for all four conditions in

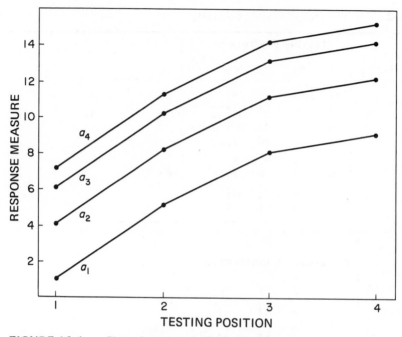

FIGURE 16-1.   Plot of the data in Table 16-2.

Fig. 16-1. An inspection of the figure reveals a marked practice effect, but one that is the same for each treatment condition. That is, there is *no interaction* between testing position and treatments. Numerically, the same treatment effects are found at each of the testing positions.

The absence of interaction between position and treatments is critical in a within-subjects design. Let's see why. Consider the interaction depicted in Fig. 16-2. You can see that differences among the treatment conditions tend to diminish during the course of testing. When the four tasks are given as first tasks in the four different sequences, the differences among the treatments are at a maximum. In contrast, when the four tasks are given as the last tasks in the different sequences, the differences very nearly disappear. Given this particular outcome, we still might be willing to generalize these findings in spite of the interaction. If the interaction had exhibited *reversals* where the ordering of conditions changed from test to test, however, an overall *F* test of the main effect of treatments would be relatively meaningless.

It is always possible to analyze the data from the first testing session separately from those from the other sessions. Performance at this point is completely uncontaminated by the effects of prior testing. Of course, such an analysis involves a retreat to a single-factor design with independent groups of subjects, and we lose the advantages of the within-subjects design. We will also be left with a relatively impoverished experiment—i.e., small numbers of subjects in each experimental condition—and quite low power. It might be possible to use portions of the data

374

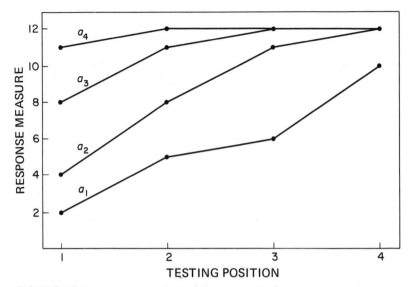

FIGURE 16-2.   An example of a Treatment × Position interaction.

matrix in which the interaction is absent. In this example, we might base an analysis on the first two testing sessions, changing the design from the original within-subjects design in which each subject receives all treatments to one in which subjects receive only two.[1]

In many cases, the presence of differential practice effects simply rules out the within-subjects design for use in the study of a particular phenomenon. In other cases, however, differential practice effects have become the *object* of study, with experiments designed to shed light on the reasons for their occurrence. As an example, consider the early studies of short-term memory in which subjects were asked to recall nonsense syllables after varying amounts of time ranging from 3 to 18 seconds. The amazing finding was an extremely rapid drop in recall from 90 percent after 3 seconds to 10 percent after 18 seconds. Keppel and Underwood (1962) showed that differential effects were operating in this sort of experiment, the short retention intervals showing very little change as a function of testing position and the long retention intervals showing a dramatic drop in performance. An example of this finding is presented in Fig. 16-3, which charts performance for subjects tested after 3 seconds and for those tested after 18 seconds as a function of when in a sequence of tests they were tested. Clearly an interaction is present: forgetting is not observed between 3 seconds and 18 seconds on the very first test, but it appears on the second test and continues to increase on later tests. The effect seems to stabilize toward the end of testing.

Empirical and theoretical interest in this Treatment × Position interaction has

---

[1]This modified design is called an *incomplete block design,* where a block refers to a subject or group of subjects receiving a particular sequence. Kirk (1968, Chap. 11) provides a comprehensive discussion of this sort of design.

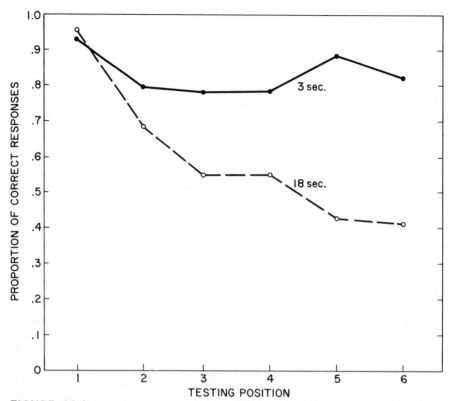

FIGURE 16-3.   Retention as a function of testing position and length of retention interval. (From Keppel, G. and Underwood, B. J. Proactive inhibition in short-term retention of single items. *Journal of Verbal Learning and Verbal Behavior*, 1962, *1*, 153–161. Copyright 1962 by Academic Press, Inc. Reprinted by permission.)

been immense. The increase in forgetting has been attributed to a process known as *proactive inhibition* specifically created by the previous tests. Subsequent research has focused on the nature of proactive inhibition: Under what other circumstances does it occur? What factors influence its size? Are there situations where it can be eliminated? What began as a questioning of methodology introduced a new phenomenon that itself became the object of study and speculation.

Constructing Latin Squares

Special attention should be given to the construction of a Latin square design when repeated measures are involved. The least desirable arrangement is a cyclic square in which each subsequent row is constructed by shifting the treatments one cell to the left (or right) while keeping the basic sequence of treatments the same. Set in the context of our present example where sequence 1 consists of the order 1-2-3-4, a cyclic square is formed when sequence 2 consists of the order

2-3-4-1, sequence 3 consists of the order 3-4-1-2, and sequence 4 consists of the order 4-1-2-3. A Latin square is created, but the order of conditions is not varied at all—a_1 always follows a_4, a_2 always follows a_1, and so on.

A far better arrangement is one in which each condition precedes and follows all other conditions once, a type of Latin square that can be said to be **digram-balanced**. The Latin square shown in Table 16-2 (p. 373) is an example. An inspection of this arrangement will verify that each condition immediately precedes and follows the other three conditions once. Wagenaar (1969) discusses digram-balanced squares and a method for constructing them. Namboodiri (1972, pp. 56-57) describes an alternative method. The main problem is that digram-balanced squares are only possible with experiments possessing an even number of treatment conditions. With odd numbers of levels; digram balancing requires the use of two Latin squares. For $a = 3$, a total of six sequences are needed; for $a = 5$, ten sequences are needed; and so on. Namboodiri indicates how these special sets of sequences are obtained.

If digram balancing is not important, you should use some random method for selecting your Latin square. (See footnote 11 in Chapter 15, p. 358, for sources describing this process.) For any Latin square, however, the actual treatment conditions should be assigned randomly to the designations specifying the square, and subjects should be assigned randomly in equal numbers to the different sequences.

In Chapter 15, we saw how a Latin square design with independent groups of subjects can be analyzed statistically. A similar analysis can be extended to within-subjects designs in which Latin squares are present. The analyses can become quite complicated and as a consequence are often disregarded by researchers. This is unfortunate, however, since the inclusion of the Latin square in the statistical analysis will often result in reducing the size of the error term and provide an opportunity to assess the significance of the Treatment × Position interaction, which, as you have seen, is needed before the interpretation of treatment differences is undertaken. The refinement of the error term is accomplished quite simply, as you will see in the next chapter.

16.3 DIFFERENTIAL CARRY-OVER EFFECTS

Treatment × Position interactions can occur for reasons other than the differential effects of practice. I am referring to situations in which earlier treatments continue to have an influence after the testing is complete and thus affect the treatment conditions that follow. Most typically, such carry-over effects will vary depending on the condition being tested and the conditions preceding it in the testing sequence. I will call such occurrences **differential carry-over effects**, which when present produce a Treatment × Position interaction.

The most common way of reducing differential carry-over effects is to provide sufficient time between sessions to allow the complete dissipation of the preceding treatment condition. Methodological work is usually required to determine how effective the time separation really is. In some research, e.g., drugs, it may be necessary to distinguish between the physiological reaction to the presence of drugs in the subject's system and the subject's psychological state following a drug session. Will a subject be affected by the experience of a drug in an earlier session even though the drug itself is completely purged from the system?

A similar problem must be considered when attempts are made to change a subject's perception of a task through the use of differential instructions—a common procedure used in psychological experimentation. Let's consider some examples: If subjects are told that performance on a given task is a measure of intelligence, how will they view any future tasks that are presented to them when the "set" is changed? If subjects are told to learn a set of material by the use of one sort of strategy, will they be able to drop that method and adopt a new one when the conditions are switched? If subjects are led to believe that one thing will happen but are given another set of treatments—a technique used in so-called deception experiments—will they believe what the experimenter says under a subsequent treatment condition? If some of the experimental conditions are frightening or distasteful, how will subjects react when they are told that they will not be given a similar treatment in a subsequent condition? If they have been given an electric shock for making incorrect responses in a task, will they be unaffected by this experience when they are told they will *not* be shocked in another condition? These are all examples of situations that should not be studied in repeated-measures designs. Greenwald (1976) refers to such possibilities as "context effects" and provides a useful discussion of these sorts of problems.[2]

16.4   OTHER CONSIDERATIONS

By now you should be convinced that the design of an experiment with repeated measures requires a great deal of care and attention to detail. If practice effects are not balanced between treatment conditions or if serious differential carry-over effects are present, the within-subjects design simply will not provide data that are interpretable in any useful manner. In this section, I will examine a number of additional points that should be considered in the design and analysis of an experiment with repeated measures.

Choice of Independent Variable

Because of differential carry-over effects, some independent variables should not be manipulated in a within-subjects design. Each field of research has its list of questionable independent variables, and a great deal of effort is expended by

---

[2]Poulton and his associates, e.g., in Poulton and Freeman (1966), Poulton (1973), and Poulton (1975), have amassed considerable data concerning differential carry-over effects in within-subjects designs. Dawes (1969) discusses additional difficulties encountered when these effects are present. For an objection to the points raised by Poulton in these discussions, see Rothstein (1974) and Poulton's reply (1974).

researchers in studying the outcome of a given manipulation first as a between-subjects factor—i.e., in a completely randomized experiment—and then as a within-subjects factor.

Suppose we are designing a multifactor experiment and are thinking about using repeated measures. If differential carry-over effects are not a problem, we have the choice of either a complete within-subjects design, where subjects receive all of the treatment combinations in a counterbalanced or random order, or a mixed design, where subjects receive all of the treatments associated with one of the independent variables but only in conjunction with one level of the other independent variable. The complete within-subjects design is chosen when fatigue or boredom is not a problem and a researcher wants to study the effects of both independent variables under the conditions of increased sensitivity usually found with repeated measures. The mixed design is chosen when one of the independent variables is an obvious choice as a within-subjects manipulation—trials, for example, in a learning experiment—but the other independent variable might produce differential carry-over effects. On the other hand, the choice might be based on the importance of the two factors to the researcher, the independent variable of primary interest being selected as the within-subjects manipulation. Another basis for choice is the predicted size of the treatment effects. In this case, a researcher might assign as the within-subjects manipulation the independent variable expected to produce the smallest effect. The reason for these choices is that two error terms are used to evaluate factorial effects in this mixed design and the one used in evaluating within-subjects differences is generally much smaller than the one used in evaluating between-subjects differences. The smallest error term achieves an increased sensitivity where it is most appropriate.

Simultaneous Within-Subjects Designs

The within-subjects designs we have discussed so far have consisted of the successive administration of the different treatment conditions to the same subject. Because of the possibility of practice effects, we have to vary the order in which the treatments are presented in such a way that practice effects and treatment effects are not confounded. As you have seen, counterbalancing and the Latin square design solve this problem. Suppose we try something else and present the different conditions to the subjects *simultaneously.* A simple example will illustrate the distinction. Suppose a language teacher is interested in the relative difficulty of learning equivalent English and Italian words in the English-Italian order versus the Italian-English order. The question might be studied in a within-subjects design with half of the subjects learning a set of words in the English-Italian order followed by a different set of words in the Italian-English order, and the other half of the subjects learning the two sets in the reverse order, Italian-English followed by English-Italian. The same experiment can be conducted in a simultaneous design in which both sets of words are presented randomly as a single set to learn rather than as two clearly segregated lists of material.

The clear advantage of this latter arrangement is the elimination of practice effects because both types of pairs in effect are learned simultaneously. But there remains a problem, unfortunately: the possibility of contrast effects. As an example, consider an experiment reported by Grice and Hunter (1964) in which the effect of the loudness of a conditioned stimulus in a classical-conditioning study was investigated under two experimental situations, one a between-subjects design in which one group of subjects received the soft conditioned stimulus and another group received the loud stimulus, and the other a simultaneous within-subjects design in which the soft and loud stimuli were intermixed. The simultaneous design revealed a dramatic difference in the learning produced by the two stimuli, while the between-subjects design produced a marked reduction in the effect. A similar type of finding was reported by Postman and Riley (1957), who contrasted the learning of pairs consisting of similar or dissimilar elements and found no difference between the two types of pairs when subjects learned pairs of a single type in a between-subjects design and striking differences when subjects learned the pairs in a simultaneous within-subjects design.

Both examples illustrate the problem with simultaneous designs, namely, the possibility that subjects behave differently only because a contrast between conditions has been created by the experimental design. Said another way, the opportunity for subjects to compare different treatments produced differences in performance that were not observed when the treatments were presented singly without the possibility of comparison. At the very least, findings of this sort limit the extent to which results can be generalized and suggest that different phenomena are being studied with the two different designs.

The Statistical Comparison of Experimental Designs

It is fairly simple to compare the findings of a successive within-subjects design with the findings of a simultaneous within-subjects design. All that is necessary is to arrange the data in a factorial matrix, one factor representing the actual manipulation, e.g., the order of the English-Italian pairs, and the other factor the type of design. The former would involve repeated measurements and the latter independent groups of subjects serving in the two different designs. The analysis would be patterned after the standard "mixed" analysis of variance (Chapter 18) and the focus of attention would be the interaction between the two factors.

A comparison of either type of within-subjects design with a *between-subjects manipulation*, where subjects receive only one of the treatment conditions, also involves a factorial design, but the analysis is considerably more complicated. Erlebacher (1977) presents a worked example of how this type of analysis is conducted. The general logic of the design can be extended to even more complex types of comparisons.

The Single - Factor
Within-Subjects Design

This chapter covers the analysis of the simplest design in which repeated measures may be used, the single-factor experiment. In this case, the easiest way to think of the design is as a *factorial* experiment in which *subjects* (factor S) are treated as a second factor. In this arrangement, then, both the independent factor (factor A) and subjects (factor S) are completely crossed; that is, each subject receives each of the a treatments.

17.1 DESIGN AND NOTATION

The single-factor design and the scores and totals that we will find necessary for the analysis are presented in Table 17-1. It is convenient and accurate to refer to this as an $(A \times S)$ design. The parentheses indicate that factor A is a within-subjects manipulation. The AS matrix has the levels of factor A listed along the columns and the levels of factor S listed along the rows. Within any given row of the AS matrix appear the scores attained by a single subject (s_j) at the different levels of factor A, while in any given column are entered the scores produced by all s subjects at that particular level of factor A (a_i). Thus, each subject provides a different scores or observations in the experiment.

The notational system is identical to the one used for the single-factor experiment with independent groups of subjects. That is, the scores in the AS matrix are symbolized as AS_{ij}, where the subscript i denotes the particular level of factor A and runs from 1 to a and the subscript j denotes one of the s different subjects (factor S) and runs from 1 to s. The marginal totals needed for the analysis are also presented in the table. It is here that the notation for the $(A \times S)$ design differs from the case with independent groups. Specifically, in addition to the usual column marginal totals A_i, *row* marginal totals S_j are also calculated. The S_j terms consist of totals for each subject of the scores produced at each of the levels of factor A. Consistent with the previous notational system,

$$S_j = \sum_{i=1}^{a} AS_{ij} .$$

Table 17-1 Notational System: $(A \times S)$ Design

SUBJECTS	LEVELS OF FACTOR A				Sum
	a_1	a_2	a_3	a_4	
s_1	AS_{11}	AS_{21}	AS_{31}	AS_{41}	S_1
s_2	AS_{12}	AS_{22}	AS_{32}	AS_{42}	S_2
s_3	AS_{13}	AS_{23}	AS_{33}	AS_{43}	S_3
s_4	AS_{14}	AS_{24}	AS_{34}	AS_{44}	S_4
Sum	A_1	A_2	A_3	A_4	T

(Such a quantity was not possible in the completely randomized design, because different subjects were represented in each cell of the AS matrix.) The symbol T continues to signify the grand total of all individual AS_{ij} scores.

17.2 COMPUTATIONAL FORMULAS

I have already indicated that the $(A \times S)$ design represents a complete crossing of factors A and S. Because of this, the calculations required of this type of design follow those enumerated for the two-way design in Chapter 10. The only exception is that there is no within-groups factor in the $(A \times S)$ design—there is only *one* score in each cell of the AS matrix, and consequently, there can be no within-cell variability. I will consider the standard analysis of variance first and then indicate how the sensitivity of the statistical test can be improved by a Latin square analysis that takes advantage of the fact that the treatment conditions have been systematically counterbalanced.

The Standard Analysis

From our knowledge of the two-way factorial, we would expect to extract from the total sum of squares SS_T two main effects, SS_A and SS_S, and the interaction $SS_{A \times S}$. These sources are presented in Table 17-2. Each sum of squares is calculated from basic ratios, symbolized as brackets around capital letters. Each letter designation refers to a score, in the case of $[AS]$, or to a sum, in the case of $[A]$, $[S]$, and $[T]$; each ratio is formed by squaring and then summing all designated quantities in the AS matrix and dividing by the number of observations contributing to any one of the quantities. For T, this number is $(a)(s)$; for A, this number is s; for S, this number is a; and for AS, this number is 1 and is usually not shown in the formula. These operations are specified in the second column of the table for the first term in each formula, except in the case of the last row, where the formula for the second term, $[T]$, is presented. The df listed in the third column for each source of variance are obtained by following the usual rules. As you have seen previously, the expanded version of each df statement can be used to specify the combining patterns of the basic ratios; for example, $df_{A \times S} = (a - 1)(s - 1) = (a)(s) - a - s + 1$. (The letters and the combination of letters designate basic ratios; the numeral 1 designates $[T]$.) The computational formulas for the sums of squares are presented in the fourth column of the table. The mean squares are constructed by dividing sums of squares by corresponding df's. The only new operation specified in Table 17-2 is the selection of the error term for the MS_A. In the table, I have indicated that the interaction mean square $MS_{A \times S}$ serves this function, but the justification of this choice will require some discussion.

One way to explain this choice of error term is to turn for a moment to the completely randomized design. In this design, the total sum of squares consists

Table 17-2 Computational Formulas for the $(A \times S)$ Design

SOURCE	BASIC RATIO[a]	df	SUM OF SQUARES	MS	F[b]
A	$[A] = \dfrac{\sum A^2}{s}$	$a - 1$	$[A] - [T]$	$\dfrac{SS_A}{df_A}$	$\dfrac{MS_A}{MS_{A \times S}}$
S	$[S] = \dfrac{\sum S^2}{a}$	$s - 1$	$[S] - [T]$	$\dfrac{SS_S}{df_S}$	
$A \times S$	$[AS] = \sum (AS)^2$	$(a-1)(s-1)$	$[AS] - [A] - [S] + [T]$	$\dfrac{MS_{A \times S}}{df_{A \times S}}$	
Total	$[T] = \dfrac{T^2}{(a)(s)}$	$(a)(s) - 1$	$[AS] - [T]$		

[a]Bracketed letters represent complete terms in computational formulas; a particular term is identified by the letter(s) appearing in the numerator.
[b]Factor A is fixed.

384

entirely of between-subject differences—each observation is obtained from a different subject and each observation is independent of the others. As you saw in Chapter 2, SS_T can be divided into two parts, SS_A and $SS_{S/A}$. The first part represents variation associated with the treatment conditions and reflects treatment effects and experimental error. (Experimental error, as you know, results primarily from the random assignment of subjects to conditions.) The second part represents variation associated with subjects treated alike, a "pure" reflection of experimental error, i.e., individual differences and other uncontrolled sources of variation. Returning to the within-subjects design, you can see that a different sort of uncontrolled variation is operating to produce chance differences among the treatment conditions. This variation cannot be due to differences *between* subjects, since each subject serves in all of the conditions, but rather to the *inconsistency* with which subjects perform under the different treatments. This inconsistency is reflected by the Treatment X Subject interaction. Typically, this source of variability is considerably smaller than one that is based on uncontrolled differences between subjects.

The isolation of uncontrolled variation in the within-subjects design can be illustrated quite simply by considering the sums of squares normally extracted in the two types of single-factor designs. Both analyses isolate the treatment sum of squares from the total sum of squares. In the completely randomized design, the remaining variation,

$$SS_{S/A} = SS_T - SS_A,$$

is used to estimate error variance. In the within-subjects design, however, this variation is refined further by subtracting a sum of squares that represents the average differences *between* subjects, SS_S, which reflects the stable and consistent behavior of subjects observed in the context of the overall experiment. This residual, namely,

$$SS_{residual} = SS_{S/A} - SS_S,$$

is actually the Treatment X Subject sum of squares. Using basic ratios and a little algebra, we have

$$SS_{residual} = ([AS] - [A]) - ([S] - [T])$$
$$= [AS] - [A] - [S] + [T] = SS_{A \times S}.$$

The increased sensitivity of the within-subjects design, then, comes from the removal of between-subject differences from the within-groups estimate of unsystematic variation operating in an experiment. In most cases, this gain is considerable.

Latin Square Analysis

The matrix depicted in Table 17-1 (p. 382) displays the data in the form required for the standard analysis of variance, but does not reflect the fact that the order in which the treatments are administered is designed to counterbalance the effects of practice—a basic requirement of the within-subjects design. As I indicated in Chapter 16, this is accomplished by presenting each treatment condition equally often as the first, second, third, or fourth treatment in what is known as a Latin square design. Consider the data matrix presented in Table 17-3. This is a Latin square in which the rows represent four subjects, the columns represent the ordinal position of the testing, and the entries in the body of the matrix are the actual treatment conditions. (For clarity, I have shown the actual treatment levels, while in practice each entry would consist of an *AS* score.) As you saw in Chapter 16 (pp. 372-374), a Latin square arrangement effectively neutralizes the effects of practice in this sort of design.

While it is not immediately obvious, counterbalanced practice effects still exert an influence on the statistical analysis by contributing directly to the size of the error term $MS_{A \times S}$. The presence of a general practice effect—a main effect in the *Latin square matrix*—becomes entangled with the $A \times S$ interaction when the individual observations are *rearranged according to treatments* in the standard analysis. A consistent improvement over the course of testing, for example, emerges as a haphazard pattern of results as far as the individual subjects are concerned and, consequently, influences the magnitude of $SS_{A \times S}$. Fortunately, there is a relatively simple way to remove practice effects from the $A \times S$ interaction. Suppose we let P_1 refer to the sum of all the observations on the first test, P_2 refer to the sum of all the observations on the second test, and so on. We can then calculate a sum of squares for "practice" as follows:

$$SS_P = \frac{\Sigma P^2}{s} - \frac{T^2}{(a)(s)}.$$

The *df* for this source is $p - 1$, where p is the number of tests. (Since there are *a* different tests in this design, *p* must equal *a*.)

All we need to do now is to subtract the sum of squares for practice from the interaction sum of squares to obtain a "practice-free" sum of squares, which I will call $SS_{\text{L.S. residual}}$ to stress the fact that the sum of squares represents the residual variation remaining after the Latin square source of variation is removed. These operations are summarized in Table 17-4. This residual sum of squares, divided by

Table 17-3   Latin Square Arrangement of Testing Orders

SUBJECTS	ORDINAL POSITION OF TREATMENTS			
	P_1	P_2	P_3	P_4
s_1	a_1	a_2	a_3	a_4
s_2	a_3	a_1	a_4	a_2
s_3	a_2	a_4	a_1	a_3
s_4	a_4	a_3	a_2	a_1

Table 17-4   The Latin-Square Analysis

SOURCE	SS	df
$A \times S$	$\Sigma\,(AS)^2 - [A] - [S] + [T]$	$(a-1)(s-1)$
Position (P)	$\dfrac{\Sigma\,P^2}{s} - [T]$	$p-1$
L.S. Residual	$SS_{A \times S} - SS_P$	$(a-1)(s-1) - (p-1)$

the appropriate number of degrees of freedom—calculated by subtracting df_P from $df_{A \times S}$—is the error term with which the overall treatment effects are evaluated.

Two points should be mentioned before I turn to a numerical example. First, there is an alternative way of conducting the Latin square analysis that is particularly useful when single-df comparisons are to be performed on the treatment means . I will introduce this procedure in a later section of this chapter (see pp. 402-404). Second, I must stress the need to check on the possibility of an interaction between the treatment conditions and testing position. As you saw in Chapter 16, this can be accomplished graphically by plotting the data as a function of testing position and examining the trends for each level of factor A. Any suspicious departure from parallel functions—i.e., any interaction—should be assessed statistically by means of a fairly complicated Latin square analysis which I will not consider.[1] A sizable Treatment $\times$ Position interaction—even if not significant—should lead to a questioning of the wisdom of using a within-subjects design to study this particular phenomenon.

17.3 A NUMERICAL EXAMPLE

As a numerical example, consider the data presented in Table 17-5. The design consists of $a = 3$ levels of the treatment factor and $s = 6$ subjects. A Latin square design is used with two subjects assigned randomly to each of the three sequences of treatments. The data arranged according to testing position are presented on the left, where the specific testing sequence received by each subject is indicated on the far left of the data matrix. (In an actual experiment, the meaning of the levels, i.e., the particular treatment condition represented, would be determined by randomly assigning the treatments to the labels.) The data have been rearranged in the AS matrix on the right according to the treatment conditions in order to facilitate the calculation of sums of squares for the standard within-subjects analysis.

As a first step, I will calculate the basic ratios for the standard analysis. Using the formulas specified in Table 17-2 and the data in the AS matrix on the right in

---

[1]Myers (1979, pp. 274-278) describes and illustrates this analysis in some detail.

Table 17-5 Numerical Example

ORDER OF TREATMENTS		ORDINAL POSITION OF TREATMENTS				AS MATRIX Treatments			
		P_1	P_2	P_3		a_1	a_2	a_3	Sum
(a_1, a_2, a_3)	s_1	13	24	22	s_1	13	24	22	59
	s_2	6	30	29	s_2	6	30	29	65
(a_2, a_3, a_1)	s_3	13	23	25	s_3	25	13	23	61
	s_4	16	25	20	s_4	20	16	25	61
(a_3, a_1, a_2)	s_5	16	25	37	s_5	25	37	16	78
	s_6	12	19	30	s_6	19	30	12	61
	Sum	76	146	163	Sum	108	150	127	385

Table 17-5, we find

$$[T] = \frac{T^2}{(a)(s)} = \frac{(385)^2}{(3)(6)} = 8{,}234.72;$$

$$[A] = \frac{\Sigma A^2}{s} = \frac{(108)^2 + (150)^2 + (127)^2}{6} = 8{,}382.17;$$

$$[S] = \frac{\Sigma S^2}{a} = \frac{(59)^2 + (65)^2 + \cdots + (78)^2 + (61)^2}{3} = 8{,}317.67;$$

and

$$[AS] = \Sigma (AS)^2 = (13)^2 + (6)^2 + \cdots + (16)^2 + (12)^2 = 9{,}265.$$

These numbers are entered in Table 17-6, where they are combined in the patterns indicated to produce the appropriate sums of squares. The remainder of the analysis follows directly from the formulas given in Table 17-2 and thus requires no comment. The main effect of factor A is not significant.

For the Latin square analysis summarized in Table 17-4, we need one more basic ratio, $[P]$. From the sums presented in the left-hand matrix in Table 17-5, we find

$$[P] = \frac{\Sigma P^2}{s} = \frac{(76)^2 + (146)^2 + (163)^2}{6} = 8{,}943.50.$$

The sum of squares for testing position can now be calculated. Specifically,

$$SS_P = [P] - [T] = 8{,}943.50 - 8{,}234.72 = 708.78.$$

Finally, we can obtain the residual sum of squares by the subtraction indicated in Table 17-4:

$$SS_{\text{L.S. residual}} = SS_{A \times S} - SS_P = 799.88 - 708.78$$
$$= 91.10.$$

388

Table 17-6 Within-Subjects Analysis of Variance

SOURCE	BASIC RATIO[a]	SUM OF SQUARES		df	MS	F
A	$[A] = 8{,}382.17$	$[A] - [T] =$	147.45	2	73.73	.92
S	$[S] = 8{,}317.67$	$[S] - [T] =$	82.95	5	16.59	
A × S	$[AS] = 9{,}265$	$[AS] - [A] - [S] + [T] =$	799.88	10	79.99	
Total	$[T] = 8{,}234.72$	$[AS] - [T] = 1{,}030.28$		17		

[a]Bracketed letters represent complete terms in computational formulas; a particular term is identified by the letter(s) appearing in the numerator.

These values are entered in Table 17-7, a summary table reflecting the entire break-down of sums of squares. The analysis now shows a significant treatment effect, which was obscured in the standard within-subjects analysis by the presence of a sizable and significant practice effect.

I indicated in the last chapter that the within-subjects design is more sensitive in detecting differences among means than is a companion experiment with independent groups. Let's see how this works out in the context of the present example. We will assume for this illustration that instead of six different subjects being tested under the three conditions, we have a sample of 18 subjects, of whom six were tested at a_1, six at a_2, and six at a_3. We can calculate the within-groups sum of squares from the basic ratios already obtained. That is,

$$SS_{S/A} = [AS] - [A] = 9{,}265 - 8{,}382.17 = 882.83.$$

The df associated with the $SS_{S/A}$ are found with the usual formula:

$$df_{S/A} = a(s - 1) = 3(6 - 1) = 15.$$

The $MS_{S/A}$ is obtained by dividing the $SS_{S/A}$ by the relevant df:

$$MS_{S/A} = \frac{882.83}{15} = 58.86.$$

The resulting F ratio for the main effect of factor A now becomes

$$F = \frac{MS_A}{MS_{S/A}} = \frac{73.73}{58.86} = 1.25,$$

which is not significant ($p > .25$).

The "sensitivity" I have been talking about refers to the amount by which this "composite" mean square, $MS_{S/A}$, is reduced by extracting the main effect of *subjects* (factor S) in the standard analysis and of *practice* (factor P) *plus* subjects in the Latin square analysis. A rough index of the relative efficiency of the different designs can be obtained by forming a ratio of two error terms and multiplying by

Table 17-7   Latin Square Analysis of Variance

SOURCE	SS	df	MS	F
A	147.45	2	73.73	6.47*
S	82.95	5	16.59	
P	708.78	2	354.39	31.11**
L.S. Residual	91.10	8	11.39	
Total	1,030.28	17		

*$p < .025$.
**$p < .01$.

$100.^2$ For the comparison between the independent-groups design and the standard within-subjects design,

$$\text{relative efficiency} = \frac{MS_{S/A}}{MS_{A \times S}} \times 100$$

$$= \frac{58.86}{79.99} \times 100 = 73.6 \text{ percent.}$$

A value greater than 100 percent would indicate greater efficiency with the within-subjects design. The value of 73.6 percent is not what we would expect, since a value of less than 100 percent implies that the within-subjects design is *less* efficient than the between-subjects design. The explanation of this puzzle is the practice effect, which contributes directly to the $MS_{A \times S}$. The error term with the practice effect removed, $MS_{\text{L.S. residual}} = 11.39$, now shows the expected difference in relative efficiency between the two types of design:

$$\text{relative efficiency} = \frac{MS_{S/A}}{MS_{\text{L.S. residual}}} \times 100$$

$$= \frac{58.86}{11.39} \times 100 = 516.8 \text{ percent.}$$

The data for this example were created to show the benefits of the Latin square analysis, since most researchers fail to take advantage of the analysis. With actual data we would see considerable gain in efficiency in the first comparison, but if there is any practice effect at all, the smaller error term from the Latin square analysis will increase the attractiveness of using repeated measures to study a given phenomenon.

17.4 STATISTICAL MODEL AND ASSUMPTIONS

Linear Model

The linear model underlying the analysis of variance is usually specified by expressing the basic score AS_{ij} as a sum of a number of quantities. That is,

$$AS_{ij} = \mu + \alpha_i + \pi_j + \alpha\pi_{ij} + \epsilon_{ij}, \quad \text{where}$$

μ is the overall mean of the population;
α_i is the treatment effect at level a_i $(\mu_i - \mu)$;
π_j is the subject effect for the jth subject $(\mu_j - \mu)$;

---

[2] Kirk (1968) offers a general discussion of efficiency (pp. 8-9). He also presents a formula for relative efficiency that corrects for the differences in dfs (p. 148).

$\alpha\pi_{ij}$ is the interaction of treatment and subject at $a_i s_j$ $(\mu_{ij} - \mu_i - \mu_j + \mu)$; and ϵ_{ij} is experimental error.

From this basic statement, expected values of the mean squares normally extracted in the analysis are written in terms of population variance components. The error term for evaluating the main effect of factor A is found by locating a mean square the expectation of which matches the expected value of the main effect (except for the population treatment component, of course). More specifically, the expected values for these two mean squares are

$$E(MS_A) = \sigma_\epsilon^2 + \sigma_{A \times S}^2 + s(\theta_A^2) \quad \text{and}$$
$$E(MS_{A \times S}) = \sigma_\epsilon^2 + \sigma_{A \times S}^2.$$

You will note that the expected value of the interaction mean square contains two quantities, σ_ϵ^2 and $\sigma_{A \times S}^2$, the first of which refers to uncontrolled sources of variability, e.g., variations in the testing conditions, measurement error, etc., and the second of which refers to differential reactions of subjects to the treatment conditions (interaction). Although we can distinguish between these two sources of variability theoretically, we cannot disentangle their separate contributions in this particular design.[3]

Assumptions

In the discussion of the analyses with independent groups, I essentially dismissed as unimportant violations of the distribution assumptions of normality and homogeneity of within-group variances. Statisticians agree that the F test is robust and insensitive to such violations with these sorts of designs. The same *cannot* be said, however, for the repeated-measures design. Of critical concern are the assumptions of **homogeneity of within-treatment variances** and **homogeneity of the covariance between pairs of treatment levels**. It is convenient to consider these assumptions and the consequences of failing to meet them in the context of repeated-measures designs in general. This discussion can be found in Chapter 19. For the present, then, I will simply acknowledge that a problem exists and suggest that you refer to pp. 467–472 if you require that information now.

Missing Data

Occasionally there will be missing data; one or more AS scores sometimes will be missing for a subject (or some subjects). The least ambiguous course of action is to replace such subjects entirely and to duplicate the testing conditions for the

---

[3]The linear model underlying the analysis we have just completed is sometimes called the **nonadditive model,** which emphasizes the fact that the Treatment × Subject interaction is included in the equation. The **additive model,** in which this interaction is absent, is not a reasonable model for within-subjects designs in the behavioral sciences. Comprehensive presentations of the linear models normally adopted with repeated-measures designs can be found in Kirk (1968), Myers (1979), and Winer (1971).

new subject(s). But perhaps this is not feasible. Procedures are available by which missing data can be estimated from the data available in the AS matrix. These require the assumption that the data loss is unrelated to the differences in the treatment conditions. Kirk (1968, pp. 146-147) and Myers (1979, pp. 177-178) discuss methods for estimating missing data under these circumstances.

17.5 COMPARISONS INVOLVING THE TREATMENT MEANS

All of the types of comparisons discussed in Part II for the completely randomized single-factor design are available for the corresponding within-subjects design. There is one important difference, however, and this again lies in the selection of the error term. I will discuss this problem first and then show how the analysis is accomplished.

Error Terms for Comparisons

You have seen that the mean square used to test the main effect of factor A, $MS_{A \times S}$, is influenced by two components: experimental error and the Treatment $\times$ Subject interaction. In our evaluation of the treatment main effect, in which all a treatment means are compared, it makes intuitive sense to use an error term based on all of the scores in the experiment. But when we consider *individual comparisons*, which do *not* include all of the treatment conditions, this overall interaction mean square may no longer be appropriate. This is, it is likely that the Treatment $\times$ Subject interaction will not be the same for each comparison conducted and, thus, will not be accurately estimated by the overall $MS_{A \times S}$. For this reason, then, it may be desirable to employ as an error term one that specifically includes this *Comparison* $\times$ Subject interaction. After all, it is *this* interaction that is presumably reflecting itself in the particular set of treatment means we are considering.

Note that the construction of different error terms for each comparison among treatment means was *not* mentioned in the discussion of designs involving independent groups. There is a good reason for this. In contrast to the case of repeated measures, the error term for a single-factor experiment with independent groups, $MS_{S/A}$, is in reality an average of a independent estimates of population error variance. Thus, any and all comparisons are best evaluated by the most stable estimate of error variance, the $MS_{S/A}$. Interestingly, when the assumption of homogeneous within-treatment variances is *not* upheld, separate error terms are calculated for any analytical comparisons that are conducted. That is, we obtain error terms that are based only on those scores involved in a particular comparison.

In general, separate error terms are necessary when the homogeneity assumptions of the statistical model are violated. Statistical tests of these assumptions are available, but they are complex and usually require the use of a computer.[4] If the assumptions are met, we are free to use the overall error term to assess the significance of all analytical comparisons conducted on the treatment means. If the assumptions are not met, however, we will have to use a separate error term for each comparison. When we are not in a position to test the homogeneity assumptions, we can follow the practical strategy of constructing separate error terms for *all* cases. If we have a case where the overall error term is in fact appropriate (but we do not know this) and separate error terms are used, there will be no bias, since the overall error term and the separate error terms provide estimates of the same thing: error variance plus interaction effects.[5] On the other hand, if we have a situation where the overall error term is *inappropriate*, the need for separate error terms is obvious. On the basis of these arguments, then, the analyses presented in this section will evaluate comparisons with error terms that are calculated from the actual scores responsible for the effects.

Computational Procedures

The computational procedures we will follow in this section have been specifically devised to facilitate the calculation of the individual error terms needed for within-subjects designs. Consequently, the analysis differs considerably from that presented in Chapter 6 for the completely randomized design. The approach taken here conducts what amounts to a within-subjects analysis on the data relevant for the single-df comparison—we will work with scores and sums in a specialized matrix I will call an **AS comparison matrix**. The approach followed in Chapter 6 worked directly with the treatment means. The method we will follow here uses sums and employs the formulas for the standard within-subjects analysis. Thus, all that is needed is to construct an AS comparison matrix and to conduct what amounts to an ordinary analysis of variance on these data.

Standard Analysis. The procedure is simple. For each subject, (1) multiply the AS scores by the relevant coefficients; (2) add together the positive weighted scores and enter these sums in a column of an AS comparison matrix labeled $a_{(+)}$; and (3) add together the negative weighted scores and enter these sums (dropping the negative sign at this point) in the other column of the matrix labeled $a_{(-)}$. This AS comparison matrix is now processed exactly as we would process an $(A \times S)$ design with *two* levels of factor A. In this case, however, "factor A" is actually the single-df comparison reflected by the choice of coefficients. The presence of a true difference between means is reflected in the difference between the mean at $a_{(+)}$ and the one at $a_{(-)}$.

Pairwise comparisons between two treatment conditions are particularly simple to conduct since all we need to do is to extract the two relevant scores for

---

[4]An example of the hand calculation of these tests, which requires a knowledge of matrix algebra, can be found in Kirk (1968, pp. 139–142).

[5]There is a loss of power due to the reduction in df for the denominator term of the F ratio.

each subject and place them directly in the AS comparison matrix. As an example, suppose we wanted to compare the two means at levels a_1 and a_3 from the earlier numerical example. From the data presented in Table 17-5 (p. 388), we enter the data from a_1 in the column labeled $a_{(+)}$ in the upper portion of Table 17-8, and the data from a_3 we enter in the column labeled $a_{(-)}$ in the same table. We are now ready to perform a statistical analysis on the data in this new AS matrix.

The first step is to calculate the basic ratios, remembering that the number of treatment levels is 2, not 3, in this analysis. I will use a prime to refer to the levels associated with $A_{\text{comp.}}$; thus, $a' = 2$. From the formulas in Table 17-2 (p. 384), we have

$$[T] = \frac{T^2}{(a')(s)} = \frac{(235)^2}{(2)(6)} = 4,602.08;$$

$$[A] = \frac{\Sigma A^2}{s} = \frac{(108)^2 + (127)^2}{6} = 4,632.17;$$

$$[S] = \frac{\Sigma S^2}{a'} = \frac{(35)^2 + (35)^2 + \cdots + (41)^2 + (31)^2}{2} = 4,710.50;$$

and

$$[AS] = \Sigma (AS)^2 = (13)^2 + (6)^2 + \cdots + (16)^2 + (12)^2 = 5,095.$$

The remainder of the analysis is summarized in the lower portion of Table 17-8. The resulting F ratio, formed by dividing the comparison mean square by the special error term, is not significant.

I will now consider a more complex comparison which will require segregating positive and negative weighted AS scores for each subject. For this example, I will compare the mean at level a_2 with the mean of the other two levels combined. The coefficients I will use are the set $(1, -2, 1)$. For convenience, the original AS matrix is presented again on the upper left side of Table 17-9 (p. 397). The AS comparison matrix is presented on the right. For the first subject, the three weighted AS scores are

$$(c_1)(AS_{11}) = (1)(13) = 13;$$
$$(c_2)(AS_{21}) = (-2)(24) = -48;$$

and

$$(c_3)(AS_{31}) = (1)(22) = 22.$$

The sum of the two positive weighted AS scores, $13 + 22 = 35$, is entered in the column labeled $a_{(+)}$ in the new matrix; the single negative weighted AS score, -48, is entered in the column labeled $a_{(-)}$. Again, the negative sign is dropped at this point in the analysis. The other sets of scores are transformed in the same way. We can now use the information in the AS comparison matrix to conduct this single-df comparison.

Table 17-8 Single-df Comparison (Pairwise)

AS COMPARISON MATRIX

	$a(+)$	$a(-)$	Sum
s_1	13	22	35
s_2	6	29	35
s_3	25	23	48
s_4	20	25	45
s_5	25	16	41
s_6	19	12	31
Sum	108	127	235

SUMMARY OF THE ANALYSIS

Source	Basic Ratio[a]	Sum of Squares	df	MS	F
$A_{comp.}$	$[A] = 4{,}632.17$	$[A] - [T] = 30.09$	1	30.09	.42
S	$[S] = 4{,}710.50$	$[S] - [T] = 108.42$	5	21.68	
$A_{comp.} \times S$	$[AS] = 5{,}095$	$[AS] - [A] - [S] + [T] = 354.41$	5	70.88	
Total	$[T] = 4{,}602.08$	$[ABS] - [T] = 492.92$	11		

[a]Bracketed letters represent complete terms in computational formulas; a particular term is identified by the letter(s) appearing in the numerator.

Table 17-9   Single-*df* Comparison (Complex)

AS MATRIX

	a_1	a_2	a_3
s_1	13	24	22
s_2	6	30	29
s_3	25	13	23
s_4	20	16	25
s_5	25	37	16
s_6	19	30	12

AS COMPARISON MATRIX

	$a_{(+)}$	$a_{(-)}$	Sum
s_1	35	48	83
s_2	35	60	95
s_3	48	26	74
s_4	45	32	77
s_5	41	74	115
s_6	31	60	91
Sum	235	300	535

SUMMARY OF THE ANALYSIS

Source	Basic Ratio[a]	Sum of Squares	df	MS	F
$A_{comp.}$	$[A] = 24,204.17$	$[A] - [T] = 352.09$	1	352.09	1.32
S	$[S] = 24,412.50$	$[S] - [T] = 560.42$	5	112.08	
$A_{comp.} \times S$	$[AS] = 26,101$	$[AS] - [A] - [S] + [T] = 1,336.41$	5	267.28	
Total	$[T] = 23,852.08$	$[AS] - [T] = 2,248.92$	11		

[a]Bracketed letters represent complete terms in computational formulas; a particular term is identified by the letter(s) appearing in the numerator.

First we calculate the basic ratios. Specifically,

$$[T] = \frac{T^2}{(a')(s)} = \frac{(535)^2}{(2)(6)} = 23{,}852.08;$$

$$[A] = \frac{\Sigma A^2}{s} = \frac{(235)^2 + (300)^2}{6} = 24{,}204.17;$$

$$[S] = \frac{\Sigma S^2}{a'} = \frac{(83)^2 + (95)^2 + \cdots + (115)^2 + (91)^2}{2} = 24{,}412.50;$$

and

$$[AS] = \Sigma (AS)^2 = (35)^2 + (35)^2 + \cdots + (74)^2 + (60)^2 = 26{,}101.$$

The remaining steps in the analysis are summarized in the lower portion of Table 17-9. This comparison is not significant.

Normalizing Sums of Squares. This computational scheme was originally introduced in Chapter 14, where it was applied to the treatment sums in the *ABC* matrix. You may recall that it was necessary at that time to "normalize" sums of squares involving single-df comparisons before calculating mean squares and F ratios. The reason for this correction was the use of weighted treatment totals in the calculation of comparison sums of squares and *un*weighted scores in the calculation of the within-groups error term. This correction is not necessary with the present design, however, since *both* the numerator and denominator mean squares are based on weighted AS scores. On the other hand, if you want to subtract sums of squares found by different single-df comparisons from the overall SS_A or to add them together, you will need to use the adjustment factor. This is the factor based on the coefficients entering in the calculations, i.e.,

$$\frac{\Sigma (c_i)^2}{2},$$

and is applied by dividing each SS of interest by this factor. Generally, it is a good idea to make a habit of adjusting sums of squares whenever the analysis is based on weighted AS scores.

As an example of the need to normalize sums of squares, suppose we wanted to verify that the sum of a set of mutually orthogonal sums of squares equals the overall sum of squares. The two comparisons considered in this section, a_1 versus a_3 and a_2 versus an average of a_1 and a_3, are orthogonal since

$$\Sigma (c_i)(c_i') = (1)(1) + (0)(-2) + (-1)(1) = 1 + 0 - 1 = 0.$$

Since there are $a = 3$ treatment conditions in the original analysis, only two orthogonal sums of squares are necessary to account completely for the treatment sum of squares. Because of the use of coefficients in the analysis, however, this relationship does not hold unless the component SS's are normalized. More specifically, the sum of the uncorrected SS's,

$$\Sigma\, SS_{A\text{ comp.}} = 30.09 + 352.09 = 382.18,$$

is not equal to $SS_A = 147.45$. The correction factor for the first comparison is

$$\frac{\Sigma\,(c_i)^2}{2} = \frac{(1)^2 + (0)^2 + (-1)^2}{2} = \frac{2}{2} = 1,$$

which will leave the sum of squares for this comparison unchanged. (In general, pairwise comparisons—where the coefficients are 1, −1, 0, 0, etc.—require no correction.) The correction for the second comparison is

$$\frac{\Sigma\,(c_i)^2}{2} = \frac{(1)^2 + (-2)^2 + (1)^2}{2} = \frac{6}{2} = 3.$$

The normalized sum of squares is

$$SS_{A\text{ comp. 2}} = \frac{352.09}{3} = 117.36.$$

The sum of the adjusted component SS's now totals SS_A; i.e.,

$$\Sigma\, SS_{A\text{ comp.}} = 30.09 + 117.36 = 147.45 = SS_A.$$

Latin Square Analysis. The presence of practice effects inflates the error term obtained in the standard analysis, as you saw earlier with this particular example. In Section 17.2, you learned how the practice effect can be removed from this error term to provide a more appropriate estimate of chance factors contributing to the differences among the treatment means. This analysis turned to the Latin square and extracted a sum of squares, SS_P, which in reality is a main effect reflecting practice. Unfortunately, this relatively simple analysis does not lend itself to the calculation of separate error terms required for comparisons. What I will offer is a technique that solves this problem by subtracting the observed practice effects from the appropriate AS scores—rather than from the interaction sum of squares—thus leaving the information remaining in the data matrix free of the overall effects of practice. We then can proceed as outlined earlier in this section, by analyzing the data in terms of specialized AS comparison matrices. Let's see how this is accomplished.

From the original listing of the data according to testing position, which is presented again on the left side of Table 17-10, we calculate the overall means for the three tests. More specifically,

$$\bar{P}_1 = \frac{76}{6} = 12.67; \quad \bar{P}_2 = \frac{146}{6} = 24.33; \quad \text{and}$$

$$\bar{P}_3 = \frac{163}{6} = 27.17.$$

Table 17-10   Latin Square: Removal of Practice Effects

ORIGINAL DATA MATRIX

Order of Treatments		Ordinal Position of Treatment		
		p_1	p_2	p_3
(a_1, a_2, a_3)	s_1	13	24	22
	s_2	6	30	29
(a_2, a_3, a_1)	s_3	13	23	25
	s_4	16	25	20
(a_3, a_1, a_2)	s_5	16	25	37
	s_6	12	19	30
Sum:		76	146	163
Mean:		12.67	24.33	27.17
Practice effect:		−8.72	2.94	5.78

DATA MATRIX: PRACTICE REMOVED

		Ordinal Position of Treatment		
		p_1	p_2	p_3
	s_1	21.72	21.06	16.22
	s_2	14.72	27.06	23.22
	s_3	21.72	20.06	19.22
	s_4	24.72	22.06	14.22
	s_5	24.72	22.06	31.22
	s_6	20.72	16.06	24.22
Sum:		128.32	128.36	128.32
Mean:		21.39	21.39	21.39

The overall mean is

$$\bar{T} = \frac{385}{18} = 21.39.$$

The practice effect for each test is obtained by subtracting $\bar{T}$ from each of the test means:

$$\text{practice effect for test 1} = \bar{P}_1 - \bar{T} = 12.67 - 21.39 = -8.72;$$

$$\text{practice effect for test 2} = \bar{P}_2 - \bar{T} = 24.33 - 21.39 = 2.94;$$

and

$$\text{practice effect for test 3} = \bar{P}_3 - \bar{T} = 27.17 - 21.39 = 5.78.$$

We next remove these practice effects from the analysis by subtracting the relevant practice effect from each of the scores in the matrix. For the first test that subjects receive—the scores at p_1—we subtract -8.72 from each of the scores in the first column of the matrix. To illustrate with the first subject, the adjusted score is $13 - (-8.72) = 21.72$. For the second test, the scores at p_2, we subtract 2.94 from each of the scores in the second column of the matrix. Again for the first subject, the adjusted score is $24 - 2.94 = 21.06$. Finally, for the third test, the scores at p_3, we subtract 5.78 from the scores in the third column of the matrix. For the first subject, the adjusted score is $22 - 5.78 = 16.22$. The results of this systematic subtraction of practice effects are presented in the right-hand matrix of Table 17-10. As a check on the subtraction, we should verify that the three test means are equal (within rounding error), showing that practice effects have been eliminated from the data.

The data are now rearranged in an AS matrix according to treatment condition and subject so that the statistical analysis can proceed. This has been done in the upper portion of Table 17-11 on the left. As a check, we should verify that the column and row marginal sums are identical to those obtained with the original AS matrix (Table 17-5, p. 388); the removal of practice effects leaves treatment sums and subject sums unchanged in a Latin square design. The data are now ready for the statistical analysis.[6] I will illustrate the analysis with the comparison contrasting levels a_1 and a_3. These data have been isolated in an AS comparison matrix on the right side of Table 17-11. From the comparison matrix, we can calculate the basic ratios required for the analysis:

$$[T] = \frac{T^2}{(a')(s)} = \frac{(235)^2}{(2)(6)} = 4{,}602.08;$$

$$[A] = \frac{\Sigma A^2}{s} = \frac{(108)^2 + (127)^2}{6} = 4{,}632.17;$$

---

[6] I will demonstrate in a moment that a standard analysis applied to the data in this AS matrix will yield identical values for the sums of squares obtained previously from the Latin square analysis conducted in Section 17-3.

$$[S] = \frac{\Sigma S^2}{a'} = \frac{(37.94)^2 + (37.94)^2 + \cdots + (46.78)^2 + (36.78)^2}{2}$$

$$= 4{,}639.59;$$

and

$$[AS] = \Sigma (AS)^2 = (21.72)^2 + (14.72)^2 + \cdots + (24.72)^2 + (20.72)^2$$

$$= 4{,}736.32.$$

The remainder of the analysis is summarized in the lower portion of Table 17-11. You will notice that the comparison sum of squares (30.09) is unchanged by this analysis (see Table 17-8, p. 396), while the sum of squares for the error term (66.64) is considerably smaller than the one calculated in the earlier analysis (354.41). This reduction is due to the removal of practice effects from the error term. The df for the error term are reduced by 1 to take into consideration the information lost by removing the practice effect from the AS comparison matrix.[7] In spite of the marked reduction in the magnitude of the error term for this comparison made possible by the Latin square analysis, the F is still not significant. (As you will see in Exercise 3 at the end of this chapter, the second comparison, which was not significant under the standard analysis, is now significant when the effects of practice are taken into consideration.)

Earlier I promised to demonstrate that the use of AS scores corrected for practice effects produces the same sum of squares as the Latin square analysis conducted previously in Section 17.3. For this demonstration, I will work with the corrected AS matrix on the left side of Table 17-11. Since the marginal sums are identical to those upon which the original Latin square analysis was based (see Table 17-5, p. 388), there is no need to illustrate these calculations again. From the earlier analysis, then,

$$[T] = 8{,}234.72;$$

$$[A] = 8{,}382.17;$$

and

$$[S] = 8{,}317.67.$$

From the left side of the upper part of Table 17-11,

$$[AS] = \Sigma (AS)^2 = (21.72)^2 + (14.72)^2 + \cdots + (24.72)^2 + (20.72)^2$$

$$= 8{,}556.22.$$

---

[7]The 1 df represents the independent information "lost" when the error term for a comparison is based on AS scores from which practice effects have been removed. That is, the df for the practice effects associated with the sum of squares for a single-df comparison are equal to $p' - 1$, where $p' = 2$, the number of tests examined in the comparison. This argument applies both to pairwise comparisons, such as the one illustrated here (a_1 versus a_3), and to complex comparisons, although the logic is more clearly seen in the pairwise case.

Table 17-11 Latin Square Analysis of a Single-*df* Comparison

AS MATRIX

	Treatments			Sum
	a_1	a_2	a_3	
s_1	21.72	21.06	16.22	59
s_2	14.72	27.06	23.22	65
s_3	19.22	21.72	20.06	61
s_4	14.22	24.72	22.06	61
s_5	22.06	31.22	24.72	78
s_6	16.06	24.22	20.72	61
Sum	108	150	127	385

AS COMPARISON MATRIX

	Comparison		Sum
	$a(+)$	$a(-)$	
s_1	21.72	16.22	37.94
s_2	14.72	23.22	37.94
s_3	19.22	20.06	39.28
s_4	14.22	22.06	36.28
s_5	22.06	24.72	46.78
s_6	16.06	20.72	36.78
Sum	108	127	235

SUMMARY OF THE ANALYSIS

Source	Basic Ratio[a]	Sum of Squares	df	MS	F
$A_{comp.}$	$[A] = 4{,}632.17$	$[A] - [T] = 30.09$	1	30.09	1.81
S	$[S] = 4{,}639.59$	$[S] - [T] = 37.51$	5	7.50	
L.S. Residual	$[AS] = 4{,}736.32$	$[AS] - [A] - [S] + [T] = 66.64$	$5 - 1$	16.66	
Total	$[T] = 4{,}602.08$	$[AS] - [T] = 132.24$	$11 - 1$		

[a]Bracketed letters represent complete terms in computational formulas; a particular term is identified by the letter(s) appearing in the numerator.

These basic ratios are combined as indicated in Table 17-12 to produce the usual sums of squares. A comparison with the sums of squares presented in Table 17-7 (p. 390) indicates that they are the same. The only quantity missing in the present analysis is the practice source of variation, which was isolated previously in the Latin square analysis by calculating SS_P from the test totals and completely eliminated in the present analysis by direct subtraction. It is clear we have an option in conducting the Latin square analysis. If you do not plan to examine single-df comparisons or if you have reason to believe that separate error terms are not necessary, you will find the Latin square analysis simpler. On the other hand, if you foresee the need for separate error terms, the practice-corrected matrix is the better choice.

17.6 CORRECTIONS FOR FAMILYWISE TYPE I ERROR

Regardless of experimental design, there is always the problem of an increased probability of type I error that occurs whenever data are subjected to more than one statistical test—the so-called familywise type I error (FW). The discussions in Chapter 8, while set in the context of a completely randomized single-factor experiment, are certainly relevant to the analysis of the within-subjects design as well. I will not go over these arguments again, but will simply present the formulas for the different correction techniques adapted for use with repeated measures. The formulas will be written in a form that specifies a corrected critical value of F that must be exceeded to be declared significant under a particular test. From the logic of earlier discussions in this chapter, we should expect to calculate a separate error term for each comparison we undertake.

The formula for the Scheffé test is applicable to *any* comparison between two means—pairwise comparisons as well as more complex comparisons between combinations of means. The critical value of F for the Scheffé test, F_S, is given by the formula

$$F_S = (a - 1) F(df_A, df_{A \times S}), \qquad (17\text{-}1)$$

where $df_{A \times S} = (a - 1)(s - 1)$. When comparisons involve a single control condition, the Dunnett test is usually used. The critical value for this test, F_D, is specified by the formula

$$F_D = (q_D)^2 , \qquad (17\text{-}2)$$

where q_D refers to an entry in Table A-5 of Appendix A under k, the total number of conditions in the analysis, under df where $df = (a - 1)(s - 1)$, and under the value chosen for familywise type I error (α_{FW}). The formula for the Tukey test correction F_T is

$$F_T = \frac{(q_T)^2}{2} , \qquad (17\text{-}3)$$

Table 17-12 Alternative Latin Square Analysis

SOURCE	BASIC RATIO[a]	SUM OF SQUARES	df	MS	F
A	$[A] = 8,382.17$	$[A] - [T] = 147.45$	2	73.73	6.47*
S	$[S] = 8,317.67$	$[S] - [T] = 82.95$	5	16.59	
L.S. Residual	$[AS] = 8,556.22$	$[AS] - [A] - [S] + [T] = 91.10$	$10 - 2$	11.39	
Total	$[T] = 8,234.72$	$[AS] - [T] = 321.50$	$17 - 2$		

*$p < .025$.

[a]Bracketed letters represent complete terms in computational formulas; a particular term is identified by the letter(s) appearing in the numerator.

where q_T is found in Table A-6 under r (the number of treatment means), under df where $df = (a - 1)(s - 1)$, and under α_{FW}. The detailed procedures involved in conducting these various correction techniques were outlined in Chapter 8.

17.7 EXERCISES[8]

1. Subjects in an actual experiment (Keppel, Postman, and Zavortink, 1968) learned a list of 10 pairs of words on one day and recalled the pairs two days later. Following recall, the subjects learned a second list of pairs, and these were also recalled after a delay of two days. This cycle of learning-recall-learning-recall was continued for six lists. The independent variable was the *ordinal position* of a particular list, i.e., whether the list was learned and recalled first, or second, . . . , or sixth in the sequence. There were $s = 8$ subjects in the experiment. Their recall data for the six lists are presented in the following table:

AS MATRIX

	Ordinal Position of the Lists (A)					
Subjects (S)	a_1	a_2	a_3	a_4	a_5	a_6
s_1	7	3	2	2	1	1
s_2	4	8	3	8	1	2
s_3	7	6	3	1	5	4
s_4	8	6	1	0	2	0
s_5	7	2	3	0	1	3
s_6	6	3	3	1	1	1
s_7	4	2	0	0	0	0
s_8	6	7	5	1	3	2

(a) Perform an analysis of variance on these data.
(b) Plot the means on a graph. You will note two striking trends, namely, a general downward slope to the curve (a linear trend) and a concave-upward curvature (a quadratic trend). Is there any statistical support for these observations?

2. An experiment is conducted in which four different drugs (a_2, a_3, a_4, and a_5) and a placebo (a_1) are administered to each of five different animals. The order in which the conditions are presented is properly counterbalanced. The response measure consists of the number of discrimination problems solved within a given time limit. The data are given in the following table:

---

[8]The answers to these problems are found in Appendix B, beginning on p. 593.

	TESTING POSITION				
	p_1	p_2	p_3	p_4	p_5
s_1	a_3 9	a_2 11	a_1 11	a_4 6	a_5 7
s_2	a_2 13	a_4 10	a_5 5	a_1 8	a_3 2
s_3	a_1 13	a_5 6	a_2 9	a_3 3	a_4 4
s_4	a_4 13	a_1 12	a_3 6	a_5 6	a_2 3
s_5	a_5 13	a_3 8	a_4 9	a_2 8	a_1 7

(a) Conduct a standard analysis of variance on these data.

(b) Perform a Latin square analysis by the method of subtracting the practice sum of squares (SS_P) from $SS_{A \times S}$.

(c) Assume that the experimenter is interested in finding out more about the nature of the differences reflected in the data. One comparison of interest is between the control (a_1) and an average of the four drug conditions. Is this comparison significant? Conduct the analysis two ways, one by means of the standard analysis and the other by taking advantage of the Latin square design. Be sure to use specialized error terms for the two analyses. (In order to conduct the Latin square analysis, it will be necessary to subtract the practice effects from the individual AS scores.)

3. From the data presented in Table 17-11 (p. 403), test the significance of the second comparison mentioned in the text, i.e., between the average of conditions a_1 and a_3 and condition a_2.

18

The Mixed
Two-Factor Design

Within-subjects factorial designs are extremely popular in the behavioral sciences, and for good reason: They examine the effects of several independent variables manipulated simultaneously and offer greater sensitivity than a completely randomized between-subjects counterpart. As indicated in Chapter 16 (see Table 16-1, p. 369), two types of within-subjects designs are possible when two independent variables are manipulated factorially, namely, a design in which subjects receive all of the treatment combinations, and a design in which subjects receive only a subset of the total. In this latter case, the subset consists of all combinations of one factor—the within-subjects factor—in conjunction with only *one level* of the other factor—the between-subjects factor. This blending of within-subjects and between-subjects designs is often called a *mixed* factorial design. Mixed factorial designs are more common than "pure" within-subjects factorial designs. This chapter will cover in detail the analysis of the mixed two-factor design. Chapter 19 will consider the pure case and higher-order within-subjects designs as well.

The mixed design represents a combination of the two generic types of designs we have considered previously: independent groups, constituting the levels of one factor (factor A), and repeated measures, constituting the levels of the other factor (factor B). As you will see, the analysis of the mixed design contains features of the one-factor design with independent groups and features of the one-factor design with repeated measures. Consequently, the analysis will *not* be simple and will require a more complicated treatment of the data.

The most common example of this type of design is one in which the repeated factor represents *trials* or *successive tasks* in a learning experiment. Rarely will we be interested in an ($A \times S$) experiment in which trials make up the independent variable. The reason for this is, of course, that all we can hope to show with this type of experiment is that learning does or does not occur and, if so, what the shape of the function is over trials (i.e., the levels of the independent variable). More typically, we will want to compare the learning curves for *different treatment groups*. Under these circumstances, the various treatments (factor A) will be administered to independent groups of subjects and all subjects will receive a certain number of learning trials (factor B). Thus, the experiment becomes an $A \times (B \times S)$ design. With this particular design, it is still possible to compare the different treatment groups on performance averaged over all of the learning trials. In addition to this information, however, it is also possible to compare the *shapes* of the learning curves for the different treatment groups. To be more specific, we can ask whether or not the effects of practice (trials) are the same for the different levels of factor A—i.e., whether there is an $A \times B$ interaction (a Treatment $\times$ Trials interaction).

18.1 THE STANDARD ANALYSIS OF VARIANCE

An Overview of the Analysis

The $A \times (B \times S)$ design represents a combination of two single-factor experiments, one with independent groups (factor A) and the other with repeated measures (factor B). This description is not completely accurate, however, since the two-factor design contains an $A \times B$ interaction, which obviously cannot be present in either of the single-factor experiments. Nevertheless, the analogy is sufficiently close to give us a feel for the composite nature of the mixed design. Table 18-1 makes this point explicit. The component sources of variance for a completely randomized single-factor experiment are listed in the first column. The component sources for a single-factor experiment with repeated measures are listed in the third column. [I will refer to this independent variable as factor B and to the experiment as a $(B \times S)$ design to facilitate the comparison of the designs.] The component sources of variance for the $A \times (B \times S)$ design are listed in the middle column of the table.

An inspection of the table reveals that the completely randomized design is perfectly duplicated in the mixed design. The same could be said of the $(B \times S)$ design except that the designation of subjects is different. This comes about because factor S is a *crossed factor* in the $(B \times S)$ design, while actually it is *nested* within factor A in the mixed design. Thus, factor S becomes "S/A" in the mixed design rather than the "S" appropriate for the within-subjects single-factor design.

Computational Formulas

Design and Notation. The notational system for the mixed design is presented in Table 18-2. The ABS matrix contains the individual observations recorded in the experiment.

While there is a great deal of similarity between this ABS matrix and the ABS matrix appropriate for the completely randomized factorial design, there is one critical difference. Specifically, you should note that this example depicts a total of *six* different subjects, of whom $s = 3$ are assigned randomly to the three levels of factor B at level a_1 and the other $s = 3$ to the three levels of factor B at level a_2. This fact Table 18-2 makes explicit by denoting the subjects at each level of fac-

Table 18-1   A Comparison of the Sources of Variance in Two Single-Factor Experiments with Those in the $A \times (B \times S)$ Design

COMPLETELY RANDOMIZED DESIGN	$A \times (B \times S)$ DESIGN	$(B \times S)$ DESIGN
A	A	
S/A	S/A	S
	B	B
	$B \times S/A$	$B \times S$
	$A \times B$	

tor A with different sets of numbers. An individual score ABS_{ijk} is specified by three subscripts, the i indicating the level of factor A (the between-subjects factor), the j indicating the level of factor B (the within-subjects factor), and the k specifying a subject appearing in a particular level of factor A.

The information listed in the ABS matrix is used to create two additional matrices. The first is the AB matrix, which is identical to the AB matrix formed in the analysis of the completely randomized design and is created by summing the individual scores obtained in each of the $(a)(b)$ treatment conditions. The various totals provided by this matrix permit the calculation of the two main effects and the $A \times B$ interaction. The second matrix, the AS matrix, lists the *total score* for each subject obtained when the set of observations each subject produces is summed. The subtotal for each subject is designated AS_{ik} to indicate that it is a sum of all the scores for a particular subject s_k in a particular A treatment group a_i. The AS and ABS matrices provide the information needed to calculate the two error terms required for the statistical analysis.

Sums of Squares and Degrees of Freedom. In Chapter 10 you saw how the computational formulas for sums of squares can be constructed from df statements (see pp. 191-193). To find the df for any source of variance, we apply the following rule:

Multiply (1) the products of the df's of factors to the *left* of the diagonal by (2) the product of the *levels* of factors to the *right* of the diagonal.

To see how this rule is used, consider the sources of variation normally extracted in the mixed design as presented in the first column of Table 18-3. For the two main effects A and B, the df's are simply $a - 1$ and $b - 1$, respectively. The degrees of

Table 18-2   Notational System: $A \times (B \times S)$ Design

ABS MATRIX

Subject	a_1			Subject	a_2		
	b_1	b_2	b_3		b_1	b_2	b_3
s_1	ABS_{111}	ABS_{121}	ABS_{131}	s_4	ABS_{214}	ABS_{224}	ABS_{234}
s_2	ABS_{112}	ABS_{122}	ABS_{132}	s_5	ABS_{215}	ABS_{225}	ABS_{235}
s_3	ABS_{113}	ABS_{123}	ABS_{133}	s_6	ABS_{216}	ABS_{226}	ABS_{236}

AB MATRIX

	a_1	a_2	Sum
b_1	AB_{11}	AB_{21}	B_1
b_2	AB_{12}	AB_{22}	B_2
b_3	AB_{13}	AB_{23}	B_3
Sum	A_1	A_2	T

AS MATRIX

	a_1			a_2
s_1	AS_{11}		s_4	AS_{24}
s_2	AS_{12}		s_5	AS_{25}
s_3	AS_{13}		s_6	AS_{26}
Sum	A_1		Sum	A_2

freedom for the $A \times B$ interaction are obtained by multiplying df_A by df_B. (Since no diagonal is present, only the first part of the rule applies.) The number of degrees of freedom for the S/A source is found by multiplying the df on the left of the diagonal ($df_S = s - 1$) by the number of levels of factor A. That is,

$$df_{S/A} = (df_S)(a) = (s - 1)(a).$$

A rearranged equivalent of this df statement, $a(s - 1)$, is presented in the df column of the table. The number of degrees of freedom for the $B \times S/A$ source is obtained by multiplying the df's for factors B and S by the number of levels of factor A. In symbols,

$$df_{B \times S/A} = (df_B)(df_S)(a)$$
$$= (b - 1)(s - 1)(a).$$

The rearranged version of this formula is presented in the table. The df statement for the total variation is simply 1 less than the total number of observations $(a)(b)(s)$, namely, $(a)(b)(s) - 1$.

The degrees of freedom statements, when expanded, indicate which basic ratios are required for calculating the corresponding sum of squares and how they are combined. The formulas for the main effects, interaction, and total are presented in the fourth column of Table 18-3. Since they are identical to those presented in Chapter 10, they should require no explanation. I will work through the steps for the two new sources of variance, S/A and $B \times S/A$. For the first, the expanded df statement,

$$df_{S/A} = a(s - 1) = (a)(s) - a,$$

indicates that two basic ratios are involved, $[AS]$ and $[A]$. These ratios are calculated by performing the familiar operations of (1) squaring, (2) summing, and (3) dividing by the number of observations contributing to any one of the squared numbers. In the case of $[AS]$, this number is b, since each AS sum is obtained by adding up the individual observations for any given subject and there are b of them. In the case of $[A]$, this number is $(b)(s)$, since each A total is obtained by adding together a total of $(b)(s)$ scores. For the other new source of variance, the expanded df statement,

$$df_{B \times S/A} = a(b - 1)(s - 1) = (a)(b)(s) - (a)(b) - (a)(s) + a,$$

indicates four basic ratios, namely, $[ABS]$, $[AB]$, $[AS]$, and $[A]$. The formulas for these basic ratios are presented in the second column of Table 18-3.

Mean Squares and F Ratios. The mean squares are calculated by dividing each sum of squares by the appropriate number of degrees of freedom, as shown in the fifth column of the table. The formation of the three F ratios, which is indicated in the sixth column, does follow a logical pattern. More specifically, you will note that the error term for a factorial effect which is *not* based on repeated measures (the MS_A in this design) is the within-groups mean square $MS_{S/A}$, while

Table 18-3   Computational Formulas

SOURCE	BASIC RATIO[a]	df	SUM OF SQUARES	MS	F[b]
A	$[A] = \dfrac{\sum A^2}{(b)(s)}$	$a-1$	$[A] - [T]$	$\dfrac{SS_A}{df_A}$	$\dfrac{MS_A}{MS_{S/A}}$
S/A	$[AS] = \dfrac{\sum (AS)^2}{b}$	$a(s-1)$	$[AS] - [A]$	$\dfrac{SS_{S/A}}{df_{S/A}}$	
B	$[B] = \dfrac{\sum B^2}{(a)(s)}$	$b-1$	$[B] - [T]$	$\dfrac{SS_B}{df_B}$	$\dfrac{MS_B}{MS_B \times S/A}$
$A \times B$	$[AB] = \dfrac{\sum (AB)^2}{s}$	$(a-1)(b-1)$	$[AB] - [A] - [B] + [T]$	$\dfrac{SS_A \times B}{df_A \times B}$	$\dfrac{MS_A \times B}{MS_B \times S/A}$
$B \times S/A$	$[ABS] = \sum (ABS)^2$	$a(b-1)(s-1)$	$[ABS] - [AB] - [AS] + [A]$	$\dfrac{SS_B \times S/A}{df_B \times S/A}$	
Total	$[T] = \dfrac{T^2}{(a)(b)(s)}$	$(a)(b)(s) - 1$	$[ABS] - [T]$		

[a]Bracketed letters represent complete terms in computational formulas; a particular term is identified by the letter(s) appearing in the numerator.
[b]Factors A and B are fixed.

413

the error term for the two factorial effects which *are* based on repeated measures (MS_B and $MS_{A \times B}$) is the mean square reflecting an interaction of the repeated factor (B) with factor S ($MS_{B \times S/A}$).

The use of $MS_{S/A}$ to evaluate the significance of the A main effect is easy to understand when it is pointed out that we could take the AS sums, disregard the fact that they were obtained from a mixed factorial design, and analyze them as if they were data generated from a completely randomized, *single*-factor design. The F ratios in the two analyses would be *identical*.[1] The justification of the other error term is a bit more complicated. Consider the data in the ABS matrix at one of the levels of factor A, say, a_1. This portion of the ABS matrix can be thought of as a single-factor within-subjects design involving factor B and s subjects. The error term for evaluating the differences among the treatment means in this sub-matrix would be the $B \times S$ interaction. The same argument holds for each $B \times S$ matrix at each level of factor A. When these data are brought together in the factorial analysis, the variation among the B means at each level of factor A is reflected in the B main effect and the $A \times B$ interaction. The error term for these two factorial effects, $MS_{B \times S/A}$, is actually an *average* of the separate $B \times S$ interactions, each of which is the appropriate error term for its portion of the data. The use of an average of these individual error terms is justified if we can assume that they are roughly the same, i.e., homogeneous.

A Numerical Example

The data for a hypothetical experiment are presented in Table 18–4. For the experimental factors, the design is a 2×4 factorial with repeated measures on the second factor (B). There are $s = 4$ subjects assigned randomly to each of the two levels of factor A. The total number of subjects is $(a)(s) = (2)(4) = 8$, and the total number of observations is $(a)(b)(s) = (2)(4)(4) = 32$.

I will begin the analysis by calculating the basic quantities needed for the analysis from the computational formulas of Table 18–3. From the AS matrix,

$$[A] = \frac{\Sigma A^2}{(b)(s)} = \frac{(109)^2 + (170)^2}{(4)(4)} = 2{,}548.81;$$

and

$$[AS] = \frac{\Sigma (AS)^2}{b} = \frac{(17)^2 + (35)^2 + \cdots + (54)^2 + (32)^2}{4} = 2{,}827.25.$$

---

[1] The sums of squares would be different, however, since the denominators for the basic ratios all include b in the mixed design, which is not present, of course, in the single-factor design. The b factors cancel when the F ratio is formed, which accounts for the identical answers from the two analyses.

Table 18-4 Numerical Example: $A \times (B \times S)$ Design

ABS MATRIX

	a_1					a_2			
	b_1	b_2	b_3	b_4		b_1	b_2	b_3	b_4
s_1	3	4	7	3	s_5	5	6	11	7
s_2	6	8	12	9	s_6	10	12	18	15
s_3	7	13	11	11	s_7	10	15	15	14
s_4	0	3	6	6	s_8	5	7	11	9

AB MATRIX

	a_1	a_2	Sum
b_1	16	30	46
b_2	28	40	68
b_3	36	55	91
b_4	29	45	74
Sum	109	170	279

AS MATRIX

	a_1		a_2
s_1	17	s_5	29
s_2	35	s_6	55
s_3	42	s_7	54
s_4	15	s_8	32
Sum	109	Sum	170

From the AB matrix,

$$[T] = \frac{T^2}{(a)(b)(s)} = \frac{(279)^2}{(2)(4)(4)} = 2{,}432.53;$$

$$[B] = \frac{\Sigma B^2}{(a)(s)} = \frac{(46)^2 + (68)^2 + (91)^2 + (74)^2}{(2)(4)} = 2{,}562.13;$$

and

$$[AB] = \frac{\Sigma (AB)^2}{s} = \frac{(16)^2 + (28)^2 + \cdots + (55)^2 + (45)^2}{4} = 2{,}681.75.$$

Finally, from the ABS matrix,

$$[ABS] = \Sigma (ABS)^2 = (3)^2 + (6)^2 + \cdots + (14)^2 + (9)^2 = 2{,}995.$$

The results of these basic calculations are entered in the second column of Table 18-5. The coded representations of these quantities in the third column indicate how these terms are manipulated to produce the different sums of squares. The remaining steps in the analysis are summarized in the table.

The analysis reveals a significant main effect of factor B (that is, $p < .01$). The main effect of factor A and the $A \times B$ interaction are not significant. It is

415

Table 18-5 Summary of the Analysis

SOURCE	BASIC RATIO[a]	SUM OF SQUARES	df	MS	F
A	$[A] = 2,548.81$	$[A] - [T] = 116.28$	1	116.28	2.51
S/A	$[AS] = 2,827.25$	$[AS] - [A] = 278.44$	6	46.41	
B	$[B] = 2,562.13$	$[B] - [T] = 129.60$	3	43.20	22.38*
$A \times B$	$[AB] = 2,681.75$	$[AB] - [A] - [B] + [T] = 3.34$	3	1.11	.58
$B \times S/A$	$[ABS] = 2,995$	$[ABS] - [AB] - [AS] + [A] = 34.81$	18	1.93	
Total	$[T] = 2,432.53$	$[ABS] - [T] = 562.47$	31		

*$p < .01$.

[a]Bracketed letters represent complete terms in computational formulas; a particular term is identified by the letter(s) appearing in the numerator.

instructive to compare the sizes of the two error terms in the mixed design. This difference is considerable: $MS_{S/A} = 46.41$ and $MS_{B \times S/A} = 1.93$. The difference in the sizes of the error terms reflects the increased sensitivity of the repeated-measures portion of the mixed design in detecting the influence of independent variables. Although the data are artificial, tenfold differences are not uncommon in the literature.

The Composite Nature of the Error Terms

Both error terms are averages based on pooled sources of variability. The within-groups term $MS_{S/A}$ is an average of the within-group variances reflecting the deviation of a subject's average score, $\overline{AS}_{ik}$, from the overall mean $\overline{A}_i$ for that subject's group. To illustrate, I will calculate the two within-group variances—one at level a_1 and the other at level a_2—and average them. For the two sums of squares, we use the AS totals listed in the AS matrix of Table 18-4 as follows:

$$SS_{S/A_1} = \frac{(17)^2 + (35)^2 + (42)^2 + (15)^2}{4} - \frac{(109)^2}{(4)(4)}$$

$$= 875.75 - 742.56 = 133.19;$$

and

$$SS_{S/A_2} = \frac{(29)^2 + (55)^2 + (54)^2 + (32)^2}{4} - \frac{(170)^2}{(4)(4)}$$

$$= 1{,}951.50 - 1{,}806.25 = 145.25.$$

The two mean squares are obtained by dividing each sum of squares by the appropriate number of degrees of freedom, $s - 1$. That is,

$$MS_{S/A_1} = \frac{133.19}{4 - 1} = 44.40 \quad \text{and} \quad MS_{S/A_2} = \frac{145.25}{4 - 1} = 48.42.$$

The average of these two mean squares,

$$\frac{44.40 + 48.42}{2} = 46.41,$$

is equal to the $MS_{S/A}$ (see Table 18-5).

The repeated-measures error term $(MS_{B \times S/A})$ is an average of the separate $B \times S$ interactions at the different levels of factor A. I will calculate the two sums of squares for the $B \times S$ interaction at levels a_1 and a_2 using the data from the ABS matrix in Table 18-4. To simplify the calculations, the data have been arranged in Table 18-6 as two separate within-subjects designs; you can actually use the computational formulas for the single-factor within-subjects design to calculate sums of squares for the two $B \times S$ interactions. Specifically,

Table 18-6 Separate $B \times S$ Matrices

	b_1	b_2	b_3	b_4	Sum
s_1	3	4	7	3	17
s_2	6	8	12	9	35
s_3	7	13	11	11	42
s_4	0	3	6	6	15
Sum	16	28	36	29	109

	b_1	b_2	b_3	b_4	Sum
s_5	5	6	11	7	29
s_6	10	12	18	15	55
s_7	10	15	15	14	54
s_8	5	7	11	9	32
Sum	30	40	55	45	170

$$SS_{B \times S/A_1} = [(3)^2 + (6)^2 + \cdots + (11)^2 + (6)^2]$$
$$- \frac{(16)^2 + (28)^2 + (36)^2 + (29)^2}{4}$$
$$- \frac{(17)^2 + (35)^2 + (42)^2 + (15)^2}{4} + \frac{(109)^2}{(4)(4)}$$
$$= 949 - 794.25 - 875.75 + 742.56 = 21.56;$$

and

$$SS_{B \times S/A_2} = [(5)^2 + (10)^2 + \cdots + (14)^2 + (9)^2]$$
$$- \frac{(30)^2 + (40)^2 + (55)^2 + (45)^2}{4}$$
$$- \frac{(29)^2 + (55)^2 + (54)^2 + (32)^2}{4} + \frac{(170)^2}{(4)(4)}$$
$$= 2,046 - 1,887.50 - 1,951.50 + 1,806.25 = 13.25.$$

The number of df for each interaction is $(b - 1)(s - 1) = (4 - 1)(4 - 1) = 9$, and the mean squares are

$$MS_{B \times S/A_1} = \frac{21.56}{9} = 2.40 \quad \text{and} \quad MS_{B \times S/A_2} = \frac{13.25}{9} = 1.47.$$

The average of these two mean squares is

$$\frac{2.40 + 1.47}{2} = 1.94,$$

which is equal to the $MS_{B \times S/A}$ within rounding error (1.93).

18.2 STATISTICAL MODEL AND ASSUMPTIONS

Linear Model

The linear model on which the analysis is based can be written as follows:

$$ABS_{ijk} = \mu + \alpha_i + \pi_k + \beta_j + \alpha\beta_{ij} + \beta\pi_{jk} + \epsilon_{ijk}.$$

Several new quantities should be identified. Specifically, π_k represents the average effect for each subject, $\beta\pi_{jk}$ designates the interaction effect associated with the B treatments and subjects, and ϵ_{ijk} refers to uncontrolled sources of variability. These three components are usually assumed to be random factors. On the basis of the linear model and certain other assumptions, the expected values for the various sources of variance normally extracted in the analysis can be derived. An explanation of this procedure and a specification of the expected values for this particular design are presented in Appendix C-4 (pp. 638-641) and the left-hand portion of Table 21-4 (p. 529), respectively.

Assumptions

As I have indicated before, the assumptions under which the F ratios obtained from the analysis of designs with repeated measures are distributed according to the F distribution are more restrictive than with completely randomized designs. In addition, violations of these assumptions are more serious as well. I will discuss these topics in the next chapter.

Missing Data and Unequal Sample Sizes

The analyses in this chapter assume equal sample sizes and a complete set of test scores from each subject. Occasionally, problems arise in an experiment—e.g., equipment failure, an experimenter error, or an unexpected disturbance—that result in the loss of an observation for a particular subject. In some cases, the simplest solution is to replace the subject for whom data are missing with a new subject tested under the same circumstances as the discarded subject. In other cases, replacement subjects may not be available or may be too costly to run through the complete set of conditions. In this situation, a researcher can choose to use special procedures designed to provide estimates of the missing data or to analyze the data with unequal sample sizes. However one decides to deal with these problems, the overriding concern is whether the loss of data or subjects is related to the treatment conditions. If this possibility cannot be reasonably dismissed, then the validity of the experiment will probably be brought into question.

Assuming that the reason(s) for the data loss can be attributed to chance factors alone, there are ways available to analyze partially missing data. Kirk

(1968, pp. 281-282), for example, discusses techniques for dealing with the problem. The loss of an entire subject, or the presence of unequal sample sizes in general, also complicates the statistical analysis, but not unduly. The solution best suited to this problem is the analysis of unweighted means, which was introduced in Chapter 15 (pp. 349-351). This procedure focuses on the treatment means and applies an average sample size equally to all conditions in the calculation of the sums of squares for the factorial effects. Thus, each mean contributes equally to the factorial effects, regardless of the underlying size of the sample. The sums of squares for the two error terms are based on the actual data present in the data matrix. Illustrations of this analysis can be found in Kirk (1968, pp. 276-279) and Winer (1971, pp. 601-603).

18.3 LATIN SQUARE ANALYSIS

As you saw in the last chapter, the presence of practice effects in a repeated-measures design inflates the error term when the order of the treatment conditions is counterbalanced. A Latin square analysis provides a relatively simple way of dealing with this problem, which also occurs in the mixed design. I will consider two equivalent ways of conducting a Latin square analysis with this design. The first is easier and involves the removal of certain sources of variation due to practice effects.[2] The second involves more work—the removal of the practice effects directly from the scores of individual subjects—but is necessary when subsequent analyses require separate error terms and a researcher wishes to remove practice effects from these separate error terms as well.

Subtracting Sources of Variance

The first step in the analysis is to arrange the data according to testing position in a Latin square matrix. This has been accomplished in Table 18-7 for the data of the previous example. (It is a good idea to verify this step by taking the data from the *ABS* matrix in Table 18-4, p. 415, and rearranging the four *ABS* scores for each subject according to the Latin square arrangement presented on the far left of Table 18-7, which was used for the subjects at both levels of factor A).[3] The sums and means for each column are calculated to provide information concerning practice effects. For the analysis, the column sums are arranged in a Treatment X Position matrix (*AP* matrix) that will facilitate the calculation of the practice ef-

---

[2]Myers (1979, pp. 279-286) discusses and illustrates a more complex analysis that provides partially confounded information on interactions between testing position and treatments.

[3]It is not necessary to use the same Latin square at levels a_1 and a_2, although most researchers would probably use the same square as I did in this example. Any additional blocks of subjects should be arranged in a new, randomly chosen Latin square to provide a better opportunity for balancing practice effects.

fects present in this design. An inspection of the AP matrix indicates a systematic decline in performance from the first test subjects receive (P_1) to the fourth (P_4), but shows that there is no interaction with factor A, i.e., that this decline seems to be equivalent for both levels of factor A.

The next step is to calculate the main effects of practice (SS_P) and the interaction of factor A and practice $(SS_{A \times P})$ from this matrix. We will need four basic ratios, namely, $[T]$, $[A]$, $[P]$, and $[AP]$. The first two were obtained in the earlier analysis (see pp. 414-415) and found to be

$$[T] = 2{,}432.53 \quad \text{and} \quad [A] = 2{,}548.81.$$

The other two basic ratios are computed as follows:

$$[P] = \frac{\Sigma P^2}{(a)(s)} = \frac{(81)^2 + (68)^2 + (69)^2 + (61)^2}{(2)(4)} = 2{,}458.38;$$

and

$$[AP] = \frac{\Sigma (AP)^2}{s} = \frac{(34)^2 + (47)^2 + \cdots + (22)^2 + (39)^2}{4} = 2{,}576.25.$$

The degrees of freedom and the sums of squares are calculated next. Specifically,

$$df_P = p - 1 = 4 - 1 = 3,$$

and

$$SS_P = [P] - [T] = 2{,}458.38 - 2{,}432.53 = 25.85;$$

and

$$df_{A \times P} = (a - 1)(p - 1) = (2 - 1)(4 - 1) = 3,$$

and

$$SS_{A \times P} = [AP] - [A] - [P] + [T]$$
$$= 2{,}576.25 - 2{,}548.81 - 2{,}458.38 + 2{,}432.53 = 1.59.$$

The new error term is obtained by subtracting these two sums of squares from $SS_{B \times S/A}$ (34.81, from the previous analysis). That is,

$$SS_{\text{L.S. residual}} = SS_{B \times S/A} - SS_P - SS_{A \times P}$$
$$= 34.81 - 25.85 - 1.59 = 7.37.$$

The degrees of freedom are calculated in the same way:

$$df_{\text{L.S. residual}} = df_{B \times S/A} - df_P - df_{A \times P}$$
$$= 18 - 3 - 3 = 12.$$

The complete analysis, which combines the sums of squares and degrees of freedom we have just obtained with the information from the earlier analysis (Table

Table 18-7 Latin Square Matrix

Sequences		a_1 Testing Position (P)			
		p_1	p_2	p_3	p_4
(b_1, b_2, b_3, b_4)	s_1	3	4	7	3
(b_3, b_1, b_4, b_2)	s_2	12	6	9	8
(b_2, b_4, b_1, b_3)	s_3	13	11	7	11
(b_4, b_3, b_2, b_1)	s_4	6	6	3	0
Sum		34	27	26	22
Mean		8.50	6.75	6.50	5.50

	a_2 Testing Position (P)			
	p_1	p_2	p_3	p_4
s_5	5	6	11	7
s_6	18	10	15	12
s_7	15	14	10	15
s_8	9	11	7	5
Sum	47	41	43	39
Mean	11.75	10.25	10.75	9.75

AP MATRIX

	Testing Position				Sum
	p_1	p_2	p_3	p_4	
a_1	34	27	26	22	109
a_2	47	41	43	39	170
Sum	81	68	69	61	279

Table 18-8 Latin Square Analysis

SOURCE	SS	df	MS	ERROR TERM	F
A	116.28	1	116.28	S/A	2.51
S/A	278.44	6	46.41	—	
B	129.60	3	43.20	L. S. residual	70.82*
P	25.85	3	8.62	L. S. residual	14.13*
$A \times B$	3.34	3	1.11	L. S. residual	1.82
$A \times P$	1.59	3	.53	L. S. residual	.87
L. S. Residual	7.37	12	.61	—	
Total	562.47	31			

*$p < .01$.

18-5, p. 416), is summarized in Table 18-8. The error term for the A main effect is $MS_{S/A}$ and is unchanged in this analysis. The error term for the sources containing repeated measures—B and $A \times B$, from the standard analysis, and P and $A \times P$, from the Latin square analysis—is the error term representing residual variation remaining after practice effects are removed ($MS_{\text{L.S. residual}}$). The analysis shows two significant effects: a main effect of factor B, which was also observed in the standard analysis, and a main effect of practice.

Removing Practice Effects Directly

An alternative, but equivalent, method for removing practice effects from the within-subjects error term involves subtracting practice effects directly from the individual observations. We begin by calculating the practice effects associated with each testing position. This is done separately at each level of factor A. A practice effect is defined as the deviation of a mean for any given test position from the overall mean for the relevant data set. Consider the data at level a_1 presented in the upper portion of Table 18-7. The four test means, based on the column sums in this table, are presented on the left in Table 18-9. The overall mean for this data matrix is

$$\overline{A}_1 = \frac{109}{(4)(4)} = 6.81.$$

The practice effect for the first test is

$$\overline{AP}_{11} - \overline{A}_1 = 8.50 - 6.81 = 1.69.$$

The three other practice effects are calculated the same way. All four practice effects are presented in the last row of Table 18-9. Similar calculations are conducted with the data at level a_2. The practice effects observed with these data are presented on the right in the last row of the table.

The next step is the most tedious: subtracting the relevant practice effect from each of the scores in the experiment and entering the results in a new Latin

Table 18-9 Calculation of Practice Effects

LEVEL a_1

	Testing Position				Sum
	p_1	p_2	p_3	p_4	
Sum	34	27	26	22	109
Mean	8.50	6.75	6.50	5.50	6.81
Practice effect	1.69	−.06	−.31	−1.31	

LEVEL a_2

	Testing Position				Sum
	p_1	p_2	p_3	p_4	
Sum	47	41	43	39	170
Mean	11.75	10.25	10.75	9.75	10.63
Practice effect	1.12	−.38	.12	−.88	

square matrix. This has been accomplished in the upper portion of Table 18-10. To illustrate, for the first test given to subjects at level a_1, the practice effect of 1.69 is subtracted from each of the four *ABS* scores in that column; from the data presented in Table 18-7 in the original Latin square matrix, we find

$$3 - 1.69 = 1.31; \quad 12 - 1.69 = 10.31; \quad 13 - 1.69 = 11.31; \quad \text{and}$$

$$6 - 1.69 = 4.31.$$

For the second test, $-.06$ is subtracted from the four *ABS* scores in the second column of Table 18-7, and so on for the other two tests. Similar calculations are performed on the data appearing at level a_2. As a check, the data in each column should be summed and the mean calculated. All of the means at level a_1 should be the same (within rounding error) and equal to the overall mean, $\bar{A}_1 = 6.81$; similarly, all of the means at level a_2 should be the same and equal to $\bar{A}_2 = 10.63$. This check permits us to verify that the practice effects have been properly removed.

We now proceed with an ordinary analysis of variance. The data from the Latin square matrix must be transposed into an *ABS* matrix with factor *B* taking the place of treatment position. This has been done in the middle portion of Table 18-10. Also included are the *AB* and *AS* matrices, which will be needed for the analysis. We will first obtain the basic ratios:

$$[T] = \frac{T^2}{(a)(b)(s)} = \frac{(279.04)^2}{(2)(4)(4)} = 2{,}433.23;$$

$$[A] = \frac{\Sigma A^2}{(b)(s)} = \frac{(108.96)^2 + (170.08)^2}{(4)(4)} = 2{,}549.97;$$

$$[B] = \frac{\Sigma B^2}{(a)(s)} = \frac{(46.01)^2 + (68.01)^2 + (91.01)^2 + (74.01)^2}{(2)(4)}$$

$$= 2{,}562.82;$$

$$[AB] = \frac{\Sigma (AB)^2}{s} = \frac{(15.99)^2 + (27.99)^2 + \cdots + (55.02)^2 + (45.02)^2}{4}$$

$$= 2{,}682.91;$$

$$[AS] = \frac{\Sigma (AS)^2}{b} = \frac{(16.99)^2 + (34.99)^2 + \cdots + (54.02)^2 + (32.02)^2}{4}$$

$$= 2{,}828.41;$$

and

$$[ABS] = \Sigma (ABS)^2 = (1.31)^2 + (6.06)^2 + \cdots + (14.38)^2 + (7.88)^2$$

$$= 2{,}968.72.$$

The remainder of the analysis is summarized in Table 18-11. The degrees of freedom for the new error term are adjusted for the removal of the practice main

Table 18-10   Data Matrices for Direct Method of Removing Practice Effects

LATIN SQUARE MATRIX

Sequence		a_1 Testing Position				a_2 Testing Position			
		p_1	p_2	p_3	p_4	p_1	p_2	p_3	p_4
(b_1, b_2, b_3, b_4)	s_1	1.31	4.06	7.31	4.31	3.88	6.38	10.88	7.88
(b_3, b_1, b_4, b_2)	s_2	10.31	6.06	9.31	9.31	16.88	10.38	14.88	12.88
(b_2, b_4, b_1, b_3)	s_3	11.31	11.06	7.31	12.31	13.88	14.38	9.88	15.88
(b_4, b_3, b_2, b_1)	s_4	4.31	6.06	3.31	1.31	7.88	11.38	6.88	5.88
Sum		27.24	27.24	27.24	27.24	42.52	42.52	42.52	42.52
Mean		6.81	6.81	6.81	6.81	10.63	10.63	10.63	10.63

CORRECTED ABS MATRIX

	a_1				a_2			
	b_1	b_2	b_3	b_4	b_1	b_2	b_3	b_4
s_1	1.31	4.06	7.31	4.31				
s_2	6.06	9.31	10.31	9.31				
s_3	7.31	11.31	12.31	11.06				
s_4	1.31	3.31	6.06	4.31				
s_5					3.88	6.38	10.88	7.88
s_6					10.38	12.88	16.88	14.88
s_7					9.88	13.88	15.88	14.38
s_8					5.88	6.88	11.38	7.88

CORRECTED AB MATRIX

	a_1	a_2	Sum
b_1	15.99	30.02	46.01
b_2	27.99	40.02	68.01
b_3	35.99	55.02	91.01
b_4	28.99	45.02	74.01
Sum	108.96	170.08	279.04

CORRECTED AS MATRIX

	a_1		a_2
s_1	16.99	s_5	29.02
s_2	34.99	s_6	55.02
s_3	41.99	s_7	54.02
s_4	14.99	s_8	32.02
Sum	108.96	Sum	170.08

Table 18-11 Analysis of Variance: Practice Effects Removed

SOURCE	BASIC RATIO[a]	SUM OF SQUARES	df	MS.	F
A	$[A] = 2{,}549.97$	$[A] - [T] = 116.74$	1	116.74	2.52
S/A	$[AS] = 2{,}828.41$	$[AS] - [A] = 278.44$	6	46.41	
B	$[B] = 2{,}562.82$	$[B] - [T] = 129.59$	3	43.20	70.82*
A × B	$[AS] = 2{,}682.91$	$[AB] - [A] - [B] + [T] = 3.35$	3	1.12	1.84
L. S. Residual	$[ABS] = 2{,}968.72$	$[ABS] - [AB] - [AS] + [A] = 7.37$	12	.61	
Total	$[T] = 2{,}433.23$	$[ABS] - [T] = 535.49$	25		

*$p < .01$.

[a]Bracketed letters represent complete terms in computational formulas; a particular term is identified by the letter(s) appearing in the numerator.

effect (3 *df*) and the $A \times P$ interaction (3 *df*), which do not appear in this analy-sis.[4] They could be calculated, of course, from the original Latin square arrange-ment, as you saw in the preceding section (Table 18-8), and included in the summary. The main point to note, however, is the exact duplication of the sums of squares, mean squares, and *F* ratios obtained in the Latin square analysis.

18.4 ANALYTICAL COMPARISONS

A factorial experiment provides a rich source of analytical comparisons, which were discussed in Chapter 11 in the context of the completely randomized two-factor design. All of these analyses are available to us in assessing the results of a mixed factorial design. The main complication introduced by the use of repeated measures is the determination of the appropriate error term for the different analyses. Other-wise, the logic of the analyses remains unchanged.

Analyzing Main Effects

In the absence of a significant $A \times B$ interaction, we usually direct our atten-tion to the detailed analysis of the main effects. If the comparisons involve the nonrepeated factor (factor *A*), the computational procedures for the comparison sums of squares are identical to those presented in Chapter 11 (pp. 209–211); the error term is the within-groups mean square $MS_{S/A}$. If the comparisons involve the repeated factor (factor *B*), separate error terms are usually required; these are most easily obtained from the analysis of interaction comparisons to be considered later in this section. The sum of squares for the comparison itself is obtained from this analysis as well. If separate error terms are not assumed to be necessary, we use the formulas of Chapter 11 to calculate the comparison sum of squares and use the within-subjects error term $MS_{B \times S/A}$ or the Latin square error term $MS_{\text{L.S. residual}}$.

Analyzing Simple Effects

A significant interaction can be subjected to two different forms of analysis: an analysis of simple effects, which I will consider in this section, and an analysis of interaction comparisons, which I will consider in the next section. Both sets of procedures attempt to discover the particular treatment combinations responsible for a significant $A \times B$ interaction. The analysis of simple effects involves examin-ing the data in the *AB* matrix row by row or column by column and looking for significance attributable to the variation of one of the independent variables while

---

[4]The *df* associated with practice effects can be calculated from the original *df* statement for the source, $df_{B \times S/A} = a(b-1)(s-1)$, simply by deleting the factor $(s-1)$ from the expres-sion. Thus, the correction for practice in this design is $a(b-1) = 2(4-1) = 6$.

the other is held constant. (See pp. 220-221 for a detailed discussion of the meaning and use of an analysis of simple effects.) I will consider the two sets of analyses
separately—A at b_j and B at a_i—as the error terms are different depending on the
between-subjects or the within-subjects nature of the manipulation.

   Simple Effects Involving the Repeated Factor (B).   What specific data are to
be analyzed depends on whether the standard analysis or the Latin square analysis
is conducted. I will consider the standard analysis first. This analysis will be undertaken when the repeated factor is *not* counterbalanced, as is the case in a learning
experiment, or when practice effects are assumed (or found) not to be significant.
To calculate the sum of squares for a simple effect we treat the data in a row (or
column) of the AB matrix as if they were produced by a single-factor experiment.
Following the procedures described in Chapter 11 (pp. 215-217) and using the
data in Table 18-4 (p. 415), we find

$$SS_{B \text{ at } a_1} = \frac{(16)^2 + (28)^2 + (36)^2 + (29)^2}{4} - \frac{(109)^2}{(4)(4)}$$

$$= 794.25 - 742.56 = 51.69;$$

and

$$SS_{B \text{ at } a_2} = \frac{(30)^2 + (40)^2 + (55)^2 + (45)^2}{4} - \frac{(170)^2}{(4)(4)}$$

$$= 1,887.50 - 1,806.25 = 81.25.$$

Each simple effect is based on $b - 1 = 4 - 1 = 3$ degrees of freedom, and so

$$MS_{B \text{ at } a_1} = \frac{51.69}{3} = 17.23 \quad \text{and} \quad MS_{B \text{ at } a_2} = \frac{81.25}{3} = 27.08.$$

Separate error terms based on the $B \times S$ interactions at the different levels of
factor A are used to test the significance of these simple effects.[5] These were calculated earlier for these data in Section 18.1 (pp. 417-418). From those calculations,
we found

$$MS_{B \times S/A_1} = 2.40 \quad \text{and} \quad MS_{B \times S/A_2} = 1.47.$$

The F ratios for the two simple effects are

$$F_{B \text{ at } a_1} = \frac{MS_{B \text{ at } a_1}}{MS_{B \times S/A_1}} = \frac{17.23}{2.40} = 7.18;$$

[5]Winer (1971, pp. 527-528) suggests a procedure by which the separate error terms are pooled
if the entire set of separate mean squares—one for each level of the nonrepeated factor (factor
A)—can be shown to be homogeneous. (The pooled error term in this case is the overall within-
subjects error term, $MS_{B \times S/A}$.) Separate error terms can be used even under these circumstances, however, although the F tests are slightly conservative on account of the smaller
number of $df_{\text{denom.}}$ associated with the separate error terms than with the pooled one.

and

$$F_{B \text{ at } a_2} = \frac{MS_{B \text{ at } a_2}}{MS_{B \times S/A_2}} = \frac{27.08}{1.47} = 18.42.$$

At $df_{\text{num.}} = 3$ and $df_{\text{denom.}} = 9$, both F ratios are significant $(p < .01)$.

If the Latin square analysis is appropriate, we employ the method that subtracts the practice effect directly from each individual score and then obtain the necessary quantities from this practice-free matrix. I will first calculate the simple effects. Using the data from the corrected AB matrix in Table 18-10 (p. 426), we find

$$SS_{B \text{ at } a_1} = \frac{(15.99)^2 + (27.99)^2 + (35.99)^2 + (28.99)^2}{4} - \frac{(108.96)^2}{(4)(4)}$$

$$= 793.71 - 742.02 = 51.69;$$

and

$$SS_{B \text{ at } a_2} = \frac{(30.02)^2 + (40.02)^2 + (55.02)^2 + (45.02)^2}{4} - \frac{(170.08)^2}{(4)(4)}$$

$$= 1{,}889.20 - 1{,}807.95 = 81.25.$$

The two mean squares are

$$MS_{B \text{ at } a_1} = \frac{51.69}{3} = 17.23 \quad \text{and} \quad MS_{B \text{ at } a_2} = \frac{81.25}{3} = 27.08.$$

(You will note that these sums of squares and mean squares are identical to those obtained with the standard analysis; this is because the Latin square analysis affects the error terms and not the treatment effects.)

The next step is to obtain the separate error terms. Using the data from the ABS matrix in Table 18-10, we find

$$SS_{\text{L.S. residual } (a_1)} = [(1.31)^2 + (6.06)^2 + \cdots + (11.06)^2 + (4.31)^2]$$

$$- \frac{(15.99)^2 + (27.99)^2 + (35.99)^2 + (28.99)^2}{4}$$

$$- \frac{(16.99)^2 + (34.99)^2 + (41.99)^2 + (14.99)^2}{4}$$

$$+ \frac{(108.96)^2}{(4)(4)}$$

$$= 929.77 - 793.71 - 875.21 + 742.02 = 2.87;$$

and

$$SS_{\text{L.S. residual } (a_2)} = [(3.88)^2 + (10.38)^2 + \cdots + (14.38)^2 + (7.88)^2]$$

$$- \frac{(30.02)^2 + (40.02)^2 + (55.02)^2 + (45.02)^2}{4}$$

$$- \frac{(29.02)^2 + (55.02)^2 + (54.02)^2 + (32.02)^2}{4}$$

$$+ \frac{(170.08)^2}{(4)(4)}$$

$$= 2{,}038.95 - 1{,}889.20 - 1{,}953.20 + 1{,}807.95 = 4.50$$

Each error term is based on $(b - 1)(s - 1) = (4 - 1)(4 - 1) = 9$ degrees of freedom, *minus* $p - 1 = 4 - 1 = 3$ *df* to take into account the removal of practice effects from the data matrix. Thus,

$$MS_{\text{L.S. residual } (a_1)} = \frac{2.87}{6} = .48;$$

and

$$MS_{\text{L.S. residual } (a_2)} = \frac{4.50}{6} = .75.$$

Finally, we form the two F ratios; i.e.,

$$F_{B \text{ at } a_1} = \frac{MS_{B \text{ at } a_1}}{MS_{\text{L.S. residual } (a_1)}} = \frac{17.23}{.48} = 35.90;$$

and

$$F_{B \text{ at } a_2} = \frac{MS_{B \text{ at } a_2}}{MS_{\text{L.S. residual } (a_2)}} = \frac{27.08}{.75} = 36.11.$$

At $df_{\text{num.}} = 3$ and $df_{\text{denom.}} = 6$, both F's are significant ($p < .01$).

Simple Effects Involving the Nonrepeated Factor (A). The simple effects factor A, the nonrepeated factor, are based on what can be viewed as individual completely randomized single-factor experiments at the different levels of the repeated factor (factor B). The error term for any one of these "experiments" is based on the variability of subjects treated alike at the level of factor B for that particular experiment. As an example of the analysis, I will analyze the simple effect at level b_3. The relevant data from Table 18-4 (p. 415)—the individual scores from $a_1 b_3$ and $a_2 b_3$—are presented in Table 18-12.

Table 18-12   Simple Effect of Factor A at Level b_3

a_1	a_2
7	11
12	18
11	15
6	11
Sum: 36	55

The simple effect is calculated from the treatment sums as follows:

$$SS_{A \text{ at } b_3} = \frac{(36)^2 + (55)^2}{4} - \frac{(36 + 55)^2}{(2)(4)}$$

$$= 1{,}080.25 - 1{,}035.13 = 45.12.$$

This effect is based on $df = a - 1 = 2 - 1 = 1$, and so $MS_{A \text{ at } b_3} = 45.12$. The within-groups error term is calculated from the individual scores. That is,

$$SS_{S/A \text{ at } b_3} = [(7)^2 + (12)^2 + \cdots + (15)^2 + (11)^2] - \frac{(36)^2 + (55)^2}{4}$$

$$= 1{,}141 - 1{,}080.25 = 60.75.$$

The number of degrees of freedom associated with this particular source of variance is $a(s - 1) = 2(4 - 1) = 2(3) = 6$, and the mean square is

$$MS_{S/A \text{ at } b_3} = \frac{60.75}{6} = 10.13.$$

The F ratio becomes

$$F_{A \text{ at } b_3} = \frac{MS_{A \text{ at } b_3}}{MS_{S/A \text{ at } b_3}} = \frac{45.12}{10.13} = 4.45,$$

which with $df_{num.} = 1$ and $df_{denom.} = 6$ is not significant ($p > .05$).[6]

---

[6]Some authors recommend a pooling of the separate error terms—one from each level of factor B—if the set is homogeneous. (The pooled error term is a weighted average of $MS_{S/A}$ and $MS_{B \times S/A}$, called the **within-cell mean square**.) Separate error terms can be used even in this case, however, although the F tests are slightly conservative on account of the smaller number of $df_{denom.}$ associated with the separate error terms than with the pooled one. For a discussion of the within-cell mean square, see Kirk (1968, pp. 264–265) and Winer (1971, pp. 529–532).

Interaction Comparisons

Interaction comparisons consist of miniature factorial arrangements created from a larger, multilevel factorial design. Analytical questions, in the form of single-df comparisons, are applied to either independent variable separately or to both simultaneously to form interaction comparisons of the kind I have referred to as partial factorials. I will present an analysis procedure that facilitates the calculations required when separate error terms are considered appropriate, which is most of the time unless the restrictive statistical assumptions are fully met. Since most researchers do not test the validity of these assumptions, the best course of action is to assume that interactions of treatment comparisons and subjects are not identical for all comparisons and thus to use separate error terms generally. I will consider two situations: those in which comparisons involve only the nonrepeated factor ($A_{comp.} \times B$ interaction comparisons) and those in which they involve the repeated factor ($A \times B_{comp.}$ and $A_{comp.} \times B_{comp.}$ interaction comparisons). Because of this need for separate error terms, the approach taken here is different from the one presented in Chapter 11 for the completely randomized design.

Interaction Comparisons Involving Only the Nonrepeated Factor ($A_{comp.}$). This type of interaction comparison ($A_{comp.} \times B$) poses no special problems for the statistical analysis. You can use the computational procedures covered in Chapter 11 to obtain the comparison sums of squares (see pp. 222-227). If you decide instead to use the factorial analysis based on a comparison matrix, following in this case the procedures outlined in Chapter 14 (see pp. 320-323), you will have to normalize the sums of squares for the main effect of the comparison ($A_{comp.}$) and the $A_{comp.} \times B$ interaction. This correction, you will recall, consists of dividing the two sums of squares by $[\Sigma\,(c_i)^2]/2$. The analysis is completed by using appropriate error terms from the overall analysis of variance. For the evaluation of $A_{comp.}$, we use the $MS_{S/A}$ from the standard analysis:

$$F = \frac{MS_{A_{comp.}}}{MS_{S/A}}.$$

For the evaluation of the $A_{comp.} \times B$ interaction, we use either the repeated-measures error term if the standard analysis is conducted, that is,

$$F = \frac{MS_{A_{comp.} \times B}}{MS_{B \times S/A}},$$

or the residual error term if the Latin square analysis is conducted, that is,

$$F = \frac{MS_{A_{comp.} \times B}}{MS_{\text{L.S. residual}}}.$$

Separate error terms are not required.

Interaction Comparisons Involving Only the Repeated Factor ($B_{comp.}$). For this type of interaction comparison ($A \times B_{comp.}$), I will extend the procedure introduced in Chapter 17 to the present situation. (This approach is particularly better-suited to within-subjects designs than that presented in Chapter 11 for the completely randomized design.) The first step is to weight the individual *ABS* scores by the coefficients for the single-*df* comparison being conducted on the repeated factor (factor *B*). In the second step, we combine the positive scores for each subject and place them in the first column of a new *ABS comparison matrix*; similarly, we combine the negative scores and place them in the second column of the new matrix, dropping the sign in the process. Finally, we conduct an ordinary analysis of variance on the extracted data in the *ABS* comparison matrix. Let's see how this is accomplished.

I will consider two examples. The first illustrates a situation in which counterbalancing is used and practice effects are removed from the analysis by means of the direct method described in Section 18.3. The second illustrates the analysis appropriate for a situation in which counterbalancing is *not relevant*, e.g., when the levels of factor *B* are trials in a learning experiment where counterbalancing would make no sense.

The first example involves a comparison between levels b_1 and b_2 for which I will use 1, -1, 0, and 0 as the coefficients. This analysis concentrates on the difference between b_1 and b_2 and determines whether this difference depends on the levels of factor *A*. We begin with the practice-corrected *ABS* matrix found in Table 18-10 (p. 426). The construction of the *ABS* comparison matrix is easy in this case: we simply take the *ABS* scores from level b_1 and place them in the level labeled $b_{(+)}$ (the positive weighted *ABS* scores) and take the scores from level b_2 and place them in the level labeled $b_{(-)}$ (the negative weighted *ABS* scores). This has been done in Table 18-13. The analysis at this point follows the general procedures for the analysis of a Latin square design (see pp. 425–428). You should remember that factor *B* now consists of *two* levels rather than three in the calculations. I will use the symbol b', which here is equal to 2, to emphasize this change.

The basic ratios are calculated from the information provided in Table 18-13. Specifically,

$$[T] = \frac{T^2}{(a)(b')(s)} = \frac{(113.52)^2}{(2)(2)(4)} = 805.42;$$

$$[A] = \frac{\Sigma A^2}{(b')(s)} = \frac{(43.98)^2 + (69.54)^2}{(2)(4)} = 846.26;$$

$$[B] = \frac{\Sigma B^2}{(a)(s)} = \frac{(45.51)^2 + (68.01)^2}{(2)(4)} = 837.07;$$

$$[AB] = \frac{\Sigma (AB)^2}{s} = \frac{(15.99)^2 + (29.52)^2 + (27.99)^2 + (40.02)^2}{4} = 878.04;$$

$$[AS] = \frac{\Sigma\,(AS)^2}{b'} = \frac{(5.37)^2 + (15.37)^2 + \cdots + (23.76)^2 + (12.76)^2}{2} = 998.38;$$

and

$$[ABS] = \Sigma\,(ABS)^2 = (1.31)^2 + (6.06)^2 + \cdots + (13.88)^2 + (6.88)^2$$

$$= 1,033.57.$$

These quantities are combined in Table 18-14 to produce the various sums of squares obtained with this analysis.

The remainder of the analysis is summarized in Table 18-14. The degrees of freedom for the repeated-measures error term, which is usually equal to $a(b' - 1)$ $(s - 1) = 2(2 - 1)(4 - 1) = 6$, must be reduced because of the removal of practice effects from the original ABS scores. The correction factor for this design is $a(b' - 1) = 2(2 - 1) = 2$.[7] The number of df for the Latin square error term is $df_{\text{L.S. residual}} = 6 - 2 = 4$. The primary purpose of this analysis is to evaluate the significance of the two effects associated with factor B. Both of these mean squares, the main effect of the comparison and the interaction of the comparison with factor A, are divided by the Latin square error term. The main effect of factor A is usually not assessed in this particular type of analysis. The analysis reveals a significant main effect of the comparison between b_1 and b_2 and an interaction that is not significant.

Table 18-13 Data Matrices for Interaction Comparison

ABS COMPARISON MATRIX

	a_1				a_2		
	$b_{(+)}$	$b_{(-)}$	Sum		$b_{(+)}$	$b_{(-)}$	Sum
s_1	1.31	4.06	5.37	s_5	3.38	6.38	9.76
s_2	6.06	9.31	15.37	s_6	10.38	12.88	23.26
s_3	7.31	11.31	18.62	s_7	9.88	13.88	23.76
s_4	1.31	3.31	4.62	s_8	5.88	6.88	12.76
Sum	15.99	27.99	43.98	Sum	29.52	40.02	69.54

AB COMPARISON MATRIX

	$b_{(+)}$	$b_{(-)}$	Sum
a_1	15.99	27.99	43.98
a_2	29.52	40.02	69.54
Sum	45.51	68.01	113.52

[7] As indicated in footnote 4 (p. 423), the df associated with practice effects for this design are equal to $a(b - 1)$. The formula given here simply substitutes b' for b in this correction formula.

Table 18-14   Summary of the Analysis

SOURCE	BASIC RATIO[a]	SUM OF SQUARES	df	MS	F
A	$[A] = 846.26$	$[A] - [T] = 40.84$	1	—[b]	—[b]
S/A	$[AS] = 998.38$	$[AS] - [A] = 152.12$	6	—[b]	
$B_{comp.}$	$[B] = 837.07$	$[B] - [T] = 31.65$	1	31.65	37.24*
$A \times B_{comp.}$	$[AB] = 878.04$	$[AB] - [A] - [B] + [T] = .13$	1	.13	.15
L. S. Residual	$[ABS] = 1,033.57$	$[ABS] - [AB] - [AS] + [A] = 3.41$	$6 - 2$	.85	
Total	$[T] = 805.42$	$[ABS] - [T] = 228.15$	$15 - 2$		

*$p < .01$.
[a] Bracketed letters represent complete terms in computational formulas; a particular term is identified by the letter(s) appearing in the numerator.
[b] Not needed.

main effect of factor A is usually not assessed in this particular type of analysis. The analysis reveals a significant main effect of the comparison between b_1 and b_2 and an interaction that is not significant.

As a second example, I will consider a single-df comparison that is commonly conducted with the mixed factorial design, namely, a trend analysis. I have already mentioned that mixed designs are easily created from completely randomized single-factor experiments simply by adding a number of learning trials. An obvious analysis in this type of design is a detailed comparison of the learning curves obtained under the different treatments. The extraction of orthogonal trend components provides a precise, analytical way to characterize the shapes of the learning curves. The procedures we will follow in this analysis are no different from those we would follow with any single-df comparison.

Let's assume, then, that factor B consists of four training trials and that we are interested in examining the linear trends exhibited by the learning curves. A significant $A \times B_{\text{linear}}$ interaction would mean that the slopes of the learning curves are not the same at all levels of factor A.[8] Since counterbalancing of the B treatments—trials—is obviously not used in this type of mixed factorial, we will work with the data from the *original* data matrix (see Table 18-4, p. 415). The coefficients for linear trend are found in Table A-4 in Appendix A. They consist of the set $(-3, -1, 1,$ and $3)$. The individual ABS scores for each subject are weighted by these coefficients. Consider the four ABS scores for the second subject at level a_1. The scores, coefficients, and weighted scores for this subject are given in the following table:

	b_1	b_2	b_3	b_4
ABS scores:	6	8	12	9
Coefficients:	−3	−1	1	3
Weighted scores:	−18	−8	12	27

The weighted scores for all of the subjects in this example are presented in the upper portion of Table 18-15.

The next step is to add separately for each subject the two positive and two negative weighted scores and to place the two sums in an ABS comparison matrix. For this subject, the sum of the positive scores is $12 + 27 = 39$, and the sum of the negative scores is $-18 + (-8) = -26$. The positive sum is placed in the ABS matrix under level $b_{(+)}$ and the negative sum (sign deleted) is placed in the ABS matrix under level $b_{(-)}$. This comparison matrix is presented in the middle portion of

---

[8]More complex components could be studied as well, e.g., the quadratic and cubic components in this particular case. The linear component is usually the first one examined in a trend analysis, and the procedures for the higher-order trends are the same except for the change in coefficients.

Table 18-15 Data Matrices for Trend Analysis (Linear)

WEIGHTED *ABS* SCORES

	a_1					a_2			
	b_1	b_2	b_3	b_4		b_1	b_2	b_3	b_4
s_1	−9	−4	7	9	s_5	−15	−6	11	21
s_2	−18	−8	12	27	s_6	−30	−12	18	45
s_3	−21	−13	11	33	s_7	−30	−15	15	42
s_4	0	−3	6	18	s_8	−15	−7	11	27

***ABS* COMPARISON MATRIX**

	a_1				a_2		
	$b(+)$	$b(-)$	Sum		$b(+)$	$b(-)$	Sum
s_1	16	13	29	s_5	32	21	53
s_2	39	26	65	s_6	63	42	105
s_3	44	34	78	s_7	57	45	102
s_4	24	3	27	s_8	38	22	60
Sum	123	76	199	Sum	190	130	320

***AB* COMPARISON MATRIX**

	$b(+)$	$b(-)$	Sum
a_1	123	76	199
a_2	190	130	320
Sum	313	206	519

Table 18-15. You will note that marginal sums have also been calculated in this *ABS* matrix, the column marginal sums providing the information required for the *AB* matrix listed at the bottom of Table 18-15 and the row marginal sums providing the sums usually found in the *AS* matrix. With these various quantities, we can calculate the required basic ratios as follows:

$$[T] = \frac{T^2}{(a)(b')(s)} = \frac{(519)^2}{(2)(2)(4)} = 16{,}835.06;$$

$$[A] = \frac{\Sigma A^2}{(b')(s)} = \frac{(199)^2 + (320)^2}{(2)(4)} = 17{,}750.13;$$

$$[B] = \frac{\Sigma B^2}{(a)(s)} = \frac{(313)^2 + (206)^2}{(2)(4)} = 17{,}550.63;$$

$$[AB] = \frac{\Sigma\,(AB)^2}{s} = \frac{(123)^2 + (190)^2 + (76)^2 + (130)^2}{4} = 18{,}476.25;$$

$$[AS] = \frac{\Sigma\,(AS)^2}{b'} = \frac{(29)^2 + (65)^2 + \cdots + (102)^2 + (60)^2}{2} = 19{,}858.50;$$

and

$$[ABS] = \Sigma\,(ABS)^2 = (16)^2 + (39)^2 + \cdots + (45)^2 + (22)^2 = 20{,}699.$$

These quantities are combined as indicated in Table 18-16 to produce the necessary sums of squares.

The remaining steps in the analysis are summarized in Table 18-16. As before, the focus of attention will be the two sources of variance based on $B_{comp.}$. In this case, only the linear main effect is significant, indicating the presence of a linear trend in the overall trial means. Performance increases steadily with trials (a significant linear main effect), and this increase is approximately the same at both levels of factor A (i.e., there is no interaction).

If you wish to compare the sums of squares obtained from this analysis with sums of squares obtained from other interaction comparisons or from the original analysis, it is necessary to normalize them first. In fact, it is generally a good idea to normalize the relevant sums of squares any time this method of calculating interaction comparisons is used. As you saw in Chapter 17, this adjustment is accomplished quite simply by dividing relevant comparison sums of squares by the factor

$$\frac{\Sigma\,(\text{coefficients})^2}{2}.$$

For the first example, no adjustment is required since the correction is 1. In the present analysis, the correction factor would be

$$\frac{\Sigma\,(c_i)^2}{2} = \frac{(-3)^2 + (-1)^2 + (1)^2 + (3)^2}{2} = \frac{20}{2} = 10.$$

Applying this correction to the three critical sums of squares needed for this analysis, we find

$$SS_{B_{\text{linear}}} = \frac{715.57}{10} = 71.56,$$

$$SS_{A \times B_{\text{linear}}} = \frac{10.57}{10} = 1.06, \text{ and}$$

$$SS_{B_{\text{linear}} \times S/A} = \frac{114.36}{10} = 11.44.$$

Table 18-16 Summary of the Trend Analysis Based on Weighted *ABS* Scores

SOURCE	BASIC RATIO[a]	SUM OF SQUARES (UNADJUSTED)	df	MS	F
A	$[A] = 17,750.11$	$[A] - [T] = 915.05$	1	—[b]	—[b]
S/A	$[AS] = 19,858.50$	$[AS] - [A] = 2,108.39$	6	—[b]	
B_{linear}	$[B] = 17,550.63$	$[B] - [T] = 715.57$	1	715.57	37.54*
$A \times B_{\text{linear}}$	$[AB] = 18,476.25$	$[AB] - [A] - [B] + [T] = 10.57$	1	10.57	.55
$B_{\text{linear}} \times S/A$	$[ABS] = 20,699$	$[ABS] - [AB] - [AS] + [A] = 114.36$	6	19.06	
Total	$[T] = 16,835.06$	$[ABS] - [T] = 3,863.94$	15		

*$p < .01$.

[a] Bracketed letters represent complete terms in computational formulas; a particular term is identified by the letter(s) appearing in the numerator.

[b] Not needed.

The mean squares and F ratios become

$$F = \frac{71.56/1}{11.44/6} = \frac{71.56}{1.91} = 37.47 \text{ and}$$

$$F = \frac{1.06/1}{11.44/6} = \frac{1.06}{1.91} = .55,$$

for B_{linear} and $A \times B_{\text{linear}}$, respectively. As you can see by comparing these F ratios with the corresponding ones presented in Table 18-16, that except for rounding error, the numerical outcomes are the same.

Now that we have normalized the sums of squares, we can compare them directly with the sums of squares obtained from the original analysis. For example, the sum of squares for the main effect of this comparison ($SS_{B_{\text{linear}}} = 71.56$) can be compared with the B main effect from the overall analysis ($SS_B = 129.60$, as shown in Table 18-5) to provide a rough indication of how much of this variation can be attributed to linear trend. In this case, $71.56/129.60 \times 100 = 55.2$ per cent of the B main effect is associated with linear trend. Are any other trends present? An inspection of the overall trial means obtained from the AB matrix of Table 18-4 (p. 415)–5.75, 8.50, 11.38, and 9.25–suggests the presence of a quadratic trend (a reversal of direction) in addition to the significant linear trend we have just discovered.

Interaction Contrasts. Interaction is most precisely pinpointed by the use of interaction contrasts. You will recall from Chapter 11 (pp. 227-229) that an interaction contrast is a factorial comparison formed when both independent variables are transformed into single-df comparisons to create what amounts to a 2 × 2 factorial design, which produces a highly specific $A_{\text{comp.}} \times B_{\text{comp.}}$ interaction. The focus of such an analysis is the interaction, although comparison main effects become of interest when the interaction is not significant. The analysis is slightly different from those I have considered already in this chapter and is accomplished in two major steps. First, we calculate the repeated-measures error term, which is based on the $B_{\text{comp.}} \times S$ interaction pooled over the independent groups (factor A); $A_{\text{comp.}}$ does not enter the calculations at this point. Second, we obtain the comparison sums of squares, which requires the application of $A_{\text{comp.}}$ and $B_{\text{comp.}}$ to the matrix of treatment sums. I will present this analysis through a numerical example.

Consider the data presented in Exercise 1 at the end of this chapter (p. 448). The design is a mixed factorial with factor A consisting of three levels and factor B consisting of four levels; $s = 4$ subjects are assigned randomly to each of the three levels of the independent-groups factor (factor A). Suppose we are interested in an interaction contrast formed by crossing a comparison between level a_2 and an average of levels a_1 and a_3 with a comparison between an average of levels b_1 and b_4 and an average of levels b_2 and b_3. (This interaction contrast is not particularly informative; the one specified in Exercise 3c at the end of the chapter represents a more meaningful example of an interaction contrast.)

For the **first major step**, then, we calculate the within-subjects error term. We begin by forming an *ABS* comparison matrix, which is created by weighting the individual scores by the coefficients for factor *B* $(1, -1, -1, \text{and } 1)$. This has been accomplished in Table 18-17. (I will use the subscript c to indicate which factor is involved in creating the comparison matrix, because it can become confusing. Since factor *B* is the one involved at this point in the analysis, I will call this matrix an AB_cS comparison matrix.)

We now calculate the sum of squares for the repeated-measures error term, as we did in the earlier two examples. This is accomplished in two stages. The first extracts a sum of squares from the AB_cS comparison matrix, and the second normalizes the sum of squares to adjust for the fact that the calculations are performed on the weighted *ABS* scores. (Normalization was not necessary in the analyses presented earlier in this section because *all* critical sums of squares were based on the same weighted scores. This is not true for this analysis, however, which will require the separate normalization of each sum of squares derived from the analysis). To emphasize the fact that the sums of squares need to be normalized before the *F* ratios are formed, I will use a prime to refer to uncorrected sums of squares.

We are now ready to calculate the uncorrected repeated-measures error term $SS_{B' \times S/A}$. All of the information we need is available from the entries and the marginal sums appearing in the AB_cS comparison matrix. More specifically,

$$SS_{B' \times S/A} = \Sigma (ABS)^2 - \frac{\Sigma (AB)^2}{s} - \frac{\Sigma (AS)^2}{b'} + \frac{\Sigma A^2}{(b')(s)}$$

$$= (53)^2 + (44)^2 + \cdots + (70)^2 + (65)^2$$

$$- \frac{(190)^2 + (200)^2 + \cdots + (234)^2 + (271)^2}{4}$$

$$- \frac{(104)^2 + (90)^2 + \cdots + (132)^2 + (121)^2}{2}$$

$$+ \frac{(390)^2 + (443)^2 + (505)^2}{(2)(4)}$$

$$= 76{,}288 - 75{,}641.50 - 76{,}026.00 + 75{,}421.75 = 42.25.$$

As indicated in the preceding paragraph, we must normalize this sum of squares before it can be used in the statistical analysis. Since only $B_{\text{comp.}}$ is involved in the analysis at this point, the correction factor is

$$\frac{\Sigma (c_j)^2}{2} = \frac{(1)^2 + (-1)^2 + (-1)^2 + (1)^2}{2} = \frac{4}{2} = 2.$$

The normalized sum of squares is

$$SS_{B_{\text{comp.}} \times S/A} = \frac{SS_{B' \times S/A}}{\text{correction}} = \frac{42.25}{2} = 21.13.$$

Table 18-17 The AB_cS Comparison Matrix

a_1

	$b_{(+)}$	$b_{(-)}$	Sum
s_1	53	51	104
s_2	44	46	90
s_3	54	57	111
s_4	39	46	85
Sum	190	200	390

a_2

	$b_{(+)}$	$b_{(-)}$	Sum
s_5	46	47	93
s_6	52	57	109
s_7	57	59	116
s_8	58	67	125
Sum	213	230	443

a_3

	$b_{(+)}$	$b_{(-)}$	Sum
s_9	63	72	135
s_{10}	53	64	117
s_{11}	62	70	132
s_{12}	56	65	121
Sum	234	271	505

The degrees of freedom are $a(b' - 1)(s - 1) = 3(2 - 1)(4 - 1) = 3(1)(3) = 9$; the mean square is

$$MS_{B_{comp.} \times S/A} = \frac{21.13}{9} = 2.35.$$

These steps are summarized in Table 18-19.

For the **second major step**, we calculate the comparison sums of squares. Here we shift our attention to the AB comparison matrix on the left in Table 18-18, which I have designated the AB_c comparison matrix and which is constructed from the column marginal totals obtained from the AB_cS comparison matrix in Table 18-17. Since we have already transformed factor B into the desired comparison and recorded this information in the AB_c comparison matrix, all that remains is to translate factor A in a similar fashion. This has been accomplished in the A_cB_c comparison matrix on the right. For this comparison, I will use the coefficients, 1, -2, and 1. The entries in the row labeled $a_{(+)}$ are the sums obtained by combining the two levels of factor A with positive coefficients (levels a_1 and a_3), while the entries in the row labeled $a_{(-)}$ are the quantities from level a_2 multiplied by the single negative coefficient for this comparison (-2). (As before, the negative signs are dropped before the weighted sums are placed in the matrix.) All that is necessary now is to calculate the basic ratios in the normal fashion, remembering that the levels of both factors are $a' = 2$ and $b' = 2$ and not their actual values from the original factorial design. To illustrate,

$$[T] = \frac{T^2}{(a')(b')(s)} = \frac{(1,781)^2}{(2)(2)(4)} = 198,247.56;$$

$$[A] = \frac{\Sigma A^2}{(b')(s)} = \frac{(895)^2 + (886)^2}{(2)(4)} = 198,252.63;$$

$$[B] = \frac{\Sigma B^2}{(a')(s)} = \frac{(850)^2 + (931)^2}{(2)(4)} = 198,657.63;$$

and

$$[AB] = \frac{\Sigma (AB)^2}{s} = \frac{(424)^2 + (426)^2 + (471)^2 + (460)^2}{4} = 198,673.25.$$

The uncorrected sums of squares are calculated next:

$$SS_{A'} = [A] - [T] = 5.07;$$

$$SS_{B'} = [B] - [T] = 410.07;$$

and

$$SS_{A' \times B'} = [AB] - [A] - [B] + [T] = 10.55.$$

Table 18-18 The AB_c and A_cB_c Comparison Matrices

AB_c COMPARISON MATRIX			A_cB_c COMPARISON MATRIX		
	$b(+)$	$b(-)$		$b(+)$	$b(-)$	Sum

	$b(+)$	$b(-)$		$b(+)$	$b(-)$	Sum
a_1	190	200	$a(+)$	424	471	895
a_2	213	230	$a(-)$	426	460	886
a_3	234	271				
			Sum	850	931	1,781

To normalize these SS's, we must correct for *both* sets of coefficients since the AB sums on which the uncorrected SS's are based were weighted by the c_i's and the c_j's simultaneously. In this case, then, the correction factor is the *product* of the correction factors for each of the two sets of coefficients; i.e.,

$$\left[\frac{\Sigma (c_i)^2}{2}\right]\left[\frac{\Sigma (c_j)^2}{2}\right] = \left[\frac{(1)^2 + (-2)^2 + (1)^2}{2}\right]\left[\frac{(1)^2 + (-1)^2 + (-1)^2 + (1)^2}{2}\right]$$

$$= \left(\frac{6}{2}\right)\left(\frac{4}{2}\right) = 3(2) = 6.$$

When this is applied to the uncorrected SS's, we find

$$SS_{A\text{ comp.}} = \frac{SS_{A'}}{\text{correction}} = \frac{5.07}{6} = .85;$$

$$SS_{B\text{ comp.}} = \frac{SS_{B'}}{\text{correction}} = \frac{410.07}{6} = 68.35;$$

Table 18-19 Summary of the Analysis

SOURCE	SS	df	MS	F
$A_{\text{comp.}}$	.85	1	.85	$\dfrac{.85}{MS_{S/A}}$
S/A	$-^a$	$a(s-1)$	$\dfrac{SS_{S/A}}{df_{S/A}}$	
$B_{\text{comp.}}$	68.35	1	68.35	29.09*
$A_{\text{comp.}} \times B_{\text{comp.}}$	1.76	1	1.76	.75
$B_{\text{comp.}} \times S/A$	21.13	9	2.35	

*$p < .01$.
^{a}Obtained from Exercise 1.

and

$$SS_{A_{comp.} \times B_{comp.}} = \frac{SS_{A' \times B'}}{\text{correction}} = \frac{10.55}{6} = 1.76.$$

These sums of squares are entered in Table 18-19.

The degrees of freedom for these sources of variation are

$$df_{A_{comp.}} = a' - 1 = 2 - 1 = 1;$$
$$df_{B_{comp.}} = b' - 1 = 2 - 1 = 1;$$

and

$$df_{A_{comp.} \times B_{comp.}} = (a' - 1)(b' - 1) = (2 - 1)(2 - 1) = 1.$$

The df's are also entered in the table. The mean squares are calculated in the usual fashion. The error term for the main effect of $A_{comp.}$ is the within-groups mean square from the *original* analysis, $MS_{S/A}$, which is not calculated here but is left for you to calculate when you tackle Exercise 1. The error term for the main effect of $B_{comp.}$ and the $A_{comp.} \times B_{comp.}$ interaction is the specialized repeated-measures error term $MS_{B_{comp.} \times S/A}$, which was calculated previously. The analysis reveals that only the main effect of $B_{comp.}$ is significant.

Summary. A basic principle governs the specification of error terms in repeated-measures designs. If the comparison of interest uses only one piece of information from each of the subjects contributing to the comparison, the error term is some sort of within-groups mean square, which is based on mean squares reflecting the variability of subjects treated alike and pooled or averaged over independent groups. On the other hand, if the analysis uses more than one piece of information from the subjects involved, the error term is an interaction of the repeated factor and subjects—with the levels of the repeated factor either remaining intact in the case of a simple effect or being transformed in the case of a comparison. Table 18-20 provides a listing of the error terms for the various analytical comparisons I considered in this section.

This governing principle underlying error-term selection is easily seen with the main effects. For factor A, the data are collapsed over the repeated factor producing a single piece of information for each subject. Under these circumstances, then, the error term for the main effect and for any comparison involving the A treatment means is $MS_{S/A}$ from the overall analysis, a within-groups mean square. For factor B, the data are collapsed over the between-subjects factor, but each subject continues to supply more than one piece of information. The MS_B involves all of the individual scores obtained from each of the subjects, and the error term consists of an interaction of $B \times S$ pooled over the independent groups. Any single-df comparison involving the B means, while using only a portion of the information available from each subject, is still based on two scores, whether they consist of individual observations or combinations of observations. Specialized error terms are required, which are based only on the data specifically contributing to the comparison. In this case, the error term consists of an interaction of $B_{comp.} \times S$ pooled over the independent groups. There is a different $B_{comp.} \times S/A$ mean square for each comparison examined in the analysis.

The $A \times B$ interaction uses all of the individual scores produced by the subjects in the experiment. The error term in this case is an interaction of factor B and subjects pooled over all independent groups ($MS_{B \times S/A}$). Analyses designed to specify the nature of this interaction use only a portion of the data available from the experiment. Simple effects, which are listed next in Table 18-20, focus on the variation of one of the independent variables with the other variable held constant. As you have seen, the analysis of simple effects effectively becomes an analysis of separate single-factor designs—one for each of the levels of the factor held constant in the analysis. If the simple effects involve the *nonrepeated factor* (factor A), the ABS matrix is literally subdivided into a number of *completely randomized* single-factor designs, a different one for each level of factor B; the error term for the simple effect of factor A in each analysis is a within-groups mean square based on the individual scores found in the ABS matrix at the relevant level of factor B. Following a significant simple effect, additional comparisons are usually conducted (simple comparisons). The error term for these analyses is the same as that used to evaluate the overall simple effect.

If the simple effects involve the *repeated factor* (factor B), the ABS matrix is again subdivided into a number of separate single-factor experiments, but this time they consist of single-factor *within-subjects* designs, a different one for each level of factor A. The error term for the simple effect of factor B in each analysis is an interaction of factor B and subjects obtained from the data appearing in the ABS matrix at the appropriate level of factor A. Simple comparisons, which use only a portion of the information available in this data matrix, require separate

Table 18-20 Error Terms for Analytical Comparisons in the $A \times (B \times S)$ Design

	SOURCE	ERROR TERM
Main Effects	A	S/A
	$A_{comp.}$	S/A (p. 428)
	B	$B \times S/A$
	$B_{comp.}$	$B_{comp.} \times S/A$ (p. 428)
Interaction	$A \times B$	$B \times S/A$
Simple Effects	A at b_j	S/A at b_j (pp. 431–432)
	$A_{comp.}$ at b_j	S/A at b_j
	B at a_i	$B \times S$ at a_i (pp. 429–431)
	$B_{comp.}$ at a_i	$B_{comp.} \times S$ at a_i
Interaction Comparisons	$A_{comp.} \times B$	$B \times S/A$ (p. 433)
	$A \times B_{comp.}$	$B_{comp.} \times S/A$ (pp. 434–441)
	$A_{comp.} \times B_{comp.}$	$B_{comp.} \times S/A$ (pp. 441–446)

error terms, just as analytical comparisons do in an actual single-factor within-subjects design.

Interaction comparisons represent a second major way that interaction is analyzed analytically. The characteristic feature of all interaction comparisons is the formation of smaller factorial designs from which the information required for the analysis is obtained. If the comparison defining the smaller factorial involves the *nonrepeated factor only*—that is, an $A_{comp.} \times B$ factorial—the error terms come from the original analysis, $MS_{S/A}$ for the comparison main effect and $MS_{B \times S/A}$ for the comparison interaction. In contrast, if the *repeated factor is involved* in defining the smaller factorial, either alone as an $A \times B_{comp.}$ interaction comparison or in conjunction with an $A_{comp.}$ as an $A_{comp.} \times B_{comp.}$ interaction comparison (that is, an interaction contrast), it becomes necessary to calculate a separate error term to evaluate the two sources based on repeated measures, $B_{comp.}$ and the interaction. The procedure outlined in this chapter uses a specialized *ABS* comparison matrix in which the individual *ABS* scores have been multiplied by the relevant coefficients and combined according to the sign of the coefficients. For the $A \times B_{comp.}$ interaction comparison, the entire analysis then becomes a standard $A \times (B \times S)$ analysis of variance, which is conducted on the weighted data appearing in the *ABS* comparison matrix. For the $A_{comp.} \times B_{comp.}$ analysis, the *ABS* comparison matrix is used to calculate the repeated-measures error term and a specialized *AB* comparison matrix, which contains *AB* treatment sums weighted by *both* comparisons, is used to calculate the two comparison main effects and the interaction.[9]

18.5 EXERCISES[10]

(Note: Taken together, Exercises 1 to 3 represent a comprehensive analysis of a set of data. While the amount of work required to complete these problems is considerable, you should keep in mind that the time spent on calculations is quite small when compared with the time consumed in designing an actual experiment and collecting the real data! The purpose of the problems is to work toward discovering the locus of the significant $A \times B$ interaction.)

1. Subjects are given a digit-cancellation task under three conditions of motivation. The subjects in a_1 are simply asked to do their "best." Subjects in a_2, on the other hand, are given highly motivating instructions, while subjects in a_3 are offered $5 if they perform at some predetermined level. Each subject (there are four subjects per incentive group) is given four 30-second trials (factor *B*). The response measure consists of the number of digits canceled from a long series of

[9]In any of these analyses, you should adopt the practice of normalizing all sums of squares that are calculated from comparison matrices where the data have been weighted by coefficients. While this procedure is not necessary for all comparison sources derived from comparison matrices, it will help to avoid the serious mistake of failing to normalize comparison sums of squares when it *is* required.

[10]The answers to these problems are found in Appendix B, beginning on p. 595.

digits within the time period. The data from this experiment are given below. Analyze these results.

ABS MATRIX

	a_1					a_2					a_3			
	b_1	b_2	b_3	b_4		b_1	b_2	b_3	b_4		b_1	b_2	b_3	b_4
s_1	23	24	27	30	s_5	15	20	27	31	s_9	23	34	38	40
s_2	20	21	25	24	s_6	18	25	32	34	s_{10}	19	32	32	34
s_3	23	29	28	31	s_7	24	26	33	33	s_{11}	24	32	38	38
s_4	14	22	24	25	s_8	22	31	36	36	s_{12}	18	28	37	38

2. The $A \times B$ interaction in the last problem was significant. One useful way to study interaction is by means of simple effects. There two sets of simple effects, of course, one examining the effects of the different conditions of motivation (simple effects of A) and the other examining the effects of practice trials (simple effects of B). Both sets of simple effects might be of interest in this study.
   (a) Analyze the simple effects of the three motivating conditions. What have you learned from this analysis?
   (b) Analyze the simple effects of trials. What does this analysis tell you about the $A \times B$ interaction?
3. Another way to approach the analysis of a significant interaction is through the use of partial factorials and interaction comparisons. Both independent variables in Exercise 1 yield potentially informative single-df comparisons.
   (a) Factor B consists of a quantitative independent variable (trials). Perform a trend analysis on the data from Exercise 1. What has this analysis told you about the nature of the significant $A \times B$ interaction?
   (b) Factor A is a qualitative independent variable which yields a number of useful single-df comparisons: e.g., a comparison between the two incentive conditions—strongly motivating instructions (a_2) versus monetary incentive (a_3)—and a comparison between the baseline control condition (a_1) and an average of the other two conditions. Conduct both of these interaction comparisons on these data. What have you learned from these analyses?
   (c) Now that you have viewed the $A \times B$ interaction through partial factorials involving the separate analysis of the two independent variables, what might an analysis of interaction contrasts tell you about the interaction? Try one of them, the interaction of Acomp. (control versus the combined motivation groups) with Bcomp. (linear trend).
4. In this experiment, 12 subjects (small nonhuman mammals) were randomly assigned to one of three treatment conditions. Condition a_1 was a control group that was prepared for surgery and given anesthetic but not operated on. Condition a_2 consisted of a group of subjects that were operated on and had an area of the brain critical to the interest of the researcher removed. Condition a_3 consisted of a group of subjects that were also operated on but had an area of the brain removed that was thought to be unrelated to the behavior under study. The second factor in the experiment was a battery of four different tests. We will not be concerned with the exact nature of the tests except to note that they were relevant to the research. Each of the subjects was tested on the four tests; the tests were administered in the counterbalanced order indicated below. The

following data were obtained:

	a_1 (Control)					a_2 (Critical Area)					a_3 (Noncritical Area)			
	Testing Position					*Testing Position*					*Testing Position*			
	P_1	P_2	P_3	P_4		P_1	P_2	P_3	P_4		P_1	P_2	P_3	P_4
s_1	6	7	10	6	s_5	7	7	4	0	s_9	11	7	10	6
s_2	12	11	7	12	s_6	14	6	8	7	s_{10}	11	14	10	10
s_3	18	12	15	14	s_7	16	14	10	13	s_{11}	15	14	10	12
s_4	18	20	13	9	s_8	10	13	13	10	s_{12}	11	12	14	3

LATIN SQUARE ARRANGEMENT

	Subjects			*Testing Position*			
				P_1	P_2	P_3	P_4
s_1	s_5	s_9		b_1	b_2	b_3	b_4
s_2	s_6	s_{10}		b_2	b_4	b_1	b_3
s_3	s_7	s_{11}		b_3	b_1	b_4	b_2
s_4	s_8	s_{12}		b_4	b_3	b_2	b_1

(a) Perform a standard analysis of variance with these data, disregarding any practice effects that might be present.

(b) Perform a Latin square analysis on these data using the procedure of subtracting the practice effect from each individual test score. Compare your results with the other method of analysis, in which sums of squares reflecting practice effects are subtracted from the repeated-measures error term.

(c) Our next step in the analysis would be to try to make some sense of the significant $A \times B$ interaction. An examination of the AB matrix suggests that the first two tests (b_1 and b_2) do not discriminate among the three groups of animals, while the other two tests (b_3 and b_4) do. Focusing on these two tests, you can see that the fourth test seems to detect a particularly large deficit for the subjects with the critical area removed—a finding of particular interest to the researcher, presumably. To substantiate this observation, however, the researcher would have to analyze a number of partial factorials. Can you list and describe them?

(d) Picking only one of these partial factorials as an example, determine whether the test at b_4 discriminates between the two operated groups (a_2 and a_3) while the test at b_3 does not. (Note: the analysis should be conducted on the practice-corrected ABS scores obtained in part b.)

19

Other Common Within-Subjects Designs

In this chapter, I will consider additional within-subjects designs that are commonly used in the behavioral sciences. As you saw in the last chapter, the same factorial effects and analytical comparisons that can be extracted from a completely randomized two-factor design can be obtained from a corresponding mixed factorial. In general, this will always be the case—the number of independent variables combined factorially in an experiment will determine the nature of the information available to analyze in an experiment. The fact that repeated measures are involved makes no difference in this regard. Where repeated measures enter the picture is in the determination of the error terms used to evaluate systematic variation and additional complications such as the need to counterbalance practice effects; the need to avoid the occurrence of differential carry-over effects which if present might lead to a questioning of the findings of the experiment; and the need to consider the possibility that the special assumptions associated with repeated-measures designs are violated and what this implies for the interpretation of the F tests.

The most common example of within-subjects designs is a completely randomized design that includes repeated applications of the same treatments in the form of learning trials. The value of such designs is the unique information provided by this particular within-subjects factor, namely, information that offers the opportunity to study the standard factorial effects—main effects and interactions—collapsed over trials (the repeated factor) and to determine whether these effects interact with trials. There are other reasons why higher-order designs contain within-subjects factors in addition to trials. For example, a researcher may be particularly interested in detecting differences associated with a certain independent variable and may choose to manipulate that variable as a within-subjects factor to take advantage of the increased sensitivity such a factor usually enjoys. In other cases, a researcher turns to within-subjects designs in order to reduce the total number of subjects required. In the first section of this chapter, I will discuss the general form of the analysis of higher-order within-subjects designs. As you will see, the procedures are relatively simple extensions of the analyses we covered in the preceding two chapters.

19.1 GENERAL RULES FOR ANALYZING WITHIN-SUBJECTS DESIGNS

Although the analysis of within-subjects designs is more complicated than the analysis of completely randomized designs, it is possible to reduce confusion considerably by mastering a set of rules that applies to the analysis of all factorial designs. In this section, I will present these rules and general principles. You will find out how to determine the sources of variability normally extracted in an analysis of variance, how to write the *df* statement from which computational formulas for *SS*'s, *df*'s, and *MS*'s are obtained, and how to locate the appropriate error terms for forming F ratios. In subsequent sections, I will illustrate the use of these rules in the analysis of the more common within-subjects designs encountered in the literature. My intent is to provide you with a general plan with which you will be able to determine the analysis for any design with which you may become involved.

Identifying Sources of Variance

The Rule. We can identify the various sources of variance obtained from any factorial design by applying the following rule:

1. List the *independent* factors and all possible interactions of these factors; and
2. Add factor S *plus* all interactions with factor S except those in which letters are duplicated.

As you will see, the first part of the rule generates the sources of variance reflecting treatment effects—main effects and interactions—while the second part of the rule generates sources of variance reflecting chance, or random, effects. It is from this second list that we find the error terms needed to evaluate the significance of the treatment effects obtained by the application of the first part of the rule.

One Within-Subjects Factor. To see how this rule works, let's first examine designs with one within-subjects factor. I have discussed two of these already, the $(A \times S)$ design, where the effects of a single independent variable are studied, and the $A \times (B \times S)$ design, where two independent variables are manipulated factorially. Table 19-1 summarizes the results of applying the rule to these two designs. For the $(A \times S)$ design, the first part of the rule produces only A and the second part produces S (factor S in this design) and $A \times S$. For the $A \times (B \times S)$ design, the first part of the rule produces A, B, and $A \times B$. The second part requires the specification of factor S, which in this case is S/A, and the formation of interactions in which letters are not duplicated. The only interaction where this requirement is met is $B \times S/A$. (Interactions that produce duplicated letters—$A \times S/A$ and $A \times B \times S/A$ in this case—refer to impossible sources of variance; i.e., a factor cannot be nested in a factor—S/A—and cross with it as well.) The complete set of sources extracted in this design, then, consists of A, B, and $A \times B$ (from part 1) and S/A and $B \times S/A$ (from part 2).

To generalize to a slightly more complicated design, imagine a two-factor completely randomized design (an $A \times B$ factorial) in which a third factor (factor C) is introduced as a within-subjects manipulation. This means that each subject receives a particular $a_i b_j$ treatment combination in conjunction with all levels of factor C. This design is symbolized as $A \times B \times (C \times S)$. Application of the first part of the rule yields the sources of variance normally obtained from a three-factor design—three main effects, three two-way interactions, and a three-way interaction. These sources are enumerated in the last column of Table 19-1. Factor S in this design is S/AB, the variability of the combined test scores for the independent

Table 19-1 Source of Variance for Three Designs with One Within-Subjects Factor

		TYPE OF DESIGN	
	$(A \times S)$	$A \times (B \times S)$	$A \times B \times (C \times S)$
Part 1	A	$A, B, A \times B$	$A, B, C, A \times B,$ $A \times C, B \times C,$ $A \times B \times C$
Part 2 Factor S: Interactions:	S $A \times S$	S/A $B \times S/A$	S/AB $C \times S/AB$

groups of subjects assigned to each of the $a_i b_j$ treatment combinations. An application of the second part of the rule produces $C \times S/AB$ as the only interaction with factor S that does not repeat letters. Rather than continue this process with additional examples, I will assume that you can apply this rule to all higher-order factorials in this particular "family" defined by the presence of one within-subjects factor.

Two Within-Subjects Factors. Let's consider next factorial designs with *two* within-subjects factors. The simplest example in this family is the $(A \times B \times S)$ design, in which each subject serves in *all* of the $(a)(b)$ treatment combinations. Table 19-2 summarizes the results of applying the source rule to this design. The first part again enumerates the factorial treatment effects of interest to the researcher, A, B, and $A \times B$. In this design, factor S is symbolized as S since there is no nesting of subjects: each subject serves in all of the treatment conditions. The second rule produces three interactions with factor S, namely, $A \times S$, $B \times S$, and $A \times B \times S$. As you will see, these interactions are used as error terms in the analysis of this particular design.

Continuing with this family of designs, we come next to the $A \times (B \times$

Table 19-2 Sources of Variance for Two Designs with Two Within-Subjects Factors

	TYPE OF DESIGN	
	$(A \times B \times S)$	$A \times (B \times C \times S)$
Part 1	$A, B, A \times B$	$A, B, C, A \times B,$ $A \times C, B \times C,$ $A \times B \times C$
Part 2 Factor S: Interactions:	S $A \times S,$ $B \times S,$ $A \times B \times S$	S/A $B \times S/A,$ $C \times S/A,$ $B \times C \times S/A$

454

$C \times S$) design, in which factor A is a between-subjects factor and factors B and C are within-subjects factors. The design can be described as consisting of separate ($B \times C \times S$) experiments conducted with independent groups of subjects at the different levels of factor A. Part 1 of the rule generates the factorial treatment effects normally associated with a three-factor design. These are enumerated in Table 19-2. Factor S in this design is S/A; that is, an independent group of subjects is present at each level of factor A—subjects are nested in factor A. An application of part 2 of the rule again produces three interactions with factor S, which are listed in the table.

The method of generalizing the rule to higher-order factorials in this particular family of within-subjects designs should be obvious. A four-factor design, for example, introduces two between-subjects factors (A and B) and two within-subjects factors (C and D) and is symbolized as $A \times B \times (C \times D \times S)$. Factor S in this case would be S/AB. The sources listed under part 1 would reflect the normal yield from a four-way factorial, while the sources listed under part 2 would consist of factor S and three interactions with the two within-subjects factors and factor S, that is, $C \times S/AB$, $D \times S/AB$, and $C \times D \times S/AB$.

More Complicated Families of Designs. You now possess the ability to specify the sources of variance for more complicated families of within-subjects designs. Consider, for example, a three-factor design in which subjects receive all $(a)(b)(c)$ treatment combinations, a design symbolized as ($A \times B \times C \times S$). Part 1 of the rule will produce the factorial effects associated with any three-way factorial. Part 2 starts with factor S, which is S in this design, and produces an interaction of S with each of the factorial effects listed in part 1, that is, $A \times S$, $B \times S, \cdots, B \times C \times S$, and $A \times B \times C \times S$. Each of these interactions serves as an error term for a different source of variance. Adding between-subjects factors to this design changes the factorial yield from part 1; e.g., the addition of a single between-subjects factor results in a *four*-way factorial design, $A \times (B \times C \times D \times S)$. Part 2, on the other hand, will produce the same set of interactions with factor S; the only change will be the nesting of subjects. In the four-factor design, factor S is S/A, since independent groups of subjects receive the $(b)(c)(d)$ treatment combinations at the different levels of factor A. As an example of this particular design, and a test of your newly acquired knowledge, see Exercise 3 at the end of this chapter.

Summary. The sources of variance normally extracted in an analysis of variance are determined by two factors: the factorial complexity of the independent variables (part 1 of the rule) and the arrangement of the subject factor (part 2 of the rule). Within-subjects designs are conveniently grouped as families defined by the number of within-subjects factors present in the designs. If there are no within-subjects factors, the family consists of the completely randomized factorial designs. Designs from this family have one error term, the within-groups source of variance. As I have indicated, designs from families containing within-subjects factors have several error terms. The number of error terms is determined by family "membership," i.e., the number of within-subjects factors. The reason for spending a great deal of time discussing and illustrating the application of the rule for generating the sources of variance is that the remainder of the statistical analysis can be specified from a listing of the sources. As you will see, the letters designating each source can be used to write the *df* statement, which, as you know, identifies the basic ratios required to calculate the sum of squares. With these two quantities, *df* and *SS*, we have the mean squares. Finally, the rule for specifying the error term for the *F* ratio will also be given in terms of the letters used to designate the sources of variance.

Specifying Degrees of Freedom

The *df* statement for any source of variance is obtained by applying a rule that is based on the letters designating a given source. If the source contains no nested factors, the rule states:

Multiply the *df*'s associated with the factors listed in the source.

For the $A \times B \times C$ interaction, for example, the source is identified as $A \times B \times C$ and the *df* statement consists of the product formed by multiplying the *df*'s for all three factors. That is,

$$(df_A)(df_B)(df_C) = (a - 1)(b - 1)(c - 1).$$

If the source contains nested factors, the rule distinguishes between letters appearing to the *left* of the diagonal (nested factors) and letters appearing to the *right* of the diagonal (factors within which the nesting occurs). More specifically, the rule states:

Multiply (1) the product of the *df*'s of factors listed to the *left* of the diagonal by (2) the product of the *levels* of factors listed to the *right* of the diagonal.

As an example, consider the two nested factors listed in Table 19-1 for the $A \times (B \times S)$ design, that is, S/A and $B \times S/A$. Applying the rule, we find

$$df_{S/A} = (df_S)(a) = (s - 1)(a);$$

and

$$df_{B \times S/A} = (df_B)(df_S)(a) = (b - 1)(s - 1)(a).$$

For the two nested sources in the three-factor design, $A \times B \times (C \times S)$ factorial also considered in this table, the rule produces

$$df_{S/AB} = (df_S)(a)(b) = (s - 1)(a)(b);$$

and

$$df_{C \times S/AB} = (df_C)(df_S)(a)(b) = (c - 1)(s - 1)(a)(b).$$

Computing Sums of Squares

As you have seen on numerous occasions, computational formulas for sums of squares can be constructed from df statements. That is, we are given sufficient information from an expanded df statement to construct the basic ratios entering into the calculations and to specify the patterns in which these ratios are combined to produce the complete computational formula. These steps were explained in detail in Chapter 10 (pp. 191-194). Another piece of information provided by the expanded df statements is an indication of the different summary matrices needed to obtain the different quantities specified by the formulas. The term $(a)(b)(c)(s)$, for example, indicates scores or sums contained within the four-way classification of factors A, B, C, and S–i.e., the $ABCS$ matrix. Similarly, the $(b)(c)(s)$ indicates the quantities contained within the three-way classification of factors B, C, and S– the BCS matrix.

As an example, consider the $A \times B \times (C \times S)$ design. The sources listed in Table 19-1 have been entered in column 1 of Table 19-3. The factorial treatment effects (main effects and interactions) contain no nested factors, which means that the df statements are formed entirely from the df's of the factors listed in each source. The df statements for these effects are listed in column 2 of the table. The df statements for the two nested sources, S/AB and $C \times S/AB$, are obtained by applying the rule as follows:

$$df_{S/AB} = (df_S)[(a)(b)] = (s - 1)(a)(b);$$

and

$$df_{C \times S/AB} = [(df_C)(df_S)][(a)(b)] = (c - 1)(s - 1)(a)(b).$$

These statements, rearranged slightly in the more common format, are also presented in column 2.

The basic ratios, which specify some of the calculations required for the sums of squares, can be determined from expanded versions of the df statements. I will not illustrate this particular procedure, since you have been exposed to this operation many times before. I will simply note that the basic ratios needed to calculate the various sums of squares are specified in column 3 of Table 19-3. The expanded df statement also indicates the pattern in which the basic ratios are combined to calculate each sum of squares. These patterns are indicated in column 4 of the table. A numerical example of this particular design is provided by Exercise 4 at the end of this chapter.[1]

---

[1]Worked examples of this particular design are found in a variety of sources, e.g., Kirk (1968, pp. 284-287), Myers (1979, pp. 214-217), and Winer (1971, pp. 563-567).

Table 19-3 Computational Formulas for the $A \times B \times (C \times S)$ Design

(1) SOURCE	(2) df STATEMENT	(3) BASIC RATIO	(4) SUM OF SQUARES
A	$a - 1$	$\dfrac{\Sigma A^2}{(b)(c)(s)}$	$[A] - [T]$
B	$b - 1$	$\dfrac{\Sigma B^2}{(a)(c)(s)}$	$[B] - [T]$
C	$c - 1$	$\dfrac{\Sigma C^2}{(a)(b)(s)}$	$[C] - [T]$
$A \times B$	$(a-1)(b-1)$	$\dfrac{\Sigma (AB)^2}{(c)(s)}$	$[AB] - [A] - [B] + [T]$
$A \times C$	$(a-1)(c-1)$	$\dfrac{\Sigma (AC)^2}{(b)(s)}$	$[AC] - [A] - [C] + [T]$
$B \times C$	$(b-1)(c-1)$	$\dfrac{\Sigma (BC)^2}{(a)(s)}$	$[BC] - [B] - [C] + [T]$
$A \times B \times C$	$(a-1)(b-1)(c-1)$	$\dfrac{\Sigma (ABC)^2}{s}$	$[ABC] - [AB] - [AC] - [BC]$ $+ [A] + [B] + [C] - [T]$
S/AB	$(a)(b)(s-1)$	$\dfrac{\Sigma (ABS)^2}{c}$	$[ABS] - [AB]$
$C \times S/AB$	$(a)(b)(c-1)(s-1)$	$\Sigma (ABCS)^2$	$[ABCS] - [ABC] - [ABS] + [AB]$
Total	$(a)(b)(c)(s) - 1$	$\dfrac{T^2}{(a)(b)(c)(s)}$	$[ABCS] - [T]$

Selecting Error Terms

The error terms for the different sources of variance can be found by means of the following principle:[2]

If a source contains no repeated factors, the error term is factor S.

If a source contains a repeated factor or factors, the error term is an interaction of factor S with the repeated factor or factors.

I will consider the first part of this rule first. You have seen in the $A \times (B \times S)$ design that the error term for the MS_A, which contains no repeated factor, is the $MS_{S/A}$—factor S in this design (see Table 19-1). This rule holds for any design in which repeated and nonrepeated factors are mixed—sources coming from that part of the experiment represented by independent groups of subjects are evaluated by factor S, which in fact is the within-groups mean square. The second part of the rule, on the other hand, pertains to sources of variance based on repeated factors. In the examples I considered in Chapters 17 and 18, the error term has always been an interaction of factor S and the repeated factor involved. In the case of the $(A \times S)$ design, for example, the error term was $MS_{A \times S}$, an interaction of factor $S(S)$ and the repeated factor (A). In the case of the $A \times (B \times S)$ design, the error term was $MS_{B \times S/A}$, again, an interaction of factor S (S/A) and the repeated factor (B).

Now, let's apply the rule to designs we have not examined in detail. Consider first a three-factor design with one within-subjects factor—the $A \times B \times (C \times S)$ design—which was used to illustrate the generation of computational formulas for the df's, basic ratios, and SS's displayed in Table 19-3. As a first step, we identify factor S, which in this case is S/AB. Next, we locate all of the factorial treatment effects containing no repeated factors, which would be A, B, and $A \times B$ in this design. The first part of the rule applies to these factors and indicates that S/AB, factor S, is the error term for each of them. This step is summarized in the first column of Table 19-4. Next, we segregate the factorial treatment effects according to the repeated factor (or factors) contained in the source. In this design, there is only one repeated factor (factor C), so that the remaining factorial treatment effects, which all involve factor C, are C, $A \times C$, $B \times C$, and $A \times B \times C$. Applying the second part of the rule to these sources, we find that the error term is the interaction of factor S and the repeated factor, namely, $MS_{C \times S/AB}$. This fact is also recorded in the first column of the table. Taken together, Table 19-3 and Table 19-4 specify the standard analysis of variance for this design, which was generated entirely on the basis of the three sets of rules presented in this section.

Let's extend the rule to two other relatively common within-subjects designs. The first is a two-factor design containing only repeated measures, i.e., the $(A \times B \times S)$ design. The sources of variance for this design were presented in Table 19-2. Factor S is S in this particular design. There are no between-subjects factors,

---

[2]These rules assume the fixed-effects model, which is the model appropriate for most experiments in the behavioral sciences. If random effects are present, see Chapter 21 (pp. 520–524) and Appendix C-4 (pp. 641–642) for a discussion of the complications.

Table 19-4 Identification of Error Terms for Three Within-Subjects Designs

$A \times B \times (C \times S)$ DESIGN (FACTOR $S: S/AB$)		$(A \times B \times S)$ DESIGN (FACTOR $S: S$)		$A \times (B \times C \times S)$ DESIGN (FACTOR $S: S/A$)	
Source	Error Term	Source	Error Term	Source	Error Term
No Repeated Factors		No Repeated Factors		No Repeated Factors	
A	S/AB	None		A	S/A
B	S/AB				
$A \times B$	S/AB	One Repeated Factor		One Repeated Factor	
One Repeated Factor		A	$A \times S$	B	$B \times S/A$
				$A \times B$	$B \times S/A$
C	$C \times S/AB$	B	$B \times S$		
$A \times C$	$C \times S/AB$			C	$C \times S/A$
$B \times C$	$C \times S/AB$	Two Repeated Factors		$A \times C$	$C \times S/A$
$A \times B \times C$	$C \times S/AB$	$A \times B$	$A \times B \times S$	Two Repeated Factors	
				$B \times C$	$B \times C \times S/A$
				$A \times B \times C$	$B \times C \times S/A$

which means that the first part of the rule is not applicable. Two sources of variance contain one repeated factor, namely, A and B. Applying the second part of the rule, we find the error terms to be $A \times S$ and $B \times S$, respectively—in both cases, interactions between the factor listed in the source (A or B) and factor S. The final remaining source, $A \times B$, contains both repeated factors; the rule indicates that the error term is the $A \times B \times S$ interaction. These steps are summarized in the middle column of Table 19-4.

The second example is a three-factor design containing one nonrepeated factor and two repeated factors, the $A \times (B \times C \times S)$ design. The sources of variance for this design can be found in Table 19-2 also. Factor S is S/A. There is one source that contains no repeated factors: A, for which the $MS_{S/A}$ is the error term. Four sources of variance contain one repeated factor. Specifically, B and $A \times B$ involve factor B, and C and $A \times C$ involve factor C. The error term for the first two factorial sources is the interaction of the repeated factor (B) and factor S, $B \times S/A$, while the error term for the second two factorial sources is the interaction of the other repeated factor (C) and factor S, $C \times S/A$. Finally, two sources contain both repeated factors, $B \times C$ and $A \times B \times C$. In this case, the error term is the interaction of the two repeated factors and factor S, that is, $B \times C \times S/A$. These steps are summarized in the third column of Table 19-4.

Latin Square Analysis

Generally, the order in which the repeated treatments are administered will be varied for different subjects in such a way that practice effects are spread equally over the levels of the repeated factor (or factors). Usually this is accomplished by some form of Latin square arrangement of the repeated treatments. If more than one repeated factor is involved, the Latin square will probably be based on the treatment *combinations* formed by crossing the repeated factors. Suppose the design were a 3 × 2 factorial with both factors repeated; each subject would receive (3)(2) = 6 treatment conditions. A Latin square would be used with six test positions (first, second, third, and so on) and six sequences conforming to an appropriate Latin square. In other words, we would treat the treatment combinations as if they represented the levels of a single repeated factor. You will note that this Latin square requires a minimum of $s = 6$ subjects to achieve proper counterbalancing; any additional subjects would be added in multiples of 6. If the number of treatment combinations exceeds the number of available subjects, you should randomly order the treatments separately for each subject as a way of spreading practice effects evenly over the treatment conditions.

Counterbalancing does present some difficulties for statistical analysis. If practice effects are present, these systematic changes in performance become "deposited" in the repeated-measures error terms, as you have seen in Chapters 17 and 18. A Latin square analysis can be undertaken to remove these effects statistically so that the error terms reflect only those chance factors that are also affecting the variation associated with the treatment sources of variance.

The Latin square analysis of higher-order within-subjects designs can be quite complex. Since in most cases you will be interested in conducting analytical comparisons that require separate error terms, I recommend using the method that subtracts the practice effects from the scores of the individual subjects. To use this method, you arrange your data in a Latin square matrix in which test position replaces the repeated factor as the basis of classification. (See Table 18-7, p. 422, for an example with the two-factor mixed design.) If more than one repeated factor is involved, testing position will probably refer to the position of the treatment *combinations,* as I suggested previously. Practice effects are calculated from the means obtained from this matrix and subtracted from the scores of the individual subjects in the manner illustrated in the last two chapters (see pp. 399–404 and 423–428). After the practice effects have been removed, a standard analysis of variance is then performed on these "corrected" data.

There is one slight complication that I should mention, however. You must remember to adjust the degrees of freedom for the information "lost" by removing practice effects from the data. This adjustment can be easily calculated for any repeated-measures error term simply by deleting the quantity $(s - 1)$ from the df statement for the appropriate error term in the standard analysis. That is,

$$df_{\text{L.S. residual}} = df_{\text{error}} - df_{\text{correction}}, \tag{19-1}$$

where

$$df_{\text{correction}} = \frac{df_{\text{error}}}{s - 1}. \tag{19-2}$$

As an example, consider the $A \times B \times (C \times S)$ design. The df for the repeated-measures error term are

$$df_{C \times S/AB} = a(b)(c-1)(s-1).$$

The correction for practice effects removed from the individual scores is found by substituting the *df* statement in Eq. (19-2); i.e.,

$$df_{C \times S/AB \text{ correction}} = \frac{a(b)(c-1)(s-1)}{s-1}$$

$$= a(b)(c-1).$$

The degrees of freedom for the Latin square error term are then obtained by substituting in Eq. (19-1).

Let's take a more complicated example, the $(A \times B \times S)$ design, in which there are three repeated-measures error terms, $A \times S$, $B \times S$, and $A \times B \times S$. Assuming that the $(a)(b)$ treatment conditions are arranged in a Latin square with $(a)(b)$ test positions and that practice effects have been subtracted from the individual *ABS* scores, the *df* correction for each error term is

$$df_{A \times S \text{ correction}} = \frac{(a-1)(s-1)}{s-1} = a-1;$$

$$df_{B \times S \text{ correction}} = \frac{(b-1)(s-1)}{s-1} = b-1;$$

and

$$df_{A \times B \times S \text{ correction}} = \frac{(a-1)(b-1)(s-1)}{s-1} = (a-1)(b-1).$$

Each of these corrections is entered in Eq. (19-1) to obtain the degrees of freedom for the Latin square error terms.

Analytical Comparisons

All analytical comparisons appropriate for a completely randomized factorial design can be conducted with its repeated-measures counterpart. The only complication is, of course, the probable need for separate error terms. The procedures followed in the last two chapters can be generalized to the analysis of higher-order designs. A simple rule to remember is that you can never go wrong if you base your error term for a comparison on the data matrix specifically involved in the comparison.

Nested Independent Variables

The most common example of nesting in psychology experiments is the nesting that occurs when subjects are assigned randomly to different treatment groups. As you saw in Chapter 12 (pp. 256-257), however, independent variables can be nested as well. Lists of nonsense syllables arranged in different serial orders, instances of different types of problems, and small groupings of subjects are examples of nesting that were considered in Chapter 12.

Similar types of manipulations are also found in the psychological literature as nested within-subjects factors. Suppose, for example, that we were interested in the speed with which subjects would react to nouns or to verbs flashed on a screen. Assume that a set of nouns and a set of verbs are obtained and presented in scrambled order to a group of subjects. The design as described consists of two independent variables; one, which we can call factor *A,* represents the type of word flashed on the screen (noun versus verb) and the variable of primary interest, and the other, which we can call factor *B/A,* represents the words contained within the two different sets. This latter variable is nested within the first factor—the set of nouns is completely unrelated to the set of verbs—and both independent variables are within-subjects factors.

Designs of this type are quite common in certain areas of contemporary research (see Clark, 1973). Not only do such nested factors represent within-subjects manipulations, but they often are viewed as random, as opposed to fixed, factors as well. These two features of these manipulations, repeated measures and random factors, cause major problems for the statistical analysis and interpretation of the data. I will discuss these and other problems in Chapter 21.

19.2 ANALYSIS OF THE (*A* X *B* X *S*) DESIGN

This section illustrates the application of the general principles of analysis summarized in the last section to the simplest form of factorial with *two* repeated factors, the (*A* X *B* X *S*) design. In this particular design, each subject receives all of the (*a*)(*b*) treatment combinations. The reason for choosing this design as an illustration of the rules is that it provides a first glimpse at the proliferation of repeated-measures error terms found in the standard analysis of factorial designs with two or more within-subjects factors.

Identifying Sources of Variance

Applying the rule for identifying sources of variance (p. 453), we list first the independent factors and all possible interactions and obtain

$$A, B, \text{and } A \times B,$$

which represent the factorial treatment effects, and then add factor *S* which is *S* in this design—there is no nesting of subjects—and all interactions with factor *S* that contain no duplicated letters, which gives us

$$S, A \times S, B \times S, \text{and } A \times B \times S.$$

These sources are listed in column 1 of Table 19-5.

Specifying Degrees of Freedom

The rule for specifying *df* statements is easy to apply in this design since there are no nested factors (see p. 456). Thus, the *df* for any source is the product of the *df*'s associated with each of the factors listed in the source. The *df* statements for all sources of variance are presented in column 2 of the table.

Computing Sums of Squares

Expanded df Statements. The sums of squares are calculated in two steps—basic ratios first and then the *SS*'s themselves, which are based on different combinations of basic ratios. Expanding each *df* statement and substituting *T* for 1 provides us with the information necessary to form the basic ratios and the sums of squares as well. Column 3 of Table 19-5 lists the expanded *df* statements for each source.

Notation. Each letter or combination of letters refers to a unique quantity calculated from the data. To make these operations explicit, I have enumerated the notational system in Table 19-6. The *ABS* matrix lists the basic scores obtained in the experiment. Each of the $s = 3$ subjects contributes a total of $(a)(b) = (2)(3) = 6$ scores, one under each of the treatment conditions in the experiment. The *AB* matrix is formed in the usual manner by summing the *ABS* scores in each treatment combination; the sums in this matrix provide the information necessary for calculating the *SS*'s for the factorial treatment effects. The other two matrices provide a convenient way of obtaining the additional sums needed for the analysis. The *AS* matrix contains sums obtained by collapsing over the *b* treatments. For example, AS_{11} represents the sum of the three *ABS* scores for s_1 obtained under level a_1; and AS_{23} represents the sum of the three *ABS* scores for s_3 obtained under level a_2. In symbols,

$$AS_{11} = ABS_{111} + ABS_{121} + ABS_{131}$$

and

$$AS_{23} = ABS_{213} + ABS_{223} + ABS_{233} \ .$$

Except for the fact that the *AS* matrix contains *AS* sums, based on *b* observations, the matrix is identical to that formed with the $(A \times S)$ design. The *BS* matrix contains sums obtained by collapsing over the *a* treatments. As an example, BS_{23} refers to the sum of the two *ABS* scores for s_3 obtained under level b_2. In symbols,

$$BS_{23} = ABS_{123} + ABS_{223}.$$

This matrix can be viewed as a single-factor design also, with factor *B* representing the within-subjects factor; in this case, the matrix contains *BS* sums based on *a* observations.

Basic Ratios and Sums of Squares. Basic ratios are formed by squaring and then summing members of a set of quantities having the same letter designation

Table 19-5 Computational Formulas for the $(A \times B \times S)$ Design

(1) SOURCE	(2) df STATEMENT	(3) EXPANDED df STATEMENT	(4) BASIC RATIO	(5) SUM OF SQUARES	(6) F RATIO
A	$a-1$	$a-1$	$[A] = \dfrac{\Sigma A^2}{(b)(s)}$	$[A]-[T]$	$\dfrac{MS_A}{MS_{A \times S}}$
B	$b-1$	$b-1$	$[B] = \dfrac{\Sigma B^2}{(a)(s)}$	$[B]-[T]$	$\dfrac{MS_B}{MS_{B \times S}}$
$A \times B$	$(a-1)(b-1)$	$(a)(b)-a-b+1$	$[AB] = \dfrac{\Sigma (AB)^2}{s}$	$[AB]-[A]-[B]+[T]$	$\dfrac{MS_{A \times B}}{MS_{A \times B \times S}}$
S	$s-1$	$s-1$	$[S] = \dfrac{\Sigma S^2}{(a)(b)}$	$[S]-[T]$	
$A \times S$	$(a-1)(s-1)$	$(a)(s)-a-s+1$	$[AS] = \dfrac{\Sigma (AS)^2}{b}$	$[AS]-[A]-[S]+[T]$	
$B \times S$	$(b-1)(s-1)$	$(b)(s)-b-s+1$	$[BS] = \dfrac{\Sigma (BS)^2}{a}$	$[BS]-[B]-[S]+[T]$	
$A \times B \times S$	$(a-1)(b-1)(s-1)$	$(a)(b)(s)-(a)(b)-(a)(s)$ $-(b)(s)+a+b+s-1$	$[ABS] = \Sigma (ABS)^2$	$[ABS]-[AB]-[AS]-[BS]$ $+[A]+[B]+[S]-[T]$	
Total	$(a)(b)(s)-1$	$(a)(b)(s)-1$	$[T] = \dfrac{T^2}{(a)(b)(s)}$	$[ABS]-[T]$	

and dividing by the number of observations contributing to any one of the members in the set. These operations are specified in column 4 of Table 19-5 for the first term listed for each source in column 3 except for the last source, which indicates the basic ratio based on the grand total T. Column 5 specifies the patterns of combination required to calculate each sum of squares; this pattern corresponds to the patterns of letters provided by the expanded df statements.

Selecting Error Terms

Mean squares are calculated by dividing each sum of squares by the appropriate number of degrees of freedom. This obvious step is not indicated in the table. The rule for selecting error terms depends on the blend of within- and between-subjects factors in a particular source of variance (see p. 459). Since all factorial treatment effects contain within-subjects factors, the error term for each source is simply the interaction of factor S with the repeated factor (or factors) listed in the source. As indicated in column 6 of Table 19-5, the error term for the main effect of factor A is the $A \times S$ interaction; the error term for the main effect of factor B is the $B \times S$ interaction; and the error term for the $A \times B$ interaction is the $A \times B \times S$ interaction.

Table 19-6　　Notational System: $(A \times B \times S)$ Design

	ABS MATRIX					
	a_1			a_2		
Subject	b_1	b_2	b_3	b_1	b_2	b_3
s_1	ABS_{111}	ABS_{121}	ABS_{131}	ABS_{211}	ABS_{221}	ABS_{231}
s_2	ABS_{112}	ABS_{122}	ABS_{132}	ABS_{212}	ABS_{222}	ABS_{232}
s_3	ABS_{113}	ABS_{123}	ABS_{133}	ABS_{213}	ABS_{223}	ABS_{233}

	AS MATRIX				BS MATRIX			
	a_1	a_2	Sum		b_1	b_2	b_3	Sum
s_1	AS_{11}	AS_{21}	S_1	s_1	BS_{11}	BS_{21}	BS_{31}	S_1
s_2	AS_{12}	AS_{22}	S_2	s_2	BS_{12}	BS_{22}	BS_{32}	S_2
s_3	AS_{13}	AS_{23}	S_3	s_3	BS_{13}	BS_{23}	BS_{33}	S_3
Sum	A_1	A_2	T	Sum	B_1	B_2	B_3	T

	AB MATRIX			
	b_1	b_2	b_3	Sum
a_1	AB_{11}	AB_{12}	AB_{13}	A_1
a_2	AB_{21}	AB_{22}	AB_{23}	A_2
Sum	B_1	B_2	B_3	T

To justify the use of these error terms, let's consider first the main effect of factor A. In the discussion of the $(A \times S)$ design in Chapter 17, it was argued that we usually suspect the presence of a Treatment $\times$ Subject interaction in most behavioral studies, which means that the MS_A contains this interaction and error variance, in addition to any treatment effects that might be present. This posed no problem for the evaluation of the significance of factor A, however, since the interaction mean square $MS_{A \times S}$ contains the interaction and error variance.

The same argument applies to the present situation. Consider the AS matrix in Table 19-6. This matrix displays the results of what may be viewed as an $(A \times S)$ experiment. The main effect of factor A contains a Treatment $\times$ Subject interaction, error variance, and a treatment effect. In this case, the error term is the $MS_{A \times S}$, because it reflects the interaction and error variance. Similarly, the BS matrix enumerates a $(B \times S)$ experiment. By the same logic offered to justify the use of $MS_{A \times S}$ as the error term for the MS_A in the $(A \times S)$ design, the main effect of factor B contains a Treatment $\times$ Subject interaction, error variance, and treatment effects. The interaction in this case, however, is one involving the BS matrix. Thus, the appropriate error term for the MS_B is the $MS_{B \times S}$, which is assumed to reflect the relevant interaction and error variance. Finally, we have the $MS_{A \times B}$, which can also be thought to contain three components, a possible $A \times B$ interaction, an $A \times B \times$ Subjects interaction, and error variance. The mean square for the $A \times B \times S$ interaction contains the last two components—$(A \times B \times$ Subjects) and error variance—and, thus, is an appropriate error term with which to test the significance of the $A \times B$ interaction.

Numerical Examples

I will not work through a numerical example of this analysis formally, since the procedures are straightforward and duplicate the operations performed in other chapters of this book. If you wish to conduct an analysis on your own, you might try Exercise 5 at the end of this chapter or look up a worked example in Keppel (1973, pp. 429–430).

19.3 HOMOGENEITY ASSUMPTIONS

The statistical analysis of within-subjects designs operates under the same distribution assumptions required of completely randomized designs, namely, normality, homogeneity of within-treatment variances, and independence. In addition, however, certain assumptions are made concerning the correlations between the multiple measures obtained from the same subjects. I will describe these new assumptions first and then indicate the consequences when they are violated as they often are in the behavioral sciences. Finally, I will discuss various courses of action that can be taken to deal with these problems.

The Assumptions

The homogeneity assumptions consist of two parts, one relevant to mixed within-subjects designs and the other relevant to all within-subjects designs. Let's consider the latter assumption in the context of the simplest design with repeated measures, the $(A \times S)$ design. Since each subject receives all of the treatment conditions, it is possible to arrange the data in terms of all possible pairs of treatment conditions. For each pair of treatments, suppose we subtract the two scores for each of the subjects and then calculate variances based on these difference scores. There will be a variance of difference scores for each unique pair of treatment conditions. If $a = 3$, for example, there will be three variances, one based on difference scores obtained from levels a_1 and a_2, another from levels a_1 and a_3, and another from levels a_2 and a_3. The assumption is that these three variances of differences are equal in the population.[3] With two or more repeated factors, this assumption applies to each data matrix involving the repeated factors. For the $(A \times B \times S)$ design, the assumption applies to the variances of differences obtained from the AS, BS, and ABS matrices.

With mixed factorials, there is the added assumption of the equality of the variances of differences obtained with the repeated factor at the levels of the independent factor (or factors). With the $A \times (B \times S)$ design, there would be a different set of variances of differences obtained from the pairs of B treatments at each level of the nonrepeated factor, factor A.

Tests of these homogeneity assumptions are described by Huynh and Feldt (1970), Huynh and Mandeville (1979), and Rouanet and Lépine (1970), but they are complicated and beyond the scope of this book. Keselman, Rogan, Mendoza, and Breen (1980) have shown that the test for equal variances of differences is extremely sensitive to departures from these assumptions, and since most experiments in the behavioral sciences will violate these assumptions anyway, they suggest that researchers omit testing the validity of the homogeneity assumptions and direct their efforts instead to dealing directly with the problems resulting from the generally assumed violations of these assumptions.

Implications of Violations of the Homogeneity Assumptions

You have seen with the completely randomized designs that assumptions concerning the nature of the distributions of treatment populations are not critical in the evaluation of F tests. Only severe violations of the assumptions of homogeneity

---

[3]This assumption is usually stated in terms of population within-treatment variances and of correlations between pairs of treatments and is referred to as the **assumption of compound symmetry**. Huynh and Feldt (1970) have shown that the assumption of equal variances of differences is the correct assumption to make and that the assumption of compound symmetry is too stringent. Myers (1979, pp. 163–174) provides a useful discussion of the statistical model and assumptions for the single-factor within-subjects design.

of population variances call for some concern, and then only when unequal sample sizes or certain single-df comparisons are involved. In contrast, violations of the homogeneity assumptions with repeated-measures designs can seriously affect our interpretation of F ratios. More specifically, these violations produce sampling distributions of the F ratio that are not distributed as F when the null hypothesis is true, which means that standard F tables cannot be used to judge directly the significance of an observed F. Since it is known that the actual sampling distribution shifts to the right of the central F distribution when violations are present, the critical values of F obtained from the tabled values of the F distribution are *too small*. That is, the actual critical values we should be using, which would be based on the correct sampling distribution, are larger than those listed in the F table.

Under these circumstances, the F test is said to be biased in a *positive* direction. It could be the case, for example, that the tabled value of F at $\alpha = .05$ actually represents a significance level that is *greater* than .05—for example, $\alpha = .10$. If we do not make an adjustment in our rejection procedure, we will in effect be operating at a more "lenient" significance level than we had set originally. As a consequence, we will reject the null hypothesis falsely a greater percentage of the time than our statements of significance would imply.

As an illustration, consider the demonstration reported by Collier, Baker, Mandeville, and Hayes (1967) in which the computer and Monte Carlo procedures were used to provide an estimate of the magnitude of the bias in the standard analysis. Briefly, these investigators built different degrees of heterogeneity into separate populations of scores, then sampled randomly from these populations and performed statistical analyses on the sets of sampled scores. All of the populations had the same mean. Thus, if a large number of such "experiments" were conducted, the resulting sampling distribution of F should approximate the theoretical distribution when the homogeneity assumptions are fully met. That is, 5 percent of the empirical F ratios should exceed the critical value of F at $\alpha = .05$. When violations of these assumptions are introduced, the extent to which empirical F ratios exceed the 5 percent value would provide an indication of the extent of the positive bias.

Collier et al. varied a number of characteristics of the distributions of scores to determine the effect on the empirical α level for the main effects and for the $A \times B$ interaction in the $A \times (B \times S)$ design. They obtained this information for 15 different conditions of heterogeneity, some clearly more deviant than would ever be expected in actual experimentation. The results of these determinations on the *nonrepeated factor, A,* indicated that approximately 5 percent of the F ratios exceeded the critical value of F. Thus, conclusions concerning the significance of the main effect of A are essentially uninfluenced by these severe violations of the homogeneity assumptions. As expected by theory, positive biases *did* appear for the comparisons involving *repeated measures.* If we take an average over the 15 different conditions of their study, we find for the main effect of factor B that 6.8 percent of the obtained F ratios exceeded the α level when $s = 5$ and 7.5 percent when $s = 15$. The corresponding values for the $A \times B$ interaction were slightly higher, 8.0 percent and 8.2 percent, respectively.

Solving the Problem of the Biased *F* Test

Several ways of solving the problem of bias have been proposed in the literature, including doing nothing (Keppel, 1973, pp. 466–467). The justification for this seemingly irresponsible recommendation is the fact that the positive bias in actual research applications—such as those studied by Collier et al.—is probably of the order of 2 to 3 percent and that most experimenters will still pay close attention to an *F* that is significant at α equal to .06 to .08, which is about what may be the case if decision rules are based on an uncorrected *F* nominally set at $\alpha = .05$. But statistical solutions are available that specifically take steps to eliminate or greatly reduce the positive bias. I will consider three.

The Geisser-Greenhouse Correction. One solution to this problem is to perform the usual analysis of variance but to evaluate observed *F* ratios based on repeated measures against a new critical value that for statistical convenience assumes the presence of *maximal heterogeneity*. In practice, this is accomplished easily by decreasing the numerator and denominator *df*'s associated with the original *F* ratios and then using these new values in consulting the *F* table. The correction is made simply by dividing the original numerator and denominator *df*'s by a factor equal to the *df* associated with the repeated factor (or factors). In symbols, the two corrected *df*'s are

$$df_{\text{num.}} = \frac{df_{\text{effect}}}{df_{\text{repeated factors}}} \quad \text{and} \quad df_{\text{denom.}} = \frac{df_{\text{error term}}}{df_{\text{repeated factors}}} .$$

These corrections were introduced by Geisser and Greenhouse (1958). It is important to note that the *mean squares* obtained from the analysis are still based on the usual *df*'s and *not* on these corrected ones. The corrected *df*'s are used only when searching the *F* table to find critical values.

As an example, consider the corrections for the two-factor mixed design, $A \times (B \times S/A)$. There is no adjustment required for the evaluation of the main effect of factor *A* because no repeated factors are involved. Thus,

$$F = \frac{MS_A}{MS_{S/A}}$$

continues to be evaluated with

$$df_{\text{num.}} = a - 1 \quad \text{and} \quad df_{\text{denom.}} = a(s - 1).$$

The *df*'s are changed for the other two *F* ratios because of the presence of repeated factors. More specifically,

$$F = \frac{MS_B}{MS_{B \times S/A}}$$

is evaluated with

$$df_{\text{num.}} = \frac{b - 1}{b - 1} = 1$$

and

$$df_{\text{denom.}} = \frac{a(b - 1)(s - 1)}{b - 1} = a(s - 1);$$

and

$$F = \frac{MS_{A \times B}}{MS_{B \times S/A}}$$

is evaluated with

$$df_{\text{num.}} = \frac{(a - 1)(b - 1)}{b - 1} = a - 1$$

and

$$df_{\text{denom.}} = \frac{a(b - 1)(s - 1)}{b - 1} = a(s - 1).$$

To see how the critical values change under the Geisser-Greenhouse correction, let's consider an experiment in which $a = 3$, $b = 3$, and $s = 5$. The original df's associated with the first F ratio are $df_{\text{num.}} = b - 1 = 3 - 1 = 2$ and $df_{\text{denom.}} = a(b - 1)(s - 1) = 3(3 - 1)(5 - 1) = 24$. The uncorrected critical value of $F(2, 24)$ is 3.40 at $p = .05$. The corrected df's are $df_{\text{num.}} = 1$ and $df_{\text{denom.}} = a(s - 1) = 3(5 - 1) = 12$; the corrected value of $F(1, 12)$ is 4.75 at $p = .05$. This means, then, that an F must equal or exceed 4.75 to be significant under the Geisser-Greenhouse correction rather than the 3.40 associated with the uncorrected test. For the interaction, the uncorrected value of F is 2.78 for $df_{\text{num.}} = (a - 1)(b - 1) = (3 - 1)(3 - 1) = 4$ and $df_{\text{denom.}} = a(b - 1)(s - 1) = 3(3 - 1)(5 - 1) = 24$. The corrected value of F is 3.89 for $df_{\text{num.}} = a - 1 = 3 - 1 = 2$ and $df_{\text{num.}} = a(s - 1) = 3(5 - 1) = 12$.

The main difficulty with this correction is that it tends to *overcorrect*, leading to a reduction in the number of null hypotheses falsely rejected as expected by theory. In other words, the adjusted F ratios are now biased in a *negative* direction. (This negative bias was confirmed in the Monte Carlo study of Collier et al. They found that only about 2 percent of the F ratios exceeded the corrected critical values at $\alpha = .05$.) In short, then, if we proceed in the normal fashion and use an uncorrected value of F when there is heterogeneity, the test is positively biased; if we use the correction, the test is probably negatively biased.

The Box Correction. Box (1954) introduced a method for adjusting numerator and denominator df's by a factor that reflects the degree of heterogeneity actually present in an experiment. This factor, ϵ, is estimated from covariance matrices that list within-treatment variances and between-treatment correlations (expressed in terms of covariance).[4] Examples of the calculations required to obtain the adjustment factor $\hat{\epsilon}$, which are complex but manageable, can be found in Myers (1979, pp. 173-174) and Winer (1971, pp. 523-524). In a mixed factorial design, the variances and covariances are obtained by averaging over the nonrepeated factor (or factors). Huynh and Feldt (1976) introduce a related correction factor, $\tilde{\epsilon}$, which they recommend should be used when ϵ is less than .75 (see pp. 75-76 of their article for the formulas). The correction factor is multiplied by the numerator and denominator df's to provide the adjusted df's that are used to obtain the critical value of F from the standard F tables. Theoretically, the factor ranges between $\epsilon = 1.0$ when the homogeneity assumptions are met and $1/df_{\text{repeated factors}}$ when they are maximally violated. The former situation results in the use of the usual numerator and denominator df's, while the latter represents the Geisser-Greenhouse correction.

Given the computational demands required to use the Box correction, I recommend using the testing strategy advocated by Greenhouse and Geisser (1959), which was designed to avoid calculating $\hat{\epsilon}$ except when logically necessary. The strategy consists of the following steps: First, F is evaluated with df's obtained from the Geisser-Greenhouse procedure. If the F is significant under this overly *stringent* criterion, we reject the null hypothesis. If the F is not significant, we next evaluate the F with the uncorrected df's. If the F is not significant under this generally too *lenient* criterion, we do not reject the null hypothesis; on the other hand, if the F is significant, we turn to the Box correction to resolve the ambiguity posed by the different outcomes from the two tests. You can also avoid these complicated calculations by using a computer.

Multivariate Procedures. Multivariate procedures can be used to analyze the data from within-subjects designs. Their advantage is a reduction in the number of restrictive assumptions required for the analysis. McCall (1970) and McCall and Appelbaum (1973) provide useful, nontechnical discussions of multivariate techniques. A more demanding introduction can be found in Myers (1979, Chapter 18). Tatsuoka (1971) offers a discussion of multivariate analysis of variance in a form consistent with the analyses considered here.

Homogeneity Assumptions and Single-*df* Comparisons

The problems discussed in the preceding two sections are applicable only when the repeated factor consists of more than two levels. If there are only two levels of a repeated factor, there is only one variance of differences and obviously

---

[4]Covariance is defined as follows: Covariance $= r_{XY}(s_X)(s_Y)$, where r_{XY} is the product-moment correlation between two sets of scores X and Y obtained from the same subjects, s_X is the standard deviation of one of the sets, and s_Y is the standard deviation of the other set.

no problem of homogeneity. The same argument holds true when single-*df* comparisons are conducted on a repeated factor—there are only two levels and one variance of differences. For this reason, then, single-*df* comparisons conducted on repeated factors are immune to the problems addressed earlier (see, for example, Kirk, 1968, p. 263; and Rogan, Keselman, and Mendoza, 1979, pp. 277–278). It would still be necessary, of course, to calculate separate error terms for each of the single-*df* comparisons evaluated.

19.4 EXERCISES[5]

1. Consider the following interrelated studies reported as they might have appeared in an actual article.[6] Each describes a specific experiment conducted with different combinations of between- and within-subjects factors. The details of the manipulations are not important for this exercise. In each case, (a) identify the factorial—i.e., the nature of each independent variable, the levels of each factor, and sample size—and (b) list the sources of variance you would expect to isolate in the statistical analysis. (c) Indicate also the error term for each factorial treatment effect.

   Experiment A: Twenty-four subjects served in a 2 X 2 X 5 factorial. The main variable (generate versus read) was between subjects, as was the presentation rate (timed versus self-paced). The variable *rules* was within subjects.

   Experiment B: Participants were 12 subjects. The design was a 2 X 2 X 5 factorial with generate versus read as a within-subjects factor, informed versus uninformed about a test as a between-subjects factor, and rules, again, as a within-subjects factor.

   Experiment C: Participants were 24 subjects, employed in a 2 X 2 X 2 factorial design. The generate versus read variable was within subjects, the stimulus-versus-response recognition variable was between subjects, and a third variable of informed versus uninformed of a test was also between subjects.

   Experiment D: Participants were 12 subjects. A "pure" within-subjects design was employed, consisting of a 2 X 3 X 5 factorial with generate versus read, rules, and 5 learning trials all as within-subjects factors.

   Experiment E: Participants were 24 subjects. The design was a 2 X 2 X 5 factorial with generate versus read as a within-subjects variable, stimulus-versus-response recall as a between-subjects variable, and the 5 trials as a within-subjects variable.

2. The following are descriptions of two actual experiments reported in the literature concerned with the effects of marijuana on memory. On the basis of the information provided, (a) identify the independent variables, indicating which represent between-subjects manipulations and which represent within-subjects manipulations; (b) identify the sources of variance normally extracted from this sort of design; and (c) indicate the error terms for each of the factorial treatment effects.

---

[5]The answers to these problems are found in Appendix B, beginning on p. 603.

[6]These descriptions are based on experiments reported by Slamecka and Graf (1978).

Experiment A:[7] Forty male volunteers were recruited for the study. Upon arrival in the laboratory, subjects were assigned to a marijuana (M) or placebo (P) condition. Taped instructions indicated that they would hear a series of word lists with one word presented every 3 seconds. A given list of words was presented three times. Immediately following each presentation, they were required to write down as many words as they could remember. Two lists of 35 words each were obtained from standard norms. An answer sheet was provided with the initial letter of each word in the list printed in the order of presentation at the top. These letters served as cues for recall. In the cued condition, subjects were told that these cues would be available during presentation of the lists and during the retention test, and could be used in any way they wished in order to help them organize their thoughts for recall. In the uncued condition, the same instructions were given except that subjects were told that the recall cues would be removed prior to the recall test. The order of the cueing conditions was counterbalanced within the M and P groups.

Experiment B:[8] Sixteen male volunteers served as subjects. In each of the four sessions, subjects smoked a single marijuana cigarette containing one of three dosage levels of tetrahydrocannabinol (THC), or a placebo cigarette from which all THC had been exhausted. All sessions were separated by a 1-week interval. The design was counterbalanced by assigning four subjects to each of four possible orders of dosage. On arrival in the laboratory, subjects were randomly assigned to a dosage condition. In successive sessions, the dosage was changed so that each subject was eventually run under all treatment conditions. Following smoking, subjects were presented with two 40-item word lists. One list was presented at a 2-second rate and the other at a 4-second rate. New lists were used in each session and both lists and presentation rates were counterbalanced as equally as possible from session to session. Following presentation of each list, an immediate recall test was administered during which the subjects were required to write down all the words they could remember in any order. Subjects were allowed 2 minutes to recall each list. Following the recall interval, a new list was immediately presented.

3. Consider the following experiment reported by Slobin (1966). Subjects were presented pictures depicting some sort of activity together with a sentence describing the objects in the pictures. The subjects' task was to indicate whether or not the sentence accurately described the picture. There were four independent variables in the experiment, three of which involved repeated measures and one of which involved independent groups. Thus, the design could be represented as an $A \times (B \times C \times D \times S)$ factorial.

The three independent variables based on repeated measures were (a) 4 types of sentences (factor B), (b) the truth or falsity of the descriptive sentences (factor C), and (c) the reversibility or nonreversibility of the subject and object depicted in the picture (factor D). For this latter independent variable, *reversibility* referred to situations in which the ". . . object of action could also serve as the subject. . ." and *nonreversibility* referred to situations in which ". . . the object could not normally serve as the subject" (p. 219). Factor A

---

[7] Based on an experiment reported by Miller, Cornett, Brightwell, McFarland, Drew, and Wikler (1976).

[8] Based on an experiment reported by Miller and Cornett (1978).

consisted of groups of subjects drawn from five different age groups—i.e., groups of subjects whose average ages were 6, 8, 10, 12, and 20 years.

In short, then, the experiment was a "mixed" design, with four independent variables, three of which involved repeated measures, and it contained a total of $(a)(b)(c)(d) = (5)(4)(2)(2) = 80$ treatment combinations. There were $s = 16$ subjects in each of the age groupings. Your task is to identify the treatment sources of variance and the appropriate error terms with which to evaluate their significance.

4. The influence of two variables, meaningfulness and intertrial spacing, is studied in a learning experiment. The design is a 2 X 4 X 5 factorial, the first variable consisting of two levels of meaningfulness (factor A), the second variable consisting of four levels of intertrial spacing (factor B), and the third variable consisting of five learning trials (factor C). Each of the $(a)(b) = (2)(4) = 8$ meaningfulness-spacing conditions contains $s = 3$ subjects and each subject receives all five of the learning trials. Thus, the design represents a so-called mixed design—i.e., an $A \times B \times (C \times S)$ design. The scores for each of the subjects on each of the learning trials are given in the accompanying $ABCS$ matrix. Analyze the results of the experiment.

ABCS MATRIX

	a_1						a_2				
	c_1	c_2	c_3	c_4	c_5		c_1	c_2	c_3	c_4	c_5
					b_1						
s_1	3	1	4	6	7	s_4	3	3	5	7	7
s_2	1	2	5	5	5	s_5	0	1	3	2	4
s_3	4	6	7	7	8	s_6	2	5	6	6	7
					b_2						
s_7	0	4	4	7	8	s_{10}	1	3	6	5	6
s_8	2	3	5	7	8	s_{11}	0	4	6	7	6
s_9	0	4	4	4	8	s_{12}	2	2	3	5	7
					b_3						
s_{13}	1	3	3	4	4	s_{16}	2	3	5	7	8
s_{14}	1	3	3	5	6	s_{17}	0	4	5	8	8
s_{15}	1	4	7	7	8	s_{18}	1	4	5	7	7
					b_4						
s_{19}	3	5	8	7	6	s_{22}	1	4	4	5	8
s_{20}	0	2	3	6	4	s_{23}	1	2	4	6	8
s_{21}	2	1	2	5	5	s_{24}	2	5	6	7	7

5. The data for a hypothetical experiment are presented in the accompanying matrix. For the experimental factors, the design is a 2 X 4 factorial with repeated measures on both factors. There are $s = 5$ subjects, each of whom served in all of the $(a)(b) = (2)(4) = 8$ treatment combinations. Conduct an analysis of variance on these data.

ABS MATRIX

	a_1				a_2			
	b_1	b_2	b_3	b_4	b_1	b_2	b_3	b_4
s_1	3	5	9	6	5	6	11	7
s_2	7	11	12	11	10	12	18	15
s_3	9	13	14	12	10	15	15	14
s_4	4	8	11	7	6	9	13	9
s_5	1	3	5	4	3	5	9	7

6. The data for this problem were selected from an experiment reported by Postman (1964).[9] The main purpose of the experiment was to study the transfer of verbal habits as a function of a number of different independent variables. Each subject received three transfer "cycles," each containing two learning tasks; of primary interest was the performance on the second task. There were two types of second tasks (factor A), one in which there was no possibility of the transfer of specific habits from task 1 to task 2 (level a_1) and the other in which a subject could use the habits learned on the first task to help with the learning of the second task (level a_2). I have mentioned already that each subject received three transfer cycles (factor B). Within each of these cycles a subject received the same sort of transfer task (a_1 or a_2) that he or she had been receiving previously; the actual learning tasks themselves were different from cycle to cycle. The final independent variable was trials on task 2 (factor C). Specifically, all subjects were given $c = 4$ trials on each of the transfer tasks in the three cycles.

ABCS MATRIX

	Cycle 1 (b_1)				Cycle 2 (b_2)				Cycle 3 (b_3)			
	c_1	c_2	c_3	c_4	c_1	c_2	c_3	c_4	c_1	c_2	c_3	c_4
						Task a_1						
s_1	1	3	6	6	3	5	6	6	2	4	6	7
s_2	2	4	4	5	2	4	6	7	2	4	6	6
s_3	3	3	4	6	1	2	5	7	3	4	5	7
s_4	2	4	5	7	2	5	6	7	3	4	5	6
s_5	3	4	6	7	4	6	6	7	2	5	5	6
s_6	2	4	4	6	2	4	5	6	1	4	5	6
						Task a_2						
s_7	4	5	6	6	4	4	7	6	5	6	7	8
s_8	1	2	4	5	2	4	5	6	4	6	7	7
s_9	1	3	3	5	2	4	4	4	2	4	5	5
s_{10}	2	4	4	5	3	5	5	6	3	7	7	7
s_{11}	2	3	4	3	3	6	5	6	4	5	6	7
s_{12}	2	4	5	5	4	6	7	6	5	5	6	6

[9] The data were generously made available by Dr. Leo J. Postman. The data presented in the problem are a random sample of the subjects actually serving in the experiment; this was done to reduce the labor of calculation.

One group of subjects received the a_1 transfer task and a different group of subjects received the a_2 transfer task. All subjects received the four trials on task 2 in all three transfer cycles. Thus, the design was an $A \times (B \times C \times S)$ factorial. The dependent variable was the number of correct responses given on each trial of task 2. The questions being asked were: Would subjects differ on the two transfer tasks? Would they differ by the same amount on each of the transfer trials? Would these differences change as subjects gained experience over the three transfer cycles? For the data given in the accompanying $ABCS$ matrix at the bottom of p. 476, there are $s = 6$ subjects in each of the two transfer tasks. Perform an analysis of variance on these data.

VI

ADDITIONAL TOPICS: ANALYSIS OF COVARIANCE AND GENERALIZING RESULTS

This last major section of the book covers two topics that I feel are best appreciated after one has been exposed to the design and analysis of a wide variety of experimental plans. The first topic consists of a procedure that is intended to reduce the size of the error term and to increase the sensitivity of an experiment by using the methods of linear regression. This procedure is known as the *analysis of covariance* and is considered in Chapter 20. Chapter 21 provides a systematic examination of the statistical models underlying the analyses covered in the preceding chapters and emphasizes the problems encountered when we attempt to generalize the results of our research beyond the confines of a specific experiment or study.

20

Analysis of Covariance

The primary function of an experimental design is to create a setting in which observations can be related to variations in treatments in an unambiguous and unequivocal manner. The major problem is, of course, the unavoidable presence of error variance, which introduces uncertainty into the outcome of any experiment. Different types of designs have been created to reduce the magnitude of this uncertainty by exerting varying degrees of control on the operation of unsystematic, or chance, variability. The completely randomized design minimizes confounding and bias through the random assignment of subjects to treatments but does so at the expense of a relatively insensitive experiment—i.e., a large error term. Other types of design attempt to reduce the size of this uncontrolled variation in a number of different ways. We have considered two methods already, namely, the Treatments × Blocks design and within-subjects designs. I will examine a third method in this chapter. Before I begin, let's see how these different designs achieve a reduction in error variance.

20.1   CONTROLLING ERROR VARIANCE

In the analysis of any experiment, whatever the design, the significance of a main effect or an interaction is assessed with reference to an error term. In the behavioral sciences, large error terms are common, and anything that can be done to reduce their size directly increases the sensitivity of the experiment in detecting treatment differences. One approach is to use a homogeneous pool of subjects, but there is a possible loss of generality when an experiment is conducted with a highly selected group of subjects. There are other approaches, however, that do not suffer from this potentially serious shortcoming. In general, these methods achieve a reduction in the magnitude of uncontrolled variability either directly through experimental design or indirectly through statistical calculations. I will consider these approaches briefly.

Direct Control

Direct control is achieved by identifying important sources of nuisance variables, including them in the experimental design, and removing their influence directly in the partitioning of the total sum of squares. In the Treatments × Blocks design (pp. 247–253), for example, subjects are segregated into blocks on the basis of some characteristic that is known or suspected to influence the behavior under study and then randomly assigned from each block to the different treatment conditions. Variation associated with blocks (the main effect and interactions) is isolated in the statistical analysis; these sources of variation would contribute to error variance in the completely randomized design. The net result, then, is a reduction in the size of the error term and an increase in the sensitivity of the experiment.

Within-subjects designs achieve a reduction in error variance by using the same subjects in all or in some selected subset of the treatment conditions. In the simplest design, subjects are tested under all treatment conditions in a single-factor experiment. As you saw in Chapter 17, this arrangement permits the removal of consistent individual differences (the main effect of subjects) from the within-groups error term to produce a new error term (the $A \times S$ interaction) that is greatly reduced in magnitude, again increasing the sensitivity of the experiment.

Statistical Control

The topic of this chapter is a procedure that reduces experimental error by statistical, rather than by experimental, means. This is accomplished by using a statistical procedure to adjust the results of an experiment for differences existing among subjects *before* the start of the experiment. This method is known as the **analysis of covariance** and requires the measurement of subjects on some relevant ability or characteristic prior to the administration of the experimental treatments. I will call this information the **covariate**.[1] Following the administration of the experimental treatments and the collection of the data, this information is used to accomplish two important adjustments: (1) to refine estimates of experimental error and (2) to adjust treatment effects for any differences between the treatment groups that existed before the start of the experiment. As you will see, the magnitude of these adjustments depends on two factors: the degree of linear correlation between the covariate and the dependent variable, and the differences actually observed on the covariate. Assuming that subjects have been randomly assigned to the treatment conditions, we would expect to find relatively small differences among the treatments on the covariate and considerably larger differences among the subjects within the different treatment conditions. Thus, the analysis of covariance is expected to achieve its greatest benefits by reducing the size of the *error term*; any correction for preexisting differences produced through random assignment will be small by comparison.

20.2 THE BASIS FOR STATISTICAL CONTROL: LINEAR REGRESSION

Linear regression consists of a statistical technique for establishing a linear function—a straight line—relating two variables. With this line, or a regression equation describing this line mathematically, it is possible to identify a certain portion of the variation on the dependent variable that is associated with the covariate. This variability, which is systematically related to the covariate, is subtracted from the variation associated with the dependent variable, leaving a residual variation that is used to estimate the operation of experimental error in the experiment.

[1] You will find the covariate also referred to as the **control variable** and the **concomitant variable**.

The Linear Regression Equation

Let's see how the linear function is established for a single set of scores, e.g., the scores of subjects in one of the treatment conditions of a completely randomized single-factor experiment, and then how it is used to reduce the variability of the subjects on the dependent variable. We start with the formula for a straight line:

$$Y = a + (b)(X),$$

where X is a score on the covariate, a and b are constants, and Y is the corresponding score on the dependent variable. The constant a is called the **Y intercept** and consists of the value of Y when $X = 0$. The other constant, b, represents the **slope**, or tilt, of the line and reflects the change in Y associated with a given change in X. The sign of the slope indicates the direction of the linear relationship. A positive slope means that the two variables change in the same direction—as X increases Y increases and as X decreases Y decreases—while a negative slope means that the two variables change in opposite directions—as X increases Y decreases and as X decreases Y increases.

The Linear Regression Line.   The two constants required to specify a straight line, the slope and the intercept, must be estimated from a set of data consisting for each subject of an X score and a corresponding Y score. In the context of the analysis of covariance, the X scores will be obtained before the experimental treatments are introduced and the Y scores will be the responses observed after they are administered. The procedures we follow in estimating these two constants produce an equation for the line that keeps the sum of the squared discrepancies of the actual data from the line at a minimum value. This line is called a **regression line** and is often described as the best-fitting straight line obtained by applying the **criterion of least squares.**

Estimating Slope.   The slope of a line can be defined as follows:

$$\text{slope} = \frac{\text{rate of change in } Y}{\text{rate of change in } X}.$$

With data that describe a straight line perfectly, e.g., temperatures measured on the Celsius and Fahrenheit scales, slope can be determined by choosing any two pairs of X, Y scores, for example, X_1, Y_1 and X_2, Y_2, and relating the change in Y associated with a change in X as follows:

$$\text{slope} = \frac{Y_2 - Y_1}{X_2 - X_1}.$$

With behavioral data, linear relationships will not be perfect, which means that no two sets of X, Y pairs can be guaranteed to give the slope of the regression line. What is needed is a formula that estimates the best-fitting straight line to data that contain random fluctuation. Such a formula is the following:

$$\text{slope} = \frac{\text{covariation of } X \text{ and } Y}{\text{variation of } X}.$$

Covariation of X and Y refers to the degree to which two variables *covary,* that is, *vary together,* and represents the change in Y associated with a change in X; variation in X refers to the variability of the X scores.

Variation in X can be expressed in terms of the variance of the X scores; i.e.,

$$\text{variance } (X) = \frac{\Sigma (X_i - \bar{X})^2}{df} = \frac{SS_x}{df}.$$

This is the familiar formula for the variance of a set of scores. The covariation of X and Y can be expressed in terms of a quantity called **covariance**, which represents a blending of the deviation of X scores from their mean $(X_i - \bar{X})$ with corresponding deviations of Y scores from their mean $(Y_i - \bar{Y})$. In symbols,

$$\text{covariance } (X, Y) = \frac{\Sigma (X_i - \bar{X})(Y_i - \bar{Y})}{df}.$$

Covariance is large when deviations on the two variables tend to be of the same magnitude—large with large, medium with medium, and small with small. Covariance is zero when the pairing of the two magnitudes tends to be inconsistent. The value of covariance can be either positive or negative depending on the direction of slope; positive covariance (and slope) is present when the signs of the pairs of deviations tend to be the same, and negative covariance (and slope) is present when the signs tend to be different. I will refer to the numerator term as the sum of products of corresponding deviations on the X and Y variables, or more simply, as the **sum of products**, abbreviated *SP.* Thus,

$$\text{covariance } (X, Y) = \frac{SP}{df}.$$

The computational formulas for SS_x and SP involve relatively simple operations. For the sum of squares,

$$SS_x = \Sigma (X)^2 - \frac{(\Sigma X)^2}{s}. \tag{20-1}$$

For the sum of products,

$$SP = \Sigma (X)(Y) - \frac{(\Sigma X)(\Sigma Y)}{s}. \tag{20-2}$$

These two sets of calculations are easily understood in the context of an example. Consider the data presented in Table 20-1. For each of $s = 8$ subjects, an X score and a Y score are listed. From the X scores we calculate

$$SS_x = [(10)^2 + (6)^2 + \cdots + (9)^2 + (12)^2] - \frac{(63)^2}{8}$$

$$= 547 - \frac{3,969}{8} = 547 - 496.13 = 50.87.$$

In order to calculate the SP, we need the products of each pair of X and Y scores as well as the product of the sum of each set of scores. More specifically,

$$SP = [(10)(15) + (6)(1) + \cdots + (9)(7) + (12)(13)] - \frac{(63)(56)}{8}$$

$$= (150 + 6 + \cdots + 63 + 156) - \frac{3,528}{8} = 533.00 - 441.00 = 92.00.$$

We can now obtain the slope—known as the **regression coefficient**—of the best-fitting straight line relating the covariate and the dependent variable. You will recall that

$$b \text{ (slope)} = \frac{\text{covariance } (X, Y)}{\text{variance } (X)},$$

which becomes

$$b = \frac{SP/df}{SS_x/df} = \frac{SP}{SS_x}, \tag{20-3}$$

when we simplify the numerator and denominator terms. Substituting the two quantities we have just calculated into Eq. (20-3), we find

$$b = \frac{92.00}{50.87} = 1.81.$$

Table 20-1   Pairs of Scores for Eight Subjects

SUBJECT	X	Y
1	10	15
2	6	1
3	5	4
4	8	6
5	9	10
6	4	0
7	9	7
8	12	13
	$\Sigma X = 63$	$\Sigma Y = 56$
	$\bar{X} = 7.88$	$\bar{Y} = 7.00$
	$\Sigma (X)^2 = 547$	$\Sigma (Y)^2 = 596$

This value of slope means that if the covariate X changes by one unit, the linear regression line predicts a change in the same direction of 1.81 units on the dependent variable (Y).

Estimating the Intercept. The Y intercept, a, is obtained quite easily by substitution in the formula

$$a = \bar{Y} - (b)(\bar{X}). \tag{20-4}$$

Entering the relevant data from Table 20-1 and the value of $b = 1.81$, we compute

$$a = 7.00 - (1.81)(7.88) = 7.00 - 14.26 = -7.26.$$

This value of a indicates that the linear regression line predicts a value of $Y = -7.26$ when $X = 0$, a value that may not make sense logically but is necessary to specify this particular line of best fit.

The Regression Equation. We are now able to write the equation for the regression line by substituting the estimates of the slope and the Y intercept in the equation for a straight line as follows:

$$Y' = a + (b)(X) = -7.26 + (1.81)(X),$$

where Y' refers to the value of Y predicted by the regression line for any given value of X. What I will now do with the regression equation is to show how a knowledge of the linear relationship between the covariate and the dependent variable can be used to reduce the estimate of uncontrolled variability of the Y scores.

Uncontrolled (or Residual) Variation

The pairs of X and Y scores from Table 20-1 have been plotted in Fig. 20-1. The horizontal line on the graph represents the value of the mean of the Y scores, $\bar{Y} = 7.00$. The deviation of each data point from this line is also indicated. These deviations when squared, summed, and divided by the degrees of freedom produce a quantitative value for the variance of the Y scores. That is,

$$\text{variance } (Y) = \frac{\Sigma (Y_i - \bar{Y})^2}{df}.$$

Suppose we use the regression equation to give a value of Y for each subject (Y') that is based on information available before the start of the experiment, namely, each subject's X score. This has been done in column 4 of Table 20-2. To illustrate for the first subject,

$$Y'_1 = -7.26 + (1.81)(X_1)$$
$$= -7.26 + (1.81)(10) = -7.26 + 18.10 = 10.84.$$

The regression line, which can be drawn once two values of Y' have been calculated, is presented in Fig. 20-2 together with the original eight data points.

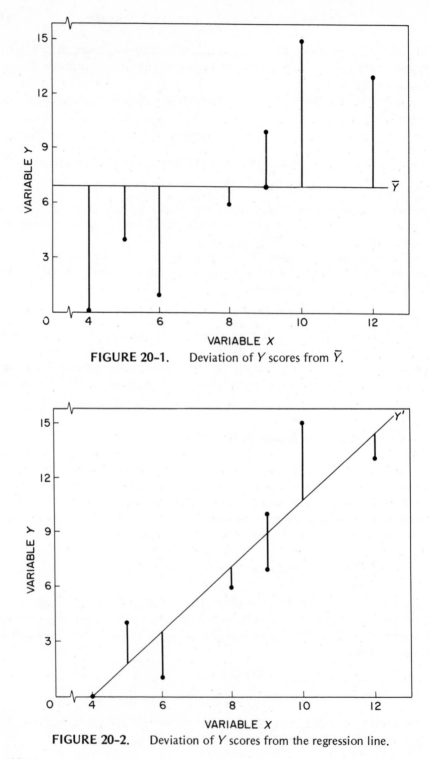

FIGURE 20-1.   Deviation of Y scores from $\bar{Y}$.

FIGURE 20-2.   Deviation of Y scores from the regression line.

Consider the regression line for a moment. Notice how much more closely it approaches the data points than did the line drawn at $\bar{Y} = 7.00$ (see Fig. 20-1). In the absence of a linear relationship between the two variables, the regression line becomes $Y' = \bar{Y}$ and the two lines are identical.[2] When a linear relationship is present, however, the two lines are different and the regression line will always provide a closer fit to the data than will the horizontal line drawn through $\bar{Y}$. What this means, therefore, is that if the discrepancies between the data points and the regression line are used to calculate a new variance—one reflecting truly uncontrolled (or unpredicted) variability—this new variance will be *smaller* than will the variance based on the horizontal line drawn at $\bar{Y}$.

Let's see how this works out in practice. To obtain the variance of the Y scores, first calculate the sum of squares:

$$SS_y = \Sigma (Y)^2 - \frac{(\Sigma Y)^2}{s}$$

$$= [(15)^2 + (1)^2 + \cdots + (7)^2 + (13)^2] - \frac{(56)^2}{8}$$

$$= 596 - 392.00 = 204.00.$$

Then divide by the degrees of freedom:

$$\text{variance } (Y) = \frac{SS_y}{s-1} = \frac{204.00}{8-1} = 29.14.$$

The sum of squares based on the deviation of each subject's Y score from Y'—the value of Y predicted for that subject from the value of X—can be calculated from the entries in column 5 of Table 20-2, where the discrepancy between the actual Y score and that predicted by linear regression $(Y - Y')$ has been calculated for each

Table 20-2 Analysis of Predicted Y Scores (Y')

(1) SUBJECT	(2) X	(3) Y	(4) Y'	(5) $Y - Y'$
1	10	15	10.84	4.16
2	6	1	3.60	−2.60
3	5	4	1.79	2.21
4	8	6	7.22	−1.22
5	9	10	9.03	.97
6	4	0	−.02	.02
7	9	7	9.03	−2.03
8	12	13	14.46	−1.46

[2]You can verify this point by setting $b = 0$, the value taken by b when covariance is zero, and solving for a. From Eq. (20-4), $a = \bar{Y} - (b)(\bar{X}) = \bar{Y} - (0)(\bar{X}) = \bar{Y}$. The regression line becomes $Y' = \bar{Y} + (0)(X) = \bar{Y}$.

subject. Again, for the first subject, this discrepancy is

$$Y_1 - Y_1' = 15 - 10.84 = 4.16.$$

Squaring and summing these differences gives us

$$
\begin{aligned}
SS_{y(\text{adj.})} &= \Sigma\,(Y_i - Y_i')^2 \\
&= (4.16)^2 + (-2.60)^2 + \cdots + (-2.03)^2 + (-1.46)^2 \\
&= 37.63.
\end{aligned}
$$

The variance based on these difference scores has 1 less degree of freedom than does a variance based on the Y scores because the slope of the regression line has been estimated from the data. Thus,

$$
\begin{aligned}
\text{variance}\,(Y_{\text{adj.}}) &= \frac{SS_{y(\text{adj.})}}{s - 2} \\
&= \frac{37.63}{8 - 2} = 6.27.
\end{aligned}
$$

These calculations verify what our eyes could see in Fig. 20-1 and Fig. 20-2, namely, that the variability is much smaller when the deviations are based on the regression line, i.e., 6.27, than the value resulting when they are based on the mean of the Y scores, i.e., 29.14.

The adjusted sum of squares can be obtained more simply by means of a formula that includes quantities we have already computed in determining the slope of the regression line. More specifically,

$$
\begin{aligned}
SS_{y(\text{adj.})} &= SS_y - SS_{\text{lin. regr.}} \\
&= SS_y - \frac{(SP)^2}{SS_x}.
\end{aligned}
\tag{20-5}
$$

The adjusted sum of squares is found by subtracting from SS_y a sum of squares that reflects the degree to which variation in Y is associated with the linear relationship between the covariate and the dependent variable (X and Y, respectively). This latter quantity can also be written as $(b)(SP)$.[3] Taking advantage of the calculations we have completed already, we find

$$
\begin{aligned}
SS_{y(\text{adj.})} &= 204.00 - \frac{(92.00)^2}{50.87} \\
&= 204.00 - 166.38 = 37.62,
\end{aligned}
$$

---

[3]The deviations reflecting the $SS_{\text{lin. regr.}}$ are the differences between the predicted score (Y', the points on the regression line) and the mean of the Y scores (the horizontal line drawn at $\bar{Y}$). You can verify this fact by calculating these differences ($Y' - \bar{Y}$) for each subject, squaring them, and then summing the squares. In symbols, $SS_{\text{lin. regr.}} = \Sigma\,(Y_i' - \bar{Y})^2$.

which is equal within rounding error the value value of 37.63 we obtained by squaring and then summing the differences between Y and Y' for each subject. The adjustment formula specified in Eq. (20-5) forms the basis of the analysis of covariance, in which the within-group sum of squares will be adjusted separately for each treatment group and then pooled to create the error term for the F ratio. If the reduction in the sizes of these SS's approaches the amount observed in this example for the variances (29.14 to 6.27), the gain in the sensitivity of the statistical analysis can be considerable.

Estimating Treatment Effects

A secondary purpose of the analysis of covariance is to obtain a more precise estimate of treatment effects. As you know, a major source of error in estimating treatment effects occurs as a result of randomly assigning subjects to conditions, which inevitably produces treatment groups that are imperfectly matched at the outset. When covariate scores are available, however, we have information about differences between treatment groups that existed before the start of the experiment. As you will see, the analysis of covariance again uses linear regression to produce an adjusted treatment mean square that takes these chance differences on the covariate into consideration.

It is important to note that this adjustment for group differences can either increase *or decrease* the size of the treatment mean square. The nature of the actual adjustment is complex and depends on two factors: (1) the direction of the relationship between the group means on the covariate and the dependent variable, and (2) the direction of the relationship between the two variables observed for the individual subjects in the different treatment conditions.[4] The adjustment should be minor, however, in comparison with the reduction in the size of the error term normally associated with an analysis of covariance.

20.3 THE COMPLETELY RANDOMIZED SINGLE-FACTOR EXPERIMENT

I will present the computational procedures of the analysis of covariance in the context of the completely randomized single-factor design. This design represents the simplest example of the analysis. It can be generalized readily to more complex factorial arrangements, as you will see in Section 20.4.

---

[4]To be more specific, when the differences between the group means on the covariate and the dependent variable are in the *same direction,* a positive correlation between the two measures for subjects will tend to decrease the size of the treatment effects, while a negative correlation will tend to increase the size of the effects. On the other hand, when the differences between the group means are in the *opposite direction,* a positive correlation will tend to increase the size of the treatment effects, while a negative correlation will tend to decrease the size of the effects.

The analysis of covariance possesses many elements of similarity with an ordinary analysis of variance. In fact, the first step actually consists of calculating three familiar sums of squares—SS_A, $SS_{S/A}$, and SS_T—in the usual manner separately for the scores obtained on the covariate and for the scores obtained on the dependent variable. Moreover, corresponding sums of products—SP_A, $SP_{S/A}$, and SP_T—are calculated from analogous computational formulas that are based on the X, Y pairs rather than on the X or Y scores considered separately. The second step consists of the adjustment of the treatment and within-groups sums of squares for differences observed on the covariate. This adjustment is similar to the one presented in Section 20.2 for one treatment group. Finally, we obtain the adjusted estimates of the treatment population means, which can then be used for conducting analytical comparisons among selected treatment conditions.

The Covariate

The main criterion for a covariate is a high linear correlation with the dependent variable. In most cases, the scores on the covariate are obtained *prior* to the initiation of the experimental treatment. There may be a formal pretest of some sort administered to all potential participants in the experiment, or the scores may be available from records of the subjects. Achievement scores, IQ determinations, and grade-point averages are common examples. Occasionally, the scores on the covariate are gathered *after* the experiment is completed. Such a procedure is defensible only when it is certain that the experimental treatment did *not* influence the covariate. For relatively "permanent" subject abilities (e.g., reading ability) this may be a reasonable assumption, but for labile tendencies (e.g., anxiety, ego involvement) it may be an untenable position to take. The analysis of covariance is predicated upon the availability of information that is *independent* of the experimental treatment. Therefore, any determination that is taken following the end of the experiment should be scrutinized carefully.

Computational Formulas

In this design, we are assuming that there are a treatment conditions and that s subjects have been randomly assigned to each of the treatment conditions. Each of the subjects provides us with two scores, one from the covariate (X) and the other from the dependent variable (Y).

I should say a few words about notation at this point. The basic notation is the same as that used for the completely randomized single-factor design, where AS_{ij} refers to a particular subject (the jth subject) in a particular treatment (the ith condition), A_i refers to the treatment sum for the ith condition, and T refers to the grand total of all the scores. In the analysis of covariance, these symbols continue to have the same meaning except that it is necessary to add a subscript to distinguish between scores or sums based on the covariate (the X variable) from those based on the dependent variable (the Y variable). This is accomplished quite simply by adding an x or a y to the subscript. Thus, $AS_{21(x)}$ refers to the score on the covariate of the first subject in condition a_2, and $AS_{21(y)}$ refers to the score on the dependent variable of the same subject. The symbols for sums work the same way. For example, $A_{2(x)}$ is the sum of the scores on the covariate for condition a_2 and $A_{3(y)}$ is the sum of the scores on the dependent variable for condition a_3; similarly, T_x is the grand sum of the scores on the covariate, while T_y is the grand sum of the scores on the dependent variable. Cross products are designated by means of parentheses. For example, $(AS_{21(x)})(AS_{21(y)})$ is the product of the X and Y scores for the first subject in condition a_2; $(A_{1(x)})(A_{1(y)})$ is the product of the group totals for condition a_1 on the two variables; and $(T_x)(T_y)$ is the product of the two grand sums.

Calculating SS's and SP's. It is convenient to consider the analysis of covariance in two major steps. The first step consists of the calculation of basic sums of squares and sums of products for the X and Y variables. For the single-factor experiment there are two sources of variance in which we are interested: A and S/A. The computational formulas for the sums of squares and of products for these two sources are given in Table 20-3. The formulas for the sums of squares should pose no problem, as they are the standard ones we have been using all along for the calculation of the SS_A and the $SS_{S/A}$. The only additions to the formulas are the x and y subscripts to indicate whether the scores are from the covariate or the dependent variable.

The formulas for the sums of products may take a while to comprehend. Consider the formula for the calculation of the SP_A. In the numerator of the first term we are asked to multiply each "treatment" sum for the covariate by the corresponding treatment sum for the dependent variable. The single summation sign in the numerator indicates that all of the possible products are summed in this operation. In the numerator of the second term, we multiply the grand total of the scores on the covariate, T_x, by the grand total of the scores on the dependent variable, T_y. The denominators are the same as those specified for the corresponding quantities in the computational formulas for either sum of squares. The final new term appears in the formula for the $SP_{S/A}$ as the first and indicates that the two scores for each subject are multiplied and then summed over all of the subjects in the experiment.

As a numerical example, assume that we have three levels of factor A with $s = 8$ subjects in each condition. Further, let's assume that the subjects were given a pretest before the start of the experiment and were assigned randomly to the three experimental conditions. Thus, we have no reason to believe that the experimental treatments exerted any influence on the pretest scores. The pairs of AS_{ij} scores are presented in an AS matrix in Table 20-4.

An inspection of the data suggests a positive correlation between the two sets of scores within each of the treatment conditions: The larger the score on the covariate, the larger the score on the dependent variable. The presence of any within-group correlation implies that the adjusted error term will be smaller than

Table 20-3 Computational Formulas: Sums of Squares and Sums of Products

SOURCE	CONTROL VARIABLE (X)	CROSS PRODUCTS (X)(Y)	DEPENDENT VARIABLE (Y)
A	$\dfrac{\sum (A_x)^2}{s} - \dfrac{(T_x)^2}{(a)(s)}$	$\dfrac{\sum (A_{i(x)})(A_{i(y)})}{s} - \dfrac{(T_x)(T_y)}{(a)(s)}$	$\dfrac{\sum (A_y)^2}{s} - \dfrac{(T_y)^2}{(a)(s)}$
S/A	$\sum (AS_x)^2 - \dfrac{\sum (A_x)^2}{s}$	$\sum (AS_{ij(x)})(AS_{ij(y)}) - \dfrac{\sum (A_{i(x)})(A_{i(y)})}{s}$	$\sum (AS_y)^2 - \dfrac{\sum (A_y)^2}{s}$

the unadjusted one. The $A_{i(y)}$ totals indicate a numerical difference among the conditions and the $A_{i(x)}$ totals suggest relative comparability of the three groups on the covariate.

The first step is to substitute these data into the computational formulas for the sums of squares and of products given in Table 20-3. As in the preceding chapters, we perform these operations in two substeps, first calculating the basic terms entering into the computational formulas and then adding and subtracting these terms in the actual determination of the various sums of squares and products. Working first with the scores on the covariate, we find

$$[T_x] = \frac{(T_x)^2}{(a)(s)} = \frac{(180)^2}{(3)(8)} = 1{,}350.00;$$

$$[A_x] = \frac{\Sigma (A_x)^2}{s} = \frac{(63)^2 + (64)^2 + (53)^2}{8} = 1{,}359.25;$$

and

$$[AS_x] = \Sigma (AS_x)^2 = (10)^2 + (6)^2 + \cdots + (6)^2 + (8)^2 = 1{,}464.$$

Identical operations on the scores on the dependent variable produce

$$[T_y] = \frac{(T_y)^2}{(a)(s)} = \frac{(240)^2}{(3)(8)} = 2{,}400.00;$$

$$[A_y] = \frac{\Sigma (A_y)^2}{s} = \frac{(56)^2 + (88)^2 + (96)^2}{8} = 2{,}512.00;$$

Table 20-4   Numerical Example: AS Matrix

	a_1		a_2		a_3	
	X	Y	X	Y	X	Y
	10	15	4	6	7	14
	6	1	8	13	8	9
	5	4	8	5	7	16
	8	6	8	18	3	7
	9	10	6	9	6	13
	4	0	11	7	8	18
	9	7	10	15	6	13
	12	13	9	15	8	6
Sum:	63	56	64	88	53	96
Mean:	7.88	7.00	8.00	11.00	6.63	12.00

$$T_x = 63 + 64 + 53 = 180; \overline{T}_x = 7.50$$
$$T_y = 56 + 88 + 96 = 240; \overline{T}_y = 10.00$$

and

$$[AS_y] = \Sigma\,(AS_y)^2 = (15)^2 + (1)^2 + \cdots + (13)^2 + (6)^2 = 3{,}010.$$

Finally, we perform analogous calculations on the cross products:

$$[T_{xy}] = \frac{(T_x)(T_y)}{(a)(s)} = \frac{(180)(240)}{(3)(8)} = 1{,}800.00;$$

$$[A_{xy}] = \frac{\Sigma\,(A_{i(x)})(A_{i(y)})}{s} = \frac{(63)(56) + (64)(88) + (53)(96)}{8}$$

$$= 1{,}781.00;$$

and

$$[AS_{xy}] = \Sigma\,(AS_{i(x)})(AS_{i(y)}) = (10)(15) + (6)(1) + \cdots + (6)(13)$$
$$+ (8)(6) = 1{,}912.$$

These three sets of quantities are combined in Table 20-5 to produce the desired sums of squares and sums of products.

Adjusting the Sums of Squares. The next step in the analysis of covariance is to bring together the appropriate quantities to provide the adjustment for the linear effect of the covariate. The computational formula for the within-groups sum of squares $SS_{S/A}$ is essentially the same as Eq. (20-5), p. 490, which we used to adjust the sum of squares based on a single set of scores. More specifically,

$$SS_{S/A\,\text{(adj.)}} = SS_{S/A(y)} - \frac{(SP_{S/A})^2}{SS_{S/A(x)}}. \tag{20-6}$$

Substituting the values from Table 20-5 in Eq. (20-6), we find

$$SS_{S/A\,\text{(adj.)}} = 498.00 - \frac{(131.00)^2}{104.75} = 334.17.$$

The adjustment of the treatment sum of squares SS_A is conducted indirectly. That is,

$$SS_{A\,\text{(adj.)}} = SS_{A(y)} - \left[\frac{(SP_T)^2}{SS_{T(x)}} - \frac{(SP_{S/A})^2}{SS_{S/A(x)}}\right]. \tag{20-7}$$

An inspection of Eq. (20-7) indicates that the two quantities involved in the adjustment and enclosed within the brackets—the first specifying the *total* sum of products and sum of squares and the second specifying the *within-groups* sum of products and sum of squares—when subtracted do provide an adjustment that involves the treatment component; i.e.,

treatment = total − within-groups.[5]

---

[5]See Kirk (1968, p. 464) for an explanation of this particular adjustment.

Table 20-5 Numerical Example: Sums of Squares and Sums of Products[a]

SOURCE	CONTROL VARIABLE (X)	CROSS PRODUCTS (X)(Y)	DEPENDENT VARIABLE (Y)
A	$[A_x] - [T_x] = 9.25$	$[A_{xy}] - [T_{xy}] = -19.00$	$[A_y] - [T_y] = 112.00$
S/A	$[AS_x] - [A_x] = 104.75$	$[AS_{xy}] - [A_{xy}] = 131.00$	$[AS_y] - [A_y] = 498.00$
Total	$[AS_x] - [T_x] = 114.00$	$[AS_{xy}] - [T_{xy}] = 112.00$	$[AS_y] - [T_y] = 610.00$

[a]Bracketed letters represent complete terms in the computational formulas; a particular term is identified by the letter(s) appearing in the numerator.

497

From Table 20-5, we calculate

$$SS_{A \text{ (adj.)}} = 112.00 - \left[\frac{(112.00)^2}{114.00} - \frac{(131.00)^2}{104.75} \right]$$

$$= 112.00 - (110.04 - 163.83) = 165.79.$$

The Analysis of Covariance. The computational formulas for the complete analysis of covariance are presented in Table 20-6. The degrees of freedom for the error term are the same as those associated with the $MS_{S/A}$ in the corresponding analysis of variance, *minus* 1. The loss of this df is due to the estimation of the population slope in the calculation of the adjusted within-groups sum of squares. The degrees of freedom associated with the adjusted sum of squares for treatments are identical to those associated with the unadjusted sum of squares. A df is *not* lost in the calculation of this adjusted sum of squares, since the regression line for the *means* was not used in the computation of this sum of squares.

The remaining steps in the analysis involve the calculation of the adjusted mean squares and the F ratio. As indicated in Table 20-6, the F ratio is formed by dividing the adjusted mean square for the treatment effects by the adjusted mean square for error. The significance of the F ratio is evaluated against the tabled value of F corresponding to the adjusted df's.

To complete the numerical example, the adjusted sums of squares calculated previously are entered in Table 20-7. The calculation of the adjusted df's and the adjusted mean squares is straightforward. The resultant F test indicates a significant value when evaluated against the tabled value of $F(2, 20)$.

It is instructive to see what this analysis of covariance has accomplished. If we calculate the F on the *unadjusted* scores, we find that the differences among the three means are not significant. That is,

$$F = \frac{SS_{A(y)}/df_A}{SS_{S/A(y)}/df_{S/A}}$$

$$= \frac{112.00/2}{498.00/21} = \frac{56.00}{23.71} = 2.36,$$

Table 20-6   Computational Formulas for the Analysis of Covariance

SOURCE	SUM OF SQUARES	df	F
A	$SS_{A \text{ (adj.)}} = SS_{A(y)} - \left[\dfrac{(SP_T)^2}{SS_{T(x)}} - \dfrac{(SP_{S/A})^2}{SS_{S/A(x)}} \right]$	$a - 1$	$\dfrac{MS_{A \text{ (adj.)}}}{MS_{S/A \text{ (adj.)}}}$
S/A	$SS_{S/A \text{ (adj.)}} = SS_{S/A(y)} - \dfrac{(SP_{S/A})^2}{SS_{S/A(x)}}$	$a(s - 1) - 1$	

Table 20-7   Summary of the Analysis

SOURCE	$SS_{adj.}$	df	$MS_{adj.}$	F
A	165.79	2	82.90	4.96*
S/A	334.17	20	16.71	

*$p < .025$.

a value that lies between the 10 and 25 percent levels of significance. The larger F from the analysis of covariance was the result of *two* changes: (1) a *decrease* in the size of the within-groups mean square, which we expected from the correlation between the two sets of scores, and (2) an *increase* in the size of the main effect of factor A. This latter adjustment "corrects" for chance differences between groups on the control variable. (See p. 500 for an explanation.)

Comparisons Involving Adjusted Means

Adjustment of Treatment Means. If any comparisons are to be conducted among the treatment groups, they must be made with the adjusted treatment means. The adjustments are performed by substituting the means from the X and Y variables in an equation relating the predicted (or adjusted) means to differences among the means on the covariate. This relationship is given by the formula

$$\bar{A}'_{i(y)} = \bar{A}_{i(y)} - b_{S/A}(\bar{A}_{i(x)} - \bar{T}_x), \qquad (20\text{-}8)$$

where $\bar{A}'_{i(y)}$ is the adjusted treatment mean and $b_{S/A}$ is the average within-groups regression coefficient. This latter quantity is given by the formula

$$b_{S/A} = \frac{SP_{S/A}}{SS_{S/A(x)}}. \qquad (20\text{-}9)$$

If you look closely at Eq. (20-8), you see that the adjusted mean of a treatment group, $\bar{A}'_{i(y)}$, is found by subtracting from the observed mean $\bar{A}_{i(y)}$ a value that takes into consideration the deviation of the group from the overall mean on the covariate—that is, $(b_{S/A})(\bar{A}_{i(x)} - \bar{T}_x)$. It should be noted that the regression coefficient is based on the linear regression obtained from groups of subjects that are treated alike—i.e., an average or pooled within-groups coefficient. Actually, $b_{S/A}$ is an average that weights each group coefficient by the variability of the groups on the covariate. (I will demonstrate this fact when I consider the regression assumptions—see pp. 507-508.)

Since we will usually want to obtain all of the adjusted means, it is convenient to arrange the application of Eq. (20-8) as a series of steps. This has been done in Table 20-8. The covariate means $(\bar{A}_{i(x)})$ and the unadjusted treatment means $(\bar{A}_{i(y)})$ are entered in the first two rows of the table. The *deviation* of each group mean from the total mean on the covariate is given in the third row. Using level a_1

Table 20-8 Calculation of Adjusted Treatment Means

STEPS	a_1	a_2	a_3
$\bar{A}_{i(x)}$	7.88	8.00	6.63
$\bar{A}_{i(y)}$	7.00	11.00	12.00
$\bar{A}_{i(x)} - \bar{T}_x$	.38	.50	−.87
$b_{S/A}(\bar{A}_{i(x)} - \bar{T}_x)$	.48	.63	−1.09
$\bar{A}'_{i(y)} = \bar{A}_{i(y)} - b_{S/A}(\bar{A}_{i(x)} - \bar{T}_x)$	6.52	10.37	13.09

as an example,

$$\bar{A}_{1(x)} - \bar{T}_x = 7.88 - 7.50 = .38.$$

In order to complete the operations specified in the fourth row, we must calculate the within-groups regression coefficient $b_{S/A}$. From Eq. (20-9) and using the relevant numbers from Table 20-5, we have

$$b_{S/A} = \frac{SP_{S/A}}{SS_{S/A(x)}} = \frac{131.00}{104.75} = 1.25.$$

To continue with the adjustment,

$$b_{S/A}(\bar{A}_{1(x)} - \bar{T}_x) = (1.25)(.38) = .48.$$

The final step in the adjustment indicated in the fifth row produces the adjusted means. For this example,

$$\bar{A}'_{1(y)} = \bar{A}_{1(y)} - b_{S/A}(\bar{A}_{1(x)} - \bar{T}_x) = 7.00 - .48 = 6.52.$$

The steps in calculating the other two adjusted treatment means are indicated in Table 20-8.

You can see that the adjustments for the linear effect of the covariate have spread out the treatment means. This has happened because (1) there is a positive correlation within the groups and (2) the differences among the groups on the covariate are in a direction *opposite* to the outcome of the experiment. Any adjustment of these chance differences must *increase* the estimated treatment effects. (See footnote 4, p. 491, for a statement of the relationship between the direction of the correlation within groups and the direction of the correlation between groups.)

Single-df Comparisons. We may perform any of the comparisons on the adjusted means that we would consider with unadjusted data from a single-factor experiment. These techniques and procedures were discussed in detail in Part II. In all of these single-*df* comparisons, we calculate the sum of squares for the particular comparison in exactly the same fashion as we would for the analysis of variance, except that we use *adjusted* treatment means. For instance, the general formula for this type of comparison is translated as

$$SS_{A \text{ comp.(adj.)}} = \frac{s[\Sigma (c_i)(\bar{A}'_{i(y)})]^2}{\Sigma (c_i)^2}. \qquad (20\text{-}10)$$

The main change in the analysis is in the calculation of the error term. In the one-factor analysis of variance, we would use the $MS_{S/A}$. For the analysis of covariance we must perform an additional operation on the adjusted error term before comparisons among groups are conducted. I will refer to this mean square as the MS'_{error}, which is calculated as follows:[6]

$$MS'_{error} = MS_{S/A \text{ (adj.)}} \left[1 + \frac{SS_{A (x)}/(a-1)}{SS_{S/A (x)}} \right]. \qquad (20\text{-}11)$$

An inspection of Eq. (20-11) reveals that the MS'_{error} will always be at least as large as the $MS_{S/A \text{ (adj.)}}$ and that the size of the adjustment called for is directly related to the differences among the treatment conditions on the *covariate*. It will generally be the case, however, that MS'_{error} will still be smaller than the unadjusted error term.

As an example, let's compare the adjusted mean at level a_1 with the combined adjusted means at levels a_2 and a_3. The coefficients for this comparison and the adjusted means from Table 20-8 are given below:

	a_1	a_2	a_3
c_i:	2	−1	−1
$\bar{A}'_{i(y)}$:	6.52	10.37	13.09

The sum of squares for this comparison is obtained from Eq. (20-10). That is,

$$
\begin{aligned}
SS_{A \text{ comp.(adj.)}} &= \frac{s[\Sigma (c_i)(\bar{A}'_{i(y)})]^2}{\Sigma (c_i)^2} \\
&= \frac{8[(2)(6.52) + (-1)(10.37) + (-1)(13.09)]^2}{(2)^2 + (-1)^2 + (-1)^2} \\
&= \frac{8(-10.42)^2}{6} = \frac{868.61}{6} = 144.77.
\end{aligned}
$$

The next step is to calculate the error term for the comparison. Substituting the needed quantities from Table 20-5 ($SS_{A (x)} = 9.25$ and $SS_{S/A(x)} = 104.75$) and

---

[6]This formula can be used to calculate the error term for any comparison between means. An alternative formula, which is presented on p. 502, is frequently used for planned comparisons. This latter formula takes into consideration the specific nature of each comparison and adjusts the error term accordingly.

Table 20-7 ($MS_{S/A(\text{adj.})} = 16.71$), we have

$$MS'_{\text{error}} = 16.71\left[1 + \frac{9.25/(3-1)}{104.75}\right]$$

$$= 16.71\left[1 + \frac{4.63}{104.75}\right]$$

$$= 16.71(1 + .04) = 17.38.$$

The F ratio for this comparison becomes

$$F = \frac{MS_{A\text{comp.(adj.)}}}{MS'_{\text{error}}} = \frac{144.77}{17.38} = 8.33.$$

This F is evaluated with $df_{\text{num.}} = 1$ and $df_{\text{denom.}} = df_{S/A(\text{adj.})}$, which in this example is 20. This comparison is significant, $p < .01$.

An alternative formula for the error term is often recommended when comparisons are *planned* (see Winer, 1971, p. 779). This formula substitutes $SS_{A\text{comp.}(x)}$ for the quantity $\dfrac{SS_{A(x)}}{a-1}$ in Eq. (20-11). In this example,

$$SS_{A\text{comp.}(x)} = \frac{s[\Sigma (c_i)(\overline{A}_{i(x)})]^2}{\Sigma (c_i)^2}$$

$$= \frac{8[(2)(7.88) + (-1)(8.00) + (-1)(6.63)]^2}{(2)^2 + (-1)^2 + (-1)^2}$$

$$= \frac{8(1.13)^2}{6} = \frac{10.22}{6} = 1.70.$$

Substituting 1.70 for 4.62 in the previous calculation, we have

$$MS'_{\text{error}} = 16.71\left[1 + \frac{1.70}{104.75}\right]$$

$$= 16.71(1 + .02) = 17.04,$$

and the F becomes

$$F = \frac{144.77}{17.04} = 8.50,$$

which is slightly larger than the F obtained with the first formula. Snedecor (1956, pp. 401-402) indicates that we may use Eq. (20-11), which involves less work, especially when several comparisons are involved, if the $df_{S/A(\text{adj.})} > 20$ and the differences among the treatment groups on the control variable are not significant.

Assumptions Underlying the Analysis of Covariance

The assumptions underlying the analysis of *variance* continue to be applicable to the corresponding analysis of covariance. Several other assumptions concern the analysis of covariance in particular.[7] I will consider them briefly.

The Assumptions. The first assumption specifies an independence of the covariate from the treatment effects. I discussed this fundamental requirement in Section 20.1. The most common way to guarantee that this assumption is met is to collect the scores on the covariate before the start of the experiment and to assign subjects randomly to the treatment conditions in complete ignorance of these preexperimental scores. If there is any possibility that the treatments may have affected the scores on the control variable, the analysis of covariance is inappropriate.

The next two assumptions concern regression. One of these is the assumption of **linear regression**. More formally, the assumption is that the deviations from regression—i.e., the adjusted or residual scores—are normally and independently distributed in the population, with means of zero and homogeneous variances. (Since these assumptions concerning the distribution of the residuals will generally not hold if the true regression is not linear, it is accurate to refer to them as an assumption of linear regression.) Presumably, if linear regression is used in the analysis while the true regression is of another form (e.g., curvilinear), adjustments will not be of great benefit. More important, however, we could question the meaning of the treatment means, which are also adjusted on the assumption of linear regression.[8]

The final assumption specifies **homogeneity of regression** coefficients for the different treatment populations. As you will see, individual within-group regression coefficients are averaged in the analysis, and adjustments are made on the basis of this average regression line. The assumption of homogeneous within-group regression is critical for a meaningful interpretation of the results of the F test in the analysis of covariance. (This problem is discussed in detail by Huitema, 1980, pp. 103-104.) The statistical effects of violating this assumption have been studied in Monte Carlo experiments which generally have shown the presence of a *negative* bias, i.e., a reduction in the sensitivity of the F test, when heterogeneity is present. I will consider the test of this assumption next.

Test for Homogeneity of Regression. The adjustment for the linear effect of the covariate involves an average within-groups regression coefficient, namely, $b_{S/A}$. As I have noted, a critical assumption of the analysis of covariance is that regression coefficients based only on the data from each treatment group ($b_{S/A\,i}$) are the same, i.e., homogeneous. This assumption is tested by contrasting two sources of variance: (1) a source reflecting the deviation of the *group* regression

---

[7]Useful discussions are found in Elashoff (1969), Glass, Peckham, and Sanders (1972), and Huitema (1980, Ch. 6).

[8]Discussions of the statistical test of this assumption can be found in Kirk (1968, pp. 470–471) and Winer (1971, pp. 774–775).

coefficients from the *average* regression coefficient, and (2) a source reflecting the deviation of *individual subjects* from their own *group* regression lines. The first source is actually a sort of *between-groups* source of variance, but one involving group regression coefficients rather than group means. I will refer to the sum of squares associated with this source as the **between-groups regression sum of squares** ($SS_{bet.regr.}$). The second source is a sort of *within-groups* source of variance, but one involving the deviation of subjects from their group regression coefficients. I will refer to the sum of squares associated with this source as the **within-groups regression sum of squares** ($SS_{w.regr.}$).

The computational formulas for these two quantities are given in Table 20-9. The first thing to note is that

$$SS_{bet.regr.} + SS_{w.regr.} = SS_{S/A(adj.)}, \qquad (20\text{-}12)$$

which may be verified by adding the sums of squares in the first two rows of the table. It will also be noted that the two computational formulas together contain three unique terms and that we have dealt with two of these already in the calculation of the adjusted within-groups sum of squares. Thus, there is only one new quantity we need to discuss, which is

$$\Sigma \left[\frac{(SP_{S/A_i})^2}{SS_{S/A\,i(x)}} \right].$$

The quantity within the brackets is related to the regression coefficient for any one of the treatment groups, i.e.,

$$b_{S/A_i} = \frac{SP_{S/A_i}}{SS_{S/A\,i(x)}}.$$

It represents the amount by which the sum of squares for any group can be adjusted by removing the linear relationship from the data. This adjustment is based on the data for an individual treatment group, however, while the adjustment applied in the analysis of covariance is based on an averaging of the individual regression coefficients. What the $SS_{bet.regr.}$ reflects, then, is the variability of the individual regression coefficients—actually the individual adjustments for linear regression—about the average regression coefficient.

The *df* for the different sources of variance are also given in Table 20-9. The *df* for the source representing the variation among the group regression coefficients—i.e., between-groups regression—is simply 1 less than the number of coefficients: $df_{bet.\,regr.} = a - 1$. The *df* for the source representing the variation of subjects about their group regression lines—i.e., within-groups regression—equals the number of subjects (s) minus 2, summed over the a treatment groups: $df_{w.\,regr.} = a(s - 2)$. An additional *df* is lost by estimating a different regression coefficient for each group.

The test of the hypothesis that the group regression coefficients are equal is indicated in the last column of the table. The numerator reflects the degree to

Table 20-9 Test of the Assumption of Homogeneity of Regression

SOURCE	SUM OF SQUARES	df	F
Between regression	$\Sigma\left[\dfrac{(SP_{S/A_i})^2}{SS_{S/A_i(x)}}\right] - \dfrac{(SP_{S/A})^2}{SS_{S/A(x)}}$	$a-1$	$\dfrac{MS_{\text{bet. regr.}}}{MS_{\text{w. regr.}}}$
Within regression	$SS_{S/A(y)} - \Sigma\left[\dfrac{(SP_{S/A_i})^2}{SS_{S/A_i(x)}}\right]$	$a(s-2)$	
Adjusted S/A	$SS_{S/A(y)} - \dfrac{(SP_{S/A})^2}{SS_{S/A(x)}}$	$a(s-1)-1$	

which the group regression coefficients deviate from each other—i.e., are not "accounted" for by the average coefficient. The denominator reflects the degree to which the separate coefficients fail to predict the actual scores on the dependent variable. When the null hypothesis is true, the expected value of the ratio is approximately 1.0 and the ratio is distributed as F with $df_{\text{num.}} = a - 1$ and $df_{\text{denom.}} = a(s-2)$.

We are ready for a numerical example. We have already calculated two of the unique quantities in Table 20-9, namely, the unadjusted within-groups sum of squares and the correction for the linear effect of the covariate. The next step, then, is to calculate the remaining quantity, the sum of the individual group adjustments. For the covariate sums of squares, we obtain the separate within-group sums of squares with the usual computational formula. Working with the data in Table 20-4 (p. 495) and using condition a_1 as an example, we have

$$SS_{S/A_1(x)} = \Sigma\,(AS_{1j(x,}))^2 - \frac{(A_{1(x)})^2}{s}$$

$$= [(10)^2 + (6)^2 + \cdots + (9)^2 + (12)^2] - \frac{(63)^2}{8}$$

$$= 547 - 496.13 = 50.87$$

This calculation and those for the other conditions are summarized in the second column of Table 20-10. As an illustration of the calculations for the corresponding sums of products, we find for condition a_1:

$$SP_{S/A_1} = \Sigma\,(AS_{1j(x)})(AS_{1j(y)}) - \frac{(A_{1(x)})(A_{1(y)})}{s}$$

$$= [(10)(15) + (6)(1) + \cdots + (9)(7) + (12)(13)] - \frac{(63)(56)}{8}$$

$$= 533 - 441.00 = 92.00.$$

Table 20-10   Basic Calculations for the Homogeneity Assumption

SOURCE	COVARIATE	CROSS PRODUCTS
S/A_1	$547 - 496.13 = 50.87$	$533 - 441.00 = 92.00$
S/A_2	$546 - 512.00 = 34.00$	$728 - 704.00 = 24.00$
S/A_3	$371 - 351.13 = 19.87$	$651 - 636.00 = 15.00$
Total	104.74	131.00

The calculations for all three sums of products are given in the third column of the table.

As a computational check, we can verify that the sum of these component sums of squares equals the respective $SS_{S/A}$. That is,

$$\Sigma\, SS_{S/A_i(x)} = 50.87 + 34.00 + 19.87 = 104.74,$$

which agrees within rounding error with the value listed in Table 20-5, $SS_{S/A(x)} = 104.75$. There is a similar check for the sum of products:

$$\Sigma\, SP_{S/A_i} = 92.00 + 24.00 + 15.00 = 131.00 = SP_{S/A}.$$

We can now calculate the two component sums of squares:

$$SS_{\text{bet. regr.}} = \left[\frac{(92.00)^2}{50.87} + \frac{(24.00)^2}{34.00} + \frac{(15.00)^2}{19.87}\right] - \frac{(131.00)^2}{104.75}$$

$$= (166.38 + 16.94 + 11.32) - 163.83 = 30.81;$$

and

$$SS_{\text{w. regr.}} = 498.00 - \left[\frac{(92.00)^2}{50.87} + \frac{(24.00)^2}{34.00} + \frac{(15.00)^2}{19.87}\right]$$

$$= 498.00 - (166.38 + 16.94 + 11.32) = 303.36.$$

Again, as a computational check,

$$SS_{\text{bet. regr.}} + SS_{\text{w. regr.}} = 30.81 + 303.36 = 334.17 = SS_{S/A(\text{adj.})}.$$

These two sums of squares are entered in Table 20-11.

The df for the deviation among regression coefficients are 1 less than the number of coefficients: $df_{\text{bet. regr.}} = a - 1 = 3 - 1 = 2$. The df for the deviation of individual subjects from the group regression lines are given by the equation $df_{\text{w. regr.}} = a(s - 2) = 3(8 - 2) = 18$. The result of the F test, summarized in the table, indicates that the hypothesis of homogeneity of group regression coefficients is tenable. Some authors [e.g., Kirk (1968)] suggest that we use a significance level much larger than usual, say $\alpha = .10$ or $.25$, in evaluating the significance of this F test. The reasoning behind this recommendation is that since it is in our interest to

Table 20-11 Summary of the Homogeneity Analysis

SOURCE	SS	df	MS	F
Between regression	30.81	2	15.41	<1
Within regression	303.36	18	16.85	
S/A(adj.)	334.17	20		

accept the null hypothesis, we should, under these circumstances, worry about committing a type II error. (A type II error, in this case, would consist of failing to recognize an actual violation of a statistical assumption.) A direct way of decreasing the type II error is to increase the α level. In the present example, of course, there is no ambiguity, since $F < 1$.

At the beginning of this chapter, I presented a regression analysis on a single set of scores to show how information on the covariate can be used to reduce variability on the dependent variable (see pp. 487–491). (The actual data set came from the group of subjects at level a_1 in Table 20-4, p. 495.) It is informative to perform this same analysis on each of the treatment groups. While we could use Eq. (20-3) to calculate these coefficients, I will use instead the same formula written in the context of the single-factor design, namely,

$$ b_{S/A_i} = \frac{SP_{S/A_i}}{SS_{S/A_i(x)}}. \tag{20-13} $$

Substituting values from Table 20-10 in Eq. (20-13), we have

$$ b_{S/A_1} = \frac{92.00}{50.87} = 1.81, \qquad b_{S/A_2} = \frac{24.00}{34.00} = .71, $$

$$ b_{S/A_3} = \frac{15.00}{19.87} = .75. $$

(The hypothesis we have just tested is that these regression coefficients are equal.) The *average* within-groups coefficient is given by Eq. (20-9):

$$ b_{S/A} = \frac{SP_{S/A}}{SS_{S/A(x)}} = \frac{131.00}{104.75} = 1.25. $$

As mentioned earlier, the within-groups coefficient is actually a weighted mean of individual group coefficients. For this example,

$$ b_{S/A} = \frac{(SS_{S/A_1(x)})(b_{S/A_1}) + (SS_{S/A_2(x)})(b_{S/A_2}) + (SS_{S/A_3(x)})(b_{S/A_3})}{SS_{S/A_1(x)} + SS_{S/A_2(x)} + SS_{S/A_3(x)}}. $$

In words, the group coefficients are weighted by the corresponding within-group sum of squares on the covariate, summed, and divided by the sum of the weights. From the values calculated on p. 507 and from Table 20-10, we find with this alternative formula:

$$b_{S/A} = \frac{(50.87)(1.81) + (34.00)(.71) + (19.87)(.75)}{50.87 + 34.00 + 19.87}$$

$$= \frac{131.12}{104.74} = 1.25.$$

While I am on the subject, another useful index of the relationship between the coviariate and the dependent variable is the within-groups **correlation coefficient**. This index is obtained by combining quantities with which we are already familiar:

$$r_{S/A} = \frac{SP_{S/A}}{\sqrt{(SS_{S/A(x)})(SS_{S/A(y)})}}. \tag{20-14}$$

From Table 20-5 (p. 497),

$$r_{S/A} = \frac{131.00}{\sqrt{(104.75)(498.00)}} = \frac{131.00}{228.40} = .57.$$

The precision afforded by covariance is directly related to the magnitude of the within-groups correlation.

Multiple Covariates

Occasionally, even greater precision may result if additional covariates are included in the analysis. The analysis is not overly complicated with two covariates, although the computational effort is approximately twice that required for the analysis with a single covariate. There is often little gain in precision with the addition of three or more covariates, provided that the first two are reasonably correlated with the dependent variable and uncorrelated with each other.

The adjustment made with two covariates essentially involves the separate adjustments of the $SS_{A(y)}$ and $SS_{S/A(y)}$ for the linear effects of the two covariates. Winer (1971, pp. 809–812) discusses the analysis of a number of covariates, while Kirk (1968, pp. 472–475) provides a worked example of a one-factor analysis of covariance. At this point you will probably not be interested in hand calculation, however, and will turn to the computer to process the analysis, which is facilitated by the fact that most analysis-of-variance packages include the analysis of covariance as an option. You might also be interested in viewing the analysis of covariance in terms of a general linear regression model and as a problem of multiple regression. Cohen and Cohen (1975, Chapter 9), Edwards (1979, Chapter 12), and Huitema (1980, Chapter 4) provide useful discussions of this approach.

20.4 GENERAL COMPUTATIONAL RULES

The analysis of covariance is easily extended to factorial designs. For completely randomized designs, which I will consider first, all sums of squares are adjusted for the linear effects of the covariate. The adjustment of the error term again involves removing from an individual's score on the dependent variable that part which is predictable from a knowledge of his or her covariate score and of the linear relationship between the covariate and the dependent variable. The adjustment of factorial effects uses the average within-groups regression coefficient—for example, $b_{S/AB}$ for the $A \times B$ design and $b_{S/ABC}$ for the $A \times B \times C$ design—and discrepancies among the relevant treatment means on the covariate to make corrections for chance differences between groups produced by the random assignment of subjects to conditions. (See Huitema, 1980, for a comprehensive coverage of the analysis of covariance and other procedures designed to increase the sensitivity of experiments.)

Completely Randomized Designs

The computational scheme is surprisingly simple. Consider first the adjustment of the sum of squares for error variance, presented in the upper portion of Table 20-12. *Error variance* refers to any source of variance that will be used as the denominator in a test of significance. It is clear that the correction is identical in form to the one specified in Eq. (20-6), p. 496, for the single-factor design. To illustrate with the two-factor design, we require three quantities:

$SS_{S/AB(y)}$ = the unadjusted sum of squares from the normal analysis of variance;

$SS_{S/AB(x)}$ = the corresponding sum of squares based on the covariate scores;

and

$SP_{S/AB}$ = the sum of products based on the pairs of scores from both the covariate and the dependent variable.

Substituting in the general computational formula, we obtain

$$SS_{S/AB(\text{adj.})} = SS_{S/AB(y)} - \frac{(SP_{S/AB})^2}{SS_{S/AB(x)}}.$$

The degrees of freedom for the error term are specified in the lower portion of the table. These df are the same as those associated with the error term in the corresponding analysis of variance, *minus* 1. The loss of this df is due to the estimation of the overall within-group regression coefficient.

The adjustment of treatment sums of squares is accomplished "indirectly," as you saw in the single-factor design (see pp. 496–498). An inspection of the upper

Table 20-12 General Computational Formulas for the Analysis of Covariance

ADJUSTED SUMS OF SQUARES

Source	Adjusted Sum of Squares $(SS_{adj.})$
Treatment effect	$SS_{effect(adj.)} = SS_{effect(y)} - \left[\dfrac{(SP_{effect} + SP_{error})^2}{SS_{effect(x)} + SS_{error(x)}} - \dfrac{(SP_{error})^2}{SS_{error(x)}} \right]$
Error	$SS_{error(adj.)} = SS_{error(y)} - \dfrac{(SP_{error})^2}{SS_{error(x)}}$

SUMMARY OF THE ANALYSIS

Source	$SS_{adj.}$	df	$MS_{adj.}$	F
Treatment effect	$SS_{effect(adj.)}$	df_{effect}	$\dfrac{SS_{effect(adj.)}}{df_{effect}}$	$\dfrac{MS_{effect(adj.)}}{MS_{error(adj.)}}$
Error	$SS_{error(adj.)}$	$df_{error} - 1$	$\dfrac{SS_{error(adj.)}}{df_{error} - 1}$	

portion of Table 20-12 indicates that two quantities—the two ratios within the brackets—are involved in the adjustment, the first combining the sums of squares (or products) for the treatment effect *and* for error, and the second consisting of the error-term adjustment factor. For the single-factor design, the numerator of the first term is $(SP_A + SP_{S/A})^2$ and the denominator is $(SS_{A(x)} + SS_{S/A(x)})$.[9] Applying this formula to the A main effect in a two-factor design, we obtain

$$SS_{A(adj.)} = SS_{A(y)} - \left[\frac{(SP_A + SP_{S/AB})^2}{SS_{A(x)} + SS_{S/AB(x)}} - \frac{(SP_{S/AB})^2}{SS_{S/AB(x)}} \right].$$

The adjustments of the B main effect and the $A \times B$ interaction follow this same pattern, namely, treatment effect plus error. The degrees of freedom associated with the adjusted sums of squares for treatment effects are identical to those associated with the unadjusted sums of squares.

The remaining steps in the analysis are summarized in the lower portion of Table 20-12. The F ratio is formed by dividing the adjusted mean square for the treatment effect by the adjusted mean square for error. The significance of the F ratio is evaluated against the tabled value of F corresponding to the adjusted df's.

The computational scheme outlined in Table 20-12 can be extended to any factorial design. The adjusted mean squares for treatment effects are evaluated by the same error terms (adjusted, of course) as would be used in the usual analysis of variance. It will be noted that over *three times* as much computational effort is

[9]In Eq. (20-7) (p. 496) I expressed these two sums as $(SP_T)^2$ and $SS_{T(x)}$, respectively; the two sets of expressions are identical.

required for the analysis of covariance as for the standard analysis of variance. In essence, we must obtain the same set of sums of squares for the scores on the covariate, the scores on the dependent variable, and the products of these two sets of scores. The gain in precision can be considerable, however, and this increased efficiency may justify the extra computational effort.

For a numerical example of the analysis of covariance applied to a two-factor design, you might work through Exercise 2 at the end of this chapter. A worked example can be found in Winer (1971, pp. 788–792).

Designs with Repeated Measures

As you have seen, repeated-measures designs can greatly increase the sensitivity of an experiment. In effect, one can view the within-subjects design as a way to avoid the need for the analysis of covariance, since the adjustment process is accomplished about as well as possible by the within-subjects analysis. Under certain circumstances, however, the analysis of covariance can be used to increase the sensitivity of within-subjects designs. First, and most common, is the use of the analysis of covariance in conjunction with the *between-subjects factors* in mixed repeated-measures designs. What is done is to obtain scores on the covariate for all the subjects before any testing begins and to use this information to adjust sources of variance that represent only between-subjects differences; the within-subjects portion of the analysis remains unchanged. As you will see in a moment, this particular analysis is identical to that conducted with completely randomized designs. A second example is the use of the covariate to adjust *within*-subject sources as well, but this requires obtaining a different covariate score immediately before the administration of *each* of the treatments given to a subject. I will consider both cases briefly.

Between-Subjects Factor. With a single covariate score available for each subject, the analysis of covariance permits adjustments only for sources of variance involving differences between subjects. In the $A \times (B \times S)$ design, for example, where factor A is represented by independent groups of subjects and factor B is represented as a within-subjects manipulation, adjustments will be possible for the main effect of factor A and the between-subjects error term, S/A; none of the other sources—B, $A \times B$, and $B \times S/A$—will be affected by the analysis. The reason for this is that all of the scores obtained from any given subject on the dependent variable are associated with the *same* score on the covariate. Hence, there are no differences on the covariate to adjust for sources of variance in which repeated measures are involved.

The analysis of the mixed design is conducted by entering the X score b times in the ABS matrix, but focusing only on the quantities needed to adjust the adjustable sources of variance, in this case, A and S/A. If you prefer to perform the complete analysis of covariance on the entire set of scores, you will quickly discover that the various adjustment factors listed in the upper portion of Table 20-12 will equal zero for all of the within-subjects sources, i.e., for B, $A \times B$ and $B \times S/A$.

Winer (1971, pp. 796–805) discusses this point and illustrates the analysis with a useful numerical example. The attractiveness of this analysis is the possibility of increasing the sensitivity of that portion of the mixed design that normally does not benefit from a reduction in error variance in the standard repeated-measures analysis.

Within-Subjects Factor.   In the second situation, a covariate score is obtained before each of the treatments a subject receives. A common use of this type of arrangement is in the case when researchers feel that a subject's "resting" state, or before-test state, fluctuates unpredictably and adds "noise" to the critical determinations taken on the dependent variable under the experimental treatments. Analysis of covariance is then employed to remove as much of this variation from the Y scores as permitted by the linear relationship between the covariate and the dependent variable. This analysis follows the procedures summarized in Table 20-12. *All* sources of variance will be adjusted in this analysis, including each of the different error terms, since each Y score is now associated with a different X score. For worked examples of this type of analysis of covariance, see Myers (1979, pp. 424–428) and Winer (1971, pp. 805–808).

20.5 AN EVALUATION OF THE DIFFERENT CONTROL PROCEDURES

I began this chapter by drawing a distinction between two methods for increasing the precision of an experiment, namely, direct (or experimental) and statistical. As a reminder, the direct method achieves control of error variance by isolating sources normally included in the error term of the completely randomized design and removing them in the statistical analysis. In the Treatments × Blocks design, the introduction of the blocking factor into an experiment—e.g., IQ, reading-proficiency scores, socioeconomic status, sex, and so on—permits the removal from the error term of the blocking factor and its interactions with the treatment variables. In the within-subjects design, *subjects* become a blocking factor for which matching is perfect since the same subject is used in the different conditions. Statistical control, as exemplified by the analysis of covariance, uses *regression analysis* to achieve the increase in precision. I will now compare these procedures on a number of criteria.

Precision

Since the primary reason for turning to these methods is the hope of increasing precision, mainly in the refinement of the error term, it is reasonable to compare the different approaches on this important criterion. In most circumstances, within-subjects designs offer the most effective way of increasing the precision of an experiment. If the choice is between blocking and the analysis of covariance, Feldt (1958) has shown that blocking is more precise when the correlation between the covariate and the dependent variable is less than .4, while the analysis of covariance is more precise with correlations greater than .6. Since we rarely obtain correlations of this latter magnitude in the behavioral sciences, we will not find a unique advantage in the analysis of covariance in most research applications.

Assumptions

Both within-subjects designs and analyses of covariance require a number of specialized statistical assumptions. With the former, homogeneity of between-treatment differences and the absence of differential carry-over effects are assumptions that are critical for an unambiguous interpretation of the results of an experiment. With the latter, the most stringent is the assumption of homogeneous within-group regression coefficients. Both the analysis of covariance and the analysis of within-subjects designs are sensitive only to the *linear* relationship between *X* and *Y*, in the first case, and between pairs of treatment conditions in the second case. In contrast, the Treatments X Blocks design is sensitive to any type of relationship between treatments and blocks—not just linear. As Winer puts it, the Treatments X Blocks design "is a function-free regression scheme" (1971, p. 754). This is a major advantage of the Treatments X Blocks design. In short, the Treatments X Blocks design does not have restrictive assumptions and, for this reason, is to be preferred for its relative freedom from statistical assumptions underlying the data analysis.

Assessment of the Treatment X Block Interaction

While the presence of a Treatment X Block interaction can invalidate an analysis of covariance by producing heterogeneous within-group regression coefficients, the Treatments X Blocks design is capable of assessing the presence of an interaction directly. On the other hand, the analysis of covariance does permit us to test for the presence of heterogeneous regression coefficients and to study the heterogeneity as well. The corresponding interaction in the within-subjects design is the Treatment X Subject interaction, which is normally used as the error term in the statistical analysis. Tukey (1949) has developed a test for determining the presence of such interaction, although the test is not sensitive to all forms of interaction (Myers, 1979, pp. 185-186).[10] Another possibility is to design a within-subjects experiment with replication of treatments, i.e., one in which each subject is given two or more tests under each treatment condition. In this case, the Treatment X Subject interaction is evaluated with an error term based on the variation observed over the different replications (see Hays, 1973, pp. 546-550, for a discussion of this type of analysis).

[10]For a discussion and illustration of the Tukey test, known as the **test for nonadditivity**, see Kirk (1968, pp. 137-139) and Myers (1979, pp. 183-186). Winer (1971, pp. 473-478) discusses the test in the context of a completely randomized factorial design.

Estimating Treatment Effects

In comparison with the completely randomized designs, all three methods increase the precision with which treatment effects are estimated. The direct methods achieve this increase either through matching (in the Treatments X Blocks design) or by using the same subject in all of the treatment conditions (in the within-subjects design). The analysis of covariance, on the other hand, accomplishes this increase statistically by adjusting the treatment means for differences observed among groups on the covariate. As I mentioned earlier in this chapter, this aspect of the analysis of covariance is not expected to produce large changes in the analysis, especially when the sample size is reasonably large and the random assignment of subjects has had an "opportunity" to bring the groups close together prior to the start of the experiment.

But suppose the groups *do* differ widely on the covariate, so much so that these differences are significant when an analysis of variance is performed on them. Our interpretation of such an occurrence is to attribute the differences to the randomization procedure, since we do expect to find significant differences a known proportion of the time (i.e., α). Nevertheless, most researchers will still be suspicious of the results of the experiment itself—i.e., the scores on the dependent variable—or at least of the group or groups which apparently are the "deviant" ones. The analysis of covariance is a technique designed to adjust for chance differences among the groups, but for many researchers the adjustment of significant differences is still a cause for concern.

Another situation in which the analysis of covariance is questioned occurs frequently in educational research, where it is often convenient to assign the different experimental treatments to entire classes of school children. It would be rare for these intact groups to be equated on characteristics considered important for performance on the experimental task. Classes in school are usually not equated on such factors as IQ or grade-point average. Typically, useful information is available for each subject prior to the start of the experiment, so that the analysis of covariance appears to be an attractive means for adjusting differences among groups. Offhand, this use of the analysis of covariance seems appropriate. Unfortunately, it usually is not. That is, unless the intact groups are constituted randomly originally and treated identically during the period preceding the experiment, we can never be sure that differences among intact groups reflect a freedom from *systematic* bias. It is always possible, for example, that the groups differ on a number of uncontrolled variables for which we have no measure. We avoid this problem in a completely randomized experiment, since uncontrolled variables exert an *unsystematic* influence on the response measure and their influence is reflected in the estimate of error variance.[11]

---

[11]Useful discussions of the problem of using the analysis of covariance to adjust for differences in preexisting groups can be found in articles by Elashoff (1969), Lord (1967, 1969), Overall and Woodward (1977), and Weisberg (1979). An interesting debate on this issue has also appeared in the literature. See, for example, Evans and Anastasio (1968), Harris, Bisbee, and Evans (1971), Maxwell and Cramer (1975), and Sprott (1970). Huitema (1980, Ch. 7) offers a comprehensive treatment of this general problem.

514

Finally, the analysis of covariance covered in this chapter adjusts only for the *linear* effects of the covariate, although it is possible to extend the analysis to include adjustments for higher-order relationships between the covariate and the dependent variable (see Cohen and Cohen, 1975, Chapter 9 and Huitema, 1980, Chapter 9). When the relationship between X and Y is not linear, the interpretation of the adjusted treatment effects is very much open to question.

20.6 EXERCISES[12]

1. The subjects for this experiment were assigned randomly to the $a = 3$ different levels of the independent variable. The covariate scores were obtained prior to the administration of the experimental treatments. The AS matrix is given below.

AS MATRIX

a_1		a_2		a_3	
X	Y	X	Y	X	Y
2	11	5	15	2	12
1	8	3	12	2	9
4	8	1	16	5	8
1	9	3	19	1	11
3	7	3	16	3	7
5	9	5	20	1	7

   (a) Perform an analysis of covariance on these data.
   (b) Do you feel that the experimenter benefited from the introduction of the covariate into the statistical analysis? Be specific.
2. Consider the following factorial design and the scores produced by the $s = 4$ subjects in each of the treatment conditions. The covariate scores were obtained before the start of the experiment, and the subjects were assigned randomly to the conditions without knowledge of these scores.

ABS MATRIX

ab_{11}		ab_{12}		ab_{13}		ab_{21}		ab_{22}		ab_{23}		ab_{31}		ab_{32}		ab_{33}	
X	Y	X	Y	X	Y	X	Y	X	Y	X	Y	X	Y	X	Y	X	Y
2	11	5	9	2	12	4	15	6	19	3	8	3	12	2	11	1	10
1	8	5	7	3	7	5	12	4	16	4	9	2	9	3	7	5	9
5	8	1	9	4	6	3	16	3	20	4	7	5	8	4	7	3	7
4	7	3	10	1	11	4	14	5	15	1	10	2	10	3	9	4	11

   (a) With the help of Table 20–12 (p. 510), construct the computational formulas necessary to conduct an analysis of covariance with this particular experiment.
   (b) Perform an analysis of covariance on these data.

[12]The answers to these problems are found in Appendix B, beginning on p. 607.

21

Generalizing Results and Other Theoretical Considerations

The primary focus of this chapter is a consideration of the theoretical basis for generalizing the results of an experiment. Central to this process is the concept of random factors, which I discussed briefly in connection with nested experimental designs in Chapter 12. As you will see, the presence of random factors in an experiment complicates the evaluation process by changing the way F tests are constructed. I will begin by discussing the generalization process. Next, I will define fixed and random factors and demonstrate why a change of error term is required in the statistical analysis of experiments with random factors. I will then show how we can determine which source or combination of sources satisfies the criteria required for an error term in the analysis of variance.

21.1 GENERALIZING RESULTS

The results of nearly any experiment can be extended beyond the specific boundary conditions under which it is conducted. On the other hand, however, there are definite limits to the "length" of these generalizations, and you should understand the factors restricting the scope of an experiment. In a very real sense, every experiment is unique; no two experiments are ever alike. How can a science build on such highly specific findings to create generalizations that apply to wide ranges of situations, settings, and individuals? I will consider two bases for generalizing results: statistical and nonstatistical.

Nonstatistical Generalization

Experiments are designed to fit in with a tradition of research on a particular topic. While no two experiments are ever exactly the same, it is also the case that they tend to differ in ways that researchers have found are not critical for the study of a given phenomenon. In a memory experiment, for example, the length of the list, the rate of presentation, the time of day, and the sex of the subjects are probably not critical, in the sense that changes in the setting of these and many other factors do not influence the basic outcome of the results. Stated more formally, noncritical factors are factors that are known not to interact with the manipulations under study. A researcher's knowledge of these apparently nonfunctional differences among experiments permits an extension of a set of findings beyond the particular set of conditions existing for a single study. Occasionally, nonstatistical generalizations of this sort are found to be incorrect, at which time the critical factors are identified and often become the object of study in subsequent experiments.

Nonstatistical generalization depends on the results of related experiments that vary in a number of different ways. The greater the variation among experiments in which the outcome remains the same, the greater the generalization provided to other situations and settings. Unfortunately, there is an understandable tendency for researchers to reduce the variation from study to study, to duplicate procedures, to use the same manipulations—in short, to *standardize* the nonessential features of an experiment. Some years ago, Irion (1959, pp. 546-549) argued that the absence of standardization of experiments was responsible for the slow progress of research in certain fields. Obviously, some sort of balance must be achieved between standardization, which limits generalization, and variation among experiments, which increases generalization.[1]

A common solution to the problem of deciding between standardization and variation is to introduce systematic variation into an experiment as additional independent variables—control factors, as I have called them—and to determine directly whether these factors interact with the independent variables of primary interest. The absence of interactions between the control factors and the factors of systematic interest means that any conclusion drawn from the study generalizes over the control factors included in the experiment. A significant interaction, on the other hand, means that the results are associated with a particular combination of treatment and control factors, an outcome that severely limits the generality of the findings. That is, the presence of an interaction between stimulus sets or presentation orders, for example, indicates that conclusions drawn from the experiment must be more circumscribed than they are already. This is the case if a given effect appears and disappears with different sets of materials, or the size of an effect varies with the different presentation orders. I discussed this type of experimental design in Chapter 15 (pp. 339-340).

Statistical Generalization

A less common, but increasingly popular, way of increasing the generalizability of results is the use of random factors and statistical theory to generalize the findings of an experiment. As an example, consider an experiment in which a researcher is interested in studying the reading comprehension of subjects under varying degrees of alcohol intoxication. Suppose that several passages are included in the experimental design as a crossed factor, i.e., each passage is presented to subjects an equal number of times under the different treatment conditions. A test of the passages X treatments interaction would determine whether the results generalize across the passages tested in the experiment. However, most researchers would be interested in a more far-reaching generalization, namely, generalizing the results across passages *in general*. This is where random factors and statistical generalization enter the picture. If the passages can be properly viewed as representing a *random sample* drawn from a large population of passages, then statistical theory provides a procedure for generalizing to the larger population. The remainder of this chapter is primarily concerned with this type of statistical analysis.

---

[1] The role of replications in experimentation was discussed in Chapter 4 (pp. 73-76).

Distinction between Fixed and Random Factors

The distinction between fixed and random factors centers on the manner in which one conceptualizes the population of treatment conditions and the way in which the levels of the independent variable are selected from the population. To qualify as a **fixed factor**, the levels of an independent variable are selected arbitrarily and systematically, and are assumed to represent the entire population of treatment conditions in which a researcher has theoretical interest. Thus, statistical generalizations are limited to the treatment effects observed with these particular treatment conditions. In contrast, to qualify as a **random factor**, the levels of an independent variable are selected either *randomly* or *unsystematically* from a larger pool of possible levels and are assumed to represent a *random sample* obtained from this larger population of treatment conditions. In this case, then, statistical generalization extends beyond those levels included in the experiment.

In spite of this apparently important difference in the generalizability of results, most independent variables manipulated in the behavioral sciences are treated as *fixed* by researchers in the statistical analyses reported in the journals. Any extension of findings to conditions not included in an experiment is based on nonstatistical rather than on statistical considerations and arguments. There are two major reasons for this. First, for many independent variables, the levels included in an experiment effectively exhaust the pool of possible levels. There may be only two or three drugs that produce a particular effect or only a handful of teaching methods that can be considered realistic alternatives to be used in a classroom. Under these circumstances, there is no need to generalize, since as far as the researcher is concerned, *all* of the levels of the factor are included in the experiment.

A second and related point is that a researcher usually chooses the levels to be *representative* of the independent variable. Suppose we are varying the intensity of background noise in a psychophysical investigation and we decide to include four levels of this variable in our experiment. If we consider the potential levels of the variable that we could use in our experiment, the number is exceedingly large. Even so, most researchers would not select the four levels randomly from this pool of potential levels. Instead they would be influenced by some or all of the following considerations: (1) whether to represent the full extent of the effective stimulus dimension in the experiment; (2) whether to choose levels that are expected to produce a reasonably large difference between adjacent levels; and (3) whether to attempt to "hit" points of inflection—points where there might be a change in the direction of the functional relation. *These* are the overriding considerations in the selection of the four levels, and they certainly are *not* met by a random selection procedure, which gives equal weight to all possible levels of the variable. With random selection there is no guarantee that the important points along the dimensions will be represented in the experiment.

In most of the examples of random factors found in statistics books, it is clear that the variable is not to be *manipulated* but to be *sampled,* and that the interest centers around statistical generalization. For instance, an educator who wants to try out a number of methods of teaching reading (a fixed factor) in the second grade may choose as a second independent variable *schools* within a particular city or state. Although not all the second-graders in question can be included in the experiment, the researcher clearly wants to extend any conclusions to the total population of students. Thus, schools become a random factor. Other examples of random factors might include (1) a sampling of the personalities of different experimenters, (2) the order of presenting a large set of material, (3) hospitals in a particular locality, and (4) raters and ratees from different political parties.

It is important to point out that we do not have fixed or random factors in the world, but rather different structural models we impose on the world when we design an experiment. Thus, the independent variable schools becomes a fixed or a random factor only in the context of an actual experiment where decisions are made to include all or only a portion of the potential levels in the study. In addition, you should keep in mind that the structural model adopted for an experiment usually only approximates the formal statistical model on which it is based. It will frequently be the case that even when the levels of an independent variable are not chosen randomly, the factor may still be viewed as random by a researcher since the experimental situation does represent a reasonably close approximation of the random model and the researcher wishes to generalize his or her results to the levels of the factor not included in the study.

The Effect of Random Factors on the Analysis

In Sections 21.2 and 21.3, I will discuss in detail the analysis of experiments with random factors. At this point, however, I simply want to show that the analyses are different and to offer some intuitive arguments why. I will present the discussion in the context of research in which investigators study the influence of semantic and linguistic factors on such cognitive processes as perception, learning, memory, problem solving, and thinking. An early paper by Coleman (1964) introduced the problem in the context of a repeated-measures design in which the control and treatment factors cross. Clark (1973), in a widely read and influential paper, extended the problem to designs in which control factors are nested. Both papers, which together provide a useful introduction to the issues, have sparked debate and controversy.[2] Santa, Miller, and Shaw (1979) point out that random control factors are found in major fields of psychology outside the cognitive area, e.g., clinical, developmental, educational, and social psychology (see pp. 37–40 of that article for examples and discussion). In short, the topic is current and of general interest to researchers in the behavioral sciences. I will consider the analysis of experiments with nested and crossed random factors separately.

---

[2]See the paper by Wike and Church (1976) and the discussion of this paper and the general problem by Clark (1976), Cohen (1976), Keppel (1976), and Smith (1976).

Nested Random Factors. The Clark article (1973) concentrated on a hypothetical experiment comparing reading speeds for two types of words, nouns and verbs. From a dictionary, a random sample of each word type is selected. The words in each sample constitute a second independent variable that happens to be nested within word type—the set of nouns is completely unrelated to the set of verbs. Assume for the moment that the null hypothesis is true, i.e., that nouns and verbs in the population do not differ in the speed with which they can be read by subjects. While we would expect to find no difference in the reading speeds for the two types of words when averaged over many independent experiments in which different random samples were obtained, we would certainly expect to find a difference between nouns and verbs in a single experiment. That is, we would expect *random sampling* to produce a set of nouns that on the average will be either easier to read than a set of verbs or more difficult to read. There is nothing mysterious about this process, just the operation of chance factors favoring one of the conditions over the other. Stated another way, the random selection of words introduces a *confounding* of the materials chosen for the experiment with the treatment factor.

The problem, then, is to compare the variation observed between nouns and verbs with an error term that specifically includes this particular sampling factor. To anticipate, this is accomplished by analyzing the data at the individual word level, using the variation among words of the same type to provide an estimate of the sampling error that is influencing to some extent the difference observed between the overall mean for the nouns and the overall mean for the verbs. You may recall a similar argument when I considered nested factors in Chapter 12 (pp. 262–263). I will discuss the analysis of three different experimental designs adapted to this hypothetical study in Section 21.3.

Crossed Random Factors. Let's return to the example of reading comprehension and levels of intoxication (factor A). In this case, the second independent variable (factor B), passages, crosses with the factor of primary interest. We start with the linear model for this design, presented originally in Chapter 10 as

$$ABS_{ijk} = \mu + \alpha_i + \beta_j + \alpha\beta_{ij} + \epsilon_{ijk},$$

where μ is the overall mean, α_i is the main effect of factor A at level a_i, β_j is the main effect of factor B at level b_j, $\alpha\beta_{ij}$ is the interaction effect at the treatment combination $a_i b_j$, and ϵ_{ijk} is experimental error. A critical requirement of a fixed factor is that the sum of the separate treatment effects (deviations) equals zero. For example, factor A is a fixed factor if

$$\Sigma_i (\mu_i - \mu) = 0.$$

Since μ is the mean of all of the μ_i's and since all of the levels of factor A are included in the experiment (and thus all of the μ_i's are included also), the sum of the deviations of the μ_i's from the overall mean μ must equal zero. In an $A \times B$ experiment with both factors fixed,

$$\Sigma\, (\mu_i - \mu) = \Sigma\, \alpha_i = 0,$$

$$\Sigma\, (\mu_j - \mu) = \Sigma\, \beta_j = 0,$$

and

$$\Sigma\, (\mu_{ij} - \mu_i - \mu_j + \mu) = \Sigma\, \alpha\beta_{ij} = 0.$$

Additionally, the interaction effects sum to zero for any row and for any column; otherwise, they would become part of a main effect. In symbols,

$$\sum_{i=1}^{a} \alpha\beta_{ij} = 0 \quad \text{and} \quad \sum_{j=1}^{b} \alpha\beta_{ij} = 0. \tag{21-1}$$

Under these assumptions, then, the $MS_{S/AB}$ is the appropriate error term for evaluating the significance of the two main effects and the $A \times B$ interaction.

A different situation exists for an experiment with a random factor present. Staying within the context of a two-way factorial, we can think of an AB matrix in which all possible levels of factor A are listed in one direction and all possible levels of factor B are listed in the other direction. Included in the cells of this matrix are the population interaction effects (the $\alpha\beta_{ij}$ terms). For this *potential AB* matrix, Eq. (21-1) holds both for rows and for columns. If both independent variables are fixed factors, the potential AB matrix and the AB matrix actually represented in the experiment are the same. This is not true, however, if one or both of the factors are random.

Let's assume that the passages are selected randomly from linguistic sources. This means that we would select at random b levels of factor B from the total population of levels present in the potential AB matrix, while we would include all of the levels of factor A. Suppose we examine the consequences of crossing a random factor (factor B) with a fixed factor (factor A). A potential AB matrix is presented in the upper portion of Table 21-1. (For convenience the potential number of levels of factor B has been made small.) Entered in the body of the matrix are numbers representing the $\alpha\beta_{ij}$ interaction effects. Notice that for each row and column of this matrix, the sum of the effects equals zero. For purposes of this discussion, I will assume that there are no main effects in the population; thus, interaction effects are all that should be present. What this means is that we can specify the population cell means (the μ_{ij}'s) by simply knowing the appropriate $\alpha\beta_{ij}$ interaction effect and the overall mean μ. That is,

$$\mu_{ij} = \alpha\beta_{ij} + \alpha_i + \beta_j + \mu$$

$$= \alpha\beta_{ij} + 0 + 0 + \mu$$

$$= \alpha\beta_{ij} + \mu.$$

If we set $\mu = 10$ and then add this quantity to all of the $\alpha\beta_{ij}$'s, we obtain an AB matrix of population means (the μ_{ij}'s). This matrix appears in the middle portion of Table 21-1. If we include *all levels* of the two factors in our experiment, both

Table 21-1 A Potential AB Matrix Contrasted with an Actual AB Matrix

POTENTIAL AB MATRIX: $\alpha\beta_{ij}$ INTERACTION EFFECTS

Potential Levels of Factor A	Potential Levels of Factor B					Sum
	b_1	b_2	b_3	b_4	b_5	
a_1	3	2	−1	−2	−2	0
a_2	3	−1	1	−5	2	0
a_3	1	−2	3	−1	−1	0
a_4	−7	1	−3	8	1	0
Sum	0	0	0	0	0	

POTENTIAL AB MATRIX: POPULATION MEANS (μ_{ij})

Potential Levels of Factor A	Potential Levels of Factor B					Mean
	b_1	b_2	b_3	b_4	b_5	
a_1	13	12	9	8	8	10
a_2	13	9	11	5	12	10
a_3	11	8	13	9	9	10
a_4	3	11	7	18	11	10
Mean	10	10	10	10	10	

ACTUAL AB MATRIX: POPULATION MEANS (μ_{ij})

Levels of Factor A	Levels of Factor B[a]			Mean
	$b_1(b_2)$	$b_2(b_3)$	$b_3(b_5)$	
a_1	12	9	8	9.7
a_2	9	11	12	10.7
a_3	8	13	9	10.0
a_4	11	7	11	9.7
Mean	10.0	10.0	10.0	

[a]Corresponding levels in the AB matrix are indicated in parentheses.

main effects will be zero; this is because all of the row means are equal (the μ_i's) and all of the column means are equal (the μ_j's). On the other hand, there will be an interaction present. (We knew this from the upper matrix.)

In our example, however, we are going to sample randomly from the potential levels of factor B, but include *all* levels of factor A. One of the possible AB matrices is presented in the lower portion of Table 21-1. In this matrix I have simply taken three entire columns from the AB matrix of μ_{ij}'s given in the middle portion of the table. Consider what will happen to the main effects in this new matrix. For the random independent variable (factor B) the column marginal means are still equal, and therefore, the main effect will be zero. For the fixed independent variable (factor A), on the other hand, the row marginal means are *not* equal; consequently, a main effect will be observed.

This demonstration shows us that with a random independent variable present in a two-factor design, the $\alpha\beta_{ij}$ interaction effects will *intrude* upon the main effect of the other independent variable. If the situation had been reversed, with factor B fixed and factor A random, the main effect of factor B would have been affected by any interaction effects present. If both factors had been random, both main effects would have been affected by the interaction effects. The practical conclusion from this demonstration is that with random factors present, the expected values of main effects will contain the interaction component in addition to the components for the main effect and experimental error. This means that we will have to search for new error terms, since the expected value of the within-group mean square ($MS_{S/AB}$ in this example) will continue to be σ_ϵ^2.

Comment

The issue frequently arises that control factors are not fixed, in the sense that they do not enumerate all levels of interest to the researcher, but are not randomly selected from some clearly defined population, either. It is at this point that you remind yourself that, in the world of experimentation, structural models only approximate any given experimental application and that it is up to you to determine whether it is better to view the factor as random or as fixed. Myers (1979, pp. 193-194) offers useful advice by suggesting that a control factor should be classified as random if independent investigators could have selected other sets of material and that each set in such an admittedly poorly defined population has an equally likely chance of being included in the experiment. Again, it will be a matter of judgment whether any particular study reasonably fits these two criteria.

Even if random sampling has not been followed but the levels chosen clearly do not constitute the population, it is probably a good idea to treat the factor as random nevertheless. The reason for this advice is that there is a real possibility that the "random" factor will still intrude on treatment effects of interest, and this real possibility should be assessed statistically. Thus, from a practical point of view, error terms appropriate for random effects might be required even though the extent of the statistical generalization possible is limited by the failure to sample randomly. In any case, random factors, or "quasi-random" factors, pose serious problems for the statistical analysis and evaluation of treatment effects.

I will now turn to the details of the statistical analyses required when random factors are present. Section 21.2 examines the analysis of designs in which the random factor is crossed, and Section 21.3 covers the analysis of designs in which the random factor is nested.

21.2 ANALYSIS OF DESIGNS WITH CROSSED RANDOM FACTORS

Most of the analyses we have considered in this book have assumed that the independent variables represent fixed effects. This assumption, which is appropriate for the vast majority of the research conducted in the behavioral sciences, has permitted the use of fairly simple rules specifying the details of the statistical analysis, including the selection of appropriate error terms. The introduction of random factors into an experiment can change the theoretical basis of the analysis sufficiently that the rules I have presented in earlier chapters no longer apply and a new strategy must be adopted. This strategy involves examining the expected values of the mean squares normally obtained in a standard analysis of variance in the search for appropriate error terms to evaluate treatment sources of variance. In all cases, however, the goal is to create a ratio having the form

$$\frac{treatment + error}{error},$$

in which *treatment* refers to the treatment effects of interest—i.e., the null-hypothesis component—and *error* refers to unsystematic sources of variability. The whole problem is to figure out exactly what is meant by *error*, and this is precisely where a specification of expected values becomes useful.

Criterion for Selection

The basic criterion for selecting an error term can be stated as follows:

A mean square qualifies as an error term if its expected value matches the expected value of the MS_{effect} in all respects except the null-hypothesis component.

To aid in this selection, authors usually present tables showing the expected values for the different sources. Sometimes they actually list the variance components for the different arrangements of fixed and random independent variables. A more efficient display consists of a listing of the variance components that remain or drop out depending upon the nature of the different independent variables [see Winer (1971, p. 346) for a comprehensive example with a three-factor design]. In whatever way the expected values are listed, the selection procedure is the same: The variance components of the different sources are compared with the variance components of the effect, and an error term is discovered when a source matches the expectation of the effect except for the component reflecting the effect.

Since it is not practical to present such tables for higher-order factorials, most authors offer some sort of mechanical scheme for actually writing the expected values for each term listed in the analysis-of-variance summary table.[3] You will find such a scheme in Appendix C-4 if you are curious about the inner workings of this sort of system or if you need to obtain expected values for mean squares not covered in the reference books at your disposal.

Examples

Completely Randomized Two-Way Factorial Design. As our first illustration, consider the possible arrangements of fixed and random independent variables in the completely randomized two-way factorial design specified in Table 21-2. In the first case, both factors are fixed. You will notice that the expected value for each factorial effect consists of two terms, error variance (σ_ϵ^2) and the null-hypothesis component; the expected value of the within-groups source $MS_{S/AB}$ is σ_ϵ^2. It is obvious that this latter source is the appropriate error term for each of the factorial effects.

The next two cases are examples in which one factor is fixed and the other is random. In the first of these, the random factor is B. You should note several changes in the expected values occurring with this model. First, the symbol used to designate the null-hypothesis component for the MS_B is σ_B^2 rather than θ_B^2, indicating that this factor is random. Second, the null-hypothesis component for the $A \times B$ interaction represents a random effect rather than a fixed effect. In general, any interaction involving one or more random factors is random. Finally, the expected value of the A main effect consists of *three* terms: error variance, the null-hypothesis component, *and* the null-hypothesis component for the interaction. Because of this third term, the within-groups mean square is no longer appropriate as an error term for evaluating this factorial effect, but the interaction mean square is. That is, the expected value of the interaction exactly matches the expected value of the A main effect except for the null-hypothesis component, satisfying the criterion for the F test.

In the third case, factor A is random and factor B is fixed. An inspection of Table 21-2 shows a pattern similar to the second case. That is, the B main effect now contains the interaction component, requiring the use of the interaction mean square as the error term for assessing the significance of this effect.

In the final case, both factors are random.[4] Under these circumstances, the expected values of the two main effects contain the interaction component in addition to experimental error and the null-hypothesis component. The error

---

[3]See, for example, Glass and Stanley (1970, pp. 479–481), Kirk (1968, pp. 208–212), Lindman (1974, pp. 151–154; 180–181), Myers (1979, pp. 205–206), and Winer (1971, pp. 371–375).

[4]The two "pure" cases—all fixed factors or all random factors—are often called the **fixed-effect** and **random-effect** models, respectively. The "heterogeneous" cases are often called mixed models, but this terminology is easily confused with certain repeated-measures designs in which both between-subjects and within-subjects factors are present and which are also called *mixed* designs.

Table 21-2 Expected Values of Mean Squares for Special Cases of the Completely Randomized $A \times B$ Factorial Design

(1) BOTH FACTORS FIXED

Source	$E(MS)$	Error Term
A	$\sigma_\epsilon^2 + b(s)(\theta_A^2)$	S/AB
B	$\sigma_\epsilon^2 + a(s)(\theta_B^2)$	S/AB
$A \times B$	$\sigma_\epsilon^2 + s(\theta_{A \times B}^2)$	S/AB
S/AB	σ_ϵ^2	

(2) FACTOR A FIXED; FACTOR B RANDOM

Source	$E(MS)$	Error Term
A	$\sigma_\epsilon^2 + s(\sigma_{A \times B}^2) + b(s)(\theta_A^2)$	$A \times B$
B	$\sigma_\epsilon^2 + a(s)(\sigma_B^2)$	S/AB
$A \times B$	$\sigma_\epsilon^2 + s(\sigma_{A \times B}^2)$	S/AB
S/AB	σ_ϵ^2	

(3) FACTOR A RANDOM; FACTOR B FIXED

Source	$E(MS)$	Error Term
A	$\sigma_\epsilon^2 + b(s)(\sigma_A^2)$	S/AB
B	$\sigma_\epsilon^2 + s(\sigma_{A \times B}^2) + a(s)(\theta_B^2)$	$A \times B$
$A \times B$	$\sigma_\epsilon^2 + s(\sigma_{A \times B}^2)$	S/AB
S/AB	σ_ϵ^2	

(4) BOTH FACTORS RANDOM

Source	$E(MS)$	Error Term
A	$\sigma_\epsilon^2 + s(\sigma_{A \times B}^2) + b(s)(\sigma_A^2)$	$A \times B$
B	$\sigma_\epsilon^2 + s(\sigma_{A \times B}^2) + a(s)(\sigma_B^2)$	$A \times B$
$A \times B$	$\sigma_\epsilon^2 + s(\sigma_{A \times B}^2)$	S/AB
S/AB	σ_ϵ^2	

term for both main effects is $MS_{A \times B}$; the error term for the interaction continues to be $MS_{S/AB}$.

Completely Randomized Three-Way Factorial Design. A second illustration considers two arrangements of fixed and random factors in the completely randomized three-way factorial design. The first is the typical situation in which all three independent factors are fixed. The expected mean squares for each source of variance normally obtained in the analysis of variance for this case are presented on the left side of Table 21-3. The expected value for each factorial effect consists of σ_ϵ^2 and the relevant null-hypothesis component; the expected value of $MS_{S/ABC}$ is σ_ϵ^2. As you can see, the within-groups mean square is the appropriate error term for all of the factorial effects in the analysis.

The second example specifies factor A random and the other two factors fixed. If you examine the expected mean squares closely, you will see that factorial effects involving factor A (A, $A \times B$, $A \times C$, and $A \times B \times C$) consist of σ_ϵ^2 and the null-hypothesis component. Since $E(MS_{S/ABC}) = \sigma_\epsilon^2$, the within-groups mean square serves as the error term for these sources of variance. Each of the remaining factorial effects (B, C, and $B \times C$) contains a *third* component, the interaction of the effect with factor A. The intrusion of interactions with the random factor into these expected values means that the within-groups mean square cannot be used as the error term for these sources of variance. As indicated in Table 21-3, the error terms consist of mean squares reflecting the interaction of the relevant source with the random factor—i.e., B is tested by $A \times B$; C is tested by $A \times C$; and $B \times C$ is tested by $A \times B \times C$.

Repeated Measures. Our final example considers two possible arrangements of fixed and random factors in the most common repeated-measures design—the $A \times (B \times S)$ design, in which independent groups of subjects are assigned to the different levels of factor A but are given all combinations of that level with the levels of factor B. The first case represents the model assumed in Chapter 18, namely, the model in which both factors are fixed. The expected values of the standard sources of variance extracted for this design are presented on the left in Table 21-4.

As you will recall, this design requires the use of two error terms, one to assess between-subjects differences ($MS_{S/A}$) and the other to assess within-subjects differences ($MS_{B \times S/A}$). An inspection of the expected mean squares indicates why. The expected mean square for the within-subjects error term contains two components, σ_ϵ^2 and $\sigma_{B \times S/A}^2$. The first is often referred to as *measurement error*, the variability that one would expect if a subject were repeatedly tested in the same treatment condition, together with so-called nuisance factors that vary randomly in an experiment. The second reflects the interaction of the B treatments with subjects. In the usual design, these two components cannot be disentangled, even though they are assumed to exist apart theoretically. The expected values for the two factorial effects involving repeated measures, B and $A \times B$, contain these two error components plus the relevant null-hypothesis component, which indicates why $MS_{B \times S/A}$ is the error term for these two sources of variance.

Table 21-3 Expected Values of Mean Squares for Two Special Cases of the Completely Randomized $A \times B \times C$ Factorial Design

	ALL FACTORS FIXED		FACTOR A RANDOM; FACTORS B AND C FIXED	
Source	Expected Mean Square		Expected Mean Square	Error Term
A	$\sigma_\epsilon^2 + b(c)(s)(\theta_A^2)$		$\sigma_\epsilon^2 + b(c)(s)(\sigma_A^2)$	S/ABC
B	$\sigma_\epsilon^2 + a(c)(s)(\theta_B^2)$		$\sigma_\epsilon^2 + c(s)(\sigma_{A \times B}^2) + a(c)(s)(\theta_B^2)$	$A \times B$
C	$\sigma_\epsilon^2 + a(b)(s)(\theta_C^2)$		$\sigma_\epsilon^2 + b(s)(\sigma_{A \times C}^2) + a(b)(s)(\theta_C^2)$	$A \times C$
$A \times B$	$\sigma_\epsilon^2 + c(s)(\theta_{A \times B}^2)$		$\sigma_\epsilon^2 + c(s)(\sigma_{A \times B}^2)$	S/ABC
$A \times C$	$\sigma_\epsilon^2 + b(s)(\theta_{A \times C}^2)$		$\sigma_\epsilon^2 + b(s)(\sigma_{A \times C}^2)$	S/ABC
$B \times C$	$\sigma_\epsilon^2 + a(s)(\theta_{B \times C}^2)$		$\sigma_\epsilon^2 + s(\sigma_{A \times B \times C}^2) + a(s)(\theta_{B \times C}^2)$	$A \times B \times C$
$A \times B \times C$	$\sigma_\epsilon^2 + s(\theta_{A \times B \times C}^2)$		$\sigma_\epsilon^2 + s(\sigma_{A \times B \times C}^2)$	S/ABC
S/ABC	σ_ϵ^2		σ_ϵ^2	

Table 21-4 Expected Values of Mean Squares for Two Special Cases of the $A \times (B \times S)$ Design

	BOTH FACTORS FIXED		FACTOR A RANDOM; FACTOR B FIXED	
Source	Expected Mean Square	Error Term	Expected Mean Square	Error Term
A	$\sigma_\epsilon^2 + b(\sigma_{S/A}^2) + b(s)(\theta_A^2)$	S/A	$\sigma_\epsilon^2 + b(\sigma_{S/A}^2) + b(s)(\sigma_A^2)$	S/A
S/A	$\sigma_\epsilon^2 + b(\sigma_{S/A}^2)$		$\sigma_\epsilon^2 + b(\sigma_{S/A}^2)$	
B	$\sigma_\epsilon^2 + \sigma_{B \times S/A}^2 + a(s)(\theta_B^2)$	$B \times S/A$	$\sigma_\epsilon^2 + \sigma_{B \times S/A}^2 + s(\sigma_{A \times B}^2) + a(s)(\theta_B^2)$	$A \times B$
$A \times B$	$\sigma_\epsilon^2 + \sigma_{B \times S/A}^2 + s(\theta_{A \times B}^2)$	$B \times S/A$	$\sigma_\epsilon^2 + \sigma_{B \times S/A}^2 + s(\sigma_{A \times B}^2)$	$B \times S/A$
$B \times S/A$	$\sigma_\epsilon^2 + \sigma_{B \times S/A}^2$		$\sigma_\epsilon^2 + \sigma_{B \times S/A}^2$	

The expected mean square for the between-subjects error term $(MS_{S/A})$ also contains two components, σ_ϵ^2 and $b(\sigma_{S/A}^2)$. The first is measurement error and the second is the variability among the subjects in the treatment populations assumed to exist for each level of factor A. Again, these two components cannot be disentangled. As you can see from the table, this mean square qualifies as the error term for the A main effect, since the two sets of expected values are matched except for the null-hypothesis component for A.

The second example in Table 21-4 assumes that factor A is random and factor B is fixed. As you would suspect from the two-factor case considered previously (Table 21-2, case 3), the main complication will be the intrusion of the $A \times B$ interaction into the expected value of the *fixed* factor, MS_B. The consequence of adding this component to the expected value of the B main effect is to change the error term from $MS_{B \times S/A}$ to $MS_{A \times B}$, for it is with this new error term that the expected values are matched except for the null-hypothesis component for the main effect of factor B.

Comment. The selection of error terms is a relatively simple matter, provided you have a table of expected mean squares handy! In fact, it is even possible to devise schemes that lead to the correct error term for any source, bypassing the specification of expected mean squares completely. In the earlier edition of this book, I presented three charts that performed this function, one for completely randomized factorial designs (Table 16-2, p. 340), one for completely randomized nested designs (Table 18-9, p. 384), and one for repeated-measures designs (Table 21-3, p. 468). The problem with that system is that it finds only those error terms consisting of single sources of variance—such as the examples we have considered in this section. The system does not help a researcher when the error term consists of some *combination* of two or more mean squares, as can happen when several random factors are included in an experiment, and particularly when random factors are introduced in repeated-measures designs. It is at this point that you will need some way of determining the expected values of the mean squares obtained in your analysis. I will consider examples of this special sort of error term next.

Quasi *F* Ratios

In Table 21-4, you saw how the error term for the main effect of factor B changes from $MS_{B \times S/A}$—the usual error term when both factors are fixed—to $MS_{A \times B}$ when factor A is random and factor B is fixed. Consider what happens when the situation is reversed and factor B is random and factor A is fixed. The expected values for the different sources of variance are presented in Table 21-5. Let's determine the error term for the A main effect. From the two previous examples presented in Table 21-4, we would expect to use $MS_{S/A}$ or perhaps $MS_{A \times B}$. An inspection of the expected value for the A main effect listed in Table 21-5 indicates that *four* terms must be matched by the expected value of a source of variance if it is to serve as an error term, namely,

$$\sigma_\epsilon^2, \quad \sigma_{B \times S/A}^2, \quad s(\sigma_{A \times B}^2), \quad \text{and} \quad b(\sigma_{S/A}^2).$$

A further inspection of the expected values of the remaining sources in the table reveals that *none* provides this necessary match. An *F* test cannot be found.

Two solutions are possible. The first is to test the $A \times B$ interaction for significance. If it is *not* significant, we might be willing to drop the interaction term from the $E(MS_A)$ and then use the $MS_{S/A}$—which now provides the necessary match—as the error term. On the other hand, if the *F is* significant, more attention will be directed toward the analysis of the *interaction* than toward the main effects and the problem with the error term will seemingly be avoided. I do not recommend this particular strategy, for several reasons. First, there is no agreement concerning the conditions under which a term can be dropped from a statistical model. Usually, one is expected to have available strong evidence from independent research that the interaction is either quite small or does not exist. Second, a researcher may have an interest in testing the *A* main effect regardless of the significance of the interaction. In this case, the problem of the error term still remains. Finally, there is a more acceptable procedure, which I will now consider.

While we are unable in this design to find a single term to provide the matching of terms, we can find a match by combining several of them. More specifically, the $E(MS_{S/A})$ does include three of the four terms needed, and the $E(MS_{A \times B})$ contains the remaining term. If we add these two mean squares, we will have a new mean square that contains the four critical terms and two repeats, that is, σ_ϵ^2 and $\sigma_{B \times S/A}^2$. These two extra terms can be eliminated by subtracting $MS_{B \times S/A}$ from the sum. That is,

$$
\begin{aligned}
E(MS_{\text{denom.}}) &= E(MS_{S/A}) + E(MS_{A \times B}) - E(MS_{B \times S/A}) \\
&= [\sigma_\epsilon^2 + \sigma_{B \times S/A}^2 + b(\sigma_{S/A}^2)] \\
&\quad + [\sigma_\epsilon^2 + \sigma_{B \times S/A}^2 + s(\sigma_{A \times B}^2)] \\
&\quad - [\sigma_\epsilon^2 + \sigma_{B \times S/A}^2] \\
&= \sigma_\epsilon^2 + \sigma_{B \times S/A}^2 + b(\sigma_{S/A}^2) + s(\sigma_{A \times B}^2),
\end{aligned}
$$

which equals the expected value of MS_A except for the null-hypothesis component. We have an error term. On the basis of these arguments, then, we can form a ratio,

Table 21-5 Expected Values of Mean Squares for a Special Case of the $A \times (B \times S)$ Design (Factor *A* Fixed; Factor *B* Random)

SOURCE	EXPECTED MEAN SQUARE
A	$\sigma_\epsilon^2 + \sigma_{B \times S/A}^2 + s(\sigma_{A \times B}^2) + b(\sigma_{S/A}^2) + b(s)(\theta_A^2)$
S/A	$\sigma_\epsilon^2 + \sigma_{B \times S/A}^2 + b(\sigma_{S/A}^2)$
B	$\sigma_\epsilon^2 + \sigma_{B \times S/A}^2 + a(s)(\sigma_B^2)$
$A \times B$	$\sigma_\epsilon^2 + \sigma_{B \times S/A}^2 + s(\sigma_{A \times B}^2)$
$B \times S/A$	$\sigma_\epsilon^2 + \sigma_{B \times S/A}^2$

F', to evaluate the significance of the A main effect. That is,

$$F' = \frac{MS_A}{MS_{S/A} + MS_{A \times B} - MS_{B \times S/A}} . \tag{21-2}$$

The F ratio specified in Eq. (21-2) is called a **quasi F**—a statistic that is not distributed as F. As a consequence, we are not able to use the F table in any simple way to determine the critical values for the statistical test. Satterthwaite (1946) has provided a formula for calculating adjusted degrees of freedom that then permits the straightforward use of the F table. This adjustment formula can be used to calculate the degrees of freedom for any term that is a combination of mean squares; the df for terms representing single sources of variance are calculated in the usual way without an adjustment. The adjustment formula consists of a ratio in which the numerator contains the combination of mean squares, which is squared, and the denominator contains the sum of a set of ratios each of which is based on the mean squares contributing to the combination. More specifically, each ratio is obtained by squaring the mean square and dividing by the appropriate number of degrees of freedom. If the combination involves some combination of mean squares represented arbitrarily as MS_U, MS_V, MS_W, etc., the adjustment formula becomes

$$df_{\text{adj.}} = \frac{(\text{combination of } MS_U, MS_V, MS_W, \cdots)^2}{(MS_U)^2/df_U + (MS_V)^2/df_V + (MS_W)^2/df_W + \cdots} . \tag{21-3}$$

(The value obtained from this formula is rounded to the nearest whole number.) Applied to the present example, where the denominator of the quasi F ratio consists of $MS_{B/A} + MS_{S/A} - MS_{B \times S/A}$, Eq. (21-3) becomes

$$df_{\text{adj.}} = \frac{(MS_{B/A} + MS_{S/A} - MS_{B \times S/A})^2}{(MS_{B/A})^2/df_{B/A} + (MS_{S/A})^2/df_{S/A} + (MS_{B \times S/A})^2/df_{B \times S/A}} .$$

Thus, we can test the significance of the A main effect by calculating the quasi F specified in Eq. (21-2) and finding the critical value of this statistic in the F table under $df_{\text{num.}} = df_A$ and $df_{\text{denom.}} = df_{\text{adj.}}$.

While the quasi F specified by Eq. (21-2) is preferred by some authors (see Myers, 1979, p. 192), there is the possibility of obtaining a denominator with a negative value, which can happen if the third mean square is larger than the sum of the other two mean squares. To avoid this potential problem, several statisticians recommend an alternative quasi F that avoids subtraction and negative numbers altogether. Consider, for example,

$$F'' = \frac{MS_A + MS_{B \times S/A}}{MS_{S/A} + MS_{A \times B}} . \tag{21-4}$$

Turning back to Table 21-5, we find

$$E(MS_A + MS_{B \times S/A})$$
$$= \left[\sigma_\epsilon^2 + \sigma_{B \times S/A}^2 + s(\sigma_{A \times B}^2) + b(\sigma_{S/A}^2) + b(s)(\theta_A^2) \right] + \left[\sigma_\epsilon^2 + \sigma_{B \times S/A}^2 \right] ;$$

and

$$E(MS_{S/A} + MS_{A \times B})$$
$$= \left[\sigma_\epsilon^2 + \sigma_{B \times S/A}^2 + b(\sigma_{S/A}^2) \right] + \left[\sigma_\epsilon^2 + \sigma_{B \times S/A}^2 + s(\sigma_{A \times B}^2) \right].$$

A resorting of the terms for the numerator and denominator expected values will reveal a perfect match except for the null-hypothesis component, $b(s)(\theta_A^2)$, in the numerator of F''. That is,

$$E(MS_A + MS_{B \times S/A}) = 2\sigma_\epsilon^2 + 2\sigma_{B \times S/A}^2 + s(\sigma_{A \times B}^2) + b(\sigma_{S/A}^2) + b(s)(\theta_A^2);$$

and

$$E(MS_{S/A} + MS_{A \times B}) = 2\sigma_\epsilon^2 + 2\sigma_{B \times S/A}^2 + s(\sigma_{A \times B}^2) + b(\sigma_{S/A}^2).$$

This means that F'' will be approximately 1.0 when the null hypothesis is true and greater than 1.0 when it is false. This quasi F test is distributed approximately as F if the numerator and denominator degrees of freedom are adjusted by means of Eq. (21-3). For the numerator, this adjustment is

$$df_{\text{adj.}} = \frac{(MS_A + MS_{B \times S/A})^2}{(MS_A)^2/df_A + (MS_{B \times S/A})^2/df_{B \times S/A}} ;$$

and for the denominator, it is

$$df_{\text{adj.}} = \frac{(MS_{S/A} + MS_{A \times B})^2}{(MS_{S/A})^2/df_{S/A} + (MS_{A \times B})^2/df_{A \times B}} .$$

Not too much is known about the sensitivity of the quasi F test to violations of the assumptions required for the standard F tests in the analysis of variance. The studies that have been reported, e.g., Forster and Dickinson (1976) and Santa, Miller, and Shaw (1979), suggest that the quasi F is reasonably robust to all but the most serious violations, while remaining relatively sensitive in detecting treatment effects.

21.3   ANALYSIS OF DESIGNS WITH NESTED RANDOM FACTORS

Nested factors usually represent subsets of levels drawn from large populations of levels, e.g., orderings of stimulus materials, sets of problems, lists of words, and sub-groupings of subjects (sections or classes in a school, wards in a hospital, schools in a large school system, etc.). Typically, researchers are not interested in these factors per se, but in the larger population. Thus, it frequently is the case that the intention of the researcher and the method of selecting the levels included in the experiment will suggest that a nested factor is more appropriately viewed as random than as fixed. You will recall a previous example in which the average reading speeds of sets of nouns and verbs were compared. Each set was randomly chosen from a listing of nouns and verbs available to the researcher. Presumably the researcher was interested in the average reading speeds of nouns and verbs *in general* and not in the particular sets of words actually tested in the study. Moreover, the words were chosen unsystematically. Consequently, the two sets of words are best classified as random.

I will illustrate the selection of error terms with this study. There are two independent variables in the experiment: word type (noun versus verb) and random samples of words within each type. Word type (factor A) is fixed, and the variable words within type (factor B/A) is random. I will discuss the analysis of this simple experiment in the context of three different experimental designs. You should take careful note of how the error term for evaluating the main effect of word type changes in each of these designs.

The first experiment is a completely randomized design in which subjects are assigned randomly to read only *one* of the words, either a noun or a verb. There is a different group of subjects for each of the words in the experiment—an uneconomical and unrealistic example, but one that illustrates the effect of a nested random factor most clearly. Three sources of variation are extracted from this design: word type (A), word instances pooled over word type (B/A), and subjects (S/AB).[5] The expected values for these three sources are presented in Table 21-6. The expected value for factor A consists of three terms: error variance (σ_ϵ^2), the confounding introduced by the nested random factor ($\sigma_{B/A}^2$), and the effects of the treatments (θ_A^2). (The nested component reflects the fact that random samples of nouns and verbs will introduce a certain amount of distortion into this mean square, a point that was discussed in Section 21.1, pp. 520-521.) The expected value for word instances (B/A) consists of the first two terms listed for factor A and thus becomes the error term for evaluating the significance of any difference observed between nouns and verbs. The $MS_{B/A}$ reflects the joint influence of two sets of chance factors, those stemming from the random assignment of subjects to individual words (σ_ϵ^2) and those stemming from the random selection of words from the dictionary ($\sigma_{B/A}^2$).

Two other important points can be made with this design. First, consider

Table 21-6   Expected Mean Squares and Error Terms for a Completely Randomized Design

SOURCE	EXPECTED MEAN SQUARE	ERROR TERM
A	$\sigma_\epsilon^2 + s(\sigma_{B/A}^2) + b(s)(\theta_A^2)$	B/A
B/A	$\sigma_\epsilon^2 + s(\sigma_{B/A}^2)$	S/AB
S/AB	σ_ϵ^2	

[5]Technically, this term could be written $S/B/A$—subjects are nested within words and words in turn are nested in word type—but this rearrangement does not change the nature of the nesting with regard to factor S. That is, the source refers to the pooled variability of subjects receiving a particular word of a particular type. In any case, S/AB represents a source with which we are already familiar.

what would happen if the within-groups mean square ($MS_{S/AB}$) were used as the error term for the treatment effects. An inspection of the expected values of the two mean squares, MS_A and $MS_{S/AB}$, indicates a positive bias in this F test and an anticipated increase in type I error. Monte Carlo studies verify the presence of this bias (e.g., Forster and Dickinson, 1976; Santa, Miller, and Shaw, 1979). Moreover, this bias increases as subject sample size increases; this relationship is indicated by the coefficient s appearing with the nested term $\sigma_{B/A}^2$ in the expected value of MS_A.

Second, consider the relative effectiveness on the power of rejecting the treatment null hypothesis of increasing the number of subjects versus increasing the number of words in each sample. An increase in subject sample size—the usual way of increasing power in this sort of design—has *no major effect* on power, since the subject coefficient s influences both numerator and denominator terms of the F ratio. Levels of the nested factor, b, on the other hand, affect only the *numerator* term of the F ratio. Thus, an increase in the size of the word sets will result in a sharp increase in power.[6] From the point of view of experimental design, therefore, it makes far more sense to increase the levels of the nested factor than to increase the number of subjects per group. In general, this recommendation holds true for all three nested designs I will be considering.

The next two designs introduce repeated measures into the experiment. A common way to design this particular experiment is to test one group of subjects on all of the nouns and another group of subjects on all of the verbs. The result is a "mixed" or "split-plot" design that includes both between-subjects variation and within-subjects variation. The sources of variance normally obtained from this design and the expected values for these sources are presented in Table 21–7.

An examination of the terms in the expected value of the A main effect indicates that the source contains four terms that must be matched by an error

Table 21-7 Expected Mean Squares and Error Terms for a "Mixed" Repeated-Measures Design

SOURCE	EXPECTED MEAN SQUARE	ERROR TERM
A	$\sigma_\epsilon^2 + \sigma_{B \times S/A}^2 + s(\sigma_{B/A}^2) + b(\sigma_{S/A}^2) + b(s)(\theta_A^2)$	F'
S/A	$\sigma_\epsilon^2 + \sigma_{B \times S/A}^2 + b(\sigma_{S/A}^2)$	
B/A	$\sigma_\epsilon^2 + \sigma_{B \times S/A}^2 + s(\sigma_{B/A}^2)$	$B \times S/A$
$B \times S/A$	$\sigma_\epsilon^2 + \sigma_{B \times S/A}^2$	

$$F' = \frac{MS_A}{MS_{S/A} + MS_{B/A} - MS_{B \times S/A}}$$

[6]It is true that sample size does affect the accuracy of the estimate of the treatment component θ_A^2, but the result is not as direct as is the effect of the size of the word samples, indexed by the b coefficient.

term. None of the other sources listed in Table 21-7 can serve this function. It is necessary, therefore, to attempt to construct a quasi F ratio in which mean squares are combined in such a way as to provide a matching of the expected values for the numerator and denominator terms except for the null-hypothesis component in the numerator. One quasi F that satisfies this requirement is indicated at the bottom of Table 21-7. An alternative quasi F, which avoids the possibility of negative values, is given by the formula

$$F'' = \frac{MS_A + MS_{B \times S/A}}{MS_{S/A} + MS_{B/A}}.$$

You will recall that quasi F ratios require the adjustment of df's when mean squares are combined to form either the numerator or the denominator of the ratio. (See pp. 532-533 for a discussion of this adjustment procedure.)

The final design is the one discussed in detail by Clark (1973), an experiment in which each subject is tested on *all* of the words in the study. The sources of variance and expected mean squares extracted from this particular design are presented in Table 21-8. Again, you can see that no single source can serve as an error term for evaluating the A main effect. A quasi F that will provide a solution to this problem is presented at the bottom of the table. An alternative quasi F is

$$F'' = \frac{MS_A + MS_{B \times S/A}}{MS_{B/A} + MS_{A \times S}}.$$

Again, adjusted df's must be calculated for the denominator term of F' and for both terms of F''.

Table 21-8   Expected Mean Squares and Error Terms for a "Pure" Repeated-Measures Design

SOURCE	EXPECTED MEAN SQUARE	ERROR TERM
A	$\sigma_\epsilon^2 + \sigma_{B \times S/A}^2 + b(\sigma_{A \times S}^2) + s(\sigma_{B/A}^2) + b(s)(\theta_A^2)$	F'
B/A	$\sigma_\epsilon^2 + \sigma_{B \times S/A}^2 + s(\sigma_{B/A}^2)$	$B \times S/A$
S	$\sigma_\epsilon^2 + \sigma_{B \times S/A}^2 + a(b)(\sigma_S^2)$	
$A \times S$	$\sigma_\epsilon^2 + \sigma_{B \times S/A}^2 + b(\sigma_{A \times S}^2)$	
$B \times S/A$	$\sigma_\epsilon^2 + \sigma_{B \times S/A}^2$	

$$F' = \frac{MS_A}{MS_{B/A} + MS_{A \times S} - MS_{B \times S/A}}$$

Comment

There is no denying the logic of the statistical analysis required when words are actually drawn at random from a large pool of instances. On the other hand, there are many cases where this description of stimulus selection is completely inappropriate. These are situations where words are not chosen at random, but with careful matching on dimensions known to influence the behavior under study—reading speed in this case. For example, a researcher might *match* nouns and verbs on the frequency with which the words occur in written and spoken prose, on the number of syllables, on the number of letters, and so on. The goal is not to study the reading speed of nouns and verbs as they exist in the linguistic environment, which presumably is the intent when one selects words randomly, but to study the cognitive effects of *nounness* versus *verbness* with all other characteristics held constant.

This type of experimental design calls for a different kind of statistical analysis, one that substitutes *matched pairs* or *matched blocks of words* for random samples of words. Instead of the nested factor *B/A* (words within word type), we would have a factor *B* (blocks of words) that *crosses* with factor *A*. While this type of design still involves a random factor (blocks of words) and has to be analyzed with that assumption in mind, the analysis will generally result in a more sensitive assessment of the main independent variable (nounness versus verbness) than that provided by the nested design and the random selection of words.[7] This occurs because variability among words is isolated from the analysis in the crossed design as the *B* main effect, but remains unanalyzed in the error term in the nested design. For this reason, then, the matched design will often prove to be a better choice in this type of investigation.

---

[7]The analysis of experiments with crossed random factors was discussed in Section 21-2.

22

Concluding Remarks

I have come to the end of the formal presentation. It might be fruitful, at this time, to indicate where we are in our discussion of the design and analysis of experiments. In the process of doing so, I will consider briefly directions that you might take to increase your understanding of the general area of study.

I have focused on a particular form of statistical analysis, namely, hypothesis testing by means of analysis-of-variance techniques. The justification for this emphasis is that these are the procedures used by most researchers in the experimental areas of the behavioral sciences. But there are other ways to examine the results of an experiment. For example, Tukey (1977), in a creative and provocative book, argues convincingly for the use of procedures particularly suited to exploring relationships in a set of data. He distinguishes between **confirmatory procedures** and **exploratory data analysis**. The analysis of variance is a comfirmatory procedure designed to assess the status of research hypotheses articulated before the start of an experiment. Exploratory data analysis, on the other hand, is decidedly post hoc—guided by the data and new flexible ways of discerning trends and outcomes not expected by a researcher, but often interesting and thought-provoking nevertheless. While experienced researchers go far beyond their original plans for analyzing a set of data, the procedures introduced by Tukey are different and certainly worthy of study and contemplation. A useful introduction to Tukey's book is provided by an inexpensive monograph by Hartwig and Dearing (1979).

A second area you should consider exploring is **multiple regression and correlation**. As many have pointed out, the analysis of variance is actually a special case of these procedures, although the two analysis traditions have until recently coexisted independently since the 1930s.[1] Cohen

[1]Two interesting accounts of the history of the analysis of variance appeared within a year of each other in different journals and different countries (Lovie, 1979; Rucci and Tweney, 1980).

(1968) provides a strong case for the adoption of these techniques as a general analytic tool for the behavioral sciences. The primary factor working against this suggestion—the complex and time-consuming calculations—is no longer a problem, on account of the widespread availability of high-speed computers and useful programs. At this point, it is a matter of preference whether one uses analysis of variance or multiple regression and correlation to analyze a set of data. Analysis of variance can be done by hand with the assistance of an inexpensive electronic calculator. The training of most researchers has been and continues to be in this tradition. What is needed is convincing arguments in favor of the correlational techniques and books that provide the cross-referencing of analyses during the transition period. Edwards (1979) offers a short introduction to multiple regression and correlation. Cohen and Cohen (1975) and Kerlinger and Pedhazur (1973) present a comprehensive coverage of analysis of variance from the correlational framework, while Myers (1979) offers a similar coverage from the point of view of experimental design and analysis of variance.

A related and important topic is the **multivariate analysis of variance.** Multivariate procedures, which permit the study of more than one *dependent* variable in an experimental design, are finding application in research areas in which a number of dependent variables have been identified and are of interest to study jointly. Multivariate analyses are often recommended with repeated-measures designs where the variance-covariance assumptions are greatly violated. A widely cited introduction to multivariate procedures is a book by Anderson (1958). Tatsuoka (1971) offers a useful discussion of these procedures in a context that is particularly compatible with the approach taken here. Winer has included a discussion of multivariate analysis of variance in the second edition of his book (1971, pp. 232-240). McCall (1970) presents a nontechnical introduction to multivariate techniques with references drawn from developmental psychology.

Finally, I have given no mention to **nonparametric or distribution-free statistics.** The interest in nonparametric statistics is twofold: (1) their freedom from assumptions about the distribution of the scores in the population and (2) their simplicity, especially when compared with the analysis of variance. Researchers sometimes turn to these procedures when there is a particularly high degree of variability associated with one or more treatment conditions. Nonparametric tests can occasionally detect treatment differences when the F test is heavily influenced by error variance. On the negative side, however, nonparametric statistics are not as flexible with regard to the types of hypotheses that may be tested as is the analysis of variance. In addition, they are not as powerful and provide less information from the data when the assumptions underlying the analysis of variance are met. Moreover, nonparametric procedures have not been developed for the higher-order factorial designs that are so widely represented in the current experimental literature. If you want to pursue the topic, various excellent discussions are available. Both Kirk (1968, Chapter 13) and Winer (1971, pp. 848-855), for example, provide brief discussions. An excellent introduction to the topic has been published by

Bradley (1972). Siegel (1956) is still a popular reference for many researchers, although several more recent books have become available, e.g., Bradley (1968) and Edgington (1969). A more demanding book by Marascuilo and McSweeney (1977) offers an authoritative and comprehensive coverage of the various nonparametric techniques available to the researcher in the behavioral sciences.

You will undoubtedly find it necessary to consult a number of statistics books when you come across a problem that demands special treatment. When relevant, I have provided specific page references to the primary statistical source books written for psychologists, Kirk (1968) and Winer (1971), where more detailed and technical explanations are given. As mentioned already, the most recent edition of Myers (1979) offers in one volume an extensive coverage of analysis of variance and an introduction to multiple regression-correlation and to multivariate statistics. Myers' treatment of Latin square design with repeated measures is particularly useful to the psychologist. Lindman (1974) provides a thorough discussion of complex experimental designs, including an excellent chapter on nested designs. The classic book by Lindquist (1953), which is probably out of print, still offers useful advice on designing experiments. Finally, I should mention Hays (1973), who makes accessible to the nonmathematically trained researcher the theory that lies behind the more common statistical procedures and tests.[2]

An important region toward which your future study perhaps should point is that of *experimental design*. A study of general principles of experimental design is useful in forcing us to examine our methods and procedures with a highly critical eye. Two older, but excellent, sources may be recommended: a discussion by Campbell and Stanley, which originally appeared as a chapter in a book (1963) but has been reprinted as a separate monograph (1966), and a book by Underwood (1957) in which Chapters 4 and 5 are particularly relevant. A more recent book by Cook and Campbell (1979) offers advice and guidance in designing field research. Another book that considers issues relevant to the broad research needs of the behavioral scientist is by Neale and Liebert (1980). Finally, I should mention a book by Webb, Campbell, Schwartz, and Sechrest (1966), *Unobtrusive Measures*, which discusses the role of experimentation in changing the actual behavior under study.

General discussions which focus on experimental design or on the statistical analysis of experiments are only a first step, however—you still must apply them in the laboratory. The success of any research attempt will depend in large part on the skill with which you accomplish this translation.

---

[2]Bruning and Kintz (1977) have prepared a useful chart providing cross-references to a number of widely used statistics texts for a variety of experimental designs and procedures (pp. 301–304).

Appendix A

Statistical Tables

Table A-1 Critical Values of the F Distribution

df FOR NUMERATOR

df FOR DENOM.	α	1	2	3	4	5	6	7	8	9	10	12	15	20	24	30	40	60	∞
1	.25	5.83	7.50	8.20	8.58	8.82	8.98	9.10	9.19	9.26	9.32	9.41	9.49	9.58	9.63	9.67	9.71	9.76	9.85
	.10	39.9	49.5	53.6	55.8	57.2	58.2.	58.9	59.4	59.9	60.2	60.7	61.2	61.7	62.0	62.3	62.5	62.8	63.3
	.05	161	200	216	225	230	234	237	239	240	242	244	246	248	249	250	251	252	254
	.025	648	800	864	900	922	937	948	957	963	969	977	985	993	997	1001	1006	1010	1018
	.01	4052	5000	5403	5625	5764	5859	5928	5982	6022	6056	6106	6157	6209	6235	6261	6287	6313	6366
	.001	4053*	5000*	5404*	5625*	5764*	5859*	5929*	5981*	6023*	6056*	6107*	6158*	6209*	6235*	6261*	6287*	6313*	6366*
2	.25	2.57	3.00	3.15	3.23	3.28	3.31	3.34	3.35	3.37	3.38	3.39	3.41	3.43	3.43	3.44	3.45	3.46	3.48
	.10	8.53	9.00	9.16	9.24	9.29	9.33	9.35	9.37	9.38	9.39	9.41	9.42	9.44	9.45	9.46	9.47	9.47	9.49
	.05	18.5	19.0	19.2	19.3	19.3	19.3	19.4	19.4	19.4	19.4	19.4	19.4	19.5	19.5	19.5	19.5	19.5	19.5
	.025	38.5	39.0	39.2	39.3	39.3	39.3	39.4	39.4	39.4	39.4	39.4	39.4	39.5	39.5	39.5	39.5	39.5	39.5
	.01	98.5	99.0	99.2	99.3	99.3	99.3	99.4	99.4	99.4	99.4	99.4	99.4	99.5	99.5	99.5	99.5	99.5	99.5
	.001	999	999	999	999	999	999	999	999	999	999	999	999	999	1000	1000	1000	1000	1000
3	.25	2.02	2.28	2.36	2.39	2.41	2.42	2.43	2.44	2.44	2.44	2.45	2.46	2.46	2.46	2.47	2.47	2.47	2.47
	.10	5.54	5.46	5.39	5.34	5.31	5.28	5.27	5.25	5.24	5.23	5.22	5.20	5.18	5.18	5.17	5.16	5.15	5.13
	.05	10.1	9.55	9.28	9.12	9.01	8.94	8.89	8.85	8.81	8.79	8.74	8.70	8.66	8.64	8.62	8.59	8.57	8.53
	.025	17.4	16.0	15.4	15.1	14.9	14.7	14.6	14.5	14.5	14.4	14.3	14.2	14.2	14.1	14.1	14.0	14.0	13.9
	.01	34.1	30.8	29.5	28.7	28.2	27.9	27.7	27.5	27.4	27.2	27.0	26.9	26.7	26.6	26.5	26.4	26.3	26.1
	.001	167	148	141	137	135	133	132	131	130	129	128	127	126	126	125	125	124	124
4	.25	1.81	2.00	2.05	2.06	2.07	2.08	2.08	2.08	2.08	2.08	2.08	2.08	2.08	2.08	2.08	2.08	2.08	2.08
	.10	4.54	4.32	4.19	4.11	4.05	4.01	3.98	3.95	3.94	3.92	3.90	3.87	3.84	3.83	3.82	3.80	3.79	3.76
	.05	7.71	6.94	6.59	6.39	6.26	6.16	6.09	6.04	6.00	5.96	5.91	5.86	5.80	5.77	5.75	5.72	5.69	5.63
	.025	12.2	10.6	9.98	9.60	9.36	9.20	9.07	8.98	8.90	8.84	8.75	8.66	8.56	8.51	8.46	8.41	8.36	8.26
	.01	21.2	18.0	16.7	16.0	15.5	15.2	15.0	14.8	14.7	14.6	14.4	14.2	14.0	13.9	13.8	13.8	13.6	13.5
	.001	74.1	61.2	56.2	53.4	51.7	50.5	49.7	49.0	48.5	48.0	47.4	46.8	46.1	45.8	45.4	45.1	44.8	44.0

*Multiply these entries by 100.

5	.25	1.69	1.85	1.88	1.89	1.89	1.89	1.89	1.89	1.89	1.89	1.89	1.89	1.88	1.88	1.88	1.88	1.87	1.87
	.10	4.06	3.78	3.62	3.52	3.45	3.40	3.37	3.34	3.32	3.30	3.27	3.24	3.21	3.19	3.17	3.16	3.14	3.10
	.05	6.61	5.79	5.41	5.19	5.05	4.95	4.88	4.82	4.77	4.74	4.68	4.62	4.56	4.53	4.50	4.46	4.43	4.36
	.025	10.0	8.43	7.76	7.39	7.15	6.98	6.85	6.76	6.68	6.62	6.52	6.43	6.33	6.28	6.23	6.18	6.12	6.02
	.01	16.3	13.3	12.1	11.4	11.0	10.7	10.5	10.3	10.2	10.0	9.89	9.72	9.55	9.47	9.38	9.29	9.20	9.02
	.001	47.2	37.1	33.2	31.1	29.8	28.8	28.2	27.6	27.2	26.9	26.4	25.9	25.4	25.1	24.9	24.6	24.3	23.8
6	.25	1.62	1.76	1.78	1.79	1.79	1.78	1.78	1.78	1.77	1.77	1.77	1.76	1.76	1.75	1.75	1.75	1.74	1.74
	.10	3.78	3.46	3.29	3.18	3.11	3.05	3.01	2.98	2.96	2.94	2.90	2.87	2.84	2.82	2.80	2.78	2.76	2.72
	.05	5.99	5.14	4.76	4.53	4.39	4.28	4.21	4.15	4.10	4.06	4.00	3.94	3.87	3.84	3.81	3.77	3.74	3.67
	.025	8.81	7.26	6.60	6.23	5.99	5.82	5.70	5.60	5.52	5.46	5.37	5.27	5.17	5.12	5.07	5.01	4.96	4.85
	.01	13.8	10.9	9.78	9.15	8.75	8.47	8.26	8.10	7.98	7.87	7.72	7.56	7.40	7.31	7.23	7.14	7.06	6.88
	.001	35.5	27.0	23.7	21.9	20.8	20.0	19.5	19.0	18.7	18.4	18.0	17.6	17.1	16.9	16.7	16.4	16.2	15.8
7	.25	1.57	1.70	1.72	1.72	1.71	1.71	1.70	1.70	1.69	1.69	1.68	1.68	1.67	1.67	1.66	1.66	1.65	1.65
	.10	3.59	3.26	3.07	2.96	2.88	2.83	2.78	2.75	2.72	2.70	2.67	2.63	2.59	2.58	2.56	2.54	2.51	2.47
	.05	5.59	4.74	4.35	4.12	3.97	3.87	3.79	3.73	3.68	3.64	3.57	3.51	3.44	3.41	3.38	3.34	3.30	3.23
	.025	8.07	6.54	5.89	5.52	5.29	5.12	4.99	4.90	4.82	4.76	4.67	4.57	4.47	4.42	4.36	4.31	4.25	4.14
	.01	12.2	9.55	8.45	7.85	7.46	7.19	6.99	6.84	6.72	6.62	6.47	6.31	6.16	6.07	5.99	5.91	5.82	5.65
	.001	29.2	21.7	18.8	17.2	16.2	15.5	15.0	14.6	14.3	14.1	13.7	13.3	12.9	12.7	12.5	12.3	12.1	11.7
8	.25	1.54	1.66	1.67	1.66	1.66	1.65	1.64	1.64	1.63	1.63	1.62	1.62	1.61	1.60	1.60	1.59	1.59	1.58
	.10	3.46	3.11	2.92	2.81	2.73	2.67	2.62	2.59	2.56	2.54	2.50	2.46	2.42	2.40	2.38	2.36	2.34	2.29
	.05	5.32	4.46	4.07	3.84	3.69	3.58	3.50	3.44	3.39	3.35	3.28	3.22	3.15	3.12	3.08	3.04	3.01	2.93
	.025	7.57	6.06	5.42	5.05	4.82	4.65	4.53	4.43	4.36	4.30	4.20	4.10	4.00	3.95	3.89	3.84	3.78	3.67
	.01	11.3	8.65	7.59	7.01	6.63	6.37	6.18	6.03	5.91	5.81	5.67	5.52	5.36	5.28	5.20	5.12	5.03	4.86
	.001	25.4	18.5	15.8	14.4	13.5	12.9	12.4	12.0	11.8	11.5	11.2	10.8	10.5	10.3	10.1	9.92	9.73	9.33
9	.25	1.51	1.62	1.63	1.63	1.62	1.61	1.60	1.60	1.59	1.59	1.58	1.57	1.56	1.56	1.55	1.54	1.54	1.53
	.10	3.36	3.01	2.81	2.69	2.61	2.55	2.51	2.47	2.44	2.42	2.38	2.34	2.30	2.28	2.25	2.23	2.21	2.16
	.05	5.12	4.26	3.86	3.63	3.48	3.37	3.29	3.23	3.18	3.14	3.07	3.01	2.94	2.90	2.86	2.83	2.79	2.71
	.025	7.21	5.71	5.08	4.72	4.48	4.32	4.20	4.10	4.03	3.96	3.87	3.77	3.67	3.61	3.56	3.51	3.45	3.33
	.01	10.6	8.02	6.99	6.42	6.06	5.80	5.61	5.47	5.35	5.26	5.11	4.96	4.81	4.73	4.65	4.57	4.48	4.31
	.001	22.9	16.4	13.9	12.6	11.7	11.1	10.7	10.4	10.1	9.89	9.57	9.24	8.90	8.72	8.55	8.37	8.19	7.81

Table A-1 (Cont.)

df FOR DENOM.	α	1	2	3	4	5	6	7	8	9	10	12	15	20	24	30	40	60	∞
10	.25	1.49	1.60	1.60	1.59	1.59	1.58	1.57	1.56	1.56	1.55	1.54	1.53	1.52	1.52	1.51	1.51	1.50	1.48
	.10	3.29	2.92	2.73	2.61	2.52	2.46	2.41	2.38	2.35	2.32	2.28	2.24	2.20	2.18	2.16	2.13	2.11	2.06
	.05	4.96	4.10	3.71	3.48	3.33	3.22	3.14	3.07	3.02	2.98	2.91	2.85	2.77	2.74	2.70	2.66	2.62	2.54
	.025	6.94	5.46	4.83	4.47	4.24	4.07	3.95	3.85	3.78	3.72	3.62	3.52	3.42	3.37	3.31	3.26	3.20	3.08
	.01	10.0	7.56	6.55	5.99	5.64	5.39	5.20	5.06	4.94	4.85	4.71	4.56	4.41	4.33	4.25	4.17	4.08	3.91
	.001	21.0	14.9	12.6	11.3	10.5	9.92	9.52	9.20	8.96	8.75	8.45	8.13	7.80	7.64	7.47	7.30	7.12	6.76
11	.25	1.47	1.58	1.58	1.57	1.56	1.55	1.54	1.53	1.53	1.52	1.51	1.50	1.49	1.49	1.48	1.47	1.47	1.45
	.10	3.23	2.86	2.66	2.54	2.45	2.39	2.34	2.30	2.27	2.25	2.21	2.17	2.12	2.10	2.08	2.05	2.03	1.97
	.05	4.84	3.98	3.59	3.36	3.20	3.09	3.01	2.95	2.90	2.85	2.79	2.72	2.65	2.61	2.57	2.53	2.49	2.40
	.025	6.72	5.26	4.63	4.28	4.04	3.88	3.76	3.66	3.59	3.53	3.43	3.33	3.23	3.17	3.12	3.06	3.00	2.88
	.01	9.65	7.21	6.22	5.67	5.32	5.07	4.89	4.74	4.63	4.54	4.40	4.25	4.10	4.02	3.94	3.86	3.78	3.60
	.001	19.7	13.8	11.6	10.4	9.58	9.05	8.66	8.35	8.12	7.92	7.63	7.32	7.01	6.85	6.68	6.52	6.35	6.00
12	.25	1.46	1.56	1.56	1.55	1.54	1.53	1.52	1.51	1.51	1.50	1.49	1.48	1.47	1.46	1.45	1.45	1.44	1.42
	.10	3.18	2.81	2.61	2.48	2.39	2.33	2.28	2.24	2.21	2.19	2.15	2.10	2.06	2.04	2.01	1.99	1.96	1.90
	.05	4.75	3.89	3.49	3.26	3.11	3.00	2.91	2.85	2.80	2.75	2.69	2.62	2.54	2.51	2.47	2.43	2.38	2.30
	.025	6.55	5.10	4.47	4.12	3.89	3.73	3.61	3.51	3.44	3.37	3.28	3.18	3.07	3.02	2.96	2.91	2.85	2.72
	.01	9.33	6.93	5.95	5.41	5.06	4.82	4.64	4.50	4.39	4.30	4.16	4.01	3.86	3.78	3.70	3.62	3.54	3.36
	.001	18.6	13.0	10.8	9.63	8.89	8.38	8.00	7.71	7.48	7.29	7.00	6.71	6.40	6.25	6.09	5.93	5.76	5.42
13	.25	1.45	1.55	1.55	1.53	1.52	1.51	1.50	1.49	1.49	1.48	1.47	1.46	1.45	1.44	1.43	1.42	1.42	1.40
	.10	3.14	2.76	2.56	2.43	2.35	2.28	2.23	2.20	2.16	2.14	2.10	2.05	2.01	1.98	1.96	1.93	1.90	1.85
	.05	4.67	3.81	3.41	3.18	3.03	2.92	2.83	2.77	2.71	2.67	2.60	2.53	2.46	2.42	2.38	2.34	2.30	2.21
	.025	6.41	4.97	4.35	4.00	3.77	3.60	3.48	3.39	3.31	3.25	3.15	3.05	2.95	2.89	2.84	2.78	2.72	2.60
	.01	9.07	6.70	5.74	5.21	4.86	4.62	4.44	4.30	4.19	4.10	3.96	3.82	3.66	3.59	3.51	3.43	3.34	3.17
	.001	17.8	12.3	10.2	9.07	8.35	7.86	7.49	7.21	6.98	6.80	6.52	6.23	5.93	5.78	5.63	5.47	5.30	4.97

14	.25	1.44	1.53	1.53	1.52	1.51	1.50	1.49	1.48	1.47	1.46	1.45	1.44	1.43	1.42	1.41	1.41	1.40	1.38
	.10	3.10	2.73	2.52	2.39	2.31	2.24	2.19	2.15	2.12	2.10	2.05	2.01	1.96	1.94	1.91	1.89	1.86	1.80
	.05	4.60	3.74	3.34	3.11	2.96	2.85	2.76	2.70	2.65	2.60	2.53	2.46	2.39	2.35	2.31	2.27	2.22	2.13
	.025	6.30	4.86	4.24	3.89	3.66	3.50	3.38	3.29	3.21	3.15	3.05	2.95	2.84	2.79	2.73	2.67	2.61	2.49
	.01	8.86	6.51	5.56	5.04	4.69	4.46	4.28	4.14	4.03	3.94	3.80	3.66	3.51	3.43	3.35	3.27	3.18	3.00
	.001	17.1	11.8	9.73	8.62	7.92	7.43	7.08	6.80	6.58	6.40	6.13	5.85	5.56	5.41	5.25	5.10	4.94	4.60
15	.25	1.43	1.52	1.52	1.50	1.49	1.48	1.47	1.46	1.46	1.45	1.44	1.43	1.41	1.41	1.40	1.39	1.38	1.36
	.10	3.07	2.70	2.49	2.36	2.27	2.21	2.16	2.12	2.09	2.06	2.02	1.97	1.92	1.90	1.87	1.85	1.82	1.76
	.05	4.54	3.68	3.29	3.06	2.90	2.79	2.71	2.64	2.59	2.54	2.48	2.40	2.33	2.29	2.25	2.20	2.16	2.07
	.025	6.20	4.77	4.15	3.80	3.58	3.41	3.29	3.20	3.12	3.06	2.96	2.86	2.76	2.70	2.64	2.59	2.52	2.40
	.01	8.68	6.36	5.42	4.89	4.56	4.32	4.14	4.00	3.89	3.80	3.67	3.52	3.37	3.29	3.21	3.13	3.05	2.87
	.001	16.6	11.3	9.34	8.25	7.57	7.09	6.74	6.47	6.26	6.08	5.81	5.54	5.25	5.10	4.95	4.80	4.64	4.31
16	.25	1.42	1.51	1.51	1.50	1.48	1.47	1.46	1.45	1.44	1.44	1.43	1.41	1.40	1.39	1.38	1.37	1.36	1.34
	.10	3.05	2.67	2.46	2.33	2.24	2.18	2.13	2.09	2.06	2.03	1.99	1.94	1.89	1.87	1.84	1.81	1.78	1.72
	.05	4.49	3.63	3.24	3.01	2.85	2.74	2.66	2.59	2.54	2.49	2.42	2.35	2.28	2.24	2.19	2.15	2.11	2.01
	.025	6.12	4.69	4.08	3.73	3.50	3.34	3.22	3.12	3.05	2.99	2.89	2.79	2.68	2.63	2.57	2.51	2.45	2.32
	.01	8.53	6.23	5.29	4.77	4.44	4.20	4.03	3.89	3.78	3.69	3.55	3.41	3.26	3.18	3.10	3.02	2.93	2.75
	.001	16.1	11.0	9.00	7.94	7.27	6.81	6.46	6.19	5.98	5.81	5.55	5.27	4.99	4.85	4.70	4.54	4.39	4.06
17	.25	1.42	1.51	1.50	1.49	1.47	1.46	1.45	1.44	1.43	1.43	1.41	1.40	1.39	1.38	1.37	1.36	1.35	1.33
	.10	3.03	2.64	2.44	2.31	2.22	2.15	2.10	2.06	2.03	2.00	1.96	1.91	1.86	1.84	1.81	1.78	1.75	1.69
	.05	4.45	3.59	3.20	2.96	2.81	2.70	2.61	2.55	2.49	2.45	2.38	2.31	2.23	2.19	2.15	2.10	2.06	1.96
	.025	6.04	4.62	4.01	3.66	3.44	3.28	3.16	3.06	2.98	2.92	2.82	2.72	2.62	2.56	2.50	2.44	2.38	2.25
	.01	8.40	6.11	5.18	4.67	4.34	4.10	3.93	3.79	3.68	3.59	3.46	3.31	3.16	3.08	3.00	2.92	2.83	2.65
	.001	15.7	10.7	8.73	7.68	7.02	6.56	6.22	5.96	5.75	5.58	5.32	5.05	4.78	4.63	4.48	4.33	4.18	3.85
18	.25	1.41	1.50	1.49	1.48	1.46	1.45	1.44	1.43	1.42	1.42	1.40	1.39	1.38	1.37	1.36	1.35	1.34	1.32
	.10	3.01	2.62	2.42	2.29	2.20	2.13	2.08	2.04	2.00	1.98	1.93	1.89	1.84	1.81	1.78	1.75	1.72	1.66
	.05	4.41	3.55	3.16	2.93	2.77	2.66	2.58	2.51	2.46	2.41	2.34	2.27	2.19	2.15	2.11	2.06	2.02	1.92
	.025	5.98	4.56	3.95	3.61	3.38	3.22	3.10	3.01	2.93	2.87	2.77	2.67	2.56	2.50	2.44	2.38	2.32	2.19
	.01	8.29	6.01	5.09	4.58	4.25	4.01	3.84	3.71	3.60	3.51	3.37	3.23	3.08	3.00	2.92	2.84	2.75	2.57
	.001	15.4	10.4	8.49	7.46	6.81	6.35	6.02	5.76	5.56	5.39	5.13	4.87	4.59	4.45	4.30	4.15	4.00	3.67

Table A-1   (Cont.)

df FOR DENOM.	α	1	2	3	4	5	6	7	8	9	10	12	15	20	24	30	40	60	∞
																df FOR NUMERATOR			
19	.25	1.41	1.49	1.49	1.47	1.46	1.44	1.43	1.42	1.41	1.41	1.40	1.38	1.37	1.36	1.35	1.34	1.33	1.30
	.10	2.99	2.61	2.40	2.27	2.18	2.11	2.06	2.02	1.98	1.96	1.91	1.86	1.81	1.79	1.76	1.73	1.70	1.63
	.05	4.38	3.52	3.13	2.90	2.74	2.63	2.54	2.48	2.42	2.38	2.31	2.23	2.16	2.11	2.07	2.03	1.98	1.88
	.025	5.92	4.51	3.90	3.56	3.33	3.17	3.05	2.96	2.88	2.82	2.72	2.62	2.51	2.45	2.39	2.33	2.27	2.13
	.01	8.18	5.93	5.01	4.50	4.17	3.94	3.77	3.63	3.52	3.43	3.30	3.15	3.00	2.92	2.84	2.76	2.67	2.49
	.001	15.1	10.2	8.28	7.26	6.62	6.18	5.85	5.59	5.39	5.22	4.97	4.70	4.43	4.29	4.14	3.99	3.84	3.51
20	.25	1.40	1.49	1.48	1.47	1.45	1.44	1.43	1.42	1.41	1.40	1.39	1.37	1.36	1.35	1.34	1.33	1.32	1.29
	.10	2.97	2.59	2.38	2.25	2.16	2.09	2.04	2.00	1.96	1.94	1.89	1.84	1.79	1.77	1.74	1.71	1.68	1.61
	.05	4.35	3.49	3.10	2.87	2.71	2.60	2.51	2.45	2.39	2.35	2.28	2.20	2.12	2.08	2.04	1.99	1.95	1.84
	.025	5.87	4.46	3.86	3.51	3.29	3.13	3.01	2.91	2.84	2.77	2.68	2.57	2.46	2.41	2.35	2.29	2.22	2.09
	.01	8.10	5.85	4.94	4.43	4.10	3.87	3.70	3.56	3.46	3.37	3.23	3.09	2.94	2.86	2.78	2.69	2.61	2.42
	.001	14.8	9.95	8.10	7.10	6.46	6.02	5.69	5.44	5.24	5.08	4.82	4.56	4.29	4.15	4.00	3.86	3.70	3.38
22	.25	1.40	1.48	1.47	1.45	1.44	1.42	1.41	1.40	1.39	1.39	1.37	1.36	1.34	1.33	1.32	1.31	1.30	1.28
	.10	2.95	2.56	2.35	2.22	2.13	2.06	2.01	1.97	1.93	1.90	1.86	1.81	1.76	1.73	1.70	1.67	1.64	1.57
	.05	4.30	3.44	3.05	2.82	2.66	2.55	2.46	2.40	2.34	2.30	2.23	2.15	2.07	2.03	1.98	1.94	1.89	1.78
	.025	5.79	4.38	3.78	3.44	3.22	3.05	2.93	2.84	2.76	2.70	2.60	2.50	2.39	2.33	2.27	2.21	2.14	2.00
	.01	7.95	5.72	4.82	4.31	3.99	3.76	3.59	3.45	3.35	3.26	3.12	2.98	2.83	2.75	2.67	2.58	2.50	2.31
	.001	14.4	9.61	7.80	6.81	6.19	5.76	5.44	5.19	4.99	4.83	4.58	4.33	4.06	3.92	3.78	3.63	3.48	3.15
24	.25	1.39	1.47	1.46	1.44	1.43	1.41	1.40	1.39	1.38	1.38	1.36	1.35	1.33	1.32	1.31	1.30	1.29	1.26
	.10	2.93	2.54	2.33	2.19	2.10	2.04	1.98	1.94	1.91	1.88	1.83	1.78	1.73	1.70	1.67	1.64	1.61	1.53
	.05	4.26	3.40	3.01	2.78	2.62	2.51	2.42	2.36	2.30	2.25	2.18	2.11	2.03	1.98	1.94	1.89	1.84	1.73
	.025	5.72	4.32	3.72	3.38	3.15	2.99	2.87	2.78	2.70	2.64	2.54	2.44	2.33	2.27	2.21	2.15	2.08	1.94
	.01	7.82	5.61	4.72	4.22	3.90	3.67	3.50	3.36	3.26	3.17	3.03	2.89	2.74	2.66	2.58	2.49	2.40	2.21
	.001	14.0	9.34	7.55	6.59	5.98	5.55	5.23	4.99	4.80	4.64	4.39	4.14	3.87	3.74	3.59	3.45	3.29	2.97

df	α																		
26	.25	1.25	1.28	1.29	1.30	1.31	1.32	1.34	1.35	1.37	1.37	1.38	1.39	1.41	1.42	1.44	1.45	1.46	1.38
	.10	1.50	1.58	1.61	1.65	1.68	1.71	1.76	1.81	1.86	1.88	1.92	1.96	2.01	2.08	2.17	2.31	2.52	2.91
	.05	1.69	1.80	1.85	1.90	1.95	1.99	2.07	2.15	2.22	2.27	2.32	2.39	2.47	2.59	2.74	2.98	3.37	4.23
	.025	1.88	2.03	2.09	2.16	2.22	2.28	2.39	2.49	2.59	2.65	2.73	2.82	2.94	3.10	3.33	3.67	4.27	5.66
	.01	2.13	2.33	2.42	2.50	2.58	2.66	2.81	2.96	3.09	3.18	3.29	3.42	3.59	3.82	4.14	4.64	5.53	7.72
	.001	2.82	3.15	3.30	3.44	3.59	3.72	3.99	4.24	4.48	4.64	4.83	5.07	5.38	5.80	6.41	7.36	9.12	13.7
28	.25	1.24	1.27	1.28	1.29	1.30	1.31	1.33	1.34	1.36	1.37	1.38	1.39	1.40	1.41	1.43	1.45	1.46	1.38
	.10	1.48	1.56	1.59	1.63	1.66	1.69	1.74	1.79	1.84	1.87	1.90	1.94	2.00	2.06	2.16	2.29	2.50	2.89
	.05	1.65	1.77	1.82	1.87	1.91	1.96	2.04	2.12	2.19	2.24	2.29	2.36	2.45	2.56	2.71	2.95	3.34	4.20
	.025	1.83	1.98	2.05	2.11	2.17	2.23	2.34	2.45	2.55	2.61	2.69	2.78	2.90	3.06	3.29	3.63	4.22	5.61
	.01	2.06	2.26	2.35	2.44	2.52	2.60	2.75	2.90	3.03	3.12	3.23	3.36	3.53	3.75	4.07	4.57	5.45	7.64
	.001	2.69	3.02	3.18	3.32	3.46	3.60	3.86	4.11	4.35	4.50	4.69	4.93	5.24	5.66	6.25	7.19	8.93	13.5
30	.25	1.23	1.26	1.27	1.28	1.29	1.30	1.32	1.34	1.35	1.36	1.37	1.38	1.39	1.41	1.42	1.44	1.45	1.38
	.10	1.46	1.54	1.57	1.61	1.64	1.67	1.72	1.77	1.82	1.85	1.88	1.93	1.98	2.05	2.14	2.28	2.49	2.88
	.05	1.62	1.74	1.79	1.84	1.89	1.93	2.01	2.09	2.16	2.21	2.27	2.33	2.42	2.53	2.69	2.92	3.32	4.17
	.025	1.79	1.94	2.01	2.07	2.14	2.20	2.31	2.41	2.51	2.57	2.65	2.75	2.87	3.03	3.25	3.59	4.18	5.57
	.01	2.01	2.21	2.30	2.39	2.47	2.55	2.70	2.84	2.98	3.07	3.17	3.30	3.47	3.70	4.02	4.51	5.39	7.56
	.001	2.59	2.92	3.07	3.22	3.36	3.49	3.75	4.00	4.24	4.39	4.58	4.82	5.12	5.53	6.12	7.05	8.77	13.3
40	.25	1.19	1.22	1.24	1.25	1.26	1.28	1.30	1.31	1.33	1.34	1.35	1.36	1.37	1.39	1.40	1.42	1.44	1.36
	.10	1.38	1.47	1.51	1.54	1.57	1.61	1.66	1.71	1.76	1.79	1.83	1.87	1.93	2.00	2.09	2.23	2.44	2.84
	.05	1.51	1.64	1.69	1.74	1.79	1.84	1.92	2.00	2.08	2.12	2.18	2.25	2.34	2.45	2.61	2.84	3.23	4.08
	.025	1.64	1.80	1.88	1.94	2.01	2.07	2.18	2.29	2.39	2.45	2.53	2.62	2.74	2.90	3.13	3.46	4.05	5.42
	.01	1.80	2.02	2.11	2.20	2.29	2.37	2.52	2.66	2.80	2.89	2.99	3.12	3.29	3.51	3.83	4.31	5.18	7.31
	.001	2.23	2.57	2.73	2.87	3.01	3.15	3.40	3.64	3.87	4.02	4.21	4.44	4.73	5.13	5.70	6.60	8.25	12.6
60	.25	1.15	1.19	1.21	1.22	1.24	1.25	1.27	1.29	1.30	1.31	1.32	1.33	1.35	1.37	1.38	1.41	1.42	1.35
	.10	1.29	1.40	1.44	1.48	1.51	1.54	1.60	1.66	1.71	1.74	1.77	1.82	1.87	1.95	2.04	2.18	2.39	2.79
	.05	1.39	1.53	1.59	1.65	1.70	1.75	1.84	1.92	1.99	2.04	2.10	2.17	2.25	2.37	2.53	2.76	3.15	4.00
	.025	1.48	1.67	1.74	1.82	1.88	1.94	2.06	2.17	2.27	2.33	2.41	2.51	2.63	2.79	3.01	3.34	3.93	5.29
	.01	1.60	1.84	1.94	2.03	2.12	2.20	2.35	2.50	2.63	2.72	2.82	2.95	3.12	3.34	3.65	4.13	4.98	7.08
	.001	1.89	2.25	2.41	2.55	2.69	2.83	3.08	3.31	3.54	3.69	3.87	4.09	4.37	4.76	5.31	6.17	7.76	12.0

Table A-1   (Cont.)

		df FOR NUMERATOR																
df FOR DENOM.	α	1	2	3	4	5	6	7	8	9	10	12	15	20	24	30	40	60	∞
120	.25	1.34	1.40	1.39	1.37	1.35	1.33	1.31	1.30	1.29	1.28	1.26	1.24	1.22	1.21	1.19	1.18	1.16	1.10
	.10	2.75	2.35	2.13	1.99	1.90	1.82	1.77	1.72	1.68	1.65	1.60	1.55	1.48	1.45	1.41	1.37	1.32	1.19
	.05	3.92	3.07	2.68	2.45	2.29	2.17	2.09	2.02	1.96	1.91	1.83	1.75	1.66	1.61	1.55	1.50	1.43	1.25
	.025	5.15	3.80	3.23	2.89	2.67	2.52	2.39	2.30	2.22	2.16	2.05	1.94	1.82	1.76	1.69	1.61	1.53	1.31
	.01	6.85	4.79	3.95	3.48	3.17	2.96	2.79	2.66	2.56	2.47	2.34	2.19	2.03	1.95	1.86	1.76	1.66	1.38
	.001	11.4	7.32	5.79	4.95	4.42	4.04	3.77	3.55	3.38	3.24	3.02	2.78	2.53	2.40	2.26	2.11	1.95	1.54
∞	.25	1.32	1.39	1.37	1.35	1.33	1.31	1.29	1.28	1.27	1.25	1.24	1.22	1.19	1.18	1.16	1.14	1.12	1.00
	.10	2.71	2.30	2.08	1.94	1.85	1.77	1.72	1.67	1.63	1.60	1.55	1.49	1.42	1.38	1.34	1.30	1.24	1.00
	.05	3.84	3.00	2.60	2.37	2.21	2.10	2.01	1.94	1.88	1.83	1.75	1.67	1.57	1.52	1.46	1.39	1.32	1.00
	.025	5.02	3.69	3.12	2.79	2.57	2.41	2.29	2.19	2.11	2.05	1.94	1.83	1.71	1.64	1.57	1.48	1.39	1.00
	.01	6.63	4.61	3.78	3.32	3.02	2.80	2.64	2.51	2.41	2.32	2.18	2.04	1.88	1.79	1.70	1.59	1.47	1.00
	.001	10.8	6.91	5.42	4.62	4.10	3.74	3.47	3.27	3.10	2.96	2.74	2.51	2.27	2.13	1.99	1.84	1.66	1.00

Table A-2   Power Functions for Analysis of Variance (Fixed-Effects Model)

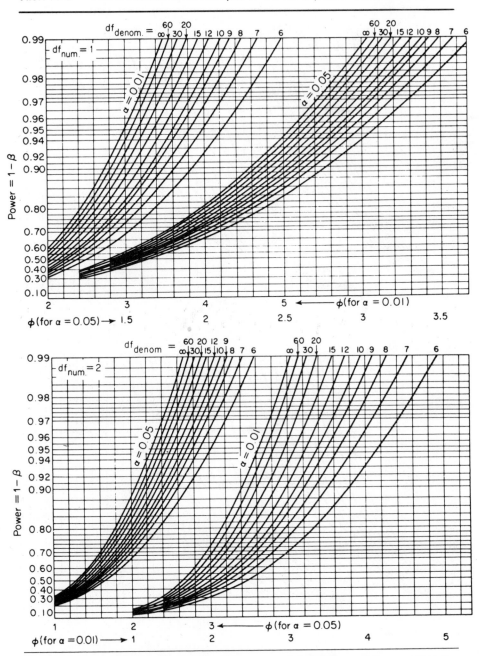

These charts are reproduced from E. S. Pearson and H. O. Hartley, Charts of the power function for analysis of variance tests, derived from the non-central F distribution, *Biometrika*, 1951, *38*, 112–130, by permission of the *Biometrika* Trustees.

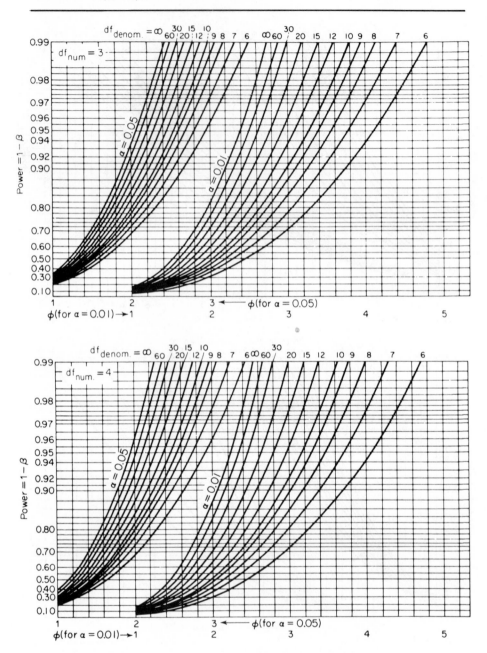

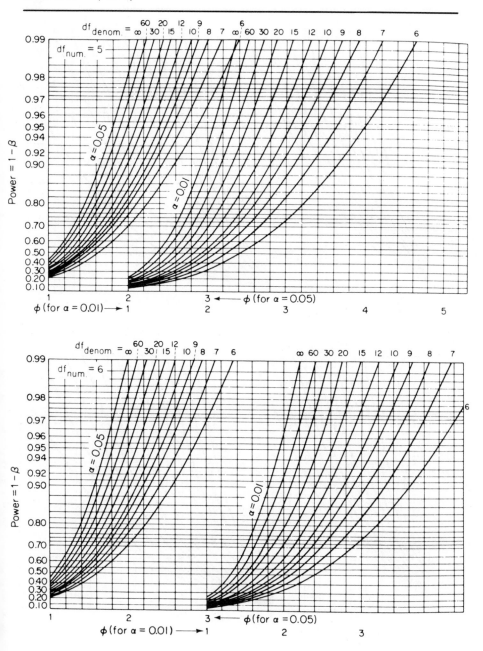

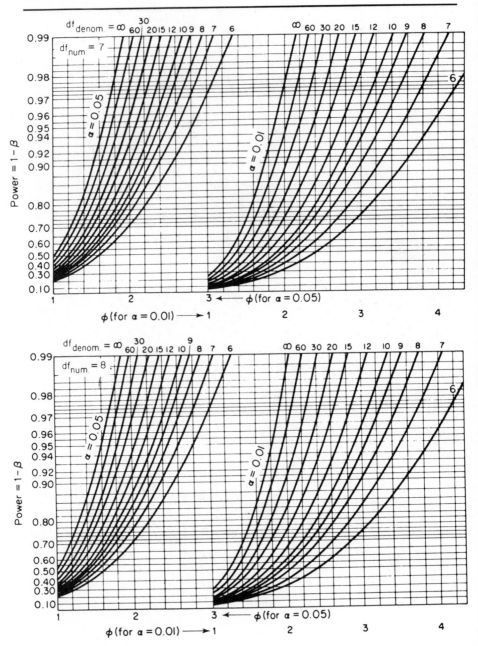

Table A-3   Selected Values from the *t* Distribution

df	$\alpha = .05$	$\alpha = .01$	df	$\alpha = .05$	$\alpha = .01$
1	12.71	63.66	18	2.10	2.88
2	4.30	9.92	19	2.09	2.86
3	3.18	5.84	20	2.09	2.84
4	2.78	4.60	21	2.08	2.83
5	2.57	4.03	22	2.07	2.82
6	2.45	3.71	23	2.07	2.81
7	2.36	3.50	24	2.06	2.80
8	2.31	3.36	25	2.06	2.79
9	2.26	3.25	26	2.06	2.78
10	2.23	3.17	27	2.05	2.77
11	2.20	3.11	28	2.05	2.76
12	2.18	3.06	29	2.04	2.76
13	2.16	3.01	30	2.04	2.75
14	2.14	2.98	40	2.02	2.70
15	2.13	2.95	60	2.00	2.66
16	2.12	2.92	120	1.98	2.62
17	2.11	2.90	∞	1.96	2.58

This table is abridged from Table 12 in E. S. Pearson and H. O. Hartley (Eds.), *Biometrika tables for statisticians* (3rd ed., Vol. 1), Cambridge University Press, New York, 1970, by permission of the *Biometrika* Trustees.

Table A-4   Coefficients of Orthogonal Polynomials

NUMBER OF LEVELS	POLYNOMIAL	COEFFICIENTS										$\Sigma(c_i)^2$
3	Linear	−1	0	1								2
	Quadratic	1	−2	1								6
4	Linear	−3	−1	1	3							20
	Quadratic	1	−1	−1	1							4
	Cubic	−1	3	−3	1							20
5	Linear	−2	−1	0	1	2						10
	Quadratic	2	−1	−2	−1	2						14
	Cubic	−1	2	0	−2	1						10
	Quartic	1	−4	6	−4	1						70
6	Linear	−5	−3	−1	1	3	5					70
	Quadratic	5	−1	−4	−4	−1	5					84
	Cubic	−5	7	4	−4	−7	5					180
	Quartic	1	−3	2	2	−3	1					28
	Quintic	−1	5	−10	10	−5	1					252
7	Linear	−3	−2	−1	0	1	2	3				28
	Quadratic	5	0	−3	−4	−3	0	5				84
	Cubic	−1	1	1	0	−1	−1	1				6
	Quartic	3	−7	1	6	1	−7	3				154
	Quintic	−1	4	−5	0	5	−4	1				84
8	Linear	−7	−5	−3	−1	1	3	5	7			168
	Quadratic	7	1	−3	−5	−5	−3	1	7			168
	Cubic	−7	5	7	3	−3	−7	−5	7			264
	Quartic	7	−13	−3	9	9	−3	−13	7			616
	Quintic	−7	23	−17	−15	15	17	−23	7			2,184
9	Linear	−4	−3	−2	−1	0	1	2	3	4		60
	Quadratic	28	7	−8	−17	−20	−17	−8	7	28		2,772
	Cubic	−14	7	13	9	0	−9	−13	−7	14		990
	Quartic	14	−21	−11	9	18	9	−11	−21	14		2,002
	Quintic	−4	11	−4	−9	0	9	4	−11	4		468
10	Linear	−9	−7	−5	−3	−1	1	3	5	7	9	330
	Quadratic	6	2	−1	−3	−4	−4	−3	−1	2	6	132
	Cubic	−42	14	35	31	12	−12	−31	−35	−14	42	8,580
	Quartic	18	−22	−17	3	18	18	3	−17	−22	18	2,860
	Quintic	−6	14	−1	−11	−6	6	11	1	−14	6	780

This table is abridged from Table 47 in E. S. Pearson and H. O. Hartley (Eds.), *Biometrika tables for statisticians* (3rd ed., Vol. 1), Cambridge University Press, New York, 1970, by permission of the *Biometrika* Trustees.

Table A-5 Critical Values of the Dunnett Test for Comparing Treatment Means with a Control

		TWO-TAILED COMPARISONS								
		k = number of treatment means, including control								
df_{error}	α_{FW}	2	3	4	5	6	7	8	9	10
5	.05	2.57	3.03	3.29	3.48	3.62	3.73	3.82	3.90	3.97
	.01	4.03	4.63	4.98	5.22	5.41	5.56	5.69	5.80	5.89
6	.05	2.45	2.86	3.10	3.26	3.39	3.49	3.57	3.64	3.71
	.01	3.71	4.21	4.51	4.71	4.87	5.00	5.10	5.20	5.28
7	.05	2.36	2.75	2.97	3.12	3.24	3.33	3.41	3.47	3.53
	.01	3.50	3.95	4.21	4.39	4.53	4.64	4.74	4.82	4.89
8	.05	2.31	2.67	2.88	3.02	3.13	3.22	3.29	3.35	3.41
	.01	3.36	3.77	4.00	4.17	4.29	4.40	4.48	4.56	4.62
9	.05	2.26	2.61	2.81	2.95	3.05	3.14	3.20	3.26	3.32
	.01	3.25	3.63	3.85	4.01	4.12	4.22	4.30	4.37	4.43
10	.05	2.23	2.57	2.76	2.89	2.99	3.07	3.14	3.19	3.24
	.01	3.17	3.53	3.74	3.88	3.99	4.08	4.16	4.22	4.28
11	.05	2.20	2.53	2.72	2.84	2.94	3.02	3.08	3.14	3.19
	.01	3.11	3.45	3.65	3.79	3.89	3.98	4.05	4.11	4.16
12	.05	2.18	2.50	2.68	2.81	2.90	2.98	3.04	3.09	3.14
	.01	3.05	3.39	3.58	3.71	3.81	3.89	3.96	4.02	4.07
13	.05	2.16	2.48	2.65	2.78	2.87	2.94	3.00	3.06	3.10
	.01	3.01	3.33	3.52	3.65	3.74	3.82	3.89	3.94	3.99
14	.05	2.14	2.46	2.63	2.75	2.84	2.91	2.97	3.02	3.07
	.01	2.98	3.29	3.47	3.59	3.69	3.76	3.83	3.88	3.93
15	.05	2.13	2.44	2.61	2.73	2.82	2.89	2.95	3.00	3.04
	.01	2.95	3.25	3.43	3.55	3.64	3.71	3.78	3.83	3.88
16	.05	2.12	2.42	2.59	2.71	2.80	2.87	2.92	2.97	3.02
	.01	2.92	3.22	3.39	3.51	3.60	3.67	3.73	3.78	3.83
17	.05	2.11	2.41	2.58	2.69	2.78	2.85	2.90	2.95	3.00
	.01	2.90	3.19	3.36	3.47	3.56	3.63	3.69	3.74	3.79
18	.05	2.10	2.40	2.56	2.68	2.76	2.83	2.89	2.94	2.98
	.01	2.88	3.17	3.33	3.44	3.53	3.60	3.66	3.71	3.75
19	.05	2.09	2.39	2.55	2.66	2.75	2.81	2.87	2.92	2.96
	.01	2.86	3.15	3.31	3.42	3.50	3.57	3.63	3.68	3.72
20	.05	2.09	2.38	2.54	2.65	2.73	2.80	2.86	2.90	2.95
	.01	2.85	3.13	3.29	3.40	3.48	3.55	3.60	3.65	3.69
24	.05	2.06	2.35	2.51	2.61	2.70	2.76	2.81	2.86	2.90
	.01	2.80	3.07	3.22	3.32	3.40	3.47	3.52	3.57	3.61
30	.05	2.04	2.32	2.47	2.58	2.66	2.72	2.77	2.82	2.86
	.01	2.75	3.01	3.15	3.25	3.33	3.39	3.44	3.49	3.52
40	.05	2.02	2.29	2.44	2.54	2.62	2.68	2.73	2.77	2.81
	.01	2.70	2.95	3.09	3.19	3.26	3.32	3.37	3.41	3.44
60	.05	2.00	2.27	2.41	2.51	2.58	2.64	2.69	2.73	2.77
	.01	2.66	2.90	3.03	3.12	3.19	3.25	3.29	3.33	3.37

Table A-5 (Cont.)

TWO-TAILED COMPARISONS

k = number of treatment means, including control

df_{error}	α_{FW}	2	3	4	5	6	7	8	9	10
120	.05	1.98	2.24	2.38	2.47	2.55	2.60	2.65	2.69	2.73
	.01	2.62	2.85	2.97	3.06	3.12	3.18	3.22	3.26	3.29
∞	.05	1.96	2.21	2.35	2.44	2.51	2.57	2.61	2.65	2.69
	.01	2.58	2.79	2.92	3.00	3.06	3.11	3.15	3.19	3.22

This table is abridged from C. W. Dunnett, New tables for multiple comparisons with a control, *Biometrics*, 1964, *20*, 482–491, by permission of the author and the editor.

ONE-TAILED COMPARISONS

k = number of treatment means, including control

df_{error}	α_{FW}	2	3	4	5	6	7	8	9	10
5	.05	2.02	2.44	2.68	2.85	2.98	3.08	3.16	3.24	3.30
	.01	3.37	3.90	4.21	4.43	4.60	4.73	4.85	4.94	5.03
6	.05	1.94	2.34	2.56	2.71	2.83	2.92	3.00	3.07	3.12
	.01	3.14	3.61	3.88	4.07	4.21	4.33	4.43	4.51	4.59
7	.05	1.89	2.27	2.48	2.62	2.73	2.82	2.89	2.95	3.01
	.01	3.00	3.42	3.66	3.83	3.96	4.07	4.15	4.23	4.30
8	.05	1.86	2.22	2.42	2.55	2.66	2.74	2.81	2.87	2.92
	.01	2.90	3.29	3.51	3.67	3.79	3.88	3.96	4.03	4.09
9	.05	1.83	2.18	2.37	2.50	2.60	2.68	2.75	2.81	2.86
	.01	2.82	3.19	3.40	3.55	3.66	3.75	3.82	3.89	3.94
10	.05	1.81	2.15	2.34	2.47	2.56	2.64	2.70	2.76	2.81
	.01	2.76	3.11	3.31	3.45	3.56	3.64	3.71	3.78	3.83
11	.05	1.80	2.13	2.31	2.44	2.53	2.60	2.67	2.72	2.77
	.01	2.72	3.06	3.25	3.38	3.48	3.56	3.63	3.69	3.74
12	.05	1.78	2.11	2.29	2.41	2.50	2.58	2.64	2.69	2.74
	.01	2.68	3.01	3.19	3.32	3.42	3.50	3.56	3.62	2.67
13	.05	1.77	2.09	2.27	2.39	2.48	2.55	2.61	2.66	2.71
	.01	2.65	2.97	3.15	3.27	3.37	3.44	3.51	3.56	3.61
14	.05	1.76	2.08	2.25	2.37	2.46	2.53	2.59	2.64	2.69
	.01	2.62	2.94	3.11	3.23	3.32	3.40	3.46	3.51	3.56
15	.05	1.75	2.07	2.24	2.36	2.44	2.51	2.57	2.62	2.67
	.01	2.60	2.91	3.08	3.20	3.29	3.36	3.42	3.47	3.52
16	.05	1.75	2.06	2.23	2.34	2.43	2.50	2.56	2.61	2.65
	.01	2.58	2.88	3.05	3.17	3.26	3.33	3.39	3.44	3.48
17	.05	1.74	2.05	2.22	2.33	2.42	2.49	2.54	2.59	2.64
	.01	2.57	2.86	3.03	3.14	3.23	3.30	3.36	3.41	3.45
18	.05	1.73	2.04	2.21	2.32	2.41	2.48	2.53	2.58	2.62
	.01	2.55	2.84	3.01	3.12	3.21	3.27	3.33	3.38	3.42

Table A-5   (Cont.)

k = number of treatment means, including control

df_{error}	α_{FW}	2	3	4	5	6	7	8	9	10
19	.05	1.73	2.03	2.20	2.31	2.40	2.47	2.52	2.57	2.61
	.01	2.54	2.83	2.99	3.10	3.18	3.25	3.31	3.36	3.40
20	.05	1.72	2.03	2.19	2.30	2.39	2.46	2.51	2.56	2.60
	.01	2.53	2.81	2.97	3.08	3.17	3.23	3.29	3.34	3.38
24	.05	1.71	2.01	2.17	2.28	2.36	2.43	2.48	2.53	2.57
	.01	2.49	2.77	2.92	3.03	3.11	3.17	3.22	3.27	3.31
30	.05	1.70	1.99	2.15	2.25	2.33	2.40	2.45	2.50	2.54
	.01	2.46	2.72	2.87	2.97	3.05	3.11	3.16	3.21	3.24
40	.05	1.68	1.97	2.13	2.23	2.31	2.37	2.42	2.47	2.51
	.01	2.42	2.68	2.82	2.92	2.99	3.05	3.10	3.14	3.18
60	.05	1.67	1.95	2.10	2.21	2.28	2.35	2.39	2.44	2.48
	.01	2.39	2.64	2.78	2.87	2.94	3.00	3.04	3.08	3.12
120	.05	1.66	1.93	2.08	2.18	2.26	2.32	2.37	2.41	2.45
	.01	2.36	2.60	2.73	2.82	2.89	2.94	2.99	3.03	3.06
∞	.05	1.64	1.92	2.06	2.16	2.23	2.29	2.34	2.38	2.42
	.01	2.33	2.56	2.68	2.77	2.84	2.89	2.93	2.97	3.00

This table is reproduced from C. W. Dunnett, A mulitple comparison procedure for comparing several treatments with a control, *Journal of the American Statistical Association*, 1955, *50*, 1,096–1,121, by permission of the author and the editor.

Table A-6 Critical Values of the Studentized Range Statistic

r = number of means (Tukey test) or number of steps between ordered means (Newman-Keuls test)

df_{error}	α_{FW}	2	3	4	5	6	7	8	9	10	11	12	13	14	15	16	17	18	19	20	α_{FW}	df_{error}
5	.05	3.64	4.60	5.22	5.67	6.03	6.33	6.58	6.80	6.99	7.17	7.32	7.47	7.60	7.72	7.83	7.93	8.03	8.12	8.21	.05	5
	.01	5.70	6.98	7.80	8.42	8.91	9.32	9.67	9.97	10.24	10.48	10.70	10.89	11.08	11.24	11.40	11.55	11.68	11.81	11.93	.01	
6	.05	3.46	4.34	4.90	5.30	5.63	5.90	6.12	6.32	6.49	6.65	6.79	6.92	7.03	7.14	7.24	7.34	7.43	7.51	7.59	.05	6
	.01	5.24	6.33	7.03	7.56	7.97	8.32	8.61	8.87	9.10	9.30	9.48	9.65	9.81	9.95	10.08	10.21	10.32	10.43	10.54	.01	
7	.05	3.34	4.16	4.68	5.06	5.36	5.61	5.82	6.00	6.16	6.30	6.43	6.55	6.66	6.76	6.85	6.94	7.02	7.10	7.17	.05	7
	.01	4.95	5.92	6.54	7.01	7.37	7.68	7.94	8.17	8.37	8.55	8.71	8.86	9.00	9.12	9.24	9.35	9.46	9.55	9.65	.01	
8	.05	3.26	4.04	4.53	4.89	5.17	5.40	5.60	5.77	5.92	6.05	6.18	6.29	6.39	6.48	6.57	6.65	6.73	6.80	6.87	.05	8
	.01	4.75	5.64	6.20	6.62	6.96	7.24	7.47	7.68	7.86	8.03	8.18	8.31	8.44	8.55	8.66	8.76	8.85	8.94	9.03	.01	
9	.05	3.20	3.95	4.41	4.76	5.02	5.24	5.43	5.59	5.74	5.87	5.98	6.09	6.19	6.28	6.36	6.44	6.51	6.58	6.64	.05	9
	.01	4.60	5.43	5.96	6.35	6.66	6.91	7.13	7.33	7.49	7.65	7.78	7.91	8.03	8.13	8.23	8.33	8.41	8.49	8.57	.01	
10	.05	3.15	3.88	4.33	4.65	4.91	5.12	5.30	5.46	5.60	5.72	5.83	5.93	6.03	6.11	6.19	6.27	6.34	6.40	6.47	.05	10
	.01	4.48	5.27	5.77	6.14	6.43	6.67	6.87	7.05	7.21	7.36	7.49	7.60	7.71	7.81	7.91	7.99	8.08	8.15	8.23	.01	
11	.05	3.11	3.82	4.26	4.57	4.82	5.03	5.20	5.35	5.49	5.61	5.71	5.81	5.90	5.98	6.06	6.13	6.20	6.27	6.33	.05	11
	.01	4.39	5.15	5.62	5.97	6.25	6.48	6.67	6.84	6.99	7.13	7.25	7.36	7.46	7.56	7.65	7.73	7.81	7.88	7.95	.01	
12	.05	3.08	3.77	4.20	4.51	4.75	4.95	5.12	5.27	5.39	5.51	5.61	5.71	5.80	5.88	5.95	6.02	6.09	6.15	6.21	.05	12
	.01	4.32	5.05	5.50	5.84	6.10	6.32	6.51	6.67	6.81	6.94	7.06	7.17	7.26	7.36	7.44	7.52	7.59	7.66	7.73	.01	
13	.05	3.06	3.73	4.15	4.45	4.69	4.88	5.05	5.19	5.32	5.43	5.53	5.63	5.71	5.79	5.86	5.93	5.99	6.05	6.11	.05	13
	.01	4.26	4.96	5.40	5.73	5.98	6.19	6.37	6.53	6.67	6.79	6.90	7.01	7.10	7.19	7.27	7.35	7.42	7.48	7.55	.01	
14	.05	3.03	3.70	4.11	4.41	4.64	4.83	4.99	5.13	5.25	5.36	5.46	5.55	5.64	5.71	5.79	5.85	5.91	5.97	6.03	.05	14
	.01	4.21	4.89	5.32	5.63	5.88	6.08	6.26	6.41	6.54	6.66	6.77	6.87	6.96	7.05	7.13	7.20	7.27	7.33	7.39	.01	
15	.05	3.01	3.67	4.08	4.37	4.59	4.78	4.94	5.08	5.20	5.31	5.40	5.49	5.57	5.65	5.72	5.78	5.85	5.90	5.96	.05	15
	.01	4.17	4.84	5.25	5.56	5.80	5.99	6.16	6.31	6.44	6.55	6.66	6.76	6.84	6.93	7.00	7.07	7.14	7.20	7.26	.01	

df	α																			
16	.05	3.00	3.65	4.05	4.33	4.56	4.74	4.90	5.03	5.15	5.26	5.35	5.44	5.52	5.59	5.66	5.73	5.79	5.84	5.90
	.01	4.13	4.79	5.19	5.49	5.72	5.92	6.08	6.22	6.35	6.46	6.56	6.66	6.74	8.82	6.90	6.97	7.03	7.09	7.15
17	.05	2.98	3.63	4.02	4.30	4.52	4.70	4.86	4.99	5.11	5.21	5.31	5.39	5.47	5.54	5.61	5.67	5.73	5.79	5.84
	.01	4.10	4.74	5.14	5.43	5.66	5.85	6.01	6.15	6.27	6.38	6.48	6.57	6.66	6.73	6.81	6.87	6.94	7.00	7.05
18	.05	2.97	3.61	4.00	4.28	4.49	4.67	4.82	4.96	5.07	5.17	5.27	5.35	5.43	5.50	5.57	5.63	5.69	5.74	5.79
	.01	4.07	4.70	5.09	5.38	5.60	5.79	5.94	6.08	6.20	6.31	6.41	6.50	6.58	6.65	6.73	6.79	6.85	6.91	6.97
19	.05	2.96	3.59	3.98	4.25	4.47	4.65	4.79	4.92	5.04	5.14	5.23	5.31	5.39	5.46	5.53	5.59	5.65	5.70	5.75
	.01	4.05	4.67	5.05	5.33	5.55	5.73	5.89	6.02	6.14	6.25	6.34	6.43	6.51	6.58	6.65	6.72	6.78	6.84	6.89
20	.05	2.95	3.58	3.96	4.23	4.45	4.62	4.77	4.90	5.01	5.11	5.20	5.28	5.36	5.43	5.49	5.55	5.61	5.66	5.71
	.01	4.02	4.64	5.02	5.29	5.51	5.69	5.84	5.97	6.09	6.19	6.28	6.37	6.45	6.52	6.59	6.65	6.71	6.77	6.82
24	.05	2.92	3.53	3.90	4.17	4.37	4.54	4.68	4.81	4.92	5.01	5.10	5.18	5.25	5.32	5.38	5.44	5.49	5.55	5.59
	.01	3.96	4.55	4.91	5.17	5.37	5.54	5.69	5.81	5.92	6.02	6.11	6.19	6.26	6.33	6.39	6.45	6.51	6.56	6.61
30	.05	2.89	3.49	3.85	4.10	4.30	4.46	4.60	4.72	4.82	4.92	5.00	5.08	5.15	5.21	5.27	5.33	5.38	5.43	5.47
	.01	3.89	4.45	4.80	5.05	5.24	5.40	5.54	5.65	5.76	5.85	5.93	6.01	6.08	6.14	6.20	6.26	6.31	6.36	6.41
40	.05	2.86	3.44	3.79	4.04	4.23	4.39	4.52	4.63	4.73	4.82	4.90	4.98	5.04	5.11	5.16	5.22	5.27	5.31	5.36
	.01	3.82	4.37	4.70	4.93	5.11	5.26	5.39	5.50	5.60	5.69	5.76	5.83	5.90	5.96	6.02	6.07	6.12	6.16	6.21
60	.05	2.83	3.40	3.74	3.98	4.16	4.31	4.44	4.55	4.65	4.73	4.81	4.88	4.94	5.00	5.06	5.11	5.15	5.20	5.24
	.01	3.76	4.28	4.59	4.82	4.99	5.13	5.25	5.36	5.45	5.53	5.60	5.67	5.73	5.78	5.84	5.89	5.93	5.97	6.01
120	.05	2.80	3.36	3.68	3.92	4.10	4.24	4.36	4.47	4.56	4.64	4.71	4.78	4.84	4.90	4.95	5.00	5.04	5.09	5.13
	.01	3.70	4.20	4.50	4.71	4.87	5.01	5.12	5.21	5.30	5.37	5.44	5.50	5.56	5.61	5.66	5.71	5.75	5.79	5.83
∞	.05	2.77	3.31	3.63	3.86	4.03	4.17	4.29	4.39	4.47	4.55	4.62	4.68	4.74	4.80	4.85	4.89	4.93	4.97	5.01
	.01	3.64	4.12	4.40	4.60	4.76	4.88	4.99	5.08	5.16	5.23	5.29	5.35	5.40	5.45	5.49	5.54	5.57	5.61	5.65

This table is abridged from Table 29 in E. S. Pearson and H. O. Hartley (Eds.), *Biometrika tables for statisticians* (3rd ed., Vol. 1), Cambridge University Press, New York, 1970, by permission of the *Biometrika* Trustees.

Appendix B

Answers to
the Chapter Exercises

CHAPTER 2

1. (**a,** b)

	a_1	a_2	a_3	a_4	a_5
A_i:	80	60	70	120	100
$\sum_j^s (AS_{ij})^2$:	684	426	600	1,524	1,096
$\bar{A}_i$:	8.00	6.00	7.00	12.00	10.00

(c)

$$[T] = \frac{T^2}{(a)(s)} = \frac{(80 + 60 + 70 + 120 + 100)^2}{(5)(10)} = \frac{184,900}{50} = 3,698.00;$$

$$[A] = \frac{\sum A^2}{s} = \frac{(80)^2 + (60)^2 + (70)^2 + (120)^2 + (100)^2}{10} = \frac{39,300}{10}$$

$$= 3,930.00;$$

$$[AS] = \sum (AS)^2 = 684 + 426 + 600 + 1,524 + 1,096 = 4,330.$$

$$SS_A = [A] - [T] = 232.00;$$

$$SS_{S/A} = [AS] - [A] = 400.00;$$

and

$$SS_T = [AS] - [T] = 632.00.$$

Check: $SS_A + SS_{S/A} = SS_T;$

$$232.00 + 400.00 = 632.00.$$

CHAPTER 3

1. (a) $F(4, 30) = 2.69, p = .05.$
   (b) $F(1, 120) = 11.4, p = .001.$
   (c) $df_{num.} = a - 1 = 7 - 1 = 6; df_{denom.} = a(s - 1) = 7(5 - 1) = 7(4)$
       $= 28; F(6, 28) = 2.00, p = .10.$
   (d) $df_{num.} = a - 1 = 3 - 1 = 2; df_{denom.} = a(s - 1) = 3(9 - 1) = 3(8)$
       $= 24; F(2, 24) = 1.47, p = .25.$

2.

SOURCE	CALCULATIONS	SS	df	MS	F
A	374.00 − 365.07 =	8.93	2	4.47	.37
S/A	518 − 374.00 =	144.00	12	12.00	
Total	518 − 365.07 =	152.93	15		

should be 14?

3.

SOURCE	CALCULATIONS	SS	df	MS	F
A	3,930.00 − 3,698.00 =	232.00	4	58.00	6.52*
S/A	4,330 − 3,930.00 =	400.00	45	8.89	
Total	4,330 − 3,698.00 =	632.00	49		

*$p < .01.$

4. (a)

SOURCE	CALCULATIONS	SS	df	MS	F
A	640.00 − 563.33 =	76.67	5	15.33	3.14*
S/A	757 − 640.00 =	117.00	24	4.88	
Total	757 − 563.33 =	193.67	29		

*$p < .05.$

(b) The formula for a within-group variance is calculated in two steps, the sum of squares and then the division by the degrees of freedom. For any one group,

$$\hat{o}_i^2 = \frac{SS_{S/A\,i}}{df_{S/A\,i}},$$

where $SS_{S/A\,i} = \sum_{j=1}^{s} (AS_{ij})^2 - \frac{A_i^2}{s}$ and $df_{S/A\,i} = s - 1$.

The steps in the analysis are enumerated in the following table:

GROUPS	A_i	$\sum_{j=1}^{s} (AS_{ij})^2$	$SS_{S/A\,i}$	$\hat{o}_i^2$
a_1	15	65	20.00	5.00
a_2	10	35	15.00	3.75
a_3	25	130	5.00	1.25
a_4	35	275	30.00	7.50
a_5	25	150	25.00	6.25
a_6	20	102	22.00	5.50

The average variance is found by summing the individual within-group variances obtained in the preceding calculations and dividing by the number of variances:

$$\hat{o}_{S/A}^2 = \frac{\Sigma \hat{o}_i^2}{a} = \frac{29.25}{6} = 4.88.$$

This average variance is identical to the $MS_{S/A}$ calculated in part (a) of this question. The equality indicates that the within-groups mean square is an average of the separate within-group variances.

CHAPTER 4

1. (a) If we let $\mu_1 = 10$, $\mu_2 = 10$, $\mu_3 = 14$, $\mu_4 = 16$, and $\mu_5 = 15$; $\mu = \Sigma \mu_i/a = 65/5 = 13$. Then,

$$\Sigma (\alpha_i)^2 = (10 - 13)^2 + (10 - 13)^2 + (14 - 13)^2 + (16 - 13)^2 + (15 - 13)^2$$
$$= 32.$$

From Eq. (4-1),

$$\phi_A^2 = \frac{s'(32)/5}{15} = .43s'; \quad \phi_A = \sqrt{.43s'} = .66\sqrt{s'}.$$

If we try $s' = 7$, we find $\phi_A = (.66)(2.65) = 1.75$, $df_{\text{denom.}} = 5(7 - 1) = 30$, and power $= .83$. Any smaller sample size gives power $<.80$.

(b) If we try $s' = 10$, we find $\phi_A = (.66)(3.16) = 2.09$, $df_{denom.} = 5(10 - 1)$ $= 45$, and power $= .86$. On the other hand, $s' = 9$ produces ϕ_A $= (.66)(3.00) = 1.98$, and power $= .78$.

2. In these estimates all we need is to calculate ϕ_A^2 from Eq. (4-1). This is accomplished by expressing each proposed situation in terms of population treatment means and solving for $\Sigma (\mu_i - \mu)^2$. The other necessary information is given in the problem; the power estimate is obtained from the power functions found in Table A-2 of Appendix A, in the chart labeled $df_{num.} = 7$.

Minimum variability. The μ_i's are 5, 8.5, 8.5, 8.5, 8.5, 8.5, 8.5, and 12; $\Sigma (\mu_i - \mu)^2 = 24.50$; $\phi_A^2 = 1.00$; $\phi_A = 1.00$; and power $= .45$.

Intermediate variability. The μ_i's are 5, 6, 7, 8, 9, 10, 11, and 12; $\Sigma (\mu_i - \mu)^2 = 42.00$; $\phi_A^2 = 1.71$; $\phi_A = 1.31$; and power $= .72$.

Maximum variability. The μ_i's are 5, 5, 5, 5, 12, 12, 12, and 12; $\Sigma (\mu_i - \mu)^2$ $= 98.00$; $\phi_A^2 = 4.00$; $\phi_A = 2.00$; and power $> .98$. If this were a real situation, the researcher could probably afford to reduce sample size, since power is so high in this particular case.

3. With the information provided, $\phi_A^2 = (.35)(s')$ and $\phi_A = .59 \sqrt{s'}$. A value of $s' = 16$ gives $\phi_A = (.59)(4.00) = 2.36$ and power $= .90$.

CHAPTER 5

1. (a)

	A_i	$\hat{\sigma}_i$	$\hat{\sigma}_M$	$t(\hat{\sigma}_M)$	95% CONFIDENCE INTERVAL
a_1	3.00	2.24	1.00	2.78	$.22 \leqslant \mu_1 \leqslant 5.78$
a_2	2.00	1.94	.87	2.42	$-.42 \leqslant \mu_2 \leqslant 4.42$
a_3	5.00	1.12	.50	1.39	$3.61 \leqslant \mu_3 \leqslant 6.39$
a_4	7.00	2.74	1.22	3.39	$3.61 \leqslant \mu_4 \leqslant 10.39$
a_5	5.00	2.50	1.12	3.11	$1.89 \leqslant \mu_5 \leqslant 8.11$
a_6	4.00	2.35	1.05	2.92	$1.08 \leqslant \mu_6 \leqslant 6.92$

(b) The 95 percent confidence interval of the mean consists of a range of values that is constructed in such a way that it will contain the population mean 95 percent of the time.

2. (a)

$$\hat{\omega}_A^2 = \frac{210.00 - (2)(14.17)}{380.00 + 14.17} = .461; \quad \hat{\epsilon}_A^2 = \frac{210.00 - (2)(14.17)}{380.00} = .478.$$

(b) The experimental treatments account for nearly 50 percent of the total variability in the experiment. Using Cohen's (1977) terminology, this finding represents a "large" effect.

3. (a)

$$\hat{\omega}_A^2 = \frac{8.93 - (2)(12.00)}{152.93 + 12.00} = -.091.$$

(b) The presence of a negative value is interpreted to mean the absence of a treatment effect. (Negative values are obtained when $F < 1$.)

4. (a)

$$\hat{\omega}_A^2 = \frac{233.33 - (2)(17.90)}{609.33 + 17.90} = .315; \quad \hat{\omega}_A^2 = \frac{233.33 - (2)(17.90)}{1,790.63 + 17.90} = .109.$$

(b) As revealed by the F tests, the statistical conclusions drawn from the two experiments are the same, but the relative strengths of the treatment effects are quite different. With other factors held constant, a stronger treatment effect is associated with the experiment having the *smaller* sample size ($s = 8$ versus $s = 30$).

CHAPTER 6

1. (a)

SOURCE	CALCULATIONS	SS	df	MS	F
A	$5,117.25 - 4,651.25 =$	466.00	4	116.50	3.15*
S/A			15	37.00	

*$p < .05$.

(b)

	Coefficients and Sums of Weighted Means						
	a_1	a_2	a_3	a_4	a_5		
$\bar{A}_j$:	15.00	13.75	8.00	16.50	23.00	$\hat{\psi}_A$	$\Sigma (c_j)^2$
Comp. 1:	4	-1	-1	-1	-1	-1.25	20
Comp. 2:	0	1	1	-1	-1	-17.75	4
Comp. 3:	0	1	-1	0	0	5.75	2
Comp. 4:	0	0	0	1	-1	-6.50	2

(c) (Comp. 1) $\times$ (Comp. 2):

$$(4)(0) + (-1)(1) + (-1)(1) + (-1)(-1) + (-1)(-1) = 0;$$

(Comp. 1) $\times$ (Comp. 3):

$$(4)(0) + (-1)(1) + (-1)(-1) + (-1)(0) + (-1)(0) = 0;$$

$$\cdots$$

(Comp. 3) $\times$ (Comp. 4):

$$(0)(0) + (1)(0) + (-1)(0) + (0)(1) + (0)(-1) = 0.$$

(d) Substituting the values from the table into Eq. (6–5), we have

$$SS_{A\ \text{comp. 1}} = \frac{4(-1.25)^2}{20} \; ; \quad SS_{A\ \text{comp. 2}} = \frac{4(-17.75)^2}{4} \; ;$$

$$SS_{A\ \text{comp. 3}} = \frac{4(5.75)^2}{2} \; ; \quad \text{and} \quad SS_{A\ \text{comp. 4}} = \frac{4(-6.50)^2}{2} \; .$$

The remainder of the analysis is summarized as follows:

SOURCE	SS	df	MS	F
A	(466.0000)	(4)		
Comp. 1	.3125	1	.3125	<1
Comp. 2	315.0625	1	315.0625	8.52*
Comp. 3	66.1250	1	66.1250	1.79
Comp. 4	84.5000	1	84.5000	2.28
S/A		15	37.00	

*$p < .025$.

The analysis indicates that the main outcome of the experiment was a difference between the two drugs.

(e)

$$.3125 + 315.0625 + 66.1250 + 84.5000 = 466.0000 = SS_A .$$

2. This problem has various answers. One solution is as follows:

	a_1	a_2	a_3	a_4	a_5
			(a)		
Comp. 3	0	1	1	0	−2
Comp. 4	0	1	−1	0	0
			(b)		
Comp. 3	0	0	−1	−1	2
Comp. 4	−1	4	−1	−1	−1
			(c)		
Comp. 3	1	0	−1	−1	1
Comp. 4	−1	4	−1	−1	−1
			(d)		
Comp. 3	1	−1	0	0	0
Comp. 4	0	0	1	0	−1

3. (a)

SOURCE	SS	df	MS	F
Comp. 1	162.45	1	162.45	12.03*
Comp. 2	44.10	1	44.10	3.27
Comp. 3	3.60	1	3.60	<1
Comp. 4	.10	1	.10	<1

*$p < .01$.

The main conclusion is that performance is significantly better when the material is presented all at once rather than exposed one word at a time.

(b)

$$SS_A = 3,460.40 - 3,226.24 = 234.16.$$

$$\sum SS_{A \text{ comp.}} = 162.45 + 44.10 + 3.60 + .10 = 210.25.$$

If we replace the fourth comparison with one that is orthogonal to the other three, $(-1, -1, 4, -1, -1)$, $SS_{A \text{ comp. 4}'} = 24.01$. Now, the four sums of squares sum to SS_A; i.e.,

$$\Sigma SS_{A \text{ comp.}} = 162.45 + 44.10 + 3.60 + 24.01 = 234.16.$$

On the other hand, this substitute comparison does not represent a meaningful comparison in this experiment (see pp. 122–123).

4. (a)

$$SS_{A \text{ set}} = \frac{(48)^2 + (53)^2 + (47)^2}{10} - \frac{(48 + 53 + 47)^2}{(3)(10)}$$

$$= 732.20 - 730.13 = 2.07.$$

$$MS_{A \text{ set}} = \frac{2.07}{2} = 1.04; \quad F_{\text{set}} = \frac{1.04}{4.11} = .25.$$

The three incentives did not influence performance differentially.

(b) The average for the control condition is 3.20 problems and for the combined incentive conditions is $(4.8 + 5.3 + 4.7)/3 = 4.93$ problems. To avoid fractions we can use the following set of coefficients to determine the sum of squares for this comparison: $(-1, -1, -1, 3)$.

$$SS_{A \text{ comp.}} = \frac{10(-5.20)^2}{12} = 22.53.$$

$$F = \frac{22.53}{4.11} = 5.48, p < .05.$$

While equally effective, the incentive conditions did facilitate problem solving in this experiment.

(c)

$$SS_A = \frac{(48)^2 + (53)^2 + (47)^2 + (32)^2}{10} - \frac{(48 + 53 + 47 + 32)^2}{(4)(10)}$$

$$= 834.60 - 810.00 = 24.60.$$

$$MS_A = \frac{24.60}{3} = 8.20; \quad F = \frac{8.20}{4.11} = 2.00, p > .10.$$

This problem illustrates the advantage of planned comparisons. The omnibus F test assesses the average or overall differences among the treatment means and can "water down" specific differences present in the data. In this case, the fact that the three incentive conditions did not differ helped to "average out" the significant single-df comparison between the control and the combined incentive conditions. The set of planned comparisons represented by parts (a) and (b) reflects a meaningful and logical way to analyze this experiment.

CHAPTER 7

1. (a) You should be able to detect the presence of both a linear trend (a general rise in the function) and a quadratic trend (a downward curvature).

 (b) *Linear component:*

$$\hat{\psi}_{\text{linear}} = (-3)(1.52) + (-2)(2.64) + (-1)(4.28) + (0)(3.86) + (1)(3.86)$$
$$+ (2)(2.79) + (3)(3.70) = 6.42;$$

$$SS_{A \text{ linear}} = \frac{(14)(6.42)^2}{28} = 20.61; \quad F = \frac{20.61}{5.84} = 3.53, p > .05.$$

 Quadratic component:

$$\hat{\psi}_{\text{quadratic}} = (5)(1.52) + (0)(2.64) + (-3)(4.28) + (-4)(3.86) + (-3)(3.86)$$
$$+ (0)(2.79) + (5)(3.70) = -13.76;$$

$$SS_{A \text{ quadratic}} = \frac{14(-13.76)^2}{84} = 31.56; \quad F = \frac{31.56}{5.84} = 5.40, p < .025.$$

2. (a)

SOURCE	SS	df	MS	F
A	31.37	5	6.27	7.55*
S/A	20.00	24	.83	
Total	51.37	29		

*$p < .01$.

 (b) Theoretical considerations justify examining the quadratic trend component regardless of the outcome of the omnibus F test.

$$\hat{\psi}_{\text{quadratic}} = (5)(.80) + (-1)(1.60) + (-4)(3.40) + (-4)(3.60)$$
$$+ (-1)(3.20) + (5)(2.80) = -14.80;$$

$$SS_{A\,\text{quadratic}} = \frac{5(-14.80)^2}{84} = 13.04; \quad F = \frac{13.04}{.83} = 15.71, p < .01.$$

An examination of the data indicates that a strong linear trend is present. Since this component was not specified ahead of time, we should first test the significance of the residual variation to see whether it is justified statistically to assess the linear component.

$$SS_{A\,\text{residual}} = SS_A - SS_{A\,\text{quadratic}} = 31.37 - 13.04 = 18.33;$$

$$df_{A\,\text{residual}} = df_A - df_{A\,\text{quadratic}} = 5 - 1 = 4;$$

$$MS_{A\,\text{residual}} = \frac{18.33}{4} = 4.58; \quad \text{and} \quad F = \frac{4.58}{.83} = 5.52, p < .01.$$

Since the residual variation is significant, it is appropriate to examine the linear component:

$$\hat{\psi}_{\text{linear}} = (-5)(.80) + (-3)(1.60) + (-1)(3.40) + (1)(3.60)$$
$$+ (3)(3.20) + (5)(2.80) = 15.00;$$

$$SS_{A\,\text{linear}} = \frac{5(15.00)^2}{70} = 16.07; \quad \text{and} \quad F = \frac{16.07}{.83} = 19.36, p < .01.$$

(c) The theoretical expectations were supported by the experiment with a significant concave downward trend relating anxiety and backward memory span. In addition, there is a significant tendency for memory span to increase as a function of the anxiety level of the subjects.

CHAPTER 8

1.

COMPARISON	VERBAL STATEMENT
1	Do the two control conditions differ?
2	Do the combined control conditions differ from the combined drug conditions?
3	Does drug B differ from the combined control conditions?
4	Do the combined drug A conditions differ from the combined control conditions?
5	Do the combined drug conditions differ from the first control?
6	Does drug B differ from the first control?
7	Do the combined drug A conditions differ from the first control?
8	Do the combined drug conditions differ from the second control?
9	Does drug B differ from the second control?
10	Do the combined drug A conditions differ from the second control?
11	Does the drug A_1 condition differ from the combined control conditions?
12	Does the drug A_2 condition differ from the combined control conditions?

13	Does the drug A_1 condition differ from the first control?
14	Does the drug A_2 condition differ from the first control?
15	Does the drug A_1 condition differ from the second control?
16	Does the drug A_2 condition differ from the second control?
17	Do the two drug A conditions differ?
18	Do the combined drug A conditions differ from drug B?
19	Does the drug A_1 condition differ from drug B?
20	Does the drug A_2 condition differ from drug B?

2. (a) The first step is to determine the "acceptable" familywise type I error rate for planned comparisons. From Eq. (8-3), $\tilde{\alpha}_{FW\,planned} = (4)(.05) = .20$. Next, we can calculate the per comparison probability to be used with the planned comparisons ($\tilde{\alpha}_{planned}$). From Eq. (8-4), $\tilde{\alpha}_{planned} = .20/c$. This probability will be calculated for each of the possible plans listed in Table 8–5. That is,

$$\text{for comp. 1 (n.s.), comp. 17 (n.s.), } \tilde{\alpha}_{planned} = \frac{.20}{6} = .033;$$

$$\text{for comp. 1 (sign.), comp. 17 (n.s.), } \tilde{\alpha}_{planned} = \frac{.20}{9} = .022;$$

$$\text{for comp. 1 (n.s.), comp. 17 (sign.), } \tilde{\alpha}_{planned} = \frac{.20}{7} = .029;$$

and

$$\text{for comp. 1 (sign.), comp. 17 (sign.), } \tilde{\alpha}_{planned} = \frac{.20}{10} = .020.$$

(b) The critical value of F is obtained in three steps. First, we determine the value of z for one of the tails in the normal distribution, i.e.,

$\frac{1}{2}(\tilde{\alpha}_{planned})$. Calculating these in order, we find

$\frac{1}{2}(.033) = .017$, and $z = 2.12$; $\frac{1}{2}(.022) = .011$, and $z = 2.29$;

$\frac{1}{2}(.029) = .015$, and $z = 2.17$; and $\frac{1}{2}(.020) = .010$, and $z = 2.33$.

The second step involves Eq. (8-5), which gives us the approximate value of the critical value of t. For the first plan,

$$t(45) = 2.12 + \frac{(2.12)^3 + 2.12}{4(45 - 2)} = 2.12 + .07 = 2.19.$$

For the remaining three, $t(45) = 2.37$, 2.24, and 2.42, respectively. The final step involves squaring t to obtain the critical value of F. The four values are $F(1, 45) = 4.80$, 5.62, 5.02, and 5.86, respectively.

3. (a)

SOURCE	CALCULATIONS	SS	df	MS	F
A	$28{,}463.88 - 27{,}789.03 =$	674.85	7	96.41	3.35*
S/A			120	28.75	

*$p < .01$.

(b) Critical $\bar{C}$-$\bar{E}$ difference is

$$\bar{d}_D = \frac{2.65\sqrt{2(28.75)}}{\sqrt{16}} = \frac{(2.65)(7.58)}{4} = 5.02.$$

Thus,

	E_1	E_2	E_3	E_4	E_5	E_6	E_7
$\bar{C} - \bar{E}$:	1.19	3.00	.63	6.13*	4.75	5.25*	5.69*

*$p < .05$.

(c) $F_S = (8 - 1)(2.09) = 14.63$. If we consider the largest difference, C versus E_4, and translate this comparison into a sum of squares, we have

$$SS_{A\,comp.} = \frac{16(6.13)^2}{2} = 300.62.$$

The $F = 300.62/28.75 = 10.46$ does not exceed $F_S = 14.63$. Thus, none of the control-experimental differences is significant, which demonstrates the marked advantage of specifying a restricted set of comparisons with multiple-comparison techniques.

An alternative way to approach this problem is to express the Scheffé correction in terms of a *critical mean difference*. In this case,

$$\bar{d}_S = \frac{\sqrt{F_S}\sqrt{2(MS_{S/A})}}{\sqrt{s}} = \frac{\sqrt{14.63}\sqrt{2(28.75)}}{\sqrt{16}}$$

$$= \frac{(3.82)(7.58)}{4} = 7.24.$$

Again, none of the C-E differences exceeds this critical value.

4. (a and b) The Fisher test first assesses the significance of the omnibus F:

SOURCE	CALCULATIONS	SS	df	MS	F
A	$122{,}754.43 - 112{,}770.88 =$	9,983.55	7	1,426.22	24.32*
S/A			48	58.65	

*$p < .01$.

Since the omnibus F is significant, the Fisher test permits the assessment of all pairwise differences without correction for FW error. The critical value, $\bar{d}_F$, is the same as that used to evaluate planned comparisons where no corrections are made either. In this example,

$$\bar{d}_F = \frac{t(48) \sqrt{2(MS_{S/A})}}{\sqrt{s}} = \frac{(2.02)\sqrt{2(58.65)}}{\sqrt{7}}$$

$$= \frac{(2.02)(10.83)}{2.65} = 8.26.$$

In the table presented below, any pairwise difference between means that equals or exceeds this critical value is declared significant by the Fisher test.

The critical difference for the Tukey test is

$$\bar{d}_T = \frac{q_T \sqrt{MS_{S/A}}}{\sqrt{s}} = \frac{4.52 \sqrt{58.65}}{\sqrt{7}} = \frac{(4.52)(7.66)}{2.65}$$

$$= 13.06.$$

Any pairwise difference that equals or exceeds this critical value is declared significant by the Tukey test.

$\bar{A}_j$:	a_7 17.57	a_6 32.43	a_3 43.86	a_1 45.14	a_2 47.57	a_4 53.29	a_5 56.86	a_8 62.29
$\bar{A}_7 = 17.57$	–	14.86[a,b]	26.29[a,b]	27.57[a,b]	30.00[a,b]	35.72[a,b]	39.29[a,b]	44.72[a,b]
$\bar{A}_6 = 32.43$		–	11.43[a]	12.71[a]	15.14[a,b]	20.86[a,b]	24.43[a,b]	29.86[a,b]
$\bar{A}_3 = 43.86$			–	1.28	3.71	9.43[a]	13.00[a]	18.43[a,b]
$\bar{A}_1 = 45.14$				–	2.43	8.15	11.72[a]	17.15[a,b]
$\bar{A}_2 = 47.57$					–	5.72	9.29[a]	14.72[a,b]
$\bar{A}_4 = 53.29$						–	3.57	9.00[a]
$\bar{A}_5 = 56.86$							–	5.43
$\bar{A}_8 = 62.29$								–

[a]$p < .05$, Fisher test.
[b]$p < .05$, Tukey test.

(c) For any comparison significant with the Tukey test (b superscript), reject H_0; for any comparison not significant with the Tukey test but significant with the Fisher test (a superscript), suspend judgment; and for any comparison not significant with the Fisher test, do not reject H_0.

CHAPTER 9

1. (a) No interaction present; (b) no interaction present; (c–f) interactions present.
2. (a) 37, 43, 49.

(b) $37 + X$, $43 + X$, $49 + X$, where X is any number except 0.

(c) 49, 43, 37.

(d) There are many answers. Three conditions must be met: (1) the sum of the three means at b_2 must equal 129 (the sum of the three means at b_1), (2) the column sums must be different (if they are equal, there is no A main effect), and (3) the means at b_2 cannot be equal to the corresponding means at b_1 (if they are equal, there is no interaction).

CHAPTER 10

1. (a)

SOURCE	CALCULATIONS	SS	df	MS	F
A	$12{,}892.00 - 12{,}701.01 =$	190.99	4	47.75	7.70**
B	$13{,}125.20 - [T] =$	424.19	2	212.10	34.21**
$A \times B$	$13{,}454.00 - [A] - [B] + [T] =$	137.81	8	17.23	2.78*
S/AB	$13{,}826 - [AB] =$	372.00	60	6.20	
Total	$[ABS] - [T] =$	1,124.99	74		

*$p < .025$.

**$p < .01$.

(b)

$$\hat{\omega}_A^2 = \frac{SS_A - (df_A)(MS_{S/AB})}{SS_T + MS_{S/AB}} = \frac{190.99 - (4)(6.20)}{1{,}124.99 + 6.20} = .147;$$

$$\hat{\omega}_A^2 = \frac{SS_B - (df_B)(MS_{S/AB})}{SS_T + MS_{S/AB}} = \frac{424.19 - (2)(6.20)}{1{,}124.09 + 6.20} = .364;$$

and

$$\hat{\omega}_{A \times B}^2 = \frac{SS_{A \times B} - (df_{A \times B})(MS_{S/AB})}{SS_T + MS_{S/AB}} = \frac{137.81 - (8)(6.20)}{1{,}124.99 + 6.20} = .078.$$

2. (a)

SOURCE	CALCULATIONS	SS	df	MS	F
A	$4{,}525.13 - 4{,}440.20 =$	84.93	2	42.47	11.51*
B	$4{,}510.56 - [T] =$	70.36	4	17.59	4.77*
$A \times B$	$4{,}766.33 - [A] - [B] + [T] =$	170.84	8	21.36	5.79*
S/AB	$4{,}877 - [AB] =$	110.67	30	3.69	
Total	$[ABS] - [T] =$	436.80	44		

*$p < .01$.

(b) $\hat{\omega}_A^2 = .176$; $\hat{\omega}_B^2 = .126$; and $\hat{\omega}_{A \times B}^2 = .321$.

3. First, convert the means to sums and calculate the treatment SS's. The resultant AB matrix is given below:

	a_1	a_2	a_3	Sum
b_1	44	48	40	132
b_2	12	40	56	108
Sum	56	88	96	240

Since we are given the value of F for the interaction source of variance, we can solve for the $MS_{S/AB}$. That is,

$$F = \frac{MS_{A \times B}}{MS_{S/AB}} = 3.93,$$

$$MS_{S/AB} = \frac{MS_{A \times B}}{3.93} = \frac{72.00}{3.93} = 18.32.$$

With this value, we can calculate the F's for the two main effects and the $SS_{S/AB}$. These quantities are presented in the following summary table:

SOURCE	CALCULATIONS	SS	df	MS	F
A	$2,512.00 - 2,400.00 =$	112.00	2	56.00	3.06*
B	$2,424.00 - [T] =$	24.00	1	24.00	1.31
$A \times B$	$2,680.00 - [A] - [B] + [T] =$	144.00	2	72.00	3.93**
S/AB			18	18.32	

*$p < .10$.
**$p < .05$.

4. (a)

SOURCE	SS	df	MS	F
A	55.80	2	27.90	2.66
B	34.13	1	34.13	3.25
$A \times B$	4.07	2	2.04	.19
S/AB		24	10.50	

(b) To calculate power (and estimate sample size), we must estimate ϕ_B.

From Table 10-9, $\phi_B^2 = \dfrac{(a)(s')[\sum (\beta_j)^2]}{(b)(\sigma_{S/AB}^2)}$.

Estimating the two B population treatment means (5.87 and 3.73) and the overall population mean (4.80) from the data, we can calculate $\Sigma\,(\beta_j)^2 = (5.87 - 4.80)^2 + (3.73 - 4.80)^2 = 2.29$. Substituting this estimate and other information from the experiment into the formula, we find

$$\phi_B^2 = \frac{(3)(s')(2.29)}{(2)(10.50)} = (.33)(s').$$

We obtain $\phi_B = \sqrt{(.33)(s')} = .57\sqrt{s'}$. If we try $s' = 12$,

$\phi_B = .57\sqrt{12} = (.57)(3.46) = 1.97$. From the power charts—$df_{num.} = 1$, $\alpha = .05$, $\phi_B = 1.97$, and $df_{denom.} = (3)(2)(12 - 1) = 66$—power $= .80$.

CHAPTER 11

1. (a) A logical first test is to compare the three alcohol conditions. If the three conditions do not differ significantly, we might be willing to combine them and to compare this average with the control condition. If the three conditions differ significantly, there are several interesting comparisons possible. For example, we might want to compare each of the alcohol conditions separately with the control to determine whether an effect of alcohol has been obtained. We will probably want to see what sorts of differential alcohol effects were found; e.g., do the two whiskeys differ? do the two whiskeys separately or in combination differ from the "pure" alcohol condition? All of these comparisons ask meaningful questions of the data.

   (b) The main purpose of a trend analysis is to determine useful ways to analyze and to describe the relationship between aggressive behavior and the time spent in the tank. An assessment of the linear trend would answer the question whether aggressive behavior increases steadily (a positive linear trend) or decreases steadily (a negative linear trend). An assessment of the quadratic trend would determine whether there is a significant curvature to this function. Suppose the alcohol has little effect at first but then builds up quickly; this tendency will be reflected in significant linear and quadratic trends. On the other hand, suppose aggressive behavior increases, reaches a peak, and drops as the fish become heavily intoxicated; this tendency will be reflected in a significant quadratic trend.

   (c) Each set of comparisons can be applied to the interaction. If we consider the comparisons relevant to the *alcohol conditions,* we can examine the following partial interactions with the exposure variable left intact: (1) Do the three alcohol conditions show the same effects of the exposure variable? (2) If this partial interaction is not significant, we might combine the three groups and compare this average alcohol condition against the control and ask whether the average alcohol condition shows different effects of exposure to the alcohol than does the control group to the unadulterated water. (3) On the other hand, if the interaction is significant, we might then examine partial interactions involving comparisons among the alcohol conditions. For example, we might compare each alcohol condition with the control condition to see whether the exposure variable produces differential effects. Additionally, we might determine whether the two whiskey conditions show the same effects with the exposure variable or whether they show the same effects either separately or in combination as does the "pure" alcohol condition with the exposure variable.

Similarly, we might extend the analytical comparisons appropriate for the *exposure variable* to the analysis of the interaction. For example, the linear component of the interaction will indicate whether the linear slopes of the four treatment conditions differ; the quadratic component of the interaction will indicate whether the curvatures of the trends observed for the four treatment conditions differ.

It is to be hoped that you turned directly to the analysis of *interaction contrasts*, which bring together your analytical thinking about the two independent variables into the focused analysis of interaction. More specifically, each of the interactions specified for the treatment conditions in part (a) can be combined with the trend components in part (b) to form precise assessments of the interaction. For example, does the average linear slope of the combined alcohol conditions differ from that of the control condition? Do the linear slopes for the two whiskey conditions differ? And so on. Exactly the same questions can be asked about the quadratic component: Do the three alcohol conditions differ in the degree to which the curves "bend"? Is the curvature for the combined alcohol conditions different from that observed for the control condition? Are the curvatures for the two whiskey conditions the same? And so on.

2. For some of the analyses it is convenient to work with the AB matrix of sums, which is obtained easily by multiplying each cell mean by $s = 8$:

	a_1	a_2	a_3	Sum
b_1	28	32	60	120
b_2	30	62	88	180
Sum	58	94	148	300

(a) Simple effect of A at b_1: 3.50 versus 4.00 versus 7.50.

$$SS_{A \text{ at } b_1} = \frac{(28)^2 + (32)^2 + (60)^2}{8} - \frac{(120)^2}{(3)(8)} = 676.00 - 600.00 = 76.00;$$

$$df_{A \text{ at } b_1} = 3 - 1 = 2; \quad \text{and} \quad MS_{A \text{ at } b_1} = \frac{76.00}{2} = 38.00.$$

(b) Simple comparison of A at b_1: 3.50 versus 4.00.

$$c_i: (1, -1, 0); \quad \hat{\psi}_{A \text{ at } b_1} = (1)(3.50) + (-1)(4.00) + (0)(7.50) = -.50;$$

$$SS_{A \text{ comp. at } b_1} = \frac{8(-.50)^2}{2} = 1.00; df_{A \text{ comp. at } b_1} = 1;$$

and

$$MS_{A \text{ comp. at } b_1} = \frac{1.00}{1} = 1.00.$$

(c) Simple effects of B at the different levels of factor A:

B at a_1: 3.50 versus 3.75.

$$SS_{B \text{ at } a_1} = \frac{(28)^2 + (30)^2}{8} - \frac{(58)^2}{(2)(8)} = 210.50 - 210.25 = .25;$$

$$df_{B \text{ at } a_1} = 1;$$

and

$$MS_{B \text{ at } a_1} = \frac{.25}{1} = .25.$$

B at a_2: 4.00 versus 7.75.

$$SS_{B \text{ at } a_2} = \frac{(32)^2 + (62)^2}{8} - \frac{(94)^2}{(2)(8)} = 608.50 - 952.25 = 56.25;$$

$$df_{B \text{ at } a_2} = 1;$$

and

$$MS_{B \text{ at } a_2} = \frac{56.25}{1} = 56.25.$$

B at a_3: 7.50 versus 11.00.

$$SS_{B \text{ at } a_3} = \frac{(60)^2 + (88)^2}{8} - \frac{(148)^2}{(2)(8)} = 1,418.00 - 1,369.00$$
$$= 49.00;$$

$$df_{B \text{ at } a_3} = 1;$$

and

$$MS_{B \text{ at } a_3} = \frac{49.00}{1} = 49.00.$$

(d) $A_{\text{comp.}} \times B$ interaction:

	a_1	a_2	$\hat{\psi}_A$ at b_j
b_1	3.50	4.00	$-.50$
b_2	3.75	7.75	-4.00
Mean	3.63	5.88	-2.25

$$SS_{A \text{ comp.} \times B} = \left[\frac{8(-.50)^2}{2} + \frac{8(-4.00)^2}{2} \right] - \frac{2(8)(-2.25)^2}{2}$$

$$= [1.00 + 64.00] - 40.50 = 24.50;$$

$$df_{A \text{ comp.} \times B} = (1)(1) = 1;$$

and

$$MS_{A_{comp.} \times B} = \frac{24.50}{1} = 24.50.$$

3. (a)

SOURCE	SUM OF SQUARES	df	MS	F
B at a_1	$520.00 - 392.00 = 128.00$	1	128.00	6.98*
B at a_2	$976.00 - 968.00 = 8.00$	1	8.00	<1
B at a_3	$1,184.00 - 1,152.00 = 32.00$	1	32.00	1.75
S/AB		18	18.33	

*$p < .025$.

(b) From Table 10-8 (p. 200), $SS_B = 24.00$ and $SS_{A \times B} = 144.00$.

$24.00 + 144.00 = 168.00$, and $128.00 + 8.00 + 32.00 = 168.00$.

4. (a) In the first case, the analysis might show that A is significant only at b_1. In the second case, the analysis would probably show the same thing, although the significance of A at b_2 will depend on the size of the error term. In the third case, the analysis might show that both simple effects are significant.

(b) It would follow that the $A \times B$ interaction is significant, since the two simple effects are in opposite directions and significant separately.

(c) Since the two simple effects are in the same direction, the fact that they both are significant tells us nothing about the significance of the inter-action—i.e., whether the two simple effects themselves differ. We are left with the same conclusion even if we find that only the effect at b_1 is significant. We need the interaction test to assess whether the two simple effects, which are in the same direction, are significantly different.

5. (a)

SOURCE	CALCULATIONS	SS	df	MS	F
A	$5,218.40 - 5,198.40 = $	20.00	3	6.67	2.16*
B	$5,428.80 - [T] = $	230.40	1	230.40	74.56***
$A \times B$	$5,483.20 - [A] - [B] + [T] = $	34.40	3	11.47	3.71**
S/AB	$5,582 - [AB] = $	98.80	32	3.09	
Total	$[ABS] - [T] = $	383.60	39		

*$p < .25$.
**$p < .025$.
***$p < .01$.

(b) For this analysis we treat the three incentive conditions as a separate two-factor experiment. Working with the following modified AB matrix

	a_1	a_2	a_3	Sum
b_1	72	65	69	206
b_2	48	53	47	148
Sum	120	118	116	354

we find

$$SS_{A_{set} \times B} = \frac{(72)^2 + (48)^2 + \cdots + (69)^2 + (47)^2}{5}$$

$$- \frac{(120)^2 + (118)^2 + (116)^2}{(2)(5)} = \frac{(206)^2 + (148)^2}{(3)(5)} = \frac{(354)^2}{(3)(2)(5)}$$

$$= 4{,}298.40 - 4{,}178.00 - 4{,}289.33 + 4{,}177.20 = 8.27;$$

$$df_{A_{set} \times B} = 3 - 1 = 2; MS_{A_{set} \times B} = \frac{8.27}{2} = 4.14;$$

and

$$F = \frac{4.14}{3.09} = 1.34, p > .25.$$

The statistical test shows that the three incentive conditions exert roughly the same relative influence on the two types of tasks.

(c) The means for this interaction comparison are

	Combined incentive	No incentive	$\hat{\psi}_{A \text{ at } b_j}$
b_1	13.73	14.00	$-.27$
b_2	9.87	6.40	3.47
Mean	11.80	10.20	1.60

The coefficients for $A_{comp.}$ are $\frac{1}{3}$, $\frac{1}{3}$, $\frac{1}{3}$, and -1.

$$SS_{A_{comp.} \times B} = \left[\frac{5(-.27)^2}{1.33} + \frac{5(3.47)^2}{1.33} \right] - \frac{2(5)(1.60)^2}{1.33}$$

$$= [.27 + 45.27] - 19.25 = 26.29;$$

$$df_{A_{comp.} \times B} = (1)(2 - 1) = 1;$$

$$MS_{A_{comp.} \times B} = \frac{26.29}{1} = 26.29;$$

and

$$F = \frac{26.29}{3.09} = 8.51, p < .01.$$

(d) For the simple task:

$$SS_{A \text{ comp. at } b_1} = \frac{5(-.27)^2}{1.33} = .26; \quad df_{A \text{ comp. at } b_1} = 1;$$

$$MS_{A \text{ comp. at } b_1} = \frac{.27}{1} = .27; \quad \text{and} \quad F = \frac{.27}{3.09} = .09, p > .27.$$

For the complex task:

$$SS_{A \text{ comp. at } b_2} = \frac{5(3.47)^2}{1.33} = 45.27; \quad df_{A \text{ comp. at } b_2} = 1;$$

$$MS_{A \text{ comp. at } b_2} = \frac{45.27}{1} = 45.27; \quad \text{and} \quad F = \frac{45.27}{3.09} = 14.65, p < .01.$$

(e) Overall, the simple problems are easier for the students to solve than are the complex ones. The three incentive conditions are equally effective in facilitating performance on the complex problems; incentives have no effect on the simple problems.

6. (a)

SOURCE	SUM OF SQUARES		df	MS	F
A	$1,244.70 - 1,243.23 =$	1.47	3	.49	< 1
B	$1,407.25 - [T] =$	164.02	1	164.02	33.89**
$A \times B$	$1,458.20 - [A] - [B] + [T] =$	49.48	3	16.49	3.41*
S/AB	$1,613 - [AB] =$	154.80	32	4.84	
Total	$[ABS] - [T] =$	369.77	39		

*$p < .05$.
**$p < .01$.

(b)

	a_1	a_2	a_3	a_4	$\hat{\psi}_{A \text{ linear}}$	$\hat{\psi}_{A \text{ quadratic}}$	$\hat{\psi}_{A \text{ cubic}}$
b_1	5.80	8.40	9.20	7.00	4.40	-4.80	-1.20
b_2	4.80	3.00	2.40	4.00	-3.00	3.40	1.00
Mean	5.30	5.70	5.80	5.50	.70	$-.70$	$-.10$

SOURCE	SUM OF SQUARES		df	MS	F
Linear	$\left[\dfrac{5(4.40)^2}{20} + \dfrac{5(-3.00)^2}{20}\right] - \dfrac{2(5)(.70)^2}{20}$	$= 6.84$	1	6.84	1.41
Quadratic	$\left[\dfrac{5(-4.80)^2}{4} + \dfrac{5(3.40)^2}{4}\right] - \dfrac{2(5)(-.70)^2}{4}$	$= 42.02$	1	42.02	8.68*
Cubic	$\left[\dfrac{5(-1.20)^2}{20} + \dfrac{5(1.00)^2}{20}\right] - \dfrac{2(5)(-.10)^2}{20}$	$= .60$	1	.60	<1
S/AB			32	4.84	

*$p < .01$.

(c) For facilitating pretraining (b_1):

$$SS_{A\,\text{quadratic at } b_1} = \frac{5(-4.80)^2}{4} = 28.80; \quad df_{A\,\text{quadratic at } b_1} = 1;$$

$$MS_{A\,\text{quadratic at } b_1} = \frac{28.80}{1} = 28.80; \quad \text{and} \quad F = \frac{28.80}{4.84} = 5.95, p < .025.$$

For interfering pretraining (b_2):

$$SS_{A\,\text{quadratic at } b_2} = \frac{5(3.40)^2}{4} = 14.45; \quad df_{A\,\text{quadratic at } b_2} = 1;$$

$$MS_{A\,\text{quadratic at } b_2} = \frac{14.45}{1} = 14.45; \quad \text{and} \quad F = \frac{14.45}{4.84} = 2.99, p < .10.$$

Only the quadratic trend at b_1 is significant.

7. (a)

SOURCE	CALCULATIONS	SS
A	$745.00 - 722.50$	22.50
B	$785.00 - [T]$	62.50
$A \times B$	$930.00 - [A] - [B] + [T]$	122.50

(b)

	a_1b_1	a_1b_2	a_2b_1	a_2b_2	
Means:	3.00	4.00	8.00	2.00	$\hat{\psi}$
A:	1	1	−1	−1	−3.00
B:	1	−1	1	−1	5.00
$A \times B$:	1	−1	−1	1	−7.00

$$SS_A = \frac{10(-3.00)^2}{4} = 22.50; \quad SS_B = \frac{10(5.00)^2}{4} = 62.50; \quad \text{and}$$

$$SS_{A \times B} = \frac{10(-7.00)^2}{4} = 122.50.$$

CHAPTER 12

1. (a)

SOURCE	SUM OF SQUARES	df	MS	F
A	$3,930.00 - 3,698.00 = 232.00$	4	58.00	8.79*
B	$3,747.00 - [T] = 49.00$	4	12.25	1.86
$A \times B$	$4,165.00 - [A] - [B] + [T] = 186.00$	16	11.63	1.76
S/AB	$4,330 - [AB] = 165.00$	25	6.60	
Total	$[ABS] - [T] = 632.00$	49		

*$p < .01$.

(b) The main gain from this analysis is the assurance that the same treatment effects were obtained by the five experimenters—revealed by the non-significant interaction. A second gain is the small reduction in the error term (6.60 versus 8.89), which came about by isolating the effects of the experimenters. The only loss is a reduction in the denominator df (25 versus 45); the small loss of power resulting from the reduction in df is easily compensated for by the reduction in the size of the error term.

2. (a) I will designate the nested factor, classes within methods, B/A, and factor S, S/AB, although this latter term is more accurately designated $S/B/A$.

SOURCE	df	ERROR TERM
A	2	B/A
B/A	3	S/AB
S/AB	120	None
Total	125	

(b) The main disadvantage is the low power associated with the F test ($df_{\text{denom.}} = 3$). The researcher could increase the *number of classes* involved in the study. Another possibility is to use a *crossed* design with students in each class randomly assigned in equal numbers ($s = 7$) to the three methods. Under these circumstances the error term for the main effect of A would be the $A \times$ Class interaction. (See Chapter 21, pp. 525–528, for an explanation.) The crossed design would provide an increase in error df, i.e., $df_{A \times B} = (3 - 1)(6 - 1) = 10$, and provide a way of controlling differences between classes, which are permitted to vary randomly in the nested design.

3. (a) Three sources of variance are isolated: problem type (A), instances of problems (B/A), and factor S (S/AB). I will calculate the sum of squares for the nested factor two ways, the first pooling the two separate sums of squares (disjunctive instances and conjunctive instances) and the second calculating the separate sums of squares and then pooling.

$$[A] = \frac{(31)^2 + (51)^2}{(5)(2)} = 356.20; \quad [T] = \frac{(82)^2}{(2)(5)(2)} = 336.20;$$

$$[AB] = \frac{(2)^2 + (5)^2 + \cdots + (12)^2 + (20)^2}{2} = 479.00; \quad \text{and}$$

$[ABS] = 511$ (given).

SOURCE	SUM OF SQUARES	df	MS	ERROR TERM	F
A	$356.20 - 336.20 = 20.00$	1	20.00	B/A	1.30
B/A	$479.00 - [A] = 122.80$	8	15.35	S/AB	4.80*
S/AB	$511 - [AB] = 32.00$	10	3.20	None	
Total	$[ABS] - [T] = 174.80$	19			

*$p < .025$.

The separate sums of squares,

$$SS_{B/A_1} = \frac{(2)^2 + (5)^2 + (2)^2 + (8)^2 + (14)^2}{2} - \frac{(31)^2}{(5)(2)}$$

$$= 146.50 - 96.10 = 50.40 \quad \text{and}$$

$$SS_{B/A_2} = \frac{(6)^2 + (7)^2 + (6)^2 + (12)^2 + (20)^2}{2} - \frac{(51)^2}{(5)(2)}$$

$$= 332.50 - 260.10 = 72.40,$$

give us $SS_{B/A}$ when pooled; i.e., $50.40 + 72.40 = 122.80$.

(b) Something must be done about the marked differences observed among problems of the same type. You might go back to the original definition of the two types of problems and see whether some extraneous factor was allowed to enter in the construction of the problems. It would be wise to control all extraneous features. It might also be a good idea to increase the number of problems, but the main difficulty appears to be marked problem heterogeneity. Until this difficulty is solved, the prognosis for the experiment is poor.

4. The original analysis isolated three sources of variance: treatments (A), list orders, which were nested within treatments (B/A), and the within-groups source (S/AB). All that we need to do is to analyze the A effects more completely. One way to do this is to work with the A treatment means and conduct single-df comparisons that isolate the two main effects of meaningfulness and similarity and their interaction. This is accomplished as follows:

	a_1	a_2	a_3	a_4	
Means:	29.18	19.27	42.57	25.86	$\hat{\psi}$
Meaningfulness:	1	−1	1	−1	26.62
Similarity:	1	1	−1	−1	−19.98
Interaction:	1	−1	−1	1	−6.80

$$SS_{\text{meaningfulness}} = \frac{(10)(10)(26.62)^2}{4} = 17{,}715.61;$$

$$SS_{\text{similarity}} = \frac{(10)(10)(-19.98)^2}{4} = 9{,}980.01; \text{ and}$$

$$SS_{\text{interaction}} = \frac{(10)(10)(-6.80)^2}{4} = 1{,}156.00.$$

As a check, let's verify that the sum of these three sums of squares equals SS_A from the original analysis. That is,

$$\Sigma \, SS_{A\text{ comp.}} = 17{,}715.61 + 9{,}980.01 + 1{,}156.00 = 28{,}851.62 = SS_A.$$

Completing the analysis, we have

SOURCE	SS	df	MS	ERROR TERM	F
Meaningfulness	17,715.61	1	17,715.61	B/A	76.59**
Similarity	9,980.01	1	9,980.01	B/A	43.15**
Interaction	1,156.00	1	1,156.00	B/A	5.00*
Order/treatments (B/A)	8,326.42	36	231.29	S/AB	1.25
Within-groups (S/AB)	66,615.60	360	185.04	None	
Total	103,793.64	399			

*$p < .05$.
**$p < .01$.

CHAPTER 13

1.

	THREE-WAY INTERACTIONS	TWO-WAY INTERACTIONS	MAIN EFFECTS
Example 1:	No	None	A
Example 2:	No	None	A and B
Example 3:	No	None	A, B, and C

	THREE-WAY INTERACTIONS	TWO-WAY INTERACTIONS	MAIN EFFECTS
Example 4:	No	$A \times B$	None
Example 5:	No	$A \times B$	C[a]
Example 6:	No	$B \times C$	A[a]
Example 7:	No	$A \times B$ and $A \times C$	—
Example 8:	Yes	—	—
Example 9:	Yes	—	—
Example 10:	Yes	—	—

[a]This main effect is interpretable, since it does not enter the two-way interaction.

2.

(a)

c_1	a_1	a_2		c_2	a_1	a_2
b_1	30	20		b_1	30	20
b_2	30	20		b_2	30	20

(b)

c_1	a_1	a_2		c_2	a_1	a_2
b_1	30	20		b_1	25	15
b_2	40	30		b_2	35	25

(c)

c_1	a_1	a_2		c_2	a_1	a_2
b_1	30	20		b_1	30	20
b_2	20	30		b_2	20	30

(d)

c_1	a_1	a_2		c_2	a_1	a_2
b_1	30	20		b_1	40	30
b_2	20	30		b_2	30	40

(e)

c_1	a_1	a_2		c_2	a_1	a_2
b_1	30	20		b_1	20	30
b_2	20	30		b_2	30	20

(f)

c_1	a_1	a_2		c_2	a_1	a_2
b_1	30	20		b_1	10	20
b_2	20	30		b_2	20	10

3. (a)

SOURCE	CALCULATIONS	SS	df	MS	F
A	$2,540.75 - 2,222.22 = 318.53$		2	159.27	91.01**
B	$2,431.25 - [T] = 209.03$		2	104.52	59.73**
C	$2,242.28 - [T] = 20.06$		1	20.06	11.46**
A × B	$2,762.00 - [A] - [B] + [T] = 12.22$		4	3.06	1.75
A × C	$2,575.83 - [A] - [C] + [T] = 15.02$		2	7.51	4.29*
B × C	$2,456.00 - [B] - [C] + [T] = 4.69$		2	2.35	1.34
A × B × C	$2,815.50 - [AB] - [AC] - [BC]$				
	$+ [A] + [B] + [C] - [T] = 13.73$		4	3.43	1.96
S/ABC	$2,910 - [ABC] = 94.50$		54	1.75	
Total	$[ABCS] - [T] = 687.78$		71		

*$p < .05$.
**$p < .01$.

(b) Since the three-way interaction is not significant, we can look at the two-way interactions and certain main effects for an adequate description of these results. For a more detailed comment on this problem, see Exercise 1 at the end of Chapter 14, where this example is examined further (pp. 332–333).

4. (a)

SOURCE	CALCULATIONS	SS	df	MS	F
A	$8,643.40 - 8,534.53 = 108.87$		3	36.29	19.51*
B	$8,851.40 - [T] = 316.87$		2	158.44	85.18*
C	$8,624.67 - [T] = 90.14$		1	90.14	48.46*
A × B	$9,006.60 - [A] - [B] + [T] = 46.33$		6	7.72	4.15*
A × C	$8,765.33 - [A] - [C] + [T] = 31.79$		3	10.60	5.70*
B × C	$9,076.40 - [B] - [C] + [T] = 134.86$		2	67.43	36.25*
A × B × C	$9,311.60 - [AB] - [AC] - [BC]$				
	$+ [A] + [B] + [C] - [T] = 48.21$		6	8.04	4.32*
S/ABC	$9,490 - [ABC] = 178.40$		96	1.86	
Total	$[ABCS] - [T] = 955.47$		119		

*$p < .01$.

(b) Since the three-way interaction is significant, attention would be directed toward the detailed analysis of this effect. Examples of such analyses conducted on this problem can be found in Exercise 2 at the end of Chapter 14 (p. 333).

CHAPTER 14

1. (a)

SOURCE	CALCULATIONS	SS	df	MS	F
C at a_1	$301.42 - 301.04 =$	.38	1	.38	<1
C at a_2	$555.33 - 522.67 =$	32.66	1	32.66	18.66*
C at a_3	$1{,}719.08 - 1{,}717.04 =$	2.04	1	2.04	1.17
S/ABC			54	1.75	

*$p < .01$.

As a check, $\Sigma\, SS_{C \text{ at } a_i} = 35.08$ and $SS_{A \times C} + SS_C = 35.08$.

(b)

	b_1	b_2	b_3	$\hat{\psi}_B$	$\Sigma (c_j)^2$
$\bar{B}_j$:	7.92	4.79	3.96		
Comp. 1:	$-\frac{1}{2}$	1	$-\frac{1}{2}$	-1.15	1.5
Comp. 2:	1	0	-1	3.96	2

$$SS_{B_{\text{comp. 1}}} = \frac{(3)(2)(4)(-1.15)^2}{1.5} ; \text{ and}$$

$$SS_{B_{\text{comp. 2}}} = \frac{(3)(2)(4)(3.96)^2}{2} .$$

SOURCE	SS	df	MS	F
Comp. 1	21.16	1	21.16	12.09*
Comp. 2	188.18	1	188.18	107.53*
S/ABC		54	1.75	

*$p < .01$.

2. For these simple interactions, it is most convenient to form AB matrices at each level of factor C:

AB MATRIX AT LEVEL c_1

	a_1	a_2	a_3	a_4	Sum
b_1	35	46	49	55	185
b_2	42	51	55	62	210
b_3	29	40	45	49	163
Sum	106	137	149	166	558

AB MATRIX AT LEVEL c_2

	a_1	a_2	a_3	a_3	Sum
b_1	37	49	56	65	207
b_2	40	38	44	42	164
b_3	27	23	19	14	83
Sum	104	110	119	121	454

$$SS_{A \times B \text{ at } c_1} = \frac{(35)^2 + (42)^2 + \cdots + (62)^2 + (49)^2}{5}$$

$$- \frac{(106)^2 + (137)^2 + (149)^2 + (166)^2}{(3)(5)}$$

$$- \frac{(185)^2 + (210)^2 + (163)^2}{(4)(5)} + \frac{(558)^2}{(4)(3)(5)}$$

$$= 5,373.60 - 5,317.47 - 5,244.70 + 5,189.40 = .83,$$

$$SS_{A \times B \text{ at } c_2} = \frac{(37)^2 + (40)^2 + \cdots + (42)^2 + (14)^2}{5}$$

$$- \frac{(104)^2 + (110)^2 + (119)^2 + (121)^2}{(3)(5)}$$

$$- \frac{(207)^2 + (164)^2 + (83)^2}{(4)(5)} + \frac{(454)^2}{(4)(3)(5)}$$

$$= 3,938.00 - 3,447.87 - 3,831.70 + 3,435.27 = 93.70.$$

SOURCE	SS	df	MS	F
$A \times B$ at c_1	.83	6	.14	<1
$A \times B$ at c_2	93.70	6	15.62	8.40*
S/ABC		96	1.86	

*$p < .01$.

As a check,

$$\Sigma \, SS_{A \times B \text{ at } c_k} = 94.53 \quad \text{and} \quad SS_{A \times B \times C} + SS_{A \times B} = 94.54.$$

3. The first step is to construct an ABC comparison matrix. Using the coefficients, $(1, -\frac{1}{2}, -\frac{1}{2})$ for c_i, $(1, -1, 0)$ for c_j, and $(1, -\frac{1}{2}, -\frac{1}{2})$ for c_k, we obtain:

SINGLE LANGUAGE $(c_{(+)})$			COMBINED BILINGUAL $(c_{(-)})$		
	Control $(a_{(+)})$	Combined Drugs $(a_{(-)})$		Control $(a_{(+)})$	Combined Drugs $(a_{(-)})$
Low frequency $(b_{(+)})$	45	40	Low frequency $(b_{(+)})$	45	20
High frequency $(b_{(-)})$	45	40	High frequency $(b_{(-)})$	45	40

From the ABC comparison matrix, we can form the three two-way matrices also needed for the analysis:

AB COMPARISON MATRIX			
	$a(+)$	$a(-)$	Sum
$b(+)$	90	60	150
$b(-)$	90	80	170
Sum	180	140	320

AC COMPARISON MATRIX			
	$a(+)$	$a(-)$	Sum
$c(+)$	90	80	170
$c(-)$	90	60	150
Sum	180	140	320

BC COMPARISON MATRIX			
	$b(+)$	$b(-)$	Sum
$c(+)$	85	85	170
$c(-)$	65	85	150
Sum	150	170	320

The analysis summarized below produces sums of squares that need to be corrected for the use of weighted sums. For this example, each sum of squares is normalized by dividing by

$$\left(\frac{\Sigma\,(c_i)^2}{2}\right)\left(\frac{\Sigma\,(c_j)^2}{2}\right)\left(\frac{\Sigma\,(c_k)^2}{2}\right) = \left(\frac{1.5}{2}\right)\left(\frac{2}{2}\right)\left(\frac{1.5}{2}\right) = .5625.$$

SOURCE	BASIC RATIO	SUM OF SQUARES		df
		Unadjusted	*Normalized*	
$A_{comp.}$	$[A] = 2{,}600.00$	40.00	71.11	1
$B_{comp.}$	$[B] = 2{,}570.00$	10.00	17.78	1
$C_{comp.}$	$[C] = 2{,}570.00$	10.00	17.78	1
$A_{comp.} \times B_{comp.}$	$[AB] = 2{,}620.00$	10.00	17.78	1
$A_{comp.} \times C_{comp.}$	$[AC] = 2{,}620.00$	10.00	17.78	1
$B_{comp.} \times C_{comp.}$	$[BC] = 2{,}590.00$	10.00	17.78	1
$A_{comp.} \times B_{comp.} \times C_{comp.}$	$[ABC] = 2{,}660.00$	10.00	17.78	1
Between group[a]	$[T] = 2{,}560.00$	100.00		7

[a]The formula for this source is $SS_{bg} = [ABC] - [T]$; this sum of squares serves as a computational check.

4. Linear analysis

	AB LINEAR MATRIX				BC LINEAR MATRIX		
	$a(+)$	$a(-)$	Sum		c_1	c_2	Sum
b_1	328	414	742	b_1	387	355	742
b_2	346	413	759	b_2	387	372	759
b_3	361	419	780	b_3	387	393	780
Sum	1,035	1,246	2,281	Sum	1,161	1,120	2,281

	AC LINEAR MATRIX		
	$a(+)$	$a(-)$	Sum
c_1	538	623	1,161
c_2	497	623	1,120
Sum	1,035	1,246	2,281

SOURCE	BASIC RATIO	SS^a	df	MS	F
A_{linear}	$[A] = 29,152.68$	247.34	1	247.34	166.00***
B	$[B] = 28,917.42$	12.08	2	_b	_b
C	$[C] = 28,914.68$	9.34	1	_b	_b
$A_{linear} \times B$	$[AB] = 29,171.57$	6.81	2	3.41	2.29*
$A_{linear} \times C$	$[AC] = 29,171.36$	9.34	1	9.34	6.27**
$B \times C$	$[BC] = 28,938.83$	12.07	2	_b	_b
$A_{linear} \times B \times C$	$[ABC] = 29,219.67$	17.35	2	8.68	5.83***
Between group^c	$[T] = 28,905.34$	314.33	11		
S/ABC			252	1.49	

*$p < .25$.
**$p < .025$.
***$p < .01$.
^{a}Since $\Sigma (c_i)^2 = 2$, no correction is needed.
^{b}Quantities left blank are not needed for this analysis.
^{c}The formula for this source is $SS_{bg} = [ABC] - [T]$; this sum of squares serves as a computational check.

Quadratic analysis

AB QUADRATIC MATRIX	$a(+)$	$a(-)$	Sum
b_1	742	752	1,494
b_2	759	750	1,509
b_3	780	788	1,568
Sum	2,281	2,290	4,571

BC QUADRATIC MATRIX	c_1	c_2	Sum
b_1	783	711	1,494
b_2	773	736	1,509
b_3	781	787	1,568
Sum	2,337	2,234	4,571

AC QUADRATIC MATRIX	$a(+)$	$a(-)$	Sum
c_1	1,161	1,176	2,337
c_2	1,120	1,114	2,234
Sum	2,281	2,290	4,571

SOURCE	BASIC RATIO	SUM OF SQUARES Unadjusted	SUM OF SQUARES Normalized[a]	df	MS	F
$A_{quadratic}$	$[A] = 116,078.46$	.45	.15	1	.15	<1
B	$[B] = 116,129.02$	51.01	_b	2	_b	_b
C	$[C] = 116,136.94$	58.93	_b	1	_b	_b
$A_{quad.} \times B$	$[AB] = 116,133.10$	3.63	1.21	2	.61	<1
$A_{quad.} \times C$	$[AC] = 116,139.84$	2.45	.82	1	.82	<1
$B \times C$	$[BC] = 116,238.83$	50.88	_b	2	_b	_b
$A_{quad.} \times B \times C$	$[ABC] = 116,245.40$	.04	.01	2	.01	<1
Between group[c]	$[T] = 116,078.01$	167.39		11		
S/ABC				252	1.49	

[a]Since $\Sigma (c_i)^2 = 6$, the correction factor is 3.
[b]Not needed for this analysis.
[c]The formula for this source is $SS_{bg} = [ABC] - [T]$; this sum of squares serves as a computational check.

CHAPTER 15

1.

		a_1	a_2	a_3	a_4
	Sum	150	52	80	67
	s_j	20	16	12	10
	$\bar{A}_i$	7.50	3.25	6.67	6.70
$\displaystyle\sum_{j=1}^{s_j} (AS_{ij})^2$		1,374	210	650	517
	SS_{S/A_i}	249.00	41.00	116.67	68.10
	df_{S/A_i}	19	15	11	9

$$SS_{S/A} = 249.00 + 41.00 + 116.67 + 68.10 = 474.77;$$

$$df_{S/A} = 19 + 15 + 11 + 9 = 54;$$

$$s_h = \frac{4}{1/20 + 1/16 + 1/12 + 1/10} = \frac{4}{.05 + .06 + .08 + .10} = 13.79;$$

$$\bar{T}' = \frac{7.50 + 3.25 + 6.67 + 6.70}{4} = 6.03;$$

and

$$SS_A = (13.79)[(7.50 - 6.03)^2 + (3.25 - 6.03)^2 + (6.67 - 6.03)^2$$

$$+ (6.70 - 6.03)^2]$$

$$= (13.79)(2.16 + 7.73 + .41 + .45) = 148.24.$$

SOURCE	SS	df	MS	F
A	148.24	3	49.41	5.62*
S/A	474.77	54	8.79	

*$p < .01$.

2. (a)

	a_1b_1	a_2b_1	a_3b_1	a_1b_2	a_2b_2	a_3b_2
Sum	106	176	90	122	263	227
s_{ij}	10	12	8	15	18	12
$\overline{AB}_{ij}$	10.60	14.67	11.25	8.13	14.61	18.92
$\sum_{k=1}^{s_{ij}} (ABS_{ijk})^2$	1,172	2,624	1,034	1,046	3,923	4,325
$SS_{S/AB_{ij}}$	48.40	42.67	21.50	53.73	80.28	30.92
$df_{S/AB_{ij}}$	9	11	7	14	17	11

	a_1b_3	a_2b_3	a_3b_3
Sum	51	64	43
s_{ij}	5	6	4
$\overline{AB}_{ij}$	10.20	10.67	10.75
$\sum_{k=1}^{s_{ij}} (ABS_{ijk})^2$	533	708	469
$SS_{S/AB_{ij}}$	12.80	25.33	6.75
$df_{S/AB_{ij}}$	4	5	3

$$SS_{S/AB} = 48.40 + 42.67 + \cdots + 25.33 + 6.75 = 322.38;$$
$$df_{S/AB} = 9 + 11 + \cdots + 5 + 3 = 81;$$

and

$$s_h = \frac{(3)(3)}{1/10 + 1/12 + \cdots + 1/6 + 1/4}$$
$$= \frac{9}{.10 + .08 + .13 + .07 + .06 + .08 + .20 + .17 + .25} = 7.89.$$

AB' MATRIX

	a_1	a_2	a_3	Sum
b_1	83.63	115.75	88.76	288.14
b_2	64.15	115.27	149.28	328.70
b_3	80.48	84.19	84.82	249.49
Sum	228.26	315.21	322.86	866.33

SOURCE	CALCULATIONS	SS	df	MS	F
A	$10,802.64 - 10,569.32 = 233.32$	233.32	2	116.66	29.31*
B	$10,701.88 - [T'] = 132.56$	132.56	2	66.28	16.65*
$A \times B$	$11,244.20 - [A'] - [B'] + [T'] = 309.00$	309.00	4	77.25	19.41*
S/AB		322.38	81	3.98	

*$p < .01$.

(b) To get you started, $SS_{B \text{ at } a_1} = \dfrac{(83.63)^2 + (64.15)^2 + (80.48)^2}{7.89}$

$- \dfrac{(228.26)^2}{(3)(7.89)}$.

SOURCE	CALCULATIONS	SS	df	MS	F
B at a_1	$2,228.93 - 2,201.21 = 27.72$	27.72	2	13.86	3.48*
B at a_2	$4,280.51 - 4,197.61 = 82.90$	82.90	2	41.45	10.41**
B at a_2	$4,734.76 - 4,403.83 = 330.93$	330.93	2	165.47	41.58**
S/AB			81	3.98	

*$p < .05$.
**$p < .01$.

CHAPTER 17

1. (a)

SOURCE	CALCULATIONS	SS	df	MS	F
A	$588.00 - 444.08 = 143.92$	143.92	5	28.78	10.32*
S	$498.33 - [T] = 54.25$	54.25	7	7.75	
$A \times S$	$740 - [A] - [S] + [T] = 97.75$	97.75	35	2.79	
Total	$[AS] - [T] = 295.92$		47		

*$p < .01$.

(b) Linear analysis:

SOURCE	CALCULATIONS	SS^a	df	MS	F
A_{linear}	$19,472.00 - 15,376.00 = 4,096.00$	4,096.00	1	4,096.00	78.98*
S	$16,673.00 - [T] = 1,297.00$	1,297.00	7	185.29	
$A_{\text{lin.}} \times S$	$21,132 - [A] - [S] + [T] = 363.00$	363.00	7	51.86	
Total	$[AS] - [T] = 5,756.00$		15		

*$p < .01$.
[a]It is not necessary to normalize the sums of squares for this analysis since all calculations are based on weighted AS scores. The correction in any case is $[\Sigma (c_i)^2]/2 = 70/2 = 35$.

Quadratic analysis:

SOURCE	CALCULATIONS	SS[a]	df	MS	F
$A_{quadratic}$	$16{,}198.63 - 15{,}190.56 = 1{,}008.07$		1	1,008.07	6.16*
S	$16{,}563.50 - [T] = 1{,}372.94$		7	196.13	
$A_{quad.} \times S$	$18{,}717 - [A] - [S] + [T] = 1{,}145.43$		7	163.63	
Total	$[AS] - [T] = 3{,}526.44$		15		

*$p < .05$.

[a]It is not necessary to normalize the sums of squares for this analysis since all calculations are based on weighted AS scores. The correction in any case is $[\Sigma\ (c_i)^2]/2 = 84/2 = 42$.

2. (a)

SOURCE	CALCULATIONS	SS	df	MS	F
A	$1{,}690.80 - 1{,}632.16 = 58.64$		4	14.66	1.19
S	$1{,}646.00 - [T] = 13.84$		4	3.46	
$A \times S$	$1{,}902 - [A] - [S] + [T] = 197.36$		16	12.34	
Total	$[AS] - [T] = 269.84$		24		

(b)

	CALCULATIONS	SS	df	MS	F
Position	$1{,}804.00 - [T] = 171.84$		4	42.96	20.17*
L. S. residual	$197.36 - 171.84 = 25.52$		12	2.13	

*$p < .01$.

The treatment main effect is now significant:

$$F = \frac{14.66}{2.13} = 6.88, p < .01.$$

(c) For this analysis, I used the coefficients $(4, -1, -1, -1, -1)$.[1]

Standard analysis:

SOURCE	CALCULATIONS	SS	df	MS	F
$A_{comp.}$	$12{,}883.40 - 12{,}602.50 = 280.90$		1	280.90	2.33
S	$12{,}690.50 - [T] = 88.00$		4	22.00	
$A_{comp.} \times S$	$13{,}453 - [A] - [S] + [T] = 481.60$		4	120.40	
Total	$[AS] - [T] = 850.50$		9		

[1]It is not necessary to normalize the sums of squares for these two analyses since all calculations are based on weighted AS scores. The correction in any case is $[\Sigma\ (c_i)^2]/2 = 20/2 = 10$.

Latin square analysis (note: practice effect is 4.12, 1.32, −.08, −1.88, and −3.48 for testing position 1 to 5, respectively:

SOURCE	CALCULATIONS	SS	df	MS	F
$A_{comp.}$	$12{,}883.40 - 12{,}602.50 = 280.90$		1	280.90	80.95*
S	$12{,}686.76 - [T] = 84.26$		4	21.07	
$A_{comp.} \times S$	$12{,}978.06 - [A] - [S] + [T] = 10.40$		$4-1$	3.47	
Total	$[AS] - [T] = 375.56$		$9-1$		

*$p < .01$.

3.

SOURCE	CALCULATIONS	SS[a]	df	MS	F
$A_{comp.}$	$24{,}204.17 - 23{,}852.08 = 352.09$		1	352.09	19.19*
S	$24{,}133.31 - [T] = 281.23$		5	56.25	
$A_{comp.} \times S$	$24{,}558.78 - [A] - [S] + [T] = 73.38$		$5-1$	18.35	
Total	$[AS] - [T] = 706.70$		$11-1$		

*$p < .01$.
[a]It is not necessary to normalize the sums of squares for this analysis since all calculations are based on weighted AS scores.

CHAPTER 18

1.

SOURCE	CALCULATIONS	SS	df	MS	F
A	$37{,}710.88 - 37{,}296.75 = 414.13$		2	207.07	6.17*
S/A	$38{,}013.00 - [A] = 302.12$		9	33.57	
B	$38{,}449.17 - [T] = 1{,}152.42$		3	384.14	114.67**
$A \times B$	$38{,}993.50 - [A] - [B] + [T] = 130.20$		6	21.70	6.48**
$B \times S/A$	$39{,}386 - [AB] - [AS] + [A] = 90.38$		27	3.35	
Total	$[ABS] - [T] = 2{,}089.25$		47		

*$p < .025$.
**$p < .01$.

2. (a)

SOURCE	CALCULATIONS	SS	df	MS	F
A at b_1	$4{,}924.25 - 4{,}920.75 =\quad 3.50$		2	1.75	<1
S/A at b_1	$5{,}053 - 4{,}924.25 = 128.75$		9	14.31	
A at b_2	$8{,}874.00 - 8{,}748.00 = 126.00$		2	63.00	4.81*
S/A at b_2	$8{,}992 - 8{,}874.00 = 118.00$		9	13.11	
A at b_3	$12{,}056.25 - 11{,}844.08 = 212.17$		2	106.09	12.44**
S/A at b_3	$12{,}133 - 12{,}056.25 =\quad 76.75$		9	8.53	
A at b_4	$13{,}139.00 - 12{,}936.33 = 202.67$		2	101.34	13.21**
S/A at b_4	$13{,}208 - 13{,}139.00 =\quad 69.00$		9	7.67	

*$p < .05$.
**$p < .01$.

There are two useful arithmetical checks you should take advantage of:

$$\Sigma\,SS_{A\text{ at }b_j} = SS_A + SS_{A \times B} \quad \text{and} \quad \Sigma\,SS_{S/A\text{ at }b_j} = SS_{S/A} + SS_{B \times S/A}.$$

For the first, $3.50 + 126.00 + 212.17 + 202.67 = 544.34$ and $414.13 + 130.20 = 544.33$. For the second, $128.75 + 118.00 + 76.75 + 69.00 = 392.50$ and $302.12 + 90.38 = 392.50$.

This analysis indicates that the incentive manipulation is not effective on the first trial, but emerges on subsequent training trials.

(b)

SOURCE	CALCULATIONS[a]	SS	df	MS	F
B at a_1	$9{,}633.00 - 9{,}506.25 = 126.75$		3	42.25	12.76*
S	$9{,}615.50 - [T] = 109.25$		3	36.42	
$B \times S$ at a_1	$9{,}772 - [B] - [S] + [T] =\quad 29.75$		9	3.31	
B at a_2	$12{,}746.25 - 12{,}265.56 = 480.69$		3	160.23	52.36*
S	$12{,}402.75 - [T] = 137.19$		3	45.73	
$B \times S$ at a_2	$12{,}911 - [B] - [S] + [T] =\quad 27.56$		9	3.06	
B at a_3	$16{,}614.25 - 15{,}939.06 = 675.19$		3	225.06	61.32*
S	$15{,}994.75 - [T] =\quad 55.69$		3	18.56	
$B \times S$ at a_3	$16{,}703 - [B] - [S] + [T] =\quad 33.06$		9	3.67	

*$p < .01$.
[a]For convenience, I have treated each analysis as if it were a separate ($B \times S$) experiment for which the level of factor A was held constant.

As in part (a), there are two useful arithmetical checks you should conduct at this point:

$$\Sigma\, SS_{B\ \text{at}\ a_i} = SS_B + SS_{A\times B} \quad \text{and} \quad \Sigma\, SS_{B\times S\ \text{at}\ a_i} = SS_{B\times S/A}.$$

For the first, $126.75 + 480.69 + 675.19 = 1{,}282.63$ and $1{,}152.42 + 130.20 = 1{,}282.63$. For the second, $29.75 + 27.56 + 33.06 = 90.37$ and $SS_{B\times S/A} = 90.38$.

This analysis does not help to pinpoint the locus of the significant $A\times B$ interaction, since all we have discovered is that each simple effect of factor B (trials) is significant. What is needed is an analysis that is directed at identifying the factor (or factors) responsible for the significant interaction.

3. (a) I will present the analysis of all three trend components, although in an actual analysis a researcher might decide to test for residual trend effects after each new trend component is calculated (see pp. 139–140). To conserve space, I will work through the analysis of the linear component in detail and summarize the outcomes of the quadratic and cubic analyses. The coefficients for the linear analysis are $(-3, -1, 1, 3)$.

SOURCE	CALCULATIONS	SS[b]	df	MS	F
A	$286{,}848.75 - 284{,}272.67 =$	$2{,}576.08$	2	—[a]	—[a]
S/A	$289{,}282.00 - [A] =$	$2{,}433.25$	9	—[a]	—[a]
B_{linear}	$294{,}940.83 - [T] =$	$10{,}668.16$	1	$10{,}668.16$	$233.49*$
$A\times B_{\text{lin.}}$	$298{,}495.50 - [A] - [B] + [T] =$	978.59	2	489.30	$10.71*$
$B_{\text{lin.}}\times S/A$	$301{,}340 - [AB] - [AS] + [A] =$	411.25	9	45.69	
Total	$[ABS] - [T] = 17{,}067.33$		23		

$*p < .01.$
[a]Not needed.
[b]These SS's have not been adjusted for the use of weighted ABS scores.

In the analyses that follow, I have normalized the sums of squares for the different trend components. This step is not necessary for calculating the F ratios, but does allow verification that the sum of the component sums of squares equals the overall sum of squares. For the B main effect, $1{,}066.82 + 85.34 + .27 = 1{,}152.43$, while $SS_B = 1{,}152.42$; for the interaction, $97.86 + 24.54 + 7.81 = 130.21$, while $SS_{A\times B} = 130.20$; and for $B\times S/A$, $41.13 + 21.13 + 28.13 = 90.39$, while $SS_{B\times S/A} = 90.38$.

SOURCE	SUM OF SQUARES		df	MS	F
	Unadjusted	Normalized[a]			
B		$1{,}152.42$	3		
Linear	$10{,}668.16$	$1{,}066.82$	1	$1{,}066.82$	$233.44**$
Quadratic	170.67	85.34	1	85.34	$36.31**$
Cubic	2.66	$.27$	1	$.27$	<1

SOURCE	SUM OF SQUARES Unadjusted	SUM OF SQUARES Normalized[a]	df	MS	F
$A \times B$		130.20	6		
Linear	978.59	97.86	2	48.93	10.71**
Quadratic	49.08	24.54	2	12.27	5.22*
Cubic	78.09	7.81	2	3.91	1.25
$B \times S/A$		90.38	27		
Linear	411.25	41.13	9	4.57	
Quadratic	42.25	21.13	9	2.35	
Cubic	281.25	28.13	9	3.13	

*$p < .05$.
**$p < .01$.
[a]Linear correction $= {}^{20}\!/_2 = 10$; quadratic correction $= {}^{4}\!/_2 = 2$; and cubic correction $= {}^{20}\!/_2 = 10$.

The analysis indicates that the interaction can be fairly well characterized as due to differences in the linear slopes associated with the different incentive conditions although a small quadratic component is present.

(b) Since no numerical example of this type of interaction comparison was given in the text, I will provide more detail in this answer. The analysis does not require specialized error terms, and consequently, we can work directly with the AB matrix to obtain the weighted sums needed to calculate $SS_{A\,comp.}$ and $SS_{A\,comp.} \times B$. Using the coefficients, 0, 1, and -1 for the first comparison, we obtain the following AB comparison matrix:

	$a_{(+)}$	$a_{(-)}$	Sum
b_1	79	84	163
b_2	102	126	228
b_3	128	145	273
b_4	134	150	284
Sum	443	505	948

Basic ratios extracted from this matrix are as follows:

$$[T] = \frac{(948)^2}{(2)(4)(4)} = 28{,}084.50;$$

$$[A] = \frac{(443)^2 + (505)^2}{(4)(4)} = 28{,}204.63;$$

$$[B] = \frac{(163)^2 + (228)^2 + (273)^2 + (284)^2}{(2)(4)} = 29{,}217.25; \quad \text{and}$$

$$[AB] = \frac{(79)^2 + (102)^2 + \cdots + (145)^2 + (150)^2}{4} = 29,360.50.$$

The two critical sums of squares are

$$SS_A' = [A] - [T] = 120.13; \text{ and}$$

$$SS_{A' \times B} = [AB] - [A] - [B] + [T] = 23.12.$$

The next step is to normalize these sums of squares, which in this case is not necessary since the correction is $[\Sigma (c_i)^2]/2 = 2/2 = 1$. The two comparison sums of squares are entered in an analysis summary table given on p. 600.

For the second comparison, I will use as coefficients 2, −1, and −1. With these coefficients, the following AB comparison matrix is obtained:

	$a_{(+)}$	$a_{(-)}$	Sum
b_1	160	163	323
b_2	192	228	420
b_3	208	273	481
b_4	220	284	504
Sum	780	948	1,728

The basic ratios are

$$[T] = \frac{(1,728)^2}{(2)(4)(4)} = 93,312.00;$$

$$[A] = \frac{(780)^2 + (948)^2}{(4)(4)} = 94,194.00;$$

$$[B] = \frac{(323)^2 + (420)^2 + (481)^2 + (504)^2}{(2)(4)} = 95,763.25; \text{ and}$$

$$[AB] = \frac{(160)^2 + (192)^2 + \cdots + (273)^2 + (284)^2}{4} = 96,966.50.$$

The unadjusted sums of squares are

$$SS_{A'} = [A] - [T] = 882.00; \text{ and}$$

$$SS_{A' \times B} = [AB] - [A] - [B] + [T] = 321.25.$$

The correction factor for this comparison is $6/2 = 3$. The normalized sums of squares become

$$SS_{A \text{ comp.}} = \frac{882.00}{3} = 294.00 \text{ and } SS_{A \text{ comp.} \times B} = \frac{321.25}{3} = 107.08.$$

These two quantities are entered in the analysis summary table on p. 600.
The remainder of the analysis is straightforward. The two error terms

come from the overall analysis; $MS_{S/A}$ is the error term for the two comparison main effects and $MS_{B \times S/A}$ is the error term for the two comparison interactions.

SOURCE	SS	df	MS	F
A	(414.13)	(2)		
$A_{\text{comp. 1}}$	120.13	1	120.13	3.58
$A_{\text{comp. 2}}$	294.00	1	294.00	8.76*
S/A		9	33.57	
$A \times B$	(130.20)	(6)		
$A_{\text{comp. 1}} \times B$	23.12	3	7.71	2.30
$A_{\text{comp. 2}} \times B$	107.08	3	35.69	10.65**
$B \times S/A$		27	3.35	

*$p < .025$.
**$p < .01$.

Since the two comparisons are orthogonal, we can take advantage of the fact that the sum of a complete set of component sums of squares equals the overall sum of squares to provide ourselves with an arithmetic check on the calculations. That is,

$$120.13 + 294.00 = 414.13 \quad \text{and} \quad SS_A = 414.13;$$

and

$$23.12 + 107.08 = 130.20 \quad \text{and} \quad SS_{A \times B} = 130.20.$$

This analysis reveals that a major component of the interaction consists of the comparison between the control and average incentive conditions and that very little variation is associated with a comparison between the two forms of incentive or motivation.

(c) The calculations for the sums of squares are performed in two major steps: first the calculations required for the repeated-measures error term, and then those required for the main effects and interaction of the comparisons themselves. The first step has already been accomplished in part (a), p. 597, where the $SS_{B\text{lin.} \times S/A}$ was calculated for the analysis of the linear trend. All that is necessary is to correct this sum of squares for the use of weighted ABS scores in the calculations. In this case, the correction is $20/2 = 10$ and $SS_{B\text{lin.} \times S/A} = {}^{411.25}/_{10} = 41.13$. The other error term, S/A, comes from the original analysis (see p. 595) and is not corrected since it was obtained from unweighted data.

For the remaining sums of squares, we need to construct an $A_c B_c$ comparison matrix. We can begin with the AB_c matrix that was obtained in part (a) for the linear trend and then weight these once-weighted AB sums by coefficients reflecting $A_{\text{comp.}}$. If we use as coefficients $1, -\frac{1}{2}$, and $-\frac{1}{2}$, we obtain the following doubly-weighted $A_c B_c$ comparison matrix needed for the analysis:

	$a(+)$	$a(-)$	Sum
$b(+)$	434	562.50	996.50
$b(-)$	336	358.50	694.50
Sum	770	921	1,691

The three unadjusted sums of squares are

$$SS_{A'} = 180{,}142.63 - 178{,}717.56 = 1{,}425.07;$$
$$SS_{B'} = 184{,}417.81 - [T] = 5{,}700.25;$$

and

$$SS_{A' \times B'} = 186{,}545.13 - [A] - [B] + [T] = 702.25.$$

The correction factor for these sums of squares is $\left(\frac{1.5}{2}\right)\left(\frac{20}{2}\right) = 7.50$. The analysis is summarized below:

SOURCE	SS	df	MS	F
$A_{comp.\,2}$	190.01	1	190.01	5.66*
S/A		9	33.57	
B_{linear}	760.03	1	760.03	166.31**
$A_{comp.\,2} \times B_{lin.}$	93.63	1	93.63	20.49**
$B_{lin.} \times S/A$	41.13	9	4.57	

*$p < .05$.
**$p < .01$.

4. (a)

SOURCE	CALCULATIONS	SS	df	MS	F
A	$5{,}506.50 - 5{,}461.33 =$	45.17	2	22.59	<1
S/A	$5{,}885.50 - [A] =$	379.00	9	42.11	
B	$5{,}532.33 - [T] =$	71.00	3	23.67	3.61*
$A \times B$	$5{,}662.00 - [A] - [B] + [T] =$	84.50	6	14.08	2.15
$B \times S/A$	$6{,}218 - [AB] - [AS] + [A] =$	177.00	27	6.56	
Total	$[ABS] - [T] =$	756.67	47		

*$p < .05$.

(b)

LATIN SQUARE ANALYSIS: DIRECT REMOVAL OF PRACTICE EFFECTS

Source	Calculations	SS	df	MS	F
A	$5{,}510.10 - 5{,}464.75 =$ 45.35		2	22.68	<1
S/A	$5{,}889.10 - [A] =$ 379.00		9	42.11	
B	$5{,}535.75 - [T] =$ 71.00		3	23.67	6.36**
A × B	$5{,}665.60 - [A] - [B] + [T] =$ 84.50		6	14.08	3.78*
L. S. residual	$6{,}111.60 - [AB] - [AS] + [A] =$ 67.00		$27 - 9^a$	3.72	
Total	$[ABS] - [T] =$ 646.85		$47 - 9^a$		

*p < .025.
**p < .01.
$^a df_P + df_{A \times P} = 3 + 6 = 9.$

LATIN-SQUARE ANALYSIS: REMOVAL OF SUMS OF SQUARES

Source	Calculations^a	SS	df	MS	F
B	(From part (a))	71.00	3	23.67	6.31**
A × B	(From part (a))	84.50	6	14.08	3.75*
Practice (P)	$5{,}562.50 - [T] =$ 101.17		3	33.72	8.99**
A × P	$5{,}616.50 - [A] - [P] + [T] =$ 8.33		6	1.39	<1
L. S. residual	$177.00 - 101.17 - 8.33 =$ 67.50		18	3.75	

*p < .025.
**p < .01.
$^a[A]$ and $[T]$ were obtained from part (a).

(c) There are various approaches to this analysis. One of these focuses on two partial factorials formed from the A manipulation, namely, a comparison designed to assess the effects of removing the noncritical area (a_1 versus a_2) and a comparison focusing directly on the removal of the critical area (a_2 versus a_3). Presumably the researcher is primarily interested in the second comparison and less interested in the first. Under these circumstances, as the researcher you might proceed as follows: (1) Form a partial factorial consisting of the second comparison (a_2 versus a_3) and all four levels of factor B. A significant interaction would indicate that the difference between the two operated groups depends on the particular test given. (2) Form several interaction contrasts to identify the particular test or combination of tests that shows the effects of removing the critical area. For example, a contrast formed by crossing this comparison with the first two tests (b_1 versus b_2) would probably reveal no interaction, while a comparison of the second two tests (b_3 versus b_4)

might. On the other hand, if neither interaction is significant, you might look at an interaction contrast involving an average of the first two tests compared with an average of the last two tests.

The purpose of this problem was to encourage you to think of analytical questions and the form that they take in an actual analysis. The analysis discussed in the last paragraph was post hoc, relying on the outcome of the experiment to dictate the next question or analysis. Most researchers would feel that some correction for familywise error should be made at this point. Of course, it would be far better to have formed some speculations concerning which tests would detect differences and which would not and to have incorporated these ideas into a series of planned comparisons.

(d) (Note: There is no need to normalize sums of squares in this analysis because both comparisons give a correction factor of 1.)

SOURCE	CALCULATIONS	SS	df	MS	F
$A_{comp.}$ S/A	$1,513.38 - 1,483.02 = 30.36$ (From part (b))		1 9	30.36 42.11	<1
$B_{comp.}$ $A_{comp.} \times B_{comp.}$ $B_{comp.} \times S/A$	$1,508.02 - [T] = 25.00$ $1,542.38 - [A] - [B] + [T] = 4.00$ $3,272.98 - 3,068.48 - 3,223.67$ $+ 3,026.98 = 7.81$		1 1 $9-1$	25.00 4.00 .98	25.51** 4.08*

*$p < .10$.
**$p < .01$.

As you can see from this analysis, the statistical support is weak for the conclusion that test 4 discriminates between the two operated groups while test 3 does not.

CHAPTER 19

1. *Experiment A:* An $A \times B \times (C \times S)$ design, where

   A consists of two levels (generate versus read);
   B consists of two levels (timed versus self-paced);
   C consists of five levels (rules); and
   $s = 6$ subjects in each of the $(a)(b) = 4$ independent groups.

SOURCE	ERROR TERM
A	S/AB
B	S/AB
$A \times B$	S/AB
S/AB	—
C	$C \times S/AB$
$A \times C$	$C \times S/AB$
$B \times C$	$C \times S/AB$
$A \times B \times C$	$C \times S/AB$
$C \times S/AB$	—

Experiment B: An $A \times (B \times C \times S)$ design, where

A consists of two levels (informed versus uninformed);
B consists of two levels (generate versus read);
C consists of five levels (rules); and
$s = 6$ subjects in each of the $a = 2$ independent groups.

SOURCE	ERROR TERM
A	S/A
S/A	—
B	$B \times S/A$
$A \times B$	$B \times S/A$
$B \times S/A$	—
C	$C \times S/A$
$A \times C$	$C \times S/A$
$C \times S/A$	—
$B \times C$	$B \times C \times S/A$
$A \times B \times C$	$B \times C \times S/A$
$B \times C \times S/A$	—

Experiment C: An $A \times B \times (C \times S)$ design, where

A consists of two levels (stimulus-versus-response recognition);
B consists of two levels (informed versus uninformed);
C consists of two levels (generate versus read); and
$s = 6$ subjects in each of the $(a)(b) = 4$ independent groups.

The analysis is the same as that enumerated for Experiment A.

Experiment D: An $(A \times B \times C \times S)$ design, where

A consists of two levels (generate versus read);
B consists of three levels (rules);
C consists of five levels (trials); and
$s = 12$ subjects.

SOURCE	ERROR TERM
A	$A \times S$
$A \times S$	—
B	$B \times S$
$B \times S$	—
C	$C \times S$
$C \times S$	—
$A \times B$	$A \times B \times S$
$A \times B \times S$	—
$A \times C$	$A \times C \times S$
$A \times C \times S$	—
$B \times C$	$B \times C \times S$
$B \times C \times S$	—
$A \times B \times C$	$A \times B \times C \times S$
$A \times B \times C \times S$	—

Experiment E: An $A \times (B \times C \times S)$ design, where

A consists of two levels (stimulus-versus-response recall);
B consists of two levels (generate versus read);
C consists of five levels (trials); and
$s = 12$ subjects in each of the $a = 2$ independent groups.

The analysis is the same as that enumerated for Experiment B.

2. *Experiment A:* An $A \times (B \times C \times S)$ design, where

A consists of two levels (marijuana versus placebo);
B consists of three levels (trials);
C consists of two levels (cued versus uncued); and
$s = 20$ subjects in each of the $a = 2$ independent groups.

The analysis is identical to that enumerated for Experiment B, Exercise 1.

Experiment B: An $(A \times B \times S)$ design, where

A consists of four levels (placebo and three dosages);
B consists of two levels (rate of presentation); and
$s = 16$ subjects.

SOURCE	ERROR TERM
A	$A \times S$
$A \times S$	—
B	$B \times S$
$B \times S$	—
$A \times B$	$A \times B \times S$
$A \times B \times S$	—

3.

TREATMENT SOURCE	ERROR TERM	TREATMENT SOURCE	ERROR TERM
No Repeated Factors		Two Repeated Factors	
A	S/A	$B \times C$	$B \times C \times S/A$
		$A \times B \times C$	$B \times C \times S/A$
One Repeated Factor		$B \times D$	$B \times D \times S/A$
B	$B \times S/A$	$A \times B \times D$	$B \times D \times S/A$
$A \times B$	$B \times S/A$		
		$C \times D$	$C \times D \times S/A$
C	$C \times S/A$	$A \times C \times D$	$C \times D \times S/A$
$A \times C$	$C \times S/A$		
		Three Repeated Factors	
D	$D \times S/A$		
$A \times D$	$D \times S/A$	$B \times C \times D$	$B \times C \times D \times S/A$
		$A \times B \times C \times D$	$B \times C \times D \times S/A$

(Note: From this outline of the analysis, you should be able to write the *df* statements for each source of variance and to generate the corresponding computational formulas from these statements.)

SOURCE	CALCULATIONS	SS	df	MS	F
A	$2,306.47 - 2,305.63 =$ .84		1	.84	<1
B	$2,306.07 - [T] =$ .44		3	.15	<1
A × B	$2,320.80 - [A] - [B] + [T] =$ 13.89		3	4.63	<1
S/AB	$2,424.80 - [AB] =$ 104.00		16	6.50	
C	$2,737.75 - [T] =$ 432.12		4	108.03	109.12*
A × C	$2,740.33 - [A] - [C] + [T] =$ 1.74		4	.44	<1
B × C	$2,751.00 - [B] - [C] + [T] =$ 12.81		12	1.07	1.08
A × B × C	$2,784.67 - [AB] - [AC] - [BC]$				
	$+ [A] + [B] + [C] - [T] =$ 17.20		12	1.43	1.44
C × S/AB	$2,952 - [ABC] - [ABS] + [AB] =$ 63.33		64	.99	
Total	$[ABCS] - [T] =$ 646.37		119		

*$p < .01$.

5.

SOURCE	CALCULATIONS	SS	df	MS	F
A	$3,181.30 - 3,132.90 =$ 48.40		1	48.40	30.44*
S	$3,522.75 - [T] =$ 389.85		4	97.46	
A × S	$3,577.50 - [A] - [S] + [T] =$ 6.35		4	1.59	
B	$3,308.60 - [T] =$ 175.70		3	58.57	45.05*
B × S	$3,714.00 - [B] - [S] + [T] =$ 15.55		12	1.30	
A × B	$3,360.40 - [A] - [B] + [T] =$ 3.40		3	1.13	2.31
A × B × S	$3,778 - [AB] - [AS] - [BS]$				
	$+ [A] + [B] + [S] - [T] =$ 5.85		12	.49	
Total	$[ABS] - [T] =$ 645.10		39		

*$p < .01$.

6.

SOURCE	CALCULATIONS	SS	df	MS	F
A	$3,017.01 - 3,015.84 =$ 1.17		1	1.17	<1
S/A	$3,057.08 - [A] =$ 40.07		10	4.01	
B	$3,047.27 - [T] =$ 31.43		2	15.72	17.09*
A × B	$3,064.88 - [A] - [B] + [T] =$ 16.44		2	8.22	8.93*
B × S/A	$3,123.25 - [AB] - [AS] + [A] =$ 18.30		20	.92	

SOURCE	CALCULATIONS	SS	df	MS	F
C	$3{,}260.36 - [T] =$ 244.52		3	81.51	169.81*
A × C	$3{,}271.94 - [A] - [C] + [T] =$ 10.41		3	3.47	7.23*
C × S/A	$3{,}326.33 - [AC] - [AS] + [A] =$ 14.32		30	.48	
B × C	$3{,}292.75 - [B] - [C] + [T] =$ .96		6	.16	<1
A × B × C	$3{,}321.17 - [AB] - [AC] - [BC]$				
	$+ [A] + [B] + [C] - [T] =$ .40		6	.07	<1
B × C × S/A	$3{,}419 - [ABC] - [ABS] - [ACS]$				
	$+ [AB] + [AC] + [AS] - [A] =$ 25.14		60	.42	
Total	$[ABCS] - [T] =$ 403.16		143		

*$p < .01$.

CHAPTER 20

1. (a)

SOURCE	CALCULATIONS	$SS_{adj.}$	df	$MS_{adj.}$	F
A	$225.33 - (13.92 - .05) =$ 211.46		2	105.73	20.37*
S/A	$72.67 - .05 =$ 72.62		14	5.19	

*$p < .01$

(b) It is obvious that little or no adjustment was applied to the within-groups error term. This fact clearly indicates that no precision was gained from the introduction of a covariate into the analysis. This lack of gain is reflected in the near-zero within-groups correlation between the covariate and the dependent variable. That is,

$$r_{S/A} = \frac{-1.33}{\sqrt{(36.00)(72.67)}} = -.03.$$

2. (a) The computational formulas are found in Table B-1. Table B-2 gives an even more detailed specification of the calculations of the different sums of squares and sums of products.

(b)

SOURCE	CALCULATIONS	$SS_{adj.}$	df	$MS_{adj.}$	F
A	$160.06 - (.65 - 21.66) =$ 181.07		2	90.54	30.48*
B	$45.39 - (8.61 - 21.66) =$ 58.44		2	29.22	9.84*
A × B	$124.44 - (6.44 - 21.66) =$ 139.66		4	34.92	11.76*
S/AB	$99.00 - 21.66 =$ 77.34		26	2.97	

*$p < .01$.

Table B-1 Analysis of Covariance: $A \times B$ Design

SOURCE	ADJUSTED SUM OF SQUARES	df	F
A	$SS_{A(y)} - \left[\dfrac{(SP_A + SP_{S/AB})^2}{SS_{A(x)} + SS_{S/AB(x)}} - \dfrac{(SP_{S/AB})^2}{SS_{S/AB(x)}} \right]$	$a - 1$	$\dfrac{MS_A \text{(adj.)}}{MS_{S/AB}\text{(adj.)}}$
B	$SS_{B(y)} - \left[\dfrac{(SP_B + SP_{S/AB})^2}{SS_{B(x)} + SS_{S/AB(x)}} - \dfrac{(SP_{S/AB})^2}{SS_{S/AB(x)}} \right]$	$b - 1$	$\dfrac{MS_B\text{(adj.)}}{MS_{S/AB}\text{(adj.)}}$
$A \times B$	$SS_{(A \times B)(y)} - \left[\dfrac{(SP_{(A \times B)} + SP_{S/AB})^2}{SS_{(A \times B)(x)} + SS_{S/AB(x)}} - \dfrac{(SP_{S/AB})^2}{SS_{S/AB(x)}} \right]$	$(a-1)(b-1)$	$\dfrac{MS_{(A \times B)}\text{(adj.)}}{MS_{S/AB}\text{(adj.)}}$
S/AB	$SS_{S/AB(y)} - \dfrac{(SP_{S/AB})^2}{SS_{S/AB(x)}}$	$(a)(b)(s-1) - 1$	

Table B-2 Sums of Squares and Products: Two-Factor Analysis of Covariance

SOURCE	CONTROL VARIABLE (X)	CROSS PRODUCTS (XY)	DEPENDENT VARIABLE (Y)
A	$\dfrac{\Sigma (A_x)^2}{(b)(s)} - \dfrac{(T_x)^2}{(a)(b)(s)}$	$\dfrac{\Sigma (A_{i(x)})(A_{i(y)})}{(b)(s)} - \dfrac{(T_x)(T_y)}{(a)(b)(s)}$	$\dfrac{\Sigma (A_y)^2}{(b)(s)} - \dfrac{(T_y)^2}{(a)(b)(s)}$
B	$\dfrac{\Sigma (B_x)^2}{(a)(s)} - [T_x]$	$\dfrac{\Sigma (B_{j(x)})(B_{j(y)})}{(a)(s)} - [T_{xy}]$	$\dfrac{\Sigma (B_y)^2}{(a)(s)} - [T_y]$
$A \times B$	$\dfrac{\Sigma (AB_x)^2}{s} - [A_x] - [B_x] + [T_x]$	$\dfrac{\Sigma (AB_{ij(x)})(AB_{ij(y)})}{s} - [A_{xy}] - [B_{xy}] + [T_{xy}]$	$\dfrac{\Sigma (AB_y)^2}{s} - [A_y] - [B_y] + [T_y]$
S/AB	$\Sigma (ABS_x)^2 - [AB_x]$	$\Sigma (ABS_{ijk(x)})(ABS_{ijk(y)}) - [AB_{xy}]$	$\Sigma (ABS_y)^2 - [AB_y]$
Total	$[ABS_x] - [T_x]$	$[ABS_{xy}] - [T_{xy}]$	$[ABS_y] - [T_y]$

APPENDIX C-3

1. (a)

SOURCE	CALCULATIONS	SS	df	MS	F
A	$5,194.05 - 4,878.02 = 316.03$		2	158.02	25.65*
S/A	$5,545 - [A] = 350.95$		57	6.16	
Total	$[AS] - [T] = 666.98$		59		

*$p < .01$.

(b)

	a_1	a_2	a_3	$\Sigma (c_i)(\bar{A}_i)$	$\Sigma (c_i)^2$
$\bar{A}_i$:	12.05	8.50	6.50		
c_{1i}:	−7.67	−3.67	11.33	−49.97	200.67
c_{2i}:	28.43	−35.97	7.53	85.78	2,158.81

SOURCE	SS	df	MS	F
A	(316.03)	(2)		
Linear	248.87	1	248.87	40.40*
Quadratic	68.17	1	68.17	11.07*
S/A		57	6.16	

*$p < .01$.

(Note: $\Sigma SS_{A\text{comp.}} = 248.87 + 68.17 = 317.04$ and $SS_A = 316.03$; the discrepancy is the rounding error introduced in the calculation of the coefficients.)

APPENDIX C-4

1.

SOURCE	EXPECTED MEAN SQUARE	ERROR TERM
B	$\sigma_\epsilon^2 + s(\sigma_{A/B}^2) + a(s)(\theta_B^2)$	A/B
A/B	$\sigma_\epsilon^2 + s(\sigma_{A/B}^2)$	S/AB
S/AB[a]	σ_ϵ^2	—

[a]More accurately, this source is written $S/A/B$; on the other hand, S/AB is equivalent and more familiar.

2.

SOURCE	EXPECTED MEAN SQUARE	ERROR TERM
B	$\sigma_\epsilon^2 + s(\sigma_{A/BC}^2) + a(c)(s)(\theta_B^2)$	A/BC
C	$\sigma_\epsilon^2 + s(\sigma_{A/BC}^2) + a(b)(s)(\theta_C^2)$	A/BC
$B \times C$	$\sigma_\epsilon^2 + s(\sigma_{A/BC}^2) + a(s)(\theta_{B \times C}^2)$	A/BC
A/BC	$\sigma_\epsilon^2 + s(\sigma_{A/BC}^2)$	S/ABC
S/ABC[a]	σ_ϵ^2	—

[a]More accurately, this source is written $S/A/BC$, but S/ABC is equivalent and more familiar.

3. (a) The experimental design, diagramed below, shows factor C nested in the different combinations of the levels of factors A and B, i.e., C/AB.

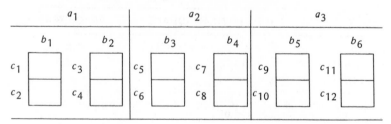

SOURCE	EXPECTED MEAN SQUARE	ERROR TERM
A	$\sigma_\epsilon^2 + s(\sigma_{C/AB}^2) + c(s)(\sigma_{A \times B}^2) + b(c)(s)(\theta_A^2)$	$A \times B$
B	$\sigma_\epsilon^2 + s(\sigma_{C/AB}^2) + a(c)(s)(\sigma_B^2)$	C/AB
$A \times B$	$\sigma_\epsilon^2 + s(\sigma_{C/AB}^2) + c(s)(\sigma_{A \times B}^2)$	C/AB
C/AB	$\sigma_\epsilon^2 + s(\sigma_{C/AB}^2)$	S/ABC
S/ABC[a]	σ_ϵ^2	—

[a]More accurately, this source is written $S/C/AB$, but S/ABC is equivalent and more familiar.

(b) The experimental design, diagramed below, shows factor C continuing to be nested as before (i.e., C/AB) but factor B now nested in factor A (i.e., B/A). That is, the school systems receiving one book are different from the systems receiving the other two books.

SOURCE	EXPECTED MEAN SQUARE	ERROR TERM
A	$\sigma_\epsilon^2 + s(\sigma_{C/AB}^2) + c(s)(\sigma_{B/A}^2) + b(c)(s)(\theta_A^2)$	B/A
B/A	$\sigma_\epsilon^2 + s(\sigma_{C/AB}^2) + c(s)(\sigma_{B/A}^2)$	C/AB
C/AB	$\sigma_\epsilon^2 + s(\sigma_{C/AB}^2)$	S/ABC
S/ABC[a]	σ_ϵ^2	—

[a]More accurately, this source is written $S/C/AB$, but S/ABC is equivalent and more familiar.

4. The sources of variance, expected mean squares, and error terms are given below:

SOURCE	EXPECTED MEAN SQUARE	ERROR TERM
A	$\sigma_\epsilon^2 + b(s)(\sigma_{C/A}^2) + b(c)(s)(\theta_A^2)$	C/A
B	$\sigma_\epsilon^2 + s(\sigma_{B \times C/A}^2) + a(c)(s)(\theta_B^2)$	$B \times C/A$
$A \times B$	$\sigma_\epsilon^2 + s(\sigma_{B \times C/A}^2) + c(s)(\theta_{A \times B}^2)$	$B \times C/A$
C/A	$\sigma_\epsilon^2 + b(s)(\sigma_{C/A}^2)$	S/ABC
$B \times C/A$	$\sigma_\epsilon^2 + s(\sigma_{B \times C/A}^2)$	S/ABC
S/ABC	σ_ϵ^2	—

SOURCE	CALCULATIONS	SS	df	MS	ERROR TERM	F
A	$1{,}582.20 - 1{,}560.60 =$	21.60	1	21.60	C/A	<1
B	$1{,}687.30 - [T] =$	126.70	2	63.35	$B \times C/A$	33.17*
$A \times B$	$1{,}765.60 - [A] - [B] + [T] =$	56.70	2	28.35	$B \times C/A$	14.84*
C/A	$2{,}142.00 - [A] =$	559.80	8	69.98	S/ABC	13.72*
$B \times C/A$	$2{,}356.00 - [AB] - [AC] + [A] =$	30.60	16	1.91	S/ABC	<1
S/ABC	$2{,}509 - [ABC] =$	153.00	30	5.10	—	
Total	$[ABCS] - [T] =$	948.40	59			

*$p < .01$.

The nature of the variation contributing to the nested factor, *problems*, can be understood by calculating separate sums of squares at each level of factor A and *then* pooling them. For the main effect of problems (C/A), I will calculate the variation due to the problems at a_1 and at a_2 separately as follows:

$$SS_{C/A_1} = 1{,}226.17 - 974.70 = 251.47;$$

and

$$SS_{C/A_2} = 915.83 - 607.50 = 308.33.$$

The sum of these two SS's, $\Sigma SS_{C/A_i} = 251.47 + 308.33 = 559.80$, is equal to $SS_{C/A}$ calculated above.

For the interaction of problems and feedback (factor B), I will calculate the separate $B \times C$ interactions at levels a_1 and a_2. This can be accomplished easily by treating each BC matrix as if it contained data from a two-factor design. That is,

$$SS_{B \times C/A_1} = 1{,}427.50 - 1{,}148.30 - 1{,}226.17 + 974.70 = 27.73;$$

and

$$SS_{B \times C/A_2} = 928.50 - 617.30 - 915.83 + 607.50 = 2.87.$$

The sum of these two SS's, $\Sigma SS_{B \times C/A_i} = 27.73 + 2.87 = 30.60$, is equal to the $SS_{B \times C/A}$ calculated above.

Appendix C-I

A Comparison of Notational Systems

Most of you were probably brought up on "standard notation," which uses either an X or a Y and multiple summation signs—both with identifying subscripts—to designate all of the arithmetical operations required in a statistical analysis. Unfortunately, very few authors of more advanced statistics books use this form of notation, because it is awkward when applied to the analysis of variance and confusing to beginners. As you will soon discover, if you have not already, no two authors use the same notational system to express calculations. The system adopted for this book uses unique symbols (letters and combinations of letters) to designate the different quantities entering into computational formulas. In this appendix, I will summarize the principles underlying my notational system and then present a comparison of the different systems adopted by the authors of some of the more widely used books. I hope that this overview will help you in adapting to my system and in translating the systems of others.

A SUMMARY OF THE PRESENT NOTATIONAL SYSTEM

1. **Capital letters**, either singly or in combination with other letters, refer to *data*—i.e., the individual observations and the various sums obtained from a systematic processing of these observations. In the completely randomized two-way factorial, for example, the symbol ABS represents the *individual observation*. The three letters do *not* specify multiplication, but rather they emphasize the fact that a basic observation is produced by a particular subject (the S in the designation) in a particular treatment combination derived from the factorial arrangement of the two

independent variables, factor A (the A in the designation) and factor B (the B in the designation). When a set of ABS scores are summed for any given treatment combination, we obtain a subtotal that is designated by the symbol AB. Again, this designation emphasizes the fact that this *sum* comes from a treatment condition formed by a combination of factor A (the A in the designation) and of factor B (the B in the designation). Combining the AB sums over the levels of factor B produces totals that are called A sums; there is one A sum for each of the levels of factor A. Combining the AB sums over the levels of factor A produces B sums; here too, there is one B sum for each of the levels of factor B. Finally, there is the grand total of all the observations in the experiment, which is designated T.

   2. **Subscripts** are added when it is necessary to specify a particular observation or a particular subtotal. The subscripts are identified by the symbol for a basic observation in the experiment. For the two-factor design, for example, ABS_{ijk} indicates that $i =$ the levels of factor A, $j =$ the levels of factor B, and $k =$ the levels of factor S. Numerical subscripts are used to specify a particular quantity. Thus, the score ABS_{124} refers to the score of the fourth subject (factor S) receiving the treatment combination formed by pairing level a_1 with level b_2, with the order of the subscripts corresponding to the order of the three capital letters—A treatment first, B treatment second, and the subject third. If any subscripts run over 9, commas are introduced to keep the subscripts separate and distinct.

   3. **Summation signs** are used without additional notation when the summation is conducted on *all* the quantities in a set of similar quantities. Subscripted summation signs and multiple summation signs are used only when a particular quantity is to be summed over some but not all of the subscripts. These situations will be made clear by the context in which they appear. In general, most summation is *implicit* in this notation, with capital letters—e.g., AB, A, B, and T—representing different sums, which minimizes the need for the subscripted multiple summation signs required by most other systems of notation.

   4. **The levels of a factor** are designated by the lower-case version of the letter representing the factor. In the example I have been considering, $a =$ the levels of factor A, $b =$ the levels of factor B, and $s =$ the levels of factor S, i.e., sample size. Subscripts are used to designate particular levels. Contrary to what I said about the symbols for scores and sums, combinations of lower-case letters *do* imply multiplication. This fact is emphasized by the use of parentheses. That is, the total number of treatment combinations in the two-factor design is $(a)(b)$—the product obtained by multiplying the number of levels of factor A by the number of levels of factor B. The symbol AB, on the other hand, refers to the *sum* of the scores in one of the treatment combinations. Similarly, the total number of observations in this design is given by $(a)(b)(s)$; ABS designates one of the scores in the experiment.

   5. **Squaring operations** are performed on scores and sums in the analysis of variance. The square of any score or sum involving more than one capital letter will be designated by placing parentheses around the relevant symbol to avoid any confusion about the operation specified. That is, $(ABS)^2$ refers to the square of an in-

dividual observation and $\Sigma (ABS)^2$ refers to the sum of all the squared individual observations in the experiment.

A COMPARISON OF DIFFERENT SYSTEMS

I will begin by comparing the present system with two versions of standard notation. The five sets of quantities entering into the analysis of a completely randomized two-way factorial design are listed in column 1 of Table 1. Column 2 gives the letter symbols used in this book to distinguish the quantities in any given set from those in the other sets. Standard notation, presented in the next two columns, uses a single symbol, X_{ijk}, to represent the different quantities. In column 3, subscripted summation signs are used to perform this task. A cell sum, for example, requires the summation of all X_{ijk} scores in one of the treatment groups. Since the k subscript refers to the subject classification, $\Sigma_k X_{ijk}$ tells us to sum these scores over k only, beginning with $k = 1$ (assumed) and ending with $k = s$ (the last, or sth, score in the group). Symbolically,

$$\sum_k X_{ijk} = X_{ij1} + X_{ij2} + \cdots + X_{ijs}.$$

The grand sum, at the other extreme, requires the summation of all X_{ijk} scores in the experiment. This operation is specified by three summation signs—one for each subscript—namely, $\Sigma_i \Sigma_j \Sigma_k X_{ijk}$, where the summation sign on the right (Σ_k)

Table 1   A Comparison of the Present Notational System with Standard Notation

(1) DESIGNATED QUANTITY	(2) PRESENT SYSTEM	(3) *Standard Notation* COMPLETE	(4) ABBREVIATED
Basic score	ABS_{ijk}	X_{ijk}	X_{ijk}
Cell sum	AB_{ij}	$\sum_k X_{ijk}$	$X_{ij.}$
A sum	A_i	$\sum_j \sum_k X_{ijk}$	$X_{i..}$
B sum	B_j	$\sum_i \sum_k X_{ijk}$	$X_{.j.}$
Grand sum	T	$\sum_i \sum_j \sum_k X_{ijk}$	$X_{...}$

produces the treatment sums for each of the $(a)(b)$ groups, the one in the middle (Σ_j) combines these sums over the levels of factor B, and the sign on the left (Σ_i) completes the process by summing these last subtotals.

An abbreviated version of standard notation is given in column 4 of Table 1. The main feature of this alternative is the use of a *dot* that replaces any subscript over which a summation occurs. The group sum becomes $X_{ij\cdot}$, the dot replacing the k subscript "active" in this operation, and the grand sum becomes $X_{\cdot\cdot\cdot}$, since all three subscripts are involved in defining this quantity.

Table 2 compares six notational systems used by different authors. Columns 2 and 3 list the different symbols used in this book and by Winer (1971). Except for only minor differences, the two sets of symbols are the same. This close correspondence should facilitate switching back and forth between these two books. The next two columns list systems that are examples of standard notation, but with Y's instead of X's. A subtle difference, however, is the use of the i subscript for the subject classification, rather than k as in the other systems we have examined. You will have to watch this difference carefully when you turn to Hays (1973) or Myers (1966, 1972) as a reference. In column 6, I have presented the new system adopted by Myers in his third edition (1979), which, as you can see, is the abbreviated version of standard notation summarized in Table 1. Again, you should note that the i subscript continues to refer to the subject classification. In the final column is the system employed by Kirk (1968), which is unlike all of the others and requires close study to understand.

The fact that each notational system is different is a constant source of an-

Table 2   A Comparison of Six Notational Systems

(1) DESIGNATED QUANTITY	(2) PRESENT SYSTEM	(3) WINER (1971)	(4) HAYS (1973)	(5) MYERS (1966, 1972)	(6) MYERS (1979)	(7) KIRK (1968)
Basic score	ABS_{ijk}	X_{ijk}	y_{ijk}	Y_{ijk}	Y_{ijk}	ABS_{ijm}
Cell sum	AB_{ij}	AB_{ij}	$\sum\limits_{i} y_{ijk}$	$\sum\limits_{i}^{n} Y_{ijk}$	$T_{\cdot jk}$	AB_{ij}
A sum	A_i	A_i	$\sum\limits_{k}\sum\limits_{i} y_{ijk}$	$\sum\limits_{i}^{n}\sum\limits_{k}^{b} Y_{ijk}$	$T_{\cdot j\cdot}$	$\sum\limits_{1}^{q} A$
B sum	B_j	B_j	$\sum\limits_{j}\sum\limits_{i} y_{ijk}$	$\sum\limits_{i}^{n}\sum\limits_{j}^{a} Y_{ijk}$	$T_{\cdot\cdot k}$	$\sum\limits_{1}^{p} B$
Grand sum	T	G	$\sum\limits_{j}\sum\limits_{k}\sum\limits_{i} y_{ijk}$	$\sum\limits_{i}^{n}\sum\limits_{j}^{a}\sum\limits_{k}^{b} Y_{ijk}$	$T_{\cdot\cdot\cdot}$	$\sum\limits_{1}^{N} ABS$

noyance and irritation to students and researchers alike. Eventually the complaints reduce in number and intensity as the individual develops a familiarity with the operations that are represented in coded form by a given notational system. I hope that Tables 1 and 2 will help speed the translation process. The simplest way to understand how any particular notational system works is to follow the symbols through a numerical example—especially an analysis with which you are reasonably comfortable. The actual processing of the numbers usually will shed light on an unfamiliar notational system more quickly than will a detailed discussion of its formal characteristics.

Appendix C-2

Orthogonality of Sources of Variance

At various points I have asserted that the sources of variance normally extracted in the analysis of variance are mutually orthogonal. It is possible to demonstrate the orthogonality of these sources of variance, but the demonstration is complicated and a little tedious. I will include such an illustration, nevertheless, because students frequently express an interest in the problem and their understanding of the analysis of variance seems enhanced when it is presented to them. The general plan will be to devise a set of coefficients that are mutually orthogonal and that reflect the sources of variance being extracted. These coefficients will then be applied to actual data to produce corresponding sums of squares. Finally, the sums of squares associated with each set of coefficients will be added together to produce values that are numerically identical to the sums of squares obtained for the same sources of variance with the usual computational formulas.

COMPARISONS AND ORTHOGONALITY: A REVIEW

The notion of comparisons was first introduced in Chapter 6. Briefly, a comparison is produced by applying weights (or coefficients) to the different treatment means and then calculating the sums of squares associated with the comparison. More specifically, a comparison must satisfy the requirement that

$$\Sigma \left(c_i \right) = 0, \tag{1}$$

where the c_i terms are the coefficients for a particular comparison. Suppose we have four groups in a single-factor experiment and we want to make the following comparisons: (1) the group at a_1 versus the group at a_3, (2) the group at a_2 versus the group at a_4, and (3) the average of the groups at a_1 and a_3 versus the average of the groups at a_2 and a_4. These comparisons are reflected by the coefficients of combination (c_i) listed for each group:

	LEVELS OF FACTOR A			
	a_1	a_2	a_3	a_4
Means:	$\bar{A}_1$	$\bar{A}_2$	$\bar{A}_3$	$\bar{A}_4$
Comparison 1:	1	0	−1	0
Comparison 2:	0	1	0	−1
Comparison 3:	1	−1	1	−1

The requirement specified in Eq. (1) is met with each of these comparisons.

Two comparisons are orthogonal if the sum of the products of corresponding coefficients equals zero. In symbols,

$$\Sigma \, (c_i)(c_i') = 0, \tag{2}$$

where c_i represents the coefficients for one comparison and c_i' represents the corresponding coefficients for the other comparison. The three comparisons listed above are mutually orthogonal:

(1) vs. (2): $(1)(0) + (0)(1) + (-1)(0) + (0)(-1) = 0,$

(1) vs. (3): $(1)(1) + (0)(-1) + (-1)(1) + (0)(-1) = 0,$

(2) vs. (3): $(0)(1) + (1)(-1) + (0)(1) + (-1)(-1) = 0.$

I will consider a numerical example in which there are $s = 4$ subjects in each of the four groups. The scores and summary calculations are presented in Table 1. The three sets of coefficients are also entered in the table. The computational formula for the sums of squares associated with a comparison is

$$SS_{A \, \text{comp.}} = \frac{s \, (\hat{\psi}_A)^2}{\Sigma \, (c_i)^2}, \tag{3}$$

where $\hat{\psi}_A = \Sigma \, (c_i)(\bar{A}_i)$, the sum of the weighted treatment means. This sum is listed to the right of the coefficients for each of the three comparisons. As an example, the sum of the weighted means for comparison 3 is found as follows:

$$\hat{\psi}_{A \, \text{comp. 3}} = (1)(5.0) + (-1)(3.0) + (1)(7.0) + (-1)(10.0) = -1.0.$$

Table 1   Orthogonal Comparisons and the Single-Factor Design

	a_1	a_2	a_3	a_4		
	3	1	8	10		
	5	3	6	9		
	7	6	5	14		
	5	2	9	7		
Sum:	20	12	28	40		
Mean:	5.0	3.0	7.0	10.0	$\hat{\psi}_A$	$\Sigma\,(c_i)^2$
Comp. 1:	1	0	−1	0	−2.0	2
Comp. 2:	0	1	0	−1	−7.0	2
Comp. 3:	1	−1	1	−1	−1.0	4

Substituting in Eq. (3), we find the following sums of squares:

$$SS_{A\,\text{comp. 1}} = \frac{4(-2.0)^2}{2} = 8.0;$$

$$SS_{A\,\text{comp. 2}} = \frac{4(-7.0)^2}{2} = 98.0;$$

and

$$SS_{A\,\text{comp. 3}} = \frac{4(-1.0)^2}{4} = 1.0.$$

As noted in Chapter 6, the SS_A can be partitioned into a set of orthogonal comparisons, the number of which is equal to the df_A—that is, $a - 1$. To show this property with the present data, we must calculate the SS_A:

$$SS_A = \frac{\Sigma\,(A)^2}{s} - \frac{(T)^2}{(a)(s)}$$

$$= \frac{(20)^2 + (12)^2 + (28)^2 + (40)^2}{4} - \frac{(20 + 12 + 28 + 40)^2}{(4)(4)}$$

$$= 732.0 - 625.0 = 107.0.$$

As verification of the additivity property,

$$SS_A = \Sigma\,SS_{A\,\text{comp.}},$$
$$107.0 = 8.0 + 98.0 + 1.0 = 107.0.$$

This breakdown of the SS_A into a set of orthogonal comparisons illustrates the meaning of degrees of freedom: the number of degrees of freedom specifies the
620

number of *orthogonal comparisons* that may be constructed from a given set of data. We are now ready to use this property to show that the SS_A and the $SS_{S/A}$ are themselves orthogonal.

ORTHOGONALITY OF THE SS_A AND THE $SS_{S/A}$ IN THE SINGLE-FACTOR DESIGN

In the analysis of variance, the total variability among subjects (SS_T) is partitioned into two orthogonal sources, the SS_A and the $SS_{S/A}$. I will demonstrate this orthogonality by dividing the total sum of squares into $(a)(s) - 1$ orthogonal comparisons, $a - 1$ of which will reflect the SS_A, and $a(s - 1)$ of which will reflect the $SS_{S/A}$. If all these comparisons are mutually orthogonal, then I will have demonstrated that *two subsets* of the comparisons, the SS_A and the $SS_{S/A}$, are orthogonal also.

For this illustration I will use the individual scores as the basic entry. In the single-factor experiment these are designated AS_{ij}. These scores have been listed at the top of Table 2. There are four AS scores ($s = 4$) for each treatment condition, and a total of $(a)(s) = (4)(4) = 16$ scores are listed across the table. The first step is to write a complete set of coefficients representing orthogonal comparisons, one comparison for each of the total number of df available in the experiment: $df_T = (a)(s) - 1 = (4)(4) - 1 = 15$. This has been accomplished in the 15 rows below the actual scores.

Consider, initially, the first three comparisons and the coefficients presented in the table. It will be noted that these comparisons are the numerical equivalents of the three comparisons listed in Table 1. Comparison, 1, for example, combines the four scores at level a_1 and contrasts them with the four scores at level a_3. This is exactly what is specified in Table 1, except that we are operating on the treatment means; i.e., the four AS scores have been combined already. The next two comparisons in Table 2 correspond to comparisons 2 and 3 in Table 1. Thus, if we apply the formula for the sums of squares to these data, we will extract the same quantities from Table 2 as we were able to extract from Table 1. A formula for a comparison, modified to fit this situation, is

$$SS_{AS\text{comp.}} = \frac{\hat{\psi}_{AS}^2}{\Sigma\,(c_{ij})^2}, \tag{4}$$

where $\hat{\psi}_{AS} = \Sigma\,(c_{ij})(AS_{ij})$, the sum of the weighted AS scores, and c_{ij} represents the coefficients for the jth subject in the ith treatment condition. Since we are dealing with single AS scores, s does not appear as a multiplier in the numerator of Eq. (4). The sums of the weighted AS scores for these three comparisons are given to the right of the coefficients. Substituting in Eq. (4), we find

$$SS_{AS\text{comp. 1}} = \frac{(-8)^2}{8} = 8.0;$$

Table 2   A Complete Set of Orthogonal Comparisons for the Single-Factor Design

	a_1				a_2				a_3				a_4				$\hat{\psi}_{AS}$	$\Sigma(c_{ij})^2$
	AS_{11}	AS_{12}	AS_{13}	AS_{14}	AS_{21}	AS_{22}	AS_{23}	AS_{24}	AS_{31}	AS_{32}	AS_{33}	AS_{34}	AS_{41}	AS_{42}	AS_{43}	AS_{44}		
Score:	3	5	7	5	1	3	6	2	8	6	5	9	10	9	14	7		
Comp. 1	1	1	1	1	0	0	0	0	−1	−1	−1	−1	0	0	0	0	−8	8
Comp. 2	0	0	0	0	1	1	1	1	0	0	0	0	−1	−1	−1	−1	−28	8
Comp. 3	1	1	1	1	−1	−1	−1	−1	1	1	1	1	−1	−1	−1	−1	−4	16
Comp. 4	3	−1	−1	−1	0	0	0	0	0	0	0	0	0	0	0	0	−8	12
Comp. 5	0	2	−1	−1	0	0	0	0	0	0	0	0	0	0	0	0	−2	6
Comp. 6	0	0	1	−1	0	0	0	0	0	0	0	0	0	0	0	0	2	2
Comp. 7	0	0	0	0	3	−1	−1	−1	0	0	0	0	0	0	0	0	−8	12
Comp. 8	0	0	0	0	0	2	−1	−1	0	0	0	0	0	0	0	0	−2	6
Comp. 9	0	0	0	0	0	0	1	−1	0	0	0	0	0	0	0	0	4	2
Comp. 10	0	0	0	0	0	0	0	0	3	−1	−1	−1	0	0	0	0	4	12
Comp. 11	0	0	0	0	0	0	0	0	0	2	−1	−1	0	0	0	0	−2	6
Comp. 12	0	0	0	0	0	0	0	0	0	0	1	−1	0	0	0	0	−4	2
Comp. 13	0	0	0	0	0	0	0	0	0	0	0	0	3	−1	−1	−1	0	12
Comp. 14	0	0	0	0	0	0	0	0	0	0	0	0	0	2	−1	−1	−3	6
Comp. 15	0	0	0	0	0	0	0	0	0	0	0	0	0	0	1	−1	7	2

$$SS_{AS\,comp.\,2} = \frac{(-28)^2}{8} = 98.0;$$

and

$$SS_{AS\,comp.\,3} = \frac{(-4)^2}{16} = 1.0.$$

These sums of squares are identical to those obtained from the treatment means and Eq. (3), and as we have seen, collectively they constitute the SS_A.

I will now construct a set of orthogonal comparisons that will permit the calculation of the within-groups sum of squares. Consider the coefficients constituting the next three orthogonal comparisons in Table 2. As you can verify easily, these comparisons are mutually orthogonal and orthogonal to comparisons 1 to 3. The choice of this set of coefficients was entirely arbitrary and was made only to facilitate enumeration. You can also see that the four different sets of three comparisons each extract the within-group sum of squares for levels a_1, a_2, a_3, and a_4. These comparisons, too, are orthogonal to all other comparisons in the table. Thus, I have constructed a total of 15 orthogonal comparisons, completely using up the degrees of freedom that are available. No additional orthogonal comparisons can be added to this set.

I will now obtain the separate within-group sums of squares and from these the pooled within-groups sum of squares, $SS_{S/A}$. The sum of the weighted AS scores appears on the right-hand side of the table. Applying Eq. (4) to the comparison listed for level a_1, we have

$$SS_{AS\,comp.\,4} = \frac{(-8)^2}{12} = 5.3;$$

$$SS_{AS\,comp.\,5} = \frac{(-2)^2}{6} = .7;$$

and

$$SS_{AS\,comp.\,6} = \frac{(2)^2}{2} = 2.0.$$

Calculated in the usual manner, the within-group sum of squares is given by the formula

$$SS_{S/A_1} = \Sigma\,(AS_{1j})^2 - \frac{(A_1)^2}{s}$$

$$= [(3)^2 + (5)^2 + (7)^2 + (5)^2] - \frac{(3 + 5 + 7 + 5)^2}{4} = 8.0.$$

This value is identical to that obtained by summing the sums of squares for the three orthogonal comparisons:

$$\Sigma\, SS_{AS_{comp.}} = 5.3 + .7 + 2.0 = 8.0.$$

The sums of squares for the orthogonal comparisons, the within-group sum of squares, and the verification of additivity for the remaining three levels of factor A will now be given. For a_2:

$$SS_{AS_{comp.\ 7}} = \frac{(-8)^2}{12} = 5.3;$$

$$SS_{AS_{comp.\ 8}} = \frac{(-2)^2}{6} = .7;$$

$$SS_{AS_{comp.\ 9}} = \frac{(4)^2}{2} = 8.0;$$

$$SS_{S/A_2} = [(1)^2 + (3)^2 + (6)^2 + (2)^2] - \frac{(1 + 3 + 6 + 2)^2}{4}$$

$$= 14.0;$$

and

$$\Sigma\, SS_{AS_{comp.}} = 5.3 + .7 + 8.0 = 14.0.$$

Next, for a_3, we have

$$SS_{AS_{comp.\ 10}} = \frac{(4)^2}{12} = 1.3;$$

$$SS_{AS_{comp.\ 11}} = \frac{(-2)^2}{6} = .7;$$

$$SS_{AS_{comp.\ 12}} = \frac{(-4)^2}{2} = 8.0;$$

$$SS_{S/A_3} = [(8)^2 + (6)^2 + (5)^2 + (9)^2] - \frac{(8 + 6 + 5 + 9)^2}{4}$$

$$= 10.0;$$

and

$$\Sigma\, SS_{AS_{comp.}} = 1.3 + .7 + 8.0 = 10.0.$$

Finally, for a_4:

$$SS_{AS_{comp.\ 13}} = \frac{(0)^2}{12} = 0.0;$$

$$SS_{AS_{\text{comp. 14}}} = \frac{(-3)^2}{6} = 1.5;$$

$$SS_{AS_{\text{comp. 15}}} = \frac{(7)^2}{2} = 24.5;$$

$$SS_{S/A_3} = [(10)^2 + (9)^2 + (14)^2 + (7)^2] - \frac{(10 + 9 + 14 + 7)^2}{4}$$

$$= 26.0;$$

and

$$\Sigma \, SS_{AS_{\text{comp.}}} = 0.0 + 1.5 + 24.5 = 26.0.$$

The remaining step in this illustration is to show that the sum of the four within-group sums of squares equals the $SS_{S/A}$. Calculating this latter quantity directly, we have

$$SS_{S/A} = \Sigma \, (AS)^2 - \frac{\Sigma \, (A)^2}{s}$$

$$= [(3)^2 + (5)^2 + \cdots + (14)^2 + (7)^2] - \frac{(20)^2 + (12)^2 + (28)^2 + (40)^2}{4}$$

$$= 58.0.$$

This value is also found when the individual within-group sums of squares are combined:

$$\Sigma \, SS_{S/A_i} = 8.0 + 14.0 + 10.0 + 26.0 = 58.0.$$

Summary

You have seen that it is possible to construct a set of comparisons that contains as many orthogonal comparisons as there are degrees of freedom. Moreover, these comparisons may be selected to reflect sources of variance that are of interest—i.e., one may select comparisons contributing to the between-groups sum of squares (SS_A) and comparisons contributing to the within-groups sum of squares $(SS_{S/A})$. Since the comparisons constituting these two quantities are mutually orthogonal, these two sums of squares are orthogonal as well.

ORTHOGONALITY OF MAIN EFFECTS AND INTERACTION IN THE TWO-FACTOR DESIGN

I will now consider an $A \times B$ design and demonstrate that the three sums of squares normally isolated in the analysis—the SS_A, the SS_B, and the $SS_{A \times B}$—are orthogonal. I will do this by writing a different single-df comparison for each degree of freedom associated with the variability of the $(a)(b)$ treatment means. We will concern our-selves only with the between-groups variability in this example. (I could also show that the two main effects and the interaction are orthogonal to the within-groups sum of squares, $SS_{S/AB}$, by the procedures followed in the last section.)

The design is a 3×2 factorial, and the data come from an experiment that we analyzed in Chapter 10 (see Table 10-8, p. 200). The six treatment means and the coefficients for a set of $(a)(b) - 1 = (3)(2) - 1 = 5$ orthogonal comparisons are presented in Table 3. (In this example, there are $s = 4$ subjects in each treat-ment condition.) The orthogonality of these comparisons can be verified by sum-ming the cross products of corresponding coefficients for all possible pairs of comparisons.

The first two comparisons represent a set of contrasts which, when translated into sums of squares and then added together, will equal the SS_A. It will be noted that for each of these comparisons, the same patterns of coefficients operating on the three levels of factor A are repeated at each of the two levels of factor B. In comparison 1, for example, the basic pattern is $2, -1, -1$, while in comparison 2 the pattern is $0, 1, -1$. Since the patterns are repeated at each level of factor B, we are in essence collapsing across the B classification and obtaining sums of squares reflecting only the variation among the A means.

The next comparison involves the B means. Since there are two levels of fac-tor B in this example, only one comparison is possible, and the sum of squares ob-tained with this comparison must equal the SS_B. In this particular case, you will note that the same pattern of coefficients operating on the two levels of factor B (1 and -1) is repeated at each of the levels of factor A. The repetition of this pat-tern results in a collapsing across the A classification and a comparison involving the B means.

The last two sets of coefficients represent orthogonal components of the $A \times B$ interaction. They are usually formed by multiplying each set of coefficients for factor A by each set of coefficients for factor B, which creates **interaction contrasts**—as they are called—that reflect the interaction of comparisons involving factor A with comparisons involving factor B. In this example, there are two orthogonal interaction contrasts: comparison 4, which is created by multiplying corresponding coefficients of comparisons 1 and 3, and comparison 5, which is created similarly from comparisons 2 and 3.

I will now compute the two main effects and the interaction by means of these orthogonal comparisons. The computational formula for a comparison sum of squares is

$$SS_{AB_\text{comp.}} = \frac{s\,(\hat{\psi}_{AB})^2}{\Sigma\,(c_{ij})^2},\tag{5}$$

where $\hat{\psi}_{AB} = \Sigma\,(c_{ij})(\overline{AB}_{ij})$, the sum of the weighted treatment means, and c_{ij} repre-sents the coefficients associated with the $(a)(b)$ treatment conditions. The sums of the products obtained by multiplying the coefficients and the treatment means,

Table 3   Orthogonal Comparisons and the Two-Factor Design

	a_1b_1	a_1b_2	a_2b_1	a_2b_2	a_3b_1	a_3b_2	$\hat{\psi}_{AB}$	$\Sigma(c_{ij})^2$
MEAN:	3.0	11.0	10.0	12.0	14.0	10.0		
Comp. 1:	2	2	-1	-1	-1	-1	-18.0	12
Comp. 2:	0	0	1	1	-1	-1	-2.0	4
Comp. 3:	1	-1	1	-1	1	-1	-6.0	6
Comp. 4:	2	-2	-1	1	-1	1	-18.0	12
Comp. 5:	0	0	1	-1	-1	1	-6.0	4

and the sums of the squared coefficients appear in Table 3 to the right of the coefficients.

Using Eq. (5) and the information in the last two columns of Table 3, we can calculate the two sums of squares that collectively constitute the SS_A. Specifically,

$$SS_{AB\,\text{comp. 1}} = \frac{4(-18.0)^2}{12} = 108.0 \quad \text{and} \quad SS_{AB\,\text{comp. 2}} = \frac{4(-2.0)^2}{4} = 4.0.$$

From the analysis presented in Table 10-8, $SS_A = 112.0$, which is what we obtain when we sum the SS's found with the first two comparisons:

$$108.0 + 4.0 = 112.0.$$

Turning next to the comparison for SS_B, we find

$$SS_{AB\,\text{comp. 3}} = \frac{4(-6.0)^2}{6} = 24.0,$$

which is equal, of course, to the SS_B obtained from the standard formula.

The sums of squares for the last two comparisons collectively add up to the $SS_{A \times B}$. To show this,

$$SS_{AB\,\text{comp. 4}} = \frac{4(-18.0)^2}{12} = 108.0 \quad \text{and} \quad SS_{AB\,\text{comp. 5}} = \frac{4(-6.0)^2}{4} = 36.0.$$

The sum of these two comparisons,

$$108.0 + 36.0 = 144.0,$$

agrees with the value obtained in Table 10-8, $SS_{A \times B} = 144.0$.

SUMMARY

Similar demonstrations may be conducted for more complicated designs, but the point has been made with the two examples considered in this appendix. When we use orthogonal comparisons in an *actual* analysis, we do not make up just *any* set of comparisons. Instead, we consider comparisons that make *meaningful* contrasts among the treatment conditions. In so doing, we would probably not even want to construct a complete set of orthogonal comparisons. In an interaction, for example, we might only be interested in one or two of the orthogonal components—not the complete set. The purpose of these demonstrations, of course, was not the extraction of meaningful comparisons. Specifically, they were presented to show that the different sources of variance, into which we usually partition the total sums of squares (in the single-factor case) and the between-groups sum of squares (in the two-factor case), do in fact represent independent pieces of information.

Appendix C-3

Calculating Orthogonal Polynomial Coefficients

In Chapter 7, I discussed the analysis of experiments in which the independent variable represents a quantitative dimension (see pp. 128–132). The analysis consisted of a division of the SS_A into orthogonal components of trend. The sums of squares associated with each trend component were calculated by substituting the treatment means $(\overline{A}_i)$ and the orthogonal polynomial coefficients (c_i) in the general formula for a comparison, Eq. (6–5). Each set of coefficients reflects a different type of trend in its pure form—linear, quadratic, cubic, and so on. As long as the levels of the independent variable are equally spaced, we can obtain the orthogonal polynomial coefficients from tables, such as Table A–4 of Appendix A. However, as noted in Chapter 7, often we will *not* want to use equally spaced intervals in an experiment. Nevertheless, trend analyses are still possible with data obtained from such experiments. The only troublesome feature is that the sets of orthogonal polynomial coefficients must be calculated for the *specific spacings* represented in each individual experiment.

The sets of coefficients are calculated in a series of steps. We start with the linear coefficients, using information about the spacing of the levels of the independent variable and the general property of comparisons —namely, that the coefficients sum to zero—to allow the determination of a single unknown in the formulas. The quadratic coefficients are calculated next. The computational effort is more involved, as there are now *two* unknowns for which solutions must be found. The information needed for these determinations comes from the spacing of the levels, the general property of comparisons, and the requirement of orthogonality of comparisons —i.e., that the sum of pairs of corresponding coefficients equal zero.

I will construct sets of coefficients for an example with *equal* spacing so that we can compare the results with the values tabled in Appendix A. An example with unequal spacing can be found in Exercise 1 at the end of this appendix. In any case, the procedures are the same regardless of the nature of the spacing. The general procedure I will follow assumes equal sample sizes for the various treatment groups.[1]

LINEAR COEFFICIENTS

I will begin by constructing a set of linear coefficients. As an example, let's assume that the independent variable is represented by four points on a quantitative dimension with values of 2, 4, 6, and 8. We begin with the following formula representing any one of the linear coefficients:

$$\alpha_1 + X_i, \tag{1}$$

where α_1 is a constant and X_i stands for the numerical values of the *independent variable*. Next, we write this expression out for each of the four levels. This has been done in column 2 of Table 1. (Some authors recommend that the X_i values be reduced to smaller multiples, X_i'. In the present case, X_i' would be 1, 2, 3, and 4. The reason for this suggestion is to reduce the magnitude of the numbers which are encountered in the calculations, especially with the higher-degree coefficients.)

We now have the four coefficients, represented by numbers, and one unknown, α_1. We can solve for the unknown by employing the general requirement of a set of coefficients that they sum to zero. That is, we will add the four coefficients and set the sum equal to zero. This will give us one equation and one unknown—sufficient information to permit us to solve for α_1. More formally, we start with

$$\Sigma c_i = 0. \tag{2}$$

Substituting the four coefficients in Table 1 in this equation, we have

$$(\alpha_1 + 2) + (\alpha_1 + 4) + (\alpha_1 + 6) + (\alpha_1 + 8) = 0,$$
$$4\alpha_1 + 20 = 0.$$

[1] Even with unequal sample sizes, I still recommend conducting an unweighted-means analysis, in which each mean is treated equally and normal coefficients are used in the analysis. This is because our interest generally is in detecting the presence of trend components, and it makes most sense to use an analysis that permits each point on the stimulus dimension—i.e., each level of the independent variable—to contribute *equally* to the determination of this functional relationship. On the other hand, procedures are available for constructing coefficients that do take into consideration unequal sample sizes (e.g., Gaito, 1965; Kirk, 1968, pp. 513–517; and Myers, 1979, pp. 441–445).

Table 1   Calculating Linear Coefficients

(1) X_i	(2) $\alpha_1 + X_i$	(3) SUBSTITUTION	(4) c_{1i}
2	$\alpha_1 + 2$	$-5 + 2 =$	-3
4	$\alpha_1 + 4$	$-5 + 4 =$	-1
6	$\alpha_1 + 6$	$-5 + 6 =$	1
8	$\alpha_1 + 8$	$-5 + 8 =$	3

Solving for α_1, we get

$$4\alpha_1 = -20,$$

$$\alpha_1 = -\frac{20}{4} = -5.$$

If we now substitute $\alpha_1 = -5$ in the formulas representing the four coefficients, we will obtain numerical values for the linear coefficients (c_{1i}). These substitutions are shown in column 3, and the final coefficients are given in column 4. As a check, we should verify that the coefficients sum to zero and that the coefficients form a straight line when plotted against the independent variable.

QUADRATIC COEFFICIENTS

In order to calculate the quadratic coefficients, we begin with a formula representing one of these coefficients:

$$\alpha_2 + (\beta_2)(X_i) + (X_i)^2, \tag{3}$$

where α_2 and β_2 are constants and X_i refers to the values of the independent variable. These formulas are written for each coefficient in column 2 of Table 2. Again we can apply Eq. (2) and set the sum of the four coefficients to zero. That is,

$$(\alpha_2 + 2\beta_2 + 4) + (\alpha_2 + 4\beta_2 + 16) + (\alpha_2 + 6\beta_2 + 36) + (\alpha_2 + 8\beta_2 + 64) = 0,$$

$$4\alpha_2 + 20\beta_2 + 120 = 0. \tag{4}$$

This time, however, we have *one* equation and *two* unknowns, α_2 and β_2, which do not amount to sufficient information to allow us to solve for the unknowns. We need another equation involving these constants. This equation comes from the additional requirement of these coefficients that the set be *orthogonal* to the set of linear coefficients we have constructed already. This property is stated as

$$\Sigma\,(c_{1i})(c_{2i}) = 0. \tag{5}$$

Table 2 Calculating Quadratic Coefficients

(1) X_i	(2) $\alpha_2 + (\beta_2)(X_i) + (X_i)^2$	(3) c_{1i}	(4) $(c_{1i})(c_{2i})$	(5) SUBSTITUTION	(6) c_{2i}
2	$\alpha_2 + 2\beta_2 + 4$	-3	$-3\alpha_2 - 6\beta_2 - 12$	$20 - 20 + 4 =$	4
4	$\alpha_2 + 4\beta_2 + 16$	-1	$-1\alpha_2 - 4\beta_2 - 16$	$20 - 40 + 16 =$	-4
6	$\alpha_2 + 6\beta_2 + 36$	1	$1\alpha_2 + 6\beta_2 + 36$	$20 - 60 + 36 =$	-4
8	$\alpha_2 + 8\beta_2 + 64$	3	$3\alpha_2 + 24\beta_2 + 192$	$20 - 80 + 64 =$	4

You will now see how this requirement can be used to help in the determination of the two unknowns.

We apply Eq. (5), using the linear coefficients from Table 1 (c_{1i}) and the formulas for the quadratic coefficients from Table 2 (c_{2i}). The linear coefficients are entered in column 3 of Table 2, and the products of corresponding coefficients $-(c_{1i})(c_{2i})$ or (column 2) $\times$ (column 3)—are given in column 4. From Eq. (5),

$$\Sigma\,(c_{1i})(c_{2i}) = 0.$$

Performing this summation on the products in column 4 of the table, we have

$$(-3\alpha_2 - 6\beta_2 - 12) + (-1\alpha_2 - 4\beta_2 - 16)$$
$$+ (1\alpha_2 + 6\beta_2 + 36) + (3\alpha_2 + 24\beta_2 + 192) = 0,$$
$$0\alpha_2 + 20\beta_2 + 200 = 0.$$

We can now solve for β_2:

$$20\beta_2 = -200,$$
$$\beta_2 = -\frac{200}{20} = -10.$$

The other unknown, α_2, is obtained by substituting in Eq. (4) and solving for α_2:

$$4\alpha_2 + 20\beta_2 + 120 = 0,$$
$$4\alpha_2 + 20(-10) + 120 = 0,$$
$$4\alpha_2 - 200 + 120 = 0,$$
$$4\alpha_2 = 200 - 120 = 80,$$
$$\alpha_2 = \frac{80}{4} = 20.$$

The final steps involve substituting the values of the two unknowns into the original formulas (column 2) and completing the arithmetic. These two operations are enumerated in columns 5 and 6, respectively, of Table 2. It will be noted

632

that these coefficients are all multiples of 4. We can divide each coefficient by 4 and not change the nature of the comparison represented by the coefficients (see p. 112 for a justification of this procedure). The coefficients become

$$1, \quad -1, \quad -1, \quad \text{and} \quad 1.$$

We can compare the linear and quadratic coefficients we have just constructed with those listed in Table A-4 of Appendix A. They are identical.

COMPUTING HIGHER-DEGREE COEFFICIENTS

The calculation of the higher-degree orthogonal polynomial coefficients is accomplished in the same manner as the quadratic coefficients in our two examples:

1. Apply the general formula for the coefficients to each value of X_i. The formula for the cubic coefficients is

$$\alpha_3 + (\beta_3)(X_i) + (\gamma_3)(X_i)^2 + (X_i)^3,$$

and for the quartic coefficient is

$$\alpha_4 + (\beta_4)(X_i) + (\gamma_4)(X_i)^2 + (\delta_4)(X_i)^3 + (X_i)^4.$$

2. Set the sum of these formulas equal to zero [Eq. (2)]. This step gives us one equation and several unknowns.
3. Additional equations involving these unknowns are obtained by ensuring that the requirement of orthogonality holds [Eq. (5)] for each of the sets of coefficients constructed for the lower-degree components. For the cubic coefficients there are two equations (linear $\times$ cubic and quadratic $\times$ cubic), and for the quartic coefficients there are three (linear $\times$ quartic, quadratic $\times$ quartic, and cubic $\times$ quartic).
4. Solve for the different unknowns by using the sets of equations obtained in steps 2 and 3. There will be sufficient information to allow the solution of the unknowns; e.g., for the cubic coefficients there will be three equations and three unknowns, and for the quartic coefficients there will be four equations and four unknowns.
5. Substitute the constants into the original formulas for the coefficients (step 1) to obtain the desired coefficients.

EXERCISES[2]

1. An experiment is conducted in which the effect on the recall of a list of words is studied as a function of the number of trials subjects receive on a second list of unrelated words. There are three basic groups of subjects, one group receiving one trial on the second list, another receiving five trials on the second list, and a third receiving 20 trials. There are $s = 20$ subjects in each treatment condition.

---

[2]The answers to this problem are found in Appendix B, p. 609.

The following set of data was obtained:

NUMBER OF TRIALS:	1 TRIAL	5 TRIALS	20 TRIALS
Treatment sums (A_i):	241	170	130

In addition, $\Sigma (AS)^2 = 5{,}545$.

(a) Conduct a one-way analysis of variance on these data.

(b) Conduct a trend analysis, constructing your own orthogonal polynomial coefficients. Check your result by showing that $SS_{\text{linear}} + SS_{\text{quadratic}} = SS_A$.

Appendix C-4

Analyzing Complex Designs

This appendix brings together in one place a set of rules outlining the analysis of variance for a wide variety of experimental designs and structural models. Some of these rules were presented earlier in the context of certain types of designs, but they were restricted to a particular structural model, the **fixed-effect model**. Chapter 21 introduced the **random-effect model** and the complications that arise in the statistical analysis when random factors are included in a standard experimental design. Central to this discussion was the need to examine the expected values of the sources of variance in order to determine how an F ratio or a quasi F ratio is formed. A major purpose of this appendix is to offer rules for generating expected mean squares. I will begin with the rules for identifying sources of variation.

IDENTIFYING SOURCES OF VARIATION

The key to the system considered in this appendix is the identification and proper labeling of the sources of variation relevant to any given design. I will use capital letters to represent the factors present in an experiment, which, alone or in combination with other letters, are used to represent the different sources. From such a list, you can write the df statements and generate the computational formulas for the sums of squares as well as the linear model expressing population effects influencing an individual score. I will offer a system presented by Lindman (1974, pp. 176–178) that produces this information in a simple and reliable manner.

    The system begins by listing all of the factors in an experiment, including factor S, and pretending that they all cross. Since nested factors are disregarded at this point, each factor will be represented by a single capital letter. Next, all possible main effects and interactions are formed from these factors. As an example, suppose our experiment is a two-factor design in which factor A is represented by independent groups of subjects and factor B by repeated measures taken on the same subjects. The design contains three factors, A, B, and S/A, which become A, B, and S under the temporary assumption that all three factors cross. From these factors, we obtain the following sources of variation:

$$A, \ B, \ S, \ A \times B, \ A \times S, \ B \times S, \ \text{and} \ A \times B \times S.$$

The next step is to substitute nested notation whenever a nested factor appears in the list. In this example, factor S is nested and the notation S/A is substituted for S wherever it appears. Thus, we now have

$$A, \ B, \ S/A, \ A \times B, \ A \times S/A, \ B \times S/A, \ \text{and} \ A \times B \times S/A.$$

Finally, we delete from the list impossible interactions involving nested factors—identified when the same letter (or letters) appears (or appear) on both sides of the diagonal. Applying this rule to the present design, we delete two sources from the list, namely, $A \times S/A$ and $A \times B \times S/A$, since A appears on both sides of the diagonal. Both sources are impossible interactions, of course, because factor S cannot simultaneously be nested in factor A and cross the factor A, a condition these "interactions" describe. The final list, then, becomes

$$A, \ B, \ S/A, \ A \times B, \ \text{and} \ B \times S/A,$$

which are the correct sources of variation for this particular design.

Any interaction with a nested factor maintains the original orientation of the different letters with respect to the diagonal in the designation of the interaction. Thus, the interaction of factor B and factor S in the example became $B \times S/A$, indicating that the $B \times S$ *interaction* is nested in factor A. If more than one factor is nested—I will consider an example of this case in a moment—it is possible for nested factors to interact with each other as well as with nonnested factors. This can be stated as a rule:

> **Letters appearing to the left of the diagonal in the original listing of each nested factor stay on the left of the diagonal for the interaction.**
> **Letters appearing to the right of the diagonal in the original listing of each nested factor stay on the right of the diagonal for the interaction.**

In certain nested designs, letters will be repeated on the *right* side of the interaction diagonal, in which case the letter (or letters) is (are) listed only once.

As an example, suppose we were interested in determining whether nouns are more difficult to perceive than verbs under difficult perceptual conditions and that one group of subjects is given 20 nouns to recognize and another group of subjects is given 20 verbs to recognize. There are three factors in this experiment: factor A (types of words—nouns or verbs), factor B (the set of 20 nouns and the set of 20 verbs), and factor S (the s subjects assigned randomly to either the noun or the verb condition). Two of these factors, factor B and factor S, are nested. More specifically, word sets (factor B) are uniquely defined at the two levels of factor A, one set of words being used for the noun condition and an entirely different set of words being used for the verb condition. Thus, factor B is nested within factor A, which is symbolized as B/A. Factor S is also nested in factor A, since different groups of subjects receive the two treatment conditions. This nesting is symbolized as S/A.

Let's now go through the rules to identify the sources of variation. First, we list the sources, pretending that the three factors are completely crossed:

$$A, B, S, A \times B, A \times S, B \times S, \text{ and } A \times B \times S.$$

Next, we substitute the two nested factors, B/A and S/A, to obtain

$$A, B/A, S/A, A \times B/A, A \times S/A, B \times S/A, \text{ and } A \times B \times S/A.$$

You should note carefully how the last two quantities are formed even though one of them will be deleted in the next step. From the $B \times S$ interaction, for example, we obtain an interaction between the two nested factors, that is, $B/A \times S/A$. Following the rule presented above, $B \times S$ is placed to the left of the diagonal for the interaction (first part of the rule), A is placed to the right (second part of the rule), and the repeated A is deleted. From the $A \times B \times S$ interaction, we have $A \times B/A \times S/A$ when we substitute the nested factors. $A \times B \times S$ is placed on the left of the diagonal for the "interaction" and A is placed on the right. The repeated A is deleted.

The final step in identifying the sources of variation is to delete impossible interactions involving nested factors. These are identified by the appearance of the same letter on both sides of the diagonal. Examining the potential sources enumerated in the last paragraph, we can eliminate three interactions from the list, namely, $A \times B/A$, $A \times S/A$, and $A \times B \times S/A$. The final list now includes:

A: the main effect of word type (noun versus verb)

B/A: the pooled effect of word sets (the variation among the 20 nouns plus the variation among the 20 verbs)

S/A: the pooled effect of subjects (the variation among the subjects receiving nouns plus the variation among the subjects receiving verbs)

$B \times S/A$: the pooled interaction of word sets and subjects (the interaction of the 20 nouns and subjects plus the interaction of the 20 verbs and subjects)

SPECIFYING DEGREES OF FREEDOM

Once the sources of variance are listed, it is a simple matter to write the corresponding df statements. If the source contains no nested factors, the following rule applies:

Multiply the df's associated with the different factors listed in the source.

If the source contains nested factors, the rule distinguishes between letters appearing to the *left* of the diagonal (nested factors) and letters appearing to the *right* of the diagonal. The rule states:

> **Multiply (1) the product of the *df*'s of factors listed to the *left* of the diagonal by (2) the product of the *levels* of the factors listed to the *right* of the diagonal.**

As an example, consider the three nested factors listed at the end of the last section. Applying the rule, we find

$$df_{B/A} = (df_B)(a) = (b - 1)(a);$$
$$df_{S/A} = (df_S)(a) = (s - 1)(a);$$

and

$$df_{B \times S/A} = (df_B)(df_S)(a) = (b - 1)(s - 1)(a).$$

COMPUTING SUMS OF SQUARES

Throughout this book, I have demonstrated how computation formulas for sums of squares can be constructed from *df* statements. That is, sufficient information is given in the expanded *df* statement to construct the basic ratios entering into the calculations and to specify the pattern in which these ratios are combined to produce the complete computational formula. These steps were explained in detail in Chapter 10 (pp. 191–193). As illustrated in Chapter 19 (p. 457), the expanded *df* statements also indicate the different summary matrices needed to obtain the different quantities specified by the formulas.

WRITING EXPECTED MEAN SQUARES AND SELECTING ERROR TERMS

The expected value of a mean square consists of the sum of a set of terms. These terms reflect potential sources of variation in the population. In the completely randomized single-factor design, for example, there are two sources, namely, treatment effects (α_i) and experimental error (ϵ_{ij}), which are specified by the linear model

$$AS_{ij} = \mu + \alpha_i + \epsilon_{ij}$$

adopted for the analysis. For the within-groups mean square, the expected value is

$$E(MS_{S/A}) = \sigma_\epsilon^2;$$

and for the treatment mean square, the expected value is

$$E(MS_A) = \sigma_\epsilon^2 + s(\theta_A^2)$$

if factor A represents a fixed effect and

$$E(MS_A) = \sigma_\epsilon^2 + s(\sigma_A^2)$$

if factor A represents a random effect.

Various schemes have been devised to generate expected values in complex experimental designs. These systems start with a listing of the sources of variation assumed by the linear model, translate these sources into corresponding θ^2's and σ^2's depending on the nature of the effect represented, add coefficients when appropriate, and provide rules by which these terms are assigned to each mean square to form its expected value. You should understand at the outset that none of these systems, including the one I will present, provides an important insight into the inner workings of statistical theory or even into the mathematical derivation of expected values. What these systems do offer is a reliable device for writing expected values for most of the designs you will encounter in the behavioral sciences. This is particularly valuable when the expected values for a design you are considering cannot be found in the statistical reference books you have available and you need this information to work out the pattern of statistical tests appropriate for your design.

Forming Component Terms

Expected values of mean squares consist of a sum of terms each of which involves a squared quantity, σ^2 or θ^2, identifying subscripts, and coefficients. To be more specific, each component term is differentiated by the following set of features:

1. **Basic symbol:** The symbol σ^2 is used to designate a random effect and θ^2 to designate a fixed effect. Interactions are considered fixed effects only if *all* of the interacting factors are fixed; otherwise, interactions are considered random.
2. **Subscripts:** The same capital letters designating the sources of variance are used to distinguish among the different terms, for example, θ_A^2 or $\sigma_{B/A}^2$.
3. **Coefficients:** Each component variance is multiplied by a set of coefficients that are represented by the letters (in lower case) that were not used as subscripts. These letters are the levels of the factors not involved in defining the component term. The product of these letters consists of the number of observations contributing to each deviation upon which either σ^2 or θ^2 is based.

As an illustration, consider the noun-verb example from an earlier section. For this design, the total number of observations is $(a)(b)(s)$, which also specifies the letters needed to identify all sources of variation. If we apply the rules of the last paragraph to each component term, we find the following:

$A = b(s)(\theta_A^2)$; the manipulation is fixed and the "unused" letters are b and s;

$B/A = s(\sigma_{B/A}^2)$; the manipulation is random—nouns and verbs were chosen randomly from a large pool of words—and the unused letter is s;

$S/A = b(\sigma_{S/A}^2)$; factor S (subjects) is always considered random and the unused letter is b;

and

$B \times S/A = \sigma_{B \times S/A}^2$; the interaction component is random and there are no unused letters.

You should study this example to make sure that you understand how the different rules operate.

Rules for Generating Expected Mean Squares

I will now consider a set of rules that specify how the terms identified in the last section are combined to produce the expected mean square for each source of variance. These rules can be stated as follows:

1. List each source of variance.
2. List σ_ϵ^2 for each source.
3. List the term identifying each source which is also known as the null-hypothesis component. (Disregard this step for the within-groups source in completely randomized designs; that is, the expected value of the MS_{wg} is σ_ϵ^2—no other terms are present.)
4. List additional terms whenever they satisfy the following *two* requirements: (a) that the subscripts of the term include *all* the letters defining the source, which includes letters on both side of the diagonal if the source is nested; *and* (b) that any additional letters to the *left* of the diagonal represent *only random effects*. (For nonnested terms, all letters are assumed to be to the left of the diagonal.)

An optional final step is to rearrange the terms for each source so that σ_ϵ^2 appears on the far left and the null-hypothesis component appears on the far right and additional terms are arranged from left to right from higher-order to lower-order effects. This type of arrangement facilitates the location of appropriate error terms and the formation of quasi F ratios when standard error terms are not possible.

The expected mean squares for the noun-verb experiment we have been considering are presented in Table 1. Let's see how the rules presented in the last paragraph are applied to this example. First, you should verify that the first three rules have been applied properly, i.e., that each source is listed together with σ_ϵ^2 and the appropriate null-hypothesis component. Next, you should work systematically from source to source determining which additional terms—if any— should be included. Consider first the effect of word type (A). Working systematically through the sources and applying rule 4, we find that we can add the B/A term,

Table 1 Expected Mean Squares for the Noun-Verb Example

SOURCE	EXPECTED MEAN SQUARE
A	$\sigma_\epsilon^2 + \sigma_{B \times S/A}^2 + s(\sigma_{B/A}^2) + b(\sigma_{S/A}^2) + b(s)(\theta_A^2)$
B/A	$\sigma_\epsilon^2 + \sigma_{B \times S/A}^2 + s(\sigma_{B/A}^2)$
S/A	$\sigma_\epsilon^2 + \sigma_{B \times S/A}^2 + b(\sigma_{S/A}^2)$
$B \times S/A$	$\sigma_\epsilon^2 + \sigma_{B \times S/A}^2$

since A is included in the term and the single letter to the left of the diagonal, B, represents a random effect. Similarly, we can add the S/A term, since A is included and the single letter to the left of the diagonal, S, represents a random effect. Finally, we can also add the last term, $B \times S/A$, because A is included in the term and the two letters to the left of the diagonal, B and S, both represent random effects. For the next two sources, B/A and S/A, only the $B \times S/A$ term is added, since it is the only term that includes the letters in the source and includes letters representing random effects to the left of the diagonal. The final source of variation, $B \times S/A$, includes no additional terms in its expected mean square.

Selecting Error Terms

The construction of an F ratio requires finding a numerator that contains the null-hypothesis component and a denominator that matches exactly the other components included with the null-hypothesis component. In symbols, our goal is to create a ratio of the form

$$\frac{\text{null-hypothesis component} + \text{error}}{\text{error}},$$

where *null-hypothesis component* refers to the treatment effect of interest and *error* refers to unsystematic sources of variability. As you saw in Chapter 21, this procedure is a simple operation once the expected values of the sources of variance have been specified. Suppose we wanted to test the significance of the nested factor in the noun-verb experiment. An examination of Table 1 reveals that $MS_{B \times S/A}$ satisfies the criteria for the error term, since the expected value of this mean square,

$$E(MS_{B \times S/A}) = \sigma_\epsilon^2 + \sigma_{B \times S/A}^2,$$

exactly matches the expected value for $MS_{B/A}$,

$$E(MS_{B/A}) = \sigma_\epsilon^2 + \sigma_{B \times S/A}^2 + s(\sigma_{B/A}^2),$$

leaving only the null-hypothesis component, $s(\sigma_{B/A}^2)$, in the numerator. Thus,

$$F = \frac{MS_{B/A}}{MS_{B \times S/A}}$$

provides an appropriate test for significant variation among the words tested in the two sets.

It should also be evident that the main effect of factor A —nouns versus verbs —has no error term, since none of the other sources of variation listed in Table 1 matches all of the terms in the expected value of A except for the null-hypothesis component. As indicated in Chapter 21 (pp. 530-533), a quasi F test is possible, however, where two or more mean squares are combined to provide an acceptable matching of numerator and denominator expected values. One such ratio is

$$\frac{MS_A}{MS_{B/A} + MS_{S/A} - MS_{B \times S/A}}.$$

More specifically, the expected value of the combination of mean squares in the denominator,

$$\begin{aligned} E(MS_{\text{denom.}}) &= E(MS_{B/A}) + E(MS_{S/A}) - E(MS_{B \times S/A}) \\ &= [\sigma_\epsilon^2 + \sigma_{B \times S/A}^2 + s(\sigma_{B/A}^2)] \\ &\quad + [\sigma_\epsilon^2 + \sigma_{B \times S/A}^2 + b(\sigma_{S/A}^2)] \\ &\quad - [\sigma_\epsilon^2 + \sigma_{B \times S/A}^2] \\ &= \sigma_\epsilon^2 + \sigma_{B \times S/A}^2 + s(\sigma_{B/A}^2) + b(\sigma_{S/A}^2), \end{aligned}$$

provides an appropriate match for the expected value of the numerator as indicated in Table 1.

The only complication at this point is the need to adjust degrees of freedom for entry in the F table when either the numerator or denominator term consists of combinations of mean squares. As discussed in Chapter 21 (pp. 532-533), the adjusted df are given by the following formula:

$$df_{\text{adj.}} = \frac{(\text{combination of } MS_U, MS_V, MS_W, \cdots)^2}{\dfrac{(MS_U)^2}{df_U} + \dfrac{(MS_V)^2}{df_V} + \dfrac{(MS_W)^2}{df_W} + \cdots},$$

where MS_U, MS_V, MS_W, etc., represent the mean square involved in the combination. In the present example, the denominator df are found by substituting:

$$df_{\text{adj.}} = \frac{(MS_{B/A} + MS_{S/A} - MS_{B \times S/A})^2}{\dfrac{(MS_{B/A})^2}{df_{B/A}} + \dfrac{(MS_{S/A})^2}{df_{S/A}} + \dfrac{(MS_{B \times S/A})^2}{df_{B \times S/A}}}.$$

EXERCISES[1]

1. A college senior plans to conduct an honors project using students in a large residence hall on campus. The student is interested in studying the effects of different background music on reading comprehension, e.g., no music, jazz, and classical music. For convenience, subjects are assigned to conditions by *rooms,* with roommates tested at the same time and under the same background condition. Let's call the background conditions factor B and the rooms factor A. We will assume that an equal number of rooms (a) are assigned randomly to each of the b treatment conditions. As described, factor A is random and nested in factor B. Assume further that there are s roommates in each room. (Factor S is always considered a random factor.)
   (a) Identify the sources of variance for this design.
   (b) Derive the expected values for each of these sources.
   (c) Indicate the error term for each source of variance.
2. Continuing with the example in Exercise 1, let's assume that the experimenter decides to compare students on the different floors of the dormitory. Let's call this new variable factor C. Again, the s subjects in each room are assigned randomly to the b treatment conditions. This time, however, the assignment is accomplished floor by floor so that an equal number of a rooms are assigned from each of the c floors to the treatment conditions.
   (a) Identify the sources of variance for this design.
   (b) Derive the expected values for each of these sources.
   (c) Indicate the error term for each source of variance.
3. Imagine that a team of educators in California is planning to evaluate the relative effectiveness of three science books for sixth-grade children developed by competing publishers. Because they want to generalize their findings to all school systems in California but cannot include them all in the study, they decide to sample randomly from the systems in the state. Furthermore, in order to reduce again the number of students tested, they plan to sample randomly sixth-grade classes from each of the systems selected. We will refer to the books as factor A, to school systems as factor B, and to the classes themselves as factor C. (We will assume that each class contains s students.) For each of the possibilities listed below, (1) indicate the sources of variance that may be obtained from the design, (2) derive the expected values for each of these sources, and (3) indicate the error term for each source of variance.
   (a) The team plans to assign randomly an equal number of classes (c) from *each* of the school systems to use each of the three books.
   (b) The team plans to assign randomly an equal number of school systems to use each of the three books, and to have *all* the classes randomly chosen within any particular system receive *only* one of the books.
4. A researcher is interested in comparing two different concept-formation tasks, one involving a disjunctive concept and the other involving a conjunctive concept, under three conditions of informative feedback—immediate knowledge of results, knowledge that is delayed by 10 seconds, and knowledge that is delayed by 30 seconds. The design, so far, is a 2 × 3 factorial. In order to increase the external validity of the experiment, the researcher includes *problems* as a third factor. The design is made explicit in the accompanying table. There are three

[1] The answers to these problems are found in Appendix B, beginning on p. 609.

feedback conditions (factor B) under the two types of conceptual tasks (factor A). In addition, there are five different examples of each of the two types of tasks (factor C). The sums presented in the ABC matrix represent the numbers of trials required to reach a criterion of performance and are based on the scores of $s = 2$ subjects in each individual cell of the matrix. For this example, $\Sigma (ABCS)^2 = 2,509$. Perform an analysis of variance on these data. (Assume that factor C is random.)

ABC MATRIX

	Disjunctive Concept (a_1)				Conjunctive Concept (a_2)		
	Feedback Intervals (B)				*Feedback Intervals (B)*		
Problems (C)	0 sec. (b_1)	10 sec. (b_2)	30 sec. (b_3)	*Problems* (C)	0 sec. (b_1)	10 sec. (b_2)	30 sec. (b_3)
c_1	2	6	14	c_6	2	4	4
c_2	5	7	9	c_7	14	17	18
c_3	2	6	12	c_8	3	4	6
c_4	8	12	24	c_9	2	4	5
c_5	14	20	30	c_{10}	16	19	17

References

Anderson, T. W. *Introduction to multivariate statistical analysis.* New York: Wiley, 1958.

Appelbaum, M. I., & Cramer, E. M. Some problems in the nonorthogonal analysis of variance. *Psychological Bulletin,* 1974, *81,* 335–343.

Birch, H. G., & Lefford, A. Visual differentiation, intersensory integration, and voluntary motor control. *Monographs of the Society for Research in Child Development,* 1967, *32* (2, Serial No. 110).

Boik, R. J. Interactions, partial interactions, and interaction contrasts in the analysis of variance. *Psychological Bulletin,* 1979, *86,* 1,084–1,089.

Box, G. E. P. Non-normality and tests on variances. *Biometrika,* 1953, *40,* 318–335.

Box, G. E. P. Some theorems on quadratic forms applied in the study of analysis of variance problems, II. Effects of inequality of variance and of correlation between errors in the two-way classification. *Annals of Mathematical Statistics,* 1954, *25,* 484–498.

Bradley, J. V. *Distribution-free statistical tests.* Englewood Cliffs, N.J.: Prentice-Hall, 1968.

Bradley, J. V. Nonparametric statistics. In R. E. Kirk (Ed.), *Statistical issues.* Monterey, Calif.: Brooks/Cole, 1972, 329–338.

Brewer, J. K. On the power of statistical tests in the *American Educational Research Journal. American Educational Research Journal,* 1972, *9,* 391–401.

Brewer, J. K. Issues of power: Clarification. *American Educational Research Journal,* 1974, *11,* 189–192.

Brown, J. Some effects of selective reporting of experimental results. Paper delivered at the meetings of the Experimental Psychology Society, Oxford, England, July, 1979.

Bruning, J. L., & Kintz, B. L. *Computational handbook of statistics* (2nd ed.). Glenview, Ill.: Scott, Foresman, 1977.

Campbell, D. T., & Stanley, J. C. Experimental and quasi-experimental designs for research on teaching. In N. L. Gage (Ed.), *Handbook of research on teaching.* Skokie, Ill.: Rand McNally, 1963, 171–246.

Campbell, D. T., & Stanley, J. C. *Experimental and quasi-experimental designs for research.* Skokie, Ill.: Rand McNally, 1966.

Carlson, J. E., & Timm, N. H. Analysis of nonorthogonal fixed-effects designs. *Psychological Bulletin,* 1974, *81,* 563–570.

Carmer, S. G., & Swanson, M. R. An evaluation of ten pairwise multiple comparison procedures by Monte Carlo methods. *Journal of the American Statistical Association,* 1973, *68,* 66–74.

Carlson, J. E., & Timm, N. H. Analysis of nonorthogonal fixed-effects designs. *Psychological Bulletin,* 1974, *81,* 563–570.

Carroll, R. M., & Nordholm, L. A. Sampling characteristics of Kelley's ϵ^2 and Hays' $\hat{\omega}^2$. *Educational and Psychological Measurement,* 1975, *35,* 541–554.

Church, J. D., & Wike, E. L. The robustness of homogeneity of variance tests for asymmetric distributions: A Monte Carlo study. *Bulletin of the Psychonomic Society,* 1976, *7,* 417–420.

Cicchetti, D. V. Extension of multiple-range tests to interaction tables in the analysis of variance: A rapid approximate solution. *Psychological Bulletin,* 1972, *77,* 405–408.

Clark, H. H. The language-as-fixed-effect fallacy: A critique of language statistics in psychological research. *Journal of Verbal Learning and Verbal Behavior,* 1973, *12,* 335–359.

Clark, H. H. Reply to Wike and Church. *Journal of Verbal Learning and Verbal Behavior,* 1976, *15,* 257–261.

Cohen, J. The statistical power of abnormal-social psychological research: A review. *Journal of Abnormal and Social Psychology,* 1962, *65,* 145–153.

Cohen, J. Multiple regression as a general data-analytic system. *Psychological Bulletin,* 1968, *70,* 426–443.

Cohen, J. Statistical power analysis and research results. *American Educational Research Journal,* 1973, *10,* 225–229.

Cohen, J. Random means random. *Journal of Verbal Learning and Verbal Behavior,* 1976, *15,* 261–262.

Cohen, J. *Statistical power analysis for the behavioral sciences* (Rev. ed.). New York: Academic Press, 1977.

Cohen, J., & Cohen, P. *Applied multiple regression/correlation analysis for the behavioral sciences.* Hillsdale, N. J.: Lawrence Erlbaum Associates, 1975.

Coleman, E. B. Generalizing to a language population. *Psychological Reports,* 1964, *14,* 219–226.

Collier, R. O., Jr., Baker, F. B., Mandeville, G. K., & Hayes, T. F. Estimates of test size for several test procedures based on conventional variance ratios in the repeated measures design. *Psychometrika,* 1967, *32,* 339–353.

Cook, T. D., & Campbell, D. T. *Quasi-experimentation: Design and analysis issues for field settings.* Chicago: Rand McNally, 1979.

Cooper, H. M., & Rosenthal, R. Statistical versus traditional procedures for summarizing research findings. *Psychological Bulletin,* 1980, *87,* 442–449.

Cornfield, J., & Tukey, J. W. Average values of mean squares in factorials. *Annals of Mathematical Statistics,* 1956, *27,* 907–949.

Dawes, R. M. "Interaction effects" in the presence of asymmetrical transfer. *Psychological Bulletin,* 1969, *71,* 55–57.

Dayton, C. M., Schafer, W. D., & Rogers, B. C. On appropriate uses and interpretations of power analysis: A comment. *American Educational Research Journal,* 1973, *10,* 231–234.

Dixon, W. J., & Massey, F. J., Jr. *Introduction to statistical analysis* (2nd ed.). New York: McGraw-Hill, 1957.

Dodd, D. H., & Schultz, R. F., Jr. Computational procedures for estimating magnitude of effect for some analysis of variance designs. *Psychological Bulletin,* 1973, *79,* 391–395.

Dooling, D. J., & Danks, J. H. Going beyond tests of significance: Is psychology ready? *Bulletin of the Psychonomic Society,* 1975, *5,* 15–17.

Dunnett, C. W. A multiple comparison procedure for comparing several treatments with a control. *Journal of the American Statistical Association,* 1955, *50,* 1,096–1,121.

Dunnett, C. W. New tables for multiple comparisons with a control. *Biometrics,* 1964, *20,* 482–491.

Dwyer, J. H. Analysis of variance and the magnitude of effects: A general approach. *Psychological Bulletin,* 1974, *81,* 731–737.

Edgington, E. S. Statistical inference and nonrandom samples. *Psychological Bulletin,* 1966, *66,* 485–487.

Edgington, E. S. *Statistical inference: The distribution-free approach.* New York: McGraw-Hill, 1969.

Edwards, A. L. *Multiple regression and the analysis of variance and covariance.* San Francisco: W. H. Freeman, 1979.

Einot, I., & Gabriel, K. R. A study of the powers of several methods of multiple comparisons. *Journal of the American Statistical Association,* 1975, *70,* 574–583.

Elashoff, J. D. Analysis of covariance: A delicate instrument. *American Educational Research Journal,* 1969, *6,* 383–401.

Erlebacher, A. Design and analysis of experiments contrasting the within- and between-subjects manipulation of the independent variable. *Psychological Bulletin,* 1977, *84,* 212–219.

Evans, S. H., & Anastasio, E. J. Misuse of analysis of covariance when treatment effect and covariate are confounded. *Psychological Bulletin,* 1968, *69,* 225–234.

Feldt, L. S. A comparison of the precision of three experimental designs employing a concomitant variable. *Psychometrika,* 1958, *23,* 335–353.

Fisher, R. A. *The design of experiments* (6th ed.). Edinburgh: Oliver and Boyd, 1951.

Fisher, R. A., & Yates, F. *Statistical tables for biological, agricultural and medical research* (4th ed.). Edinburgh: Oliver and Boyd, 1953.

Forster, K. I., & Dickinson, R. G. More on the language-as-fixed-effect fallacy: Monte Carlo estimates of error rates for F_1, F_2, F', and $min\ F'$. *Journal of Verbal Learning and Verbal Behavior,* 1976, *15,* 135–142.

Friedman, H. Magnitude of experimental effect and a table for its rapid estimation. *Psychological Bulletin,* 1968, *70,* 245–251.

Gaito, J. Unequal intervals and unequal *n* in trend analyses. *Psychological Bulletin,* 1965, *63,* 125–127.

Games, P. A. Errata for "Multiple comparisons on means," *AERJ,* 1971, 531–565. *American Educational Research Journal,* 1971, *8,* 677–678. (a)

Games, P. A. Multiple comparisons of means. *American Educational Research Journal,* 1971, *8,* 531–565. (b)

Games, P. A. A four-factor structure for parametric tests on independent groups. *Psychological Bulletin,* 1978, *85,* 661–672. (a)

Games, P. A. A three-factor model encompassing many possible statistical tests on independent groups. *Psychological Bulletin,* 1978, *85,* 168–182. (b)

Games, P. A., & Howell, J. F. Pairwise multiple comparison procedures with unequal N's and/or variances: A Monte Carlo study. *Journal of Educational Statistics*, 1976, *1*, 113–125.

Games, P. A., Keselman, H. J., & Clinch, J. J. Tests for homogeneity of variance in factorial designs. *Psychological Bulletin*, 1979, *86*, 978–984.

Games, P. A., Winkler, H. B., & Probert, D. A. Robust tests for homogeneity of variance. *Educational and Psychological Measurement*, 1972, *32*, 887–909.

Geisser, S., & Greenhouse, S. W. An extension of Box's results on the use of the *F* distribution in multivariate analysis. *Annals of Mathematical Statistics*, 1958, *29*, 885–891.

Glass, G. V, & Hakstian, A. R. Measures of association in comparative experiments: Their development and interpretation. *American Educational Research Journal*, 1969, *6*, 403–414.

Glass, G. V, Peckham, P. D., & Sanders, J. R. Consequences of failure to meet assumptions underlying the fixed effects analyses of variance and covariance. *Review of Educational Research*, 1972, *42*, 237–288.

Glass, G. V, & Stanley, J. C. *Statistical methods in education and psychology.* Englewood Cliffs, N.J.: Prentice-Hall, 1970.

Gollin, E. S. A developmental approach to learning and cognition. In L. P. Lipsitt & C. C. Spiker (Eds.), *Advances in child development and behavior* (Vol. II). New York: Academic Press, 1965, 159–186.

Grant, D. A. Analysis-of-variance tests in the analysis and comparison of curves. *Psychological Bulletin*, 1956, *53*, 141–154.

Greenhouse, S. W., & Geisser, S. On methods in the analysis of profile data. *Psychometrika*, 1959, *24*, 95–112.

Greenwald, A. G. Within-subjects designs: To use or not to use? *Psychological Bulletin*, 1976, *83*, 314–320.

Grice, G. R., & Hunter, J. J. Stimulus intensity effects depend upon the type of experimental design. *Psychological Review*, 1964, *71*, 247–256.

Guenther, W. C. *Analysis of variance.* Englewood Cliffs, N.J.: Prentice-Hall, 1964.

Harris, D. R., Bisbee, C. T., & Evans, S. H. Further comments—Misuse of analysis of covariance. *Psychological Bulletin*, 1971, *75*, 220–222.

Harter, H. L. Error rates and sample sizes for range tests in multiple comparisons. *Biometrics*, 1957, *13*, 511–536.

Hartwig, F., & Dearing, B. E. *Exploratory data analysis.* Beverly Hills, Calif.: Sage, 1979.

Hayes-Roth, B. Evolution of cognitive structures and processes. *Psychological Review*, 1977, *84*, 260–278.

Hays, W. L. *Statistics for the social sciences* (2nd ed.). New York: Holt, Rinehart and Winston, 1973.

Himmelfarb, S. What do you do when the control group doesn't fit into the factorial design? *Psychological Bulletin*, 1975, *82*, 363–368.

Huck, S. W., & Sandler, H. M. *Rival hypotheses.* New York: Harper & Row, 1979.

Huitema, B. E. *The analysis of covariance and alternatives.* New York: Wiley, 1980.

Huynh, H., & Feldt, L. S. Conditions under which mean square ratios in repeated measurements designs have exact *F*-distributions. *Journal of the American Statistical Association*, 1970, *65*, 1,582–1,589.

Huynh, H., & Feldt, L. S. Estimation of the Box correction for degrees of freedom from sample data in randomized block and split-plot designs. *Journal of Educational Statistics*, 1976, *1*, 69–82.

Huynh, H., & Mandeville, G. K. Validity conditions in repeated measures designs. *Psychological Bulletin*, 1979, *86*, 964–973.

Irion, A. L. Rote learning. In S. Koch (Ed.,) *Psychology: A study of a science. Vol. 2. General systematic formulations, learning, and special processes.* New York: McGraw-Hill, 1959, 538–560.

Johnson, E. S., & Baker, R. F. The computer as experimenter: New results. *Behavioral Science,* 1973, *18,* 377–385.

Johnson, H. H., & Solso, R. L. *An introduction to experimental design in psychology: A case approach* (2nd ed.). New York: Harper & Row, 1978.

Keppel, G. *Design and analysis: A researcher's handbook.* Englewood Cliffs, N.J.: Prentice-Hall, 1973.

Keppel, G. Words as random variables. *Journal of Verbal Learning and Verbal Behavior,* 1976, *15,* 263–265.

Keppel, G., Postman, L., & Zavortink, B. Studies of learning to learn: VIII. The influence of massive amounts of training upon the learning and retention of paired-associate lists. *Journal of Verbal Learning and Verbal Behavior,* 1968, *7,* 790–796.

Keppel, G., & Saufley, W. H., Jr. *Introduction to design and analysis: A student's handbook.* San Francisco: W. H. Freeman, 1980.

Keppel, G., & Underwood, B. J. Proactive inhibition in short-term retention of single items. *Journal of Verbal Learning and Verbal Behavior,* 1962, *1,* 153–161.

Keren, G., & Lewis, C. Partial omega squared for ANOVA designs. *Educational and Psychological Measurement,* 1979, *39,* 119–128.

Kerlinger, F. N., & Pedhazur, E. J. *Multiple regression in behavioral research.* New York: Holt, Rinehart and Winston, 1973.

Keselman, H. J., Games, P. A., & Rogan, J. C. Protecting the overall rate of type I errors for pairwise comparisons with an omnibus test statistic. *Psychological Bulletin,* 1979, *86,* 884–888.

Keselman, H. J., & Rogan, J. C. The Tukey multiple comparison test: 1953–1976. *Psychological Bulletin,* 1977, *84,* 1,050–1,056.

Keselman, H. J., Rogan, J. C., Mendoza, J. L., & Breen, L. J. Testing the validity conditions of repeated measures *F* tests. *Psychological Bulletin,* 1980, *87,* 479–481.

Kirk, R. E. *Experimental design: Procedures for the behavioral sciences.* Monterey, Calif.: Brooks/Cole, 1968.

Kirk, R. E. Classification of ANOVA designs. In R. E. Kirk (Ed.), *Statistical issues.* Monterey, Calif.: Brooks/Cole, 1972, 241–260.

Kirk, R. E. (Ed.). *Statistical issues.* Monterey, Calif.: Brooks/Cole, 1972.

Kohr, R. L., & Games, P. A. Testing complex a priori contrasts on means from independent samples. *Journal of Educational Statistics,* 1977, *2,* 207–216.

Lane, D. M., & Dunlap, W. P. Estimating effect size: Bias resulting from the significance criterion in editorial decisions. *The British Journal of Mathematical and Statistical Psychology,* 1978, *31,* 107–112.

Lindman, H. R. *Analysis of variance in complex experimental designs.* San Francisco: W. H. Freeman, 1974.

Lindquist, E. F. *Design and analysis of experiments in psychology and education.* Boston: Houghton Mifflin, 1953.

Lord, F. M. A paradox in the interpretation of group comparisons. *Psychological Bulletin,* 1967, *68,* 304–305.

Lord, F. M. Statistical adjustments when comparing preexisting groups. *Psychological Bulletin,* 1969, *72,* 336–337.

Lovie, A. D. The analysis of variance in experimental psychology: 1934–1945. *The British Journal of Mathematical and Statistical Psychology,* 1979, *32,* 151–178.

Marascuilo, L. A., & Levin, J. R. Appropriate post hoc comparisons for interaction and nested hypotheses in analysis of variance designs: The elimination of Type IV errors. *American Educational Research Journal,* 1970, *7,* 397–421.

Marascuilo, L. A., & McSweeney, M. *Nonparametric and distribution-free methods for the social sciences.* Monterey, Calif.: Brooks/Cole, 1977.

Martin, C. G., & Games, P. A. ANOVA tests for homogeneity of variance: Non-normality and unequal samples. *Journal of Educational Statistics,* 1977, *2,* 187–206.

Maxwell, S., & Cramer, E. M. A note on analysis of covariance. *Psychological Bulletin,* 1975, *82,* 187–190.

Maxwell, S. E., Camp, C. J., & Arvey, R. D. Measures of strength of association: A comparative examination. *Journal of Applied Psychology,* 1981, in press.

McCall, R. B. Addendum. The use of multivariate procedures in developmental psychology. In P. H. Mussen (Ed.), *Carmichael's manual of child psychology* (3rd ed., Vol. I). New York: Wiley, 1970, 1,366–1,377.

McCall, R. B., & Appelbaum, M. I. Bias in the analysis of repeated-measures designs: Some alternative approaches. *Child Development,* 1973, *44,* 401–415.

Meyer, D. L. Issues of power: Rejoinder. *American Educational Research Journal,* 1974, *11,* 193–194. (a)

Meyer, D. L. Statistical tests and surveys of power: A critique. *American Educational Research Journal,* 1974, *11,* 179–188. (b)

Miller, L., Cornett, T., Brightwell, D., McFarland, D., Drew, W. G., & Wikler, A. Marijuana and memory impairment: The effect of retrieval cues on free recall. *Pharmacology Biochemistry and Behavior,* 1976, *5,* 639–643.

Miller, L. L., & Cornett, T. L. Marijuana: Dose effects on pulse rate, subjective estimates of intoxication, free recall and recognition memory. *Pharmacology Biochemistry and Behavior,* 1978, *9,* 573–577.

Moses, L. E., & Oakford, R. V. *Tables of random permutations.* Stanford, Calif.: Stanford University Press, 1963.

Myers, J. L. *Fundamentals of experimental design.* Boston: Allyn and Bacon, 1966.

Myers, J. L. *Fundamentals of experimental design* (2nd ed.). Boston: Allyn and Bacon, 1972.

Myers, J. L. *Fundamentals of experimental design* (3rd ed.). Boston: Allyn and Bacon, 1979.

Namboodiri, N. K. Experimental designs in which each subject is used repeatedly. *Psychological Bulletin,* 1972, *77,* 54–64.

Neale, J. M., & Liebert, R. M. *Science and behavior* (2nd ed.). Englewood Cliffs, N.J.: Prentice-Hall, 1980.

Norton, D. W. An empirical investigation of some effects of non-normality and heterogeneity of the *F*-distribution. Unpublished doctoral dissertation, State University of Iowa, 1952.

O'Brien, R. G. A simple test for variance effects in experimental designs. *Psychological Bulletin,* 1981, *89,* 570–574.

Overall, J. E., & Dalal, S. N. Design of experiments to maximize power relative to cost. *Psychological Bulletin,* 1965, *64,* 339–350.

Overall, J. E., & Spiegel, D. K. Concerning least squares analysis of experimental data. *Psychological Bulletin,* 1969, *72,* 311–322.

Overall, J. E., Spiegel, D. K., & Cohen, J. Equivalence of orthogonal and nonorthogonal analysis of variance. *Psychological Bulletin,* 1975, *82,* 182–186.

Overall, J. E., & Woodward, J. A. Nonrandom assignment and the analysis of covariance. *Psychological Bulletin,* 1977, *84,* 588–594.

Pearson, E. S., & Hartley, H. O. Charts of the power function for analysis of variance tests, derived from the non-central *F*-distribution. *Biometrika,* 1951, *38,* 112–130.

Pearson, E. S., & Hartley, H. O. (Eds.). *Biometrika tables for statisticians* (3rd ed., Vol. 1). New York: Cambridge University Press, 1970.

Petrinovich, L. F., & Hardyck, C. D. Error rates for multiple comparison methods:

Some evidence concerning the frequency of erroneous conclusions. *Psychological Bulletin*, 1969, *71*, 43–54.

Postman, L. Studies of learning to learn: II. Changes in transfer as a function of practice. *Journal of Verbal Learning and Verbal Behavior*, 1964, *3*, 437–447.

Postman, L., & Keppel, G. Retroactive inhibition in free recall. *Journal of Experimental Psychology*, 1967, *74*, 203–211.

Postman, L., & Riley, D. A. A critique of Köhler's theory of association. *Psychological Review*, 1957, *64*, 61–72.

Poulton, E. C. Unwanted range effects from using within-subject experimental designs. *Psychological Bulletin*, 1973, *80*, 113–121.

Poulton, E. C. Range effects are characteristic of a person serving in a within-subjects experimental design—A reply to Rothstein. *Psychological Bulletin*, 1974, *81*, 201–202.

Poulton, E. C. Range effects in experiments on people. *American Journal of Psychology*, 1975, *88*, 3–32.

Poulton, E. C., & Freeman, P. R. Unwanted asymmetrical transfer effects with balanced experimental designs. *Psychological Bulletin*, 1966, *66*, 1–8.

RAND Corporation. *A million random digits with 100,000 normal deviates.* New York: Free Press, 1955.

Rogan, J. C., & Keselman, H. J. Is the ANOVA F-test robust to variance heterogeneity when sample sizes are equal?: An investigation via a coefficient of variation. *American Educational Research Journal*, 1977, *14*, 493–498.

Rogan, J. C., Keselman, H. J., & Mendoza, J. L. Analysis of repeated measurements. *The British Journal of Mathematical and Statistical Psychology*, 1979, *32*, 269–286.

Rosenthal, R. Combining results of independent studies. *Psychological Bulletin*, 1978, *85*, 185–193.

Rosenthal, R., & Gaito, J. The interpretation of levels of significance by psychological researchers. *The Journal of Psychology*, 1963, *55*, 33–38.

Rosenthal, R., & Rubin, D. B. Comparing significance levels of independent studies. *Psychological Bulletin*, 1979, *86*, 1,165–1,168.

Rothstein, L. D. Reply to Poulton. *Psychological Bulletin*, 1974, *81*, 199–200.

Rouanet, H., & Lépine, D. Comparison between treatments in a repeated-measures design: ANOVA and multivariate methods. *The British Journal of Mathematical and Statistical Psychology*, 1970, *23*, 147–163.

Rucci, A. J., & Tweney, R. D. Analysis of variance and the "second discipline" of scientific psychology: A historical account. *Psychological Bulletin*, 1980, *87*, 166–184.

Ryan, T. A. Multiple comparisons in psychological research. *Psychological Bulletin*, 1959, *56*, 26–47.

Santa, J. L., Miller, J. J., & Shaw, M. L. Using quasi *F* to prevent alpha inflation due to stimulus variation. *Psychological Bulletin*, 1979, *86*, 37–46.

Satterthwaite, F. E. An approximate distribution of estimates of variance components. *Biometrics Bulletin*, 1946, *2*, 110–114.

Shaffer, J. P. Reorganization of variables in analysis of variance and multidimensional contingency tables. *Psychological Bulletin*, 1977, *84*, 220–228.

Siegel, S. *Nonparametric statistics for the behavioral sciences.* New York: McGraw-Hill, 1956.

Slamecka, N. J., & Graf, P. The generation effect: Delineation of a phenomenon. *Journal of Experimental Psychology: Human Learning and Memory*, 1978, *4*, 592–604.

Slobin, D. I. Grammatical transformations and sentence comprehension in childhood and adulthood. *Journal of Verbal Learning and Verbal Behavior,* 1966, *5,* 219–227.

Smith, J. E. K. The assuming-will-make-it-so fallacy. *Journal of Verbal Learning and Verbal Behavior,* 1976, *15,* 262–263.

Snedecor, G. W. *Statistical methods applied to experiments in agriculture and biology* (5th ed.). Ames, Iowa: Iowa State University Press, 1956.

Sprott, D. A. Note on Evans and Anastasio on the analysis of covariance. *Psychological Bulletin,* 1970, *73,* 303–306.

Tatsuoka, M. M. *Multivariate analysis: Techniques for educational and psychological research.* New York: Wiley, 1971.

Tukey, J. W. One degree of freedom for non-additivity. *Biometrics,* 1949, *5,* 232–242.

Tukey, J. W. *Exploratory data analysis.* Reading, Mass.: Addison-Wesley, 1977.

Tversky, A., & Kahneman, D. Belief in the law of small numbers. *Psychological Bulletin,* 1971, *76,* 105–110.

Underwood, B. J. *Psychological research.* Englewood Cliffs, N.J.: Prentice-Hall, 1957.

Underwood, B. J. Ten years of massed practice on distributed practice. *Psychological Review,* 1961, *68,* 229–247.

Underwood, B. J., & Richardson, J. The influence of meaningfulness, intralist similarity, and serial position on retention. *Journal of Experimental Psychology,* 1956, *52,* 119–126.

Underwood, B. J., & Shaughnessy, J. J. *Experimentation in psychology.* New York: Wiley, 1975.

Vaughan, G. M., & Corballis, M. C. Beyond tests of significance: Estimating strength of effects in selected ANOVA designs. *Psychological Bulletin,* 1969, *72,* 204–213.

Wagenaar, W. A. A note on the construction of digram-balanced Latin squares. *Psychological Bulletin,* 1969, *72,* 384–386.

Wallace, W. P., & Underwood, B. J. Implicit responses and the role of intralist similarity in verbal learning by normal and retarded subjects. *Journal of Educational Psychology,* 1964, *55,* 362–370.

Webb, E. J., Campbell, D. T., Schwartz, R. D., & Sechrest, L. *Unobtrusive measures: Nonreactive research in the social sciences.* Chicago: Rand McNally, 1966.

Weisberg, H. I. Statistical adjustments and uncontrolled studies. *Psychological Bulletin,* 1979, *86,* 1,149–1,164.

Welch, B. L. The generalization of 'Student's' problem when several different population variances are involved. *Biometrika,* 1947, *34,* 28–35.

Wike, E. L., & Church, J. D. Comments on Clark's "The language-as-fixed-effect fallacy." *Journal of Verbal Learning and Verbal Behavior,* 1976, *15,* 249–255.

Wilson, W. A note on the inconsistency inherent in the necessity to perform multiple comparisons. *Psychological Bulletin,* 1962, *59,* 296–300.

Winer, B. J. *Statistical principles in experimental design.* New York: McGraw-Hill, 1962.

Winer, B. J. *Statistical principles in experimental design* (2nd ed.). New York: McGraw-Hill, 1971.

Author Index

Subject Index